The Father

THE
FATHER

■ ■ ■

A Life of Henry James, Sr.

A L F R E D   H A B E G G E R

Farrar, Straus and Giroux
New York

Library of Congress Cataloging-in-Publication Data
Habegger, Alfred.
The father: a life of Henry James, Sr. / Alfred Habegger. — 1st ed.
p.   cm.
Includes bibliographical references and index.
1. James, Henry, 1811–1882.   2. James family.   3. Intellectuals—
United States—Biography.   4. Religious thought—United
States—19th century.   I. Title.
B921.J24H23   1994   191—dc20   93–41823 CIP
[B]

Portraits and photographs from the Schaffer Library's collections reproduced with
the permission of the Schaffer Library, Union College, Schenectady, New York.
Page from ledger of Dr. John James reproduced with the permission of the New
York State Library. Portraits and photographs from the Houghton Library's collection reproduced with the permission of the Houghton Library, Harvard University. Portraits of Revs. Alexander and Hodge reproduced with the permission
of Princeton Theological Seminary. Photograph of Frogmore Cottage reproduced
with the permission of the Royal Archives. Copyright © 1994 Her Majesty Queen
Elizabeth II. Photograph of Campagne Gerebsoff reproduced courtesy of Centre
d'iconographie genevoise, Geneva. Photograph of the Shaws reproduced with the
permission of the Staten Island Institute of Arts and Sciences. Page from *Arcana
Coelestia* reproduced with the permission of the Swedenborg School of Religion,
Newton, Mass. Photographs of Marx Edgeworth Lazarus and Stephen Pearl An-
drews reproduced with the permission of the Labadie Collection, University of
Michigan Library. Portrait of Henry James, Sr., reproduced with the permission
of the Harvard University Art Museums. Portrait of Mrs. Samuel Gray Ward
(Anna Hazard Barker) reproduced with the permission of the Museum of Fine
Arts, Boston.

For acknowledgments of permission to quote unpublished materials, see page 507.

For
Marianna and Marden
Nellie
Simon and Eliza

Contents

■ ■ ■

The Father

Chapter 1

■ ■ ■

THE LITTLE ILIAD OF
HIS INMOST HEART

In the thousands of manuscript pages he left behind—essays and lectures and treatises and thirty-page rebuttals of unfavorable reviews—he never lets up. He is always going at some antagonist who hasn't reached first base in the spiritual world and has nothing of value to say, always setting this third-rater straight about the nature of things. "Mind well what I say here," he constantly demands.

Then again, he left hundreds of splendid personal letters, some of them more witty, charming, warm, and open than anything his gifted children were able to write. In these he seems endlessly inventive, with so much ingenuity of expression, so masterly a tonal range, and such a superb feel for the nuances of relationships that one willingly forgets that blocked and monomaniacal hierophant.

And then, but much less frequently, one comes upon documents of a third kind. These are the pages in which an embittered devil comes to life, with a piece of wood where others have flesh and feeling. He wields a pen dipped in his own bottomless well of long-distilled guilt and anger. He has a tail formed of his own lengthening invisible past, and from time to time as he writes at his desk it whips into view and stings him into madness.

THE PROBLEM

One day in 1869 Henry James, Sr., learned that some of the religious writings of his older half brother, the Reverend William James, had been published by his admirers in a memorial volume. Rev. James was well known in Presbyterian circles for his regal ways, his fervent but tolerant Calvinism, his strength as a devotional writer, and his eccentricities. Before his death the previous year at the age of seventy, he had spent long hours at his writer's desk, counseling those who were struggling to overcome their spiritual unease. Forty years earlier he had been Henry's own chosen confessor and counselor, and even a kind of second father, for the two brothers were born fourteen years apart. Henry relied on Rev. William during the long, bedridden adolescence that left the boy without his right leg, and several years later, when he underwent a religious conversion and resolved to bring his disorderly life under control, he begged his older brother to be his conscience. But when Henry broke with the Presbyterian Church, his close fraternal dependency came to an end. From then on his letters to his former mentor were painfully abrasive and arrogant. On his side William felt helpless to bring an end to this dispute "in *feeling*." The rupture never healed.

Now that William was dead, Henry's animosity and resentment gained new vigor. He made up his mind to write a final refutation of his brother's religious beliefs and publish the exposé in a magazine, and he told his daughter, Alice, of his plan. If he expected her approval he did not get it. She let him know in no uncertain terms that the attack he meditated would be a "great indelicacy." He then proposed a compromise. He would go ahead and write his article, but he would publish it anonymously, asking one of his disciples to copy and submit it (for Henry Sr. was also a religious guru, with followers of his own). That way, it would not look as if one brother was assaulting another in his grave. With this, Alice "grew furious," according to her father (to whom we are indebted for our knowledge of this episode), "& cried out for help" from William, her oldest brother. But William merely said, "Why of course he will do it. He is so little restrained by conventional considerations that if you or I or Mama were to die to night he would send off a contribution to the Daily Advertiser to morrow tearing us to pieces." Henry Sr. concluded his account of this household dispute by adding, delightedly, "This I thought very good."

At the time he recounted this story for the amusement of one of his disciples—the very one he would have asked to copy his fraternal assault—the James father had thirty years' experience in getting his injudicious and sometimes scandalous and always well-articulated opinions before the public. At times the publicity was unwelcome, as had been the case the previous year when a newspaper divulged his low opinion of Ralph Waldo Emerson's lecture on Brook Farm. By 1868 this well-known commune of the 1840s had become a symbol of a bygone radical era. James was offended with Emerson's dismissive treatment of the utopian socialist Charles Fourier, and advised a friend that the lecture was derivative and disgraceful, "intellectual slip-slop of the poorest kind." The trouble was, James and Emerson were old friends. When the *Springfield Daily Republican* reported that "Emerson knows nothing about Fourier, and has confessed to [James] that he never read his works, but only knows of them from extracts which Mrs. Emerson read to him while he was shaving," James was mortified. He dashed off an angry letter denying the remark attributed to him and assailing the press's "witless rage of gossip," which, "like the lice of Egypt, invades every secret chamber of men's personal consciousness."

As a rule, though, the older Henry James wanted the public to hear his daring and sometimes dangerous opinions. Back in the revolutionary year of 1848, after Brook Farm had collapsed and some of its leaders shifted their operations to New York (where James himself had also pitched his tent), he became a reckless propagandist for Fourier's brand of utopian socialism. Most American Fourierists tried to steer clear of the Frenchman's visionary dream of complete sexual freedom. Not James. He got hold of an uncompromising pamphlet by one of Fourier's disciples and translated it under the title *Love in the Phalanstery*, leaving his own name off the title page. The publication of this work persuaded many Americans of the time that the Fourierists really did want to undermine family life and destroy the home, just as their enemies had been saying all along. As the controversy heated up, James bravely identified himself as the translator and openly declared himself for free love—at some time in the future:

> I presume a day will come when the sexual relations will be regulated in every case by the private will of the parties; when the reciprocal affection of a man and a woman will furnish the sole and sufficient sanction of their material converse.

Public statements such as this resulted in an endless train of controversies and embarrassments for James. In the mid-1870s *Woodhull & Claflin's Weekly*, a scandalous magazine devoted to free love and socialism, published his reckless private admission that "I marry my wife under the impression that she is literally perfect, and is going to exhaust my capacity of desire ever after. Ere long I discover my mistake." This public disclosure had an effect that is still with us. After James's death, the son who bore his name set to work on a novel that attacked the women's movement and the invasion of private life by the press. Read in the context of the author's family history, *The Bostonians* records a son's deeply embarrassed entanglement in his father's twenty-five-year struggle with the free-love movement and the radical press.

One great irony in the life of Henry James, Sr., is that the man who looked forward to the inevitable demise of monogamy and the isolated family became one of the most devoted family men of all time. How many intellectual parents can point to one child as remarkable as William James the psychologist and philosopher or Henry James the novelist, let alone two? By most accounts the domestic scene in the James household was warm and stimulating, presided over by a brilliant talker of a father and a strong and supportive mother. Visitors in the 1860s loved to tell stories about the Jameses' dinnertime conversations, during which the argumentative strife among the four boys would prove so irresistible to the father that he would finally join in with unforgettable vehemence. These stories all agree in representing him as the presiding genius of this brilliant and remarkably self-sufficient group.

It is owing to James's restless intellectuality that three of his children—William, Henry, Alice—are remembered today. For better and worse, he was responsible for their larger-than-life tensions, abilities, ambitions, achievements. But he was so protean and driven (and indelicate, as Alice complained) that his survivors automatically entered into something like a conspiracy of silence concerning him after his death. His body had hardly grown cold when his sister-in-law, Catharine Walsh, began going through his papers and selectively burning them, and this process continued in his son William's posthumous edition of his papers, in Henry Jr.'s marvelous but not always trustworthy memoirs of life at home, and in the selective preservation of letters and other documents (now at Harvard's Houghton Library) by his grandson Henry III.

The first biographer to tackle James was Austin Warren in a slender book of 1934, *The Elder Henry James*. A distinguished critic and an energetic searcher for letters, Warren labored under some difficult constraints: working under the protective gaze of James's grandson, he lacked access to the expanded archival collections and other sources of information that are available today. Also, Warren gave little attention to a subject of considerable interest to later biographers: the emotional tensions within the James family. The first biographer to focus on this problem was Leon Edel, who read the fiction of Henry Jr. as a symbolic expression of his familial relationships, especially his supposed fraternal rivalry with William. Where Edel saw the father as a relatively weak figure, more recent biographers regard him as a powerful creator and destroyer. Howard M. Feinstein has argued that Henry Sr. exercised the same paternal force on his son William that his own father had visited on him. Jean Strouse has shown that Henry Sr.'s teachings on "woman" had a confusing and disabling effect on Alice and contributed to her psychosis. But it introduces great distortions to approach the man solely in relation to his children. It is time to try to understand this remarkable figure in his own right.

This biography draws on an extensive search for information on Henry Sr. and his family and friends and puts hundreds of fresh discoveries on record. In telling his story, my aim has been to keep as close as possible to the surviving evidence, scattered and fragmentary as it is, and also to be honest about the many unanswered questions concerning my subject's life. To some extent my narrative has turned out to be a double one: it is both the story of the life of an elusive and complicated man and the story of a biographer's quest for the truth about him.

There can be no doubt that James himself would have strenuously repudiated any effort to uncover and narrate his life's story. His children were well aware he had a story to tell and often urged him to write it. A close friend, Parke Godwin, once asked him to reveal the "little iliad" of his private history, and although James did not comply, he did not forget the request. Thirty years later he suddenly dredged it up, agreeing at last to satisfy his friend's curiosity—and then not doing so.

When James finally did sit down to compose his story, he protected himself in various ways. He resorted to a fictional disguise, embedded the crucial episodes in a glaze of irony and syntactic complexity, treated himself as a representative case rather than an individual, repeatedly veered off into long sermons, and broke off before getting very far. The truth of the matter is that the act of autobiographical recovery posed a major threat to his sense of well-being. Once, in a letter to his youngest son, Bob, who had grave troubles of his own, the James father confessed that he was assailed by "envy, hatred, contempt of others, ill-will, lascivious memories, unchaste nay unclean desires." The oddest item in this catalogue of temptations is the one that is noticed last of all, *memories*, sandwiched between "lascivious" and "unchaste nay unclean desires." Why memory was so dreadful to Henry Sr. is one of the chief mysteries to be solved in his life. His grandson considered him "temperamentally indifferent to the past," and he himself believed that the act of revisiting one's personal history exposed one to an intimate assault from a malignant spirit world. In fact, with his profound aversion to the basic idea of individual selfhood, it is not too much to say that James did not *believe* in memory or biography. He could not allow the premises of retrospective narration.

Of course, there are extant letters in which James suddenly recalls and reveals an old hidden passage in his life. But while these documents offer important disclosures, they inevitably hint at things still more hidden and enigmatic and perhaps inadmissible. In 1859, when Sarah Shaw wrote about her fears for her children, James was moved to reply:

> How perfectly I recall your state of mind! It was years ago however . . .
> I *did* say in my inmost heart to God incessantly . . . "take these dear
> children away before they know the evil of sin." That dreadful mystery
> of sin haunted me night and day. I have been on my knees from morning
> till night (this strictly between ourselves) sometimes determined as it were
> not to let God go, till he gave me some relief.

The reference seems to be to a time in the mid-1840s, after the birth of his second son, Henry Jr., when James experienced a complete psychological collapse. What the letter intimates about his extreme devotional practices or his feelings toward his children—wishing in his "inmost heart" that William and Henry might literally die before discovering "the evil of sin"—is probably no exaggeration. Biography wants to know what was in that "inmost heart," and how that heart expressed itself. As James himself admitted during the Civil War, expression seemed to be the most difficult point: "If by any one act I could fully express, *i.e.* satisfy, the affection I bear my wife, my child, my friend . . . my next act towards them would logically be one of extermination."

At one and the same time the man was the genius of his household and a sinister exterminating angel. His complaint about the impossibility of expressing his domestic feelings saw print in 1863, the year Sarah Shaw's son, Robert Gould Shaw, led a regiment of black soldiers from Massachusetts against the cannons of Fort Wagner, South Carolina. In that pointless assault Mrs. Shaw's one boy was killed and James's third, Wilkie, gravely injured. Could James predict historical events by looking into his monstrous inmost heart? Which was he, a terrifyingly gifted seer or a crazed metaphysician? These were among the unanswered questions that pressed on his children.

Chapter 2

■ ■ ■

"YOU WHO HAVE BEEN POOR
AND GAINED WEALTH":
WILLIAM JAMES OF ALBANY

Henry's father, William James of Albany, left a broad, turbulent wake of institutions founded and landscapes altered and courthouses and news-papers full of documentary records of his multifarious activities, so that his life is more recoverable than that of Henry's mother. Yet when the time came for his survivors to frame his epitaph, they remembered his origins and forgot all the rest:

WILLIAM JAMES,
A NATIVE OF IRELAND,
DEC. 19, 1832, AGED 63.

Years later, when the State Street Presbyterian burial ground containing William's remains was turned into valuable commercial property, and the massive brownstone memorial to him and his three wives was erected in Albany Rural Cemetery, he was given a second epitaph:

SACRED
TO THE MEMORY
OF
WILLIAM JAMES
BORN
IN IRELAND
DEC. 29 [*year flaked off*]
BECAME
A RESIDENT OF ALBANY IN 1793
DIED
DEC. 19, 1832.

Once again, the man's beginnings displaced his achievements.

These two memorials, completely silent about those deeds that would most justify a commemorative boast, are among the most revealing documents William of Albany left behind.

ULSTER AND NEW YORK

The flaked-off year of origin was 1771. The place was County Cavan, at that time the southernmost of Ulster's nine counties. William grew up in the township of Bailieborough, where his father had a twenty-five-acre farm, probably a leasehold and definitely larger than the average tilled farm in eighteenth-century Ireland. The parents were "strong" farmers, and in more than one sense, for the father, after whom William was named, and the mother, Susan McCartney, attained the ages of eighty-six and seventy-eight respectively—a riper old age than William or any of his thirteen children would reach. When an American descendant returned to the ancestral graves in 1931, the large flat tombstones struck him as "bigger and better" than all the others.

William's older brother went into business and perhaps took over the farm, too, doing sufficiently well that some silver, lace, and initialed tablespoons came down to later heirs. As for William, he got a respectable education, and when he left for America, according to family tradition, one of the few possessions he packed, along "with a very small sum of money," was a Latin grammar. He may have also taken a consignment of English merchandise. His American descendants believed that one of his reasons for emigrating was to avoid the profession his father wished him to enter, the ministry.

William must have spoken with a strong Scotch-Irish burr for the remainder of his life, since he was already a young man by the time he came to America in 1789, or 1793, or possibly even 1794 (the second epitaph notwithstanding).* The youthful adventurer did not come alone: in those years some 5,000 Irish immigrants were arriving annually, two-thirds of them from Ulster. These were not poverty-stricken Catholics, as in the mid-nineteenth century, but Presbyterians in "fairly comfortable circumstances," "substantial farmers and arti-

---

* 1789 has been the received date, going back as far as the obituary in the *Albany Evening Journal*, December 19, 1832. A close and longtime friend of one of William's firstborn twins thought the date was 1793, and a brief tribute by "one who was well acquainted" with William has 1794.

sans," many of whom had profited from the linen trade's prosperous days in the 1780s. Typically, the men of Ulster had warmly supported the American colonies' revolt from English rule, so much so that the Lord Lieutenant of Ireland once complained to London that the "Irish Presbyterians were Americans 'in their Hearts' and 'talking in all companies in such a way that if they are not rebels, it is hard to find a name for them.' " This is the sort of Irishman William must have been, for according to family tradition, his first desire after crossing the Atlantic was "to visit the field of one of the revolutionary battles."

There is no doubt that William's early years in England's first and most tragic colony left a lasting stamp on his political and social views. County Cavan had three distinct populations: a large majority of poor, illiterate, subjugated Catholic peasants; a smaller number of Scots Presbyterian farmers, artisans, and merchants; and a very small number of English, some of them gentry, who held title to the land and were empowered to levy taxes and collect tithes for the Anglican Church. When the Bailieborough parish was organized in 1778, the Jameses were no doubt forced to contribute to the incumbent's support. In the later 1780s, not long before William emigrated, two northern Presbyterian ministers challenged the legitimacy of the tithe in a fierce pamphlet debate. Precisely how William and his parents viewed such tensions can only be conjectured. Did they share the usual Presbyterian disdain for the Anglican establishment? Or does the Jameses' belief that the family had come from Wales around 1700 (rather than from Scotland at the time of the religious wars) indicate a sense of distance from Scotch-Irish attitudes?

The fierce though intermittent liberalism that William often showed was characteristic of the restive and informed middle-class population from which he stemmed. Also, he passed through youth and early manhood during the most hopeful phases of the French Revolution. His second wife was apparently Roman Catholic, judging from Mary Ann Connolly's parents' religious affiliation and her own interment in a Catholic cemetery. This surprising alliance was, if not characteristic, at least symptomatic of an era when some Ulster Presbyterians were so resentful of their inferior civil status that they saw the English rather than the Irish as the enemy. The events in France of 1789–92 led many Irish Protestants to discard what Thomas Addis Emmet called "the frequently repeated dogma, that Catholics are unfit for liberty." Indeed, soon after William emigrated, there was a remarkable revolutionary development in east Ulster and Dublin, where the more radical Dissenters began to make common cause with the Irish against the English. Some Ulster

Presbyterians took the lead in organizing secret, nonsectarian political clubs, the United Irishmen, who sought national independence, equal citizenship for Catholics and Protestants, and (taking a hint from the successful Americans) French military assistance. This movement culminated in the ill-fated armed insurrection of 1798—which happened to be the year of William and Mary Ann's nuptials. But independence was still far in the future. The United Irish revolt was crushed, its leaders executed or dispersed, and the revolutionary dream of nonsectarian fraternity sent into exile. Also, Mary Ann died in 1800, and William's third and final wife—the mother of Henry—was safely Presbyterian.

One of the most important leaders of the United Irishmen, Thomas Addis Emmet, who ended up in New York after being imprisoned for four years in Dublin and the Highlands, became a good friend and ally of William's. A successful lawyer in his adopted land, Emmet was known for his "solemn and emphatic" courtroom oratory, his resentment of slurs against the Irish, and his influence among Jeffersonians. On one occasion, he defended some Catholic residents of Greenwich Village who had been provoked by a demonstration of Orangemen. On another, he was retained by John Jacob Astor, the richest American of his time, in litigation over extensive landholdings. In 1823, after William lost a lawsuit in which some $12,000 worth of mortgaged real estate was at stake, Emmet took the case on appeal, and the eloquent Irish rebel got the decision reversed. At Emmet's death in 1827 William contributed $100 for a memorial obelisk, as did Archibald McIntyre, one of William's most trusted cronies.

Emmet's younger brother, Robert, who was hanged by the English in 1803 following another doomed Irish rising, seems to have been venerated in William's family as a heroic martyr. Young Henry once gave such a moving rendition of the famous speech Robert made after being found guilty of high treason—"When my country takes her place among the nations of the earth, then, and not till then, let my epitaph be written"—that an old shoemaker who was listening freely wept. Even Henry Jr., the novelist, who looked down on the Irish, recalled the name of Robert Emmet as "a pious, indeed . . . a glorious, tradition."

Piety and profit generally went hand in hand for William. Where there had once been a short-lived revolutionary fellowship in Ireland, there was now a loose confederation of rich Scotch-Irish Jeffersonians in New York. James McBride, importer and moneylender, with a brother and partner in Dublin, looked after some of William's operations in New York City and handled international shipping arrangements. Henry Eckford, a New York City shipbuilder who hailed from Scotland, joined with William James in 1820 to form the North River Steamboat Company. William helped a younger brother and several nephews come to America and get started in business. There was an aggressive Scotch-Irish brotherhood at work in New York State in the early 1800s, and William was part of its inner circle.

These northern British affiliations were fully compatible with the ardent patriotism William felt toward his adopted country. Shortly after a naturalization law was passed in 1802, he became a citizen, declaring on oath "that he doth absolutely and entirely renounce and abjure all Allegiances and fidelity to every foreign prince, potentate, State and Sovereignty whatsoever, and particularly to the King of Great Britain."

Chief among William's influential New York friends was DeWitt Clinton, a mayor of New York, a presidential candidate who lost to James Madison in 1812, and a four-time governer of the state of New York. Clinton had some Irish blood, was considered a "friend of Ireland," and sometimes wrote over the signature "Hibernicus." As an aristocratic Jeffersonian who had been shaped by the liberalism of the Enlightenment, he had a great deal in common with William. Both were energetic promoters of public improvements. Both inclined to be high-handed. Clinton helped establish several learned societies and proved to be the key person in getting the Erie Canal built. A farsighted statesman and a resourceful administrator, he was also austere, unbending, and sarcastic, and his refusal to conciliate enemies or, worse, reward supporters, led to some dramatic ups and downs in his long political career. He helped precipitate the bitter split in New York's Democratic-Republican Party between the Clintonians and the Albany Regency, an antagonism that underlay a long succession of political wars from 1817 to 1828. (The Regency got its name in 1824, when an Albany newspaper "spoke of 'the cabinet council of [Martin] Van Buren, or rather the regency whom he has appointed to govern the state in his absence.' ")

The key fact about William's politics is that he was a tireless champion in public and private of DeWitt Clinton. In 1818, at the beginning of Clinton's first term as governor, when the feud with Van Buren was not yet out of hand, William signed a public statement urging party loyalty. In 1820, when Clinton had made so many enemies that few state legislators supported his re-election as governor, his backers took the unusual step of convening a meeting of Albany citizens to nominate him; the meeting was chaired by William. In 1821, when the governor was struggling with debt, William got up a circular proposing private financial aid and pledged $1,000 of his own money. In 1822, according to a Clintonian insider and historian, another public meeting "was got up in Albany by

Mr. William James, Mr. Archibald M'Intyre and a few others of Mr. Clinton's staunch friends." In 1824, when Clinton suffered the crowning insult of being removed from the Erie Canal Commission, the group that was appointed to "wait . . . personally upon" him and express the public's indignation was once again headed by William, who delivered the speech that was designed to pour balm on his friend's political wounds and recapture public sympathy and with it the governorship: "It could not have been expected in this enlightened age . . . that the legislature of an intelligent republic would have rewarded fourteen years of successful and disinterested efforts in promoting the prosperity and glory of the state, by this act of most base ingratitude."

As the speech's tone suggests, William was not particularly subtle in his political operations. In the fall of 1825 he had a talk with Edward P. Livingston. Soon afterward, Livingston sent a letter to Senator Van Buren in Washington, saying that Clinton wished to be President and had given William James *carte blanche* to treat" with others. What William wanted the senator to think about was that if he backed Clinton for the White House he could have any cabinet post he desired. Van Buren wouldn't touch the deal, suavely replying, "I have no reason to doubt that Mr. J.'s views are friendly and that he was unconscious of the impropriety of his suggestions."

All serious players in New York politics were well aware that Mr. J. was an enthusiast for Clinton, and when the near-great governor died in February 1828 and was given a funeral rich in symbolism, William was one of only two pallbearers out of a total of fifteen who did not hold political office. The James home on North Pearl Street was among those opened for the accommodation of crowds of visiting mourners.

During these manifestations, which marked the end of an era in New York State's rancorous political history, William's sixteen-year-old son, Henry, was probably in bed in one of the back rooms of the house, in great pain and in peril of his life.

RIVERS, STORES, AND MERCHANDISE

Probably the chief reason William James chose to settle in Albany in the early 1790s was that the city's waterfront offered the northernmost docks for freight-bearing sloops plying the Hudson River. Before the invention of the railroad, it appeared that goods transported between New York City (or any other Atlantic port) and Vermont, western New York, the Great Lakes, and the vast, unexplored interior would have to be loaded and unloaded from Albany's piers. When an early traveler first visited the city in 1788, not long before William's arrival, one of his first acts was to go out onto the river and take soundings. Finding a depth of five or six feet, he concluded that "Albany is one of the most favorable positions in America for the future enjoyment of a vast internal commerce." Another visitor grasped the same point in 1806: "Being nearly at the head of navigation of the North or Hudson's river," Albany was the future "*depôt*" both for produce from the interior and imported merchandise. It was on this geographical promise that William James founded his career.

On arriving in the small city, William seems to have found employment as clerk in a firm well enough established to be remembered as "the old blue store." By 1795 he and a partner were able to open a "Storehouse" of their own on a "slip," a sloping rock wharf extending into the water. The unusual terms of the lease suggest that William was already a person of some means—and of some mental agility as well. He and his partner were to pay an annual rent of $64.85; there would be a sum of $500 payable in full in four years; and at the end of twelve years the *owner* would pay *them* two-thirds the appraised value of the building. Two years later William advertised the opening of a second waterfront store "for the reception of country produce." By 1805 he was in partnership with a New Yorker, John Flack, the new "store" once again being located on the river. The firm of James and Flack prospered, and by at least as early as 1813 its business office was located at 54 State Street, the broad, steep avenue leading straight up to the capitol.

As an importer, William seems to have concentrated on high-quality staples, liquor, and dry goods that were shipped from Europe or elsewhere to New York City and then up the Hudson. A lengthy advertisement in the *Albany Gazette* for October 21, 1796, announces numerous products "Landing this Day, at Mark-Lane Wharf, for Wm. James and Co." Heading the list were "28 puncheons high proof Jamaica SPIRITS," followed by rum, brandy, Teneriffe wine, and twelve quarter-casks of "excellent Malaga." As a state capital, with the machinery of state government to be lubricated, Albany required a good many barrels of fine wines and spirits, but even apart from the legislators and lobbyists, the populace was a heavy-drinking lot. In 1830 a temperance group claimed the city had over four hundred taverns and alcohol-selling groceries, with an annual trade of $100,000 in alcoholic beverages. And according to a great-grandson of Thomas Addis Emmet, William had firsthand knowledge of his spiritous wares: "Old Billy James could hold his liquor, but some of his descendants couldn't."

William sold other sorts of produce as well—rice, molasses, sugar, pepper, indigo, ginger, chocolate, coffee, various kinds of tea, and "tobacco, snuff, and segars." He carried window glass by the box, candles and soap, shoes and shoe leather, slippers, hats, and plenty of rope and tar for sailing vessels. He was careful to inform potential customers that few middlemen had been involved: "N.B. *The above being purchased from Importers and Distillers, enables the disposers to sell them at a very small advance above the new-York prices.*" One reason William was able to undersell local competitors was that he had trusted confederates in New York and elsewhere. His operations were no more confined by the horizon than was the perspective of his children and grandchildren. When Henry Sr. took his children to Europe in the 1850s to be educated, or when Henry Jr. established himself with his public by writing international fiction, they were in a way following their progenitor's tracks.

In 1816 William sponsored the transplantation of two Irish nephews and set them up in promising jobs in New York City. The reports sent back to the Old World by these youthful Americans-in-the-making provide an invaluable insight into William's energetic business practices. One nephew was put into an "Auction Store," where he had "an opportunity of seeing almost all kinds of goods for sale in this market." The other was put to work in a "Hardware store," not for the salary, which paid only for board, but because it was one of the "Houses where business was done." The young Irishmen were impressed by the "emancity [immensity] of Goods at Auction" that William himself purchased and his willingness to take a loss when unavoidable. He spent three weeks in New York City at the time the nephews arrived. Busy as he was, however, he surprised them by the frequency of his visits and his interest in hearing what they thought of their new jobs. The following summer he was again away from Albany on a business trip for ten or twelve days, and after only a week at home he left for another lengthy trip to western New York.

William introduced a number of marketing innovations. An advertisement from 1818 announces that from now on Wm. James & Co. "WILL CONSTANTLY HAVE ON HAND" various staples, spirits, and spices. This was a daring promise in an era when communication with distant suppliers and shippers was difficult, expensive, and unreliable. Buyers who remembered the shortages caused by the embargo during the War of 1812 might well take notice. Another point made by the advertisement was that William would not require cash from dealers but would sell for "approved credit." What this meant in practice was that his mercantile transactions with distant businessmen resulted in valuable bonds and mortgages passing into his hands. It so happens that about the time this ad was running he took assignment of a large mortgage in Onondaga County, New York, as collateral for $9,000 worth of merchandise sold to a local dealer. After Thomas Addis Emmet did his part in the ensuing litigation, William emerged as the proprietor of some valuable real estate.

In the latter case, William won only after appealing all the way to the New York State Court for the Trial of Impeachments and the Correction of Errors. This curious court of last resort resembled no other judicial body in the United States and was eventually abolished by the state constitution of 1846. Composed of the lieutenant-governor and senators as well as higher members of the judiciary, the Court of Errors was particularly exposed to personal and political manipulation. Not surprisingly, it frequently reversed on appeal. Thanks to this institutional remnant of colonial administration, a New Yorker with the right kind of pull had access to a remarkably powerful handle.

After William died, Henry and some of his other children had access to the same court in order to break the old man's exceptionally retentive will and divvy up his vast estate.

SOLAR EVAPORATED SALT

Steady, skillful, adventurous merchandising laid the foundation for the enormous fortune acquired by William James. Land made him even richer, land that included a solid block of Greenwich Village and over forty square miles near the Mississippi River in the newly formed state of Illinois. He bought Syracuse's chief hotel and enlarged it, built the biggest hotel Albany had seen as of 1830, invested in turnpike companies, and shortly before his death began going heavily into railroads. But William would not have become one of the two or three wealthiest Americans of his time if it were not for something else—a recently exploited natural resource, a new process for refining it, an aggressive strategy for marketing it, a new route for transporting it to market, and the building up of a new city around it. At a time when salt was not just a seasoning but the indispensable agent in preserving meat, it was brine oozing from the ground that left Henry James, Sr., leisured for life, as he put it, and that gave his two older sons, William and Henry, the freedom to build their minds.

Until the 1820s, what is now downtown Syracuse was a swampy fever district obviously unfit for human life. At nearby Salina a small industry had grown up around the salt springs. The brine tenders burned wood to boil off the water, and by 1822 most of the timber in the vicinity had been used up. Joshua Forman, an ingenious developer/engineer, brought in an expert from Cape Cod to try out a new method of extraction—solar evaporation. Forman also got the state legislature to pay a bounty of three cents for each bushel of salt, and he even got a law passed that provided for the lowering of the outlet of Lake Onondaga, thus allowing Syracuse to be drained. When the kettle tenders in the nearby village of Salina showed their resentment of the new competition, Forman got more legislative help: henceforth it would be a felony to engage in "the wilful destruction of any coarse-salt erections by fire or otherwise." It may have been owing to this resourceful promoter that on April 10, 1822, at 55 Wall Street, the Syracuse Salt Company came into being, Forman becoming the "Superintendant or acting Agent" and Henry Eckford of New York City serving as the capitalist. Forman foresaw the "probable increase" in Syracuse's population and tried to convince Eckford of the "necessity of taking advantage" of this by constructing houses and stores, but Eckford was unwilling to take the plunge.

Meanwhile, Moses DeWitt Burnet, who had married a younger sister of William's wife, was looking for something to do. He dropped in on his rich brother-in-law and offered to scout around for new investments. William feeling disposed "to go into anything with him they thought would be a speculation," Burnet called on Eckford to talk about salt. A deal was struck. On May 13, 1824, the Walton Tract, a 250-acre parcel that was about to become a city, was sold for $30,000 to William James and three other investors—James McBride, his old New York crony, and the Townsend brothers, who had an iron foundry and hardware store in Albany. The group simultaneously acquired the Syracuse Salt Company, probably for an additional $30,000. William's three partners bought three-eighths of the total, for which they each paid $8,083.27. He bought the remaining five-eighths, and once he had himself formally voted president, there were to be no more official minutes until after his death. He was clearly in charge, and he hired the best men he could trust to run things for him. Burnet, as Secretary, kept accounts and acted as William's eyes and ears in Syracuse. Forman, the brains behind the original operation, went on salary, getting $500 annually to build up and manage the salt works.

William now had himself (five-eighths of) a raw but promising village and salt-manufacturing business, and the first thing he did was invest even more. By the beginning of the summer of 1825, so many new vats had been constructed that the evaporative capacity of the Syracuse Company was more than tripled. At this time the hamlet had fifteen stores, a human population of 500, and an abundance of mud holes, stumps, and unreclaimed land. A later historian of Syracuse believed that "no city in the United States was founded in such a dismal, uninteresting, and impracticable spot." But from the time he had first arrived in Albany, thirty years earlier, William knew that rivers were the way to wealth, and ever since 1820 a canal had terminated right in the middle of the Walton Tract. The canal meant shipping, and shipping meant there was a city in the offing, and a coming city meant the value of land and houses was going to rise.

Unfortunately, Burnet fell ill in the summer and fall of 1824 and, according to the story he told a fellow Syracusan in 1835, "came to the conclusion that he couldn't and wouldn't live here for any consideration whatever." He wrote his boss of his resolve to leave. William came from Albany and spent two days in Syracuse, looking through the company books and talking things over with his rebellious agent. It was vital to have his own trusted man on the spot. Finally, as the two men were walking over the old stone bridge near the Syracuse House (the hotel William would enlarge three years later), Burnet came to a stop and emphatically declared that he had to get out of the unhealthy place. According to Orcutt's retelling of the story:

> Mr. James heard him with attention, and then said, Mr. Burnet (as he always called him) you must stay here, and walked immediately to the Syracuse House, he [Burnet] followed. They took a good whif of old Holland gin and sat down. In half an hour the packet came, and Mr. James started for home, not another word was said about his [Burnet's] going or staying or on the subject of business of any kind.

William's point man in Syracuse soon recovered his health, and eleven years later admitted that since that conversation he had been seldom out of the area "and but once out of the county."

Acting for William, Burnet now saw to it that stumps were pulled, swamps drained, hills leveled, and streets laid out for the future city. Plats were drawn and lots were sold and buildings erected and mortgages taken in such numbers that in 1846, fourteen years after William's death, when the Syracuse Company was finally broken up, Henry's share alone (about one-eighteenth of the total) amounted to three full blocks and some twenty-four isolated parcels of real estate. It was mainly because of his Syracuse properties that Henry was able to tell a federal census marshal in 1850 that he was worth $80,000 in real estate, and it was because of the income from these holdings that he could take his family

abroad for several years and look for the best European education for his
children that money could buy. In 1900 a single three-story brick building
then partly owned by Henry's two oldest sons, Henry and William, and
occupied by a dry-goods firm, a barbershop, a photographer's studio, an
American Express office, "Hartigan's credit parlors," and "the hair store
of Henry Loftie," was assessed for $72,000. Soon after, Henry wrote a
novel, *The Ambassadors*, in which the leading character is too embarrassed to admit the source of his backer's wealth.

Two years after William had bought his village and industry, the
Syracuse Company was capable of turning out 400,000 bushels of coarse
salt a year, worth twenty-five cents a bushel. William's new speculation
was one of the largest manufacturing operations in western New York,
and its innovations gave it a kind of high-tech fascination in the eyes
of visitors. An early travel guide offered a description:

> The water is brought [to Syracuse] in logs from the village of *Salina*, about
> one mile and a half distant, and emptied into the vats, which occupy
> nearly 300 acres. The vats are all covered with light roofs, which are
> moveable at pleasure, to admit the rays of the sun upon the water, or to
> prevent the rain from mingling with it.

The fact that the vats were arranged in two or three tiers did away
with the continual ladling the kettles had required. Now impurities
settled to the bottom of the upper vats before the brine entered the lower
tier for the final crystallization stage. The finished product was both
cheap and pure.

In developing the new evaporation process, William seems to have
gotten the best scientific advice then available. An Albany chemist
named Lewis C. Beck ran some key tests on the brine, and the chemist's
influential brother, Dr. T. Romeyn Beck, deposited "4 bottles cont^g Salt
made by different processes at Salina" in the Albany Institute. The collections of this learned society were housed at the Albany Academy, of
which Dr. Beck was president and William a trustee. Years later Dr. Beck
recalled how the leading minds and institutions had worked together: "In
the laboratory of the Academy were conducted the investigations directed
by the state, in regard to our salt springs and the manufacture of salt,
which, at a former day, contributed so much to the benefit of that branch
of our state resources." Science, education, the state, and private capital
all cooperated for the common good—but it was William's pockets that
got lined.

The Northern states now had a new and cheaper source of domestic salt available, but it was not identical to the "fine salt" produced by boiling. What the Syracuse Company made and sold was "coarse salt," something the public was not used to. Some felt that it was "less convenient for domestic purposes." One of William's few surviving business letters conveys a vivid sense of the arm-twisting tactics with which he overcame customer—and merchant—resistance to the new product. This particular letter was sent to John R. Williams, who had recently left Albany to go into business in Detroit, a venture financed by borrowing $5,000 from William James. The loan was dated August 20, 1822, with the final payment due July 1, 1824. As of July 22, 1825, when William penned his letter, payment had not been received.

William's letter informed the barely established merchant that, whereas pork preserved by fine salt was "soft white and clamy," that cured by coarse was "solid and red" and had a "more palatable flavour." The merchant was advised to cure some barrels of meat with the two types of salt, so that his customers could see for themselves that the coarse was not only less expensive but superior. The letter concluded with this peremptory announcement:

> We have thought of keeping a large quantity of the article constantly at your place—we shall send to your care one to two thousand barrels this fall which you will please put under a temporary shed—and sell it by the quantity at two 12/100 dollars . . . We have no doubt of your closing the consignment. I am sir, y.ʳˢ mo[st] respectfully Wm. James.

The letter had begun with a bland reminder that "habit becomes a kind of nature."

When it suited him, William James played a conspicuously polite kind of hardball. The following month he sent this merchant a second letter. On the surface it was a conventional recommendation for a certain Mr. Willspaugh, a lawyer who wanted to settle in Detroit and whose "conduct and character justifies the anticipation of his friends that he will be both useful and respectable." But just in case the merchant failed to get the point, the letter was dated August 20, 1825—three years to the day from the merchant's still unpaid note. Mr. Willspaugh's fate remains unknown, but Williams went on to redeem his note in 1827 and to enjoy a prosperous career as merchant and mayor of Detroit. There were three points to keep in mind if you were one of Billy James's "friends": you could never forget who called the shots, you had to know who else was on the team, and you would come in for some very nice payoffs.

An endless supply of salt, the best advice available on how to extract it, a state premium, a company-owned boomtown, and a far-flung string of tractable dealers—there was one thing still to be done. Since the solar salt vats did not happen to be situated on a naturally navigable watercourse, a cheap method of transportation had to be devised. Someone would have to build a river.

THE ERIE CANAL

Men were dreaming about a link between the Hudson River and Lake Erie well before William James turned his mind to salt. Much of the credit for seeing the dream through has always gone to William's old friend DeWitt Clinton, who helped draw up the original and unusually accurate cost estimate ($6 million), accompanied the survey team, and served on the Canal Commission from 1810 to 1824. So closely identified was he with the Erie Canal that its opponents sometimes ridiculed it as "Clinton's Ditch."

Back in Ireland at the time of William's emigration there had been much interest in interior navigation, and a canal had been started between Dublin and the Shannon. William was one of the signatories on an early statement advocating the Erie Canal, and in 1817 he no doubt did his part in persuading the legislature and governor of the state of New York to pass an act underwriting the costs of construction. As the digging proceeded, remote villages in the path of the new waterway—Rochester, Utica—turned into boomtowns, and Albany itself entered a period of rapid growth and prosperity. From 1820 to 1825, the year the canal was completed, the city's population grew from 12,600 to 16,000. Five years later it reached 24,200, almost doubling in a decade. A traveler found Albany "a place of great resort and bustle. That part of the town, in which was our hotel, seemed full of stages and waggons."

Well before the canal was completed, William realized that the Albany waterfront would have to be renovated. He chaired a public meeting at the Albany Chamber of Commerce (of which he was a vice president), and in short order an act was passed "authorising the construction of a basin in the city of Albany, at the termination of the Erie and Champlain Canals." He was elected president of the Albany Basin Commission, and within days the newly formed body was issuing stock. A construction crew went into operation building a lengthy "pier" out in the Hudson that ran parallel to the shoreline, thus creating an enclosed basin in which canal barges could dock. Albany's waterfront was virtually doubled. One hundred twenty-three lots were laid out on the pier, and in

July 1825, a few months before the completion of the canal, there was a grand auction of all this newly created real estate. Not only was there now more land for stores but owners would henceforth get a cut in the tolls charged to canal boats for entering the basin. William bought forty-eight lots. Once again, he had a sure thing. Although construction costs totaled $133,000, the auction alone netted the corporation $194,000. The basin was already in the black without having collected a single toll, and its stock jumped from $100 to $160. It should not be necessary to add that William was one of the largest stockholders.

As the day approached when the waters of the Atlantic and the Great Lakes would be mingled, a celebration was planned. William headed the list of names on the planning committee, which decided to place a series of cannons at intervals along the full length of the waterway, so that as one sounded within earshot of the next the successive discharges would resound from Buffalo to Albany, and back again. It was a vivid demonstration of the grand geographic strategies that had animated William's restless ventures. The public would literally hear the steady conquest of vast spaces.

On the great day itself, November 2, 1825, the cannons boomed, a decorated barge that had left Buffalo a few days earlier arrived in Albany, and an endless number of toasts and compliments were offered. The chief address of the day, delivered at the capitol and printed in the *Albany Argus*, was by William James. His private library is known to have included several collections of speeches, and this oration confirms that the man of affairs was in his way an aspiring man of letters. He quoted an "eloquent Frenchman" (as American writers are wont to do), frequently invoked the sublime, and concluded with a quotation in verse prophesying the future:

> *On Erie's banks where Tigers steal along,*
> *And the dread Indian chaunts a dismal song,*
> *There shall the flocks on thymy pastures stray*
> *And shepherds dance at summer's opening day.*

It must have been a curious spectacle, the stalwart Scotch-Irish magnate rolling his r's and invoking shepherds dancing in the dawn on Lake Erie's thymy shore.

The basic idea in William's speech was that the building of the Erie Canal represented an epochal stage in the building of the nation. The successful revolt from English tyranny had been followed by a unifying constitution. Now there was union on other levels, an integrating of the coast with the interior, and an organized deployment of "our fiscal or physical resources." "Independence and the Constitution, are the pillars of our Liberty, and the great work we this day celebrate is the splendid arch which gives elegance, durability and strength to our temple of Freedom."* Unlike the monuments of the Old World, the pyramids and mausoleums and sarcophagi built by the "slaves of superstition" and dedicated to death, the canal was a life-giving creation, a cornucopia so fecund that it would endlessly "unfold its munificence and riches as human industry and wants require them."

William's familiar sentiments about America's national destiny, his reliance on the sedate and balanced Latinisms of the early republic, his obvious assumption that poetry and oratory belong to the public world, and his continuing use of "we" rather than "I" are all slightly misleading. His speech was not, or not merely, the communal statement it pretended to be but a highly personal evocation in which a brilliantly resourceful man, standing at the peak of his success, brought out into the open his vision of things. It was a powerful man's expression of a sort of public ecstasy—a word William used twice. For the one and only time in his life, he found a way to put into words the arrogant strength with which he projected himself onto others. There is a vital continuity between William's oratory and his son's and grandsons' quests for audiences— Henry Sr.'s persistent appearances behind the lectern, Henry Jr.'s doomed effort to write for the London stage, and William's remarkable push to make philosophy public and practical. These James men all laid hands on large public spaces for their powerfully integrative visions.

Appropriately, the ancestral vision was vast and watery.† William remembered the Phoenicians and the civilizing role of trade in the Mediterranean Sea, and he predicted that the Erie Canal would transform the Great Lakes into America's own Mediterranean: "The extent of our marine coasts will be more than doubled, by the additional extent of our inland shores." "The work is finished," he exulted; "the great Lakes are united with the Oceans of the World!" There was not only no limit to the "power of mind over matter," but the mind seemed to be a second creator co-equal with God—seemed capable of effecting a basic rearrangement in the original division between the waters and dry land. As William spoke, great liquid expanses constantly rose to the surface of his oration—the Baltic, the Black Sea, the Nile, the Danube, the Elbe,

* The same metaphor showed up two years earlier at the Rochester canal celebration, when the band played the Masonic hymn "The Temple Is Completed."
† In his fictionalized autobiography, Henry Sr. had his father emigrate from Somerset County, "with its watery horizons."

the "Wolga," the "gulphs, straights, &c" of Europe, "the yet unmeasured coast of Lake Superior, the extensive region of the Rainy Lake, and the Lake of the Woods." One is reminded of all the water springing and flowing in other American writers—in Thoreau's Walden Pond, Melville's South Seas, Mark Twain's Mississippi River, Whitman's East River in "Crossing Brooklyn Ferry," and Hart Crane's Caribbean. For William James just as for these later and better writers, the act of democratic augury seemed to involve the invocation of bodies of water.

But as the world turned fluid for William, his deeply rancorous spirit lost its bearings. While praising DeWitt Clinton as the canal's chief begetter, the speaker suddenly dredged up the old political quarrel with the Regency. This was a serious mistake, and not simply because Van Buren himself was in the audience. Edwin Croswell, editor of the *Albany Argus*, the Regency's chief newspaper, could not allow William's vindictive act to pass. Acknowledging the "peculiar clearness and strength" of the speech, he scolded the speaker for allowing his "partiality for Mr. Clinton" to revive "by-gone or existing differences of opinion." The grand celebration was "not the proper occasion" for this.

NATURAL TEMPER OR CALCULATION?

A portrait of William James from 1822 shows a heavy man with a broad face, his chin firmly set. His dark shoulders and light waistcoat spreading to the sides and bottom of the canvas suggest a man solidly planted and absolutely sure of his ground. He is impressively stalwart, and yet the portraitist (Ezra Ames of Albany) was not able to exhibit very much of William's character. One thing we do not see—and which we learn about from two surviving anecdotes—is that this man was possessed of a great and righteous and truly formidable anger.

The first story comes from the autobiography of Thurlow Weed, a shrewd political journalist in Albany who helped transform the anti-Masonic furor of the late 1820s into the American Whig Party. Weed got the story from a "son of Mr. [William] James"—which son remains unknown—sometime before 1832. Although the story may be inaccurate in some respects, it shows that William was widely regarded as one whose anger must not be aroused.

In 1818 a young lawyer named James King got William's consent to marry his firstborn daughter, Ellen, the only child he'd had with Mary Ann Connolly. William insisted on one condition, that King "abstain from politics and devote himself exclusively to his profession." This was probably not the first time, and it was certainly not the last, that William tried to dictate the professions of his sons and sons-in-law. King accepted the stipulation, but when the bitter quarrel between Clinton and Van Buren broke out, the young man could not keep still. He sent a "vehement article, highly denunciatory of Governor Clinton," to the *Argus*, which published it without naming the author. When the governor demanded the writer's identity, the editor found himself in a pinch. As a gentleman, he could not refuse Clinton's request, but he also did not want to dash King's up-and-coming marriage to Ellen James. To find a way out of this dilemma, Van Buren, the future President, called together his chief advisers and confederates, among them William L. Marcy, a future governor of New York, and Benjamin Knower, another Albany bigwig:

> After much and anxious consideration, it was decided that Mr. Knower should call on Mr. Isaiah Townsend, a mutual friend of Mr. James and Governor Clinton, and endeavor, by stating some extenuating circumstances, to appease Mr. James. This, however, was no easy task, for Mr. James was of a stern and implacable disposition. But Mr. Townsend knew his man, drove him up to Waterford, drank two or three glasses of gin and water, and succeeded in smoothing over the difficulty.

On June 17, 1818, the wedding came off as planned. Ellen died five years later at the age of twenty-three, but King went on to become a prominent Albany lawyer. Indeed, the source for the next anecdote was originally kept among King's files before being turned over to the New-York Historical Society—a violation of professional trust that would have outraged William. Perhaps in the end King had his revenge for having to accede to William's high-handed ultimatum.

It seems that an indictment had been lodged against the Syracuse Salt Company. At issue, apparently, was the height of a dam and the extent of a millpond—questions which would decide whose land was to be flooded. William himself went up to Syracuse to take charge, and as he traveled he was "in great straight [sic] and doubt about . . . how I was to commence the business of defence." As the case had not yet been resolved by Saturday, William decided he had better send the company attorney a report before the mail closed down for Sunday.

The scarcely legible letter he dashed off shows even more clearly than the Erie Canal oration how William imposed himself in public affairs. He had no doubt whatever that the complainants were motivated by an old feud and the hope of defrauding him of his rightful holdings, and he seized the offense from the outset: "I replied to the common civilities of every man as soon [as] I landed, that I had come to defend myself and property against an insidious combination." Although he confessed a sly doubt as to whether his motive was "natural temper or calculation," the tactic worked: "This made a noise and excited the attention and interest of every one . . . [and] in a few hours fifty of the principal inhabitants were seen examining around the pond." If William was a forceful agitator, his being the principal local capitalist must have also had an effect. He was able to uncover so many "hidden or obscure acts" that he was certain he could prove the existence of a "wreckless conspiracy." One of the "conspirators" was Henry Seymour, a longtime enemy and anti-Clintonian whom William's agent, Moses DeWitt Burnet, had once tried without success to have removed from the Canal Commission. Three others—David S. Colvin, John Wilkinson, and Thomas T. Davis—happen to be the same men who organized Syracuse's police force a few years later.

The letter concludes with these scrawled trial notes from the man at the center of the storm:

12 oc [o'clock] testimony suspended leaving many witnesses uncalled—address to Jury from Strong done in admirable style—Davis Wilkinson and Wood disappear—Colvin braving it out—it is now 7 oc—the mail closing[—]Mr. Noxon 3 hours at his address—it will at least take 2 more—he is sifting the subject [illegible word]—will probably close with more spice—at 9 to 10—after that the District Attorney and Mr. Laurence [?] will sum up—and as it will be near the sabbath I hope the Jury will acquit themselves as honest men in two minutes . . .

Wm James

The jury seems to have decided against William. Surviving legal documents that appear to represent later phases of this case suggest that William's letter was written a few months before his death, and that his position was so weak, matters were resolved only by a financial settlement between his estate and Seymour and Colvin. One could say that William died fighting, and fighting needlessly. As the end of his life approached, he not only had not lost his quickness to defend his property, his undeviating belief in the justice of his aims, his great powers of attention and endurance, his readiness to bypass "common civilities" when necessary, and his bold "wrecklessness" in battle, but he was more grasping and aggressive than ever. The young Ulsterman who had come to America full of enthusiasm for its revolutionary defiance of George III had made of himself an arbitrary monarch, prickly, suspicious, tyrannical, restless, and unhappy.

DUTY OF BENEVOLENCE THE ONLY ENJOYMENT

In the half-fictionalized autobiography composed by Henry Sr., the narrator likes to think of all the food his parents salted away for charitable purposes: "I remember that my father was in the habit of having a great quantity of beef and pork and potatoes laid by in the beginning of winter for the needy poor, the distribution of which my mother regulated; and no sooner was the original stock exhausted than the supply was renewed with ungrudging hand." This picture of William James's domestic philanthropy is probably not overdrawn. He served on the executive committee of the Albany Colonization Society, which wanted to send free people of color back to West Africa. He was on a fund-raising committee that supported the Greeks' struggle for independence from Turkey. When cholera struck Albany in 1832, he signed a petition urging steamboat proprietors to cease offering free spirits to travelers and he gave $100 "for the relief of the Sick Poor." These benevolent causes were only a few of those to which William generously contributed. He gave because of his strong sense of public involvement and responsibility, but also because philanthropy offered the kind of outlet for his managerial genius that did not call up the organized resistance his high-handed ways increasingly aroused. Philanthropy confirmed his success and power without requiring him to defend or justify them.

There is a strange and bitter fragment of a letter in the manuscript collection of the New York Public Library that expresses the deep solace William found in public benevolence. The fragment, only a couple of sentences, appears to represent his concluding assessment of his life. His unknown correspondent evidently judged the passage as worth preserving for the writer's sake, for he carefully scissored William's signature from the end of the letter and pasted it onto the fragment.

> . . . Tell me you who have been poor and gained wealth—if your Joys or happiness realy encreased with [it] in proportion—if they have I pledge myself that it has been from duty of benevolence and from no other enjoyment . . .
>
> Wm. James

What provoked this succinct and gloomy statement? Another case of what he saw as political ingratitude, the opposition of some business cabal, a desolate sense of distance from wife and children? Such explanations seem all too likely, yet there is no need to look for a specific cause. William's angry dissatisfaction was the inevitable last stage of the supervisory, supercompetent, and restlessly jealous man he was. He had been a man of force, and now he gathered all his passionate energy for a final expression of disillusionment. Nothing else written by the amateur of oratory speaks with such eloquence, or explains so well why those whose task it was to compose his epitaph chose to say nothing about this great and miserable man except where he was born and when he first started out on the Albany waterfront.

Chapter 3

■ ■ ■

THE MOTHER:
CATHARINE BARBER JAMES

The child knows his mother without anybody's help . . . The incessant contact he has with her leaves no obscurity upon that point. But he knows his father only upon his mother's testimony. He refuses to acknowledge any one as lawful father, whom she does not first acknowledge as sole husband.

—HENRY JAMES, SR.

MOTHERS AND WARRIORS

"Ma" was what Henry Sr. called his mother long after he had grown up. In 1844, when she was sixty-two and he was married and had two children and was living on the border of one of Queen Victoria's private parks, he was flooded with recollections of his first incessant contact with his mother: "I confess to some potent pullings now and then dear Ma in your direction—'nursery' remembrances, and 'little back-room' remembrances come over me not infrequently which make Windsor Castle seem a great ghastly lie." He was determined to overcome these pullings, however, and he resolutely dismissed them as "only *feelings.*" Soon afterward he fell into a period of profound depression, self-loathing, and general helplessness.

To the end of his life, Henry had little to say about his feelings for his mother. In the brief and fragmentary fictionalized autobiography he began some years after her death, he characterized her in general terms only as "maternity itself in form," "a good wife and mother, nothing else." He believed she had no selfish life of her own and extolled her as "the most democratic person by temperament I ever knew." Although the man she married, William James of Albany, became one of New York State's makers and shakers in the second and third decades of the nineteenth century, able to count the most powerful American men of the time among his cronies, Henry couldn't help noticing "how much satisfaction she could take in chatting with her respectable sewing-women, and how she gravitated as a general thing into relations of the frankest sympathy with every one conventionally beneath her." Her boy was surprised by this apparently humble preference and, looking back, supposed "she felt a tacit quarrel with the fortunes of her life in that they had sought to make her a flower or a shrub, when she herself would so willingly have remained mere lowly grass."

Catharine's father, John Barber (1753–1836), on the other hand, seems to have thought of himself as a lordly tree. He had joined a company of Minutemen at the hot-blooded age of twenty-one, a year and a half before the colonies declared their independence. From 1776 on he served as captain in the New York Militia. In civilian life he became a gentleman-farmer, a state assemblyman, and a judge. When he moved to Albany in old age to live with his daughter's family, his grandson was unfavorably impressed by his obsession with "historic reading," apparently on military subjects. Unlike his two brothers, who attended Princeton, John Barber had not been well educated, and he bored his grandchildren by exercising his "tenacious memory" upon them. When called upon to display his prowess in formal composition, as when he drew up his father's epitaph or applied for a military pension, he achieved an effect of painfully stilted learning. Others remembered him as "tall, slender and very erect" and could never "forget the marked dignity of his demeanor as he entered the house of God or the impressive reverence that characterized his attitude as he stood in prayer." Henry's mother's father seems to have been conspicuously, alarmingly, stern and upright. In recollecting him, Henry made it a point to say he "never felt any affectionate leaning to him."

Of his mother's mother, Jennett Rea, on the other hand, Henry wrote that he cherished her memory. He got to know her well during her long winter visits to her daughter, and also in the summertime, when Catharine and her children traveled down the Hudson to spend a month on the Barber farm near Montgomery, New York. Henry remembered her "vivacious love of children" and her "gift of interesting them in conversation, which greatly endeared her society to me." He much preferred her sweetness and expressiveness to her husband's stoicism. It was not until long after her death, which took place when Henry was fourteen, that he was told of the religious doubts that disturbed and depressed her in her mature years. This disclosure threw his image of her into some confusion. Evidently she had been more of a stoic than he had realized, with her "equable front." Outside Henry's fictionalized memoir, nothing is known of this woman. After his death, when his son William edited the memoir, he did not put Jennett's name on the record even though he scrupulously identified the famous male members of her family. Perhaps the name was no longer remembered. Or perhaps William thought of his family (as have some biographers) as a group consisting of men only. Certainly, Jennett's and Catharine's apparent preference for obscure companions enabled Henry to feel all the more tender and sentimental about them—even as he continued to fight for his own place in the combative world of men.

Today the Jameses have become their own legend and the Barbers are forgotten, but in the early nineteenth century it was one of Catharine's relatives—and none of William's—who got extended treatment in the biographical encyclopedias of the day. Francis Barber's career had had all the dash and meteoric brilliance of his revolutionary era. After achieving early distinction as a scholar and educator, he enlisted in the fight against the British and, quickly rising to lieutenant colonel, saw action in several important battles. Remaining in service for seven years, he played a key role in quelling the recurring mutinies, helped Baron von Steuben train troops at Valley Forge, and was called on for several delicate assignments by General Washington. In February 1783, at war's end, shortly before a celebratory dinner with the commander in chief and other officers, the thirty-two-year-old veteran and his horse were crushed by a falling tree. For as long as the events of the Revolutionary War remained fresh in mind, Francis Barber was a byword for heroic promise tragically undone.

Catharine had had a second uncle who won renown in the war, William Barber, who served as Lafayette's Division Inspector at Yorktown. Over four decades later, when an American historian interviewed the Frenchman, he told a story about William's courage and devotion to duty. William had been sent by Lafayette to deliver a message to another French officer, and as he carried out this mission,

a cannon ball passed so near his body as to inflict a slight bruise and cause his body to swell in an extraordinary manner. "You are badly wounded," said Viomenil to him hastily. "Yes I am wounded," replied Barber. "Hasten to your quarters," said Viomenil, "and find a surgeon." "No," said Barber, remaining firm in his place, "I have an order from the General and I cannot leave the field until that is executed."

William Barber died in his early forties, when Catharine, his niece and Henry's future mother, was still single and in her teens. Thus, by the time her children were old enough to want to hear about her heroic uncles, they had become distant legends, while their one surviving brother, John, had hardened into a stubborn and bombastic old man. Catharine may well have felt that an age of splendor had been succeeded by an age of brass—that she and her father formed part of an embarrassing descent from Olympus. Her son Henry thought it was strange that she did not care to recount the military honors her uncles had won. When her children coaxed her into telling of their exploits in the Revolutionary War, "she seemed someway ashamed, as well as I could gather, of having had distinguished relations."

When the Civil War erupted decades later, Catharine's gifted grandson, Henry Jr., felt a strong sense of military obligation, even though he did not enlist. He, too, proved to be an avid reader of soldiers' memoirs, like his great-grandfather John Barber. When World War I broke out, he became, unlike his revolutionary forebears, an energetic and even jingoistic supporter of England. One of his stories, "Owen Wingrave," tells of a young man who bravely pays the ultimate price—wins a grave—for resisting his family's military heritage.

A HANDMAID'S TALE

After Catharine Barber and William James got married, according to a family anecdote, her husband "saw a lady coming up the steps of his house, rose from the table at which he was absorbed in work, went to the door and said 'he was sorry Mrs. James was not in.' But the poor lady was herself his newly married wife, and cried out to him not to be 'so absent-minded.' " The story hints at the dismal role Catharine was asked to play in life—the eternal substitute, the one who is always filling in for lamented originals. Apparently, in neither the family in which she was born nor that into which she married was Catharine able to make any strong claims for herself. Instead, she was simultaneously disregarded and depended on.

In 1796, when Catharine was still only fourteen, her future husband married Elizabeth Tillman in New York City. She died a few days after giving birth to twins, in her first year of marriage. The following year William took a second wife, Mary Ann Connolly. She died in her early twenties in her second year of marriage, leaving one child. William remained a widower for three years, and then married Catharine in 1803.

Together they had nearly three decades of married life and produced ten children in all, eight of whom survived infancy. Thriving as her predecessors had not, she would seem to be the most fortunate of William's three wives. But there was an obscure and troublesome flaw in her long marital life. As she got old, William's first two brides remained perennially young in his memory. Dying in their flower (like Catharine's brother Francis), they could have been a keen regret for William to the end of life. Catharine could not. The longer the marriage lasted, the less fresh she was for him, and vice versa.

Two of Catharine's first three children, all boys, died in infancy. When the fourth was born on June 3, 1811, yet another boy, his hold on life must have seemed terribly unsure. In christening him, his parents resurrected the name they had given their previous luckless child—Henry. It was a name much favored by the Jameses in Ireland.

Henry lived, and with him the spell was broken, for the time being. His parents produced six more children, three of each sex, and all survived into adulthood. With eight children of her own to care for, and three from her husband's two previous marriages, Catharine clearly had her work cut out for her. In 1827 her oldest daughter, Jannet (after Jennett Rea and sometimes spelled Jeannette), wrote a letter to a distant member of the family that vividly evokes the busy scene at home: "Ma says she must make a thousand apologies, for not answering your letter, but she thinks if you were in our *nursery*, for half an hour you would think an *apology* quite unnecessary."

At the time the daughter was delegated to do her mother's writing, she was only thirteen but already wrote letters like a veteran. There were two younger daughters, aged four and six, who had to be looked after, and probably a seven-year-old grandchild, Mary Ann King, whose mother had died four years earlier. In addition, Catharine's next younger sister, Janette Barber Gourlay, had died a few months earlier, and several of her eight children, ranging in age from one to sixteen, had apparently been taken into the James nursery. And as if all these children were not enough to care for, Jannet's older brother Henry had a grave leg injury that required the strictest attention. Of course there were several servants to help out, and perhaps some adult relatives as well.

Catharine's domestic duties and hardships did not let up as her children matured. Setting aside Howard, her last child, who was born in 1828, when she was forty-six, and who proved a singular burden to those who tried to manage him, she not only suffered the grief of seeing two of her five sons and all three of her daughters die before her (quite apart from the two children who died in infancy), but she had to take charge of *their* children as well. As she entered her fifties and then her sixties in her large house at 43 North Pearl Street in Albany, she seems to have been continually occupied with the numerous grandchildren who had been dumped on her. Letter-writing Jannet died in 1842, leaving a girl and two boys. A daughter-in-law died four years later, adding two more children, aged five and ten, to be taken in, along with their father, John Barber James. In the 1850s there were to be more catastrophic deaths, leaving still more bereft grandchildren to be gathered up and guarded. It is clear that Catharine paid a very heavy price for her strength, longevity, and dependability. In the eyes of her family, she was seen as the surviving caretaker and little else, so that when she finally suffered an "attack" of her own in 1857, at the age of seventy-five, her son Henry wrote (from a French seaside resort) that he had "a fixed persuasion that you will never be laid aside from the activity you like, and which has so long blessed every one about you."

The grandchildren brought up by Catharine loved to tell stories about her warmhearted unselfishness. In 1920, one of these wards, Katharine Van Buren Wilson, looked back almost three-quarters of a century to the time when her mother died and she moved into the "dear old nursery" at what she called the James Homestead. The girl was eternally grateful to her father, a son of ex-President Martin Van Buren, for not separating her from Grandma Barber, whose generosity became proverbial:

> They tell a story about her going to the door one winter afternoon, and a poor beggar was there[.] Without any hesitation she took off her flannel petticoat and gave it to her. Late in the evening she complained of being cold and her niece Miss Libby Gourlay, who lived with her[,] upon examining why she was cold said "Why Aunt James you have no flannel petticoat on. My goodness, said Dear Grandma, I forgot all about it. I gave it to a poor woman at the door.

Whenever Henry brought his own family back to Albany for a visit, Catharine's large home struck her grandchild Henry Jr., the future novelist, as "a nurseried and playroomed orphanage." He was charmed by the way "the children of her lost daughters and daughters-in-law overflowed there, mainly as girls." Although he noted how much his grandmother was taken for granted whenever "the surviving sons-in-law and sons occasionally and most trustingly looked in," he too felt perfectly at home in her large and generous household: it was like an inn where the service was exemplary and no bill was ever presented. Still, the sharp-eyed boy noted that his grandmother was always "groaning—ever so gently and dryly." She seemed to have "a resigned consciousness of complications and accretions" as she "dispensed a hospitality seemingly as joyless as it was certainly boundless." There was, however, one great pleasure still reserved for her:

> the novels, at that time promptly pirated, of Mrs. Trollope and Mrs. Gore, of Mrs. Marsh, Mrs. Hubback and the Misses Kavanagh and Aguilar, whose very names are forgotten now, but which used to drive her away to quiet corners whence her figure comes back to me bent forward on a table with the book held out at a distance and a tall single candle placed, apparently not at all to her discomfort, in that age of sparer and braver habits, straight between the page and her eyes.

It is worth noting that this woman who found such a refuge in novels written by other women did not leave behind a single extant letter.

LEGACIES

Catharine Barber James found another refuge in her four Gourlay nieces—Catharine, Margaret, Jeannette, and Elizabeth. After her husband's death, she had a trust drawn up to provide for them, and in her will she was even more generous, leaving them another $15,000 and "all and singular the household furniture and apparatus, parlor ornaments, plate, linen, wearing apparel and other property of every kind whatsoever (family portraits alone excepted)." Although her two surviving daughters-in-law might reasonably have expected some of this bounty (and one of the grandchildren always remembered the furniture and china), Catharine emphatically wanted the Gourlays to have all of it. Of course, the remnant of her estate was left to her own proper descendants, but all she had to say about the division was that it should follow "the statute of descents and distribution which may be then in force in this state." The dryness and shortness of this provision is a far cry from the laborious language and repeated codicils devoted to her nieces. Perhaps she was afraid they would be cheated of their legacy or given the cold shoulder by the proud James clan. If so, she had reason. As the four unmarried Gourlay sisters died and were buried, one by one, in the large James plot in Albany Rural Cemetery, they were treated as if they had been family retainers, placed on the very edge in two neat rows and given four identical and modest-sized brownstone markers.

Last wills and testaments can be as revealing as tombstones, and those of Catharine and William afford a startling glimpse of the inner life of their marriage. When William drew up his will not long before his death, he assigned $3,000 for the "maintenance education and advancement" of the Gourlays. Of course, it was to be expected that he would be less generous toward his in-laws than his wife would be. The shocker was his stingy treatment of Catharine herself. Apart from the "mansion house" and its belongings, all of which she got, this is the slender provision made for her from an estate worth well over a million dollars:

> Desiring that my family after my decease should live respectably, but at the same time prudently and circumspectly, I further give devise and bequeath unto my said wife for her own support and for the education and support of our children, an annuity of three thousand dollars . . . during the period of her natural life.

For a man of William's great wealth, there was something extraordinarily tight-fisted, offensive, and arrogant in these terms. Not only was $3,000 an inadequate sum for a widow accustomed to a standard of living that was more than liberal, but at the time William drew up his will Catharine still had four children fourteen or younger to support, not counting grandchildren. Most insulting of all, the annuity was a life estate, meaning that when Catharine died she would have nothing of her own to bequeath, aside from her house, furnishings, and personal effects.

After setting down her meager allowance, William added a remarkably high-handed paragraph: "The foregoing devise and bequests to my said wife are intended to be and I hereby declare them to be in lieu and full satisfaction of her dower in my estate." According to the statutes of New York State, a widow was guaranteed as a minimum a certain fraction, traditionally one-third, of her husband's estate. It was up to *her* to decide whether to take this "dower" or accept what she was willed by her husband. Catharine's presumptuous husband was trying to usurp her dower right.

William's long, complicated, and curiously retentive will was destined to undergo a fourteen-year probation in New York's courts, and in the end all its key provisions were torn to pieces in the contestatory process. But the first part to be successfully challenged was the part that concerned his wife of twenty-nine years. Within a few months of his death, Catharine decided she would rather take her dower than the $3,000 annuity. This aspect of the proceedings provoked by the will was open and shut, and the judge who had to try to settle the intricate consequences for the remainder of the document, Chancellor Reuben H. Walworth, was plainly struck by the deceased's hollow assumption of authority over his wife: "In the present case, the testator seems to have taken it for granted either that he had a right to bar the wife of her dower by a specific provision in lieu thereof, or that she would elect to receive that provision."

The testator's vain effort to dictate to his wife from beyond the grave was a public announcement that the two did not have a good understanding with each other. He seems to have regarded her as a sort of obedient handmaiden or superior domestic servant. She was the one who produced his children and ran his household, and for these services she was to be salaried for life but to get no share in the estate, which, bypassing her, would eventually go to his descendants. At a later point in his will he explicitly gave the "tuition and custody" of his children to his wife—an unusual stipulation and one which once again displays an extraordinary assumption of total domestic control.

Catharine's joylessness and constant sighing and groaning; her contestation of her husband's supervisory will; his own great bitterness during his last years: these look very much like the lingering traces of an unsatisfactory union. Certain large-scale patterns discernible in their children's lives suggest the same inference. On the rare occasions when Henry recalled his parents' relationship, a strange, dry legalism rose to the surface of his prose:

> For example. I myself am the offspring of a marriage on my father's part with three successive women; a marriage-union which was legally ratified doubtless by whatever in these new spiritual latitudes of humanity calls itself church or state. Now if this be so, then it will be safe to infer that church and state, in sanctioning my father's union with his three wives, had no intention to disobey but only to obey the Divine will in relation to marriage. And this inference again proves that, so far as the opinion of our existing church and state goes . . . marriage is *not*, in its civic aspect, the spiritual union which it is in heaven, of one and the same man with one and the same woman.

Henry's arid reasoning, his insistence that his parents' union was not a spiritual one, and his leaping generalizations about *all* unions probably reflect an old and troubling situation at home. Perhaps this particular child became famously devoted to his own wife and children in order to compensate for the coldness and distance of the home he had grown up in.

Larger patterns of growth and generational affiliation in the James clan tell the same story. Of the five sons Catharine produced, only the oldest followed William in business. (William's first marriage produced a son, Robert, who joined him in a mercantile firm and died soon after.) Looking back from the early twentieth century, Henry Jr. was struck by "our sudden collective disconnectedness" from business—*our* referring to the "whole kinship." Writing with unusual emphasis (and some exaggeration), he flatly declared that "the rupture with my grandfather's tradition and attitude was complete; we were never in a single case, I think, for two generations, guilty of a stroke of business." There is no better testimony to Catharine's quiet resentment of her forceful husband than this refusal of their sons to enter into partnership with him. Fittingly, Gus, the only one of her sons who *did* become a businessman, was remembered as being a "very rigid (& somewhat harsh!) disciplinarian." And like his father, Gus tended to play a very rough game: once he forced the president of the Mohawk and Hudson Railroad to resign by getting the board to slash his remuneration from $4,000 to $500. *

In 1845 Catharine and some other members of the James family subscribed for a large plot in the newly developed Albany Rural Cemetery. It was probably soon after this purchase that a massive brownstone monument, tall and square and topped with a draped urn, was erected to the memory of William James—and to his first two wives. William's epitaph occupied one side of the stone. His first wife's name and dates occupied another:

ELIZABETH TILLMANN
WIFE OF
WILLIAM JAMES
BORN MARCH 5, 1774
DIED JUNE 9, 1797

A third side was given to his second wife:

MARY A. CONNOLLY
WIFE OF
WILLIAM JAMES
DIED OCT. 8, 1800
IN HER 22ND YEAR†

* Gus's letters show frequent transposed spellings ("rouge" for *rogue*, "vauge" for *vague*) and lapses from correct grammar ("800 shares was sold this day"). Young Henry Jr. caught his mispronunciation of "the celebrated 'Rosseau,' " and also the derision he provoked in other family members.
† The obituary in the *Albany Register* for October 14, 1800, says she died "in her 23rd year."

The fourth side was blank, no doubt reserved for Catharine, who finally died in 1859, twenty-seven years after her husband. But instead of having her name and dates chiseled on the one free side, her few surviving children had them placed immediately beneath those of William's first wife:

CATHARINE BARBER

WIFE OF

WILLIAM JAMES

BORN

APRIL 5, 1782

DIED

AUGUST 18, 1859

Maybe the grain on the fourth side of the stone was too rotten to sustain the stonemason's chisel. Or maybe there was some other reason. Whatever the explanation may have been, the effect of this arrangement of names is blatant and unmistakable. Catharine not only occupies an inferior position, but the one salient detail regarding her and her two predecessors, aside from their having one and the same husband (whose name is repeated in full in his three wives' epitaphs), is that the second wife—the Catholic one—died "in her 22nd year."

THE ONLY ENGLISH BLOOD

Henry's second child, Henry Jr., born in 1843, arrived long after both his grandfathers had died, but he did get to know his two grandmothers. Elizabeth Walsh, who died in 1847, he barely remembered, but having reached the age of sixteen by the time Grandma James died, he felt he had a sharp impression of her. In general, young Henry Jr. was an extraordinarily retentive observer. His strong and direct impression of Catharine's unhappiness is undoubtedly to be trusted. But, strangely, he was mistaken in an important point he wished to make about his father's mother—her ancestry.

> She represented for us in our generation the only English blood—that of both her own parents—flowing in our veins . . . If I could freely have chosen moreover it was precisely from my father's mother that, fond votary of the finest faith in the vivifying and characterising force of mothers, I should have wished to borrow it.

Henry Jr. liked to think she had transmitted her fine English traits to her offspring and their descendants, tempering the family's cruder Scotch-Irish blood by a lifetime of devoted, motherly service. In actuality, the grandmother he thought he knew best had descended from Scots Presbyterians residing in the so-called Scot's Quarters, County Longford, Ireland. Her Englishness was a fable, a product, perhaps, of his own pronounced Anglophilia.

So not even Catharine's observant grandson got her right. In death as in life, she nourished others' "faith in the vivifying . . . force of mothers."

Chapter 4

■ ■ ■

GROWING UP
IN THE JAMES FAMILY

The heroine of Henry James, Jr.'s novel *The Wings of the Dove* (1902) is the sole surviving descendant of an old New York family characterized as an "immense extravagant unregulated cluster, with free-living ancestors, handsome dead cousins, lurid uncles, beautiful vanished aunts, persons all busts and curls." The novel tells us no more about this intriguing ancestry than what we get in this compressed, allusive passage. A few years after composing it, Henry Jr. hinted in a preface to the novel that he had been drawing on private memories, of which he hoped to offer a detailed exposition somewhere else. The story, however, would require considerable delicacy in the telling, the difficulties being such as "rather to defy than to encourage exact expression."

By 1912 the time to attempt exact expression had come. James set out to compose a "Family Book" that would commemorate his older brother, William, and the clan from which he had sprung, a project that evolved into the memoir *A Small Boy and Others*. Bringing back his earliest mid-century memories of his father's Albany kinship, James emphasized the break in continuity between William of Albany's devotion to business and his children's devotion to leisure and summed up their story as a "chronicle of early deaths, arrested careers, broken promises, orphaned children." But he refrained from going into much detail concerning all these tragic events. Instead, he crafted the impression that the Jameses had been a glamorous, happy-go-lucky tribe who had lived to "the sound of fiddles and the popping of corks" and that there had been nothing sinister or sordid (let alone ordinary) in their various fates. He also implied he had been too young to be trusted with the truth: as his father's siblings, nephews, and nieces one after another suddenly became "mysterious and legendary," the only explanations he was given were "unfathomed silences and significant headshakes."

But fiddles and popped champagne corks were not the only sounds James heard, or heard of. There were also racking coughs, screams of grief or pain, the sharp report of a family suicide, and all the other multiple, unrecorded sounds of a great family undergoing something it is no exaggeration to call an extended crack-up. Looking at Henry Sr. and his children, particularly William, Henry, and Alice, from our own time, we see a family distinguished by their writings. Looking at them from the first half of the nineteenth century, however, we see a small band of survivors who, through great effort and by drawing on what was darkest in their lives, turned catastrophe into achievement.

William of Albany no doubt had every reason to expect his daughters to live long and happy lives and his sons to do as he had done—labor in their professions, forge networks, pull strings for the good of all, produce wealth. Starting from scratch, he had not only created a great financial empire for them to inherit and manage but he saw to it that they were given every advantage—outstanding education, sound religious training, a great deal of freedom, and many pleasant amenities. The results were: his sons turned into fashionable gentlemen who lived in idleness, or they lost their faith and turned to strange enthusiasms, or they squandered their patrimony in New York's gambling dens or on alcohol or opium. And if there was one thing the sons and daughters most agreed on doing, it was dying in their prime: Robert at twenty-four, Ellen at twenty-two, Ellen King at twenty-six, Jannet at twenty-eight, John Barber at forty, Edward at thirty-eight, Catharine at thirty-three. At a time when the life expectancy of Englishmen who reached adulthood and lived in easy circumstances was thought to be over fifty, almost all of Henry Sr.'s brothers and sisters died shockingly early.

Compared to another famous nineteenth-century progenitor, the Reverend Lyman Beecher, William of Albany seems singularly cursed. Both of these founding fathers were orthodox Calvinists with exactly the same number of children who reached maturity, seven sons and four daughters. Beecher, however, would have had no trouble adding "& Sons" to *his* shingle. All seven of his boys followed him into the ministry, one of them, Henry Ward, becoming the best-known Congregational preacher of his time. Unlike William's daughters, two of Beecher's became spectacular achievers in their own right, Harriet writing *Uncle Tom's Cabin*, Catharine founding home economics. Where the Beecher family annals show what it was possible for a nineteenth-century patriarch to leave behind, those of the James family attest to the operation of a nemesis or doom no less awesome than the founding parent's vigor.

Thanks to Henry Sr., *doom* was not to be the final word on the James family. With the Beechers we are mostly confined to an honorable and strenuous past that has faded away like ink that turns brown and spidery (*Uncle Tom's Cabin* being the obvious exception). In the Jameses we confront forms of ambition, pretension, wild risk, instability, and dis-integration that seem endlessly productive, disturbing, ambiguous, and modern.

FREE WHITE MALES AND FREE WHITE FEMALES

Exactly what happened to the dynasty William of Albany thought he founded cannot be known with certainty. The silent headshakes that young Henry Jr. remembered, his own acts of silence in writing his memoirs or recalling his inspiration for *The Wings of the Dove*, and the burning of letters by him and other members of the family have all had an irreversible effect. There is not much evidence of Henry Sr.'s early life at home, and what little we know is strangely self-contradictory. This much seems safe to say: to grow up in the household created by William of Albany and Catharine Barber James was to live in the midst of huge forces not at all under control. Were the children meant to live for freedom and pleasure, or to submit to authority and live with a sense of guilt? Were they to take great luxuries for granted, or to be hard workers? The progeny of one of the richest and most powerful men in the nation, would they inherit their father's mantle, or suffocate under it, or what?

In 1810, the year before Henry Sr.'s birth, the federal census marshal stopped at the Jameses' house near the corner of State and Green Streets. Instead of writing down the inhabitants' names, ages, and relationships (information that was not recorded until the 1850 census), this official merely indicated the number of household residents who belonged to various categories on his census form. There was one "free white female" between the ages of ten and fifteen, who must have been Ellen, daughter of William's second wife. The "free white male" under ten was undoubt-edly Augustus, then three years old, and two of the three males between ten and fifteen were his half brothers, the twins Robert and William, both thirteen. The parents, William and Catharine, are also easily iden-tifiable. But beyond these six members of the "nuclear" family, the census marshal noted the presence of no less than eight additional people. There was a third free white male between the ages of ten and fifteen, three free white males aged sixteen to twenty-five, and a free white female under ten. Some of these unidentifiable individuals may have been employees, as William's place of business was in the same building as his home. Most were probably servants: years later, when Henry Sr. wrote his fictionalized autobiography, he recalled fraternizing with the coachman, the waiter, the cook, "the good-natured chambermaids," and the "out-door servant" who took care of the rabbits, poultry, and pigeons. After the enumerator had counted all the free whites in the prescribed age and gender categories, he wrote the number 3 in the catch-all slot, "all other persons." Some of these may have been slaves, for in 1810 the ownership of human beings was still legal in the state of New York.

Regardless of its exact composition, the James household remained a large, mixed collectivity, in some ways loosely organized, in others tightly, but in most respects very different from American families in the year 2000. The names William and Catharine gave their children, for instance, suggest a much less atomized notion of individual identity. Not only were many of the children named after grandparents and other kinfolk, but when two of the children died in infancy their names were revived and reassigned to later children, Henry and John Barber. If there was anything unusual in this, there is no evidence Henry ever reflected on his name's prior ownership. Even stranger (for us) was the chain of title for the name of his youngest sister, Ellen King. She was William's fourth and last daughter, and when she was born in 1823, she was given both the Christian *and* the married name of his first daughter, who had been born in 1800 to Mary Connolly (dead in her twenty-second year). What is most arresting about this second christening is that the second Ellen King was born a few months before the first one died. Evidently it was not only obvious but accepted that the older sister was dying.* Did her parents feel that the thrifty transfer of her name would perpetuate her memory?

Whatever the circumstances and motives behind the second Ellen's naming, the constant recirculation of first names served to remind children that they took their being not as individuals but as members of a tightly connected, multi-generational group. Prior members were subtly incorporated into one's own identity, thus considerably complicating the task of defining oneself. Henrys and Williams continued to abound in

---

* The reference to "a few days illness" in the first Ellen King's obituary does not seem trustworthy (*Albany Argus*, April 22, 1823).

the James family, and the referential difficulties we face whenever we wish to single out one or the other of them reproduce the ambiguities of designation they themselves endured. In 1913 Henry Jr. pleaded with a nephew named William not to pass his well-worn name on to a son, thus saddling him with a "tiresome and graceless 'Junior.' " The novelist had hated to wear "that tag to help out my identity for forty years."

Individual names, the limits of youthful freedom, and the continuity of family authority: the three were always closely entangled in the James family, particularly when there was a question of a daughter's exchanging her last name for another. When William compelled James King, his first daughter's fiancé, to renounce regency politics in favor of a quiet legal practice, he made it clear that he regarded the family as a unit and that its position in the world was not to be compromised. Thirteen years later there was still no compromise. When the Regency electors in Albany's first ward nominated King for alderman in 1831, those in the know, like Thurlow Weed, the editor of the *Albany Evening Journal*, accurately predicted the result: "It is rumored, however, and we believe it is true, that Mr. King will not accept."

The following year, when William's second daughter, Jannet, fell in love with the scion of a New York banking family, William H. Barker, she, too, found her father planted directly in her path. Jannet was not allowed to accept Barker's proposal of marriage until he successfully endured the scrutiny of William James, who steamed down the Hudson to grill his prospective son-in-law. Like Catherine Sloper, the heroine of Henry Jr.'s 1880 novel, *Washington Square*, Jannet did not question her father's authority to supervise her courtship, but she was so anxious she made herself sick. Also, she sent her lover a letter she feared might be improper:

As Father answered your letter immediately after receiving it, I thought it unnecessary for me to do so, especially as I was extremely indisposed, but if there has been a mistake, and you have not heard from him—I am afraid my dear William, you have thought me at least unkind, in hesitating a moment to relieve your anxiety—when a word from me could so easily do it. I am so very much disappointed this morning, in neither hearing from, or seeing you, that I cannot avoid writing—although I am not convinced entirely of the propriety of doing so—Papa did intend to go to New York tomorrow afternoon . . . I can [or "dare"?] not write a word more, nothing but the fear that you had not received Fathers letter could have induced this—good bye, do not forget me.

In the end, like James King, William Barker passed muster. He and Jannet were married in the First Presbyterian Church in Albany on November 14, 1832, a month before Father's fatal stroke.

The two other James daughters got married several years after their father's death. But it is worth noticing that both daughters selected men who were the products of eminent New York families. Catharine married Robert Emmet Temple, fourth in his class at West Point, and Ellen King married a former President's son, the retiring Smith Thompson Van Buren. Thus, all four James daughters married men who were well off and enjoyed a degree of social prominence. Like most other wives of their time—but unlike the Beecher daughters—they did not seek prominence for themselves.

William of Albany's early years in eighteenth-century Ireland must have endowed him with some strong paternalistic attitudes, so that what looks authoritarian to us may have struck him as no more than a decent expectation of deference and order. America had been a land of freedom and opportunity for him, but it was also a place where the paternal duty of handing the household gods over to the next generation was apt to prove extraordinarily frustrating. In 1819, he placed a notice in an Albany newspaper that "he had withdrawn himself from the superintendence of his commercial concerns, having relinquished that part of his business to his son, who would conduct it in future, under the firm of Robert James & Co." This did not mean that William was relinquishing control of his real-estate interests and other operations. What he was turning over to his firstborn twin son, then twenty-one years old, was the old mercantile business. But problems soon developed, and the following spring he was obliged to assure suppliers and customers that he himself would remain "accountable for any engagements of the firm." Worse, Robert died a year later "while on a visit" to Geneva, New York. His twin had been educated for the ministry, and the other sons were still too young to take over the business. When one of the Bailieborough Jameses arrived early in 1824, he reported home that "my Uncle William has had many troubles, and some of those but a short time since." That fall, soon after William invested in Syracuse and its salt springs (a plunge that seems to have reinvigorated him), another notice appeared in an Albany newspaper:

> The subscriber having discontinued the Mercantile business, he has heretofore had done under the firm of ROBERT JAMES, & Co. and removed all the accounts, etc. etc. to his dwelling, No. 70 Pearl-street—He requests

all who are indebted to, or who have demands against that firm, to call
on him and settle the same.
Oct. 29, 1824   WILLIAM JAMES

And that was that as far as his original business was concerned.

A MOST INFREQUENT EXHIBITION OF AUTHORITY

Curiously, in spite of all the energy and authority William devoted to
the task of getting his children pointed in what he considered the right
direction, his son Henry remembered him as "certainly a very easy
parent," remarkably unlike the strict, supervisory figure one is tempted
to imagine. "Strive as I may," Henry wrote, "I cannot remember anything
but a most infrequent exhibition of authority towards us on my father's
part." Henry even claimed that his father was "weakly, nay painfully,
sensitive to his children's claims upon his sympathy," as if to suggest
that he should have been *more* of a disciplinarian than he was. In the
evenings, it was true, "he was fond of hearing his children read to him,
and would frequently exercise them in their studies," but aside from
encouraging them in their schoolwork, he seems to have permitted his
children to do what they pleased: "the law of the house, within the
limits of religious decency, was freedom itself." Did his father *care for*
them? "I cannot recollect," Henry wrote, "that he ever questioned me
about my out-of-door occupations, or about my companions, or showed
any extreme solicitude about my standing in school." Yet the boy seems
to have been certain of his father's love, for in later years he insisted
that no child "can help secretly feeling a property in his parents so
absolute or unconditional as to make him *a priori* sure, do what he will,
of preserving their affection." This interesting passage says that children
can't help but think of themselves as their parents' owners or masters.
    These reflections of the domestic side of a father who is known from
other sources to have been unforgettably forceful are a little surprising.
Was Henry being less than candid when he wrote his fictionalized autobiography, or was he forgetting something? When he dropped out of
college against his father's wishes, the old man exploded in indignant
wrath. Yet Henry's portrait of William is not to be dismissed, chiefly
because of what it conveys about the son's sense of his father's attitude
toward him. Basically, Henry evokes a very powerful figure who mystifies
through both his indulgence and his general remoteness. He is sympathetic and inaccessible, so perplexingly absent that a son might well

suspect him of indifference if he didn't know better. This air of distance, of hiddenness, matches what is known from other sources about William—his rapt absorption in far-flung business interests, his impressive *highness* in directing his fellow humans, his practice of dealing with his children through delegated intermediaries. During Henry's disgraceful fall 1829 term at Union College, William got one of his powerful associates, Archibald McIntyre, to write a letter begging him to come to his senses. Similarly, in 1821, after Henry's older half brother, Rev. William, had gone abroad for an extended period of rest and study, he received a letter from another of the father's cronies, Eliphalet Nott, president of Union College, advising the young man to sustain the "honour of your family" and urging numerous moral maxims à la Polonius. It was almost as if the father wanted to guide his children without risking any involvement with them.

In Henry's imagination, Father's remote benevolence was epitomized by his dressing table's unlocked cash drawer. Its bottom was always covered with loose silver, the key was generally kept in the lock, and anyone who wanted to could have helped himself. At first, when Henry's mother would ask him to bring her some change or allow him to take his "weekly stipend," he felt "the greatest practical reverence for the sacred deposit." But around the age of seven or eight he went into debt for candy with a colored neighbor ("with whom my credit was very good") and began stealing his father's change. Years later, thinking about the inexhaustible well of money, the "sacred" or "magical" drawer, he supposed that the guilt he felt for his small depredations marked the beginning of his religious life. He even suggested a comparison between William's cash drawer and the tree of the knowledge of good and evil in the book of Genesis, whose fruit it is forbidden to taste. But Henry had not been commanded never to open the sacred drawer. Whatever William's expectations were, they remained tacit.

Did William want his children to be dependent on the enormous fortune he had accumulated or did he want them to be independent? The evidence points both ways. There is no doubt that the curious will he drew up in the summer of 1832 was designed to prevent his children from indulging their habits of prodigal expenditure. Yet he himself continued to foster those habits. That very spring, for instance, at a time when a full year's tuition at Albany Academy cost $25 or $30, William's New York partner, James McBride, billed him $13 for a hobby horse, which had probably been purchased for three-year-old Howard (who spent much of his adult life trying to dry out at expensive inebriate asylums). Later that same year, as eighteen-year-old Jannet prepared for her wedding to William Barker, the bride's expenses included $11 for a comb, $16 for a bonnet, and $90 for a veil. There was no stinting in the James household. Henry and the other children grew up taking for granted a princely standard of living. They would never see the cash drawer's bottom. Their credit would always be very good. Yet they were also supposed to study hard, work, increase their capital, keep the paternal estate intact, save not spend.

In 1860, when Henry was living in Newport, he got a letter from Rev. William, who had fallen seriously ill and was starting to wonder whether he was heading for a stroke, like their father. The letter Henry wrote in reply contains his only known reference to his father's character:

> As to what you say of the similarity of your constitution &c to Pa's, it may be or may not be: but his apoplexy was undoubtedly precipitated by habits of living so free as to leave yours out of all resemblance. No doubt you are undergoing nervous exhaustion . . .

There is no way of knowing what habits Henry had in mind—whether he thought Pa drank too much or took too many wives, or in general lived with too little self-restraint; the latter interpretation seems safest. What *is* clear is that Henry saw Pa's "living so free" as a very different thing from the next generation's "nervous exhaustion." Pa's freedom was premodern and carried a threat of death through distention and over-fullness. What bothered succeeding generations, on the other hand—Henry and William and some of their children, particularly William the philosopher, Alice, and Kitty Prince—was the fear of enervation and depletion.

Living in his father's wake, Henry saw freedom as a fearful and ambiguous thing. The question of the legitimacy of the satisfaction of desire came up for consideration again and again in his essays, lectures, and books. The theological system he finally worked out allowed him to have it both ways: the drive toward satisfaction and fulfillment would have a benevolent issue in the long run, and yet it was also an evil tendency to be stamped out no matter what. To seek our own private pleasure, Henry once advised his son Bob, "This precisely is our conception of *the devil.*"

NOT-TO-DO

If individual freedom was disturbingly ambiguous in the James household, there was a building on the corner of South Pearl and Beaver Streets that left Henry in no doubt whatever on the subject. This was the First Presbyterian Church, an elegant brick edifice built in the last year of President Washington's second term and lit by ample windows through which some worshippers could see the street from their pews. Henry and his family sat in the large square formed by pews 105 and 106, for which William paid an annual rent, in 1824, of $37. Since Sunday school had not yet been invented, what church meant for Henry was a rigid worship service featuring a long and learned sermon by his minister. The Gospel as heard by Henry may well have become familiar, but it was still painful and terrifying: All men have sinned against God. All have been condemned to eternal damnation. No one can escape unless he is humbled to the dust, putting all his hope in Jesus Christ, who died on the Cross and rose again. To believe anything else, to trust in one's own decency, is to go to hell.

In 1829 the Presbyterians were the leading Christian denomination in Albany, having six of the nineteen congregations in town. Of these six, the most fashionable was not the First but the Second, which numbered some powerful men among its members—Martin Van Buren, William L. Marcy, Benjamin Butler. The First had another sort of preeminence: of all the Presbyterian churches in Albany, it was the most austere and rationalistic, and its ministers preached the most "acute legal and logical" sermons. And it was not without clout: in the summer of 1826 the Common Council granted the First the privilege of stretching chains across a couple of streets on Sunday, so that worshippers would not be distracted by the noise of traffic. Henry did not forget those chains.

The first minister to make an impression on the boy must have been the Reverend Henry R. Weed, whose tenure ran from 1822 to 1829, thus covering the years between Henry's accident and amputation. An alumnus of Union College and Princeton Theological Seminary (the same schools Henry would attend), Weed was long remembered for his "plain, practical and scriptural" sermons, and also for the earnestness with which he "reproved certain society customs, which he regarded as sinful." It is probable that when young Henry was suffering at home, he received the benefit of this minister's pastoral attention, for Weed made a practice of "preaching the Gospel from house to house."

Weed's successor was the Reverend John N. Campbell, who guided the First Presbyterian Church for over thirty years and about whom there will be more to say. Remembered for his "regal presence," he had previously been the pastor of a church in Washington, D.C., where he called down the wrath of President Jackson by casting aspersions on the wife of one of his Cabinet officers. It was during Campbell's ministry that Henry officially joined the church, at the age of twenty-three.

Both these ministers were called to the First Presbyterian Church during Henry's father's twelve-year tenure as trustee. A great-grandson once claimed that William of Albany "sacrificed even his affections for what he considered the true faith," but it is far from clear just how stern a Presbyterian he was. In the Ireland from which he emigrated, the "more intellectual ministers were latitudinarians, consciously enlightened and eager to reconcile religion with modern thought." The one certain detail about the religious regimen in his Albany home is that there were prayers every morning. Late in life Henry told an interviewer that his father had been a "liberal-minded member" of the Presbyterian Church, and nothing William wrote counteracts this impression, although he seems to have followed the rule against traveling on Sunday.

Curiously, the published roll of members of the First Church does not list William James's name. Catharine became a member in 1805, not long after her marriage. Among her eight surviving children, Jannet was the only one besides Henry to unite with their parents' congregation, and she took this step only after having been awakened by the intense religious revival of 1830 and 1831, when she was attending a private school in New York City. American-style revivalism had not been a feature of Protestant religious life in Ireland, and one wonders how William positioned himself vis-à-vis the mass upheaval that swept away his daughter. All that is known is that in 1831, under pressure of the many new converts flocking into the First, its trustees decided to enlarge the edifice and then carried the project through without so much as convening the pew holders. Following this arrogant act, which was probably engineered by William (his docile son-in-law, James King, being a fellow trustee), an angry member of the church wrote a public letter declaring that if the congregation had been consulted, "the project would have been opposed." As long as the James father was in charge, there would be no nonsense about democratic religion.

Henry always remembered how hospitable his father's home was to the clergy (his own home was not). But there had been something missing in the religious tone, both at home and at church. Christianity had been regarded as nothing more than a "higher prudence." All religious talk had been governed by a "formal remorseless dogmatism." The chief thing seemed to be "the working out . . . of a conventionally virtuous and pious repute." No one seemed to realize that the Gospel was meant "to inflame . . . an enthusiasm of devotion, or beget anything like a passionate ardor of self-abasement." It is not easy to know how to interpret such accusations, energized as they are by the intensity of Henry's later rebellion against the sober Calvinism of high Presbyterianism. Like his sister Jannet, though to a very different purpose, he came under the influence of American Protestantism's wild democratized enthusiasms, and they furnished him with the artillery he never tired of leveling against his father's faith. There may well have been both a cut-and-dried formality and an ambiguous authority in William's faith, yet the zeal with which Henry endlessly excoriated it in his maturity reminds one of nothing so much as a hectoring evangelist or, better, a seventeenth-century Puritan appalled at the dead spiritlessness surrounding him and in him.

Aside from the conception of God as a jealous and arbitrary tyrant, the aspect of Henry's religious upbringing that outraged him most of all in his adulthood was the "ordinary paralytic Sunday routine." Although he felt fortunate in that his parents "were not so Sabbatarian as many," the James family apparently observed the prescribed rules as set forth by a Presbyterian tract on Sabbath-keeping—"that all the *children* spend the day in the bosom of the family" and that "the time not spent in public worship, be past [sic] at home in exercises becoming the sacredness of the Sabbath." As Henry remembered it, the James children were required

> not to play, not to dance nor to sing, not to read story-books, not to con over our school-lessons for Monday even; not to whistle, not to ride the pony, nor to take a walk in the country, nor a swim in the river, nor, in short, to do anything which nature specially craved . . . Nothing is so hard for a child as *not-to-do*; that is, to keep his hands and feet and tongue in enforced inactivity.

The inactivity of church deposited some curious spectacles in Henry's memory. From one corner of the James family pew a bored worshipper could look through the adjacent window and its movable blinds and observe the unchurched life outdoors. Henry would arrive early to secure this corner, and during the service he would play with the cords that moved the blinds and study the pedestrians outside. As he watched the stylish young men saunter past, smoking their cigars, he secretly envied their relaxed freedom even while piously congratulating himself with (what he later called) a "pharisaic pang" that he was not as they. For all its inconveniences, not-to-do was more likely to get you into heaven than were habits of living so free.

There was one enchanting spectacle of liberation the boy looked for most of all. It took place across the street at 9 South Pearl, the residence of John I. Ostrander, attorney, where a "shapely maid" had an interesting sabbatarian routine all her own:

> Every Sunday morning, just as the sermon was getting well under way, Mr. O——r's housemaid would appear upon the threshold with her crumb-cloth in hand, and proceed very leisurely to shake it over the side of the steps . . . She would do her work . . . in a very leisurely way, leaving the cloth . . . hanging upon the balustrade of the steps while she would go into the house, and then returning again and again to shake it, as if she loved the task, and could not help lingering over it.

The raised arms, the vigorous shaking of the crumb cloth, the indolent desultoriness with which the young woman repeatedly reemerged from indoors: it was like a mysterious exhibition out of some old Dutch genre painting, and it played itself out again and again before the boy's eyes —and the man's memory.

Henry did more than simply watch. At some point in boyhood he fell in love with a schoolgirl "who used to make the blood course through my veins like a race-horse and whose footsteps I used to pursue with actual adoring kisses."

GETTING OUT

Henry was nearly six years old when, in the spring of 1817, his father purchased the property the boy would always think of as the James family home. It occupied a large lot, almost 30 feet wide by 145 feet deep, at 70 North Pearl Street, on the east side.* Three stories high and built of brick, the house was commonly referred to as a mansion. William bought it for $12,500 from Daniel Hale, who had built it in 1813; the assessed value was $7,000. A couple of years later, William purchased from Stephen Lush, his son Robert's father-in-law, the adjoining 14-foot frontage to the north. This narrower property would eventually be identified as an office.

The family now occupied one of Albany's most expensive and comfortable homes in the city's most desirable neighborhood. A few doors

* Renumbered 62 circa 1831, and 43 circa 1839.

to the south was the home of Governor DeWitt Clinton, whose mansion, assessed at $9,000 in 1823, was the most valuable on the block. Rows of shade trees were planted in the owners' front yards, and within a few years passing travelers were impressed by the street's combined comfort and elegance. But there was none of the uniformity of twentieth-century zoning regulations. Tradesmen's shops were interspersed among the fine dwelling places, hogs ran loose, and not far from Clinton's home there stood an old Dutch building that struck at least one visitor as an eyesore, with "its yellow and ill-cemented bricks, its small windows and doors, its low body, and immensely disproportioned sloping roof, covered with tiles of all shapes and fashions." The building became known as the Dutch House, and it so impressed young Henry Jr. in the 1840s that he put it into his 1881 novel, *The Portrait of a Lady*. But no matter where people lived, on warm summer evenings in the days before air conditioning "the whole population swarmed into the streets and on the stoops."

Henry's picture of childhood at 70 North Pearl Street shows none of the pressured responsibility seen in his sister Jannet's letter about the "nursery." Instead, he has the parents' easy attitudes carrying over to the children's relationships, which he represents as relaxed, unsupervised, amicable, and unmarred by jealousies. The only quarrels would seem to have been instigated by himself: sometimes he "wantonly mocked" Jannet, and he "now and then violently repelled the overtures of a younger brother who aspired to associate himself with me in my sports and pastimes." The brother must have been John Barber, almost five years Henry's junior. How violently was he rebuffed? According to a painfully confessional letter Henry sent to the *New York Tribune* in 1851, all he did was pelt his brother with snowballs "to prevent his following me at play." The episode was remembered because it embodied the conflict between two great forces of his childhood—the powerfully centripetal authority of kinship and the no less powerful need to break away from the North Pearl Street home. Getting out, vigorously moving away, joining other boys in rough and risky play, taking chances that would be shuddered at at home: these are the movements that endlessly repeat themselves in Henry's recollections of childhood.

"I was never so happy at home as away from it," he wrote. The fun to be had elsewhere is a theme that appears even in his very first memory, which preserved the moment in 1815 when he was "carried out into the streets one night, in the arms of my negro nurse, to witness a grand illumination in honor of the treaty of peace then just signed with Great Britain." Within a few years he loved to fish and hunt, and he was so

often carried away by his headlong eagerness that he had several close
escapes "from rock and river." His energy was boundless:

> The dawn always found me on my feet; and I can still vividly recall the
> divine rapture which filled my blood as I pursued under the magical light
> of morning the sports of the river, the wood, or the field.

"On my feet." Not a casual phrase for someone whose childhood ended
with the loss of a leg.

Although Henry spoke of his "frankly humoristic" relations with his
brothers and sisters, the experiences he recorded generally took place
away from home. There was a shoemaker's shop near the Jameses' residence that was run by two brothers Henry remembered as being "un-
commonly bright, intelligent, and personable." He and the other
neighborhood boys who went there to be fitted got in the habit of
gathering in the brothers' workroom and, eager to impress the young
men, "so much older than ourselves," began stealing fruit, cakes, eggs,
and alcoholic drinks; Henry borrowed novels for their perusal and was
impressed by their judgments. The shop became a sort of revolutionary
salon for small boys: it was there that Henry's rendition of the courtroom
speech of the condemned Robert Emmet caused an old workman to shed
tears. The two young shoemakers, uninhibited and not particularly religious, gave the boy a taste of what it meant to look freely and boldly
at the world around him. At a time when Albany was without a single
theater, they belonged to an amateur theatrical society, and their "impassioned criticism" of the plays they saw there made the boy "long for
the day when I too should enter upon the romance of life." This admiring
portrait matches the recollections of a Rochester shoemaker, who saw
New York State's tramping journeymen bootmakers of the 1820s and
1830s as an unusually well-informed class of workmen—"able debaters,
close observers of character," clever impersonators of the clergy, and
shrewd gamblers.

Among the boys who raided their parents' pantries, larders, and cellars
in order to get provisions for the shoemakers' symposia were two of
Governor DeWitt Clinton's sons, probably George William and Franklin.
No doubt they had grown wilder after their mother died in the summer
of 1818. Henry remembered that "by the connivance of their father's
butler, these young gentlemen were in the habit of storing certain dainties
in their own room at the top of the house, whence they could be con-
veniently transported to the shop." In the spring of 1819, however, the
governor remarried, and it wasn't long before his new wife caught her

stepsons in the act of lowering a bottle of Madeira, wrapped in twine, from their room. Henry was not much more than eight at the time. Even so, the sessions at the shoemakers were not absolutely stopped. He and his fellow "habitués" merely resolved on "a much more discreet conduct for the future."

At least that's how he looked back at his early drinking in his fictionalized autobiography. In writing to his youngest son, however, who fell into a habit of periodic binges, Henry painted a much darker picture of the shoemakers' shop. Now liquor and cards, not talk, were the chief seductions: "When I was ten years old I was in the habit of taking a drink of raw gin or brandy on my way to school morning and afternoon. This was not an occasional thing but, as I say, habitual." Nor was it unusual, he might have added, for thanks to his father's enterprise as an importer of gin, rum, and perhaps the very bottle of Madeira heisted by the Clinton boys, the city of Albany was awash in spirits. William James not only liked good gin but he plied his son with stimulants when he was bedridden. "The demon of intemperance," as Henry called it, got a grip on him very early.

Decades later, when the youngest of Henry's five children was still a toddler, a close friend hinted more than once that he ought to stop drinking. Soon afterward, in an essay on alcoholism that appeared in the New York Tribune, Henry boastfully declared that he had done so through sheer willpower.

Chapter 5

■   ■   ■

EDUCATION

From an 1832 advertisement in an Albany newspaper by a lady who gave lessons in "Piano Fort, and Vocal Music," and who named William James among her references, we may deduce that his daughters got at least some instruction in piano or voice. Beyond this, about all we know of the daughters' education is that two of them, Catharine and Jannet, were sent to private boarding schools for young ladies for the desired mix of geography, belles lettres, French, manners, and religion.

Jannet left home at the age of fourteen for a school at 111 Hudson Street in New York City, run by a Mrs. Esther Smith. The girl was still there two years later when she learned that a daughter of James McBride had experienced a religious conversion. Convinced that her own soul was in peril, Jannet penned an agonized letter to her half brother, Rev. William, imploring him to "pray for me my dearest brother—pray earnestly—pray fervently." The confidential postscript that Mrs. Smith added to this outpouring conveys a vivid sense of the headmistress's dry orthodoxy, and also her discreet and tender watchfulness.

> This letter has been submitted to me without such a requirement . . . [Jannet] is certainly in a very interesting if not a hopeful state of mind— the excitement is only of a few days standing occasioned I believe, by reading a letter from one of Mr. McBrides daughters—who has come out from the world . . . [Jannet] will experience all the sympathy and direction from me I am capable of giving her, and I pray to be directed from above.

It may be that Mrs. Smith offered as good an education in her line as any other young ladies' mentor of the time. The striking fact, however, is what William and Catharine James chose *not* to do for their daughters' minds. At the Albany Female Academy (where Bret Harte's father taught), it was possible for young women to study Latin and calculus along with the more decorous subjects. There is no evidence that any of the James girls ever went to this pioneering institution.

For his sons' education, William wanted the best article on the market. What he secured for his firstborn twin and namesake (later Rev. William) carried an unmistakable flavor of the Old World. This boy was tutored first by his Scottish-born minister, the Reverend John McDonald, a "justly celebrated scholar and teacher," and then by the Reverend John Banks, who ran a preparatory school for boys in his home in Florida, New York. Also a Scotsman by birth, Banks had received a thorough university education in theology and ancient languages, and he was long remembered by other clergymen in America for his rigorous learning, his facility with Greek, Latin, and Hebrew, and the terrible monotony of his sermons. Unworldly, exacting, hot-tempered (it was recalled how the blood rushed to his head), Banks had a reputation as a "fearful disciplinarian." No doubt he was a better informed and more rigorous pedagogue than Jannet's Mrs. Smith, but he lacked her sympathy and suavity.

William was fourteen when he came within reach of Banks's ferule. Two years of this and he was ready to enter the sophomore class at Princeton, also staunchly Presbyterian. He went on to Princeton Theological Seminary after graduating, and in 1820 he received his license to preach. About the same time his health gave way, perhaps as a result of the rigors of his orthodox education. To recover, he traveled to the land of his tutors, spending a year or two in Glasgow and Edinburgh "in comparative retirement, conversing more with books than with men." The expenses of this period of educational rest and recuperation were probably borne by his father,* who seems to have recognized a special intellectual promise in his namesake. Certainly none of the other sons was given an education quite so advanced or theological. Rev. William never abandoned his ancestral Calvinism, yet the form in which he expressed it was surprisingly tender and undoctrinaire. Some of his sisters and brothers regarded him as an authoritative source of spiritual comfort. Jannet was not the only one who wrote him when in torment. Henry also begged for his counsel.

Like Catharine, Jannet, and William, two of the younger brothers,

* James McBride's daybooks for 1820–54, in the New York Public Library, record a debit of $93.33 on April 20, 1823, for Rev. William's "passage from Dublin."

John Barber and Edward, also left home for boarding school, attending the Berkshire Gymnasium. Founded in 1827 and located just across the state line in Pittsfield, Massachusetts, this academy was run by the Reverend Chester Dewey, one of the most important educators of his time. Dewey was a devout Calvinist, a "savant" who corresponded on botanical and other subjects, and a seminal influence in organizing the teaching of natural science in the United States. One of Governor Clinton's boys was placed in his charge at the same time the James boys were.

The best school the James boys attended was only a ten-minute walk from their home on North Pearl Street. This was the Albany Academy, which first opened its doors in 1815 and within a decade was offering what was probably the finest education to be had at any level in the state of New York. In the 1820s and 1830s, this school "had the most extensive curriculum, and the largest faculty and student body in the state. Its plant and endowment surpassed all others." All five of William and Catharine's sons went there, beginning in 1818 with Augustus, who won the first premium for bookkeeping, and concluding with Howard, who got the second certificates for spelling and penmanship. No prizes are known to have been won by the other three brothers—Henry, who apparently spent five years at the academy; John Barber, whose penmanship was positively ornamental; and Edward, who entered the same year as Herman Melville, 1830. (The Melvilles lived on the corner of Steuben and North Market Streets, two short blocks from the Jameses in the direction of the river. When Allan Melville died in January 1832, the boy had to leave Albany Academy and go to work at the New York State Bank—of which the James father had been a director from 1813 to 1829.)

William James became one of the trustees of Albany Academy soon after its incorporation, and when he died (ten months after Allan Melville) his name headed the list as "Senior Trustee." He presided over board meetings from 1826 on. To what extent he deserves credit for formulating the school's basic policies and procedures is open to conjecture. In all likelihood, as one who was in on the founding of so many Albany institutions, who played a key backstage role in Clintonian politics, and who had a great dream of what could be achieved by the integration of "fiscal or physical resources," William was a major force in the academy's early development. He was on the board when the key personnel appointments were made, and he probably had a hand in 1826 in framing the defining statement of goals, which emphasized the priority of the scientific and the practical over the classical. This statement was read by Gideon Hawley at the public investiture of Joseph Henry as

Professor of Mathematics and Natural Philosophy. (Hawley was the widely respected former state superintendent of schools; a few years later he became one of the three hardworking executors charged with administering William's will.) Speaking for the trustees, Hawley said:

> Without intending to derogate from the importance and value of the classical department, the Trustees are free to acknowledge that they cherish with peculiar favor and regard that department of study which is best fitted to prepare the greatest number of pupils for the useful pursuits of active life . . . they have, therefore, always regarded the English department with special favor, inasmuch as it is calculated to supply the wants of much the greatest number of our citizens; the classical department being designed only for those who look to the learned professions for future occupation.

In referring to the English department, Hawley was thinking of something much broader than the study of language and literature. Elsewhere called the "English School," this was the designation for a basic curricular division, one that encompassed literature, history, science, and mathematics and that was seen as the alternative to classics (Latin and Greek). Although the English School still required some Latin, the kind of education it offered was definitely more utilitarian than what William's firstborn got from Rev. John Banks. English, however, had less prestige than "the languages," as classics was often called. Which course of study did the James boys enter? If their father did indeed leave Ireland as a way of avoiding the ministry, he may well have preferred a more worldly and technical sort of schooling for some of his male progeny. His firstborn, however, was not the only son dedicated to the traditional world of learning. Henry, too, followed the classical curriculum, both at Albany Academy and at Union College.

When the boy first enrolled in the academy in 1819, it was a youthful institution still very much in flux. The sounds of construction must have broken into his recitations more than once, for although the academy building was first occupied in 1817, only the first two floors were finished by 1821, when Henry entered his third year. Designed by Philip Hooker and built of brownstone, this handsome building stood (and stands) in the middle of a public square adjoining the state capitol—a location that hints at the generous financial support the school received from both city and state. The square central structure, three stories high, is flanked by two two-story wings. The façade displays several classical elements in relief—arches over the first-floor windows and tall fluted pilasters surmounted by high-relief Ionic capitals. But there is also an unclassical, Dutch-looking double staircase mounting to the main entrance, which faces the Hudson River. As an architectural statement, the building is elegant and impressive without being rigorously "correct," in this way aptly expressing the academy's divided mission. At present the building houses the State Board of Education.

The man who ran Albany Academy, Dr. T. Romeyn Beck, was appointed principal at the youthful age of twenty-six. At a time when most academy and university presidents belonged to the clergy, he was a physician, a chemist, and a meteorologist. Whatever Henry's father may have contributed to the academy's development, it was Beck's skillful and visionary administration that was chiefly responsible for the school's eminence in the 1820s and 1830s. In addition to hiring a top-notch staff and introducing an innovative curriculum and teaching a heavy load himself, Beck actively promoted something that seems inconceivable at the elementary and preparatory levels—cutting-edge scientific research. It was at Albany Academy that Joseph Henry became a world-class physicist and initiated his epochal experiments with magnetism and electricity, building what was then the world's most powerful electromagnet. In 1830 he strung a mile or so of wire around the walls of a schoolroom and demonstrated that electricity could be conducted over long distances, thus making possible the telegraph. With Faraday, he was a co-discoverer of induced currents, and after his death, his work was commemorated by the name given the unit of inductance, the "henry."

Of course, when young Henry James began attending classes at the academy, there was a great deal of basic and traditional learning ahead of him. He entered when he was eight—the minimum age, according to the school's statutes, which further stipulated that new pupils must already know how to read English. Since the academy's records were destroyed by fire in 1888, little is known about the boy's course of study. At first he no doubt followed the elementary curriculum conducted by the English and mathematics tutor. The subjects included English grammar, penmanship, modern geography and history, arithmetic, and something called "Bookkeeping, and the principles of English Composition," and the textbooks included such old standards as *Murray's English Grammar* and *Blair's Lectures*.

One subject the trustees ranked particularly high was the art of public speaking. They required Beck to have the boys instructed every Wednesday afternoon "in the correct reading of English Prose, and Verse, and in the proper delivery of select pieces of Oratory." This branch of Henry's education made a great impression on him. When he dropped by his neighbors, the shoemakers, he found it "a huge pleasure to be able to compel their rapt attention to some eloquent defence of liberty or appeal to patriotism which I had become familiar with in my school or home reading." For much of his adult life, he continued to hope that he would eventually establish himself as a public lecturer.

Since Henry entered the classical department after completing his elementary work, he must have gotten a thorough dose of the Reverend Joseph Shaw, who was remembered for insisting on "a critical accuracy in the elementary teaching and drilling rarely found in our American schools." Like the taskmaster who had prepared Rev. William for Princeton, Rev. Shaw was a faithful "disciple of the old Scottish school, that never spared the rod." All the academy teachers, however, had recourse to the "rattan" when students failed to prepare their lessons. There was a great deal of memorization and standing up to recite, and all students were ranked relative to one another, those at the head of the class being rewarded with premiums. On the back of the school's quarterly bills for tuition, Dr. Beck notified parents of their particular responsibility (which William faithfully discharged):

> N.B. The whole system of instruction is founded on the principle of the Students reciting lessons *which they have studied at home.* Tasks are given by all the Instructors, and if these are neglected, or not sufficiently attended to, Parents may rest assured, that the Children do not make proper progress.

There was no doubt who was in charge. Looking back fifty years later, after a milder regimen had become the order of the day, one alumnus wanted it understood that Beck "was no meek, complaining creature, pleading with his class to be still and not make so much noise, but was the lord and master of his subjects."

Discipline was not confined to the classroom. It was never forgotten how Beck once laid a "double cut" on the hands of fifty boys who attacked a passing driver with snowballs. (Did this impressive spectacle help create the terrible guilt Henry felt from snowballing a younger brother?) "All class meetings, or meetings of the Students for improper purposes" were proscribed as "unlawful combinations against the government of the Academy." Each day opened and closed with prayer, students were required to go to church on Sunday, and there were only seven weeks of vacation annually. In 1819 the charge for one year's tuition in the elementary school was $16–$20. For the higher English school, the charge was $24. Classics cost the most, $32.

Professors were paid generously, tutors less so, but all were required by the 1819 statutes to spend at least six hours a day in class. If they wished to replace a prescribed textbook, they had to petition the trustees. Faculty were empowered to dismiss disobedient or disrespectful students but this was not the same as expelling them, and students could appeal to the board of trustees. And the teachers' private life was no more their own than was the students'. When the first Professor of Mathematics and Natural Philosophy, Michael O'Shannessy, helped a "notorious prostitute" to pass as a "*virtuous* and amiable Lady," he was dismissed.

In later life Henry complained about the authority of religion a great deal more than about the authority of school. Perhaps one reason for this was that, whereas the First Presbyterian Church and its sabbatarian regime seemed to be frozen, set, completely prescribed from of old, the Albany Academy was visibly in its springtime. Even a small child could see that it was engaged in producing knowledge as well as transmitting it. School had the sort of authority one wanted for oneself.

Then, too, the academy was the expression of its society's most vigorous aspirations. Albany was then the seventh or eighth largest city in the United States. As it doubled in size from 1820 to 1830 and took charge of the eastern terminus of the newly created Erie Canal, the city became, briefly, one of the nation's liveliest centers of scientific thought, politics, and commerce. In 1824 the Albany Institute was organized, and for several years thereafter this energetic scientific and literary society held meetings and published papers and expanded its collections (to which Henry contributed a copy of the Rosetta Stone in 1837). But Albany's premier institution, the one in which the city's energetic and inquiring spirit was chiefly concentrated, was the academy. It was Henry's good luck to pass through the school at the moment this infusion was taking place. Through osmosis he learned the most important lesson a child can absorb: the world is not cast in concrete, it is still completely fluid, you too can shape it.

Curiously, Joseph Henry, perhaps the greatest genius ever to be associated with Albany Academy, first entered as a student in 1819, the same year as Henry James. At the time they probably saw little of one another, for Joseph Henry was not only fourteen years older, he was already fired with his own scientific curiosity. Three years later he left the academy, probably to tutor the Van Rensselaer children. He returned, however, to assist Dr. Beck in his chemistry lectures in 1823–24. Perhaps it was then, two years before his appointment as professor, that the young scientist in some way tutored Henry James. Although in later years the two became close friends and occasional correspondents, all that is known of their academic connection is that the physicist once referred to Henry as his "former Pupil." Also, decades later, in the opening years of the twentieth century, Henry James the novelist proudly commemorated his father's "cherished, anecdotic" relation with his brilliant and "benignant tutor."

What did the youth who became Henry Sr. learn from the tutor whose name (yet *another* "Henry") now designates the unit of inductance? In his early thirties, at a point when Henry Sr.'s life seemed to be unraveling, he wondered whether he could find order and purpose by following "some commoner method—learn science and bring myself first into men's respect." Later on, in educating his sons, he encouraged William's scientific interests and placed Henry Jr., the future novelist, in a technical school for which the boy was plainly unsuited. One of the results of Henry Sr.'s schooling was that, as an adult, he invested science with magical power and prestige. What science meant for him was, variously, the system of social organization worked out by Charles Fourier, or a set of facts and discoveries that were of interest because of their spiritual symbolism, or a stage of development it was vitally necessary not to get stuck in. It is doubtful whether any of these visions of what scientists were up to would have made much sense to the investigator of magnetism and electricity. In the end, the path Henry Sr. picked out was much closer to that trod by the theological brother who preceded him, Rev. William, than to the one blazed by Dr. Beck and Professor Henry.

Chapter 6

■ ■ ■

MORBIDITY

The thing that happened next was unspeakably painful and devastating. It reeked of turpentine, burned flesh, blood, pus, rot, agony, guilt, and endless waiting, and its fluids soaked so deeply into the folds of the boy's mind that he was permanently altered. The importance of remembering the "morbid," the insistence that the ego undergo a therapeutic "mortification," the notion of an "amputated" and inaccessible yet still very real selfhood: the terrible vocabulary turns up over and over in Henry's writings. So far-reaching was the stain that it seems to have penetrated his children's minds, in particular that of William, who became convinced that only those who have been exposed to the "morbid" side of life are able to penetrate its secrets. William was fascinated with the idea that the human personality could be partitioned into separate selves, each functioning independently of the other, and Henry and Alice enacted forms of splitting and displacement peculiar to themselves. In their individual ways, these three children each exhibited simultaneous extremes of awareness and blindness. The James family cannot be understood unless one is prepared to think about the ways in which the human mind adjusts to the sickening horrors of extreme pain and gangrene.

No member of the family ever gave a lucid and reasonably complete account of Henry's accident and its consequences. The boy who loved to roam and hunt must have lost much of his pleasure and freedom when he lost his mobility, but it is not recorded that he ever complained. When he went to London in 1837 he acquired a "good Cork leg," which Joseph Henry pronounced a very interesting article, but the problems he had to surmount as he rose from a sitting position or climbed stairways or made his frequent trips in ferries, steamboats, Atlantic packets, trains, horsecars, and stages never once got mentioned. His letters are full of references to his frequent illnesses and indispositions, and he seems to have demanded a great deal of care from the woman he married, but he almost never talked about his lifelong disability.

If his stoic dignity seems remarkable, even for an age when discomfort and pain were taken for granted more than they are today, his children were protective to the point of secrecy. In the memoir written by Henry Jr., *Notes of a Son and Brother*, we are informed that the father suffered an accident in his early youth and that he was "so lamed" he walked with difficulty on uneven surfaces. But it is not made clear that a leg had actually been removed. In 1875 another well-known man without a leg, Ezra Stiles Gannett, was memorialized by his son. Henry Jr. read the book, and when he came upon a description of Gannett "clicking along the sidewalks," he pitied "the venerable subject in his extreme bereavement of privacy." The biographer had violated the "filial standpoint."

In his partly fictional memoir, "Immortal Life: Illustrated in a Brief Autobiographic Sketch of the Late Stephen Dewhurst," Henry Sr. changed the burned leg to an arm that has received a gunshot. He also confined the narration to two lengthy and highly polished sentences, framed within the context of his juvenile anxiety about his relationship with his father, as if this was more important than his physical suffering.

> He was certainly a very easy parent, and I might have been left to regard him perhaps as a rather indifferent one, if it had not been for a severe illness which befell me from a gun-shot wound in my arm, and which confined me for a long time to the house, when his tenderness to me showed itself so assiduous and indeed extreme as to give me an exalted sense of his affection. My wound had been very severe, being followed by a morbid process in the bone which ever and anon called for some sharp surgery; and on these occasions I remember—for the use of anaesthetics was still wholly undreamt of—his sympathy with my sufferings was so excessive that my mother had the greatest possible difficulty in imposing due prudence upon his expression of it.

It is the father who seems to suffer most during the horrible operations, and the son who somehow or other has the freedom of mind to look around him from the midst of his agony. While the father's openness of expression is such that it must be reined in, the son behaves in the reverse way, particularly in the act of retrospective narration: *he* shows *nothing*. Is there a phrase less expressive of the boy's horrifying realization that the procedure would have to be repeated than that light and airy "ever and anon"? Just how many operations were there?

Henry Sr.'s autobiographical narrative remained unpublished at the time of his death. When his son and literary executor, William, edited it, he appended a footnote evidently intended to clarify matters, as if the moment for candor had finally arrived: "At the age of thirteen, Mr. James had his right leg so severely burned while playing the then not usual game of fire-ball that he was confined to his bed for two years, and two thigh amputations had to be performed." William had taken a medical degree at Harvard, and his plain and matter-of-fact tone seems designed to do away with his father's ambiguities and equivocations, firmly replacing the patient's unreliable subjectivity with the doctor's professional mastery: no "ever and anon" here. Thus he reveals that there were two successive operations, and that even the first had been above the knee. Instead of being loosely confined to the house for a long but undetermined time, the boy was definitely in his bed for exactly two years. And the editor draws a very sharp scalpel line between fact and fancy: we are talking about Mr. James here and no imaginary Stephen Dewhurst.

Under scrutiny, however, William's account of the accident and amputation looks as spongy as his father's. What is this game of fire-ball, and why are we informed that the game was "then not usual"? Why was a second operation required? The fiction of a gunshot wound implied an answer to this question by allowing us to suppose that the bone was injured, but now that the shot has been replaced by a burn, the question becomes more insistent. And what about the sequence of events: was the boy in bed for two years as a result of the burn or as a result of the first operation? Most curious of all, William's account is not consistent with the meager contemporary documentation. One of the few things we know for sure is that an amputation took place on May 6, 1828, one month before Henry's seventeenth birthday. If the original injury occurred when he was thirteen, as William asserts, then the boy suffered for three and maybe four years before his parents and physicians resorted to the final solution.

Another report of the bungled operation supports the belief that this painful interval was longer than the son realized. In the summer of 1866, Caroline Dall, a Boston feminist and book reviewer, traveled to Albany and visited with Weare C. Little, a bookseller and longtime resident of the city. Little was full of stories about the Jameses, which Dall jotted down in her private journal:

When Henry was a little boy of twelve, his clothes took fire in the street, at a bonfire of some sort, and he was so badly burned that his leg had to be amputated— It was ill-done—& was amputated a second time, the little fellow bearing it bravely.

Some of the other James stories Dall got from Little are obvious strays from a more legendary world, particularly the tale of how William of Albany came from Ireland with his wife in a state of such dire poverty that they worked as day laborers and ate their "praties" (potatoes) in the open air, sitting on opposite ends of their chest. This particular story emerges from a confusion between late-eighteenth-century Scotch-Irish Presbyterian immigrants and the more desperate mid-nineteenth-century Irish Catholic transplants. But the amputation story is worth taking seriously (with the exception of Dall's uncertain reference to a bonfire). The bad burn at a relatively early age, the repeated amputation, the boy's stoic endurance: these details look trustworthy. Most important of all, Little had every opportunity to get the basic facts right about the 1828 operation (though not the original injury), since that was the year his bookstore first opened for business. That is to say, he was part of the original grapevine, and the information he passed on to Dall in 1866 reflects what was being said on State Street in 1828 about the James boy's ordeal.

The one other surviving account focuses not on the amputation but on the accident. It was written years later by Woolsey Rogers Hopkins, who also studied at Albany Academy:

On a summer afternoon, the older students would meet Professor Henry in the Park, in front of the Academy, where amusements and instruction would be given in balloon-flying, the motive power being heated air supplied from a tow ball saturated with spirits of turpentine. When one of these air-ships took fire, the ball would be dropt for the boys, when it was kicked here and there, a roll of fire. [One day when] young James had a sprinkling of this [turpentine] on his pantaloons, one of these balls was sent into the open window of Mrs. Gilchrist's stable. [James], thinking only of conflagration, rushed to the hayloft and stamped out the flame, but burned his leg.

We could hardly ask for a sharper, more detailed, more convincingly circumstantial narration. The playing around with balloons is in keeping with the state of scientific curiosity of the time, and the picture of Henry's headlong ardor is perfectly in character. Hopkins's own experience seems to have made him an ideal keeper of the facts: as a civil engineer with combat experience and antiquarian interests, he knew how to keep his eye on the ball and follow the exact causal sequence. Also, like the bookseller, he was on the spot and thus in position to get the facts straight, being four years younger than Henry and having lived in Albany from about 1822 on. It is worth noting, though, that Hopkins does not make himself an eyewitness. His narrative is probably a reconstruction, as he entered Albany Academy in 1827, three years after Henry left. The boys were not fellow students.

One detail in Hopkins's story needs to be corrected: Joseph Henry could not have been "Professor Henry" at the time. * The accident must have taken place while he was still a tutor, perhaps during the summer term near the end of his 1823–24 stint as Dr. Beck's assistant. It would be quite in order for Beck to ask his assistant to take charge of the boys' balloon play, which might well be beneath the dignity of a professor. Almost everything points to 1824 as the year in which young Henry burned himself. † This date would explain the discrepancy in age (twelve versus thirteen) in Caroline Dall's and William James's versions of the accident: 1824 was the summer Henry *turned* thirteen, being twelve up to June 3 and thirteen thereafter.

According to a medical journal of the time, one of the common folk treatments for burns was "holding the burnt part near the fire." A more enlightened procedure for easing the pain of scalds and burns was to apply various liquids—cold water, brandy, or turpentine. In treating children, it was thought best not to use turpentine by itself but to mix it with an ointment consisting of yellow wax, pitch, resin, and olive oil. Sometimes, "from the greater irritability of children, anodynes, as the elixir paregoric, or tinct[ure] of opium, become more necessary."

It has generally been assumed that the first amputation took place soon after the accident. Henry's son William wrote of the "burning, amputation and sickness" in that order, as if the years of sickness followed the amputation. In his paper "The Consciousness of Lost Limbs," he cited his father's case as that of a man who had "a thigh amputation performed at the age of thirteen years." Since a third-degree burn kills the skin and invites serious infection, drastic surgery may have been

---

* He was appointed professor in September 1826 (following O'Shannessy's dismissal). Hopkins's mistake is easily explained: entering the academy in 1827, when Joseph Henry was already a professor, the boy was not aware of the preceding stages of his career.
† The 1826 city directory was the first to show a Robert Gilchrist residing on Park Place (which ran south from the academy for a short distance). Since city directories were usually published in the middle of the preceding year, Gilchrist could have been at this location as early as the summer of 1824.

decided on rather quickly. But the documents from 1828 do not even hint at a prior operation, and a letter Henry Sr. sent another son, Bob, in the 1870s speaks of "my long sickness previous to the loss of my leg."

The worst was, the thirteen-year-old boy had almost four years of anguish and uncertainty to get through. Confined to his house and probably to his bed for much of this period, he continued to drink "all manner of stimulants with a view to keep up [his] strength." Along with the alcohol, he no doubt received a number of pastoral visits from his minister, Rev. Henry R. Weed. (Henry's lameness might explain his curious memory of arriving at the First Presbyterian Church in advance of all the other worshippers.) According to a questionnaire he filled out thirty years later, he got "private tuition," perhaps from Joseph Henry, who may have felt responsible for the accident.

Was the boy's physical growth affected by his apparently recurring infection and forced inactivity? What sort of psychic deformations was he undergoing? The meager surviving documentation sheds only the most scattered light on these pressing questions.

LETTERS, LEDGERS, AN EXECUTION, ANOTHER FIRE

Several months after the accident, Henry's older brother, Rev. William, married Marcia Ames, the daughter of the Albany portrait painter Ezra Ames, and within a few weeks the young couple moved to Clarkson, a small village near Rochester, where a Presbyterian church needed a temporary pastor. On New Year's Day, 1825, writing to Jannet James back in Albany, Marcia expressed the anxiety she and her husband felt about the sufferer: "We are very glad to hear Henry is so much better. I hope he has received the letter which your brother William sent him about two weeks ago."

The letter isn't extant, nor is any other document that sheds light on Henry's condition at this time. The boy who was never so happy at home as he was away from it may have been trapped there now, but beyond this we can say nothing about his doings and sufferings in 1825 and 1826. Was he able to hear his father's Erie Canal oration? Was it the boy's invalidism that caused the father to miss three meetings of Albany Academy's board of trustees in 1826?

One of the doctors who cared for Henry was Dr. James McNaughton, later Professor of Anatomy at the University of the State of New York. The physician in charge was probably Dr. William Bay, who was elected president of the Albany County Medical Society in January 1825 and whose daughter married Henry's older brother, Augustus, on October 16, 1827. Back in 1817 Bay had allowed some of his medical students to look after an Irish boy whose leg had been injured by a powder blast. When Thurlow Weed published an indignant paragraph in an Albany newspaper, Bay raised a storm and had Weed reprimanded by a police magistrate. But it turned out that Weed was right: the leg had been so badly neglected it had to be amputated. "For twenty or more years," Weed later wrote, the amputee's stumping around town with an awkward wooden leg "served to remind the doctors" of this error in judgment. Now Bay faced a similar dilemma with the son of the most powerful man in town.

Three years after Henry tried to stamp out the stable fire, a new consultant was called in, Dr. John James (no relation). This physician had been practicing medicine in Albany since 1819, the year he got his medical degree from the College of Physicians and Surgeons (afterward the medical school of Columbia University). Dr. James was an amateur herbalist or botanist and the author of *Sketches of Travels in Sicily, Italy, and France* (1820). On August 27, 1827, he held a consultation with Dr. McNaughton, whose home and office, at 71 North Pearl, were right across the street from the James residence. There was a lengthy examination and treatment of the patient. Afterward Dr. James turned to a fresh page of his ledger, opened an account for William James, and inked in the first entry: "*Visit, consult Dr. M:N & long attendance—$5.*" Five dollars was an exceptionally high charge for a house call, which usually cost fifty cents. The visit must have required an unusual effort in addition to lasting a long time. Parts of the leg were probably without skin. There must have been infection. The August heat could not have been much help.

Curiously, this particular torture session coincided with Albany's most memorable public execution. In May of that year John Whipple had been murdered in the old Van Rensselaer mansion, Cherry Hill, by a man bearing the Dickensian name of Strang. When Strang was hanged on August 24, "the ferry boats literally swarmed" with curious strangers and the city's streets were "filled by the passing crowds." It was estimated that thirty thousand spectators gathered to observe the execution. This noisy and sensational public event took place three days before Dr. James's "long attendance" on Henry.

The following November, after Augustus and his bride returned from their honeymoon in western New York, they were full of stories about Marcia and Rev. William, who was now the minister of the Second Presbyterian Church in Rochester. The newlyweds brought a piece of good news that moved Henry to write a letter to his brother, whom he probably had not seen for some time. This letter, written at the age of sixteen, is the boy's earliest surviving composition. Three years had passed since the fire.

It was with very great pleasure that I learned your intention of making us a visit this fall. We have been anxiously expecting you every day this week, and we regret to find that you have not yet arrived. Nothing would contribute, I assure you, more to the satisfaction of our family, than the event of your coming. While it would be a source of high gratification to us collectively, to me individually it might be productive of very eminent advantage, whether contemplated with a view to the ultimate improvement of my mind, or ~~with~~ to an immediate assistance to my spirits and resolution. You will therefore pardon me, if I press you to come down as soon as may be convenient.

The writer's polish and self-discipline seem extraordinary. Only after expressing the hopes of the entire family does he turn to what *he* wants, seeing William, which he expresses with a fine mastery of antithesis ("ultimate," "immediate") and indirection ("*if* I press"). Even then, it is emphatically not what he *desires* but rather a question involving his education, always a prime consideration in the James household. Finally, near the end of the paragraph he hints, ever so slightly, at his great trouble, and as he does so his prose makes its first stumble—"with" is wrong, he substitutes "to"—and then out comes the admission he has led up to so skillfully: his "spirits and resolution" are not holding up. Why they are failing is not even mentioned.

A line Dr. John James wrote in his account book three days later hints at the extent to which the youthful letter writer understated his sufferings: "*Vt. consult Dr McN Jr. [?] attend &c—$5.*" "Vt" stood for "visit." Judging from the fee, it had been another long, difficult, and painful session.

Was the boy's father present at the time? One guesses he was, but either way he soon found that one trouble always calls up another. The following Saturday, a fire broke out in some of the two-story warehouses on the Albany pier that he had rented out. Since the buildings themselves were fully insured, William was not at risk. However, the contents, which included 150 bales of hops belonging to a Mr. McMichael, were uninsured. According to one report, the fifty-six-year-old landlord rushed to the scene "and bailed water with great perseverance, but the buildings being of wood, were completely destroyed." Was the father imitating his son's rash heroism, or perhaps even attempting in some obscure way to put out the fire that had burned the boy three years earlier? Or was the motive simply the public call of duty? This was not the last fire to break out at a crucial moment in the James family annals. In 1861, when Henry Jr. was feeling the pressure to enlist in the Union Army, he injured himself while trying to get an antiquated hand-operated fire engine in Newport, Rhode Island, to pump water.

All the while the unhealed areas on Henry's right leg were spreading, not shrinking. Two weeks after Henry's dignified letter to his minister-brother, Jannet followed up with another to his wife:

> Henry's leg is not as well at present as it was in the Spring, instead of progressing it goes back and there is a greater space to heal now than there was before. We are all anxiously expecting Brother William down and will be very much disappointed if he does not come.

Jannet, thirteen years old at the time, was writing at the behest of her mother, who was both too busy to write and extremely worried about Henry's leg, and about his spirits as well. Her stepson's advice, comfort, presence were badly needed.

Fortunately, Rev. William found time to come down from Rochester. He appears to have been more than effective in restoring his imperiled brother's courage, for the next letter Henry wrote to him, dated December 14, shows no signs of pain, weakness, or depression whatever. Henry began:

> Since you left us, we have heard very many testimonials to the character of your Sabbath evening discourse, to the elegance of its composition, and the truth of its sentiments. One gentleman, Cashier Yates, stated that if any man of established reputation, Dr. Chalmers for instance, had preached that sermon, it would be considered one of his finest efforts.

The enthusiast was John W. Yates, cashier of the New York State Bank. Although Yates was not a man of great influence in Albany, the educated few recognized him for his taste and cultivation. One memoirist extolled him as "a man of education, of talents, of natural eloquence, and of extensive reading. He was the best classical scholar in the city—Judge Kent not excepted." To the Yankee and Scotch-Irish invaders who had taken over the city, it was a curious sight to see this product of old Dutch Albany "reading Homer with a pipe in his mouth" or "see him turn from the page of Thucydides, to talk Dutch." At a time when Henry's condition was so severe his life may have hung in the balance, he opened his letter by telling William his sermon had pleased a man of known literary taste. Nothing speaks more eloquently about the young man's aspirations—or the techniques of self-control by which he sought to deflect his attention from the horror that mired him.

One technique was to replace his private agony with public or family concerns. His letter went on to name some other eminent citizens of Albany who had been impressed with Rev. William's sermon:

> Dr. James, Harmanus Bleecker, John V.N. Yates and many other gentlemen expressed themselves in nearly the same way. Moss Kent (the chancellor's brother) who has lately returned from England and Scotland, and one of our first men, says he cannot remember of ever having heard any thing to compare with it, either in this country or abroad.

These were all men of cultivation and public influence. Harmanus Bleecker was a director of the Mechanics and Farmers Bank, and in later years the chief American representative to The Hague. John Van Ness Yates had been New York's Secretary of State. It seems bizarre, given the circumstances, how anxious Henry was to transmit the favorable reports of his brother's sermon. The letter expresses a sick boy's extraordinary attachment to the public order as embodied in respected elders. It is their voices, not his, that we hear. His voice does not exist.

Then, immediately following the passage quoted just above, we hear for the one and only time in Henry Sr.'s many surviving letters the voice of the most important elder of them all: "Papa desires me to be particular in telling you that this ought to show you the necessity of increasing ardour in your studies, and of gaining the acquaintance of his most respectable friends." Study harder and join my network of influential men and let them help you get ahead: the badly wounded boy faithfully transmits this no doubt characteristic advice without the slightest hint of resistance. In no other document is he known to have referred to his father as "Papa."

The remainder of the letter is full of family dutifulness. Jannet has come through some more "very alarming attacks of spasms."* Marcia must write often without waiting for replies, since "Mama" "has so large a charge, that she has hardly time to [do] anything but take [care] of the children." (The missing words suggest the writer's mind was elsewhere.) Only at the end does Henry say something about himself: "I am about as well as when you were here, and shall expect the books to-morrow

---

* James McBride's daybooks show that Jannet received expensive treatment in 1830 and 1832 from a Dr. Nelson of New York.

evening. If I should not receive them at that time, do dispatch them next week." The boy's resolution was once again in working order. He was applying himself with increasing ardor to the ultimate improvement of his mind. Rev. William's visit had been a success. *

Two weeks later, at St. Andrews University in Scotland, the great man whose name had been invoked by Cashier Yates, Thomas Chalmers, wrote a letter to an ambitious American boy who had sought his advice. Chalmers was known throughout the Protestant world for his versatile brilliance, having studied mathematics and chemistry before turning finally to moral philosophy and religion. According to a later student of Scots philosophy, "He made the old Calvinistic creed of Scotland look reasonable and philosophic, generous and lovable." The eloquence of his preaching, the enthusiasm he kindled in students, and his apparent success in harmonizing science with evangelical Christianity made him one of the most sought-after teachers of his time. Now someone named Henry James in the state of New York wanted Chalmers to advise him what course of study to follow. Chalmers did his best to answer the question even though he was without "all observation both of yourself and of your university opportunities." He strongly urged the young man, particularly if he had a "very powerful or aspiring talent," to concentrate on one of three large fields—theology, mathematics, or political economy. The books with which to begin were, in theology, Butler's *Analogy of Religion*; in mathematics, Euclid and an elementary treatise on algebra; and in political economy, Adam Smith's *Wealth of Nations*. "Proceed a little way in all these—but fasten only upon one as the main literary and intellectual business of your life." It must be remembered that learning should strengthen one's piety rather than weaken it. "Elegant literature" will be suitable as a restorative diversion.

Perhaps there was something in Henry's letter that led Chalmers (whose own career was striking for its interdisciplinarity) to warn him more than once to select a single intellectual pursuit. Considering that the recipient was to flounder for some twenty-five years as he struggled to define what he was interested in, and what he wished to be, Chalmers's advice seems singularly prescient. On the other hand, if he had known the young man better, he might not have urged him to adopt "fixed and regular hours of mental exertion" or recommended physical exercise. Although we can be sure Henry must have given Chalmers's letter his

---

* On February 26, 1828, Rev. William replied to a letter from a deistical brother-in-law by wondering whether nature alone, without Christianity, could supply *"the chief good"* (letter to Julius Ames at the New-York Historical Society). William's tolerant and noncontestatory tone may be an indication of the kind of help he offered Henry at this time.

most careful scrutiny when it reached him in January or February 1828, we cannot know how seriously he tried to apply its advice. The revealing fact is that he took the trouble to solicit it: nothing else puts so effectively on notice his exceptional ambition, resourcefulness, and preoccupation with his educational self-development.

A strong and aspiring will had come into existence during the boy's long season in hell. But it was a will that still conceived of itself as devoted to family, respected seniors, the world of learning. As if its survival depended precisely on never taking account of its own pain and fear, it could not speak of itself and did not know itself. The question was: could this ferocious energy become conscious of itself and its chains?

ARTERYS, TENDONS CORDS &C

Often the limb would be elevated. The operator used his fingers to press the artery and then applied a tourniquet. Some doctors considered the traditional tourniquet (which worked with a screw) "worse than useless" and used a simpler device consisting of a handkerchief and stick. As an assistant squeezed the skin and flesh away from the area to be cut, the operator made his incision and cut through the flesh down to the bone. Many operators wished to cut "a great deal at one stroke," but this was from "want of experience." It was better to go slowly, using short strokes with a small, convex knife. If the operator was careful, he left two large semicircular flaps that could be joined below the stump, thus affording a comfortable pad beneath the bone. First, however, using a retractor, he turned these flaps back and sawed through the bone. Then the flaps were "secured by sticking plasters."

Although opium was in use, it was a sedative, not an anesthetic. There were no anesthetics. Summer was the worst season in which to perform an amputation. Why this was so, no one understood, but the operation seemed to be followed with fewer complications when it was carried out in cool weather.

Around the middle of April 1828, some black spots appeared on Henry's right leg. The doctors were able to "subdue" them, but it was feared they might be "forerunners of *Mortification*." What if they returned in the heat of summer? "*Death* would be inevitable." On Monday, May 5, Doctors McNaughton, Bay, and James conferred among themselves and with some members of the family. They agreed they had no choice, and the operation was scheduled for twelve noon the next day.

That evening a large meeting was convened at Albany's Atheneum

Hall to make arrangements for a monument to the memory of DeWitt Clinton, who had died three months earlier. Herman Melville's uncle Peter Gansevoort was appointed secretary. It was resolved that subscriptions would be collected for a statue, and that all subscribers should make their payments to William James and Gideon Hawley. The report in the *Albany Gazette* does not disclose whether William was at the meeting.

The next day the operation was carried out as planned. Judging from Dr. James's account book, he was the assistant and Dr. McNaughton the chief surgeon: "*Vt. consult Dr. McNaughton.—assistance, amputating leg &c—$5.*" Afterward, hurrying to make the mail, Augustus sat down and got a note off to Rochester:

> ~~The~~ it was cut off some distance above the knee, the operation lasted (that is severing) about six minutes, but the most painful part was the securing the *Arterys, Tendons Cords* &c.
>
> He is now thank God, safely through it, and in a sound sleep, with every appearance of doing well,—
>
> It was a distressing operation, to be sure, but if it had been procrastinated, we would have been in dreadful anxiety through the summer because had these symptoms then appeared, amputation would have been out of the question, he bore it much better than we expected.

If this was indeed the operation that cost Henry his knee, his son William was mistaken in thinking that his father's "thigh amputation" took place at the age of thirteen. Augustus's letter pays close attention to the feelings of those involved but is silent about the father's unexpected demonstration of sympathetic agony—the one point the surviving patient wanted to make known years later.

The patient may have fallen asleep, but he was not doing well. Four days later, as Dr. James's ledger shows, there was another long, distressing scene in the James family nursery: "*Vt. with Dr. McNaughton dress[ing] &c—$5.*" Once again, the substantial fee tells us the visit involved more than a change of bandages. Three days later, on May 13, Doctors James and McNaughton were called in for a nocturnal visit involving a dressing and probably a good deal more, judging from the now usual charge of $5.

Dr. James's remaining fees suggest that the patient was at last on the mend. On May 14 there was a $1 visit, with "no dress." Five more house calls followed, all with dressings, from May 15 to May 20, and then the entries chargeable to William James come to an end. The last of the cutting had been performed, and in the nick of time. Summer was just around the corner.

Dr. James's total charge for all consultations, visits, procedures, and materials was $31. He was paid with correct punctuality on October 2, the beginning of the fourth quarter.

GUILT

That accidents happen can be the hardest truth of all to accept. Young Henry James had spent almost four years in bed without knowing when or how—or whether—it would all end, and then passed under the surgeon's knife twice or more without closing his eyes. Surely there was an answer.

Twenty years after the operation, Henry recalled the irrational guilt he felt in childhood:

> After my religious life dawned, my day was turned into hideous and unrelieved night, by these ghostly visitations. I not merely repented myself, as one of my theological teachers deemed it incumbent on me, of Adam's transgression, but every dirty transaction I had been engaged in from my youth up, no matter how insignificant soever, crept forth from its oblivious slime to paralyse my soul with threats of God's judgment. So paltry an incident of my youth as the throwing snow balls, and that ineffectually too, at a younger brother in order to prevent his following me at play, had power, I recollect, to keep me awake all night, bedewing my pillow with tears, and beseeching God to grant me forgiveness.

This memory of a period of extreme conscientiousness refers to a period before adulthood, for as Henry makes clear in his fictionalized autobiography, his religious life began in his childhood or youth. It seems probable that his first period of guilt was the period he spent in bed after burning his leg.

It is a bedridden child, not one who is up and active, who is going to have his day turned into night by obsessive guilt, and all Henry's remembered bouts of moral and religious terror occurred in bed: "The dark silent night usually led in the spectral eye of God, and set me to wondering and pondering evermore how I should effectually baffle its gaze." This feeling of being transfixed suggests a prior sense of having been immobilized. The boy couldn't *move*: it was when he was "upon [his] bed" that he remembered how he had repelled his brother and "wantonly mocked" his sister Jannet (whose spasms he dutifully reported in 1827), and the memory left him "fairly heartbroken with a dread of being estranged from God and all good men." It was this fear of estrangement that prompted his effort to impress the first men, like Chalmers, with his learning, or to inform Rev. William how *he* had impressed them. And guilt has its own terrible logic, especially when the boy who made his brother stay home while he himself ran away had so much leisure to reflect on the loss of his own mobility. Now *he* was the one kept at home—and who knows for how long? Running away was something he would never do again. The spectral eye had not been baffled. The injury, the amputation, had been *deserved*.

Perhaps the clearest evidence that Henry was overcome by guilt during his interminable convalescence is to be found in one of the volumes by Emanuel Swedenborg he bought in London in 1844. Penciled on the front flyleaf is a note in Henry's hand: "See . . . section 196 for some remarks on the malignity of Temptation states when based on bodily maladies." Section 196 deals with spiritual temptations. Taking a look, we find a penciled hand in the margin, drawn by James, which points toward the passage where Swedenborg explains why one is sometimes troubled by "a continual drawing forth, and bringing to remembrance, of the evils which one has committed." Such experiences, Swedenborg wrote,

> are effected by evil spirits who are present with man; and when they take place, they assume the appearance of interior anxieties and pains of conscience . . . *These temptations are most grievous when they are accompanied with bodily pains; and still more so, when these pains are of long continuance, and no deliverance is granted.*

Henry drew a vertical line and a large X in the margin opposite this passage. The sentence I have italicized he underlined with a pencil.

After 1844 Henry was convinced, following Swedenborg, that evil thoughts are caused by evil spirits from *outside* the individual. It makes perfect sense that he believed this—that is, that the boy whose long continued pain stimulated a pathological guilt would one day find a refuge in Swedenborg's calming revelations. Yet the impress of pain and guilt went too deep to be completely erased, and in spite of his new Swedenborgian gospel, Henry continued to insist all his life that pain was divinely ordained and a sign of God's love. In his most sustained confrontation with the problem, *The Nature of Evil* (1855), he argued that when the individual rejects God's love and wisdom, God does not leave the sinner to his own devices:

> [God] cannot weakly sympathize with my ignorant sensuality, and allow me to go on unchecked in a career of indulgence. On the contrary He is bound by permitting disaster and suffering to my outward interests, still solicitously to woo me, and soften my soul to the access of wisdom and tenderness from Him.

The Presbyterian minister who visited the boy's sickbed could not have put it better.

The only lifelong friend Henry made when he went to Princeton Theological Seminary in the 1830s was Parke Godwin, who seems to have sensed that the ordeal Henry's stump bluntly pointed to might somehow explain his views. Decades after Godwin asked Henry for his "morbid self-portraiture," Henry vividly recalled his friend's curiosity:

> I remember by the way that you once asked me in those old Seminary days . . . to recount to you the little iliad of my private bosom, or disclose in orderly form those sinister personal or sentimental grievances of mine which first sensibly impaired my natural pride of life, and afterward drove me to the seminary for relief. I did not at the time feel myself either free or disposed to satisfy your request, because I suppose I did not then acknowledge to myself as much as I have done since, the possible illustrative value of my particular history, nor regard it as merely typical in the main of the ruthless gangrene which is fast eating out the heart of our civilization. But I will now proceed to hold the *clinique* you then demanded, and give you my own mental or rather sentimental autopsy.

But the *clinique* was canceled. For whatever reason, Henry did not go on to perform the autopsy of his own sentimental life. Perhaps this was a task beyond his powers.

Even so, the diction with which he characterizes his inner history renders its outlines clear enough. I had been a boy reveling in the pride of life, he says, and then I was fatally injured by a sinister event. As a result, my sentimental life is dead, and its autopsy may be conducted. I tell you I feel no regret! What happened to me was only a type or allegory ("merely typical") of what must happen to our entire civilization, for there is gangrene everywhere. The pride of life must first express itself and then it must be cut away. With this line of thought, Henry gave meaning to his long and pointless ordeal.

On rare occasions, however, he wanted to make precisely the opposite point. In 1858, while living in France, he wrote an essay attacking the "process of brutal surgery" with which respectable society condemns those who have committed youthful indiscretions. " 'But surgery is good,' some one may say; 'it often saves life.' " Henry's answer:

> Doubtless; but at the expense of making the patient limp horribly all his days. It is the devil's method of dealing with disease—the method of the knife and cautery, the method of force—and has nothing of divinity about it but the Providence which directs it to good ends instead of evil. For my individual part, I would vastly rather die at once.

Lying on his bed, the boy had been afraid that the burning and severing were his just deserts. The man he turned into struggled with this verdict all his life, sometimes confirming it, sometimes fighting it. And the more he talked about the need to cut the gangrene away, the more it seemed to be a permanent part of him.

Chapter 7

■   ■   ■

UNION COLLEGE

The young man who was never so happy at home as he was away from it had been penned within its walls for almost four years, enduring an apparently endless run of pain, worry, tedium, advice, and individual tutoring. All that came to an end in September 1828, when Henry James traveled the fifteen miles between Albany and Schenectady and enrolled in Union College, entering the junior class along with sixty-five other young men. His long, compulsory retreat was finally over and done with. He was seventeen years old, with a fresh prospect of camaraderie and freedom and a brave new world to explore—new to him at least, though not to his father, who had been the school's principal investment banker during several very rocky years.

Union College, only thirty-three years old, was led by a strong, visionary president, the Reverend Eliphalet Nott, who believed that education must be practical and scientific. Nott was a dictator, a devious political lobbyist, a fast-talking, high-rolling, entrepreneurial gambler who nearly destroyed Union College in the process of building it up. His methods were reckless and improvisatory, and he amassed so much personal wealth that he left a lingering smell of corruption behind him.

At the time Henry enrolled, Nott had been president for twenty-four years (with thirty-eight still to go), and every aspect of the institution —its teaching staff, its curriculum, its personalized disciplinary practices, its risky financial footing, its ambitious building plan, its very location on a bluff overlooking the Mohawk River—bore the unmistakable thumbprint of its visionary strongman. Years later Henry told a Boston reporter that during his student days at Union he had "lived in President Nott's family." Adhering to his requirement that teachers reside in one of the two dormitories in order to supervise and encourage the students, Nott seems to have lived in the building known as South College. Henry may or may not have been installed in Nott's apartment, but the young man's room was probably within easy reach of this high-pressure administrator.

Curiously, Nott had been pastor of the Jameses' church in Albany before assuming the presidency in 1804. Unlike the ministers who succeeded him in the 1820s and 1830s, he was not much of a Calvinist. Instead of preaching that men's best efforts were as nothing in the sight of God, and that they could be saved only through faith in Christ, Nott's aim (as expressed by one of his admirers) "was to make men *wiser* and *better*, rather than to promote the sectarian interests and speculative tenets of the church." This memoirist considered Nott much superior to other clergymen in his secular attainments: he was "a mechanist, a political economist, a philosopher, and what is of more consequence in *any walk of life*, a man of keen observation and sound sense."

As "mechanist," Nott's outstanding achievement was the invention of a cast-iron stove capable of burning rocklike anthracite coal. It was as an inspirer of young men, however, that he became most famous, particularly when urging his students to think of science as the latest and best form of religion. The millennium seemed well within reach when he exhorted those who took the scientific course not "to remit their exertions until the most degraded tribes of earth shall have become regenerate." Like William of Albany in his Erie Canal oration, he was vastly impressed by man's ability to save himself "from misery as well as from guilt"—"by the help of God, to accomplish his own deliverance and to work out his own salvation." Nott even looked forward to the day when there would be an interplanetary society: "Who knows but that future generations, communicating with the nearest planets, and through them, with planets more remote, may effect an interchange of tidings, passed from world to world with the celerity of light." This was the sort of buoyant, can-do talk that passed from President Nott to Henry at his little college.

For its time, however, Union was not so little. Only Yale and Harvard enrolled more students in 1830, and no American college awarded more bachelor of arts degrees. The school grew at an unprecedented rate under Nott, chiefly as a result of two policies—his determination to go for broke in expanding the school's endowment and operating capital, and his policy of accepting students whose academic preparation was inadequate or who had been expelled elsewhere.

As a money-raiser, Nott was tireless, ingenious, and willing to take enormous gambles. In 1805 he got the New York State legislature to regard Union College as a public trust—and to grant it $80,000 through the state lottery office. In 1814 he extracted an additional $200,000, also to be raised by the sale of lottery tickets. When lotteries were outlawed by the revised state constitution of 1822, exception was made for the New York State Literature Lottery, whose principal beneficiary was Union College. When the income from the state-run lottery office failed to keep pace with Nott's expensive building program, he took two daring steps to keep the college in the black. He began borrowing large sums of money from William James against future lottery receipts (turning over as security the college's shares in the Mohawk Bank), and he persuaded the legislature to modify the statute on lotteries, so that, from 1822 on, those who were to benefit from this state monopoly were permitted to run it. Now that he had a private money tree, Nott arranged for two respected money men, John B. Yates and Archibald McIntyre, to tend and water it. McIntyre was New York State's former comptroller, known for his probity. Henceforth, whenever the Truly Lucky Office in South Market Street, Albany, or any of the state's other lottery dispensers sold a ticket, Union College grew fractionally richer.

Nott's gambles paid off in the end, though only at the cost of a great deal of anxiety. By March 1825 the college had received a total of $374,000 in appropriations from the state, mostly through lotteries. No other institution came close to this sum, Columbia College, for instance, getting only $54,755. Even so, in the winter of 1825–26 Yates and McIntyre found themselves unable to pay off the winning ticket holders and more or less compelled Nott to lend them an additional $100,000. Once again Union's president went hat in hand to William James, who demanded, as before, 6½ percent interest, and, as security, title to the college's physical plant and its remaining capital endowment. He also made clear that the whole lottery venture would have to be "materially curtailed," and soon, with all loans repaid. The following year he was made a trustee of the college and a member of its influential finance committee. Given his virtual ownership of the school, these appointments were long overdue.

By the time young Henry became a student in 1828, Nott and the lottery managers were under the impression that affairs were "evidently becoming brighter" and "drawing to a close." Although these rosy predictions were premature, the college did succeed in liquidating its massive debt obligation within four short years, so that on December 4, 1832,

William James returned all the Union College bonds and mortgages that had been signed over to him. (Eleven days later, as it happened, the financier was struck down by "apoplectic shock.")

President Nott's second tactic in his crash expansion program was to lower standards for admission and graduation. The 1828 catalogue recommended that prospective students prepare themselves by studying standard Latin authors and acquiring some Greek. Immediately following these stipulated prerequisites, however, came the sort of concession that characterized Nott's administrative style: "Less attention is paid to the particular books read, than to the amount of knowledge acquired." If this was encouragingly vague, so were the course and graduation requirements. On paper, Union College offered an exacting four-year classical curriculum that included Homer, Longinus, Sophocles, Euripides, chemistry, astronomy, and much more. In practice, virtually any academic stipulation could be waived, and most students were awarded their bachelor of arts after three years or less. No matter how inadequate a student's preparation, he began his studies at the sophomore or junior level, even if the classes he took were designated for freshmen. When a Scots minister visited Union in 1835, he was scandalized by the prevailing laxity: "Every student at the end of the course (three years) takes the degree of A.B. Some of them who deserve it, get it of course, and they who do not deserve it, get it *Speciali Gratia*; but all get it after three years." One of the college's best-known alumni, William H. Seward (the man who bought Alaska, "Seward's Folly"), felt that his education had been anything but thorough: "No volume or author was ever completed."

Nott had another policy that made Union College something of a degree mill: he accepted senior transfer students from other schools and then graduated them after a year. In 1832, for instance, a student at the University of Vermont wrote to ask whether he might take his senior year at Union. So many collegians made this kind of transfer, whether for academic or for disciplinary problems, that Union awarded more baccalaureate degrees than any other American college. In the bright lexicon of President Nott, there was no word for failure. He wanted to be the Moses of American education, opening the way for all young men, not just the elite, and leading them from the old monastic scholasticism toward the new ideal, where learning and public-spirited enterprise and enlightened state support all went hand in hand.

Although discipline was looser at Union than at, say, the College of New Jersey, it would still strike a modern observer as relatively monastic. Students were required to wear a uniform—"a gray coat, with a standing collar; gray pantaloons and overcoat: all of domestic manufacture." They were not to visit taverns or groceries, the two types of retail business that sold spirits. Nighttime seemed particularly risky, the young men being forbidden to leave their rooms, or fraternities to hold their meetings, after dark. At church, prayers, and of course classes "the most scrupulous attendance" was demanded. Students were fined one cent when absent with permission, three cents when they presented an acceptable excuse afterward, and 12½ cents if their absence couldn't be justified.

ABOUT AVERAGE

Henry attended Union College for somewhat less than two years, generally taking the standard load, three courses per term. The grades he received for his academic performances, and also for Attendance and Conduct, were entered in printed ledgers, the "Merit Rolls." At the end of each term, his grades were added together (provided he completed all three courses), and he was then ranked relative to his classmates.

The other official source of information on Henry's college career is his individual financial account as kept for him by the "College Register," or bookkeeper. Since this officer acted as the students' banker, paying their off-campus bills in addition to receiving payments for tuition and other charges, the bill books furnish a great deal of information about student life. The most striking disclosure is the inclusiveness of the care the institution furnished the collegians, most of whom had no expenses whatever outside the standard charges for meals, fuel, laundry, and so forth. Only a tiny handful of well-heeled students regularly incurred extramural bills.

Although Henry was allowed to enter as a junior, his first-term courses suggest he had a good deal of catching up to do. His rhetoric (composition) class used the same reader he had been assigned at Albany Academy, and his Latin class (Horace?) was classified as being at the freshman level. The hardest of his three classes, Graeca Majora, probably involved daily translations from the Greek historians, Herodotus and Thucydides. Henry's presence in this course indicates he was following the prestigious classical curriculum. Standards seem to have been rather lax, however, as eight of his fellow ten students received a grade of 100. Henry's grade, the second lowest, was 90. Although he did better in Latin and rhetoric, his combined grades for his first term gave him a ranking of thirty-two out of a class of sixty-five.

The college bill books show that Henry spent a substantial $10 for

"Newspapers &c" his first quarter, an outlay that testifies to his alert interest in the public press (and to his father's willingness to indulge it). All told, the young man's itemized expenses for the fall of 1828 came to four times the standard charge per term for tuition and room rent ($18.50). He was definitely not living in penury. In November, altering his dining arrangements, he began taking board at Francis Fisk's house, located just off campus on the Troy Turnpike (present-day Union Street). Fisk's weekly charge was a stiff $2.50, but the fellow diners included a son of John Townsend (one of William's partners in the Syracuse venture) and an engaging young tutor named Isaac W. Jackson. An ardent Clintonian, Jackson had attended Albany Academy and now taught mathematics and served as the college's military drillmaster. Not only was he a favorite with students, but Henry had a knack for establishing fraternal relations with slightly older men in positions of authority. In the winter of 1830, when he had an important message to send his fellow boarder, he opened with a warmly respectful salute, "My dear Captain."

One reason Henry had so many expenditures was that he had joined a new kind of student social club, the fraternity. Kappa Alpha, the first college fraternity in America, had been founded at Union in 1825 by a group that included Jackson (at that time still a student). Sigma Phi and Delta Phi were started up not long after. At first these clubs were thought of as "secret societies," somewhat like the Masons, and in fact the rise of fraternities was contemporary with Antimasonry, the populist political movement that opposed elite organizations based on vows of loyalty and secrecy. It isn't known whether Henry became a Mason, but his 1831 partnership in a small Albany sheet called *The Craftsman* shows where his sympathies lay. (Even in boyhood he had been a convivial member of the North Pearl Street neighborhood shoemakers' club.) In any case, during his first term at Union he joined the fledgling Sigma Phi, organized the previous year. Fraternity membership did not yet entail living in a house, and the main attraction may have been "creating secrets for the sole purpose of protecting them from the other fraternities." There were also dinners, at which a wealthy and sociable young man would have been most welcome. Perhaps Henry's new affiliation had something to do with his disastrous second term.

This term, running from January to April, seems to have been a restless one for the entire student body, with a spate of absences and a general falling off in grades. Henry's Attendance slipped to 91 in consequence of more than thirty absences from prayers and recitations, half of them not excused in advance. In Conic Sections, possibly taught by Jackson, he emerged with a mediocre 85. In Cicero, he fell so far behind he got a dismal 75. If he took a third course, he did so poorly the grade wasn't even recorded. He was one of only ten or so students who didn't receive a class ranking for the term.

For his third term, which ran from May to July, Henry's resolution was back in working order, perhaps as a result of a private lecture given him at his father's behest by Archibald McIntyre. Missing only one recitation, the young man ended up with the highest ranking of his college career, twenty-five in a class of seventy-five. In Graeca Majora, judging from a bill for two copies of a booklet on hexameters (he must have lost the first one), the focus had shifted from Greek history to the *Odyssey*. He earned a 90 in this course and also in Political Economy, but neither field of study made much of an impression on him. Thirty years later he called Homer a "garrulous old poet" and upbraided certain British statesmen for wasting their time on the "insufferable pedantries" of Homeric scholarship. As for Political Economy, the theories he adopted in the later 1840s would have made his instructor shudder. Henry's third course, "Dynamics, Hydros. &c," was required of all students, even those following the classical curriculum. But no topic in physics ever made much sense to Henry, in spite of all his previous tutoring from Joseph Henry. The young man's grade was 87, in the bottom third.

Henry may have been fortunate that he did no worse. He was spending more now for necessities—laundry, cleaning, oysters, cigars—and at the end of June, with examinations looming, he apparently took off for Ballston and its spa. Nevertheless, when the term ended in July, he was promoted to the senior class.

The following September, when Henry returned to Schenectady after an eight-week vacation, he found that being a senior brought several changes. The disciplines of Latin, Greek, and mathematics were at an end now, and although there was one last physics course to take, Optics, the young man was ready for Union's two famous capstone courses, Intellectual Philosophy and Elements of Criticism. The first of these was based on Dugald Stewart's *Elements of the Philosophy of the Human Mind*, which taught that the mind had certain implanted commonsense principles of perception and cognition. The second had as its textbook *Elements of Criticism* by Henry Home, Lord Kames. Thanks to these two eighteenth-century Scottish bulwarks against subjectivism and skepticism, Henry would at last be made to understand the organization of knowledge and the principles of critical inquiry—would see how the scattered fragments that comprised the world of learning as he had experienced it actually cohered.

Elements of Criticism, Nott's special baby, was largely responsible for the reputation he enjoyed with students and alumni. In his opening lecture he made it clear to the seniors ranged in front of him that *this* class was going to be utterly unlike any class they had taken:

> There are many, I have no doubt, in this class, as there are in all classes, who cannot be persuaded to think . . . I shall not give you long lessons but shall lead you to exercise your own minds . . . to inquire into the principles of the mind, the causes of the emotions you have seen in it, and the manner in which it is moved.

What Nott then proceeded to do for the rest of the term was to teach *against* the textbook—to inspire his students to question Lord Kames and all other academic authorities who assumed the mantle of learned rationality:

> It is asserted, young gentlemen . . . that man is a *reasonable* being—but such is not the fact—and I make this remark that you may not go forth into the world with a wrong opinion upon this subject. After long experience and much reflection and intercourse with man I can safely affirm that he is not a reasonable being.

It gradually became clear that what Nott was teaching was not the art of reasoned inquiry but how to attain public influence:

> If you were an editor you would not place your chief dependence on sound argument . . . Depend on it, the merest trifle which would arouse the feelings or enlist the prejudices of the public would be more serviceable than whole pages of sound logic and close reasoning.

These candid disclosures had an electrifying effect on Union's seniors. Francis Wayland (who became president of Brown University) remembered Nott's lectures as "a pleasure which no student was willing to lose. We then began to feel ourselves men, and to form judgments for ourselves . . . I think I do not exaggerate when I say that attendance on Doctor Nott's course formed an era in the life of every one of his pupils."

In the life of everyone except Henry James, whose grade for Elements of Criticism was a wretched 75. Out of eighty-four students, only eight scored lower. Whether he engaged in debate with Nott or sat there in sullen resentment or simply paid no attention, the course clearly did not make *him* feel himself a man. Judging from his grades for his other two classes, the whole term was a shambles. In Optics, he dropped to 80, and in the course devoted to Stewart (at $2.50 his most expensive textbook), he did so badly he was not even assigned a numerical grade. As was the case his second term, his scores were not added together and he did not receive a class ranking. Yet he had not skipped class excessively, having missed only six recitations in all. The reason his grade for Attendance took a drop—to 93 (the second lowest)—was that he was absent from prayers fourteen times.

While the young man took little interest in academics or devotions, he gave the closest attention to other matters, paying $1.50 for a looking glass and doubling his outlay for candles and "washing." His laundry bill for fall 1829 was $9.54, as against $4.13 for his first term. He was also making heavy use of the post office, which billed him $3.53 on October 6 and $4.69 the following January. The largest bills didn't come in until after the new year: $22.41 was owed Richard Cooke, a merchant tailor; $41.37 was owed a certain (perhaps Dr. Leonard) Sprague. An Andrews wanted $7.19, a Seymour $3.50. There was a tutor named George W. Eaton who taught at Union for that year only (and whom Henry affectionately remembered as "*maximus inter magnos*"); $13.50 was the amount of "Eatons demand." As in childhood, when Henry pilfered from his father's cash drawer to satisfy his sweet tooth, he was spending freely. And the bill books only hint at how lavishly he was dipping into his credit.

Into Pa's credit, that is, and Pa was getting steamed up, especially now that his son had apparently disgraced himself in some way. In November 1829, well before receiving Henry's dismal grades, William James prevailed on his longtime confederate Archibald McIntyre to undertake the unpleasant task of sending the boy a warning and an ultimatum. McIntyre opened with a stern declaration: "Were I not your friend I do not think that I would trouble you with any communications of mine at this time." He went on:

I have heard, and your friends generally have heard enough of your conduct to cause us much pain and solicitude for your safety and future usefulness. I consider you on the very verge of ruin, and am well satisfied that if you do not without delay stop short in the career of folly that you have for a time indulged in . . . you are lost to the world, to your parents and to yourself . . . Allow me then to entreat that you will for the future repose yourself upon your father and mother, and take their advice in every thing. Indulge in no expenses whatever that shall not be known to and approved by them . . . Some consider you already lost, irretrievably lost. I am not, however, one of those. I cannot believe that a young man of good parts,

with wealth to support him in well doing (but with none without performing his duty), with numerous and anxious friends, can be such an
idiot as to throw away all these advantages, and become a loathing to
himself and his best friends. Such, will be your case, however, (I will not
mince the matter) if you do not retrace your steps. Lose not a moment
then, my dear Henry, to convince your father, by every future act of your
life, that you repent of the past, and that you determine to act entirely
conformably to his advice and wishes.

There is no doubt the paternal breast was seriously ruffled. Years later,
Henry's second son and namesake had the impression he had been "quite
definitely 'wild' " during his college years. Although Henry Jr. was vague
about his father's misdeeds, another brother was better informed. In the
mid-1870s, hoping to persuade Robertson that he could put a stop to
his drinking sprees by an act of will, Henry Sr. offered a detailed and
ruthless "*exposé* of [his] early history." He made these disclosures "not
without shrinking," and when he was done he moaned, "My hand is so
tired I must give up—without another word. I cannot even read this
over." This uneasy, breast-baring document throws a great deal of light
on the ups and downs of his career at Union:

> No wonder then that when I emerged from my sick-room, & went to
> college, I was hopelessly addicted to the vice. In college matters became
> very much worse with me and by the time I left it I was looked upon as
> an utter victim to intemperance.

Characteristically, what the second sentence emphasizes is not Henry's
chronic drunkenness as such, though that was bad enough, but the view
of it in others' eyes. How others saw and judged him: that seems to have
been the most distressing aspect of his helpless addiction. As one who
pictured God as a giant scrutinizing eye, who bought a pricey mirror and
spent freely on his appearance, and who assumed a disguise in setting
out to write his autobiography, Henry could not endure being the abject
spectacle of others' disapproving gaze.

Henry's 1851 essay on intemperance would confess that "drunkenness
is the vice of natures like mine"—natures, he meant, that are less inclined
to practical activity than to thought and feeling. Although he did not
divulge his personal history in the essay, he seemed to be drawing on it
in his categorical assertion that "there is no mystery about drunkenness.
Like all habits, its strength lies in a diseased will." But even while he insisted
that the drunkard's only remedy lies within himself, he also argued that

society merely confirms him in his vice when it views him with disgust or reprobation. "Teach a man to believe himself at heart a sinner, and he will be sure to 'play hell,' as the phrase goes, with his teachers." Relieve him of this sinful imputation, and his manliness will once again prevail. These hard-won opinions reflected Henry's youthful self-disgust, his agonized sense of being a public reproach. But if his strong belief in the power of will helped him overcome his self-destructive addiction, this strategy also kept him from recognizing the circumstantial causes of his trouble.

Chief among these was that his drinking was a form of rebellion against his father, his instructors, in fact the whole order of advice-giving elders, ranging from the strict Presbyterian, Scotch-Irish world that had framed his childhood to the power-hungry president of Union College, with his cynical advice on how to win friends and influence people. All his life, whenever Henry outlined the normal processes of maturation, rebellion would invariably be a prominent feature. For him, certainly, it was inevitable. Following his prolonged, youthful invalidism, it must have been a huge relief to shuck off his precocious concern for minor misdeeds, the good opinion of "our first men," and "the ultimate improvement of my mind."

But Henry's rebellion had more despair in it than self-assertion, for what his drunkenness chiefly expressed was his sense of powerlessness in the face of his father's world. His second son believed his father's "sharp rupture" with William of Albany was caused by "some course he [Henry Sr.] had taken or had declined to take." The quarrel was probably on "clerical or anticlerical grounds," Henry Jr. thought. McIntyre's letter clarifies matters, as it absolutely breathes with the collective genius of quiet, arm-twisting cronyism, the same spirit the powerful father had invoked two years earlier when he asked Henry to remind Rev. William of the advantage "of gaining the acquaintance of his [father's] most respectable friends." Henry's careless disregard for this influential network may have been his greatest outrage in his father's eyes.

A close second, though, was the refusal to enter the profession Father had chosen for him. McIntyre, reluctantly mediating between parent and child, felt compelled to make the point perfectly clear:

Let your studies too as far as possible be conformable to your father's wishes. You intimated to me that you disliked the law. I regretted it, but yielded the point to you. On speaking to your father on this head, however, I found him inflexibly fixed on your studying the law, or at all events on studying one of the learned professions.

This would seem more than categorical, and yet, like everything that concerns William's paternal discipline, the passage is strangely ambiguous. At first Father is "inflexibly fixed" on the law, but then comes the concession: *any* learned profession will do. McIntyre's letter both authorizes and discredits the impression that the father required his son to study the law.

On one point, though, Father really was inflexible: Henry must not drop out of college. No learned profession would be open to a young man if he failed to take a degree. But the young man was not a James for nothing. Ignoring McIntyre's ultimatum to shape up or be disinherited, he carelessly set off to find his fortune, or at least spend his father's. This insouciant defiance in the midst of continuing financial dependency was more than the old man could take. One month after sending Henry his final warning, McIntyre received a splenetic and asyntactic communication from Albany.

> [He] has so debased himself as to leave his parents house in the character of a swindler &c. &c.—details presented to day—are the order which I enclose as a specimen of his progress in arts of low vileness—and unblushing falsehood;—Such will be practised in N.Y.—in book stores*— Taylors &c—and in the same as df^{ts} [drafts] on me &c;—all of which will meet him direct—and lodge him in a prison of some kind—directly; a fellow from Schenectady was after him to day for 50 to 60 drs [dollars]— (in a note I understand) for segars and oysters.

Ambrose Townsend, who also boarded at Fisk's, had the impression Henry was headed for Boston, but William was too suspicious to believe this report: "Deception is of no consequence—in his case,—they will find him and he will find his reward, poor being."

Henry *had* gone to New York, but by December 8 he had vanished, as President Nott mentioned in a letter to McIntyre that was chiefly concerned with bonds and lotteries. Wherever Henry might be, Nott hoped he would "get into business immediately; or else break down immediately—the sooner his business comes to a crisis: the better." The boy had to find out for himself "that money has some value, and that economy is a virtue, before he will be induced to look to his father for support or for counsel." Two weeks later, at the end of another business letter, McIntyre informed Nott that William James had recently heard from his son from Boston, where "he was about to be employed as a

---

* Four decades later an Albany bookseller told a Boston diarist that Henry "used to run up large bills for books at Mr Little's store. His father would never pay them."

Reader & Corrector of proofs." In McIntyre's eyes this was drudgery, and he pronounced the boy "no way fitted for such an employment. I cannot help thinking that he will soon be compelled . . . to submit to wholesome government, and the sooner that distress shall compel him the better." On this point McIntyre and Nott saw eye to eye, and when the latter replied on Christmas Day, he expressed surprise that the boy was still referring his creditors to the college: "He is a bright boy, but has defects of character; adversity may be of use to him— If he writes you let me know the contents."

The latest news on Henry runs like a refrain in the lottery correspondence of these calm and powerful men, who had no doubts as to the wisdom of their views. But William of Albany was gnashing his teeth and wallowing in the ironies of his predicament:

> It is difficult to conceive of the wound'd spirit of a man in my situation —my heart pities a poor unfortunate son—who has so perverted the mercies of a kind providence that with the most ambitious desires and means of making him one of the most respectable members of his family and of the community—all parental kindness only encreases his progress in guilt, and contempt.

The passage has a fascinating self-reflexiveness, in that William seems transfixed by the paradox of his own situation. Seeing himself as loving and omnipotent and for that very reason unable to save his son, he almost relishes the dramatic mystery of his paternal suffering. If his predicament resembles that of God the Father in the New Testament, helpless to avert his son's crucifixion, it seems even closer to that of Wagner's more tragic father, Wotan, who is prevented by the consequences of his own supreme power from preserving his son Siegmund. Wotan, however, shows more dignity. Wotan does not solicit Archibald McIntyre's pity. And Wotan does not have the option of granting mercy:

> If you see him, tell him, that when he finds how base he has acted,— and when deceiv'd and despised by himself and all others;—to come to me and I shall endeavour to screen him from infamy and as far as possible from reproach.

It was a characteristic move. Reversing himself at the last minute, William dropped the knife he held over the son he was about to sacrifice to that fiercest of Scotch-Irish dieties, Probity in Business.

THIS ROOM IS SACRED TO ME

The chief organ of American Unitarian thought was the *Christian Examiner*, a learned journal published six times a year in Boston. A glance at its articles for 1829–30 discloses a high regard for the capacity of man's moral nature, great faith in the power of rationality, an abhorrence of fanaticism and bigotry, and some doubts about the value of enthusiasm. A writer in the September issue was on the whole rather cool toward the current popularity of missionary societies, temperance societies, and bible societies, and was downright hostile to those organizations that wanted to prevent traveling on Sunday: religion was progressive, after all, and the law of the Sabbath was no longer binding. Another writer praised two of New England's more liberal eighteenth-century preachers, who insisted on "gospel virtue as the test of character and the condition of salvation," in this way abandoning the doctrine of faith alone. In January 1830, a contributor rejected the claim (dear to the cast-iron heart of President Nott) that America needed useful knowledge most of all. Of much greater value, in this writer's opinion, was literature that exercised the "highest faculties."

The man who ran the *Examiner* was Francis Jenks, who had graduated ten years earlier from Harvard's Divinity School but never been ordained. On January 13, 1830, from the house at 12 Hancock Street on Beacon Hill, where Jenks conducted his editorial work, Henry James drafted a long and boastful letter to Isaac Jackson back in Schenectady. The young man had defied his stern father and launched himself in the world, and he wanted to assure his former tutor that even though he was alone in what he called his pilgrimage, he was doing extremely well. He had found a comfortable berth on the first floor—not the basement, he wanted it understood—of Jenks's elegant four-story house, and the facilities for study and the cultivation of taste were a match for anything Schenectady had to offer. His bed stood in a "neat recess," there was a "handsome closet" on either side, and he was surrounded by refined comfort: "I am sitting on a snug sofa . . . On my left is a cheerful lehigh fire; under my feet a warm carpet and over my head a painting of Lorenzo de Medici, by Mrs. Jenks. This room is sacred to me." Perhaps the letter was intended for Nott's eyes. It was his invention of a movable circular grate that made that Lehigh stove so cheerful.

The prison Henry's father had foreseen had not materialized. Even better, the eighteen-year-old youth had found a livelihood and, he claimed, a profession. Jenks, a respected scholar, had offered him $200 a year, with room and board, for carrying out the necessary editorial

chores of proofreading, fact checking, and writing minor notices. Henry
was spending eight hours a day at this work. He scoffed at the suggestion
that it would ever lose interest for him—"This has been called by Mr
McIntyre drudgery!"—and anyway he had every opportunity to develop
his mind: "I now go on with the study of languages much more thoroughly
than I should have found it necessary had I remained at home. It is
indispensable that I should. My ambition is awakened."

In every way possible the young man demonstrated that he was not
an outcast adrift in the city. He even remembered religion, occasionally
going to hear the first Unitarian preacher of the day, William Ellery
Channing: there was no "higher treat than one of [his] practical sermons."
Perhaps the emphasis on practicality was meant to catch President Nott's
eye. Even more appealing was Henry's comment about the Reverend
Alonzo Potter, an Episcopal rector who had taught at Union a few years
earlier. Potter had been "exceedingly kind," evidently inviting the young
man into his home, and Henry went into gallant raptures over his wife:

> Mrs. Potter is what Eve might have been before the fall. Listening to and
> looking upon her sometimes, I am apt (as often before I have said in
> regard to some other married ladies of my acquaintance) to wish with the
> Psalmist, neither poverty nor riches, but just such a wife as Mrs. Potter;
> (by the way what a horrid name for that woman).

As Henry perfectly well knew, several years earlier Mrs. Potter's name
had been Sarah Maria Nott. Nothing the young man could have said
would be more likely to appease the president, who badly wanted his
much-loved daughter back at Union. In fact, Potter was not only appointed Professor of Rhetoric and Moral Philosophy in 1831, but he was
made vice-president, Nott's hand-picked successor. Henry may have defied his father and run away from college, but he was not above pacifying
a prominent man like President Nott.

Mentioning Mrs. Potter brought to mind the young woman, Elizabeth
Pomeroy, whom Jackson had taken to wife five months earlier. Twenty-
four years old, Elizabeth was the daughter of a successful manufacturer
from Pittsfield, Massachusetts, a man so imperious it was said "there
would be no living with Mr. Pomeroy, if he were not almost always
right." The newlyweds had been boarding at the same off-campus house
as Henry. In a passage that anticipates the teasing badinage of his mature
dealings with attractive women, the young collegian who liked to think
of Eve before the Fall now appeared to lose control of his writing
instrument:

My pen will run on until it hits Mr. Fisk's house. And now, in spite of
me, it will write Mrs Jackson, and the wilful thing won't be quiet till it
becomes the messenger of my love to her. How provoking! when the pen
will so tenaciously hold to the course which he who sits behind it en-
deavours so sedulously to avoid.

This wayward pen seemed a good deal less contented and sedentary than
the man who sat behind it claimed to be. Oh yes, the room was sacred,
it was most convenient that Henry was not "required to leave" it, and
the one-legged man was fortunate in having found employment that did
not necessitate physical mobility. Still, it might have been predicted
that this gifted scribbler would soon feel tempted to follow that pen.

Union's president was not impressed. On January 2, having received
an earlier (non-extant) letter from Henry, he roughly dismissed the young
man's boasts: "I have just heard from young James—he professes to have
got into business, but [I] fear he is not doing well— Nothing can be
done for him till he learns by experience the worth of a fathers house."

GRADUATION

Years later, one of Henry's children thought he had stayed in Boston for
"two or three months." Judging from an entry in the college account
books, he was still in the city and on his own as of late February, when
Union gave him $15 credit for the books he had left behind and reduced
his outstanding bill to $107. Soon afterward Henry gave up Jenks's sacred
room and bookcases and Lehigh stove and returned to school. What
exactly persuaded him to do so can only be conjectured. Although some
have supposed he was compelled against his will by William James, the
sheltered and unstable youth had sufficient reasons of his own for reaching
an accommodation with his father. Eight hours a day of reading proof
and checking the accuracy of quotations did not amount to an independent life. Alcohol was a standing temptation, the boy had a dark suspicion
his will was diseased, and his pen was restless and disobedient. Proofreading left the real questions unanswered. What did he want to do?
What did he want to be?

There was disease of another sort as well. By April, the first month
in which he is known to have been back at Union, the bookkeeper's
accounts inform us that he was too ill to eat his meals with others. At
some point during that month the young man was charged $5.72, with

this explanation—"Duncan for board furnished Henry at his room when sick." So not only was the Boston adventure over but Henry was confined to his room, just as in the old days. Was this a serious illness? Were his "spirits and resolution" affected? If one compares Duncan's bill to the weekly charge of $2.50 at Fisk's boardinghouse, it would seem that Henry had to stay in bed for sixteen days or so. Taking into account Fisk's relative expensiveness, the illness may have lasted even longer. What is certain is that Henry did not attend classes, for instead of paying the regular $18.50 for "Tuition, Room-Rent, use of College Library, Servants' Hire, Printing, &c," he was billed only $10 for the second term. His extended absence was not even recorded.

During his final April-to-July term, Henry seems to have felt even more detached from college than do most graduating seniors. Instead of taking Moral Philosophy as codified by William Paley, he joined five other students in an elementary German course—an unusual language to study at the time and one that does not show up in Union's surviving catalogues. Although the grammar and reader cost his father $2.50, Henry took so little interest in the subject that his grade was a shabby 70. He would have been better off conning "languages" in Jenks's sacred room.

Henry's other two courses, Blackstone and Kent, took their names from their textbooks' authors. Blackstone had written the standard four-volume exposition of English common law. The cost was $5.50, considerably more than any other college text. You did not buy Blackstone unless you were making a basic professional investment. Of course, a single class did not authorize a young man to hang up his shingle, but it at least prepared him to study with the sort of practicing attorney who coached apprentice lawyers. Henry had acceded to his father's wishes. He was going to enter the law. But he must have made up his mind to learn absolutely nothing, for his grade in Blackstone was tantamount to failure—a pathetic 50. Of the twenty-two students enrolled in the course, only one scored lower than he. This was his worst academic performance during his two years (speaking loosely) of college.

In Henry's third course, also an introduction to the law, his performance proved even more abysmal. Kent was James Kent, New York's most honored jurist and Albany's most distinguished citizen, a man whose reputation had impressed the young boy a few years earlier in his sickroom in North Pearl Street. Now that Henry was to learn what the great man had been all about, he utterly failed. Whether he chose not to appear before the examiners after doing so wretchedly in Blackstone or whether there was some other cause, Henry did not even receive a grade in Kent. If it were not for a duplicate and apparently provisional merit roll, there would be no record that he even enrolled in the course.

Henry broke another private record as well. In the past he had always been able to offer a tolerable excuse for his absences. Now, on eight separate occasions, he did not have any. Was he too hung over to make it to class? And what does it mean that Mrs. White's bill for washing shot up to its highest level ever, $13.02? Had he become something of a dandy as well as a drunk?

As the disapproving Scottish visitor said, every Union College senior received his B.A., whether he deserved it or not. In July 1830 the faculty begged "leave to Recommend the following young gentlemen members of the Senior Class as Candidates for the first degree in the Arts." Henry's name was on the list, and the list was respectfully presented to the board of trustees, and the sitting trustees who respectfully accepted it included Henry's father, New York's Chief Justice William L. Marcy, and the man who succeeded James Kent as chancellor, Reuben H. Walworth. Yale graduated seventy-one seniors that year, Harvard forty-eight, and Princeton twenty. Union graduated ninety-six. Of course, some of them may conceivably have learned something of value.

One wonders what William of Albany considered he had got for his money on September 28, 1830, the end of the third quarter for book-keeping, when he paid off his son's outstanding college balance, $157.43.

Chapter 8

■ ■ ■

DARK CORNERS: 1830–35

Looking backward, Henry saw the five-year period between his graduation from Union College and his enrollment in seminary as a barren waste. During this interval he made a feint at preparing for the law and dabbled in short-lived political and business ventures and did some heavy drinking. Then, soon after his twenty-first birthday, came a momentous event, his father's unexpected death, followed by the disclosure of the harsh will he had drawn up a few months earlier. As we shall see, the punishment this document meted out to Henry and some other members of the family did not go unresisted, but meanwhile he was at least receiving an annuity sufficient to live on. Released from the necessity of reading law, he left Albany and drifted across upper New York State, living in idleness and dissipation. The young man who had shown such terrible self-discipline when confined to his bed was free at last—and rudderless. Then, in late 1834 or early 1835, a second thunderclap sounded. This one not only reinvigorated the young man's weakened resolution but revealed his life's calling to him. His years of wandering were over, he believed.

This five-year period appears to be a chronicle of wasted youth—a chronicle tattered almost beyond recovery. No other period of Henry's life after childhood is so scantily documented. There is not one extant letter of his between 1830 and 1835, and the few surviving letters written by his siblings and friends shed no light whatever on his activities. It was this period that gave rise years later to his children's impression of his early wildness and restless movement from place to place. In Henry Jr.'s memory, all the tales his father told about his life in Albany seemed to feature dissolute young men, as if the whole generation had gone to ruin and Henry Sr. alone were alive to tell the story: "Each contemporary on his younger scene, each hero of each thrilling adventure, had, in spite of brilliant promise and romantic charm, ended badly, as badly as possible."

These tales of disaster bespoke Henry Sr.'s sense of having had a narrow escape, but they also reflected a large-scale civic and generational decline. Albany's glory days had passed, and those who remembered the stimulating expansion of the teens and twenties were struck by the conspicuous absence of eminent names in succeeding decades. One day in 1839, after Joseph Henry had moved to Princeton, a tramp begging for cast-off clothes was discovered to be the son of old Dr. Woodruff. "How many examples of this kind," wrote the self-made scientist, "have been furnished by the sons of the better classes in Albany."

THE CRAFTSMAN

After Union College, according to an interview Henry gave in old age, he "studied law in Albany." In principle, the young man was preparing himself for his new profession by having another go at Blackstone and Kent, poring over statutes and case law, and performing ordinary legal chores in the office of an attorney, one no doubt selected by his father. It may have been James King, Henry's brother-in-law, who directed him in these preparatory studies. Or maybe it was Gideon Hawley. Whoever the lawyer was, he had so little impact on Henry's life that there seems to be no record of his name.

The first solid clue to Henry's postgraduate life in Albany is to be found on the masthead of a short-lived newspaper, *The Craftsman*. For about three months, from October 29, 1831, to February 6, 1832, "H. James" was listed as a co-editor along with E. J. Roberts and I. T. Simmons, a local printer. The editorial office was at 65 State Street, the north side, a little below the New York State Bank. This was the first of several offbeat newspapers in which James took an interest, and it was the least likely of them all to succeed. *The Craftsman* defined itself as pro-Masonic and "independent," claimed to be the faithful inheritor of Clintonianism, and assailed practically all the current political persuasions in the state of New York. How Henry got involved with this maverick sheet, few issues of which survive, is one of the more intriguing mysteries in his life, particularly since he does not seem to have played much of a role in running it. Only a single article is recognizably his, a magazine notice that finds a pretext for praising the "scholarlike taste, and experience as an editor" of Henry's former employer, Francis Jenks.

Henry apparently had several other "brief ventures in law and business" in 1830–35, but *The Craftsman* is the only one that has come to light. To understand his involvement in this curious paper requires a brief glance at the confused state of New York politics around 1830, a time when the Clintonians were dispersed, the Regency was in the ascendant, and the Whig Party not yet invented. It was a moment when the powerful James family needed to find a new political base.

Back in 1826 a man by the name of William Morgan had announced the publication of a book that promised to reveal the Freemasons' secret political machinations. He was jailed, abducted from prison, and never seen again. John C. Spencer, one of New York State's most prominent and aggressive lawyers, was appointed special prosecutor, and in 1828 a celebrated trial of Morgan's apparent kidnappers and murderers was held in the village of Canandaigua. Hostility to Freemasonry grew so intense that a major new political organization, the Antimasonic Party, came into being. Animated by a populist suspicion that civic affairs had been subverted by an elitist conspiracy, this party got heavy support from the rural areas and small towns of western New York. Spencer expressed the mood of the time when he declared that "all secret and exclusive societies are . . . hostile to the spirit of our institutions." Masons came under such heavy fire that some among them felt compelled to renounce their membership. Others decided to establish a weekly that would combat the "anti-masonic fanaticism," and accordingly, in February 1829, in Rochester, New York, *The Craftsman* began its brief and agitated career. The man selected to run it, Elijah J. Roberts, was a veteran newspaperman and old Clintonian warhorse, and he proceeded to attack the enemies of Freemasonry with bristling pugnacity.

Masons liked to think of their society as an enlightened brotherhood devoted to virtue and civic progress. Benjamin Franklin, George Washington, and Chief Justice John Marshall had belonged, and DeWitt Clinton, the recognized leader of American Freemasonry, had been Grand Master for years. Clinton was undoubtedly embarrassed by the anti-Masonic fervor, which many lodge members interpreted as an underhanded campaign to dethrone him. Clinton's last big political move shortly before his death in 1828 was to join his old enemy, Martin Van Buren, in supporting Andrew Jackson's Democratic candidacy for President; Jackson was known to be a high Mason. Once again, many Clintonians felt betrayed by their leader and, refusing to follow him, voted for the rival candidates, John Quincy Adams (National Republican) or Francis Granger (Antimasonic).

With Clinton dead and his followers in disarray, William of Albany found himself gravely weakened at the very moment he was trying to launch an ambitious project involving no less an institution than the Bank of the United States. Although this Philadelphia bank was privately owned, it served as the depository for federal funds, controlled the currency, and in other ways played a central regulatory role in the nation's economy. William had amassed his fortune by identifying himself with the integration and centralization of fiscal resources. He wanted an entrée into the U.S. Bank, and he helped organize a quiet campaign to get it to open a branch in Albany. Going straight to the top, he wrote the bank's president, Nicholas Biddle, to press his case. But the tides of change were no longer with the financier. There was a popular suspicion now that banks were "monsters" of conspiratorial control (rather like the Masons), and President Andrew Jackson was convinced that this particular bank was unconstitutional. For the remainder of the decade, the fight between Jackson's Democratic Party and the U.S. Bank would dominate American political life.

Some of William's in-laws had run one of Albany's early newspapers, the Jeffersonian *Register*. Since then, the city's press had helped make Albany "a political centre for both the State and nation." The *Argus* had long been the mouthpiece of first the Regency and then the Jackson Democrats, and in March 1830 a number of influential Antimasons got the able Thurlow Weed to move to the capital and establish their own sheet, the *Evening Journal*. More than newspapers, the *Argus* and the *Evening Journal* were aggressive and effective party organs. Indeed, each party, as Weed later wrote, "confided the duty of organization and discipline to its respective editors. A sense of responsibility stimulated both." Neither paper, however, was responsible to William James.

Meanwhile, back in Rochester, *The Craftsman* was not prospering. When an important backer withdrew support, Roberts decided to shift his operation to the state capital, where the first issue appeared in July 1831. The newspaper's stated policy of "independence" meant nominal support of Jackson and undying defiance of the Democratic Party at the state level, and also, to be sure, continuing opposition to anti-Masonry. The Regency press saw *The Craftsman* as a sort of provocateur, designed to encourage "defection, treachery and intrigue" under cover of loyalty to the President, but the paper did have a positive program. In spite of its professed Jacksonianism, it strongly favored the renewed chartering of the U.S. Bank. On January 7, 1832, the paper ran an article defending the bank's constitutionality and insisting on "the indispensable necessity of such an institution, for the fiscal operations of the government."

The evidence is only circumstantial, but it looks very much as if William James was *The Craftsman*'s principal backer in Albany. In addition to having the same political interests as the paper—the great bank, federal support of local improvements—the financier offered material aid by running some real-estate advertisements in the sheet. At a time when Roberts was able to drum up little advertising revenue, William sent *The Craftsman* (but not the *Evening Journal*) a sizable list of commercial properties to be let. He also advertised the sale of a rural property. But the best reason for tagging William as the paper's angel is the appearance of his son's name on the masthead—a name the *Argus* pointed out to its readers. Henry was twenty years old and without an income of his own. He still depended on his father's support. He would not have been able to buy into *The Craftsman*, even if he had had a reason for wanting to do so. It was probably his father who financed the venture for him. The boy obviously had a way with his pen. What a lawyer he would make if he only put his mind to it! Of course, the political press hardly constituted a decent profession for a gentleman, but *The Craftsman* might occupy the boy's time, open his eyes a little, keep him off the bottle.

Tellingly, it was not long after Roberts took Henry on that *The Craftsman* got a sizable injection of capital. On January 1, 1832, in a major upgrade, the newspaper changed from a weekly to a daily and modernized its format and printing plant. * These were ambitious improvements, and the rival *Evening Journal* complimented the paper for its "neat and reputable appearance." Even the great *Argus* had been a daily for less than seven years. But the spiffy new look could not save *The Craftsman*. Instead of news it now offered little more than long extracts; a mysterious fire destroyed the subscription list and account books; and after February 6 "H. James" disappeared from the masthead, as did "E. J. Roberts" himself. The following week the editor alluded to an unexplained "domestic affliction" in making his apologies. The next day the paper died, leaving William's boy as much at loose ends as ever.

A JUST DISPOSITION OF MY PROPERTY

While Henry James apparently took little interest in the electoral contests of 1832, his brother Augustus—Gus, as he was known in the family—

---

* If Henry had a hand in this expensive change, that might help explain his unrealized dream, some fifteen years later, of founding a daily newspaper. At the time, February 1847, he was once again residing in Albany.

became an active player in opposition politics. Jackson's veto on July 10 of the bill renewing the charter of the U.S. Bank was the decisive provocation. From this moment, many bankers and merchants believed "the Democrats were no friends of internal improvements." Old Clintonians, convinced that Jackson must not be allowed a second term, were reunited by this powerful adversary. There were large public meetings at the state capitol, nominating conventions were announced, and Weed and others busily pulled strings. When the anti-Jackson electors of Albany's second ward gathered for their powwow, Gus was one of several prominent younger men appointed to the Committee of Vigilance.* All to no avail, Jackson being easily re-elected that November.

It was out of this bad anti-Masonic defeat that the Whig Party was born. Gus's early and enthusiastic support of this new political configuration confirms the traditional genealogy: the old aristocratic Clintonianism to which William had been so loyal was turning into an out-and-out business party. The Jameses' financial interests would be protected. But did any of William's sons, Gus excepted, really care?

By now the father was all but choking on his bitter sense of betrayal. If all but one of his children ignored or rejected him and everything he had built up, then perhaps others would appreciate his watchful care. On January 18, 1832, he chaired a public meeting to establish an endowment and provide a building for the Albany orphan asylum, and a few months later, putting his money where his mouth was, he bequeathed the sum of $2,500 to the institution, the largest gift by far from a private individual. William had not been this generous with any other charity.

The father made this bequest when he drew up his last will and testament in the summer of 1832. The time had come to think seriously about his own mortality—to make sure his great fortune would not be scattered with his death. It happened to be the summer of a cholera epidemic, with each day's newspaper announcing how many dead had been hauled away. For August, the total came to 284. Tarry smoke from smudge pots hung over Albany. Bleaching powder was dumped in sewers and drains. A sloop docked at the pier was fumigated, and afterward the body of a sleeping tramp was found. Everyone who could afford to left for the country, and so little business was done that someone sent a tongue-in-cheek complaint to a local newspaper: "The lawyers are suffering." Whatever William's motive may have been, recklessness or the press of business or a confident sense of well-being, he remained in town with the lawyers. Perhaps he was consulting with two of them, Gideon

---

* The previous year Gus had become a director of Albany's Commercial Bank.

Hawley and James King, as he composed his will (or revised a prior and no longer existing one). These were the attorneys, at any rate, whom he appointed as executors when he signed the instrument in Albany on July 24.

This remarkable document testifies to the fearsome gravity of William's conception of his providential powers and responsibilities. The sister of his first wife, Elizabeth Tillman, was still living. She got an annuity of $125. His younger brother, also an immigrant, had died near Syracuse two decades earlier, leaving a son and a daughter. The former got a legacy of $1,000, the latter an annuity of $100. Indeed, William looked after this fatherless niece, Charlotte James, in another way as well. On July 7, four days after the cholera reached Albany and began carrying off its citizens, William saw to it that she got married out of his North Pearl Street house. He, at least, still knew what family loyalty was all about.

It was in his provisions concerning his own children that William expressed his notion of paternal duty with the most particular and painful clarity. There was to be no nonsense about equal treatment across the board (as in his wife's will years later). One child in particular was repeatedly singled out for special consideration. Gus succeeded to William's partnership in the Syracuse saltworks and flour mills. Gus was to be the collector of rents from the vast real-estate holdings and was authorized to take a "reasonable percentage" (5 percent, as it turned out) for his trouble. After a period of years, Gus's children were to receive $50,000 in real estate, as compared to $20,000 for the others' children. And he was appointed executor along with Hawley and King.

As co-executor, Gus was given (or burdened with) an extraordinary degree of discretionary power in disposing of the estate. He became his father's appointed regent, delegated to slap his siblings' hands or make lavish handouts, as seemed appropriate. Any of William's sons or grandsons who wished to set himself up in a trade or profession or purchase real estate was entitled to a large advance—at the executors' discretion. If any of the male heirs led a "grossly immoral, idle or dishonorable life," the executors were encouraged, in fact required, to deny him a share in the estate, awarding nothing more than an annuity for life "sufficient to supply the probable actual wants." If William's female heirs did not behave "dutifully and affectionately" toward his widow and her relatives (her cranky father?), the executors were empowered to withhold the standard marriage allowance of $3,000. In making their final distribution, the executors were enjoined to give their "scrupulous attention especially to the personal merits and demerits of each individual." The father who had found it easier to discipline his children through intermediaries than face-to-face now assigned his legal stand-ins a judicial duty they must have found most unwelcome:

> Although the extensive and extraordinary power herein conferred of punishing idleness and vice and of rewarding virtue, must from its nature be in a considerable degree discretionary, and although its faithful exercise may prove to be a task at once responsible and painful, yet it is my full intention and earnest wish that it shall be carried into execution with rigid impartiality, sternness and inflexibility.

It almost seems that William was imagining some sort of Last Judgment, a grim, final reckoning whose most arresting feature would be the inevitable, if long delayed, punishment of the damned. Not only were the various legacies to be based on a strict assessment of the beneficiaries' individual delinquencies, but this final distribution was to take place in the distant future, *years* after the testator's death. Taking a hint perhaps from the *modus operandi* of the Calvinists' deity, William crafted his will in such a way that his children would have to be very industrious and very good in order to savor the delights of wealth.

And since Judgment Day is most effective if it never arrives, what William's children would mainly have to do was wait. Placing the bulk of his estate in a trust, with his executors as trustees, William ordained that the great hoard not be apportioned among his heirs "until the youngest of my children and grandchildren living at the date of this my will and attaining the age of twenty-one years shall have attained that age." The newest of William's grandchildren, Gus's son, William Augustus, had been born December 29, 1831. Thus, unless something happened to this baby before he reached the age of twenty-one (a contingency his more straitened relatives could not have helped thinking about), the old man's money bin would not be split open until December 29, 1852.

William was well aware of the onerousness of this long-postponed distribution, and he offered two justifications for it within the will itself. First, he was afraid (with reason) that his children would be corrupted if they came into possession of great wealth at an early age, and he hoped that a long probationary wait would discourage "prodigality and vice." He was particularly insistent that his male heirs "learn some one of the professions, trades or occupations usually pursued in this country as a livelihood and . . . assiduously pursue and practice the same," so as not to depend on an unearned fortune. But William had another reason for delaying his heirs' gratification: he wished "to preserve my estate from being wasted, and to insure its more judicious management." These two motives, somewhat contradictory, reveal a profound ambivalence about the ultimate value of his wealth. As Howard M. Feinstein has aptly said, "In preparing his will, William James was torn between a desire to protect his capital from his heirs and the wish to protect his heirs from the evils of capital." Money can be lethal, the will says—but even so it must be guarded at all costs. Money is a wonderful possession—yet money enjoyed is money wasted. In effect, there is only one correct thing to do with money, according to William of Albany's will, and that is to keep making more of it.

William must have given a great deal of thought to the trust he established in his will. Strange to say, however, he seems not to have consulted the top legal counsel available, John C. Spencer, for example, or one of the other two New York attorneys who had recodified New York's statutory law a few years earlier. These men could have called William's attention to the fifteenth paragraph of the first article in the First Revised Statutes 723, which restricted the length of time the power of alienation could be suspended. Perhaps William was revising an earlier will, one dating from before 1830, when the new state code took effect. Still, anyone who entered litigation as often as he did should have known better. If *he* didn't bother asking the lawyers who had codified the law to cast their hooded gaze at his precious document, then his heirs would take the trouble for him—with very different purposes and results. Maybe the cholera epidemic led William to act with more precipitation than prudence at a time when the best legal minds were out of town. Maybe his judgment was not what it used to be.

Or maybe he was overcome by an aching dissatisfaction with the two sons who had received the most advanced and expensive educations, Rev. William and Henry. If the other children could only manage to maintain good behavior for the next twenty-one years, fabulous wealth would shower down on them. But these two, William decided, had already disqualified themselves from receiving any part of the trust. They were to get no more than an annual allowance for life.

Rev. William's annuity was $2,000. Although it would have been possible to live in satisfactory comfort on this income, it was only a fraction—a fourth, a fifth—of his equal share in the estate. Worse, it was a life annuity. If he wanted to leave anything to his wife and daughter, it would have to be what he himself earned and saved. Rev. William was definitely being punished, probably for his recent professional conduct as a minister. In Rochester he had aroused the enmity of a rigidly proscriptive sabbatarian faction by traveling in a stage that operated on

Sundays. The acrimony grew so intense that he resigned his pulpit, accepting a temporary charge at the First Presbyterian Church of Schenectady in 1831. One Sunday morning, according to a diarist, the new minister failed to appear behind the pulpit:

> Expecting James every moment the people waited in anxiety till 11 o'clock, when his elders set off to his house where they found him comfortably seated in his easy chair with his feet upon the mantelpiece; "Well Mr. James" say they "are you not going to preach." "Oh no!" was the reply, "I am not going to the chapel, I have nothing to say."

As a friend delicately put it, Rev. William seemed "prone to something like a rash precipitance." Shortly before his father drew up his will, the unpredictable minister turned down the offer of a permanent position with the Schenectady congregation and moved back to Albany, partly because of "the failure of his health,"* partly because "his peculiarities of temperament were not in harmony with the uniform routine of pastoral life." His father no doubt took a simpler view. Rev. William was not "assiduously" devoted to his profession.

But of all William's children, it was Henry who ended up with the smallest slice of the estate, $1,250 a year. This was not, of course, the same as disinheritance. The young man's income would be equivalent to 5 percent interest on $25,000—ten times what William gave the orphanage and twenty-five times the nephew's bequest. Henry would have been able to live in comfortable idleness. He would not have had to work. But it was still a stinging rebuke. He got a *lot* less than the others, and he was being singled out as the worst of the children, the one whose reputation was already and irrevocably tarnished. Henry's older brother Gus was a paragon of responsibility. Jannet was serious and dutiful. John Barber, only sixteen years old, was a careless student but not (yet) in major trouble. It was Henry, just turned twenty-one, whose bad example and dissolute and spendthrift ways obsessed William James as he meted out his final judgment. His ominous invocation of the "lamentable consequences" that occur when well-to-do young persons suddenly acquire great property would have brought Henry to everyone's mind. Henry was the chief sinner on exhibit, and the will that exposed him to Albany's disapproving gaze was an uncompromisingly direct Presbyterian sermon, with a hard and final bite to it.

---

* Writing in August 1833, Catharine Barber James's father mentioned that Rev. William "has been sick for some time past."

HIS DEATH HAS SPREAD A GLOOM

The first Albany directory with a separate entry for Henry appeared that year, 1832, probably during the summer. He is shown as residing at 62 North Pearl Street, the same address given for his father. (Although this was a new street number, the county tax rolls show that the Jameses were still living in the same three-story brick mansion they had occupied for fifteen years.) The fact that Henry was listed separately does not suggest a break with his family but rather a need for his own business address. What the business was can only be conjectured. Perhaps it had something to do with the law.

That November, soon after Andrew Jackson was returned to the White House over the furious opposition of most banking interests, Henry's next younger sister, Jannet, married William H. Barker, the son of a powerful New York banker. A week or so later the news of Sir Walter Scott's death reached Albany, and a public meeting was held in his honor at the Albany Mansion House. Harmanus Bleecker, the leading citizen who had praised Rev. William's sermon back in 1827, now rose to display his own oratorical prowess by defending fiction against its lingering puritanical detractors:

> We do not think justly when we think too lightly of fictitious writing. It has been said, that when it faithfully describes human nature and human life, it cannot relate what is false; that it is therefore more true than professed histories of fact.

A letter of condolence to the writer's family was prepared, and among the fifty prominent fiction readers who signed it were two James brothers, Henry and John Barber. Scott had been one of Henry's earliest passions, the boy having once performed a moving rendition of "the prisoner's counsel at the trial scene" in *The Heart of Midlothian*. Henry had an instinct for passionate appeals to liberty. But which would the dissipated young law student turn out to be, prisoner or counsel?

On the evening of December 15, 1832, Henry's father, not quite sixty-one, suffered a massive stroke. Occurring too late in the day to get into Saturday's paper, the news was first reported the following Monday: "We regret to learn that our esteemed fellow citizen, Mr. William James[,] is not expected to survive an apoplectic shock with which he was visited on Saturday." The stricken man languished four days in all, "retaining, however, his reason and speech." He died at three in the morning on Wednesday the nineteenth.

In that day's *Albany Evening Journal*, William's death notice was the lead story. The editor patched together an account of his early commercial history during the 1790s but alluded in only the most general terms to his later operations, evidently taking for granted that readers were already familiar with them: "Mr James['s] death is a severe loss to the city of Albany. He has done more *to build up* the City than any other individual. His enterprise has, for the last ten years, furnished constant employment for hundreds of our mechanics and laborers." The deceased was said to be the second-richest man in the state, after John Jacob Astor, and his net worth was put at $3 million, a figure assumed to be accurate by all James family biographers ever since. In fact, at the time of his death William owned $800,000 in real and $500,000 in personal property. Subtracting his debts of $112,000 leaves a net worth of about $1,200,000.

The next day an anonymous writer contributed his own sketch of the deceased, stiffly praising his "high probity and excellence" and rising to a memorably lugubrious finale: "His death has spread a gloom over the city, and has produced a chasm in society, which will not be readily filled." The New York State Bank went into deep mourning, and when the funeral took place in the Jameses' home on December 20, at three o'clock, the members of the board were in attendance, suitably decorated. (Perhaps they brought the young clerk, Herman Melville, recently hired by the bank.) The board of managers of the Albany Orphan Asylum, seated as a group, made a particularly solemn impression. The eulogy delivered by Harvey Baldwin (Syracuse's first mayor) struck Joseph Henry as "well done but perhapse a little over coloured." Outside the family, the most deeply affected mourner may have been a certain Mr. Hurst, who had contracted "to do a large amount of work" for William. Hurst hired "a hundred men" to get the job done but failed to secure a written agreement, and when William died the unlucky contractor "lost every dollar he possessed."

Within the family, the unexpected death of its tyrannical founder had hundreds of disturbing repercussions. In addition to dealing with their grief and desolation, the children had to find a way to legitimize the profound relief some of them must have felt. Henry in particular was left with an intolerable burden of ambiguous and inexpressible feelings. He knew he had been a disgrace and a reproach and that his father had good reason to be angry with him. But the old man's demands had been so strict, and his brimming reservoir of rage and indignation so quick to overflow, that a satisfactory rapprochement had not been possible.

Following the stroke, William not only kept his reason and speech, but he had a brief four-day grace period in which to make peace with himself and his family. This he apparently attempted: in 1920 a descendant, Henry James III, put on record the family tradition that William had been reconciled "a few days before his death" with one of the two sons his will had singled out for punitive treatment. Unfortunately, this tantalizing disclosure doesn't say which one. We can only surmise that it would have been considerably harder to patch things up with Henry than with Rev. William, and also that if Henry was the restored prodigal his grandson would probably have chosen to say so.

One guesses, then, that the gloom created by William's death was particularly thick in Henry's vicinity. It was he who had been so respectful of "Papa" 's advice preceding the amputation of 1828, and so defiant ever since. If the young man listened to the logic of the emotions, the verdict he heard may well have been *guilty*. Guilty of your powerful father's death. *

Although there are many unanswered questions about William's stroke, the supposition that Henry felt himself to be responsible and blamable throws a startling light on the salient features of his later life and thought: the pathological guilt that overcame him from time to time, his unremitting attack on respectable "pharisaical" virtue, his recurring defense of egregious offenders against the moral code (often singling out adulterers and murderers), his belief in the absolute foulness of the individual egotistical self, and his insistence on the painfulness of any spiritual regeneration worth the name.

---

* Possibly there was a more specific motive for guilt. On December 15, the *Albany Evening Journal* ran an unusually moralistic poem, "Lines written to a Young Gentleman who had deviated from Moral Propriety." The author, identified only as EDWARDS (a reference to Jonathan Edwards?), was anxious about a promising young man who had fallen victim to a "guilty passion":

> Yet, oh! that vile, that hapless day,
> When Cupid held an overpowering sway;
> He yielded and became a slave;
> Justly condemn'd and treated as a knave.

The poem appeared the same day William had his fatal stroke.

Years later Henry issued a curiously framed declaration of innocence: "I have never *that I remember* brought myself either by look or word or deed into illicit relation with any woman living or dead whether that relation be conceived as dating *from* my own existing conjugality, or that of the opposite party" (italics mine). The writer's emphatic assertion of innocence is as bizarre as his legalistic exclusion of all relationships *preceding* his "conjugality." An impulse to confess seems to be struggling with a desire for self-exoneration.

DEMORALIZED PRETTY GENERALLY

After the funeral came the inevitable confusion, dissension, and ill feeling. When Catharine elected to decline her husband's meager allowance and take her legal third of the estate, she necessarily gave up her claim to particular bequests, including the house on North Pearl Street and everything in it, furniture, silverware, clothes, pictures, books. Technically, unless the heirs reached an out-of-court settlement, the domestic estate would have to be treated as if William had died intestate. Gus alone, the testator's favored child, seems to have taken his stand on the will and resisted alternative arrangements. In response, Rev. William filed a bill of complaint with the Court of Chancery that accused him of ignoring or denying "frequent and repeated" requests to join in an amicable agreement. Gus countered with a statement of his own, dated May 11, 1833, in which he indignantly denied the charge of "combination and confederacy" but then acceded to the family's wishes. Now that he was ready to cooperate, all the heirs united in a plea to "partition" the house and personal property. Although the chancellor expressed "some hesitation" in granting this plea, fearing that the rich widow would be forced to give up her home, the whole point of the family's maneuver was to prevent this improbable result by authorizing the children to solve the problem in a nonjudicial way. Thus, the large and comfortable house remained in the family, becoming a familiar second home to Henry's own children in the 1840s and 1850s.

On other points at issue, Gus dug in his heels. The only child to take an interest in the Syracuse operations, he had been acting as sales agent for his father's flour mills and saltworks. He wanted payment and recognition for his labors, and he petitioned his fellow executors for over $7,000 in sales commissions for the last five years. Clearly Gus did not want his interest in the estate merged with that of the other children. Foreseeing, perhaps, that the request to partition the home might lead to a rush to partition everything, including Syracuse, he wanted to get his special claims out on the table.

Meanwhile, Henry was receiving his annuity of $1,250 a year, and something more as well. Not a princely income, this was still considerably larger than what he had spent annually at Union College. Best of all, the income was assured, for unlike his younger brothers, he was not even required to avoid "prodigality and vice" in order to collect his money. The will had backfired, leaving the profligate young man free to do what he wanted and to travel wherever he pleased.

When Henry ran away from college in 1829, he sought gainful employment and for a time lived soberly and prudently. Now, fleeing Albany, his law studies, and the only profession for which he seemed remotely qualified, he acted far more desperately, throwing everything over and making a blind dash. As he put it some forty years later, "I left Albany, abandoning my studies, and my profession." Coming from a young man who had focused with great intensity on the future development of his mind in order to survive his terrible ordeals by fire and knife, these words carry a powerful charge. Henry's resolution and ambition had collapsed, done in by the double realization that he had a sufficient and dependable income for life and that he was seen as the pariah of his family.

He did not go to Boston or any other large city now but, rather, headed for Canandaigua, a village in north-central New York. Henry never left a satisfactory account of his life in this far from ordinary little town, yet it seems to have become a benchmark for him in his later years. In 1855, when he filled out an alumni questionnaire for Union College, he placed himself in "Canandaigua & ~~New York~~ Princeton 1830–'36." It is eminently characteristic of the man that he fumbled his whereabouts and got both years wrong. His time at Princeton ran from 1835 to 1837; it was well after 1830 that he went to Canandaigua; and he spent a year or two there rather than four or five. Also, he interrupted his sojourn by making a momentous stay in Buffalo. Even so, his fictitious retrospect does capture a certain truth (as Harmanus Bleecker might have said): Henry wanted to forget his life in Albany in the early 1830s, and one way of doing that was to exaggerate the length of time he spent in Canandaigua.

In old age Henry informed a son that he had been drawn to Canandaigua by a "good friend" who was living there. Just who this friend was can be deduced from a late newspaper interview, which discloses that "he was much in the company of the son of Gov. DeWitt Clinton" in the early 1830s. Unlike Henry, George W. Clinton had stayed with the law, first opening an office with Matthew Henry Webster in Albany in 1831 and then moving to Canandaigua, where he became a partner with the formidable John C. Spencer. Marrying Spencer's daughter, Laura Catherine, in 1832, he took on a series of dignified civic responsibilities, becoming a trustee of Ontario Female Seminary, delivering the Fourth of July oration for 1833, and being appointed Examiner in Chancery and Ontario County district attorney. At a time when Henry was still drifting, Clinton was a respectable citizen and family man, with a promising legal career opening ahead of him.

Yet it had not been easy for Clinton to settle on the law, natural history having been his first love. Perhaps it was because this somewhat older friend from childhood had been able to get his own life in order that Henry turned to him for help—that and his "kindly disposition and generous heart." Although the sort of institution Henry advocated some fifteen years later, "a hospital or infirmary for intemperance," did not yet exist, Clinton himself was a sort of cure, becoming active in temperance organizations in 1834, the first year Henry's presence in Canandaigua can be documented.

Another reason Henry found the village attractive was that it was a seat of wealth and cultivation a little off the beaten track. Two and a half days from Albany by stage, Canandaigua had been billed as the chief emporium of western New York before the building of the Erie Canal. A number of well-to-do New Englanders and New Yorkers had settled there, erecting stately homes and a neoclassical courthouse. In 1830 Canandaigua was one of only four locations in all New York in which the dignified *Christian Examiner* could be bought over the counter. There was none of the boomtown rawness of Rochester or Syracuse, and the well-kept wooden sidewalks made it possible for a one-legged man to get around on foot. By 1833 the village no longer had a future (in this respect resembling Henry), but, according to Thurlow Weed, it still weighed in with "a greater number of distinguished men" than any other interior city of the state. First on the list came Francis Granger, who led a Whig faction christened after his own striking head of hair, the "Silver Grays." Then there was John C. Spencer, who achieved a remarkable fusion of Whig politics and high culture criticism, not only befriending Alexis de Tocqueville but helping bring out the first American translation of *Democracy in America*. (Spencer's preface says that he and Tocqueville "discussed . . . many of the topics treated of in this book.") For all its smallness, Canandaigua was a powerhouse of Antimasonry and Whiggishness. All in all, the village was an exceedingly pleasant watering hole for old Clintonians.

When President Jackson carried out his threat and began removing federal deposits from the U.S. Bank, the "deposite question" became the hot issue for Canandaigua's freshly minted Whigs. Even the relatively nonpartisan *Ontario Repository* denounced Jackson as a dictator, "an arbitrary, arrogant and inconsiderate old man." That summer, 1834, a notice appeared in a local newspaper urging "all young men who are opposed to the corrupt measures and dangerous principles of the present National and State administration" to organize for the approaching election and appoint delegates to a county convention of young Whigs. Among the signatories was Henry James, whose name appears with those of various prominent Canandaigua scions—John A. Granger, P. E. Buell, A. H. Howell. If Henry attended the local convention a few days later, as seems likely, he would have voted for the resolution to "maintain the rights of the Bank against the maddened fury of a self-willed and misguided man."

Henry had now signed onto the same cause as his brother Gus. He was also voting with his ethnic and religious group: in the 1840s 90 percent of the Protestant Irish in America voted Whig, with 95 percent of the Catholic Irish going Democratic. But there may have been a personal element as well, an imaginative investment in the basic idea of banks and great money hoards. It seems fitting that the boy who regarded his father's cash drawer as magical and sacred first got politicized in response to President Jackson's assault on the U.S. Bank.

But stepping onto the opposition Whig bandwagon did nothing to resolve Henry's real problem—his future. With a modest income assured for his natural life, but no profession beckoning, the sociable young man drifted into a bad crowd. Years later, writing about his Canandaigua phase to his son Robertson, Henry confessed that his "decline was rapid. I fell in with professional gamblers, and became demoralized pretty generally. I scarcely ever went to bed sober, and lost my self-respect *almost* utterly."

Although this confession was couched in the familiar language of the parable of the Prodigal Son, there is no reason not to accept it as basically reliable. By the time Henry moved to Canandaigua, gambling had become a virtual mania, in the Mississippi Valley most famously but also throughout New York. According to a recent history of gambling in nineteenth-century America, it was in the 1830s that playing cards for money became "a part of daily life." The most popular game was faro, which "worked well for itinerant professionals because 'any number of persons' could play against the bank." It was a simple game: you placed your bets on a layout and then drew. The house odds were only 3 percent if the game was played honestly. But it rarely was, the point of faro being to lighten the pockets of "moneyed innocents" such as Henry James. The game's popularity was closely linked to the speculative fever of the time. After Jackson broke the U.S. Bank, smaller banks, especially in the West, issued their own currencies without restraint. Banknotes became inflated and abundant, with an extraordinary rise in the value of urban real estate in the mid-thirties. These were the celebrated "flush times," made legendary after the fact by writers like Joseph G. Baldwin. It makes sense that a banking game like faro became all the rage in the midst of the bank controversies, and that a rich young drifter with memories of his father's bottomless cash drawer got caught in a sucker's game. Would Henry have lost a good deal more if William's will had accorded him a full and immediate cut? The question prompts the speculation that if it hadn't been for the father's suspicious forethought the son might have squandered his fortune and there would be no famous grandchildren.

Perhaps Henry's drinking and gambling in Canandaigua were an attempt to recapture the pleasant, old, pre-amputation days at the shoemakers'. In the fall of 1833 a friend and fellow drinker from those days, Franklin Clinton, moved to the village. A younger brother of George, Franklin was also supposed to be studying for the law, and with the bar examinations looming, he decided he had better flee the distractions of city life for the village's "comparative quietude." Judging from the fact that he ended up in the Navy, where he died a lieutenant in 1842, only thirty years old, he would seem to have failed his exams. Maybe it was Henry as fellow drinker and gambler who helped him fail them. The cautionary stories Henry told his children decades later may well have involved this obscure son of New York's eminent early governor. When Henry Jr. harked back to these stories in the early twentieth century, he chose not to pass any of them on, but he did, tantalizingly, include "Clinton" among the four prominent family names he specified. One suspects there was a well-known family anecdote about Franklin and Henry Sr.—both practically the same age, both following the same downward path for a time.

A RESPITE FROM HIS VICE

It was in Buffalo, the westernmost point of Henry's travels, that he finally got back on the high road. Located at the far end of the Erie Canal, this rapidly growing town had a population of 15,000 by 1835. Henry's letter to Robertson accounted for his presence there only by saying, "I chanced in Buffalo where I had many friends." One such may have been his former partner, Elijah J. Roberts, who, following the collapse of the Albany *Craftsman*, had moved to Buffalo and become its city clerk and then, in the summer of 1834, started another short-lived paper, the *Daily Advertiser*. A much closer friend was James McKay, a gifted young attorney with doubts and questions of his own. McKay had a son baptized in the First Presbyterian Church in 1831, helped found the city's first Unitarian Church the following year, and presently turned with enthusiasm to Thomas Carlyle's early books. Like George Clinton, he took an active part in civic life, organizing a learned society and an academy or two. Both Roberts and McKay were active Whigs in the summer of 1834, the latter delivering a speech and heading a platform committee.

When Henry arrived in Buffalo, he put up at the Eagle Tavern, at that time one of the West's best-known hostelries. All prominent travelers made a point of stopping there for the night, and many local residents regarded it as home. Among the latter was John T. Hudson, a young lawyer who had graduated in 1829 from Union College, where he had been a charter member of Sigma Phi. The hotel was a very lively place as long as the flush times lasted. In the summer of 1835 a traveler who stayed there found that "beds are spread in all the halls . . . and ladies are compelled to sleep five and six in a room." Forty years later Henry described the Eagle Tavern as a "terrible drinking hole." This phrase probably tells us more about Henry's own sense of abandonment than about the hotel—but it is true that alcohol flowed very freely there. A local memoirist described how the dinner tables were set with "generous sized decanters of brandy, gin and rum, in pairs or *quartettes* straddling or surrounding a gallon pitcher of ale free to all."

During the winter of 1834–35 a group of influential men, acting independently of the temperance societies, began meeting weekly in order to "devise the best method for putting a stop" to the consumption of alcohol in Buffalo. It may have been a member of this pressure group— or his wife—who set out to rescue Henry from his vice. Whoever the couple was, the wife's loveliness and the drunkard's self-disgust were salient aspects of Henry's recollection of the episode:

> I had a very close intimacy with a person from New York residing in the city, and with his wife, who was a lovely amiable woman, and in their company house I spent most of my days. This gave me a casual respite to some extent from my vice, and the shame and horror it breeds got such a chance to come out and take hold of my conscience, that after much struggle and many vicissitudes, I was cured.

This act of personal reform had another source as well. There was a new idea sweeping through upper New York in the 1830s. For the first time in American history, a total repudiation of alcohol was affirmed to be the condition of true spirituality.

MOST AFFECTIONATELY AND TRULY

Now that Henry's prodigal years were over and done with, contemporary documents recording his thoughts and deeds begin to resurface. The first of them, a letter dated February 3, 1835, from Canandaigua, tells us that Henry broke his return trip to Albany by going to this village once again for at least a month. The letter is addressed to Rev. William, and it is full of the old family feeling. Henry would have been back home by now, he says, but he has been too "engaged in preparation" to set off. He is not sure he will be able to get to Rochester to see the Reverend Gilbert Morgan, as William had evidently recommended. (Morgan, class of 1818 at Princeton Theological Seminary, was an important educator and a strong supporter of Presbyterian missions.) But he wants Ma to know that he has seen Mrs. Clinton—Laura, George's wife—following the recent birth of a daughter. She looked so well and cheerful, Henry reports, that he could not bring himself to "communicate to her my intention to depart," adding, "If this looks like vanity, it was not so prompted."

At this moment, the letter writing is interrupted by a visit from a Mr. Beals, who has "of late been in the habit of coming to my room nearly every evening." This is Thomas Beals, fifty-one years old, one of Canandaigua's leading bankers and businessmen. Beals likes books (as someone else noted), is "happy in the use of language," and has a "marked individuality of character and deportment," habitually giving "brief, emphatic answers with the wave of his hand." His nightly calls show that Henry is lodging in the Franklin House, the Main Street hotel owned by Beals. This is a temperance inn, with no quartettes of brandy, gin, or rum out on the tables. Henry is definitely off the bottle, and it is perhaps to make sure he stays off that Beals drops in nearly every evening; Beals is a family man, with eleven children of his own. Presently the visitor leaves, after "scattering my epistolary materials far and wide over the limited compass of my brain." Disinclined to gather them up again, the penman signs off with unusual earnestness, "Most affectionately & truly."

But not everything had been scattered. The writer was able to express the chief thing on his mind before Beals's expected visit. Once again the young man has turned to his brother for help, only this time, in an extraordinarily direct and abject plea, he begs for the kind of steady, unblinking surveillance their father had wanted his executors to carry out. From now on everything must be exposed to the light. There must be no more dark corners, ever again.

I long to be with you. I want drilling and disciplining—I want advice and support in study—I want council in doubt, and a companion at all times—and such I know you will afford & be. I see my way much more clearly I think than when I wrote you—that is I have zealously devoted myself by prayer and watching to clearing up the dark corners of my mind and heart, and opening them broadly for the full light of the Scriptures to penetrate and purify—I have given heed to every whisper of conscience—I have sought in every way open to my knowledge the path of duty, and I have given myself up cheerfully to its pursuit for ever—and the result has been peace—rich, blessed [?], glorious, heavenly, confirmed peace—that peace which *must* come only from God—for such the world never gave me, nor yet, I trust in Him, shall it ever take from me.

These are the words of one who believes he has been saved from wretchedness and who is still in the first flush of his new life, who prays devotedly, studies the Scriptures, treads the path of duty, and makes no secret of his determination never again to deviate from what is right. Henry has been converted—has at last found "that peace which *must* come only from God."

But even as he writes this, underlining *must*, he sounds more desperate and clenched than ever, as if he remains secretly unsure how this great and apparently final gamble is going to turn out.

Chapter 9

■ ■ ■

CHURCH AND SEMINARY:
1835–37

Henry's intense inner upheaval had not taken place in a vacuum. Religious conversions and revivals were so pervasive in upper New York
State in the early 1830s that the region got a new name based on the
metaphor of a rapidly spreading conflagration—the "burned-over district." Like his sister Jannet before him, Henry was overtaken by the
flames of religious enthusiasm. This was his second fire, with as many
major, unforeseen consequences as had resulted from the one a decade
earlier in Mrs. Gilchrist's hayloft.

Canandaigua had been one of the hot spots. In 1824 a zealous young
minister, the Reverend Ansel Eddy, had arrived in the village resolved
to set loose the power of the Holy Ghost. Emphasizing basic orthodox
themes, "man's lost condition and the redemptive power of Jesus Christ,"
Eddy had an unparalleled success in building up the Congregational
Church, adding 122 new converts in the revival year of 1826 alone.
(The Presbyterians, not having a church of their own in Canandaigua,
worshipped with the Congregationalists.)

A few years later the main wave of what is sometimes called the Second
Great Awakening broke out in Rochester. It began when Josiah Bissell,
a leading Sabbatarian zealot and an implacable enemy of the more moderate Rev. William James, invited the Reverend Charles G. Finney to
come to town to do some *real* preaching. Finney's idea of preaching was
to try to bring in the millennium. He thought it was "a farce to suppose
that a literary ministry can convert the world," and he had little use for
studious preachers like Rev. William. He became America's most celebrated evangelist during the winter of 1830–31, and presently Eddy asked
him to come down to Canandaigua for a weeklong revival. While there,

Finney reaped such an abundant harvest of fresh converts that Eddy's church tallied 151 new members in 1831 and 1832. A new power was set loose in the land, and all over upper and western New York un-awakened congregations begged the evangelist to come and rouse them from their lethargy. From all reports he spoke with unusual dignity, like a lawyer, it was felt, and in response (the leading historian of the movement has written), "lawyers, real-estate magnates, millers, manufacturers, and commercial tycoons led the parade of the regenerated."

Most other itinerant preachers adopted more sensationalistic tactics to stir up their listeners. The so-called New Measures, many of which emerged within the Presbyterian Church, included extemporaneous preaching, protracted meetings, groaning. One of the most effective was the segregation of the convulsively guilt-stricken on an "Anxious Bench," where the spectacle of their inner struggle had a notable impact on duller members of the audience. Another powerful New Measure was ardent prayer—long, passionate, pleading supplication. Presently, a new sort of public devotional intensity appeared on the scene, raising popular expectations and producing a high degree of intolerance. It became an "offense against true religion" to ask God for anything other than the particular object of one's heart's desire, for to request vague benefits was to display an inferior sort of faith. Preachers who did not show enough emotion came under suspicion and reproof, and in many other ways established ecclesiastical authority found itself challenged by the popular new zeal. It was a kind of revolution, with many new prophets arising.

The Mormons were only one among the various sects and revelations that proliferated in the burned-over district. Joseph Smith's conviction that the Last Judgment had already occurred, that the "latter days" were here, showed up everywhere, especially in the new doctrine of Perfectionism—the belief that those who had been saved are made perfect and can sin no more. From this teaching, it was but a small step to the radical antinomian social experiments that began to dot New York's landscape. The most famous of these, the Oneida Perfectionists, abolished monogamy and instituted a severely regulated form of group promiscuity. In one particularly devout sect, which originated in Albany and spread from there to adjacent villages in New York and western Massachusetts, women converts who had become perfect insisted on sharing beds with men "as a bold self-sacrifice for the purpose of killing shame and defying public opinion." Such goings-on were long remembered, especially by salacious writers who knew how to make their pitch to safe mainstream pieties. After the Civil War, a scandalmongering British journalist named William Hepworth Dixon dug up the story of the Annesley sisters of Albany and snickered at them in a widely read book, *Spiritual Wives*.

Henry undoubtedly encountered a wide range of enthusiastic religion, from the carefully guided revivals in the more conservative Presbyterian congregations to the flourishing new fanaticisms that eluded institutional control. He must have heard Rev. Eddy in Canandaigua, and in Albany he was acquainted with the Annesley sisters, who belonged to the same church as the Jameses. Thirty years later, when he read *Spiritual Wives*, he found Dixon's cheap insinuations so disgusting he added an appendix to a book then in progress in order to defend the sisters' sincerity and idealism:

> I myself knew in my youth two young ladies, sisters, whose name Mr. Dixon wantonly parades to a mocking and lascivious gaze; and they were persons of such an exquisite feminine worth and loveliness . . . in spite of their religious aberrations, that no violets of the wood . . . ever owned a deeper heart of modesty.

Although there is no reason to think Henry was directly involved in the wilder extremes of the early 1830s, the reference to "prayer and watching" in his letter to Rev. William suggests he practiced one of the popular New Measures, extended private prayer. This letter sets forth Henry's version of the perfectionist goal of complete purity—giving heed "to *every* whisper of conscience," seeking the path of duty "in *every* way." One of the adjectives with which he later described his more youthful self, "ardent," was an important code word in the thirties for religious intensity. In 1852, when Henry published a revealing account of his former devotional extremism, he recalled how he had "abounded in prayer, day and night," how he was "studiously, even superstitiously pure in thought and act," and how diligently he "observed every precept of mystical and ordinary piety." He gave generously to the poor, as did his admired older brother, and tried to extirpate all emotions "but those of complete benignity towards my kind." He even (can aspiration aim higher?) "read every famous book."

The unstable young man now took orders directly from his older brother, who had himself been scarred by Calvinist travail. According to an old friend, Rev. William's private devotions "often took on a morbid cast, and always received a tinge . . . from his peculiar, I might almost say unique, intellectual and moral constitution." The friend who delivered this circumspect appraisal at William's funeral, the Reverend William B. Sprague, spoke less guardedly in private. In a letter to Professor Charles Hodge at Princeton Theological Seminary, Sprague said of William that, while "nobody doubts that he was a good man and has gone safely to Heaven, his character, his life, everything pertaining to him, was strange." Many stories were told of his absentmindedness, but this private summation by a good friend seems to put the man well beyond eccentricity. Unfortunately, William's disturbingly unusual qualities were never quite captured in language. It would be a mistake, however, to picture him as some sort of twisted fanatic. The emphasis should be on his intense devotional concentration, as studious and disciplined as it was rhapsodical. He often urged those who depended on his counsel to read certain religious books and then respond in a letter to him, and the correspondence went on and on. "God is near you, my brother, and He will ever be drawing nearer, nearer, nearer," he wrote to one of his adepts.

On balance, it seems fair to say that the religious enthusiasm of the 1830s, reinforced perhaps by Rev. William's own intensity, revived the exorbitant guilt and self-discipline of Henry's adolescent invalidism. Then he had fallen prey to a compulsive conscientiousness. Now he would settle for nothing less than perfection—utterly spotless purity.

The difference between then and now was that Henry had become so anxious about his life's calling he was eager to pledge his entire future. In his own words, "I vowed my life to the service of the gospel, and placed myself in the chief seminary of my sect with a view to the ministry." He seems to have made this momentous resolution sometime after writing his brother, for although Henry did indeed enroll in Princeton Theological Seminary in the fall of 1835, he had not yet applied at the time of the trustees' semiannual meeting on September 28, about five weeks before the commencement of the new school year. Dedicating himself to the Gospel may have been a last-minute decision, made with the sense that time was running out.

It seems unlikely that Henry's older brother pushed him to take this rash step. With his scholarly turn of mind and exacting standard of composition, Rev. William had himself become increasingly unsettled in his vocation. Instead of speaking from the spirit, as worshippers now demanded, he liked to take "the utmost care" in writing his sermons, which appealed mainly to "thoroughly disciplined minds." William was a very intellectual devotee rather than a man for all seasons, especially the new season of democratic enthusiasm. His piety had already been found deficient in Rochester, and the congregation that ordained him in 1833, Albany's Third Presbyterian Church, seemed to be mired in a dispiriting decline—even as tongues of flame descended everywhere else.

Indeed, the Presbyterian denomination as a whole was on the verge of splitting into two schisms, New School and Old School, defined in part by their response to the new evangelical furor. For Old School ministers like William, it was a demoralizing time. Finally, he resigned his Albany pastorate, taking this fateful step the same month Henry wrote him from Canandaigua. It was a change of guard: at the moment William gave up what proved to be his last charge, Henry became convinced he had a vocation for the ministry.

The young convert took another important step as well. On March 26, 1835, as the ledgers in the safe of Albany's First Presbyterian Church reveal, he made a formal application for admission and, "having been examined as to [his] Christian Knowledge & experience," was accepted as a member on his profession of faith. The examining committee met in the home of the pastor, the Reverend John N. Campbell, who lived a few doors away from the Jameses in what had formerly been DeWitt Clinton's mansion and was now Mrs. Lockwood's upscale boardinghouse. The rough minutes of the meeting show that Henry was the last of eleven successful applicants who had not previously entered the Presbyterian communion. Perhaps his case had been saved for the end, as presenting special difficulties.

The upshot was, Henry returned to the same congregational meetinghouse he had known as a child, when he sat next to the window squirming with boredom and waiting for Ostrander's pretty maid to shake out her crumb cloth. He gave two reasons for joining his family's church: he wished to affirm a "sacred obligation" and he "felt insecure of the right to appropriate the Christian hope until [he] had made a formal profession of faith." There is no doubt the young man was acting from the most solemn sense of responsibility.

Henry now fell under the spell of the most forceful and effective minister the First Church was to know, Rev. John N. Campbell. Installed in the pulpit in 1831 at the age of thirty-three, Campbell seems to have been well suited to the church, as he remained its pastor for a third of a century and stamped it with his own strong character. In the words of an awed successor, "His regal presence, his urbane manner, his versatile talents, his intellectual acquirements, his eloquence as a preacher, his knowledge of human nature, his instinct of government, his decision of character" all contributed to give him an authority very different from that of the wild new Gospel exhorters. Years later a lawyer who worshipped at the First Church gave the tall, spare clergyman the highest possible praise: "With the precision of a jurist he laid down his propositions, and then deduced the desired results." Campbell was a classic

Presbyterian divine—proper, austere, formidable, gripping. He even had a face that seemed "quite classical."

Before coming to Albany, Campbell had been pastor of the New York Avenue Church in Washington, D.C.—Andrew Jackson's church. Soon after the President's 1829 inauguration, a scandalous rumor began circulating to the effect that his Secretary of War, John H. Eaton, had impregnated his bride before her first husband's death. Years later, when Mrs. Eaton wrote her memoirs, she declared that the man chiefly responsible for this rumor was none other than Rev. Campbell, and that when she confronted him with the evidence of her innocence he refused to retract his accusation. Campbell also went head to head with the President, who angrily defended the Eatons' honor. Not long after this messy and of course politically motivated affair, Ambrose Spencer (who married two of DeWitt Clinton's sisters in succession) urged Albany's First Presbyterians to snag Mrs. Eaton's persecutor. This they did, offering him a generous salary of $1,600 at a time when William of Albany was trustee. Thus it happened that the Jeremiah who had exposed whoredom in high places was in position to assume direction of Henry's spiritual life following his conversion.

One of the topics this minister preached on again and again in the 1830s—the application of biblical prophecies to recent history—has an obvious relevance to Henry's later development. What was foretold in the Scriptures was being worked out in these latter days, Campbell taught, and with so many Irish Catholics arriving in America, he particularly wanted to identify the Roman Church with the great apostasy prophesied in the book of Daniel. He recognized Roman Catholics' right of religious liberty in the United States, but he warned against their pagan religious practices and their deep-seated authoritarianism—the history of persecution, the exaltation of the Pope, the proven opposition to civil liberty and free inquiry. Affirming that the age of miracles was over, Campbell attributed such wonders as the annual liquefaction of saints' blood to the "working of Satan." These dark suspicions sank deep in Henry's mind, often cropping up long after he had renounced Presbyterianism. Catholicism would always horrify him, and the view that modern-day miracles were real but sinister, the work of dark powers, flushed with new life when he confronted the spirit-rappers of the 1850s. Eventually, Henry's fervent pneumatology showed up in attenuated form in the writings of his sons, who dabbled in the other world in a more modern fashion, William conducting "scientific" inquiries into spirit possession and multiple personality and Henry Jr. playing with the idea of a malign ghostly invasion in The Turn of the Screw. To move from Henry Sr. to his sons is to observe a traditional Protestant demonology transform itself into a primitive kind of psychiatry.

In any case, Henry was now back in his parents' church. He had made up his mind to become a minister, was practicing an arduous devotional regime, and felt clean and blameless in all respects. His resolution had never been more pumped up. Yet even though his "lips were familiar with the traditional formulas of Christian praise and jubilee," as he put it years later, his soul, worrisomely, remained "destitute of peace." Rev. Campbell's sermons didn't seem to help, only aggravating the young man's sense of "inward remoteness from God." He talked to Campbell about this strange and unexpected emptiness, and probably to his brother as well, but "neither my clergyman nor my devout acquaintance appeared to understand my trouble."

It was in this untranquil state of mind that Henry traveled down to Princeton, New Jersey, in the fall of 1835, to begin his ministerial preparation.

PIETY AND LEARNING AT PRINCETON

Princeton Theological Seminary was the third recently established educational institution that Henry attended. By far the most conservative of the three, it had been founded twenty-three years earlier in order to raise up ministers who had both "the spirit of the primitive propagators of the Gospel" and the modern erudition required to defend the faith against heretics and freethinkers. The school was located as centrally as possible, in New Jersey, so as to attract students from North and South alike and thus promote "unity of sentiment." All these high purposes were about to undergo some very peculiar twists in Henry's fervent mind.

The prescribed course of study took three years, at the end of which the graduate would theoretically be able to read the Bible in its original Hebrew and Greek, explain the principal obscurities and difficulties, correct mistranslations, answer the Deists' arguments, defend the Westminster Confession of Faith, and compose correct and soul-saving sermons. But it was not enough for the ministers in training to attain these exalted intellectual heights. The young men were also expected to "grow continually" in their personal devoutness. Every morning and evening they were required to spend some time in "meditation, and self-recollection and examination," and on Sundays the entire day must be given over to "devotional exercises, either of a social or secret kind." In carrying out these religious practices, the young men were enjoined to avoid the two extremes of formalism and enthusiasm.

Order and discipline ruled the daily lives of students. They were expected to treat their teachers "with the greatest deference and respect," promptly rising to their feet when asked to recite. When they skipped a class, they had to obtain a leave of absence in advance. They were not to leave their rooms during the hours set aside for study. All students signed a statement declaring their adherence to "all the rules and regulations" of the institution, and for their first six months they were considered to be on probation. The faculty was authorized to dismiss anyone who proved "unsound in his religious sentiments; immoral or disorderly in his conduct; or . . . a dangerous or unprofitable member of the Institution."

To read these rules and regulations almost two centuries later is to get a picture of a kind of religious boot camp designed to prepare the young recruits for a lonely and exhausting profession. Henry's own later and largely fictitious account of the seminary gave heavy emphasis to its starched and regimented piety. But he was never very good at conveying a veracious account of institutions or settings: polemical motives and grand theories always got in the way. While seminary discipline was definitely stricter than what he had known at Union College in the late 1820s, Princeton was not out of line with the decorum and expectations of the time. Also, some rules must have been quietly overlooked, and there was a degree of freedom and ease that does not show up in official documents. In class, for instance, students were encouraged to ask "any pertinent questions," and on Sunday afternoons in the second-floor assembly room there was an informal "conference" involving the full student body and professorial staff. This was an open discussion of practical and personal matters.

Then, too, Henry had a specially complicated relationship with seminary routine and discipline. On the one hand, as he confessed in his 1835 letter to his brother, he actively sought a severe regimen of drilling and disciplining. He wanted, *needed*, strict personal and institutional surveillance. At the same time, his recent conversion and the wild spiritual energies of upstate New York combined to make him more "enthusiastic" than a conservative seminary could well stand. Most of all, his years of independence and idleness had undoubtedly habituated him to a greater degree of self-rule than his more subdued classmates expected. All of them had taken their B.A.'s in 1833, '34, or '35, in many cases moving from college to seminary without having lived on their own. Henry was the only one in his class who had graduated as long ago as 1830.

Most students were assigned rooms in the large four-story building that also housed the dining hall, chapel, library, and classrooms, but about one-third of the entering class of 1835 took private lodgings; Henry found rooms with a Mrs. Brearly. Parke Godwin, a fellow student who became a lifelong friend even though he left the seminary after his first year, also lived off campus, at Mrs. Gaston's. Judging from the placement of names on the 1840 census, her lodging house was a short walk from the main seminary building—a vital consideration for a one-legged man. For his second year Henry moved into her home, as did a New Yorker who would soon play a major role in his life, Hugh Walsh.

Henry had often made friends with men who were older or in a position of authority—the shoemakers, tutors Jackson and Eaton at Union College, George W. Clinton at Canandaigua. This pattern continued in New Jersey, where he was presently on easy terms with his old tutor from Albany Academy, Joseph Henry. The young man also cultivated the friendship of another teacher at the College of New Jersey, James Waddel Alexander, Professor of Rhetoric and Belles Lettres. Alexander was a strong Calvinist, a graceful stylist, and a copious writer of tracts and controversial essays. A few years later he co-authored an attack on German philosophy that was reprinted by the conservative New England forces arrayed against Ralph Waldo Emerson and the Transcendentalists. In the early 1840s Henry himself would show Transcendental tendencies and become friends with Emerson (again, somewhat older), but now, in the mid-1830s, it was a commonsense, Scottish-American Calvinist whom Henry got close to.

James Waddel Alexander's father, Archibald, had an even greater impact on Henry's life. He had guided the seminary from its beginning in 1812, and made it a force for Calvinist orthodoxy. An old-fashioned Virginian, he was said to have studied Latin at the age of four, Greek at six, and to be able to "shoot the head off a turkey with a flint-lock" at eleven. He was a shrewd and resourceful guardian of the faith, an embodiment of what was later known as the Old Princeton Theology. He was also conversant with English and Scottish philosophy and taught a course, Mental and Moral Science, that became a standard feature of the seminarians' education. Most of all, he was remembered for the canny spiritual counsel he gave his students and "the inimitable naturalness, freedom, and cordiality" of his public addresses. Combining an "absolute purity . . . of diction" with an easy Virginian colloquiality, Archibald

Alexander seems to have been an inspired performer in the informal Sunday-afternoon "conference." His portrait shows him sitting in a comfortable slouch, far removed from the ramrod pose of contemporary New England divines.

The other professor who had been at Princeton from the beginning, Samuel Miller, was by contrast a courtly and polished New Yorker, the kind of man who (several years later) would rather miss his train than not make his bows. Miller "wrote standing," it was remembered, and was "always calm, always accurate." His voluminous lecture notes, still preserved at the seminary library, justify his reputation for systematic and meticulous preparation. A gentleman of the old school, formal and ruled, Miller was nevertheless said to be "full of conversation, brilliant in company, rich in anecdote." The anecdotes showed up in his courses on Ecclesiastical History, which surveyed the bewildering variety of Christian sects and dogmas over the ages. In explaining Emanuel Swedenborg, for instance, Miller argued for his insanity by recounting that "whenever he sat down to dine, he had twelve plates laid also for the apostles, who were invariably present to dine with him." Two decades later Henry still remembered the story—and rebuked Miller for telling it.

Alexander and Miller were strong, personable, conservative men, still very much in charge of the seminary during Henry's years there. They made a lasting impression on him, partly because he was singled out for social favors, being one of the fortunate seminarians "who saw much of them in private intercourse, surrounded by their charming & cultivated families." The two old-style Calvinists spoke for some of the traditional gentry virtues Henry's suspicious self-made father had lacked—unpretentious cultivation, generosity, charm. Long after Henry renounced Presbyterianism, he not only respected and admired the two men but continued to cherish their "hearts of solid gold." Although he rapped Miller over the knuckles for his "complacent and puny estimate" of Swedenborg, he never lost his strong affection for his old professor, exclaiming a few years after his death, "God love and bless his honored head for ever!" Of course, as doughty Old School Presbyterians, Miller and Alexander had minds as well as hearts—they were trained for combat and knew how to set their lance in theological controversy. For this, also, Henry admired them, recalling how "their wit, their scholastic training, their intellectual refinement had an extreme fascination for us all."

There was a third Alexander—Joseph Addison, brother of James Wad-

del and son of Archibald—who also fascinated Henry. Addison, as he
was called, was a linguistic prodigy credited with over twenty languages.
He taught Hebrew and probably also Biblical Antiquities and the Greek
New Testament, and in his students' eyes was as formidable and remote
as the subjects that absorbed him. His "impetuous brevity of speech, and
the look of power in his face" reminded many of Napoleon. Parke Godwin
never forgot how Addison had terrified a class at the beginning of a term
by announcing: "All knowledge is pleasant . . . and I shall therefore
take it for granted, when I hear that any one does not like any particular
study, that he does not know any thing about it." Over thirty years later
Henry remembered being "acutely piqued by the mystery of [Addison's]
inner life. He habitually lived in the utmost personal remoteness from
the world." Not surprisingly, he was known among students as "the
solitary." The biographer and nephew of this unsocial teacher claimed
that Henry had been his "intimate acquaintance and favourite companion," but there is no independent evidence of this.

A fourth professor, a Kentuckian named John Breckinridge who taught
Pastoral Theology from 1835 to 1838, struck Henry as no more than "a
boyish, gushing good fellow . . . entirely unequipped with the higher
teaching faculty." Clearly the Napoleonic Addison was vastly preferable
to a common, undignified backslapper. But Breckinridge's thirty-two-
year-old wife, Margaret, a daughter of the patrician Samuel Miller, was
a different story, and Henry never forgot her "exquisite frankness, freedom, & grace both of person & manners."

The young seminarian's most troubled relationship was with Charles
Hodge, a lordly professor of theology who had married one of the Baches
of Philadelphia and greatly admired the awesome Duke of Wellington.
Suffering from a painful complaint in his right thigh, Hodge met his
classes in his house, situated just west of the main seminary building.
The reverse of Freud, he had his students recite "while he was on his
couch." Hodge may not yet have been in charge of systematic and
polemical theology during Henry's time, but he was already a dominant
presence at the seminary. Generations of students would remember his
magnum opus, *Systematic Theology*, which, as late as 1921, in the first
Cambridge History of American Literature, got extremely high marks for
its "strange sublimity." It was Hodge who delivered a famous summing
up of the Old Princeton Theology:

Drs. Alexander and Miller were not speculative men. They were not
given to new methods or new theories. They were content with the
faith once delivered to the saints. I am not afraid to say that a new idea

never originated in this Seminary. Their theological method was very simple. The Bible is the word of God. That is to be assumed or proved. If granted; then it follows, that what the Bible says, God says. That ends the matter.

Henry may have been drawn to Napoleonic personages, but he did not get on with this Wellingtonian figure who liked to end matters so magisterially. Years later, composing an unpublished memoir of the seminary, Henry remembered "all of our teachers . . . with unfeigned respect and affection," but then replaced "all" with "most." Also, he inserted a corrective footnote:

> I should like to be able to surround the names of our remaining professors with this tender memorial halo, if strict truth permitted. But Dr H. was far too genuine a Presbyterian in heart as well as head, to be at all picturesque in memory, and if I had ever once known him fairly to forget the Calvinist in the man, I would gladly give him the benefit of the doubt.

Maybe it was Hodge's presence that deterred Henry from visiting a friend in 1843:

> I should have run over to Princeton, had it not been for the awkwardness of meeting people there who *will not talk with* one on equal terms, about those matters which necessarily form the only staple of discourse *with them*. I cannot so far stultify my understanding of the divine order as to suppose any human being or set of beings entitled by their attainments in philosophy or devotion to pass an *a priori* judgment upon those who chance to differ from them.

ARGUMENTS AND LOSS OF TIME

Henry's years at Princeton coincided with an outbreak of controversy and rancor among American Presbyterians that was so divisive it ended in a historic schism. The insurgent fervor that made Rev. William James's tenure at Rochester intolerable was not confined to the state of New York. It spread everywhere, producing great tension between traditional authority and hot-blooded revivalists and converts. Alarmed by this turbulent new spirit, Archibald Alexander warned seminary students against all those "means and measures which produce a high degree of excitement." Alexander disapproved of the Anxious Bench, and when he read popular accounts of revivals he detected "a *cant* which greatly disgusts sensible men." He, Miller, and Hodge took a united stand against the excesses of the time.

Events went out of control, however, when nearby Philadelphia became the newest storm center. In 1835, Henry's first year at Princeton, the Philadelphia Synod suspended the Reverend Albert Barnes from his pulpit for a year for heresy. When the Assembly of 1836 reversed this judgment, the grand division between Old School and New School became irreversible, accompanied by expulsions and lawsuits and lasting enmities. The New School faction pulled out of Princeton and founded Union Theological Seminary in New York City, leaving the New Jersey Seminary more uncompromisingly Old School than ever.

This institutional rift had a tremendous impact on seminary students, who were so enlivened and emboldened by the spread of dissension that their zeal, as James Waddel Alexander put it, "sometimes demanded the cautious hand of repression and guidance." James Waddel claimed that all those attending the seminary from 1835 to 1838 would probably acknowledge that "the course of learning was pursued with uncommon ardour and satisfaction." But this bland opinion reflects a retrospective suppression of a painfully divisive period. In Henry James's case the spirit of eager disputation produced results not at all to the school's satisfaction, increasing his old tendency to ignore his classes in favor of other interests, sending him off on a wild theological tangent that cut across the Old School/New School divide, and leading him to see himself as a lonely crusader for unpopular truths.

Archibald Alexander was an old hand at calming disturbed or fractious young seminarians. Many years earlier, when Rev. William was a seminary student and became despondent over his spiritual state, Alexander gave him effective counsel, perhaps offering some version of his usual recommendation to be less introspective: "Look not so much within. Look to Christ." Now, two decades later, Henry also went to Alexander, not as a humble aspirant, however, but as a rebellious young questioner. There seems to have been at least one notable argument between the ruling patriarch and the young Turk, and when the dust settled Henry was more convinced than ever that he was in the right. Whenever he referred to this episode in later years, it was generally with the implication that he had objected to the arbitrariness of the Calvinists' deity. In old age he even gave an inquiring reporter the misleading impression he had been a kind of onlooker at the school, "an unattached student" who "failed to be converted to the high Calvinistic opinions then taught."

In fact, Henry turned into a kind of fanatic during his years at the seminary. Judging from the writings he published immediately after leaving it, he became in one important respect not less but more orthodox than his professors: he adopted an extreme version of faith alone (the doctrine that sinners are saved not by anything they do but by simply acknowledging their inescapable guilt and accepting Christ's vicarious sacrifice), and in this way reaffirmed the Protestant emphasis on God's complete sovereignty and man's subjection. But simultaneously Henry went the whole Reformation tradition one better by deciding that since the true apostolic church did not have a paid clergy, even the Protestants had deviated from institutional purity. In espousing these two views, Henry was positioning himself in such a way that he felt entitled to accuse Alexander, Miller, and Hodge of heresy. It was they who had fallen away from the true faith, not he. Thus, while the newly roused evangelicals assailed Princeton and traditional Presbyterianism for being frigidly authoritarian, Henry developed an extremely aggressive critique that seemed to come out of left field. He responded deeply to the growth in argumentative zeal, the institutional upheavals, the new mood of democratic insurgency, but only to insist on the necessity of returning to an anarchic original purity few others thought it wise to try for.

There was another consequence as well. The fact that the seminary catalogue for Henry's second year lists him once again with the newly entering class reveals that he had been held back, along with only seven other students out of an original class enrollment of forty-eight. Although it is possible his preparation had proved inadequate, it seems more likely that his performance was so erratic he was not considered ready to move on with his classmates. Certainly, he himself felt some compunction for not having applied himself. In September 1837, anticipating his return for his third year at Princeton, he informed a friend that if he missed the beginning of winter term, he would be falling into the old rut: "All this while . . . my time will be consuming, without any benefit to my seminary studies. I have had great reason to reproach myself in this and the past year for loss of time in Princeton." In this lament, the young man summed up two of the dominant themes of his life—his continuing sense of waste and his unavoidable self-reproach.

As William of Albany had feared, his gifted son was the reverse of assiduous in his professional commitment. In 1829 Henry had hoped to resolve the vocational impasse by running away to Boston and launching a new career as editorial assistant. In 1833 or 1834, realizing that he could not possibly be a lawyer, he let the whole question of vocation collapse and fled to Canandaigua, where he tried to forget it by drinking and gambling. Now, as he began to fear that his desperate wager on the ministry was also about to fail, he once again made preparations for a journey, his longest yet.

Chapter 10

■ ■ ■

COURTS

While Henry tried to get his religious life unkinked, New York State's highest courts and most contentious attorneys were engaged in a mighty effort to unsnarl his father's maddening will. Catharine's initial decision to take her widow's third of the estate had made for several complications, but these were relatively simple compared to the difficulties involving cy pres doctrine and cestuis que trusts and trust terms running for more than one life in being, which filled hundreds of pages in Wendell's Reports and Paige's Chancery Reports. The case of William James's will was said to be one of the "causes célèbres" of New York State's judicial history. It was not until 1846 that the huge mess was finally cleaned up, with all the real-estate holdings parceled out. But the fundamental legal questions had all been settled a decade earlier. By the beginning of 1837 Henry knew he was going to inherit so much wealth he would never have to work.

The two lawyers William of Albany had appointed to execute his will were Gideon Hawley and James King. One of the first things they had to deal with was a claim from their fellow triumvir that he already owned part of the estate, Gus having dug up a document that "charged and assigned" some Syracuse lots to him. A more fundamental and troubling issue was whether the will's basic provision—the trust that could not be divided until the youngest heir attained the age of twenty-one—was valid or not under New York law. By the fall of 1833 the two attorneys realized they could not resolve the "numerous doubts and difficulties" the will presented, and they filed a technical bill of complaint with the Court of Chancery against all the heirs. At the time New York had a two-track legal system. All criminal and many civil cases could be ap-

pealed to the Supreme Court, but equity cases went to the Court of
Chancery. It would be up to the chancellor, Reuben H. Walworth, to
rule on the proper construction of the will.

In learning, ability, and vision Walworth did not compare to James
Kent, the greatly admired jurist Henry was supposed to study during his
last term at Union College. It was said that before Walworth was offered
the chancellorship, every single member of the Supreme Court had declined the job. His difficulties in the present case were compounded by
the multiplicity of interested parties, who all weighed in with their own
legal representatives. Henry and Rev. William responded to Hawley and
King's bill of complaint by filing a cross bill, to the effect that the trust
was not valid in New York and that the estate must be divided equally
among the descendants. This bill was filed on July 25, 1834, the very
moment, as it happened, that Henry signed onto the Whig campaign
against Jackson. The two brothers' attorney, John C. Spencer, once a
leading Clintonian and Antimason and now a powerful Whig, resided
at this time in Canandaigua, as did Henry. (Laura Clinton, the woman
Henry visited in 1835 before returning to Albany, was Spencer's daughter.) Gus was represented by John Duer, his children by James John
Roosevelt, John Barber by both Harmanus Bleecker and John V.L. Pruyn,
and Hawley and King by Benjamin F. Butler. These men were the big
legal heavyweights of their time. Duer, Butler, and Spencer had drawn
up New York State's Revised Statutes of 1828; Butler was Attorney
General of the United States. None of the interested parties was taking
any chances, least of all Henry, who retained another lawyer, S. A.
Talcott, to defend his own individual interests.

Talcott argued that the trust was void for several reasons: its duration
was uncertain, it violated the provision against perpetuities in the Revised
Statutes, and it had other legal defects. He also called attention to one
of the ways in which Augustus could take advantage of the will's ambiguities. According to the testator's wishes, when the time eventually
came to dissolve and distribute the trust, it was to be divided into twelve
equal shares. Eight and a half of these were to go to certain named
members of the family, *not* including Henry. The other three and a half
were to be apportioned "among all or any number of those herein designated as in any event entitled to share in the ultimate disposition of
my estate." This language probably excluded Henry and Rev. William,
but who could be sure? Speaking for Henry, Talcott argued that the
provision concerning the three and a half shares should be declared void,
as it allowed the trustees "to dispose of the whole of those shares and

their accumulations . . . for the sole benefit of an adult . . . viz., Augustus James."

John Duer, attorney for the favored heir, conceded that the provision concerning the three and a half shares was probably invalid. Declaring that he was expressing Gus's wishes, Duer asked that the ambiguous clause be construed so as "to embrace all the descendants" and "to place each branch of the family on an equality, in the final division of the estate." This appearance of offering an amicable compromise was part of the lawyer's strategy, his purpose being to preserve the rest of the will, with its favorable treatment of Gus.

But John C. Spencer, the lawyer who represented Henry and Rev. William, and also Catharine James and the Gourlay orphans, acknowledged no concessions and gave no quarter. The trust William had tried to establish was illegal. It was not the kind of trust allowed by statute. The will as a whole was too defective to be remodeled. An immediate distribution of the entire estate was the only legal and practicable solution. Spencer articulated these positions in short, plain, hard-hitting sentences, punctuating his argument with brief assertions that had a gavel-like finality: "It is void," "The instrument must fail," "The testator has died intestate." The legal culture for which he spoke was one that insisted on the priority of ordinary language: "Words used by the legislature must be taken in their ordinary meaning and popular sense." The man who had denounced the Masons as an elite secret society now insisted that verbal obfuscation must not be permitted to confuse the plain intent of those who made the law.

Spencer also weighed in with the kind of extralegal argument no other attorney in the case made use of. He argued that the prohibitory statute that obviated William's trust had been designed "to affect society, both socially and politically." In England (and under the common law) William's trust would have been permitted, he said, but "the policy of our [American] law is to distribute. Primogeniture and entails were abolished by our ancestors, in furtherance of this policy, but they stopped short of the object. The legislature, in 1828, accomplished what they had left undone." Speaking as one who had codified New York's statutory law, Spencer was claiming a special authority for his interpretation of it. He was also politicizing the case by talking about the difference between aristocratic and democratic equity and inheritance law. In a hereditary aristocracy large estates remain intact from generation to generation, but in a democracy no estate can enjoy that kind of invulnerability. In England the fathers were able to bind the sons' economic choices, but in America each generation was free to hold, dispose of, or waste its inheritance. The reason the testator's will was defective, according to Spencer, was that it emerged from an older kind of social polity recently abandoned by the state of New York. *

This social (not legal) argument not only recalled William of Albany's deeply frustrated Old World dream of founding a lasting dynasty but anticipated Henry's later views on the differences between Europe's class distinctions and America's sentiment of equality. Even more, Spencer's argument echoed the book recently published by his friend from France, Tocqueville's Democracy in America.

Chancellor Walworth was not persuaded. In his decree, which took over forty pages, he aligned himself with Duer's and Butler's arguments rather than Spencer's. The judge was clearly uneasy about the sweeping implications of Spencer's construction of the Revised Statutes, which he feared would "deprive a parent of the power" of establishing a trust to provide for children still in their minorities. Appealing to canons of reasonableness and moral necessity, Walworth concluded ("with some hesitation") that the trust term was valid. In the words of a sympathetic judge, he chose to act "in the conservative spirit of the common law" rather than adhere to the possibly unsettling implications of the new state statutes. At the same time, the chancellor endorsed Duer's (and Gus's) position on the ambiguously assigned three and a half shares: this portion of the estate should be treated as if William had died intestate. In other words, seven/twenty-fourths of the great hoard should "be distributed, immediately, to the widow and next of kin." The decree to this effect was issued on July 21, 1835, three months before Henry began attending Princeton Theological Seminary. Well before beginning his ministerial study, in other words, he knew he was going to get a very substantial sum of money. His reasons for preparing for the ministry had little or nothing to do with economic pressure originating from his father. But would an independently wealthy seminarian be able to stay the course?

Only one interested party, Gus, accepted the chancellor's decree in all respects. Everyone else objected to one feature or another and appealed to the Court for the Correction of Errors, New York State's curious court of last resort, which was composed of senators as well as judges. The Jameses all brought in their hired guns once again, and the familiar battle

---

* When Spencer was Secretary of War under President Tyler, his son was tried and executed at sea for attempted mutiny. One of the officers who served on the drumhead court was a first cousin of Herman Melville. This episode lay behind the tormented and never finished "inside narrative," Billy Budd.

lines were drawn up. Henry still had Spencer fighting in his corner, but now, instead of retaining him jointly with Rev. William, Henry shared him with Jannet's husband, William H. Barker. This was a significant change, one that reflected Henry's growing acquaintance with his sister's in-laws. The Barkers, a rich and cultivated New York banking family, probably introduced a new social element into Henry's life. He was particularly impressed with his brother-in-law's sister, Anna Hazard Barker, whom Ralph Waldo Emerson once praised as the "loveliest of women." In 1840, one month after Henry got married, Anna got engaged to the scion of another family of bankers, the Wards of Boston. In the 1850s Henry would have a fervid correspondence with "darling Anna" on religious topics. But the only trace of their relationship in the mid-1830s is an envelope preserved at Harvard, its sealing wax still attached.

Up in Albany, meanwhile, Henry and William Barker's attorney presented the Court of Errors with a powerful legal argument for pronouncing the trust invalid (the anti-aristocratic rhetoric being abandoned). After listening to him and the other lawyers in the case, five members of the Court of Errors issued lengthy written opinions. In Chief Justice Nelson's view, "There can be no doubt the will must have been pronounced valid previous to the revised statutes." Now, however, the one "great and fundamental difficulty" could not be evaded: the term of the trust William had hoped to establish violated the statute on perpetuities. Justice Bronson was almost as categorical. Although he had been "strongly disposed to uphold the will," he was now "fully persuaded that it cannot be done consistently with the rules of law." The two senators who recorded their opinions took the same view. Justice Cowen dissented, preferring to follow the tradition of the common law, but he was in the minority. Thus, reversing the chancellor's decision, the Court of Errors irrevocably broke the back of William of Albany's will. This judgment not only gave Henry and his siblings, Gus excepted, everything they wanted, but it vindicated Henry's shrewdness in choosing Spencer as his legal representative. The majority opinion was not only based on the Revised Statutes Spencer had helped write but was guided by his interpretation of the pertinent clauses.

The Court of Errors issued its decree December 30, 1836, not long after Henry began his second year at Princeton. Except for a few small legacies to the Gourlays, the Orphan Asylum, and others, William of Albany was now considered to have died intestate. His vast wealth was to be carved up in accordance with the law of descents. Henry would have to return all the annuity payments and other sums that he had received during the four years since his father's death (a total of about

$17,000, apparently), but in exchange he became eligible for a full share of his father's fortune.

Some questions were yet to be adjudicated. Two years later Chancellor Walworth decided that the forty square miles out in Illinois could be parceled out and conveyed directly to the heirs, and in 1839 the widow consented to accept in lieu of dower an annuity of $18,800, six times what her husband had allowed. This amount was the equivalent of 5 percent of her rightful third of the estate. The enormous Syracuse real-estate holdings and salt and flour operations were still to be divided. But the 1836 decree by the Court of Errors meant that practically everything else was to be distributed to the heirs as soon as possible. A Master in Chancery was appointed to inspect the executors' books and issue a report, and one week after this task was carried out, on October 11, 1837, the Court of Chancery ordered $500,000 worth of stocks, securities, rents, and cash to be divvied up and paid out. * Henry's fraction, two/thirty-thirds, amounted to $30,000, and more was to come.

The second generation had triumphed (one of them, Gus, quite unwillingly) over the self-made immigrant father. But now what? If Henry was "leisured for life," as he later wrote, wasn't the problem of his future even more pressing than it had been?

---

* Rev. William seems to have been particularly short of cash at this time. On October 18, a week after the ordered distribution, he assigned a couple of mortgages to his stepmother, Catharine, in exchange for $1,038.

Chapter 11

■ ■ ■

ENGLAND AND IRELAND:
1837

In February 1837 Joseph Henry sailed for England and France on a seven-month research trip. He was seen off in New York by his friend and former pupil, who confided that he "had some idea of coming to Europe this summer to visit his relatives in Ireland." But the young man's plans seemed to change from one week to the next, and when James next wrote, on March 7, he made no mention of the projected trip. Instead, he commissioned the physicist to make some literary purchases in London—a monumental and expensive history of the province of Rajasthan in western India and complete sets of the *Edinburgh* and *Quarterly Review*. On one point at least the student's mind was made up. He was going to build a substantial scholarly library.

To pay for these bookish investments, James secured a bill of exchange from his father's old New York partner, James McBride, who arranged international banking transactions through a brother and partner in Dublin. The value of this financial instrument was $300—one-fifth Professor Henry's annual salary. Purchasing it took the restless young man back to New York for at least the second time during the current term. Perhaps another and very different purpose also drew him to the city—visiting Anna Barker and the two unmarried sisters of his fellow lodger at Mrs. Gaston's, Mary and Catharine Walsh.

In London, meanwhile, Joseph Henry bought complete sets of the journals James desired. Although the two men were on very easy terms, exchanging familiar and friendly letters and performing substantial favors for one another, the physicist must have been surprised when his rich friend sent him a second financial instrument, this one for £250 sterling, the equivalent of more than $1,200. It was an unsolicited loan, prompted by the Panic of 1837.*

This economic collapse, which occurred not long after Joseph Henry sailed out of New York Harbor, caused the $5,000 the college had promised him for "Philosophical Apparatus" (laboratory equipment) to shrink to $500. For anyone without a special entrée to banks and trading houses, it was not a good time to be traveling. Gold could not be had, and banknotes, as Charles Hodge discovered back in New Jersey, were accepted only in the vicinity of the issuing institution: "Princeton money is worth nothing ten miles from this place." In the face of this squeeze, James's spectacular generosity enabled the physicist to acquire the equipment he would use in his epochal experiments with magnetism and electricity after he returned to Princeton. One thing you were likely to be very good at, if you were a son of William James of Albany, was making lavish disbursements for philanthropic purposes. You were likely to be exceptionally grand if you were just coming into your inheritance.

In trying to explain the Panic, James and his friend diverged in characteristic ways. Joseph Henry got access to a file of papers in Paris and decided it was senseless to place the blame on the newly installed Van Buren Administration, believing instead that "the distress commenced in England and was produced in our country by the ruinous system of paper money and the consequent spirit of gambling and speculation." James, on the other hand, blamed the depression on the Democrats' destruction of the U.S. Bank and on Van Buren's refusal to take the advice of bankers and merchants. His friends in New York, he reported, "predict the establishment of a national Bank as the very first act of next Congress." These were standard Whig sentiments, freshly endorsed perhaps by the banking and trading family James's sister Jannet had married into.

Before long, the restless young man decided to skip his classes in earnest. Not even waiting for the May examinations that marked the end of winter term, he made arrangements to leave for England in mid-April. Instead of simply taking off, however, he seems to have obtained some sort of leave of absence from his professors, who probably understood that this privileged and troubled young man required an unusually long tether. Although they were not yet ready to dismiss him, and he was not yet ready to break with them, he did need to get away.

On April 20, 1837, a London packet, the *Westminster*, cleared New

---

* One of those ruined by the Panic was Herman Melville's brother and employer, Gansevoort, an Albany hatter. Herman had to get a job teaching in a common school.

York Harbor, and the young traveler was on the high seas at last, bending toward the Old World, from which his father had sailed less than half a century earlier. A black servant, Billy Taylor, accompanied him. It was a fairly quick passage, and nineteen days later, instead of waiting for the ship to reach Gravesend, or even Portsmouth, James disembarked at Plymouth, England's westernmost deep-water port. Perhaps the passage had been an uncomfortable one for the one-legged man, or maybe he was eager to set foot on English soil. Years later, when Henry Jr. took his first independent trip to Europe, James recalled his own youthful enchantment with the rural West Country landscape:

> Your enjoyment of England reminds me of my feelings on my first visit there forty years ago nearly, when I landed in Devonshire in the month of May or June and was so intoxicated with the roads and lanes and hedges and fields and cottages and castles and inns that I thought I should fairly expire with delight. *

Four days after landing, having got as far as Portsmouth, he dispatched a letter to Joseph Henry, whom he hoped to meet in London—"God willing"—in three or four days. The pious seminarian made it clear he would not be traveling on the Sabbath.

But Joseph Henry had just left London, and by the time James's letter caught up with him, the scientist was settled in Paris, near the Pantheon and the Sorbonne. The physicist at once lined up some useful contacts for his friend: William Vaughan, a key London point man for visiting American businessmen and scientists, and Alexander Dallas Bache, descendant of Benjamin Franklin and professor of science at the University of Pennsylvania. In his letter to Bache, Joseph Henry described James in terms befitting a rich young prince:

> He is a person to whom I am indebted for very special marks of Friendship and would be pleased to serve while in Europe . . . He has had the misfortune to loose one of his legs and on this account will be somewhat unplesantly situated among strangers. He is the son of the late Mr. James of Albany. I spoke to you of him while in London.

Bache and Vaughan promptly called on James, who seems to have found lodgings in a private home at 65 Albany Street, just east of Regent's

---

* This letter (the original has not been found) probably dates from the novelist's 1869–70 trip to England. The son was under the impression that his father's first trip had taken place in 1830 and probably substituted "forty years ago nearly" for whatever Henry Sr. had originally written—possibly "thirty years ago."

Park. Caught by surprise, the usually well-tailored young man "was quite overwhelmed at seeing two such great men enter my door, and in my embarrassment displayed the holes in my old coat, I presume to great advantage." He went out to dine with Vaughan and accompanied him to a couple of meetings of learned societies. However, with Bache, who was connected by marriage to Charles Hodge, the acquaintance never got off the ground. Bache was miffed that the young seminarian did not return his call, and complained to Joseph Henry: "Immediately after the receipt of yours to Mʳ Vaughan I called upon Mʳ James, but have not seen him except a glimpse (at Sᵗ Paul's) since."

This glimpse through another's eyes is all we know of James's first views of London. Henry Jr., endlessly fascinated with the city, tried again and again to capture in words its look and tone, but Henry Sr. did not, as far as is known, respond to the great urban spectacle. His mind was elsewhere.

Taking for granted that James would like to be his traveling companion in Europe, Joseph Henry urged him to come to Paris and proposed a further excursion to Belgium and possibly Switzerland. He even arranged for Bache to accompany his disabled friend across the Channel. But James was meditating a very different summer from what his friend had in mind, and when he finally responded three weeks later to the physicist's friendly offers, it was to turn down the prearranged escort. "I should like very well to go on to Paris with Bache," he wrote on June 15, long after receiving his friend's offer, "but fancy I shall be obliged to go into Ireland, and spend a few weeks with an uncles family there." This excuse had a trumped-up sound, for as the physicist himself had already pointed out, there would be plenty of time for Ireland as well as the Continent. James's tone was odd in another way as well: back in February the Irish visit had been the whole point of his contemplated passage to Britain, but now the visit was somehow up in the air—"but fancy I shall be obliged." His excuse for not going to Belgium was equally evasive: "The only things I care about seeing on the continent . . . are Venice & Rome." In fact, aside from this sentence, there is no evidence either city held much attraction for him. He never set foot in Italy in spite of various opportunities, and in 1869, when his son Henry Jr. was wandering in happy delirium through the streets of Rome, Henry Sr. mailed him a round denunciation of "that foul wart" the Papacy. He did not feel comfortable until his son was once again safely north of the Alps.

In 1913, when Henry Jr. tried to picture his father's first trip to the Old World, he focused (as have later biographers) on the encounter with the Irish Jameses in the village of Bailieborough, Ireland. But this family reunion seems to have counted for a good deal less with James than his quiet life in London, which he did not interrupt from May to August. Aside from the general financial uncertainty, one important reason why he preferred not to budge was that he was being fitted for a "good Cork leg." It undoubtedly took some time to have this device constructed and adjusted, and then to get accustomed to it. When Joseph Henry returned to London in the latter part of the summer, he wrote his wife that the new leg was "a very interesting article and adds much to [James's] appearance." This emphasis on looks rather than, say, comfort or ease may well reflect James's own sense of the matter. Looks were important to the young man who had left his measurements with Schenectady's tailors, and who was sensitive about being found in his old jacket. Now he would look more normal, move more naturally.

But James had an additional motive for staying in London—a powerful attachment to the peace and quiet of his room. Seven years earlier, when he ran away to Boston, he described his living quarters in loving detail and then wound up with the strange declaration that "this room is sacred to me." Now he once again extolled the pleasures of his temporary nest: "I feel a little homesick occasionally—but in the main do charmingly. I spend my time pretty much in my room, & am as happy generally as the day is long." When Joseph Henry returned from his energetic life in Paris, where he had picked up enough French to follow lectures at the Jardin des Plantes, he saw his younger friend as sunk in inactivity: "I have roused him from a lethargy which he has been enjoying for three months past. He has been living in London much at his ease with his books and a very few acquaintances. The time has passed very quietly and plesantly with him." On July 31 the physicist informed his wife that he had "partly persuaded" James to accompany him to Scotland. But once again it proved impossible to get the young man to move.

Perhaps the long confinement following James's accident in boyhood had inaugurated a lifelong habit. Or maybe he was conforming to the precedent set by his admired older brother. When Rev. William James fled to Scotland in 1820 or 1821 after being licensed for the profession he eventually gave up, "he lived in comparative retirement, conversing more with books than with men; and though within a few minutes' walk of some of the greatest spirits of the age, he seems to have studiously avoided even an introduction to them." This passage aptly describes Henry Sr.'s London summer. Each brother, facing a crisis that involved his religious and professional calling, fled overseas for a period of retreat and study. For the rest of his life James's strategy for satisfying both his restlessness and his domesticity was to enchamber himself away from home. A bored hotel letter his wife wrote after the Civil War reveals his fondness for private space in public hostelries: "Father of course was in his room all day & in the evening too."

There was something else that helps explain the young American's quiet retirement. The Dissenters and Evangelicals, whom he might ordinarily have sought out, had recently led the successful fight to abolish slavery throughout England's colonies and now regarded the United States the same way the entire world looked at South Africa in the 1980s—as a country disfigured by the despotic and retrograde treatment of blacks. It was not the best of times for an American Protestant—particularly one accompanied by a black valet—to try to break bread with his English brethren. When another American traveler attended the annual meeting of the London Missionary Society during the summer of 1837, he was shaken by the "strong disposition at present in England to think unfavorably and to speak disparagingly of *every thing American*." There was a stinging "condemnation" in the air.

What was James reading and thinking about all day long in his quiet room? Although nothing he wrote at the time sheds any light on this question, it is possible to make an informed guess on the basis of the volumes he donated to the seminary library when he returned to Princeton in the fall. Most of these, still carrying his original presentation inscription, were until recently on the library's open shelves. They afford a small glimpse of what was on his mind in London.

The most exotic of the donated works are W. Ward's *View of the History, Literature, and Mythology of the Hindoos* (a two-volume work published at a mission station in Serampore, India) and the book Joseph Henry was asked to pick up, James Tod's *Annals and Antiquities of Rajast'han*. More piously, James donated *Missionary Enterprizes in the South Seas* and six volumes put out by the Religious Tract Society of London on missionary efforts in Tahiti, India, China, West Africa, the West Indies, and North America. These gifts reflected the young man's strong support of Protestant missions. Indeed, they scarcely hint at his zeal, for, as he recalled fifteen years later, he "contributed profusely to missionary and similar enterprises," thus furthering a cause that had a very high priority for Albany's Presbyterian churches. It is altogether striking how conscious James remained of one of the chief goals of his church and seminary, the training and sending of missionaries to the "heathen," as he passed his first summer in worldly London. The contrast could not be greater with his son Henry Jr., who actively soaked up the city's intellectual and cultural riches during *his* first independent trip there in

1869. When *he* called London the modern Babylon, it was with a sense of irony and relief.

The most startling of James's gifts is a complete bound run, in one volume, of *The Protestant Penny Magazine*, still bearing the inscription *Presented to the Theological Seminary at Princeton N.J. By Henry James, a student in the same. 1837.* This cheap, Dublin-based, Catholic-baiting magazine was designed to "secure a general circulation . . . among the lower orders," a goal it pursued by showing graphic scenes from the Inquisition and running stories of priests who burned Protestant Bibles and extorted money from peasants. The only article that shows signs of having been read reproduces several passages from a priestly handbook that recommends torture for heretics. In the margin are four light vertical pencil lines of the sort James entered in his books in the 1840s.

Reading, reflecting, and praying in his quiet room, James was as unsecular a young man as can well be imagined. He was still strongly attached to the Presbyterian seminary as a seat of learning, and he continued to take its piety, its missionary goals, its doctrines for granted. His letters to Joseph Henry exhale a heavily conventional trust in Providence: "The distress is inconceivable all over the country, and when & how it will end the Lord only knows. That He may overrule it to our eventual welfare & his own glory in our midst is my prayer." He ends another letter with the pious wish "May Providence smile upon you now in yr absence and always, is the sincere prayer of yrs ever truly *H. James.*"

But the young man was also reaching out to some of Britain's most uncompromisingly radical dissenters. As he told a reporter forty-four years later, he bought books during his stay in England that "went to the roots of the questions" that were troubling him. So it must have been on one of his trips to the booksellers clustered around St. Paul's that he unearthed the volume that would set him off on the next phase of his odyssey— an obscure eighteenth-century book bearing the strange title *Letters on Theron and Aspasio.* Written by a little-known Scottish controversialist named Robert Sandeman, this work would get James out of the seminary, and out of his declared vocation as well.

BAILIEBOROUGH

On July 21 Joseph Henry returned to London, bringing with him vast new stores of knowledge and an intestinal complaint he blamed on Paris's drinking water. To recuperate, he moved in with young James, who

acted as both "Nurse and Physician," tending the sick man and pre-
scribing medicine. Before long, the physicist was back on his feet and
making preparations for an excursion to Edinburgh and Glasgow, to pick
the brains of all the local savants. At Liverpool, where the British Association held its annual meeting that year, he found out how risky it
was for an American to attempt to lecture the English, but he was also
treated with "marked attention" by the great Michael Faraday, his only
real rival in electrical research.

In early August, as Joseph Henry prepared to go up against the best
British scientists of the day, James and his servant left London for Bailieborough, County Cavan, to visit those Jameses who had never left
Ireland. The young man had reason to be uneasy about this much-talked-
about and long-deferred encounter. In addition to facing his unknown
relatives' curiosity about his handicap, he would have to get about on
his new cork leg, which had not yet received a real trial. He would also
have to remember he was a minister in training. As regards his purpose
in making the visit, Joseph Henry had the impression he meant to "assist
his poor relatives." Although the Bailieborough Jameses were not poor,
at least by Irish standards, James may well have wished to offer help of
some kind. His father had been a staunch support for the kinfolk overseas,
and now the depression afforded a further incentive to provide assistance.
The hand-loom weavers of Ulster were known to have been idled. There
were even reports that "starvation was making dreadful progress."

The event that commanded everyone's attention during James's August
visit was the parliamentary election. Since this was the first election
since Catholic Emancipation, it was an epochally stirring moment for
the followers of Daniel O'Connell and a gravely threatening one for
Tories. All over Ireland crowds gathered, windows were broken, and
tense standoffs developed between Catholic mobs and the police. In
Limerick, roused marchers led by flutes or bagpipes converged on the
polling place. However, no violence was reported in County Cavan,
even though it split its vote by returning both a Whig/Radical and a
Conservative.

There is no way of knowing how James responded to this historic
moment, as there is not one extant family letter of the time that so much
as mentions his visit. Three-quarters of a century later, when Henry Jr.
wrote the second volume of his autobiography, he evoked his father's
old stories about the "conjoined hospitality" of a lawyer, a doctor, and
a principal merchant, stories in which front doors stood constantly open
and tables were always set with whiskey (as at Buffalo's Eagle Tavern).
The American visitor supposedly found the offered drink "much less

tempting" than the company of a certain Barbara in a never-to-be-forgotten gooseberry patch. This is the picture the novelist gives us of his father's visit. But the picture is misleading. Henry Jr. surely underrated the problems Irish hospitality must have posed for his alcoholic father. He also misdated the trip, assigning it to his father's "nineteenth year" and imagining that he had been sent by wealthy William of Albany, then still alive. The novelist wanted to think of his parent as a dazzlingly gilded emissary suddenly appearing in a dull Irish town.

The one detail that shows up in all later recollections of the visit is the race of James's servant. In 1922 Robert James of Bailieborough, a first cousin once removed, received an inquiry from James's grandson Henry III and replied that he had "heard of your grandfather's visit and about his negro servant but I cannot recollect other particulars." Robert James's wife wrote that "William James of Belfast [a first cousin *twice* removed] says he remembers well his father telling of a relative coming over with a Negro servant & all the country people standing with their mouths open, never having seen a Negro previously." In this man's recollection, James had faded to a vague relative, but the servant remained as vivid as ever.

The American side was equally fixated on the Negro. When Henry James the novelist recalled in old age the stories his father had told about the Irish expedition, he remembered how his boyish imagination had been captivated by the image of " 'Billy Taylor,' the negro servant," who would "altogether rule from the point of view of effect." His "almost epic shape . . . singularly appealed, it was clear, to the Irish imagination, performing in a manner never to disappoint it." It is an index of Henry Jr.'s attitudes that he put Billy Taylor's name in quotation marks, as if the man's identity were somehow fictitious. He saw Taylor as disguised, a comic darky, the "inimitable clown" of the traveling American circus Henry Sr. brought to Bailieborough. Sharing the nostalgia for slavery's servile charms that was so widespread in postbellum America, Henry Jr. fondly imagined his father's servant's picturesque loyalty: "In those days, even in the North, young mastership hadn't too long since lapsed to have lost every grace of its tradition."

These images of Billy Taylor are not borne out by the one contemporary description of him that has survived. Recovering in James's rooms in London, Joseph Henry had ample opportunity to observe the capable servant:

[James] brought with him a black man from Albany as a waiter who is a very good fellow in the serving line. He attracts much attention and is

quite [a] Lion among the lower classes[,] eats with the family with whom
we lodge and would find no difficulty were he not married in getting a
white wife.

Back in Albany the color line was so strict the annual city directories
apparently italicized the names of blacks. Half-Southern Princeton was
even more divided. The physicist was surprised that the racial separation
he took for granted as a white American could be canceled in London
with so little fuss.

All these memories of Taylor's blackness notwithstanding, James's
most important acquisition in County Cavan was undoubtedly a new
sense of the complexities of his own racial and religious identity as an
American Irish Protestant. This new self-consciousness led him to make
an exceedingly odd and cryptic declaration in a note he dashed off to
Joseph Henry soon after returning to London:

> It would be impolitic to enlarge upon transAtlantic affairs in a document
> which may very probably fall into the Enemy's hands, and which coming
> from a man of my widely acknowledged Note, might, provided, of course,
> they should have gumption enough to decipher it, greatly aggravate the
> Existing embarrassments between the two countries.

There is no question but that England is the "Enemy" in this inflated
and somewhat self-mocking sentence. Perhaps the writer was afraid that
if he once again blamed Van Buren for the Panic, he might lend inadvertent comfort to the contemptuous English, who considered the President out of his depth in fiscal policy. James was registering his sense of
peripheral involvement in the troubled areas of dispute between England
and the United States. Not only were relations between the two countries
extremely ticklish at this time, but it was not unreasonable for James to
think of himself as prominent and exposed. He was the son of a man
who could still be described, in Joseph Henry's words, as "the intimate
friend of the lamented Emmet," Robert Emmet, the United Irishman
whom the English had executed thirty-four years earlier for sedition.

In any case, as the young, second-generation American returned to
London from his ancestral village, he undoubtedly brought with him a
fresh vision of his own history and identity. He had witnessed the first
election in which Ireland's Catholic electors had been able to vote, and
he had done so as a Presbyterian minister in training. He had been
exposed, sharply and unforgettably, to the bitter Old World history that
lay behind the Presbyterian ways of thinking he was already questioning.

He had also caught a whiff of the growing sentiment for Irish self-rule —the complications this would involve, the threat it would pose to Irish Presbyterians. He had discovered his tangled roots, not by enjoying a sentimental family reunion on the Old Sod or going on a lighthearted gooseberry-picking expedition with the charming Barbara, but by developing a half-ironic awareness of dangerous personal and political entanglements. "It would be impolitic" to put his thoughts down with pen and ink: this was the lesson James carried away from his first and last visit to his father's unhappy native land.

Back in London, the young traveler dispatched three letters to Joseph Henry, hoping to arrange their passage on the same Atlantic packet. But the physicist wasn't able to wrap up his business in time, and James set sail by himself on the *Ontario*, reaching New York on October 23 after a long month's voyage. He made a visit to his family and friends in Albany before returning to Princeton, and he also stopped in New York, perhaps to see the Barkers and the Walshes and others.

Chapter 12

. . .

PRINCETON RENOUNCED:
1837–38

Seen in isolation, James's life moves like a vessel guided by its own internal gyroscopes. Looked at in the context of other lives, he becomes one of a million corks companionably bobbing on immense swells.

The enthusiasms that had been stirred up by the revivals of the early 1830s proved difficult to contain, and as the decade neared its end, a new kind of blight fell on Protestant seminaries. Young ministerial candidates began to be troubled by a terminal deadness in their denominations—a failure of spirit, a lack of interest in pressing new social questions. Harvard Divinity School, the seedbed for New England's Unitarian clergy, was suddenly unable to attract qualified students, who (in the words of a historian of Transcendentalism) were full of "doubts about the viability of the profession." In 1838 Ralph Waldo Emerson preached his celebrated Divinity School address, boldly urging the graduates sitting before him to abandon their narrow and exclusive adherence to the Christian religion. Idealistic young preachers like John S. Dwight, Class of 1836, preached irregularly for a few years and then left their congregations. In the more orthodox seminaries—Yale, Princeton, Andover —the disillusionment was less overwhelming and took different forms, but the result was the same. From now on, the American pulpit no longer attracted the best young minds.

At Princeton James was not only caught up in the general vocational crisis, but he turned into a flaming rebel. We get a glimpse of the role he played from a letter written two decades later by a fellow seminarian, the Reverend Edward D. Bryan, who had stayed the course and was now pastor of a Presbyterian church in Rye, New York. Bryan remembered

James as the bright particular star in a cluster of apostates: "Had the tender & despised germs of your early piety been duly developed, what majestic proportions had it now attained! The *feeble* ones, who deflected from the right about the time you did I have seldom tho! of—but I have often in fancy traced your unhappy way." This overheated lament gives testimony to James's ability to command and hold others' attention.

One of the feeble ones Bryan had in mind was James A. Platt. Five years younger than James, Platt had joined the Second Presbyterian Church of Albany about the same time James joined the First Church. He arrived at Princeton one year after James, in 1836, and when he dropped out he was, according to his own account, "following in the footsteps of two of his classmates, after reading Sandeman's Letters, holding the belief therein inculcated, that a special order, such as the clergy, was not needed in the Church of Christ." Seminary records suggest Platt left during the summer of 1838. Having abandoned what he would later call "barbaric superstition," he apparently ended up in the liberal wing of the Friends.

Another classmate who deflected from the right was Hugh Walsh, the well-to-do young New Yorker with whom James roomed at Mrs. Gaston's. Walsh attended in 1835 and 1836. The next year he registered but never showed up: an asterisk by his name in the 1837–38 catalogue tells us he was "absent." Official minutes note that he "did not return to the Seminary, in the course of the present session" (winter 1837–38) and was "not expected to return." Walsh went on to enroll in medical school, first in Boston and then in New York, where he earned an M.D. degree in 1841. In 1857 his lungs were so "seriously diseased" that he sailed for Madeira. He died two years later at the age of forty-three. Walsh's and James's impact on each other is difficult to assess because of the complete and rather mystifying absence of Walsh family letters. Perhaps the papers that were destroyed by Catharine Walsh, a sister, immediately after James's death in 1882 included Hugh's correspondence. Or was there a serious breach? It seems odd that Henry Jr.'s memoirs, which have so much to say about other relatives on both the Walsh and James sides, do not mention the uncle who introduced Henry Sr. to his future wife.

There are two conflicting versions of James's departure from the seminary. In the newspaper interview he gave the year before his death, the number of students who had been converted to his views had grown from two to "some half-dozen." He also gave the impression that, in spite of his disruptiveness, he was so greatly favored by his professors that one of them—Archibald Alexander?—"was ready to wink at his heresy rather than lose the presence of one whose bright thought and good spirit seemed alike desirable." James, however, was "unwilling to make further trouble" and withdrew. In the other version, recorded by an alumni officer at Albany Academy, James dropped out after "the effect of his unorthodox opinions upon other students [was] objected to."

What little evidence there is definitely suggests that James came in for special treatment. When the board of directors met on September 25, 1837, his name was not included among those declared absent during summer term, even though he had missed all of it. He was evidently classed with those who "failed to answer to their names" at examinations but whose absence was excused as resulting from "sickness, or other unavoidable circumstances." Homeward bound on the *Ontario*, James was still in good standing.

The newspaper interviewer was clearly in error in suggesting that James quit the seminary *before* sailing to England. As his letter bemoaning his "loss of time in Princeton" reveals, he intended to return and did so in October, at which time he registered for the year, gave sixteen volumes to the library, and probably began attending classes. Exactly when he dropped out is uncertain. At the conclusion of winter term, May 1838, a librarian's report identified him as "late a student." A letter of Joseph Henry's written in March discloses that he had "been in Albany for some months past but is expected in Princeton in a few days." He was probably back in Albany on May 30 to sign a petition in chancery. On balance, it seems that James dropped out late in 1837 and then spent most of the winter and spring in his mother's home. Yet in spite of the physical inconveniences involved in traveling, he could not stay away from Princeton. The seminary was no longer "his intellectual headquarters," as the Boston interviewer correctly noted, but James's attention was still fixed on it as the seat of religious learning. Breaking away from Calvinist Presbyterianism was easier said than done.

If Albany, New York, and Princeton remained the chief stops on the restless young man's circuit, they were not the only ones. During Van Buren's term of office (1837–41), James and a younger unmarried sister, Ellen King James, went to Washington, D.C., where they were invited to a state dinner. James declined to go, and in his absence his sister was handed in by one of the Chief Executive's sons, Smith Thompson Van Buren, a retiring man less interested in politics than in elegant country life. In 1842 these two dinner partners became husband and wife, and in 1920, when one of their aged offspring recalled this now antediluvian social affair, she attributed James's absence to his youth and his known dislike of formal dinners.

SANDEMAN

In July 1838 James was in New York putting the finishing touches on an edition of the curiously titled religious book he had discovered in London, Robert Sandeman's *Letters on Theron and Aspasio*, first published in 1757. But while the young man's body was in New York, his mind kept darting back to Princeton, particularly as he wrote a short, unsigned, fire-breathing preface questioning the theological acumen of his former mentors and blasting the accommodating professionalism of the Presbyterian clergy. This work, James's first, was a cannon shot across the bow of American Presbyterianism. His long and aggressive campaign against established religion had begun. Although it would take him many years to realize the fact, he had found the only calling he would ever have.

James's reasons for putting *Letters on Theron and Aspasio* in circulation—"at his own expense"—cannot be understood unless one gets a feel for the spirit of this obscure volume, and also of the book to which James's preface unfavorably compared it, David Russell's *Letters, Practical and Consolatory*.

Robert Sandeman (1718–71) was a Scotsman who had broken with the Presbyterian Church a century earlier and organized independent congregations in Scotland and England, and also in New England, where he spent the last seven years of his life. The book James republished consisted of six lengthy letters nominally attacking James Hervey's *Theron and Aspasio* (1755). But the real target of Sandeman's wrathful book was much broader. He wanted to prove that there was no basis in Scripture for pastoral authority, and he robustly denounced all denominations and clergymen alike, established, dissenting, or revivalist, assailing them all with such contempt and rancor that George Whitefield called him "the British *Ishmael*—His hand was against *every man*." The Scotsman believed that all Christendom had fallen away from the original apostolic church, which he sought to revive in all its pristine purity. This restorative project was begun by his father-in-law, John Glas. In Sandeman's "Glasite" congregations, communion was observed every week, members shared a Love Feast, or fellowship meal, at one another's houses, and pastors were ordinary individuals with no professional training. (As Samuel Miller condescendingly put it in his course on Ecclesiastical History, the sect's pastors were "generally engaged in trade.") Sandeman's vision of the church ruled out all practices that did not derive from a close reading of the New Testament. This was the sole authority, he insisted, for any gathering that claimed to be Christian.

For James, the most attractive feature of Sandeman's zealous return to origins was his aggressively stripped-down version of justification by faith. Like the early leaders of the Reformation, Sandeman vigorously asserted man's depravity, God's sovereignty, and the sufficiency of Christ's atonement. All Protestant Churches, he insisted, had corrupted these doctrines by surreptitiously replacing faith with works. All clergymen deluded churchgoers into supposing they had to *do* something to be saved—perform devotional practices, listen to sermons, struggle inwardly, feel guilty—and as a result many poor sinners spent years "straining hard to . . . feel some impression on their hearts."

In effect, the Scotsman wiped out all the psychologies of conversion that Protestant divines had laboriously worked out, beginning with the Puritans and their painful stages of Preparation and continuing down to contemporary revivalist practices, such as the New Measures of the 1830s. In Sandeman's view, these hard emotional disciplines were pointless and absurd. Their chief result was an anxious, anticipatory state of mind that had nothing to do with a correct faith. Protestant psychology was a gigantic hoax. In its place Sandeman substituted calm, cognitive assent to a plain proposition, an act he called "belief."

Because the Gospel was so plain and "belief" so rational, quick, and easy, there was no need for a trained, professional clergy. Sandeman's chief point in *Letters on Theron and Aspasio* was that doctrinal and institutional corruption worked hand in glove: the clergy's chief technique for justifying its existence was to replace the straightforwardness of belief with the painful intricacies of faith. It was because ecclesiastics and evangelical revivalists wanted honor, power, and steady wages that they had made the conversion process so tortuous and subtle and in need of expert guidance. "The popular doctrine is so contrived," in Sandeman's words, "as to keep the people in constant dependance [sic] on the preachers, for their comfort, and in continual expectation of the season of power." In attacking this dirty system, the Scotsman did not feign a polite distance from his readers and antagonists or follow an orderly plan of exposition. Instead, rambling and bitterly sarcastic, he waged a direct and total assault on Protestant Christendom—all in the interest of Gospel purity:

> We Protestants have laid aside the crucifix; we reserve no fragments of the wood of the cross. But what have we got instead of these? We have got a perverted gospel. We have got some insipid sentiment about the cross of Christ . . . By this perverted gospel, many teachers tantalize the

souls of men, leading those whose conscience is most easily touched, through a course of the most gloomy kind of anxieties.

For someone who had gone through the upheaval of conversion but then failed to experience a deep, settled peace, and who then sought to quiet his gloomy anxieties by becoming a devotee and ministerial student, Sandeman's teaching was extraordinarily liberating. It not only released James from his strenuous quest for perfect righteousness but authorized him to break off his training for a profession he no longer cared to enter—and to take the high moral ground in doing so. And if Princeton suspected he was abandoning the ministry out of a rich man's preference for a life of ease, his edition of Sandeman would set them straight in no uncertain terms. In his resentful and argumentative preface, he made the strange claim that there were "probably no two sentiments of any moment at variance" in Sandeman's and Russell's books and that anyone who considered Russell an exponent of orthodox Presbyterianism was a "dull theologian." This was a direct challenge, aimed not only at the young Presbyterian minister James chose to name, Henry A. Boardman, but at a mentor and friend he did not—James Waddel Alexander.

David Russell was the Scottish minister whose *Letters, Practical and Consolatory* had come into vogue among cultivated Presbyterians shortly before James's arrival at the seminary. In 1834 Alexander warmly recommended a friend to "get, *own*, put on your table, and study" Russell's *Letters*. "I have read no human production," he wrote, "which comes nearer my views of Calvinism: it is . . . purity without one note of ecclesiastical harshness." In 1841, when James was married and living in New York and three full years had passed since he had attended Princeton, he was still in touch with Alexander. In all likelihood, it was this professor of rhetoric who first put Russell's *Letters* into his hands and persuaded him to take the book to heart.

Russell cast his book as a noncontroversial manual of pastoral advice on standard religious topics. In treating regeneration, however, he quietly echoed certain Sandemanian themes, particularly when insisting "that no complicated process is to be gone through in order to our acceptance; that no holy preparation is requisite; and that no perplexing course of discipline is required." Those who think that "a particular preparatory course of tormenting dread must necessarily precede faith in Christ" are misguided. To take this view is to seek "to be justified by works of law, under the name of faith." It is nothing more than "a refined way of perverting the gospel." Russell did not share Sandeman's views on the clergy, but what he said about conversion and justification nicely matched both the doctrine and the language of the "British Ishmael."

When an American edition of Russell's *Letters* came out in 1836, it had a long introduction by the man James named in his preface, Henry A. Boardman. Minister of the large and wealthy Tenth Presbyterian Church of Philadelphia, Boardman was everything James was not— established, successful, "uncompromisingly orthodox," and a leading voice of Old School Presbyterianism. Boardman was characteristically forceful and obtuse in his introductory remarks on conversion, praising *"those Letters which relate to 'the method of coming to Christ'* " but then quoting with approval a coarse, high-pressure English evangelist, John Angell James (no relation), who called up the same tormenting dread Russell had repudiated:

> You are just arousing from your long slumber of sin and spiritual death, and will now either rise up and run the race that is set before you, or soon sink back again . . . into a deeper sleep than ever . . . And should your solicitude subside altogether, it may probably never be revived.

This harsh and arrogant passage exemplified the terror tactics used by evangelical preachers. By letting this frightening voice hold forth in his introduction, Boardman effectively vitiated Russell's message.

James was outraged that a spokesman for the clerical establishment could coopt the gentle Russell with such ease, and he drew a lesson he would never forget: No matter how *fortiter in re* you were, you would accomplish nothing if you did it *suaviter in modo*. If you meant to be heard, he decided, you had to smite the church with all your strength. It took Sandeman's "severity of censure," not Russell's gentleness, to get the unadorned truth before the public. So saying, James registered his conviction that the only kind of writing that could make a difference was the kind that engaged in dire combat. With his first publication, in other words, the ex-seminarian had begun to find his voice—that rich vituperation that became so recognizable to some of his contemporaries.

Beyond defying enemies like Boardman, James's preface also announced a solemn rupture with former friends. His concluding words resonate with the young man's profound identification with Sandeman:

> DR. RUSSELL holds sentiments which are eschewed by all the standard writers of his church . . . but has not thought it his duty to carry his difference . . . to the point of separation. SANDEMAN entertaining the

same difference, sought in another communion a more cordial fellowship in the truth, and of course stood condemned by all whom he deserted.

Thinking of himself as well as Sandeman, James was bidding farewell to church and seminary and preparing to join a more cordial congregation, a step for which he expected to be anathematized by teachers, associates, friends. If, as seems likely, one of these was James Waddel Alexander, the tone of regret reflects the young man's disappointment that his distinguished friend wouldn't acknowledge the radicalism of a book, Russell's, that had meant so much to both of them.[*]

The republication of Sandeman's *Letters* was James's way of setting off on a spiritual journey into the wilderness. Just as Sandeman had been the British Ishmael, so there was now an American version of this legendary outcast, who went into the desert and whose hand was raised against all men.

THE VALUE OF PSYCHOLOGY

After James's death in 1882, his oldest son felt a gnawing remorse for having resisted his father's teachings. Confiding to one of his brothers that "Father's cry was the single one that religion is real," William resolved to pick up the fallen torch and carry it on. In 1885 he brought out an edition of some writings by his father that had not appeared in book form, and in 1901–2, in lectures that appeared under the title *The Varieties of Religious Experience*, he constructed an ambitious and quasiscientific interpretation of his father's message to the world.

William had never gone through a religious conversion and did not believe in any literal way in the transcendent or the supernatural, but he hoped his lectures would make religious belief possible and intellectually respectable (though not, like his father, compulsory). The son's strategy for rehabilitating belief was to transport religious talk into a psychological register—to focus on religious *experience*, which could then be explained by invoking the intense turn-of-the-century interest in incubation, the subconscious, the mind's "subliminal regions." (William James was one of the earliest American psychologists to take an interest in Freud.) What happened in conversion, according to *The Varieties of Religious Experience*, was that your cognitive and emotional field went through an instant recrystallization, with center and periphery being

[*] Alexander often desponded over his failure to inspire students and parishioners. He was said to have a "shattered nervous constitution."

comprehensively reorganized. Culture, institutional continuity, the tangled skeins of cause and effect in personal history, and the power of ideas: all these were definitely secondary. If you wanted to understand conversion, what you had to pay attention to was the psychology of extreme emotional states.

If the father of 1838 could have been fast-forwarded to 1901, so as to listen to his future son's lectures in Edinburgh, he would have considered them quite off the mark and, rising to his feet during the question period (with no little difficulty), vigorously denounced the speaker's culpable blindness. To be a Sandemanian was to insist on the purely cognitive aspect of conversion and to deny the pertinence of guilt, joy, paternal pride, or any other feeling. Young Henry Sr. of 1838–40 and his aging philosopher-son of 1901–2 each vigorously asserted what was fundamentally wrong for the other. The son's lectures honored—and obliterated —the father's "single cry."

By the early 1840s Henry Sr. no longer considered himself a Sandemanian Calvinist, yet he never gave up some of the convictions he acquired during this phase. To his dying day he persisted in attacking the clergy of all denominations. He also continued to devalue the significance of feelings, sentiment, psychology. This insistence on the peripheralness of feeling put James in an impregnable position for criticizing the many softheaded fads that came and went in his time. Also, it conferred on him the sort of aloofness generally expected of metaphysicians and prophets. But the rejection of psychology had the disadvantage of causing James to ignore emotional cues, his own as well as others', and to become somewhat despotic. Because real suffering was all too likely to be dismissed as "only *feelings*," he was repeatedly troubled, as were some of his children after him, by psychic distresses that seemed gratuitous and mystifying. Willpower more than self-understanding was regarded as the key to sanity in the James family.

James's blindness to his own and others' feelings must have made him a very trying parent at times. This maddening obliviousness helps explain why William searched for answers in the psychic regions—the emotions—that his father had been authorized by Sandeman to pay no attention to. With tremendous relief, the son turned to the systematic investigation of the irrational and disturbing regions of the mind, and in the process helped create the late-nineteenth-century science of psychology.

Chapter 13

■ ■ ■

DISCIPLESHIP AND MARRIAGE: 1838–40

There is no evidence that James's children ever really grasped the nature of the swerve he took between seminary and marriage, when, instead of proceeding to secularize himself, he became a more fanatical Calvinist than ever. Although he discarded the Presbyterians' regulatory machinery of church order and discipline, he proclaimed with increased vehemence the Calvinist doctrines of depravity, justification by faith, divine election. Years later, when William compiled a posthumous bibliography of his father's writings, he did not include the edition of Robert Sandeman's *Letters on Theron and Aspasio*. Did the son actively suppress his father's embarrassing reaffirmation of Calvinist thought? Certainly William was capable of shielding some aspects of his father's inner history from the public. Yet it is well to remember that children are rarely well informed about the events leading up to the courtship and marriage of their parents.

If it were not for two letters written in the later 1830s by a professor of rhetoric at the College of New Jersey, we would know almost nothing about a bellicose phase in the life of James that was at one and the same time radical and reactionary, temporary and lastingly consequential.

On October 19, 1838, soon after James's reissue of Sandeman's *Letters*, James Waddel Alexander informed his good friend John Hall of the latest doings of a well-known troublemaker.

Henry James has re-gone to England. He and H[ugh] Walsh, and Platt, all once together in the Seminary, have become Sandemanians, and joined the Scotch Baptists, in New York, a little sect, headed by Buchanan, H.B.M. Consul. They have no preaching, but assemble on Sundays, when the "elders" and others expound and pray. James has issued a tract which

I will try to keep for you, intituled "The Gospel Good News to Sinners,"
and Walsh another, "The True Grace of God." These are in many points
quite good, and their chief mistake is that they have found out something.
All they say about the *object* of faith is just what Russell says, and just
what I say myself. But they add other things.

The second trip to England in 1838–39, the issuing of James's tract, and
his worshipping with the Scotch Baptists constitute a major suppressed
chapter in James's life. In later years no member of his family ever alluded
in public or in any extant letter to any of these events. Henry was able
to divulge his youthful drunkenness to his son Bob. His resurgent Calvinist extremism he kept to himself.

TRACTS AND PAMPHLETS

Although the pamphlet Alexander attributed to Hugh Walsh, *The True
Grace of God*, does not seem to have survived as a separate publication,
it appears in a book published anonymously in 1839, *Seven Tracts on
Scriptural Subjects*. The author of these tracts was John Walker (1768–
1833), an extreme Irish Separatist who had resigned his fellowship at
Trinity College, Dublin, because of his religious views. The evidence
suggests that the American edition of *Seven Tracts* was brought out by
Walsh. If so, it was probably James who unearthed these obscure pamphlets at a London bookseller's with the idea of republishing them in
New York. The two ex-seminarians did not succeed in making Walker's
writings much better known on this side of the Atlantic than they had
been, but they pushed him so devotedly they made *themselves* into his
leading American exponents.

Incisive, caustic, and with a very well-trained mind, Walker was
Sandeman's most distinguished nineteenth-century inheritor. While he
did not share Sandeman's rough anti-intellectualism, he agreed with him
on essentials and greatly admired the Scotsman's bold defiance of well-
established errors. This was precisely the spirit that Walsh and James
admired in Walker's *Seven Tracts*, which address the reader directly and
solemnly and, while setting forth the Sandemanian construction of Calvinism, make their case by appealing to Scripture only. No non-biblical
writer is cited and the author never mentions his own experience. The
tracts are remarkably self-disciplined, but if they reject Sandeman's wild
rhetoric, they adhere very closely to his radical anticlericalism. Walker
doesn't give an inch as he sets forth the Calvinist doctrines of human

sinfulness, God's rightful wrath, and Christ's propitiation. His basic idea is that the Gospel is so offensive, so contrary to human nature, that it can never attract more than a tiny number of believers. It is always and inevitably coopted and corrupted. All so-called Christian churches are "founded on a systematic rejection of the apostolic precepts," he asserts, and for that reason every true believer must renounce his or her denominational affiliation. All "modern preachers" are false, especially those evangelists who attract large, frightened auditories. Because their sermons do not at once "comfort and gladden the heart" of sinners, they fail the one sure test by which to determine whether any preaching or doctrine is true to the Gospel.

James insisted on the identical test in the title of his fifty-page tract, *The Gospel Good News to Sinners.* Any sermon that grieves or perplexes the sinner's heart is in certain error. The Gospel is good news, not for those who consider themselves upright and dutiful, but for those with a bad conscience. The point seems ordinary enough, yet it carries a decidedly hostile subtext: the Gospel is very bad news for the righteous teachers of religion at places like Princeton.

Unlike Walsh, James did more than merely issue his tract. Although his name is not on the title page, the style, the autobiographical references, and the account of disputes alluded to elsewhere in his writings confirm Alexander's implication that he wrote this little book, even though in later years he never acknowledged or even mentioned the pamphlet. Feeling as many writers do about their fledgling publications, he apparently wished to disown it. He very nearly succeeded.

Like Sandeman's and Russell's books, *The Gospel Good News to Sinners* takes the form of letters, in this case nominally addressed to a "dear friend," about whom we learn nothing except that he is a man with two young children. This friend had recently sent the author a letter which prompted him to conclude that certain "considerations based upon the word of God . . . have evidently not had their due influence in the regulation of your religious character." Following this priggish announcement, James begs his friend to pay careful attention and then sets forth his understanding of the orthodox cycle of sin and salvation—man's depravity, his inability to save himself, the Gospel's message of salvation. Insisting that his only guide is the Bible, James cites chapter and verse for many of his contentions, tries to maintain a plain and unpretentious style, and never mentions Sandeman or Walker. At the end, sounding very much like a student who has been criticized for his sprawling compositions, he hopes he has "expressed himself" clearly and managed "to adhere closely to his theme." He takes no interest in the book's reception, he says. His only wish is to leave "his offering without anxiety at the feet of his Saviour, to be honored or set aside as his glory may prompt."

If James truly believed he wrote his little book in this humble and unaspiring mood, he was greatly deceived. Its pages bristle with Sandemanian rancor, with a great and angry desire to assail Presbyterian orthodoxy and embarrass its apologists. He was determined to expose certain errors that "extensively pervade churches," "to disentangle the minds of Christ's children [from] some of the webs, which man's ingenuity has spun around the great question of a sinner's justification with God." Like Sandeman and Walker, James was especially concerned to unmask the subtle doctrine of works that had crept into mainstream Protestantism, which falsely taught "that the spirit of God works a change in the sinner *before* he can believe the gospel." When he mentioned—though not by name—the author of a certain Presbyterian tract on justification by faith, he went for the jugular. This unnamed writer had fallen into the egregious error of requiring sinners to perform certain duties " '*prior to our justification,*' " and James corrected him with the energy of a young man out to nail his elders, giving page numbers, waxing sarcastic, employing the close reasoner's edged weapons: "Let us look a little further," "But hold," "Here, then, we learn," "No quarter is left." As James perfectly well knew, the author of the tract in question was none other than Archibald Alexander. The ex-seminarian was still carrying on his debate with the chief exemplar of Old-School Presbyterian learning.

This debate must have gotten lodged in James's very marrow, for forty years later, when he was interviewed by a reporter, he recalled Alexander's vain attempt to "explain the doctrine of justification by faith." The reporter's statement that James "thought he saw the weak spot" neatly catches his youthful argumentative stridency.

In the fifth and final letter James's tract became abruptly confessional, exposing "a certain form of error which long had possession of my mind." The purpose of this very revealing autobiographical digression was to illustrate the tenacity with which the human heart clings to the illusion of its own goodness and worth. Our natural self-conceit is so persistent, James argues, that if a man is "driven from one strong-hold" of vanity, he "will betake himself to another and another, until at length, beaten from all the more substantial ones, he dies wrapping himself about with a shadow, and the shadow of a shadow." James's rather rarefied confession concerns one of these shadows of a shadow. Looking back from his present state of wisdom, he sees that his purpose in his most rigorous religious practices was to make himself worthy of God's grace: "My solicitude constantly was to know whether I had *believed aright*, whether I *truly*

trusted, hoped, rejoiced." Unconsciously fixated on his own pious performances, he was still trapped in the closed circle of pride and vanity. His
failure to find perfect peace proved so tormenting that he eventually
resolved on an audacious and hazardous step. " 'Yes, I will pray,' " he
had vowed, " 'and if I be not answered before, up to the gates of death,
I will go on to pray—pray—pray for this inestimable boon.' " The excruciating irony, as he now sees, was that in making this resolution, he
"made prayer my Saviour—centered all my hope in pertinacity of prayer,
instead of the finished work of Jesus."

This strange confession is to be taken literally. At some point before
he learned from Sandeman and Walker that his strenuous program of
self-purification was misconceived, James became so compulsive that he
began to pray uninterruptedly to God, to "besiege him night and day"
until peace was finally granted. *Pray—pray—pray. Up to the gates of death.*
Here, more emphatically than in anything else he wrote, we see the
drivenness, the suicidal intensity, of James's religious life. He was dead
set on getting himself right, yet the more he thought about and tried to
correct his diseased subjectivity, the more he was on the wrong track.
His terrible lunges for supreme self-consciousness and final self-correction
were inevitably canceled by a monstrous self-blindness he could discern
only in retrospect.

James's son William, who would also exhaust himself on this treadmill,
chose a very different way to get off it. He drew back and thought about
the mind's capacity for harboring opposed states, for fracturing itself, and
he eventually fixed on the notion of multiple selves. This idea not only
seemed to fit laboratory observations, it helped him make sense of his
and his father's disturbing simultaneity of blindness and insight. As for
prayer, William decided that that was essentially a private exchange
between the individual's conscious and subliminal powers. Understood
in this way, prayer became the defining religious act for William. He
himself, however, did not pray. The contrast with his father is striking.
Not only did Henry Sr. pray—too often, too long, and too exhaust-
ingly—but he felt afterward that his praying had been a colossal mistake.
He was saved by a simple, rational discovery.

Saved for a few years, that is. One of many ironies is that even as
James expressed his huge relief at having finally seen through the heart's
vain shows, the relief was only temporary. A few years would pass, and
he would once again be thrashing in the depths. In 1835 he had recklessly
proclaimed his attainment of "glorious, heavenly, confirmed peace."
That passed. Then in 1837 or 1838 he realized that the work was already
finished and that he had been trying too hard—in his own metaphor,

wrapping himself with the shadow of his own pride. Each time he detected his shadow, he confidently proclaimed that he had attained a final and serene self-understanding. But each successive proclamation, however humble, was also a boastful expression of the heart's ineradicable pride. James's fundamental problem was how to escape himself for good—how to terminate the series of devastating self-insights that formed one of the patterns of his life.

Intellectually, James's deep instability reflected a built-in wobble in the Protestant doctrine of justification by faith. If one cannot do anything to attract divine mercy, then, to the extent that believing is doing something, one cannot even believe. If nothing one can do is of any value, then even one's act of faith will prove to be a vain show. The Sandemanian solution to this problem was simple and drastic: belief (in James's words) "depends wholly upon evidence, and so is involuntary." "We cannot withhold our belief of a truth when we see evidence sufficient to establish it. Evidence *compels* belief." That is to say, the believing mind is wholly passive. Instead of acting, it is being acted *upon*—invaded by evidence. One of the fascinating aspects of James's intellectual de-velopment is that long after he stopped thinking of himself as a San-demanian Calvinist, he continued to insist on this solution. For the remainder of his life he was convinced that individual human agency is a pernicious illusion. * And all the while he never ceased trying to *compel* others' belief in the most muscular way imaginable.

But James's instability was also the result of a long personal history and a well-established psychological situation. Although he did not ex-plicitly acknowledge such causes, he touched on one of them in a highly revealing passage. Intending to defend the Sandemanian construction of belief, he brought up, very abstractly, very dryly, an example from his and perhaps his dear friend's past:

> Again, suppose I credibly report to you the death of my father; the fact will affect you precisely according to its nature—it is one in which you are little interested, and it will therefore produce little effect upon you. Suppose, however, that I credibly report to you the death of your father; this intelligence will also be found to affect you precisely according to *its* nature; that is, as you are closely interested in it, it will affect you closely.

This passage says, very understatedly, that hearing of the death of one's father marks an epoch in one's life. This is James's only known reference

---

* Thirty-two years later William James would try to escape from his own intellectual and psycho-logical troubles by vigorously asserting the opposite position, insisting on the will to believe.

to the moment when he was first informed that his father was dying or dead. How curious that we find it in a tract concerned with good news.

We may conjecture that if the announcement of William of Albany's death had been welcome news in some ways, it was also unmitigated bad news, a cause of guilt so painful and protracted that it continued to inform the son's obsessive religious quest. Perhaps the reason Henry was still harping on the death of fathers was that he wished to obliterate the final sound of a gavel. He himself was the great sinner who needed to hear the Gospel's good news of unconditional pardon and somehow accept and find comfort in it.

GOD'S CHURCH ON CANAL STREET

But James's religious quest involved a good deal more than his tortured private life. Unlike his son William, for whom the religious life was essentially individualistic and emotional, Henry Sr. conceived of religion as being inescapably collective and public. As one who had grown up among the first men of his time, he was not about to vanish into private life. He was searching for a wholly new society, one in which he might possibly play a leading role, and this was partly why he began worshipping with a tiny "Scotch Baptist" gathering in New York. It was this group he had in mind when he alluded to a "more cordial fellowship" in his introduction to Sandeman's *Letters*.

James's new congregation was headed by James Buchanan—not the future President but rather Her Majesty's consul in New York. For two decades this man had not only represented the mother country in business and diplomatic affairs but also functioned as the crucial link between radical congregational separatists in Britain and America. If the tiny Anglo-American movement to restore the primitive church had a pope, it must have been Buchanan, who was nearing the end of a remarkable life by the time young James came within his reach. Starting out in northern Ireland thirty years earlier, he had established a pioneering breakaway congregation and a large nonsectarian school for both Protestant and Catholic children. In some respects, his vision was similar to that of the early Reformation Anabaptists and Mennonites: he advocated passive obedience of one's king, adult baptism, and a believers' church modeled on the New Testament reports of the earliest Christian gatherings. "I close my labors," he wrote in old age, "by calling on all to come out from every system of worship in which *the authority of Man* in any manner, or way, has place." He opposed all forms of coercion in religion, he favored Catholic emancipation in Britain, and he denounced the "separation of castes" in "the slave-holding states of America." But Buchanan was no leveler: he aligned himself with big-money interests, extolled New York State's liberal banking laws, and argued against every kind of restrictive governmental intervention in the economy. He was a free-market missionary who proclaimed "the principle of free agency and self-dependence," and yet he was also a Tory who spoke out against democracy, universal suffrage, education of the lower classes, the weakening of parental authority. Proud of his own virility, he boasted of having fathered seventeen children. He recommended that seduced women be transported to asylums in distant colonies.

Self-taught, opinionated, and armed with a remedy for every evil, Her Majesty's consul now took on the additional task of regulating young Henry James. Meeting at 183 Canal Street, Buchanan's congregation sanctioned only those practices that were explicitly ordained by New Testament precedent. Every prayer had to be on those "subjects mentioned by the apostles." Because Christ did not die for those who depend on their own good deeds, there were no rules requiring members "to believe they must abstain from Balls, Theatres, and gross violations of rules of morality" before taking Communion. (The Sandemanians' tolerant view of the stage helps explain why James, breaking with the custom of his class, took his children to numerous plays in the late 1840s and early 1850s.) Every worship service included a collection designed to transfer money from rich to poor members. Instead of a sermon, there was an "exhortation and teaching." Any brother who had a gift to speak was encouraged to do so, always remembering to be plain and simple and avoid "the sermonizing, logic, and display of learning, by which so many [clergymen] get their living."

An ordinary municipal guidebook from 1839, *New-York As It Is*, vividly captures the marginality of James's new fellowship. In the long section that lists Manhattan's many churches, the Presbyterians proudly lead off with thirty-four congregations. They are the dominant sect, followed by the Episcopalians, the Methodists, the Baptists, and so forth. Finally, there is a catch-all category, "Miscellaneous," which includes a New Jerusalem Church and a Floating Bethel. At the absolute end of the list of Gotham's houses of worship comes James's church—"Primitive Christians, 183 Canal, Mr. Buchanan." Other congregations were led by a man with a "Rev." in front of his name. The son of William and Catharine James had traveled very far from his childhood moorings.

But a voluntary society as strenuously plain as Mr. Buchanan's, and so tightly structured that each word and gesture had to be anxiously checked against scriptural authority, could not have satisfied James for long. Classically educated and passionately eager to straighten himself and others out, he must have taken charge of the exhortation and teaching on occasion. One guesses that he proved disruptive and even resisted the consul's firm leadership, for the young man had a proven capacity for challenging those in power. The Primitive Christians may not have had a pastor, but they had an elderly leader with strong, inflexible opinions and thirty years' experience in running separatist bodies. On April 20, 1841, when James was in his first year of marriage and residing at 5 Washington Place, Buchanan drafted a letter "to the Church of God assembling in Houston Street," vigorously urging them to correct "the abuse of the privilege of teaching." Those who stood up to exercise this function must remember that "controversy and contention about doctrines should not be indulged in" during worship. This Houston Street group may have been the same congregation that had worshipped on Canal Street two years earlier, or it may have consisted of some of Walker's followers, who generally identified themselves as the Church of God. Either way, one likes to imagine that Buchanan's letter, written in imitation of Paul's New Testament epistles, was aimed at Henry James.

If so, it is doubtful that Buchanan managed to rein in the young man's zeal. James had crossed the Atlantic Ocean and unearthed in London the precious Sandemanian critiques of the corrupt Presbyterian order. He had brought out an edition of Sandeman's *Letters*, and then he had written and published his own proclamation of the Gospel. He had led two friends out of Princeton Theological Seminary, one of whom, Hugh Walsh, had reprinted Walker's tracts. All three, James, Walsh, and Platt, had united with the one congregation in all of Gotham that claimed to resurrect the apostolic church. It was no easy task holding back these energetic young converts. They were not about to tolerate tiny deviations. They had not seen the troubles the aging northern Irishman had weathered.

MARY ROBERTSON WALSH

It was while Henry James was in his state of revolutionary fervor that he fell in love with, courted, and married his collaborator's sister Mary Walsh. Like most marriages, this one was the product of mutual attraction. But the marriage was also forged in the crucible of an intense religious crusade. Henry and Mary came together as members of a select group of friends who aimed at nothing less than reconstituting the original church on the basis of the New Testament's faint blueprints. More than perhaps any other family in American literature and philosophy (that of Jonathan Edwards excepted), the James family was founded on the *Word*. All the same, it is not clear whether the bride fully participated in her husband's zealotry or merely lived in its glow.

Born in 1810, one year before Henry, Mary Walsh lived at home with her widowed mother, her sister Catharine, and at least one of her four brothers. Although her father had died in 1820 in Richmond, Virginia, while away on a business trip, the family remained well off. The mother, Elizabeth Walsh, had a personal estate worth $25,000 in 1838, and her fine, three-story brick house on the north side of Washington Square, New York's most fashionable neighborhood, was assessed at $18,000.

Mary's future husband must have been introduced to her as a friend of her brother Hugh, his fellow lodger at Princeton. But another member of James's family had already entered her life. In 1823, when she was twelve years old, the Presbyterian church at which her mother worshipped hired a temporary minister—Rev. William James, fresh from his studious retreat in Scotland. He preached for six months (earning $125). In the later 1830s, when Henry first entered the Walsh household, he would have been seen as doubly clerical—not just a minister in training but the product of a ministerial family. Henry was clothed in spiritual authority the moment he walked in the door.

The Walshes worshipped at the Murray Street Church, one of Manhattan's most formidable and rock-ribbed Scots Presbyterian bodies. This was also known as Dr. Mason's Church, after the famous but failing minister whose shoes Reverend William tried to fill; Mason also ran Columbia College for a time. As late as 1912, when the serenely un-churched Henry Jr. began his memoirs, he could still remember hearing about the eminent minister under whom his mother "had 'sat' " (a privilege that cost her mother the substantial sum of $32.50 a year in pew rent, according to church books). When Mary was nineteen, the Murray Street Church served as the venue for a prestigious series of Sunday-evening sermons by the leading Calvinist divines of the time. The lavish volume in which these discourses were collected and published conveys a sense of the congregation's wealth, prominence, and piety. But the church was also known for its practical philanthropy. Mary's mother's father, Alexander Robertson (1733–1816), furnished the endowment for the church's free school for poor children. In 1904–5, when Henry James, Jr., made his first visit in twenty years to New York, he discovered that the Robertson School was still a going concern.

In the eyes of his descendants, Alexander Robertson was the great forebear and founder, just as William James of Albany was for his own. A native of Scotland and a staunch Presbyterian, Robertson engaged in many speculative mercantile ventures and became a very wealthy man. He was hardworking, forceful, and direct, and if the sketch of his career left by one of his descendants can be trusted, he at one time "controlled the linen trade between New York and other ports in Scotland and Ireland." But he was not above profiteering: a few years before the Revolutionary War broke out, a patriot caught him in the act of violating a New York embargo.

It is a measure of Alexander Robertson's patriarchal weight that each of his four children bestowed his full name upon his or her firstborn male child. Two weeks before his death, this dynastic founder singled these four grandchildren out for special consideration, bequeathing to them a 600-acre parcel in the Beaverkill district of northern Sullivan County. The dying man also handed his faith down to his descendants:

> I wish to give this public Testimony that my hopes of future happiness are founded solely on the mercy of God through the merits of my redeemer to whom I cheerfully commit the keeping of my Soul, firmly believing in a resurrection and in its reunion with the body.

There is no comparable declaration in William of Albany's will.

Mary Walsh, whose middle name was—what else?—Robertson, grew up in the midst of her firm progenitor's multiple legacies. Unlike the James family, with its excesses, contradictions, and flagrant disorders, hers had a very cohesive and staid tradition. There was no break, as yet, between the generations. At some point in her early womanhood, well before meeting Henry, she joined her family's church and (according to a first cousin nine years her junior) clothed herself in an "old-fashioned, high-church Presbyterian piety." Her brother Hugh and her sister Catharine did the same. All three became "rigidly devout," refusing on principle to attend operas, plays, even "oratorio concerts."

All this starch and piety faced a severe trial when Mary's brother Hugh introduced energetic Henry James into the family circle. The only known source of information on the conflict he precipitated is the discursive family genealogy published sixty-five years later by William Walsh, Mary's first cousin. The value of this document lies in the probability that it was based on firsthand observation: having entered an Episcopal seminary in New York in 1839, this cousin seems to have been an eyewitness to some of the events he recorded. It is thus worth noting how, in recollecting his cousin Mary's courtship, he insists that James was not to blame for the Walsh family turmoil. The Walshes had "doubtless . . . heard from Hugh of the doubts and difficulties at Princeton." It was "understood that Mr. James did not enter the family as a proselytor." These sentences suggest that James was not the first to utter the names of Sandeman, Walker, and Buchanan in the Walshes' parlors. The controversy had already been touched off by Hugh. What James did was resolve it, and in the process give the respectable Walshes a taste of something better—his "superior intellect, easy and affable manners, and his fine personality." He "brought a new element into [the family's] social life."

These recollections hint at certain qualities in James that would be well documented in his later years—his *savoir faire*, his great gifts as a conversationalist and monologuist, his flirtatiousness with women, and his fascinating charm. James was knowing and complicated and had been around, and the no-nonsense Walsh sisters were swept off their feet:

> There is such a thing in human life as a strong attraction taking place between parties on a short acquaintance. Such seems to have been the case with Mr. James and Mary and Catharine Walsh. They listened to his teaching and his arguments for the position of himself and their brother Hugh, which they adopted and withdrew from the Presbyterian Church. It was a grief to their mother, who having lost her husband was to lose in a certain sense her daughters, but it was never a bar to their reciprocal affection. In time Mr. James married Mary Walsh.

The statement that a "strong attraction" sprang up quickly between James and the two sisters is decidedly ambiguous, especially in light of the fact that in later years Catharine often resided in Mary and Henry's household. But William Walsh was not a careful writer, nor was he concerned to ward off twentieth-century suspicions. The kind of attraction he was talking about did not have an unavoidable erotic focus. His point was that the two sisters were at once persuaded by the arguments of the likable stranger. There was no long period of debate or painful doubt, but rather an almost instantaneous change of loyalty, such that the bond between the mother and her two daughters felt a painful strain. Writing seventy-five years later, Henry Jr. also recalled his mother's marriage as causing an unhappy rupture in her family. What he stressed, however, was not the break between two generations of women but the abandonment of the patriarchal tradition represented by Mary's grandfather Alexander Robertson.

If Mary was converted by Henry's Sandemanian gospel, it seems likely that she (and Catharine) also chose to worship with Mr. Buchanan's Primitive Christians in Canal Street. Would James have married her if she had not joined him in this new affiliation? John Walker had discouraged his followers from yoking themselves with non-Separatists, and Mary was twenty-eight years old in 1838, well past the age at which most women first entered matrimony. Perhaps she felt an obscure private urgency in her rapid conversion to the views of her very impressive and slightly younger visitor.

There can be no doubt that Mary was sensitive about her age. In 1848 a friend who knew how to butter her up supposed she would be "constantly mistaken" for her husband's daughter. In 1850, when the federal census marshal walked up the steps of the Jameses' house in New York City, she passed herself off as five years younger than she was. She did the same in 1855, when the state of New York conducted its own census, again making herself out to be not one year older but four years younger than her husband. This amusing deception may have been prompted by a wish to affirm his authority. Or perhaps it was female vanity, of a kind that would have led her to tell a bigger whopper yet if she hadn't been married. Her sister Catharine, still single at thirty-eight, was not satisfied to chop a mere five years off her age. She got the 1850 enumerator to write down that she was twenty-six.

Yet Mary's age and unromantic nature may have been her strong suits as far as Henry was concerned. Unstable, closely attached to his dear ma, and fond of paying gallant compliments to other men's wives, he was looking for a steady caretaker. Whatever may have been the nature of his interest in Anna Barker, two years his junior, a fragile and beautiful creature who required special handling would not have been the right mate for him. Late in life James told one of his children that he would have been lost if he had not been able "to run to the bosom of your mother" whenever he was in distress. What he needed was a solidly planted woman who could support his weight, soothe and cradle him in his need, listen attentively to his harangues.

In spite of Mary's quick conversion to the teachings of her apostolic suitor, at least two years passed before the wedding took place. Henry's strange new faith must certainly have been a major impediment. Elizabeth Walsh was already disturbed by her daughters' religious defection, and she may have tried to cool Mary's romantic interest and even impose certain conditions. As a daughter of Alexander Robertson, she would have been particularly anxious about the young man's uncertain future. Indeed, when she drew up her will on July 8, 1839, she stipulated that whatever she bequeathed to her two daughters could not be encumbered by their future husbands' debts. Yes, Elizabeth could understand that Sandeman provided her daughter's suitor with a clean exit from the ministry. But what came next? What profession did Mr. James propose to enter?

Here Henry was, in his late twenties, with marriage looming on the horizon, and he was still unable to declare his vocation. *Nothing* had been resolved after all by his fervent devotion to Sandeman. As had happened so often, the young man found that what looked like a step forward turned out to be a treacherous slide all the way back to square one.

MICHAEL FARADAY

A trip to Europe was getting to be the regular James family remedy for unsettled plans and prospects. On October 12, 1838, James embarked for England on the *Wellington*, accompanied by a nephew, Robert W. James, and two younger brothers, John Barber and Edward. There is no evidence that James's children ever became aware of the trip, his last transatlantic passage powered by sail.

In 1827 James had asked Dr. Thomas Chalmers of Edinburgh to advise him on his course of study. Now one of his chief purposes in going to London was to consult with the great English electromagnetic physicist, Michael Faraday, to whom he carried a letter of introduction from Joseph Henry: "Mr. James has some peculiar motives for wishing your acquaintance. Of these however I am but partially informed and must therefore refer you to himself for an exposition of them." The letter seems to have been written against Joseph Henry's better judgment, as if he feared that his unscientific friend would only waste Faraday's time. James had clearly been warned not to do so. As for the exact nature of his "peculiar motives" for seeking this interview, there is one very good hint in a deleted passage in Joseph Henry's rough draft: "He is of a generous and ardent temperament and wishes to devote his life to objects of philanthropy and benevolence." This strongly suggests that James believed himself to be on the track of a definite vocation and that he wanted Faraday to confirm him in this. The rich young man had already paid Joseph Henry's research expenses during a lean season. Perhaps the man Joseph Henry regarded as the "first living Experimental Philosopher" would be able to show the well-heeled drifter how to transform his wealth into a respectable calling.

Why ask Faraday? Although the great man was extremely private in his religious practices, avoiding public display and controversy, he had in fact been born into a Separatist family and by the later 1830s was undoubtedly the world's most eminent practicing Sandemanian. For James, who tended to think of science as a modern and very superior form of magic, Faraday had a unique double authority. He was in the van of scientific progress, but he was also a humble member of the tiny, apostolic church. Surely this man would be able to help the ex-seminarian reconnect the loose ends of his life. What James did not foresee was that Faraday maintained an absolute separation between his religion and his science.

An American interviewer who once tried to describe Faraday reported that he seemed to be "upon wires," having "the most lively, restless black eyes I ever saw in the head of man, or woman either." James himself (also wired) did not anticipate an oracle of this character. It happened that before he had a chance to deliver the letter of introduction, he worshipped at the Sandemanian meetinghouse in Paul's Alley, Barbican. Faraday was a deacon at the time. Two of the elders were grave and serious, but the third was "youthful looking, volatile, and lively." That evening, being told that he had been in the presence of the great man, James assumed he must have been one of the two more dignified leaders. The next morning, to James's "utter astonishment," Faraday proved to be the man on wires. *

Several months later, tardily thanking Joseph Henry for his letter, James reported on the interview in the blandest and least informative terms imaginable. Faraday had been extremely kind. He had invited James to follow his lectures and visit him at home. He even made his library available. Although James did not take up these offers, as he was afraid he "might divert [Faraday's] attention from his regular avocations," he did see the scientist "two or three times and had very pleasant intercourse with him." James's report is all serene affability, with no trace of the urgent motives that had carried him across the Atlantic on a late-season passage. Thirty years after the event, an enterprising London journalist and Swedenborgian named William White sent James a letter designed to ferret out the truth about his meeting with Faraday: "You had some curious intercourse with him which I wish you would place on record." When James refused to satisfy his curiosity, White tried again: "What you write about Faraday quite confirms the conception [?] I had formed of his intellectual religious condition. I still think it would be worth while for you to place on record your reminiscences however

* The teller of this anecdote did not identify the American visitor as James and confused Sandeman with Swedenborg. That his source was Joseph Henry, however, identifies the traveler as James.

slight." James's persistent refusal to supply any particulars of his sought-after meeting with Faraday strongly suggests that it did not turn out as he had hoped. The advice he wanted was not forthcoming.

Leaving his inflated hopes and his brothers behind (as we read in a letter sent to one of them—"I suppose Henry has left you some time ago"), James crossed the Channel on his own and went to Paris. This was his first venture outside the Anglo-American world, and he seems to have found the experience a very unpleasant one. When Joseph Henry first went to Paris the previous year, he kept a detailed record of the scenes that caught his eye—"men harnessed to carts . . . women engaged in many occupations followed only by men in America, such as watch-making street-cleaning and even shoe-making." James's report was much less detailed and sweepingly judgmental: Paris had been "a comfortless residence compared with London, from my unskilfulness in the language, and my disrelish for the peculiar ways, of the French people."

What French customs did the young traveler object to? The best indication is to be found in an unsigned editorial written thirteen years later by James. Reacting to a recent exposé of American democracy by a French conservative, Xavier Marmier, he retaliated by recalling the two worst aristocratic transgressions he had observed in France. These recollections probably refer to his first winter in Paris:

> We shared the *coupe* of a diligence one winter's night from Paris to Havre with a French gentleman of manifest high-breeding . . . The night was bitter cold, but we had not got out of the barriers before our companion lighted his cigar, and simply asking us whether we would take one, kept the *coupe* in such a smother of smoke at intervals during the entire night, that we were glad to purchase relief even at the risk of a severe cold, by letting down the glass. We said to ourselves, this man no doubt stands very well with Louis Philippe and his Court, but it will be a long time before his name is announced at the Court of Heaven, unless he mends his manners. Our other experience was the repeated vision of the most offensive natural operations going on under the light of a brilliant noon-day sun, at the edge of the sidewalk on the *boulevards* in Paris, frequented by throngs of foot-passengers and by the gayest equipages of the capital, and yet apparently provoking no interference of the police.

The enclosed outdoor *pissoirs* for men (since removed) had not yet been constructed.

As often happens with travelers abroad, James saw a great deal of a friend he had known back home, Thomas Hun, once a fellow pupil at Albany Academy. Now a medical student, Hun had been living in Paris for several years. One of the subjects they talked about was homeopathy, which James hoped Hun would "fall in love with." Based on the principle that like cures like, homeopathy taught that the body should be stimulated into healing itself by means of medicines that produce the symptoms of disease. Although rejected by the medical profession as a whole, this unorthodox system was beginning to win adherents in England and America. James, one of its earliest defenders, now had a second opposition theory to fight for.

The depression that seems to have overcome the young traveler in Paris may have reflected his realization that his second trip to Europe would not resolve his deep unsettledness. Science, however, was still marching on, and when he recrossed the Atlantic in April 1839, from England, he booked passage on a famous steamer then in its second year of operation, the *Great Western*. The ship was overbooked by fifty passengers, the crude machinery undoubtedly produced a great deal of smoke and noise, and there were rough spring gales for the entire two weeks. But the trip took only half as long as James's previous westerly crossing, and he felt, elatedly, that he had participated in a significant experiment. The passage, he informed Joseph Henry, had been "the most important one I presume yet achieved in respect to the question of the feasibility of steam navigation."

JOHN WALKER

Although James returned to America without a firm vocational identity, he had a clearer idea than ever of what he was *not*, as he proclaimed in an irritated postscript to Joseph Henry:

> I beg of you dont honour my poor name with the prefix of Rev^d . . . It would perplex me much to tell what I should be held in reverence for; and as to the custom of distinguishing certain officers in a church from their fellows, by that title, the laws of the churches of Christ delivered to us in the New Testament leave us in no darkness as to its origin—in the silly pride of the human heart. If you will therefore substitute the word "Unrev^d." it will not only be more consonant to the truth of things, but will provoke no remonstrances on my part.

James was utterly convinced of his new gospel. This, at least, was settled, and ten months later, in February 1840, when he made a visit to Princeton and talked to James Waddel Alexander, he came on like a classic true believer. Afterward, Alexander sent his friend a report:

> I send herewith, if possible, ——'s penultimate publication. I hope you will carefully read it. He has been here [Princeton], and is as strongly fixed in his opinions as if he were inspired. Sandeman is not now his leader, but the late John Walker of Ireland . . . I have been reading this Walker, who is a reasoner of singular power. The sect in Ireland is called "Separatists."

The blanked-out visitor and publishing writer was Henry James. According to an obituary in the newspaper that knew him best, he brought out a pamphlet in 1840 called *Remarks on the Apostolic Gospel.* * This lost work maintained the divinity of Christ but denied the doctrine of the Trinity—the idea that God is one substance but three persons. This denial would be consistent with a brief anti-trinitarian paragraph in *The Gospel Good News to Sinners*, which dismisses the Trinity as unscriptural and "incomprehensible." These were also the positions taken by John Walker, who regarded the doctrine as a barren, man-made topic of theological speculation.

The best reason for filling Alexander's blank with James's name is to be found on the library shelves of Princeton Theological Seminary, where the only known North American copy of John Walker's *Essays and Correspondence*, published in London in 1838, bears this inscription:

THEOLOGICAL SEMINARY

PRINCETON, N.J.

PRESENTED BY

HENRY JAMES

1840

This book was published shortly after James's first trip to London. He evidently found it there on his second trip, paid £1, 10 shillings for it (equivalent to at least one hundred dollars today), and packed it on the *Great Western*, and when he went to Princeton in February 1840 he deposited the apostolic volume in the seminary library (the gift being duly recorded three months later in the librarian's semiannual report). It was two years since he had left the seminary, and he had *still* not given

---

* The *Boston Evening Transcript* also attributed this pamphlet to James. William did not include it in the bibliography of his father's works in *Literary Remains*.

up the hope of showing the Presbyterians exactly where they had gone astray.

The fervency with which James talked Walker up may have misled Alexander into thinking the young man had renounced Sandeman. Although the orthodox saw these two British Separatists as antitypes of Ishmael, Walker's hand was by no means raised against Sandeman. The chief difference between the two men was that, while Sandeman had been self-educated, Walker was a man of learning, the author of treatises on Tacitus and the philosophy of arithmetic. Alexander was not alone in being impressed by the Irishman's "singular power" of reasoning. Even his most tenacious opponent conceded that there was "a fascinating attraction . . . in the masculine energy of his diction, the transparent clearness of his reasoning and the metaphysical acuteness of his thinking." Bold, severe, and uncompromising, the masculine Walker not only condemned all established churches but denounced evangelical practices as no more than a "*devout* path to *hell*." Like Sandeman, he abhorred ministers of every stripe as "the official ringleaders maintaining the antichristian corruptions." Every last clergyman did far more damage than the despoiler proverbially regarded as the ultimate in destructiveness, "the person who poisons a spring."

James's new master felt the greatest respect for Jonathan Edwards's "deeply thinking and well-informed mind" and would have identified himself as a Calvinist if Christians were not forbidden from "distinguishing themselves, by the names of *human* leaders." Walker saw himself as no more than a consistent defender of the authority of Scripture, the sovereignty of God, the pure doctrine of justification by faith. But he was so rigorous in spelling out these doctrines that he horrified most of his Protestant contemporaries, who saw him as a "thinking machine," a "theological automaton," a "man without a heart." Of those who tried to excise the last trace of human pride, nobody cut deeper than Walker, who considered all humans, *even the saved*, as absolutely depraved: a "murderer dying at the gallows" was "not a whit worse than myself," and "an *Apostle*, finishing his course with joy," was "not one whit better."

Walker's corrosive intelligence left an indelible mark on James. Just as the Irishman had assailed the "*soi-disant* church," James would castigate the "*soi-disant* new church" in his obsessive and endless quarrel with Swedenborgian groups. In time (and partly as a result of Swedenborg), Walker's extreme understanding of depravity got transformed in James's mind into the fervently held belief that only our *common* human nature possesses any dignity. As for our *individual* human nature, "the subjective element in us, the personal element," that is so utterly foul, he decided, that it is necessary for all of us to "*defecate ourselves* of private or subjective ambition" (italics mine). (This odd reflexive usage harks back to an older transitive meaning of *defecate—to free from impurities*.) He was certain that "the subjective element (the *me*) is a purely phenomenal or waste element in consciousness." Our individuality, selfhood, ego, all is fecal matter and must be evacuated.

But this strange and extreme anti-individualism reached its climax in James's later years. In 1839 and 1840, when he still swore by Walker's interpretation of depravity and justification, his anti-individualism articulated itself differently, as we see from a desiccating letter he wrote his sister-in-law Marcia Ames James. This letter, the only document in James's hand from the twelve months preceding his marriage, is an uncompromising expression of Walker's harsh impersonality.

A faculty wife James had been fond of at Princeton had died in 1838 at the age of thirty-five. When *A Memorial of Mrs. Margaret Breckinridge* appeared in 1839, Marcia, who liked reading "christian biography," supposed that Henry might enjoy the book. It contained a sketch of Breckinridge's life, the stark funeral sermon on submission by Archibald Alexander, and some formal letters of advice to the bereaved children from Samuel Miller (the dead woman's father). The memorial volume was an epitome of Princeton manners, thought, feelings, and piety. It summed up much of what Henry wanted to, had to, leave behind.

Henry had admired the dead woman "most highly for her various accomplishments of mind, and the winning graces of her manners," and he spent the afternoon of September 30, 1839, reading about her. Then he took a large sheet of paper from the desk he still kept in his mother's home on North Pearl Street in Albany and filled it with his critique, writing in an unusually small, tight hand. His remarks, he prefaced, would not deal with the state of Breckinridge's soul. That was now beyond man's praise or blame. He was concerned only with the way she was presented in the *Memorial*, where, he regretted to say, she did not exhibit "one unequivocal trace of genuine discipleship to Jesus." She should have testified to a simple "belief . . . that Jesus was the Christ, the Son of God, putting away sin by his own sacrifice, and . . . justifying the ungodly," but instead all she showed was "a hesitating doubtful persuasion that she had undergone some inward change." She did not know the happiness and peace the Gospel always brings. She did not know true humility. She could not even give herself to her husband's missionary work. Her "diligent cultivation of some private spirit" proved she was not a Christian (at least insofar as she was characterized in the book). Would a Christian feel a "*settled and habitual timidity*" in the face of death?

Could someone who was afraid to die truly believe that Christ had abolished death? James thought not. He briefly recapitulated his own earlier errors and then concluded by ominously reminding his sister-in-law that the last great day "draws on apace" and encouraging her to place all her hope in "the name" revealed by the Gospel, the "Just God & the Saviour."

The rigidity, the judgmentalism, the repeated invocation of a particular sacred name and certain exact verbal formulas, the snide implication that Marcia remains quite ignorant of basic Christian doctrine: these features render this letter one of the least palatable ever written by James. Its recipient apparently suffered from some recurring nervous trouble following the birth of her first child in the mid-1820s,* trouble so severe that family tradition reported her as simply "insane." James might have defended his letter by declaring that, like Walker, he was determined not to allow merely private considerations to influence him. But the fact that Marcia was the wife of Rev. William James, whose "drilling and disciplining" Henry had humbly supplicated four years earlier, alerts us to his unadmitted personal motives. Henry wanted to make good his everlasting rejection of Rev. William's guidance, and beyond that he wanted to get out from under the massive weight of family tradition, the Old Princeton theology, and his pathological guilt. In order to break free from that kind of past, he had to be ruthless and stern and coldly fanatical. If he was ever going to defecate himself of Princeton and Presbyterianism and his intense older brother, he had to become a man without a heart.

A CIVIL CONTRACT

Not only is nothing known about Henry and Mary's courtship, which probably had a tormenting drama all its own, but all we know of his emotional condition during the year preceding their marriage is what we can discern in the heartless letter about Margaret Breckinridge's lost soul. This document exhibits a terminally rigid insistence on correct thinking and feeling and prompts the suspicion the writer may have made similar demands of the woman he would soon wed: Mary would have to be right where Margaret had been wrong. One also suspects that a man so prescriptive and clenched could not have had a very good sense of the

---

* The James family genealogy omits this child, Tabitha, who died in infancy. See Caroline Spencer to Julius Ames, February 9, 1826, Misc. Spencer, New-York Historical Society.

feelings, stresses, and changes that married life would bring. That we can do no more than guess at Henry's heart-history may be a hint of the disciplinary rigors he had imposed on his feelings. That is to say, maybe he knew almost as little about them as we do.

One of the troubles that was probably eating at James was of a practical nature. If you reject the validity of the clergy, there is no way to solemnize a marriage except by means of a civil ceremony. But how do you get your prospective wife's mother—conservative, Presbyterian, anxious about losing her daughter—to consent to the kind of wedding she probably regards as no wedding?

John Walker had raised the question whether marriage should be consecrated by a minister and had worked out the obvious and categorical answer: since all organized churches and clergies were a foul corruption, it was "*absolutely inconsistent with our allegiance to Christ*" to be married in a religious ceremony. For Walker's disciples, marriage was "essentially a *civil* contract." What this meant in England, given that country's restrictive marriage laws, was that Walkerite couples had to travel to Scotland if their union was to have any legal standing.

In the city and state of New York civil weddings were recognized, but they were widely regarded as a cheap legal pretext for making a seduced woman honest. When the liberal *New York Tribune* declared that "being married by a Justice of the Peace or other political functionary always had an awkward, coarse, material look in our eyes," it expressed the community standard. But what other choice did Henry and Mary have? They could not violate the unchanging laws of the churches of Christ.

Once again, Henry was not a James for nothing. He did not need to call in a justice of the peace or any other political functionary. Accustomed from his earliest years to the society of the most eminent men of his time, he got the mayor of New York City, Isaac L. Varian, a Democrat remembered even by the opposition as "discharging every duty with integrity," to tie the knot. On July 28, 1840, in the Walsh family parlors on Washington Square, Mr. Varian solemnized Henry and Mary's union. The bride, dressed for hot weather, wore light India muslin. She also had a "wondrous gold headband."

This glaringly respectable secular ritual meant exactly the reverse of what anybody would ordinarily assume. For those in the know, it signified the strict purity of the couple's religious belief, not its relaxed liberalism. The James family originated in an enormous paradox deriving from Sandeman's strict interpretation of justification by faith: only that which is openly secular and nonreligious can put forth any claim to be truly spiritual. The only true saints are invisible saints. Saints you can see are devils. Although Henry Jr. would recall how his family lived and breathed contradiction, even he never got a clear view of the bizarre footings on which the household stood. There was to be no easy equivalence between signs and things signified in the Jameses' house. Those who came in late, the children, could never know just how things stood. They had to work very hard to try to understand.

Henry Sr. may have pacified his mother-in-law, but the James family Bible shows that at least one member of his own family could not be reconciled to the civil wedding, which is not entered on the page for marriages. Perhaps it was Catharine Barber James who was responsible for this stark omission. Even with Mayor Varian there to guarantee the couple's respectability before the law and public opinion, the ceremony represented a defiant break with family and community pieties.

As Elizabeth Robertson Walsh had lost her daughters, so Catharine Barber James now lost her son. The generational bonds between mothers and their children were ruptured by John Walker, now seven years dead, whose masculine ghost presided over the wedding ceremony. Six years later, following the birth of her fourth son, Mary began to wonder why the "undiluted masculine" principle was so strongly represented in her progeny.

Chapter 14

■ ■ ■

AROUSED FROM HIS
SELFISH TORPOR: 1840–43

Henry's letters to Mary have apparently all been burned. Of her letters to him only one survives, dating from a time when their children had grown up. Solid documentation of their first years together is so sparse that it is extremely difficult to make an accurate assessment of their early conjugal relationship. After Mary's death Henry told his novelist son that Mary "really did arouse my heart, early in our married life, from its selfish torpor . . . And this she did altogether unconsciously . . . solely by the presentation of her womanly sweetness and purity." But how much trust should one place in this kind of mellow retrospect?

Although it is probably true that Mary helped humanize John Walker's flinty disciple, James's later theories of male selfishness and female devotion led him to exaggerate his wife's responsibility for the profound changes he went through during his first few years of married life. Many other individuals and intellectual currents contributed to jump-start the man's severely rationalized heart. From Germany and France there came a new kind of philosophy that challenged the old Scottish commonsense school, withering the authority of all that logic and literalism and close biblical reading that had made Sandeman and Walker possible. Up in Massachusetts, in Concord and West Roxbury, new visions of human possibility burst forth with incredible richness, and from out of the old Puritan stronghold stepped a beautiful and serene new prophet, Ralph Waldo Emerson, who came down to New York City for a major lecture series in the spring of 1842, soon after the birth of James's first son.

James's long, impassioned letters to Emerson did not get burned. If these documents, the richest emotional outpourings he left behind, are not love letters, it is hard to know what to call them. They show James torn, almost like a Renaissance sonnet writer, between the extremes of attraction and repulsion, struggling to express his inmost feelings to the self-possessed new friend and passionately reproaching him for his elusiveness, his coolness, his refusal to reveal his inmost self. For the first time in his life, the headlong ardor James had put into his religious quest was now turned in the direction of a fellow thinker and writer. The fresh yet august New Englander seemed to embody everything that was most vital. He was charged with life and wisdom, and James strove mightily to take complete possession of him.

Mary touched Henry's heart, but it was Emerson who touched both his heart and his mind and brought about a painful kind of rebirth. Although the relationship between these two vigorous and independent men eventually proved dissatisfying to both of them, it opened James up and brought him into productive contact with the best minds and ideas of his time. Before Emerson, James had been entrenched in a remote and embattled redoubt of the Scotch-Irish Presbyterian mind. After Emerson, he abandoned this odd corner and began to make his way (though always fighting) into the larger, contemporary, nonsectarian intellectual world.

HIS OWN THINGS IN HIS OWN HOME

When the Astor House opened in 1836, it was the grandest American hotel yet built, renowned for both its magnificence and its taste. With its five granite-faced stories, it fronted a solid block on lower Broadway and was able to accommodate five hundred guests. Its large dining room became a center of New York fashion.

Looking back from 1912, Henry Jr. had the impression his parents passed their first winter together at the Astor House. An early issue of the *New York Herald* shows that a Mr. and Mrs. James of Albany checked into the hotel on Valentine's Day, 1841, a Sunday. If these were the Henry Jameses, their arrival, copied from the register by one of the newspaper's junior reporters, indicates that the couple's stay in New York's premier hotel was at best intermittent—and also that the husband signed in as coming from Albany. Perhaps he and Mary had lived there the preceding summer and fall. Nevertheless, New York was clearly the couple's home now, as James's one surviving letter from 1841, a relaxed note written in spring to Joseph Henry, suggests he and Mary had been living in the city "all winter."

When James wrote this note on March 15, he and Mary were out of the hotel and living in a rented house at 5 Washington Place. Situated in the fashionable area between Broadway and Washington Square, their new home must have been fairly luxurious, as the assessor appraised the building and lot at $14,000 (and also listed Henry James as "Occupt"). One of James's reasons for writing his former tutor was to press him to come and inspect the ex-seminarian's new quarters:

> I want to see you very much in my own house, at my own tea table or dinner table, with my own wife, and all of my own things around me, and have been much disappointed that I have not had the pleasure of so doing all winter. Come along then soon—and confess that next to your own house, and your own wife, and your own things, you would certainly be best satisfied with mine.

Now that James's years of homeless wandering seemed to be at an end, he wanted to show off his cozy domestic interior. As usual, however, with his passion for extremes, he couldn't help expressing the dark side of his hospitable urge. His house and his wife, his wife and his tea table—the letter speaks of these possessions as if they were all on the same level. All are offered for the friend to sample and enjoy, and then to compare with his own possessions.

Henry and Mary's first child was conceived about a month after this letter was written. Born January 11, 1842, the baby was given the same name as the paternal grandfather he would never know. Assigning this name to the latest arrival was a way of enrolling him in his father's generations—a symbolic act the first-time mother may have seen as an absolute duty. Thirty years later, when Mary's first male grandchild, Edward Holton James, was born, she was offended that the daughter-in-law who had "the naming" did not call the baby Henry. To choose any other name than that of the paternal grandfather, Mary felt, showed a weak "conjugal sentiment." Although Mary's children inherited this intense family piety, it proved oddly compatible with a chronic inexactness as to birth dates and ages. Henry and Mary's second child put January 9 as William's birthday (in a book originally conceived as a tribute to this brother), and when William produced a laboriously edited posthumous volume of his father's papers, he had Henry Sr. born on June 2 rather than the correct June 3.

According to Henry Jr.'s frequently inaccurate memoirs, William came into the world, not at 5 Washington Place, where his parents had been living, but at the Astor House. Yet on March 3, two months later, the family was still living at no. 5, this being the return address in Henry

Sr.'s first letter to Emerson. The fact of the Astor House birth, accepted by all James family biographers, may be questioned. In an age when mothers gave birth at home, Mary can hardly be imagined as wanting to return to the hotel for her first delivery. It only adds to the mystery that on January 8, three days before this birth, the father-to-be signed the contract that gave him possession of a house just up the street.

The assessor's book for 1842 identifies Henry Sr. as the occupant of this newly purchased home at 21 Washington Place. A handsome brick structure, three stories high and twenty-five feet wide, it was located just to the east of the recently built and impressively castellated building that housed New York University. Henry bought the property from his spendthrift younger brother, John Barber, who had purchased a choice estate at Rhinebeck (where he had a spectacular view of a bend in the Hudson River and occupied himself planting fancy roses). John sold no. 21 for the same price he had given a year and a half earlier—$18,000. For the next quarter century, no residence purchased by Henry would cost even half so much. One reason he was able to swing the deal was that he assumed John's $10,000 mortgage—meaning that little more than $8,000 actually changed hands. Even so, it was a daring plunge for a first-time home buyer with a checkered past. It was also a public announcement that the young father meant to settle down at last and raise his family.

A little over a year later, on April 15, 1843, Henry and Mary's second boy was born in this house. Like William, Henry Jr. also got his name from the father's side of the family. In caring for the baby, Mary must have had the help of several female servants, whose rooms were in the "finished attics" (to quote an advertisement for the house). There was also a wonderful modern convenience on the second floor—a "bathing room" supplied with running water piped in through the basement from New York's new municipal water system, the Forty-second Street Croton Reservoir, which had gone into operation the previous year. The whole house, in fact, was "in perfect and admirable order throughout." It was an ideal property for "a family contemplating a permanent residence in the city."

HEAVEN-GIFTED SPIRITS

But, for the father, settling down was easier said than done. There were pressing questions and contradictions in his mind, and he was reaching out restlessly in all directions to resolve them. In 1841 a couple of anonymous articles on the strange eighteenth-century Swedish visionary, Emanuel Swedenborg, appeared in John A. Heraud's *Monthly Magazine*, published in England. They were written by James John Garth Wilkinson, a versatile young physician who preferred to talk and scribble metaphysics rather than dole out drugs from his small London surgery. According to Wilkinson's son, these articles caught James's eye and led to his acquaintance with the author. Whatever the exact chain of events, within three years Wilkinson had become James's closest friend and Swedenborg his newest gospel.

Although Swedenborg stressed God's total sovereignty, it was not the kind of sovereignty that generated harsh abstract doctrines of universal depravity and salvation by faith alone. Swedenborg's universe was more organic and couldn't be understood unless one thought in images and glimpsed the celestial point of view. The divine life flowed down through man, and as it cascaded into his mind, he had the illusion of thinking for himself. Logical argument and literal biblical interpretation, as practiced by John Walker, were emphatically not the path to wisdom for Swedenborg. Yet in expounding his visionary system, this improbable seer was as dry, dispassionate, and orderly as could well be imagined. In fact, he had been a scientist who ceased writing technical treatises in mid-life and began recording his spiritual insights. Having failed to get what he wanted from Joseph Henry and Michael Faraday, James was still looking for a scientist willing to endorse a visionary account of reality. Wilkinson's articles may have given him his first cloudy glimpse of the palmy land he had to find.

Another new acquaintance, William Henry Channing, also took an interest in Swedenborg. After following his famous uncle, the Reverend William Ellery Channing, into the Unitarian pulpit, Channing had decided that this denomination was too unresponsive to social reform and the new ways of thinking. He left his Unitarian congregation in Cincinnati and, moving to New York, preached to a small but select group of independent worshippers, first in a rented hall in Brooklyn, then at the Stuyvesant Institute at Broadway and Bond, and finally in a small, plain room on Crosby Street. His listeners included Horace Greeley, the newspaperman, and Christopher Pearse Cranch, an ex-minister turned artist. In his sermons Channing expressed the new philosophical tendencies, but he also thundered against slavery and the exploitation of the urban poor. "All the other preaching in New York was tame in comparison with his," wrote his biographer, and Cranch agreed, extolling him as "prophet, thinker, eloquent speaker, pure and heaven-gifted spirit." Thoreau, on the other hand, saw Channing as a "concave man" and concluded from "his attitude and the lines of his face that he [was] retreating from himself and from yourself, with sad doubts."

James's opinion of the minister lay between these two extremes. During the months when Channing held forth at the Stuyvesant Institute, James was reportedly "in frequent attendance." His pilgrimage had taken him from Mr. Buchanan's primitive apostolic church to Channing's more socially engaged and intellectually up-to-date following. But once the preacher organized his listeners into a church, sometime around April 1843, James seems to have broken contact, telling a common friend in May that Channing had been "very busy with his church matters—& I with my matters, and although I should well like to lay hands upon him often, I have never ventured to his house, knowing not his habits nor surroundings." Liberal and enlightened and impassioned as Channing may have been, he was too closely tethered to ecclesiastical tradition to satisfy James, who no longer hoped to find a heaven-gifted spirit behind the pulpit of a Protestant church.

MY BOSOM GLOWED WITH MANY A TRUE WORD

By this time many informed Americans felt that the real religious and intellectual action was in eastern Massachusetts, where the Unitarian left wing had recently been transformed into a remarkable new movement, one that spilled over in the richest ways into social reform, literature, and philosophy.

Although Unitarianism repudiated the Calvinist notions of human depravity and regeneration through faith, it still generally insisted that Christ was divine, historical, and unique, and that the religion he founded contained spiritual truths available from no other source. Beginning around 1830, some of the most advanced and ardent Unitarian ministers had become uneasy with these claims of exclusiveness and historical particularity. These restive clergymen, as social historian Anne C. Rose has shown, cast loose from historical Christianity in search of the perennial, the universal, the intuitive, the egalitarian. No one book and no one tradition could pretend to monopolize the truth. All Christ did was to bear testimony to truths theoretically discoverable by anybody. He was eminent because of his rare insight, not his divinity.

The career of the Reverend George Ripley illustrates the pattern. As a young man, he was orthodox and rather priggish, a committed evangelical firmly locked into his elders' safe universe. By 1834 he decided that Christ was merely "the chosen vessel in whom the Spirit of God was to dwell *without measure.*" In 1837, when James was turning back to Sandeman's eighteenth-century message that the church must detach itself from all human institutions, Ripley was looking forward to a time of perfect integration, "when religion, philosophy, & politics will be united in a holy Trinity." A few years later he quit the ministry.

Ralph Waldo Emerson, minister of Boston's Second Unitarian Church, had been one of the first to step down. In 1830 he told his congregation that Christ became the Saviour, not because he was a self-sacrificing god whose death canceled the divinely imposed penalty for man's transgression, but because he was the first person who declared "fully and intelligibly those truths on which the welfare of the human soul depends." This, however, was a little vague, and two years later, when Emerson's church refused to let him celebrate Communion without using bread and wine, he resigned.

At the end of the 1830s a vigorous counterattack was mounted on these renegade ministers and they were pejoratively labeled "Transcendentalists." The term, which stuck, reflected their affinity with German idealistic philosophers, Platonists of various periods, and certain ancient non-Western writers. In Channing's sketch of the movement, Transcendentalism "was a pilgrimage from the idolatrous world of creeds and rituals to the temple of the Living God in the soul. It was a putting to silence of tradition and formulas, that the Sacred Oracle might be heard through intuitions of the single-eyed and pure-hearted." But even as this embrace of the eternal and the immanent gathered itself into a thrilling new movement, the defenders of orthodoxy marshaled themselves for battle. Andrews Norton, a conservative Unitarian who condemned Transcendentalism as the latest form of infidelity, joined forces with James's old Princeton mentor, James Waddel Alexander, who tried to refute the Continental philosophers (Victor Cousin, Benjamin Constant) undergirding the new heresy. Never before had Unitarians and conservative Presbyterians been able to act in concert.

Emerson and Ripley and the others had been the respected voices of their communities. Now, isolated and under siege, they began asking some important new questions of themselves. What kind of vocation could they substitute for the ministry? How could they integrate their spiritual intuitions with their daily and professional life? If society itself was "hostile to the teachings of religion" (in Rose's words), shouldn't society be ventilated with fresh spiritual breezes?

One way to answer questions like these was to get together and talk, and accordingly, under Emerson's lead, the Transcendentalists instituted a discussion club and founded a major new magazine, *The Dial,* which ran from 1840 to 1844. Another way was to devise a reconstituted society. The same year *The Dial* was started, Ripley drafted a prospectus for a revolutionary community, one that would "ensure a more natural union between intellectual and manual labor than now exists . . . combine the thinker and the worker, as far as possible, in the same individual . . . do away with the necessity of menial services . . . and thus . . . prepare a society of liberal, intelligent, and cultivated persons." In 1841 this projected commune came into being in West Roxbury, near Boston. Called Brook Farm, it had thirty-two members who hoped that collective farming might afford them sufficient leisure for personal and intellectual development. Hoping as well to wipe out caste distinctions, they took turns waiting on one another and performing other services usually relegated to servants.

If Ripley embodied the social and practical aims of Transcendentalism, Emerson spoke for the individualistic and literary/philosophical side of the movement. He moved to Concord, some twenty miles west of Boston, and, thanks in part to his first wife's money, became a poet and thinker. He kept his thoughts in his journal and mined it from time to time to compose his lectures, which presently afforded him an adequate livelihood. At a time when the lecture was both a secular sermon and a popular form of entertainment, Emerson's speeches became famous as a new thing under the sun: mind-bendingly speculative, chiseled and witty and brilliantly figurative, almost impossible to understand, and probably dangerous. The man's spare, serene appearance and manner of delivery contributed to the overall effect. Those who heard him for the first time were often surprised. They struggled to put into words the spell he cast. When Fredrika Bremer sailed to the New World and came face-to-face with Emerson, she confessed to her Swedish readers that she felt "a little desire for combat with him; for I never see a lion in human form without feeling my lion-heart beat." "What sentences!" Emma Wilkinson exclaimed one night in her sleep. When asked to explain by her husband, she said:

> It is Emerson lecturing! He is in a square hall, with a gallery round it, clothed in a Roman toga. Now he has just uttered a sentence, and walks round the gallery while all the people repeat it after him, that they may gain its meaning. He then goes out at a door, and reappears at another door, to utter forth a new sentence.

On March 3, 1842, Emerson made his first public appearance in New York, inaugurating a series of six lectures before large and steadily growing audiences at the New York Society Library. This was the voice the city's lonely dreamers had been waiting for. After the first night's talk, William Greene, a reader of mystic literature, called at the speaker's hotel. Rebecca Black, an ex-Presbyterian, came forward, as did Albert Brisbane, who explained the utopian social theories of Charles Fourier in a tedious monologue. In the evening Emerson visited Brisbane's boardinghouse, where there was an "animated conversation" on the old topic "Omnipotence of Arrangements versus Power of the Soul."

The most impassioned member of Emerson's first-night audience may have been Henry James. When the lecture was over, he returned to the house he still rented at 5 Washington Place and sat down at his desk:

> I listened to your address this evening, and as my bosom glowed with many a true word that fell from your lips & felt ere long fully assured that before me I beheld a man who in very truth was seeking the realities of things, I said to myself I will try when I go home how far this man follows reality—how far he loves truth and goodness. For I will write to him that I too in my small degree am coveting to understand the truth which surrounds me and embraces me, am seeking worthily to apprehend—or to be more worthily apprehended of—the love which underlies and vivifies all the seeming barrenness of our most unloving world.

James continued to address the lecturer in the third person, in this way maintaining a polite distance, but the substance of his communication was that he wished to grapple Emerson to his soul. He, too, wanted to embrace—and be embraced by—truth and love. With each step, however, he found himself "severed from friends and kindred," so much so that he was now entirely alone. "To talk familiarly" with another brave questioner had never been his lot "for one half hour even." If he could just "once feel the cordial grasp of a fellow pilgrim," he would always remember "the cheering God-speed and the ringing laugh with which he bounded on from my sight at parting." James claimed he was not seeking guidance, since to do so would insult each man's independence as a seeker,* but he did ask for help in deciphering "some of the hieroglyphics" that had baffled him. Would Emerson please call at his convenience?

The two men met the next day, not in Washington Place, however, but in Emerson's room at the Globe Hotel. Perhaps James was too im-

---

* When Henry Jr. excerpted this letter for his memoirs, he picked up the letter's one suggestion of critical detachment—"I will tell him [i.e., you, Emerson] that I do not value his substantive discoveries, whatever they may be, perhaps half so largely as he values them . . ."—and omitted everything that testified to his father's warmly enthusiastic response.

patient to await the lecturer's call. The visit proved to be a long one, as Emerson told his wife in one of his frequent letters home, and he was left with a strong first impression of James's "manlike thorough seeing" character. Encountering Brisbane on the premises, the visitor put the doctrinaire Fourierist in his place with a directness Emerson admired but could not emulate. Of all the New Yorkers he had met, James was "the best apple on the tree." Writing Margaret Fuller, Emerson offered what both understood as the highest encomium: James was a "very intelligent person," an "independent right minded man."

At some point during this trip to New York, Emerson called at 5 Washington Place, where he was "'taken upstairs' " to see two-month-old William. Perhaps this was a painful moment for the lecturer, whose beloved five-year-old son had died a month earlier. The memory of this encounter between two American philosophers, the older of whom gave "his blessing" to the younger, was treasured by the next generation of Jameses. Henry Jr. seems to have regarded the visit as an act of succession or legitimation—a laying on of hands. Typically, he moved the scene from 5 Washington Place to the majestic Astor House.

The productive encounter, however, was between Emerson and Henry Sr. As the last flower of generations of learned Congregational ministers, Emerson represented the best of New England culture at the moment of ripeness, when it abandoned its sectarian confines and boldly took all previous and contemporary thought as its rightful province. With his unruffled catholicity, the ex-preacher seemed able to turn everything to account—the homeliest details of village life no less than the ancient Hindu religious texts then making their way among a few adventurous American readers. He played with metaphors, ideas, and systems, usually without jeopardizing his own finely balanced point of view. Like James, he attached a supreme value to acute vision, independence, intrepidity. He also liked to sing the praises of self-reliant capitalist adventurism, of which James had enjoyed a ringside seat from infancy to his father's death.

In effect, the product of Hudson Valley Presbyterianism met the product of Boston Congregationalism on a kind of summit formed by the religious and philosophical enthusiasms of the day. James had reached this summit by a far more laborious path than the one Emerson took. Where the New Englander was the culminating product of a steadily liberalizing trend running for several decades and through more than one generation, the New Yorker's history was full of ruptures and zigzags, a strangely splintered Calvinism, and hot religious passions. If there was an abiding sense of privilege and empowerment, there were also scourges and chains. The two men were able to share an intense Transcendental high in 1842, and this encounter formed the basis of a lifelong friendship. But the friendship would be subject to great strain.

And there was something else. Evelyn Barish's recent biography of Emerson's early life has disclosed the strength of his distant fascination with an older Harvard student named Martin Gay. In his notebooks the young Emerson saw a connection between his interest in Gay and the "intemperate fondness" for men that historians had condemned in King James I. The word "homosexual" was not yet invented, but it is clear that early in life Emerson sensed the appeal, and the danger, of homosexual feelings and acts—"misery to himself & seed." There is no evidence James attained this kind of self-awareness.

A LECTURE SERIES OF HIS OWN

Like the early Transcendentalists, who struggled to integrate labor and intellect, economic life and speculative philosophy, James still needed to identify his vocation. If Emerson had successfully negotiated the move from pulpit to lectern, perhaps the un-Revd Henry James could do the same. Through the winter of 1842–43 he sat at his desk and worked on an ambitious lecture series. The time had come to offer instruction to New York's fellow religious seekers. By January 23 he felt he was ready.

On that date the New York *Evening Post* announced among its advertisements that Henry James would deliver a lecture later that week at the Stuyvesant Institute. His subject would be "LITERAL CHRISTIANITY, or . . . the doctrine of Jesus, as the suitable outgrowth and completion of the Jewish economy." Unlike Emerson, who cleared $200 from his first New York lecture series, James stated in his advertisement that there would be no charge for admission. He wanted an audience, and he got an opening-night boost from an old seminary friend, Parke Godwin, now one of the *Post*'s editors: "This evening, it will be remembered, Mr. Henry James lectures . . . He is an accomplished scholar, a profound thinker, and one who has given much study to the subject of which he treats."

Following the lecture, Godwin continued to use his paper to try to work up interest in the lecturer's unpromising material: "The peculiar doctrine he unfolded we shall not now attempt to explain; suffice it to say, that the lecturer exhibited unusual power and fearlessness of thought." Intense and perhaps somewhat rushed, James "spoke rapidly, but distinctly." The *Post's* notice was at once picked up by James's home-town Whig newspaper and reprinted at the head of the editorial column, with an attention-getting hand pointing in from the margin, as if to say, "Look! One of Billy James's boys is showing a strange kind of enterprise down in New York."

In spite of his announced title, James probably did not argue for the literal truth of the Christian religion. Neither did he set forth the gospel according to John Walker, as in the letter he had sent Marcia James four years earlier. Instead, he was (in Godwin's words) "liberal and comprehensive." Aggressively exposing "the defects of the prevailing religious system," he tried to "enlarge our conceptions of the scope of Christianity," probably reinterpreting it as something allegorical and non-literal and all-inclusive, something he no doubt opposed to the "Jewish economy" of his title. (If one can judge from his later writings, James interpreted Judaism in the usual Christian fashion, as a superseded legalism.) All in all, it seems clear that the thirty-one-year-old pilgrim was well along in his difficult traverse from Calvinism to a more universal, intuition-based, and up-to-date kind of thinking.

At one point in his talk James intimated he would give an entire "course of lectures" if there was sufficient demand. Apparently he thought there was, for during the next two weeks he gave three more talks under the general title INWARD REASON OF CHRISTIANITY. This title shows how far he had moved from Walker's detailed biblical exegesis and relentless logic. The Irishman's powerful reasoning could now be set aside as no more than "outward" (roughly equivalent to the late-twentieth-century "linear"). Superior thought moved inward rather than outward, was centripetal and unified, immediate and intuitive. From now on, James would aim at the "inward reason" of things, as is evident from the title of his concluding talk, "UNITY OF GOD AND MAN." To choose that kind of billing was to jettison the Calvinists' insistence on the vast distance between God and man. It was to make—or contemplate making—the daring Transcendental plunge into the inner heart of things.

James's most interesting titles, however, are those he gave his second and third lectures. A few years earlier, when he withdrew from the seminary, he had engaged in an intensely focused study of the Scriptures, the original first-century Church, and the nature of regeneration. Now, still fixated on the Bible, the "thorough seeing" questioner moved from Romans and Acts and other New Testament books all the way back to Genesis, turning in this way from the origins of Christianity to the origins of being. On his second night he spoke about "the man of the *first* chapter of Genesis, and the man of the *second* chapter; or the CREATED man and the MADE man." A few days later he continued to expound this contrast under the title "The Two Adams."

Thirty-six years later, looking back at these early efforts, James remembered feeling that he had made an "important discovery," one which would have a major impact on theology. This discovery, he said, was "that the book of Genesis was not intended to throw a direct light upon our natural or race history, but was an altogether mystical or symbolic record of the laws of God's *spiritual* creation." His first course of lectures was meant to develop this interpretation, which substituted an allegorical reading of the creation story for the usual literal understanding. But this retrospective account, screened by James's later theology, probably distorts his adventurous early thought. The advertised titles of his second and third lectures suggest that the earnest religious student had begun to think about the discrepancies between the two creation stories found in the book of Genesis. In Chapter 1 God creates man both male and female, but in Chapter 2 he forms man out of the dust and afterward makes woman from one of his ribs. The pioneers of nineteenth-century textual criticism deduced that early compilers of the Pentateuch had stitched together two different traditional creation myths. Lacking the historical and linguistic sophistication this discovery presupposed, and also continuing (unlike the Transcendentalists) to regard the Bible as the primal repository of sacred wisdom, James resolved the discrepancies by fashioning an allegorical reading in which the two different creation stories reveal two different orders of being, or stages of development.

Although we can only guess what James understood in 1843 by his distinction between the "CREATED man" of Chapter 1 and the "MADE man" of Chapter 2, he had evidently begun to work out his peculiar notion of creation. He had also found his basic method of reading— "inward" allegorizing of the sacred text. One reason he adopted this interpretative practice was that it enabled him to put Sandeman and Walker behind him. To obviate their powerful reasoning and enter the larger world, James had to take the drastic step of making reason itself subjective. This was how he saved himself—at the cost of being able to persuade others. From now on there would be a strange obscurity in all his speculations.

James thought so well of his discovery that he decided to turn his lecture series into an essay on "the *super*natural constitution of morality." As he told Emerson, the projected essay would demonstrate that man's moral life presupposed a "foreign genesis," meaning "some such interference with human history as the special manifestation of Deity in humanity which the Scriptures assign to the Christ." This statement shows that James stopped short of becoming a genuine Transcendentalist, holding instead to some basic Christian beliefs. He still thought salvation had a history rather than being equally available at all times. The Bible was still the supreme text of texts. Man was definitely insufficient in himself, and for true spirituality to be possible there had to be a divine incursion into time. James worked out these ideas by generalizing from the familiar Calvinist doctrines of Depravity and Justification, and by attributing a quasi-Gnostic character to God's "interference." Instead of being a literal incarnation, an apotheosis in the flesh, God's descent had been "logical, through a Logos or word." As such, it was conditioned on "*our understanding*." Thus, the theater of supernatural activity became the conscious mind. For James, this idea was both old and new—old in its allegiance to the rational character of a saving belief, new in its daring blend of philosophical idealism and history.

Dead set on turning his course of lectures into a little book, James was going against the obvious indications. Years later he claimed he had enjoyed "good audiences," but in fact the lectures were so unappealing his listeners dropped away. Simultaneously, on February 10, the *Post* announced that a *real* talker was coming to town, Ralph Waldo Emerson, with a portfolio of fresh material. Anticipating his arrival, the unhappy James manfully confessed his own failure: "I came to night from my lecture a little disposed to think from the smart reduction of my audience that I had about as well not prepared my lectures, especially that I get no tidings of having interested one of the sort (the religious) for whom they were wholly designed." He had conceived of his talks, he said, as the first step in his "outgoing to the world." They were an attempt to end his isolation and establish a public vocation analogous to the ministry. But the lecture platform had turned into a pillory. He had not been able to communicate his wonderful insights, and the unsolved problem of his future once again stared him in the face. Could Emerson afford him a half hour of his valuable time?

In the letter James had sent Emerson a year earlier, opening their correspondence, he presented himself as a fellow pilgrim, hale and independent, bent on following his solitary path. Now he was almost abject:

Here am I thirty one years in life ignorant in all outward science, but having patient habits of meditation which never know disgust or weariness, and feeling a force of impulsive love toward all humanity which will not let me rest wholly mute . . . What shall I do? Shall I get me a little nook in the country and communicate with my *living* kind—not my talking kind—by life only . . . Or shall I follow some commoner method—learn science and bring myself first into men's respect? . . . Can [you] . . . further me, or at least *stay* me?*

What was the secret of Emerson's success? Did he ignore those concerns that preoccupy other men and "write only by inward pressure and light," or did he consciously try to correct some particular "prevailing wrong in man's thought"? With his Presbyterian background, James had run the gauntlet of polemical theology and strictly rational demonstrations, and he couldn't help wondering whether his new friend was indifferent to logic and intellect. Didn't Emerson share James's conviction that there was nothing in life that was not first in the intellect? Didn't he care for *laws*, central *facts, orderly* understanding (underlining the considerations that pressed so hard on himself)? Where was the real man keeping himself? Impishly addressing the "Invisible Emerson," the writer pleaded with him to be frank and direct and impart the counsel James could no longer do without. "I know," he wrote, "you have the same wants as I have, deep down in your bosom hidden from my sight."

This strange pleading letter was a throwback to James's 1835 request to Rev. William for the strictest drilling and disciplining. In each case, the writer seemed to want to annul his own separateness—to establish a close union with an older male guide.

Emerson had been warned, and soon after he came to New York his passionate friend got hold of him. Afterward the New Englander reported to Thoreau: "I see W. H. Channing & Mr James at leisure & have had what the Quakers call 'a solid season,' once or twice. With Tappan a very happy pair of hours & him I must see again." Writing to his wife, Emerson took the same discreet tone: "I see Mr James a good deal & William Tappan who is a nonpareil." From the sound of this, Tappan was a delight but James was heavy, frequent, demanding, contestatory. A solid season was not a time of pleasant relaxation.

At the end of February James's friend Godwin started up an ambitious New York weekly called the *Pathfinder*. The second issue had a long, unsigned critique of Emerson's recent lectures that looks as if it was written by James. Although the reviewer had followed the series with the greatest interest, he devoted most of his space to certain complaints. Emerson does not speak *to* others. He does not argue. "He does not appeal to the logical faculty of his auditors. . . . He is . . . careful to

---

* Quoting this undated letter in *Notes of a Son and Brother*, Henry Jr. supposed it was written in 1842 and thus failed to realize that his father's desperate unsettledness was contemporaneous with his own birth.

avoid every symbol which the ordinary understanding of man recognizes as expressive of moral truth." (In his letter James had asked, "Can you not report your life by some intellectual symbols which my intellect appreciates to me?") The critic was particularly grated by Emerson's assertion that, since Jesus was "defeated," Christianity did not embody mankind's highest point of development. It isn't certain that James wrote this critique, but it nicely sums up what he found most maddening in Emerson.

Still, the friendship deepened, and after Emerson had returned to Concord, he recalled "with lively pleasure our free conversations, cheered to me by the equal love, courage, & intelligence I met." He flatteringly asked James whether he had anything for *The Dial.* He announced Thoreau's visit to New York, warning James in advance of the young man's "village pedantry" but praising his profundity and magnanimity. He also dropped the tantalizing suggestion that James might "enjoy the society" of Emerson's closest friends in Concord. A little too oblique and hypothetical to be a true invitation, this was followed by a curious admonition: "I live in Concord, & value my nest, yet I will not promise to myself or another that I shall not in a year or two flee to Berkshire from so public & metropolitan a place as this quietest of country towns." The message seemed to be: Yes, I would like to see you here, but if you're thinking of moving to Concord to be close to me, don't count on my staying here.

James was never very good at fielding such messages. In his reply, drafted immediately, he confessed he had been thinking continually about Emerson and had often been moved to write, if only to articulate "an inward yearning which frequently haunts me towards you." He was struggling to understand the reason why Emerson caused him such "intense pain":

> It evades me when I set myself deliberately to grasp it—and so I will not intrude my rash and impertinent guesses upon you. Something or other disturbs the deep serene of my rejoicing in you . . . It would be miraculous if I did not for the present regard it as a defectiveness in you . . . All that I can at present say is that being better satisfied with you than any man I ever met, I am worst satisfied.

Attributing the trouble to "some lurking narrowness" within himself, James trusted he would soon outgrow it. As he developed this idea he went back to the image he had first employed in *The Gospel Good News to Sinners*: "Every narrowness I have ever grown out of I have first hugged

and hugged as if it were a blanket for eternity—in perfect good faith for
the time mind you." In his anonymous tract of five years earlier, this
image illustrated the persistence of human vanity. Now he applied the
image to his strenuous endeavor to make his Calvinism accommodate
his newly expanding consciousness. What he was wondering was, should
he stretch his old intellectual garments or should he get rid of them
entirely?

It was because this question pressed on James that he responded so
fervently to Thomas Carlyle's *Sartor Resartus* (in English, the tailor re-
tailored), which worked out the philosophy of clothes—the mind's
clothes. A former Calvinist who had turned to the new forms of German
philosophy, Carlyle had blazed the trail so many American ex-clerics
eagerly followed. When Ripley read the Scotsman's epochal book, his
"heart leaped up with the response, 'This unknown being is my brother.' "
James McKay, James's friend out in Buffalo, found Carlyle's books an
"aid and comfort," and James himself praised the writer as "the very best
interpreter of spiritual philosophy . . . *for this age*, the age of transition
and conflict. And what renders him so is his natural birth- and education-
place. Just to think of a *Scotchman* with a heart widened to German
spiritualities!" By contrast, Emerson's great flaw, James frankly advised
him, was that he did not take Calvinism seriously. The true man of the
hour would have to be a "Jonathan Edwards redivivus."

When Emerson arranged for the American publication of Carlyle's
latest book, *Past and Present*, James eagerly looked forward to reading it.
The Germanized Scotsman was already looming on the horizon as James's
next wisdom-master, and from a distance he naïvely imagined the cranky
sage as generous and ardent and unreserved. Unlike Emerson, Carlyle
would not hold back. He would give full measure and more, dishing out
his thought until it was "heaped up to topheaviness and inevitable
lopsidedness."

But why was *Emerson* so stinting a provisioner? "Oh you man without
a handle!" James broke out, courting and complaining in his finest style,
"shall one never be able to help himself out of you, according to his
needs, and be dependent only upon your fitful tippings-up?"

QUIET DESPERATION

1844 was the year the millennium would begin, according to Father
Miller, and his followers were not the only ones who believed the last
days were at hand. The enthusiastic revivalism of the early 1830s had

grown and spread, metamorphosing into strange messianic hopes and radical utopian experiments and also generating a more fervent push for the abolition of slavery. There was a widespread expectation among American Protestants that 1843 would bring "some grand event." For Henry James as well, this was to be a year of apocalyptic dreams and obscure collapses.

As summer approached and Thoreau came to New York to take charge of the education of Emerson's brother's children, James invited the young man to call at 21 Washington Place. Although Thoreau did not record his opinion of James's home, probably the most luxurious he had ever been in, he pronounced the quiet and exclusive neighborhood "a pleasant part of the city"—his only known compliment to New York. To Emerson he sent a frank report of his session with James, which must have been an extremely solid season.

> I have been to see Henry James, and like him very much. It was a great pleasure to meet him. It makes humanity seem more erect and respectable. I never was more kindly and faithfully catechised. It made me respect myself more to be thought worthy of such wise questions. He is a man, and takes his own way, or stands still in his own place. I know of no one so patient and determined to have the good of you. It is almost friendship, such plain and human dealing . . . I had three hours' solid talk with him.

"A catechism . . . as good as a bath" was Emerson's amused summation of his young protégé's encounter. The reason James put his visitor through this bracing ordeal (cold baths were standard) was that Thoreau represented a way to get at Emerson. But the young man was a puzzler in his own right, being as hard and self-contained as he was visionary, and at one point James openly mused, "Well, you Transcendentalists are wonderfully consistent. I must get hold of this somehow!" He was still trying to find the handle, to grasp the "law" followed by these elusive Concord thinkers. For his part, Thoreau did not think his host would "write or speak inspiringly," and he was even more impressed by another disability. Writing to his parents, the robust young philosopher characterized James quite simply as a "lame man." "Almost friendship" indeed.

James was paying close attention to *The Dial* now, and when he looked at the issue for April 1843 he was greatly irritated by an article that extolled Bronson Alcott's genius and reproached Boston for failing to honor it. In James's eyes, Alcott was too egotistical, self-conscious, and histrionic to be a true prophet. Instead of honestly lamenting "the blindness of his generation to that truth which is their life" (as Sandeman and Walker had done, paying the price of obscurity), Alcott staged eloquent performances. A true Jeremiah must be more possessed, more artless.

In September of that year, *The Dial*'s brilliant editor, Margaret Fuller, returning from a vacation to the Great Lakes, made a rapid visit to New York and briefly entered James's life, and also his wife's. Although Fuller had met Rev. William James a few years earlier, greatly impressing him, it was to Emerson that Henry was indebted for this newest Transcendental acquaintance. "The dear noble woman!" he effused after first talking to her. Although the friendship was cut short by his sailing to England, he punningly anticipated "fuller conferences & sympathies" in the future. She in turn looked forward to seeing Mrs. James again and hoped Mr. James would end up preferring America's "pure waters" to Europe's "historic glories." In England she gave Wilkinson the impression that James's letters were "things of accredited value in the selectest circles." But neither the fuller conferences nor the closer sympathies materialized. Fuller died in a shipwreck in 1850, and as James read her heavily edited *Memoirs* a couple of years later, he condemned her "inordinate self-esteem." The one Transcendentalist he cared for was Emerson.

Although the new revelations originating in Concord held James's attention, he continued to spend long hours of study on biblical and theological subjects. He had detached himself from the Sandemanian and Walkerite laws of the churches of Christ, but only to devote himself to the quest for a supreme, all-embracing explanation of the laws of life in general. Unlike Emerson, who eluded systematic thought with stunning nonchalance, James had to have a completely unified account of science and religion, nature and supernature. Finally, he resolved to consult his old oracle.

Writing Joseph Henry on July 9, James said he had often wished to see him during the past year in order to ask a certain question. Was there some book that explained "the *fundamental unity* of the different sciences"? That set forth the principles that made all sciences "*one at bottom*"? Admitting his complete ignorance, James beseeched his old friend to provide a unified theory of gravitation, heat, electricity, and so forth. "Surely," he pleaded, "there must be the closest family relation among all the facts of true science."

James's purpose in sending this strange coaxing letter had nothing to do with the sciences as such, which were merely "bewildering heaps of facts" as far as he was concerned. What he was seeking was confirmation for his fixed belief "that all the phenomena of physics are to [be] explained and grouped under laws *exclusively spiritual*—that they are in fact only the material expression of spiritual truth—or as Paul says the visible forms of invisible substance. Heb[rews]. 11.3." Had the physicist's research into the physical brought him as yet "to the *moral*"? James was serious. He had groped for the invisible Emerson, lurking somewhere within his maddening tolerance for ambiguity and contradiction, and he was now reaching with equal desperation for the confirmation of his grand mania. He wanted the nation's most eminent physicist to name the text that would exhibit the spiritual unity of the sciences. If James was ever going to make good his claim that God had descended as a Logos, he had to be able to hold this unity in his mind. Nothing would make any sense at all unless religion, history, science, the whole works could be squeezed into a crystalline essence instantly penetrable by the intellect.

Joseph Henry calmly replied that the kind of book James was looking for didn't exist. Science was not some aggregate of "facts" but a systematic *"Knowledge of the Laws of Phenomena."* He predicted that the connections between the different branches of physics would become evident in the future. This answer was misinterpreted by James, who confidently announced eight years later that "science is not a record or aggregation of simple facts. It is a perception of the harmony which embeds all facts, of the unity which subtends all variety."

Two years earlier James had urged Joseph Henry to come and inspect his wife and household. But this latest letter, written three months after the second child's birth, follows a different pattern, the same one that can be observed in James's other personal writings from the troubled year of 1843: struggling to bare his inmost mind, he completely ignores Mary, William, and Henry Jr. And yet, strangely, James harps on the metaphor of warm family unity. The sciences *must* reveal the "closest family relation." There *has* to be a "brotherhood" between scientific knowledge and natural facts. *Surely* spirit is to matter as parent is to child. On every level, the letter writer turns from the physical and the literal to the spiritual, to the point of forgetting his actual family in his yearning for some warm but figurative union.

The young father felt strangely distant from his wife and children. The only letter from 1843 that mentions them was written one month after the birth of Henry Jr., and here James admonishes himself for his neglect and inner distraction: "But I must stop, ere I be stopped. My wife is grateful for your remembrance, and thinks nothing would so help me as a little intercourse with Concord. Another fine little boy now lying in her lap preaches to me that I must become settled somehow at home." It is only the briefest of glimpses, but what it reveals is quite unlike the

usual picture of the loving James family. Instead, we see a worried wife
and mother, a husband and father yearning for closer contact with Emerson, and a one-month-old infant exhorter who preaches a powerful sermon on the all-sufficiency of mother's lap.

But instead of domesticating himself in his expensive new house, James
was in fact contemplating a variety of excursions. He told Thoreau he
wanted to go with his wife to Germany to study the language, a knowledge
of which was necessary for attaining the "highest culture." He told Joseph
Henry he would probably go to France for the winter, and from there
to Germany. He told Emerson he was thinking of wintering "in some
mild English climate—Devonshire perhaps," whose rural charms he had
admired back in 1837. Along with these projected journeys there is a
running mention of failing health. To Joseph Henry: "My health has
got unsteady from deprivation of fresh air and confinement to my chair."
To Emerson: "My chest is in an unsound condition someway."

It is the letters to Concord that return most frequently to the refrain
of the advantages of country living. On May 11, after getting Emerson's
cool non-invitation to come and visit, James dropped some strategic
hints in a revealing postscript: "I have advertised my house for sale—
with a view either to go to France & Germany for a few years, or to
pitch my tent in the country. I know not what is best for me to do. If
your wisdom could resolve me do write us." Emerson's antennae were
too fine not to detect the unspoken plea: invite me, *now*, to live near
you in Concord. Alcott, of whom James was jealous, had already been
asked to do so, and Thoreau had grown up in the village.

It took two months for Emerson to answer this, and when he did, he
once again blew hot and cold at the same time. "I hear of your plans of
travelling with a kind of selfish alarm, as we do of the engagement of
beautiful women . . . We talked along so comfortably together, and the
madness (is it?) you find in my logic made such good antagonism, that
New York looked greatly nearer & warmer to me for your inhabitation."
But the warmth had better not get too near. Ignoring James's debate
between Europe and "the country," Emerson coolly spoke of the former
possibility as the only one under consideration: "Well, if you go to
Europe, I shall rejoice in the opening of opportunities so rich & stimulating." Tacitly refusing to "resolve" James, he merely asked to be
informed of his final decision. Not one word was said about visiting
Massachusetts. It was a masterly brush-off.

In advertising his house, James made it clear that the $10,000 mortgage
was assumable. Even so, it was not till October 3 that he was able to
announce—to Emerson—that he was preparing to move out. Six days

later the purchase agreement was signed by George Curtis, who had been renting a house on the same street and presumably liked the neighborhood. From the terms of the conveyance, it appears that James was in a hurry to unload. He had given $8,000 in cash for the property. He got $5,000. Usually it took about a month for the Commissioner of Deeds to record a purchase. This one was recorded the very next day, October 10. "From the desperate city you go into the desperate country," Thoreau would write soon afterward in *Walden*.

The Jameses now moved back into the Astor House, spending a week there, and then they embarked for Liverpool on the *Great Western*. A newspaper passenger list reveals that the entourage consisted of "Henry James, lady, two children and servant, Albany." Albany is a surprise. Did James plan to move back now that he had gotten rid of his New York house? Or did he still identify himself with the city of his birth? Mary's sister, Catharine, a native New Yorker, shows up elsewhere on the list. She, too, is said to be from Albany—an indication of the closeness of her attachment to her sister's home. Also on board was Henry Sr.'s nephew Robert W. James, who had sailed with him in 1838, and the Honorable J. J. Roosevelt, Gus's children's counsel in the donnybrook over Billy James's will.

One of James's last acts in New York before embarking on his third transatlantic passage was to send a parting letter to Emerson. In dating this document, James originally wrote 1833, going back, perhaps, to the moment ten years earlier when he gave up the legal profession and fled Albany for Canandaigua. Once again, he was fleeing for his life. His plans, he confessed, were up in the air. He didn't know where he would go or what would happen next. He had no idea whether his work in progress on the divine genesis of morality would prove "eminently vivifying" or "very slim," though he was thinking of having it printed in England. "One's destiny puts on many garments as it goes on shaping itself in secret," wrote James, reworking the same image he had used before; "let me not cling to any particular fashion." As if he had also determined not to cling to Emerson, he was businesslike and informative and said very little about his intense feelings for the man. They broke through only twice, once in the middle when à propos of nothing he abruptly apostrophized Emerson as "you man without a handle," and again at the end, where James wrote and then underlined the simplest and most powerful expression of longing that language permits: "Farewell then my dear friend—many things spring up to my lips to say besides, but they are only variations of the tune *I love you*."

James was still searching for the man who could be his neighbor, teacher, inspirer, confessor, father, and older half brother. His passionate *I love you* (with a reference to his lips) recalls his complaint about the difficulty of drinking from a handleless man. Looking at the imagery alone, one is tempted to say that James wanted to find his friend's withheld handle and drink till his thirst was satisfied. A better way to put it would be to say that what he wanted most of all was to be Emerson's closest and dearest friend, and that he knew his application was rejected.

Now that James was definitely on the point of leaving the country, it was safe for Emerson to warble a very different tune from what he'd been singing:

> But truly it is a great disappointment to lose you now, when by the tenour of your last letter, I was just assuring myself that you would come into Massachusetts & reside for a time, & perhaps in due time we should make a neighbour & a brother of you. A month ago I wrote you a long letter, which I withheld on reading it over, as I fancied my argument more pleasant than wise . . . But I quickly remembered that however keen is my own relish for friendly & cultivated society, I am yet so moody & capricious in my appetites, that I have no right to be forward in agitating the slightest plan of concert or arrangement never so simple, & should hardly dare to ask my own brother to unite with me to live here or there, lest, on the first day of meeting, I should wish to renew the dialogue of Abraham & Lot . . . Indeed all my momentary inclination to entertain the matter as a practical question, arose from my love of the dear & noble persons who had put it in my mind, & there & now we will leave it.

In Chapter 13 of Genesis the brothers Abraham and Lot come into conflict and agree to live apart from one another. Emerson's superbly nuanced letter was as candid and kindly as circumstances permitted. He *had* written the precious letter James had been angling for—had invited the "dear & noble" New Yorkers to think of moving to Concord, for health and friendship, but had then prudently realized that his own peace of mind would be destroyed. It would not do to live next door to this commanding and maniacal Calvinist. He was too thirsty, probing, insistent, reckless, and sensual. He would have shattered Emerson's village calm and ability to write. So the letter was destroyed, and the writer blamed his change of mind on his own "capricious" (goatlike) appetites. He also cut short any further discussion of the matter: "There & now we will leave it."

It took thirteen days for the *Great Western* to reach Liverpool, bulling its way through fresh gales from the northeast, "with heavy squalls." James didn't answer Emerson's letter, and a year later, when he returned

to America, he *still* wouldn't write, even though the long-delayed invitation had at last arrived. "I have written in vain to James to visit me,
or to send me tidings," Emerson complained to Carlyle on the last day
of 1844; "he sent me, without any note, the parcel you confided to him,
& has gone to Albany, or I know not whither."

Apparently it was not until 1847 that the friendship was patched up.
A lot of time had to pass before James could accept the hypocrisy of the
man who had called up such complex ardors in him.

THE ONLY STYLE OF MAN

It was 1872, and a brilliant crowd of Boston's older literary folk had
gathered in Annie and James T. Fields's home in Boston. The reader
for the evening was Henry James, a white-bearded old man now. His
announced topic was "Emerson." He thanked his hostess for the kind
opportunity she had given him to speak and then declared that the events
he was about to recall had taken place "full thirty years ago," when he
had been "domesticated" in New York and Emerson had first gone there
to read his lectures.

> These I diligently attended, and I saw much of him in private also. He
> at once took my imagination captive, and I have been ever since his loving
> bondman [i.e., slave]. I tried assiduously during the earlier years of our
> intimacy to penetrate the mystery of his immense fascination. But I never
> succeeded.

Emerson's attraction did not derive from his ideas, of which the speaker
was quite dismissive, and personally, the man was far too austere to have
any conventional charms. It was something else. The speaker had often
found himself thinking, "If this man were a woman, I should be sure to
fall in love with him." In his platform manner "no maiden ever appealed
more potently to your enamoured and admiring sympathy." He was entirely different from "the only style of man I had ever been bred to
recognize, namely: the masculine, moral, voluntary style . . . My intellect
. . . drove me insanely to attempt realizing it in myself although the
attempt was incessantly baffled, when at last my growing affection for
Emerson led me to suspect that the point of view of my intellect was
hopelessly wrong."

"We are born things, and we become persons," the speaker declared.
In the first chapter of Genesis Adam was created out of nothing, but in

the second chapter he is made from the dust. A thing is created from nothing, but a person is made or makes himself from a thing, and this person-making process is divine, ongoing, tortuous, agonizing. Emerson, the speaker declared, would seem to be unique, the only man ever to be born a person.

The elderly speaker wanted the listeners assembled in the Fieldses' parlors to understand that, until he heard Emerson, he himself had been no more than the usual thing.

Chapter 15

■ ■ ■

VASTATION: 1843–44

Midway through James's European retreat, he experienced a mysterious psychic collapse, and as he slowly recovered from it over the next two years, he came to see himself and the world with altered eyes.

Not only is there no contemporary record of this event but fifteen years passed before James made his first oblique reference to it in print:

> Occasionally the machinery gets a hitch, and the naked soul, in place of swimming in a summer sea of self-complacency, finds itself stranded upon the rocks of self-abhorrence, or what is the same thing, finds its sense of merit really yielding to that of demerit: and instantly the very fountains of life are dried up, the intellect withers upon its usurped throne, and we become puling idiots or frantic madmen.

Twenty more years passed before James finally brought out a circumstantial narrative of his breakdown, in *Society the Redeemed Form of Man*, published three years before his death:

> One day . . . towards the close of May [1844], having eaten a comfortable dinner, I remained sitting at the table after the family had dispersed, idly gazing at the embers in the grate, thinking of nothing, and feeling only the exhilaration incident to a good digestion, when suddenly—in a lightning-flash as it were—"fear came upon me, and trembling, which made all my bones to shake." To all appearance it was a perfectly insane and abject terror, without ostensible cause, and only to be accounted for, to my perplexed imagination, by some damnèd shape squatting invisible to me within the precincts of the room, and raying out from his fetid

personality influences fatal to life. The thing had not lasted ten seconds before I felt myself a wreck.

This dramatic account was given featured treatment in the posthumous selection of his writings and has sometimes been regarded as a kind of master key to James's inner life.

There is no doubt that James went to pieces in some way and that this collapse had a pivotal influence on his development. But what exactly happened? Howard M. Feinstein has argued that the thirty-five-year after-the-fact account is unreliable, and although Henry Jr. professed to admire these "strongest pages," he too had his doubts and wished he "might have caught [his father] sooner or younger." The trouble with Henry Sr.'s story is that if it is one part history it is five parts cure—not so much a reliable narrative of the breakdown as a strategy for coming to terms with his fundamental problems and the recurring crises they precipitated. We should be as skeptical of his claim that he originally pictured a filthy squatting devil as we are of the interpretation he eventually settled on—that the breakdown was a signal revelation of what all humans must go through in the course of their development. Each of these explanations reflected James's inability to see his sudden distress as *his own*—as an outcropping of his particular history and character. The fact that the thing seemed to him to come out of nowhere hints at the limits of his self-understanding.

Fortunately, it is possible to catch a glimpse of James's inner state preceding his collapse. His social life in London, his restless pursuit of a quiet country retreat, the disturbed letter he sent his mother shortly before his breakdown, and a revealing private confession he sent a good friend in 1859 ("this strictly between ourselves") all suggest a rather different, more individual, more connected story from the one James told.

Steaming away from Emerson across the Atlantic Ocean and then abandoning one promising European residence after another in rapid succession, James was on a collision course with himself. He thought the wreck took place without warning. The detached observer sees it coming a mile away.

SHY AND SKITTISH,
BUT A BRAVE HEART INTRINSICALLY

In 1838, when James undertook a long transatlantic trip in order to have a talk with the physicist Michael Faraday, the interview did not seem to lead anywhere. Now, however, thanks to Emerson, the traveler carried letters of presentation to John Sterling and Thomas Carlyle that proved much more fruitful.

Sterling was a poet and essayist with whom Emerson had been corresponding for the last three years. The letter Emerson gave James described him as one who was "proposing with his family to spend a winter in England, for health & travel, [and] thinks he has a right to see you. He is at once so manly, so intelligent, & so ardent, that I have found him excellent company."

The manliness was not much in evidence when James asked Emerson for a similar passport to Carlyle:

> I didnt mean to ask for a letter to Carlyle, not knowing whether he liked visitors, and feeling besides a visit would be scarcely anything but a stare on my part—but [William Henry] Channing tells me I needn't fear to ask and I accordingly do? If you have any the least scruple whether with reference to him or me, follow it I beseech you without any fear of my misunderstanding it.

The humble question mark, quite out of place, testifies to the writer's loss of nerve. Already thrown off balance by the impenetrability of the Sage of Concord, he now contemplated the more fearsome prospect of bearding the surly British lion. As it happened, Emerson gave James solid backing—"He is a fine companion from his intelligence valour & worth." But how would Carlyle jump? Channing's encouragement notwithstanding, the British writer did not take kindly to most of the Americans who dropped in on him. He considered them fanciful and unreal and was particularly derisive of those who were always shoving "Progress-of-the-Species" literature in his direction. The most otiose fool of all in his eyes was Bronson Alcott—who had also come with Emerson's recommendation.

When the *Great Western* reached Liverpool on November 1, James and his entourage traveled down to London, where he promptly made use of one of his letters. Sunday was the day Carlyle and his wife, Jane, received visitors at their house in Cheyne Row, Chelsea. James went and then went again, and on November 17 Carlyle sent his seal of approval across the ocean to Emerson: "James is a very good fellow, better and better as we see him more— Something shy and skittish in the man; but a brave heart intrinsically, with sound earnest sense, with plenty of insight and even humour. He confirms an observation of mine . . . that a stammering man is never a worthless one." Carlyle interpreted James's hesitancy and lack of confidence as an expression of "excess of delicacy, excess of sensibility to the presence of his fellow creature." One wonders just how unsure of himself James was.

For his part, James did not care for Carlyle's open anti-liberalism, but he still relished the Scotsman's contempt for sentimental reformers and intellectual pretenders. The American visitor took careful notes of his host's diatribes and quoted them decades later in what turned out to be his most successful lecture, one he delivered again and again and eventually brought out as an essay, "Some Personal Recollections of Carlyle." One day when he happened to be in Carlyle's library, James recounted, a parcel arrived from an admirer—*Twelve Lectures on the Natural History of Man* by Alexander Kinmont of Cincinnati. Carlyle said:

> The natural history of man, forsooth! And from Cincinnati too, of all places on this earth! We had a right, perhaps, to expect some light from that quarter in regard to the natural history of the hog; and I can't but think that if the well-disposed Mr. Kinmont would set himself to study that unperverted mystery he would employ his powers far more profitably to the world.

This humorously expressive voice, however jaundiced, appealed tremendously to James, who put the anecdote in circulation even though he probably knew its victim was not a product of frontier Cincinnati. Kinmont (like Carlyle) had come from a strict Presbyterian home in Scotland and been given a university education there. He became an early Swedenborgian, emigrated, and in later years his daughter corresponded with James.

James thought Carlyle was best explained as a descendant of "old Covenanting stock" who remained true to his ancestry even as he rejected orthodox Christianity. It was because the Scotsman still had a grim, vestigial faith in the cruel Calvinist deity that he felt such contempt for those who "believed in God's undiminished presence and power in human affairs, and were therefore full of hope in our social future." James was also full of this hope, but curiously, his recollections of Carlyle do not so much as hint that the Scotsman ever turned his famous contempt on *him*. According to James, the two reconstructed Calvinists got on beau-

This advertisement by William James of
Albany ran for several months in the Albany
Argus in 1818

1822 portrait of William James of
Albany by Ezra Ames, the date
appearing on the letter
(*Schaffer Library, Union College*)

125.   *William James*

Page from the account book of Dr. John James (no relation), who assisted with
Henry James, Sr.'s amputation in 1828 (*New York State Library*)

Miniature oil painting of
Henry James, Sr., late
1820s? (*Houghton Library,
Harvard University*)

The Reverend William James
(1797-1868), James's older
half brother. "God is near you,
my brother, and He will ever
be drawing nearer, nearer,
nearer" (*Houghton Library,
Harvard University*)

The Reverend Archibald
Alexander, remembered for his
"inimitable naturalness, freedom,
and cordiality." Portrait by John
Neagle, 1845 (*Princeton
Theological Seminary*)

The Reverend Charles Hodge.
"I am not afraid to say that a
new idea never originated in
this Seminary." Portrait by
Daniel Huntington, 1846
(*Princeton Theological Seminary*)

1860s photograph of Frogmore Cottage, Windsor, England, which the Jameses rented in the spring of 1844 (*The Royal Archives*)

Campagne Gerebsoff (or Gerebzow), Geneva. The Jameses rented the second floor in the fall of 1855 (*Centre d'iconographie genevoise*)

Henry James, Sr. and Jr., by
Mathew Brady's studio,
1854 (*Houghton Library,
Harvard University*)

Sarah (Sturgis) Shaw and her son, Robert Gould Shaw. Probably taken
in the latter 1840s, when the Jameses and the Shaws became acquainted
(*Staten Island Institute of Arts and Sciences*)

and this distinction is carefully observed in other places by the prophets, as where it is said in Jeremiah: "Again I will *build* thee, and thou shalt be *built*, O virgin of Israel" (xxxi. 4).

154. Nothing evil and false can possibly exist which is not of man's *proprium*, and thence derived; for the *proprium* of man is evil itself, and thus man is nothing but evil and falsity. This was demonstrated to me by the fact, that when the *proprium* of man is presented to view in the world of spirits, it appears so deformed that it is impossible to depict any thing more ugly (although with a difference according to the peculiarities of each individual), so that he to whom the things of his *proprium* are visibly exhibited, is struck with horror, and wishes to flee from himself as from a devil. When, however, the *proprium* of man is vivified by the Lord, it assumes a beautiful and graceful form, varying according to the nature of its life, to which the celestial principle of the Lord can be adjoined. Thus, such as have been endowed with, or vivified by, charity, appear like boys and girls with the most beautiful countenances; and those who have been endowed with, or vivified by, innocence, appear like naked infants, variously adorned with garlands of flowers encircling their bosoms, and diadems upon their heads, living and sporting in an adamantine aura, and having the most interior perception of felicity.

155. These words, that a rib was built into a woman, include more arcana than it is possible for any one ever to discover from the letter; for the Word of the Lord is so constituted, that its inmost contents regard the Lord himself and his kingdom, whence the whole Word receives life. The passage before us likewise, when viewed interiorly, refers to celestial marriage. This celestial marriage exists in the *proprium*, which, when vivified by the Lord, is called both the bride and the wife of the Lord. Such a *proprium* has a perception of all the good of love and the truth of faith, and consequently possesses all wisdom and intelligence conjoined with inexpressible felicity. The nature, however, of the vivified *proprium*, thus called the bride and wife of the Lord, cannot be readily explained; suffice it therefore to observe, that the angels perceive that they live from the Lord, although, when not reflecting on the subject, they know no other but that they live of themselves. They are all influenced by an affection of such a nature, that in the least departure from the good of love, and the truth of faith, they perceive a change; and consequently they are in the enjoy-

K 2

A page from Henry James, Sr.'s copy of Emanuel Swedenborg's *Arcana Coelestia*, Volume 1 (*Swedenborg School of Religion*)

William Henry Channing, Transcendental social activist and one of James's severest critics. From Frothingham's *Memoir of William Henry Channing* (Boston, 1886)

Samuel Irenaeus Prime, editor of the Presbyterian *New-York Observer*. "His voice was a menace and his attitude martial at once. Hands off! he cried." From *Irenaeus Letters, Second Series* (New York, 1885)

John James Garth Wilkinson, the London Swedenborgian who had an extended correspondence with James. "The knowing you so much better in heart & mind than in body, made me feel that I had a stone wall to get through, before I could get at you" (*Houghton Library, Harvard University*)

Henry James, Sr.
(*Schaffer Library,*
Union College)

Henry James, Sr.
(*Houghton Library,*
Harvard University)

tifully in spite of all their differences. Several years later, when Carlyle dropped in on a mutual friend, he had "very kind recollections" of James. But he remembered James's "Metaphysics also, & asked with terrible solicitude whether they yet persevered." James may have been one more half-crazed American system builder, but Carlyle liked him anyway.

Jane Carlyle was more acerbic about her husband's new acquaintance. At the end of the same month in which James first appeared, she complained that "these Yankees form a considerable item in the ennuis of our mortal life. I counted lately *fourteen* of them in one fortnight!" On the first Sunday of January the Jameses and some other Americans came calling. Afterward Jane regaled a cousin with their absurdities:

> There was such a drawling and *Sir*-ing!—I would have given a crown that you had been there for "it was *strange* upon *my* honour"! There was a Mr James with a wife and wifes-sister. "Not a *bad* man" (as C[arlyle] would say) "nor altogether a fool,"—but he has only one leg . . . Now a man may be as agreeable with one leg or three legs as with *two* but he needs to take certain precautions— The onelegged man, is bound in mercy to . . . use some sort of *stick* instead of trusting to Providence as this Mr James does . . . One awaits in horror to see him rush down amongst the tea-cups, or walk out thro the window-glass, or pitch himself headforemost into the grate! from which and the like imminent dangers he is only preserved by a continual miracle!

Jane Carlyle's cutting description of the "wife and wifes-sister" suggests why few memoirists had much to say about Mary James or Catharine Walsh: "Of his two women what could anybody say?—unless that they giggled incessantly, and wore *black* stockings with lightcoloured dresses." Looking at Henry, Mary, and Catharine through Jane Carlyle's cruel eyes, one sees an obnoxious cripple followed by two identical dowdies nervously aware of being out of their depth.

Having the entrée at Cheyne Row made it possible for James to meet other members of the British intelligentsia. He'd been in London little more than a week before he got Carlyle to present him to John A. Heraud as "Mr. James of New York, who wishes to see you as a genial reader does a genial author." Heraud, an avid follower of Swedenborg and the latest trends in philosophy, had until recently been in charge of the London *Monthly Magazine*. Thanks to him (according to Emerson in *The Dial*), this journal had been conducted in a "bolder and more creative" way than any rival British periodical.

The year before James died he talked to a Boston reporter about the

famous people he'd known through Carlyle. Without distinguishing between his visits of 1843–44 and 1855–56, James recalled having met
Frederick Denison Maurice, George Henry Lewes, Alfred Tennyson,
James Spedding, Baldwin Brown, and others. The old man was very
severe on these men for not being serious enough: "Life to them began
and ended in conversation, not in action. They never thought that
Christ's spiritual life among men was of any consequence. They were
cynical . . . Their talk was depraving to the last degree." There were
two exceptions to this sweeping condemnation—John Stuart Mill, who
by 1843 was no longer on close terms with Carlyle, and John Sterling.
The latter, also of Scots background, was dying of tuberculosis without
the solace of Christian faith. When James urged him to read Swedenborg's
writings, with their visionary reports of spirit transactions, Sterling flatly
refused to "allow any man . . . to bias my mind in regard to what I am
to see in the other world." James looked back on this independent thinker
as the "truest man" he had ever known, seeing him as much more
American than the usual Briton. Also, there was "a great deal of the
woman in him, a lovely person."

James met Sterling not in London* but in Ventnor on the Isle of
Wight. Formerly a fishermen's hamlet, this "small new stone-built town,"
as Sterling described it, with a climate touted as "almost Italian," had
recently become a resort for those with pulmonary complaints. The
consumptive poet was settled there for the winter. Anxious about his
own lungs and hoping to find pleasant and healthful accommodations
away from smoky London, James took his family down to Ventnor a
couple of weeks after first arriving in Britain. He knew of the charms of
the Isle of Wight from his first visit in 1837, and having Sterling close
at hand made the place that much more inviting. "Did you see an
American of the name of James, who went towards you?" Carlyle wrote
his friend, vouching for the visitor as "an estimable man, full of sense
and honest manfulness, when you get acquainted with him."

But Ventnor proved unsuitable for the estimable American, as Sterling
informed Carlyle on December 7:

> Mr. James, your New-England friend, was here only for a few days; I saw
> him several times, and liked him. They went, on the 24th of last month,
> back to London,—or so purposed,—because there is no pavement here
> for him to walk on. I want to know where he is, and thought I should be

---

* In his memoirs Henry Jr. thought his father may have been present with Sterling, Carlyle, and
Theodore Parker at a certain sepulchral dinner in Knightsbridge. In fact, Henry Sr. was absent,
the fourth American being Le Baron Russell.

able to learn from you. I gave him a note for Mill, who perhaps may have seen him.

Sterling wrote Emerson that "your friend James pleased me well. Would that he could have stayed here longer and let me know more of him!" Was James reluctant to get involved with a man about to die? He did not inform Emerson of Sterling's desperate condition, and when the dying man finally broke the news himself, vividly describing a "thick crimson" hemorrhage, Emerson got a bad shock. Sterling died the following September. The letters he'd had from Emerson were sent to Carlyle, who turned them over to James to carry back across the Atlantic. This was the parcel the repatriated traveler mailed to Concord without so much as an accompanying note.

It may have been Sterling's note to Mill that put James in touch with the philosopher. The two do not seem to have got on as well as James and Carlyle did. James could not appreciate Mill's keen powers of discernment and inference or sympathize fully with his principled liberalism. Two decades later James patronizingly hoped that Mill's "somewhat narrow systematic head will one day or other encounter the necessary enlargement." What he chiefly valued in On Liberty was the sense of an "upright human heart," particularly in the dedicatory homage to the author's late wife. James's final, rather stingy judgment was that Mill was "the most sincere man I ever met."

PRECISELY SUITABLE LODGINGS

The Isle of Wight having been ruled out, James resigned himself to wintering in London. He seems to have found lodgings on the south side of fashionable Mayfair, apparently in a house on Piccadilly. (The family may have lived on nearby Clarges Street and Half Moon Street as well.) Across Piccadilly was Green Park, with Buckingham Palace on the farther side. Sometimes, as James stared at the park's grazing sheep, he envied their stressless existence. If he followed his usual pattern, he spent a great deal of time at his desk. But the desk sent him out to London's bookshops, and Wilkinson vividly remembered the "bibliomanical propensity" that drove his American friend into "musty shops in queer places; maugre dear M.rs James's astonishment at your accumulations."

In this revealing vignette, Mary is a reluctant sharer of her husband's bookish pursuits. She was happier when the two of them drove through the suburbs in a pony chaise they bought or leased, perhaps to get some fresh air on doctor's orders. In later years she loved to recall a particular ride "one early spring morning through Hampstead." As young Henry Jr. listened in New York to his parents' and aunt's reminiscences of London, he got the impression that those months had been a "happy time." But the only detail he captured in his memoirs was the nursemaid's, Fanny's, sniffing remark on the massively colonnaded and endowed British Museum, which, for anyone privileged to know the Albany Institute of History and Art, rather "fell short." Fanny, at least, did not like being dragged to London.

Happy or not, the Jameses uprooted themselves well before the advent of good weather. As spring came on, Henry took his family to France, thus putting into action one of the plans he had ruminated the previous summer. The Channel was so rough that everyone got sick, and Willy "screamed incessantly to have 'the hair taken out of his mouth.' " It is significant that this, the first surviving family anecdote about William, makes him out to be both sick and demanding. He was a more troublesome child than Henry Jr., and he got much more attention from his father.

By now some members of the James clan had spent a good deal of time on the Continent, learning how to command its comfortable amenities and display suitably elevated tastes. Henry's nephew Robert W. James, often in Europe, had acted in 1841 as secretary to the American minister to The Hague, Harmanus Bleecker. ("I miss Mr. James very much," Bleecker wrote on Robert's departure, "and live in great solitude.") That was the year Gus and his family steamed up the Rhine to Switzerland. Edward, wintering in Paris, sent Bleecker a polite letter that evokes the retiring habits of the American "colony": "Mrs Van Rensselaer and the young ladies are here and living very quietly of course." In the spring of 1844, Robert, who was especially fond of Europe, may have been back in Paris. But for Henry and Mary James, Paris was a disaster and they did not stay long. Unfortunately, their detailed report of this visit was sent to an in-law (Smith Van Buren) and cannot be found. Henry's letter to his mother makes it sound as if this second trip to France, like his first, was best forgotten: "Smiths letter by this packet will inform you sufficiently of our Parisian experience." William was on the mend now, but the "wretched Paris excursion broke him up a little."

Recrossing the Channel on April 24, the Jameses were "delighted enough to get back again to tidy old England." They traveled as far west as Clifton, near Bristol, whose Hot Wells had been made famous by Smollett's *Humphry Clinker* and Burney's *Evelina*; Sterling had resided there for a few years. But the resort had deteriorated, and anyway, the

Jameses could not find "precisely suitable lodgings . . . except in the town." They pushed on to Windsor, dominated by the young Queen's massive castle and full of uniformed schoolboys from Eton College, and there James at last found the kind of shelter he had been looking for, comfortable and with plenty of rooms and in the country. Called Frogmore Cottage, it belonged to the residence of the Duchess of Kent, who lived nearby. It was on a public road that ran between two royal domains, the Great Park and the Little Park (today the Home Park). Adelaide Lodge, a cottage belonging to the Queen Dowager, was nearby, as was the Queen's poultry house. For the second time, James had landed close to Victoria, whom he pictured "looking down from her castle windows upon our modest residence." A few years after his brief stay at Frogmore Cottage, the road in front of the house was closed in order to give the royal family more privacy. The road is still off limits to the public, as is the house—still standing—in which James finally collapsed.

Judging from a photograph probably taken in the 1860s, Frogmore Cottage may have struck James as an ideally bucolic country retreat. Certainly the letter he wrote his mother on May 1 stressed its perfect suitability. The front yard, separated from the road by a "luxuriant hedge," was filled with flowers, trees, and a fruit garden. The first floor had a hall and dining room, a study, a kitchen, and servants' quarters. There was a drawing room on the second floor along with four more bedrooms. Of course, the family needed a great deal of space. Aunt Kate had to have her own room, and Henry required a study in which to revise his New York lectures and demonstrate the supernatural origins of the moral life.

Anxious to convince Ma that he was not living extravagantly, Henry added up his rent and cook's wages and everything else and claimed he was spending about $36 a week. Then, consulting Mary, he revised this upward to $40. Still, he boasted, he was getting by on a good deal less than his brothers and brothers-in-law, "John & Temple and Gus and Smith." Edward was no doubt spending less, as he lived at home with Ma, and Rev. William presumably had "some principle in the expenditure of his money. But clearly all the rest should blush." He jokingly proposed that Gideon Hawley, the estate lawyer who guarded the family's money and dispensed the checks, be informed of Henry's uncharacteristic economies.

It is doubtful that the lawyer would have smiled at Henry's sally. Hawley was not only a self-respecting member "of the much abused class generally called . . . conservatives" but a would-be philosopher who devoted his free hours to a long and deadly treatise on truth and knowledge. When ideas or notions are true, he explained, they "constitute knowledge." When they are not true, they are "mere mental illusions of no value in the practical affairs of life . . . It is truth, and that only, which gives value to our ideas or notions; *with that* they have gravity and substance, *without* it they are mere vacuities . . . and fictions." Privately distributed, Hawley's book set forth a view of truth utterly opposed to the pragmatic approach worked out decades later by William James—that a belief's truth depends on its practical moral consequences for the believer. If William's view of truth can be seen as a defense of the value of his and his father's vacuities and fictions, Hawley's view can be seen as a steely reproof of the undisciplined and much too wealthy family whose bank accounts he had to balance.

Could it be that the James family treasure keeper tried to throttle pragmatism before it got out of its cradle? How it would have shocked Hawley to discover that the idea of truth and knowledge worked out by those coddled spendthrifts would get into the mainstream of American thought!

A GREAT GHASTLY LIE

Ensconced in his safe rural paradise (which came provided with a gigantic rattle in case thieves tried to break in), James got to work on the great essay. Thirty-five years later, he remembered having made good progress during these weeks. He had an ideal workplace, one that combined the spaciousness of the old home on North Pearl Street with the rural freedom of his father's old farm at Albany's city limits. The agreeable month of May stretched before him, and everything conspired (as he wrote his mother) to give "further promise of a 'glorious summer' to this son of New York." He was playing with Richard III's well-known opening line in Shakespeare's play and identifying himself with royalty once again. He also liked to play with little William, who was "full of fun" and old enough to call his parents by their first names, "Henwy and Mawy." Little Harry was teething, but he still gave no trouble (he never did), being "good as the day is long, and the night on top of it." The father seemed to be settling in with his family. His children weren't preaching to him now.

Then, as James neared the end of his last page of his letter to his mother, he made an abrupt confession: the fact was, his mind was elsewhere and he had a compelling desire to flee his lovely paradise:

I confess to some potent pullings now and then dear Ma in your
direction—"nursery" remembrances, and "little back-room" remembrances come over me not infrequently which make Windsor Castle seem
a great ghastly lie, and its parks an endless sickness not to be endured a
moment longer. But these are only *feelings*, which do not commend themselves to my judgment in sober moments, and *they* therefore will not decide
the question of our return.

Comfortable, relaxed, and enjoying his family, James was caught up,
seemingly for no reason, in memories of home life in distant Albany.
This sudden return of the past was something to "confess," it seemed
entirely irrational, it went on in spite of his own preferences, and it
aroused real homesickness, fear of open space, and dread—all of which
he was determined to stifle, since they were "only *feelings*." Everything
was so perfect, and then there was this terrifying flip-flop.

A revealing feature of Henry's involuntary remembrances was their
very specific locations—the nursery and little back room in the old James
house. The nursery was clearly the children's quarter, consigned to
Henry, his younger siblings, and the Gourlays, and then to a variety of
family orphans—Kings, Van Burens, Temples. In 1920 one of Henry's
orphaned nieces, Katharine Van Buren Wilson, fondly recalled "the dear
old nursery in the James Homestead in North Pearl Street," where she
had been brought up (and where three older cousins from New York,
William, Henry Jr., and Wilkie, used to "sing old songs"). The nursery
must have been on the second or third floor. The little back room, on
the other hand, would have been at the far east end of the west-fronting
house and a few steps down from the first floor—as far from North Pearl
Street as one could get. In 1920, when the house had been turned into
a dry-goods store owned by the John G. Myers Company, one could still
find "in the store way back . . . two or three little steps remaining which
used to lead down to the 'old library.' "

This old library, or little back room, had probably been the scene of
Henry's interminable convalescence from his burn and botched amputation. A boy with incipient gangrene or an unhealed stump could not
be kept with the other children, and on warm afternoons the low, east
room would have been cooler than any other part of the house. The
room must have made a very comfortable library—the perfect place for
a teenage invalid who concentrated on his studies and his future as a
way of not thinking about a leg that refused to heal.

If James's two small boys caused him to revert to the little back room,
the configuration of Frogmore Cottage reinforced this effect. The house's

low first floor was at ground level, easily communicating with the outside. There were no intervening steps—always a problem for a one-legged person who refused to use a cane. A man writing an abstruse essay in his first-floor study would be frequently reminded that this was the month of May, and that the garden's fruit trees and flowers were in bloom, and that he could go outside at will. For part of 1824 and all of 1825, 1826, and 1827, and the first part of 1828, Henry (one guesses) had not been able to go into the back yard at will, in spite of its propinquity.

James's persistent search for exactly the right place had brought him to a house that evoked his early torment—brought him there in the same season, the same month, and the same time of the month as his amputation. May 6, 1828, had been the day the doctors cut off the sixteen-year-old boy's leg, and with it his glorious summer. Exactly sixteen years later, hoping to regain his shaky health as another summer came on, this son of New York opened his eyes on an insidiously familiar place and time. Had his restless movements in England and France returned him to the scene of his dismemberment? Was there a piece of unfinished business to be transacted, one that required him to be in a particular place at a particular time? James had no idea why the suppressed terrors of his adolescence were starting to resurface, the same old sickening breezes blowing up from hell. All he knew was that he would have to stifle them once again, or they would undo him.

But these feelings expressed themselves in the very sentences in which James proclaimed his determination to suppress them. Like his sleepwalking mother, who would "come to my bedside fast asleep with her candle in her hand, and go through the forms of covering my shoulders, adjusting my pillows, and so forth, just as carefully as if she were awake," James now performed a kind of sleepwriting. "An endless sickness not to be endured a moment longer"—the phrase supposedly describes his impatience with the Queen's beautiful parklands stretching out on both sides of Frogmore Cottage. What the phrase actually describes is Henry's old panicky impatience with his interminable suffering and confinement. How provoking when the pen does not obey the will of him who sits behind it!

According to James's account in *Society the Redeemed Form of Man*, when the collapse took place he pictured "some damnèd shape squatting invisible to me within the precincts of the room, and raying out from his fetid personality influences fatal to life." But the fetor did not emanate from a stinking devil. The source was Henry's damned stinking leg. In a sense, Henry had come to Frogmore Cottage to dig up that crooked, rotten leg.

Some damnèd shape. James does not *say* it is a devil. And the book in which the phrase is found bears a title signifying the opposite of damned—"redeemed form." The leg rots, the leg is severed and cast away, and the leg is restored.

But it was not precisely the physical aspects of his boyhood ordeal that commanded James's attention. Instead, he seems to have returned to his original psychological *reaction* to trauma—an extreme sense of guilt, a feeling that an unsleeping eye was gazing down at him. He also lapsed into the same devotional rigidity that had led him in 1835 or soon after to pray—pray—pray up to the gates of death. Once again, James's abiding temptation, a constant and suicidally exacting abeyance toward the Almighty, was upon him.

In *Substance and Shadow*, published in 1863, James recalled the fanatical zeal that preceded his breakdown:

> I . . . sought to attract [God's] approbation to me, by the unswerving pursuit of moral excellence, by studiously cultivating every method of personal purity. It was all in vain. The more I strove to indue myself in actual righteousness, the wider gaped the jaws of hell within me; the fouler grew its fetid breath. A conviction of inward defilement so sheer took possession of me, that death seemed better than life. I soon found my conscience, once launched in this insane career, acquiring so infernal an edge, that I could no longer . . . bestow a sulky glance upon my wife, a cross word upon my child, or a petulant objurgation on my cook—without tumbling into an instant inward frenzy of alarm.

James tended to conflate events from different times, and it may well be that this passage refers to his state of mind in New York as well as at Windsor. But it was in the latter place that the sense of exacting duty rose to an excruciating climax.

A private letter written fifteen years later reveals just how unhinged James was. Hoping to console Sarah Shaw, a good friend whose anxious love for her children had brought morbid thoughts to the surface, he recalled his own morbidity as a young parent:

> How perfectly I recall your state of mind! It was years ago however . . . I *did* say in my inmost heart to God incessantly, what you declare you *could* say, "take these dear children away before they know the evil of sin." That dreadful mystery of sin haunted me night and day. I have been on my knees from morning till night (this strictly between ourselves) sometimes determined as it were not to let God go, till he gave me some relief.

Although James did not identify the exact period in which he was haunted by this "inmost" prayer, he was probably harking back to his year abroad in 1843–44. It was then that he showed a new interest in his boys, revisited his own childhood, and went to pieces. His freshly renewed back-room remembrances had instilled in him the appalling conviction that his own innocent children, Willy and Harry, would be drawn into the same extremes of guilt and rigidly compensatory goodness that had disfigured his own life. This prospect was so fearful that he beseeched God—"from morning till night"—to take his children before they knew these spiritual agonies. Only if the children were sacrificed could the father find relief.

Significantly, this 1859 letter to Mrs. Shaw also contains James's earliest personal narrative of his breakdown: "What troubled me in my hereditary theology was, *the dishonour it left on the Divine name . . .* My heart revolted before my head was able to see any extrication for it. In this state of conflict, my nerves gave way, and I was obliged to abandon thought." James put all his strength as a thinker into the effort to work out a higher-order Calvinism—to construct the laws of science and revelation, to explain God's necessary "interference" in human history. This crazed intellectual pursuit of the ultimate and rational explanation of things was another form of his quest for personal perfection. He had to rebuild the world for the same reason he had to be perfect. This was what his hard boyhood stoicism had matured into. And even as he tried to reduce God, man, nature, history, and himself to a pure crystal, he found himself revisiting the horrors that had started him on his maniacal intellectual endeavor.

The great transition came as an undoing, a breaking up, a sharp fracture rapidly spreading through James's meticulously constructed and tended inner ice palace. He had to abandon thought, even though thought was what had been holding it and him up. This was the moment he had been afraid of.

I felt the greatest desire to run incontinently to the foot of the stairs and shout for help to my wife . . . but by an immense effort I . . . determined not to budge from my chair till I had recovered my lost self-possession. This purpose I held to for a good long hour, as I reckoned time, beat upon meanwhile by an ever-growing tempest of doubt, anxiety, and despair, with absolutely no relief from any truth I had ever encountered . . . I resolved to abandon the vain struggle, and communicate without more ado what seemed my sudden burden of inmost, implacable unrest to my wife.

The couple's secular rite of union in 1840 had solemnized the man's belief in Sandeman and Walker and the woman's belief in her man. Now the great deeps were broken up, the old foundation passed away, a new marriage covenant came into being. The husband discovered that the simplest tasks—going out for a walk, sleeping in a "strange bed"—took superhuman effort. The wife discovered she must now become her husband's ma.

SOPHIA CHICHESTER'S WORD

On May 13 there was a long letter in *The* (London) *Times* defending a new system of treatment technically known as hydropathy and popularly referred to as the water cure. Among the signers was one Henry C. Wright, an American who was to enjoy a successful career as a health reformer. He and his co-signers wrote from a hospital in Gräfenberg, Silesia, run by the celebrated Vincent Priessnitz. This was the Mecca of the water cure, and the undersigned wished to assure all English readers that they should not allow a recent, well-publicized death to prejudice them against this new mode of treatment. Over one thousand patients had visited Gräfenberg in 1843. Instead of posing a hazard, the "wet towells"—a sort of diaper—could be worn for months. They had proved "highly beneficial."

At the end of May or the beginning of June, James sought medical advice regarding his distressing collapse and was told that he had "doubtless overworked [his] brain." The only remedies were "time, and patience" and a general improvement in his health. The physician who gave this prescription was perhaps sympathetic to homeopathic doctrine and thus opposed to the heavy drugging then in use. In any case, the patient was recommended to try the new water cure then gaining favor.

Eighteen forty-four was the year of publication of *The Hand Book of Hydropathy; for Professional and Domestic Use*, the first "scientific" manual on the subject to appear in English. Its author, Dr. Joseph Weiss, had worked with Priessnitz and then opened his own water-cure establishment in Freiwaldau, Austria (one of his best-known patients being the future Napoleon III). Moving to England, Weiss announced the opening of a new treatment center—"a splendid establishment, which is nearly completed"—the same month as James's breakdown. Located a few miles west of London, in Petersham, on an estate known as Sudbrook Park, this water-cure facility became "the most important place connected with the history of hydropathy in England." Patients were housed in a three-story Georgian mansion, and there were a hundred acres of open and wooded grounds for walking and riding. Today, the mansion and parkland belong to the Richmond Golf Club, patronized by London's theater people. It was here that James went one hundred and fifty years ago to restore his shattered nerves. He must have been assigned a room or suite in what is now the clubhouse, there to lie sleepless on his "strange bed."

The probability is that Mary accompanied her helpless husband to Sudbrook and lived there with him. Did the two boys stay at Frogmore Cottage with Fanny and Aunt Kate, or did the whole entourage make the move? In 1850 Weiss's successor ran an illustrated advertisement on a magazine wrapper that shows a couple of children near some adult loungers in front of the mansion, thus hinting that patients were encouraged to bring their families. It is disappointing that we do not know whether the two James boys—one a future investigator of extreme mental states, the other a lover of English country seats—were in residence or not. Years later Henry Jr. would prick up his ears whenever his parents spoke of the early days in "Windsor and Richmond and Sudbrook and Ham Common," as if these names shadowed forth a story he wished he could piece together. He did not disclose what was said about the last three places, and like his parents, he never identified the water cure. Once he erroneously put it in the "neighbourhood of Windsor." But his arresting cluster of place-names shows that he knew more than he let on.

At the time James became a patient, Weiss and his staff administered the treatment in one of the nearby outbuildings, where the "Plunge Baths" and showers were installed. If the process James was subjected to resembled the usual treatment in American establishments, he was wrapped in wet sheets and cocooned in a feather bed "for twenty-five minutes to several hours." After he had worked up a sweat, he was unwrapped and cold water was "poured over him, or he was plunged into a cold bath, finally being briskly rubbed dry." The magazine advertisement promised that "all diseases curable, and many incurable by any previously known means," could be successfully treated by "the Water Cure ALONE." But James's disease did not seem to respond. He hated "living at this dismal water-cure," and he was repelled by his fellow sufferers as well, with their "endless 'strife of tongues' about diet, and regimen, and disease."

Fortunately, the pleasure grounds were also a part of the treatment, and in addition there was the huge expanse of Richmond Park in which to take the air. Carriages entering from Richmond Gate still had to show the appropriate order, but Sudbrook's patients had access through a private gate "by special permission of the Queen." This privilege meant a great deal to James. He never forgot that the water cure was located "on the borders of a famous park," to which the establishment "gave you unlimited right of possession and enjoyment." He and Mary also took drives in nearby Bushy Park, which they found so satisfying that twenty-five years later Henry Jr. went there for a "short stroll," having heard his parents speak of it so often.

Also close at hand, on Ham Common, was the experimental school known as Alcott House. Any reader of *The Dial* would have been likely to regard this institution as the center of radical intellectual ferment in England. Bronson Alcott had spent some time there in 1842, and when he returned to Concord in the fall of that year, he was accompanied by two men who had helped direct its affairs, Charles Lane and Henry Gardiner Wright. The forceful and charismatic James Pierrepont Greaves, subject of a recent essay in *The Dial*, had lived on the premises shortly before his death in 1842. Much of the financial support for the school and the reformers congregated around it came from a well-to-do enthusiast for radical causes named Sophia Chichester.* She was the daughter of Sir Francis Ford, baronet, and had been widowed for two decades; in the 1830s and early 1840s she resided with her sister at Ebworth Park, Painswick, Gloucester. In 1843 she rented a house on Park Place in Ham. A year or two later, as a document in the French National Archives indicates, she moved to another rented house, Belvedere, on Ham Common. It may have been at the Park Place address or Belvedere, or perhaps Alcott House, that James met Mrs. Chichester, who impressed him as "a very lovely sympathetic person." More up-to-date than he as a social thinker, she had translated a French book advocating the visionary socialism of Charles Fourier. Also, she subscribed to the Fourierist newspaper, *Démocratie Pacifique*. Although she was not a disciple of Emanuel Swedenborg, she was familiar with his ideas.

On one of his visits to Mrs. Chichester (James wrote fifteen years later), she began "to question me a little about my malady. Finding it was an overtasked brain, and overtasked too in the pursuit of the highest questions, she said you need Swedenborg, he is your physician, so not a word more till you go up to London, and bring him down in the shape of one or more of his ponderous books." In James's other account of this

* I am greatly in debt to Jacqueline E. M. Latham, whose detailed exploration of Chichester's involvement with British radicals, "Henry James Senior's Mrs. Chichester," has just appeared in *The Henry James Review*.

pivotal conversation, Mrs. Chichester was more specific in her diagnosis: "You are undergoing what Swedenborg calls a *vastation*; and though, naturally enough, you yourself are despondent or even despairing about the issue, I cannot help taking an altogether hopeful view of your prospects." When James asked her to explain the meaning of the Latin word, she provided a brief summary of Swedenborg's view of human regeneration, of which "vastation" was one of the stages. She felt, however, that she was "ill-qualified to expound his philosophy."

Regeneration, his own in particular, had been James's consuming interest ever since his Calvinist conversion of 1834–35. His anonymous pamphlet of 1838, *The Gospel Good News to Sinners*, had unfolded the Calvinist cycle of sin and redemption. Why it was he couldn't say, but all his intense and energetic thought on the subject had proved a total waste. Was it possible that some great clear-sighted seer had brought "into rational relief the alternate dark and bright—or infernal and celestial—phases" of the soul?

SWEDENBORG

Emanuel Swedenborg, born in 1688, had been an extremely devout child, "constantly engaged in thought about God, salvation, and the spiritual diseases of men." He became a very learned and well-traveled young man, giving his attention chiefly to natural history, astronomy, physics. Mines were his special subject. In 1744, exactly a century before James's vastation, his life abruptly altered course. He happened to be in London, dining by himself, when, according to his account, "a kind of mist spread before my eyes, and I saw the floor of my room covered with hideous reptiles." The mist cleared and he saw a man sitting in a corner who said, "Eat not so much!" The visions continued on successive nights. When the man reappeared, it became clear that he was more than a man. There were "strange dreams and phantasies, tremors, prostrations, trances, sweatings, and swoonings." Swedenborg soon realized (in the words of an enthusiastic follower) that the Bible typified the secret "history of the soul's formation, development and ultimate destiny," and he devoted the rest of his long life to a dryly systematic exposition of the inner or spiritual sense of the Scriptures, beginning with the many-volumed *Arcana Coelestia*.

Among Presbyterians, the official line on Swedenborg was that he was either a madman or an impostor, one "who set up pretensions very much like those of Mohammed, excepting that he did not appear to aspire to any station of temporal authority." At the time James attended Princeton Theological Seminary, the madman hypothesis prevailed. In the detailed lecture notes Professor Samuel Miller left behind, he praises Swedenborg for his "considerable *learning*" and "the purity of his *life*" but places the emphasis on his deluded visionary states: "A Personage in the shape of a *man*, appeared to him, in the midst of a strong *shining light*, & said— '*I am God, the Lord, the Creator & Redeemer!* I have chosen thee to explain to men the interior . . . senses of the sacred writings; I will dictate to thee what thou oughtest to write.' " To the Bible's literal or historic sense, Swedenborg added two others, the spiritual and (more interior yet) the celestial, all of which were interconnected by a "science of correspondences." This science, lost since the time of Job, had been rediscovered by Swedenborg, who believed he was the first man in modern times to discern the ancient and original meaning of the Bible. Miller's notes nicely convey the rhythm of the conclusion of the lecture James probably heard:

FINAL OPINION OF HIM—
    GREAT TALENTS
    GREAT LEARNING
    UPRIGHT INTENTIONS
    PROBABLY PIOUS—BUT
    PROBABLY *INSANE*—SERIOUS, PIOUS, PHILOSOPHIC INSANITY.

Nineteenth-century romantics, such as William Blake and Emerson, approached Swedenborg in a very different way from Professor Miller. They were less interested in consensual wisdom than in boldly individual insight. As far as they were concerned, exalted visionary states might well mean poetry, not madness, and they gladly ransacked Swedenborg's writings for whatever might prove serviceable. In time Emerson lost interest, however, coming to see Swedenborg as a mystic whose perception of the symbolic structure of all existence was "fatally narrowed" by his focus on the Bible and theology.

Most of Swedenborg's followers in the 1830s and 1840s were well-educated Protestants who were engaged in slipping their orthodox tethers. A case in point was the Presbyterian minister George Bush. Beginning as a well-indoctrinated seminary graduate, Bush developed a consuming interest in "laying open . . . the deep and dark things of the Word"— biblical symbolism, hints of the latter days, the prophetic books of Daniel and Revelation. By the mid-forties he was a committed, in fact a leading, Swedenborgian. Henry's old physician Dr. John James, who had moved from Albany to Alton, Illinois, was also drawn to Swedenborg, and one of the doctor's Western friends noticed that "quite a number of the presbyterians here" were doing the same, "although their Minister denounces him from the pulpit as a madman." Reading was a key Swedenborgian activity. There was a very long shelf of texts to master, and they required a high degree of cultivated application.

Like Bush, James had also been plunging back by stages to the deep and dark things buried among the origins. He had joined Mr. Buchanan's Primitive Christians. Then he had gone back to the first and second chapters of Genesis. Then he had reverted "from a state of firm, vigorous, joyful manhood to one of almost helpless infancy." If Swedenborg had recovered the laws of interpretation, lost since the time of Job, then perhaps he could show James how to reconstruct himself from the ground up. A man who felt he had fumbled regeneration, the inward meaning of Christianity, and the true sense of the creation stories might well be curious to see how Swedenborg had handled these matters.

Eagerly obeying Mrs. Chichester's advice, James did what he had done during his first English summer: he worked out his salvation by invading London's bookstores. The bookseller's labels still pasted on the inside covers of some of his Swedenborg books show that he went to William Newbery's shop on King Street, Holborn, where a "huge mass of tomes" was brought out and placed on the counter. From among them, he later said, he selected two relatively slender volumes, *Divine Love and Wisdom* and *Divine Providence* (the latter eventually becoming his favorite Swedenborgian text). But James's memory may have been at fault, and a scholar has suggested that he might have begun with *True Christian Religion* and a composite volume; his copies of these are inscribed "H. James, London, 1844." He also bought the twelve-volume English translation of *Arcana Coelestia*. At first, obeying Dr. Weiss's orders, he merely glanced into his new library, even though he was persuaded it held the explanation of his strange trouble. But before long, "instead of standing any longer shivering on the brink," he decided he "would boldly plunge into the stream, and ascertain, once for all, to what undiscovered sea its waters might bear me." The real plunge bath had begun.

Newbery's bookstore now became James's point of resort in London. This establishment was headquarters for the ongoing publication of Swedenborg's works, and it was also a gathering place for the more intellectual wing of his British followers. The Jameses also visited the large and wealthy New Church congregation at Argyle Square, in the process leaving a lasting impression of Mary's "radiant" face on Dr. J. J. Garth Wilkinson. Wilkinson lived in a modest home on Store Street (near the

British Museum) that doubled as his surgery. He had discovered Swedenborg a decade earlier and was now engaged in translating some of his scientific works into English. Although James did not share Wilkinson's interest in Swedenborg's pre-1744 writings (and did not even read the presentation copies the translator gave him), the two men hit it off from the start. Tall, dignified, learned, and tolerant, graceful to the point of airiness or even evasiveness and not at all preachy, Wilkinson nicely complemented James. The Englishman must have proved a comforting guide for a disturbed convert struggling to find his way. The two men had much in common domestically, both being in their fourth year of marriage and having small children. Later, Wilkinson showed real warmth in remembering the Jameses' first visits to Store Street:

> We shall never forget our delightful interchange with Mrs James and Miss Walsh. They were sunny evenings on which your faces graced our humble abode, and there was something of delicious youth in them from many circumstances. For you were new to us in country, in time of acquaintance, in sentiment, & in your acquaintance with our valued Truths.

Wilkinson was a gifted translator but lacked what Emerson called a "manifest centrality" and was not highly regarded in England. One of the reasons James exaggerated his talents and attached himself to him was that he was searching for an uncritical expositor of those newly valued Truths.

The most vivid evidence of James's ardent embrace of his new gospel is his private collection of Swedenborg texts, part of which is now stored at a Swedenborgian seminary in one of the family's steamer trunks. Many of the books have been read and marked and marked again, and because James's handwriting grew larger and more self-assured and sprawling as the years advanced, it is possible at times to detect and date his successive readings. At first he used an ordinary lead pencil, but in later years he marked the books in orange and aquamarine. He began with light vertical lines in the margins, and then the lines grew heavier, with large X's and stylized pointing hands. Many of the books have been read to pieces. The reader's comments mainly call attention to the more helpful Truths. Although these comments are almost never critical or speculative, they can be quite forceful whenever it becomes necessary to bring Swedenborg in line. Thus, when the text says that "the Most Ancient Church . . . was the first church, and the only one which was celestial, and therefore beloved by the Lord more than any other," the marginal comment insists, rather irrelevantly, on a point dear to James: "This is an apparent truth only as the Lord can not love one man or set of men more than another."

The truths James deemed preeminent he copied or indexed on the endpapers. On the advertisement page of *Divine Providence*, for example, we find this notation: "See 278 for a perfect exposure of the hypocrisy of our own ordinary profuse confessions of sin." On the back of the title page in the same book there is this note: "78 A man has nothing which is proper to himself (no proprium) but it appears to him as if it were." In some volumes the endpapers have been filled with such memoranda. In most instances there is no way to know (and no reason for trying to find out) just when James made his various scratchings. But there is one remarkable set of entries that stands alone. They are written in a relatively small hand in the first volume of the *Arcana Coelestia*, Swedenborg's massive, phrase-by-phrase exegesis of Genesis and Exodus. On the inside of the front board, at the top of the page—the place where an earnest note-taker would be likely to make his first jottings—we may have a contemporaneous record of James's initial exploratory read, when he resolved to learn the meaning of Mrs. Chichester's mysterious word:

Vastation, what? See 18.

Turning to paragraph 18, we find that it consists of Swedenborg's explanation of the mysterious second verse of Genesis:

And the earth was without form, and void; and darkness was upon the face of the deep. And the spirit of God moved upon the face of the waters.

Swedenborg explains that this passage describes the process of spiritual regeneration: " 'The face of the deep,' signifies the lusts of the unregenerate man, and the falsities thence originating, of which he consists, and in which he is totally immersed." The verse's imagery signifies "the vastation of man, frequently spoken of by the prophets, which precedes regeneration; for before man can know what is true, and be affected with what is good, there must be a removal of such things as hinder and resist their admission: thus the old man must needs die, before the new man can be conceived."

So that was what Mrs. Chichester's strange word was all about. "Vastation" and "waste": the same Latin root. The waste had to be voided before the man could be made whole. The rotten leg had been cut off, and then it had been cut a little higher, and since then there had been a series of more and more radical operations as James attempted to get rid of the guilt, the righteousness, the knot of pride, the terror. Sandeman and Walker had taught him how to defecate himself of his Presbyterian upbringing. Now he began to see, thanks to Swedenborg, that what had happened at Windsor was that he had defecated *himself*. The reason he had collapsed, and the reason that collapse was good, was that his rotten moral selfhood had to be amputated.

It would take a decade and more for James to complete this interpretation of his breakdown. Before he could do so, his own vast egotism had to go through one last flame-out in the late 1840s and early 1850s, a period in which he argued for a kind of self-expression so extreme it bordered on free love. Abandoning this dangerous position in 1853, James settled on the idea that selfhood was the principle of evil, a theory he developed in *The Nature of Evil* (1855). Only after writing this book was he able to understand (or so he thought) the strange and fearful thing that had happened to him at Frogmore Cottage. At last the terrifying past could be put away.

Chapter 16

■ ■ ■

THE LIVING MIND
CALLED FROM ITS NATURAL BED:
1844–47

On October 12, 1844, James and his entourage left Liverpool on the *Great Western*, reaching New York fourteen days later. Willy and Harry were a year older, Mary and Catharine had had their first taste of European cities, resorts, and fashions, and Fanny had seen the British Museum. Henry was still shaky. It was five months since his collapse, and although he was recovering, his "ghastly condition of mind continued," he later recalled, "with gradually lengthening intervals of relief, for two years, and even longer." Swedenborg may have shown him how to construe his inner disturbances and remodel his understanding of salvation and divine providence and the nature of revelation, and of course the weighty Swedenborgian tomes the sufferer brought back across the Atlantic made possible the long hours of directed study that were a necessity for him now. But just as was the case following his earlier epiphanies, inner peace eluded him.

James seems to have lived with his mother-in-law in New York for the better part of a year, and then he spent two years in Albany, living across the street from his own mother. As he read, studied, wrote letters, and circulated, he got his health back, he thought he saw a higher order synthesis of his deepest intuitions, and his career as lecturer and writer began to take off. He moved inward and then he set off outward on his longest and most sustained flight yet.

THE JAMESES AND THE WILKINSONS

As soon as he reached New York, James sent his "cheering voice" back across the Atlantic to Wilkinson, thus initiating a long and regular correspondence. The original understanding between the two men seems to have been that the Englishman had the greater mind. While he threw away all but a few of the letters he got from James, James kept a hundred and twenty of his. Most of these, still in their envelopes, were returned decades later at the request of one of Wilkinson's daughters. Because the letters were eventually deposited in a locked manuscript room in the basement of the Swedenborg Society in London, it is possible one hundred and fifty years later to ascertain just where the Jameses got their mail in 1845:

CARE OF WALSH AND MALLORY
PEARL STREET
NEW YORK.

Walsh was Alexander Robertson Walsh, Mary's oldest and most successful brother. His line was hardware and lumber, and he and his partner operated out of 211 Pearl Street, in the financial and mercantile section of lower Manhattan. Known as Robertson among his relatives, he was "the head of my mother's family" in the eyes of Henry Jr., who also remembered this uncle as looking after Henry Sr.'s affairs. While the Jameses were in England, Robertson and his very large family resided with his mother on Washington Square. In the winter of 1844–45 he moved into a rented house at 82 Clinton Place (today a segment of Eighth Street a little west of Fifth Avenue), and the repatriated Jameses took his place in Elizabeth Walsh's home. This arrangement ensured that the elderly woman could be cared for by her two daughters, Mary and Catharine, and provided the two grandchildren, William and Henry Jr., with ready access to a shaded public park and parade ground. "It was here," Henry Jr. recalled in his 1880 novel, *Washington Square*, "that your grandmother lived in venerable solitude, and . . . you took your first walks abroad, following the nursery-maid with unequal step, and sniffing up the strange odor of the ailanthus-trees."

There is only a single eyewitness sighting of Henry Sr. during this poorly documented year in New York. Ellery Channing, poet and friend of Thoreau, ran into him and, classing him among "Emerson's old cronies," characterized him as "a little fat, rosy Swedenborgian amateur, with the look of a broker, & the brains & heart of a Pascal." This

description suggests that James's health was on the mend; that his large
brow, spectacles, and intense gaze gave him a shrewd appearance; and
that he was making good progress through his Swedenborg library ("amateur" here being closer to "lover" than "dilettante"). It also shows that
even those who did not know James well could see at once that this
passionate and brilliant man eluded the usual categories.

Chiefly occupied with working out his own salvation, James still
yearned to instruct others. Wilkinson's wish that he could join "your
auditory at one of your preachings" implies that his American friend was
already standing up and holding forth by the end of 1844. When the
Englishman gave his own maiden lecture a few months later, he remembered James's "anticipatory trepidation" at the 1843 New York lectures.
Like Carlyle, who saw James as "shy and skittish," Wilkinson thought
the American's self-confidence needed bolstering and advised him to be
less studious and meticulous. He ought to just bang in:

> Whenever you feel ready, you cannot fail . . . to be promoted to your
> station of use, either as an Author, or as an oral Teacher. If I might
> counsel one *so much my Senior* [a joke, James being only one year older],
> I should press upon you the necessity of . . . doing something without
> being in the first instance too fastidious about the manner . . . Dont try
> to satisfy your self, but simply to do your best, & leave the result to the
> fitting judges, of which number you are *not*. Leave your reputation to
> *grow*, and dont try to produce it all at once.

Wilkinson wanted James to follow the example of the recent Swedenborgian convert George Bush, who was already publishing:

> You have been studying E.S. longer than Professor Bush, & unless his
> forehead beats yours, (which I think is impossible,) you should really be
> up and doing, as he is. I long to hear of your public life commencing: I
> long to hear that you are consigned to hard labor for the rest of your days;
> & that you are so involved in the machinery of your sacred calling, that
> retreat is impossible.

Your sacred calling. James must have given an indication of some new
sense of mission. Although he still couldn't decide whether to become
an author or an "oral Teacher," he had resolved to set forth Swedenborg's
vision of Christianity (as Bush was doing).

That James cherished a lofty vocational dream is apparent from the
letter in which Wilkinson expressed the hope that "you will do something
which shall not willingly be let die in the literature of your country."

This electrifying language, borrowed from no less a writer than John Milton, undoubtedly reflected the literary ambitions James had confided. One year after the "vastation," Wilkinson applauded James for going back to his "old papers," and trusted they would soon see print. The reference was to the 1843 lectures that James had been revising at Windsor. In *Society the Redeemed Form of Man* James would claim that this project had been abandoned, but in fact he continued to elaborate his "important discovery"—his belief that the two creation stories were an allegory for man's passage from nature to something infinitely higher.

Once James began sending Wilkinson his publications, the Englishman changed his tune, alternating between an attitude of awestruck admiration at the American's zeal and daring and an increasing impatience with his refusal to recognize conventional boundaries or his own limits. "Let me entreat you," he curtly advised, "not to attempt to worry yourself with Science at present." He tried to get James to clarify his thinking, to be less sprawling and impractical, to use fewer adjectives, to be less metaphysical, but judging from the gingerly tone he soon adopted, the advice was not well received. On the whole, the Englishman preferred to pacify his combative friend rather than lock horns with him. It wasn't easy arguing with James, who, in addition to being opaque, impractical, and insistent, was not averse to getting personal. Once, after he had torn into Wilkinson, the latter abruptly transformed himself into a small boy who dramatizes his own helplessness when whipped: "All the time I was *catching* [it] . . . I kept hollering out mentally: 'I'll never do so any more: I'll never do so any more': and right glad was I when you left off." Wilkinson would thank James profusely for his various publications and opinions, but helpful comment was infrequent. In 1848 James apparently asked his friend point-blank whether he so much as took an "interest" in his writings, and the next year Mary (preferring the indirect approach) dreamed that her husband's friend was "apathetic" about his labors. When James relayed his wife's insight to Wilkinson, the latter was characteristically evasive: "Mrs James' dream amuses me much." But the dream was on target: there was something factitious in the admiration James and Wilkinson professed to feel for one another.

One impediment to candor was the enormous inequality in wealth. In the 1840s Wilkinson wanted to write and translate rather than tend the sick, but his means were too slender to permit him to give up his practice. Believing the man to be a genius, James began sending him large and regular amounts of money in January 1846. Five years later Wilkinson revealed to his father that James had been paying him "from £100 to £130 a year in consideration for articles written for him." These benefactions, equivalent to at least $10,000 annually at the present time, enabled the Englishman to undertake a number of writing projects—and also to leave Store Street for genteel, suburban Hampstead. In thanking James for the checks, Wilkinson spoke of them as undeserved gifts, but in writing to his father he emphasized the contractual nature of the arrangement and used the word "employ."* This ambiguous dependency made the two Swedenborgians a good deal less frank in reacting to one another's thought. In effect, James's money insulated him from the expert and straightforward criticism he needed.

Unlike his English friend, who had to accommodate himself to others' views, James was accustomed to expressing himself as contentiously as he pleased. He was like other prophets from New York's Burned-Over District, being "positively fanatic" in the unorthodox views he had arrived at "by presumably foolproof processes." Thus, although he and Wilkinson were both critical of the organized New Jerusalem Church, believing that Swedenborg had not intended to found a distinct sect, they expressed this opinion in two very different fashions. Wilkinson remained a member of the Church of England and tried not to antagonize the leaders of the New Jerusalem Church. James, adhering to no denomination, ripped into all of them, the New Church most of all. Early in 1845, acting for Wilkinson, he approached the editors of the *New Jerusalem Magazine*, the official organ of institutional Swedenborgianism in America, with the proposition that they make use of the Englishman in some way. In April the magazine ran a short piece by Wilkinson on Swedenborg's scientific writings. But James, a poor diplomat and businessman, did not make a reliable intermediary, and he allowed Caleb Reed, one of the magazine's three Boston editors, to understand that Wilkinson considered them "too *Sectarian*." Reed at once asked Wilkinson to explain this unfriendly opinion, and Wilkinson dashed off a letter to James repudiating the phrase and ordering him to make amends: "When you are at Boston, will you kindly see Mr Reed, & if he has any stripes to lay on, pray receive them for me, & duly inform me of their administration. Perhaps they may do *you* good." This sharp request was written several months before Wilkinson's pen was dulled by James's money.

The next summer James went to Boston to try again. He talked to Caleb Reed and his co-adjutors, Sampson Reed and Theophilus Parsons, and arranged for Wilkinson to write a monthly letter from London for

* Acknowledging James's periodic checks became a real burden. Wilkinson once turned the chore over to his wife in these words: "If you can drop Mr James a letter to morrow, I shall be much obliged, for I am too fagged and dashed . . . to do justice to even a simple act of thanks."

the *New Jerusalem Magazine*. Wilkinson thanked James for "traveling hundreds of miles" on his behalf and begged him to go to no further trouble, leaving "the *whole* to Providence, & the public wants." But James left very little to Providence, and the letters began appearing that November (1846), running for a year and a half. Fifteen years later, recalling these negotiations with the "leaders of the sect," James scoffed at "their deplorable want of manhood." One probable reason for this contempt was that, in agreeing to publish Wilkinson, the editors accepted a subsidy from James, their fiercest critic.

On family matters, James's letters to Wilkinson were so uninformative that Emma Wilkinson became uneasy, finally complaining to her husband about the lack of news of "M.rs James, Miss Walsh & the children." Strangely, James did not disclose Mary's pregnancy until the baby, another boy, was born on July 21. (He must have been conceived shortly before or after the *Great Western* reached New York on October 26.) The Wilkinsons were surprised, but the real stunner was the announcement that James wanted to name the infant Garth Wilkinson. The Englishman replied that he didn't care for "naming babies after anybody at all" and would rather see the Jameses go to "the great urn of Saxon names, and take out one." But he gratefully acknowledged the honor and promised to do his part, whatever that was. Like his brothers before him, the baby was soon known by a nickname—Wilkie.

Mary James was a good deal less communicative than her husband. Nine months after the Wilkinsons saw the Jameses off at a London train station and the two families' "delightful interchange" ended, Emma Wilkinson had not yet heard from her American friend. She was beginning to think (her husband wrote) that " 'M.rs James does not care for her any longer.' " Wilkie's birth announcement gave Emma a pretext for being the first to write: "I hope dear Mrs James that you & Miss W[alsh] still continue your readings & *likings* for ES's [Emanuel Swedenborg's] works!" But why wouldn't Mrs. James write? Her husband had "made very nice & I will add satisfactory apologies for your not writing to me hitherto; but my dear friend I shall fear to address you again unless I am assured by yourself that you still remember me." Hearing nothing, Emma got to work that winter on a kind of gift that was new to the Jameses, a scrapbook. It was shipped April 18, 1846, and when it arrived the obligation to respond could be shirked no longer.

Mary's thank-you note, her earliest-known letter, is a model of propriety and correct style, with none of the familiar initials and common diction ("very nice") of Emma's letters. The scrapbook was "pronounced to be a most beautiful thing in its way, and will find numberless imitations here among the mammas to whom I have shown it." Taking care to reciprocate Emma's direct address with one of her own, Mary declared that "to *my* eye my dear Mrs Wilkinson it is more than beautiful, for it speaks to me of the kind heart that devised it, and is to me a most gratifying expression of your affectionate remembrance of us and ours." But there were no apologies for the long and unaccountable silence. Enclosing the recipes for Indian meal the Englishwoman had asked for, Mary cautioned her to bear in mind that "it requires *much* longer cooking than any other meal. It is quite another thing when well cooked, and I fear that an ignorance or disregard of this fact, may at first affect its favorable reception among you." No less haughty is Mary's statement that, although she has not yet given a "careful perusal" to a recent publication by C. A. Tulk, a British Swedenborgian, it strikes her so far as "unsatisfactory. I can follow him so far as he suggests difficulties, but when he comes to the solution of them he leaves me far behind." This judicious criticism (nicely matching Henry's views) was a far cry from the relaxed "readings & *likings*" that Emma expected Mary to share with her sister (not her husband).

The nuances in an old correspondence can be very elusive, yet it seems clear that Mary's thank-you note for a homemade gift all but brandished her formal correctness and learning. It's as if she meant to freeze her humble correspondent. This impression is deepened by a family letter from three decades later in which Mary sniffs that another note from Emma has just arrived:

> the flattest and also most characteristic thing you ever read— After going over as usual the old story of how and where all her children are settled, she closes with sending to Carrie [Mary's daughter-in-law] "for her photographic Album" her own photograph! Can you imagine egotism to go farther. I think the Dr could not have been cognizant of the performance.

Mary had come to see Emma as illiterate and déclassée. But what could you expect of a wife who didn't have sense enough to follow her husband's—"the Dr's"—more authoritative lead?

When Mary's favored son, Henry Jr., went to England in 1869 and paid a visit to the Wilkinsons, he sent back the sort of remark he knew his very superior mama would relish: "Mrs. W. inquired whether 'my mama read & studied much now—she used to have such a splendid head.' " The young novelist was a great deal more supple in both his prose and his social judgments than his mother could be—but he often listened to people with her exacting ears.

REDOMESTICATION IN ALBANY

It was probably in the early fall of 1845 that the Jameses left Elizabeth Walsh's home in New York and took a steamboat up the Hudson to Albany, where they would live for the next two years. Their new address was 50 North Pearl Street, a three-story brick house that had been in the family for at least fifteen years. Occupied from 1829 by Gus and his family, it was across the street from the James "homestead" (whose number, first 70, then 62, was now 43). Catharine Barber James was still at home, of course, as were her son Edward and some Gourlays and several half-orphaned grandchildren. Gus lived at no. 47, with an office at no. 45, and Rev. William, Marcia, and their children resided on Montgomery Street. Henry's sister Catharine Temple was living with her husband and growing family at 5 Clinton Square. Another married sister, Ellen King Van Buren, lived on Elk Street facing Albany Academy. (A third sister, Jannet, had died in 1842.) When John Barber came back with two children after his wife's death in February 1846 and moved into his mother's house, the James clan was largely reconstituted.

Before long the elm trees along North Pearl Street that impressed foreign travelers got imprinted on small Henry Jr., whose recollections, seventy years later, were framed by the "arching umbrage—I see it all as from under trees." He remembered his parents' house as "pinkish-red picked out with white." It was smaller and brighter than his grand-mother's larger, soberer house across the street, but it was still a very substantial dwelling (with a thirty-five-foot frontage and a valuation of $6,500). The novelist had the impression no. 50 was recessed from the street. He thought he could recall swinging on a gate that pulled itself shut "by an iron chain weighted with a big ball." With his grown-up detestation of America's wooden stoops, he hoped that the high stone steps leading up to his parents' door were made of marble.

Perhaps it was because of Elizabeth Walsh's "extreme illness," in Mary's words, that the Jameses had stayed in New York for almost a year. Aunt Kate wasn't able to join them in Albany, being "confined to [her] mother's sick room for the last six months." When Mary herself had to make several trips down the Hudson to help out, Henry and a "faithful nurse" were left in charge of the three boys. "He acquitted himself most satis-factorily," the mother reported, being "a most patient and judicious aid." Perhaps it was during one of her absences that he took Henry Jr. on the "first 'paid' visit" he could remember, to his youngest aunt, Ellen King Van Buren, whose Elk Street address evoked an image in the small visitor's mind of "beasts of the forest not yet wholly exorcised."

On August 29, 1846, Mary gave birth to her fourth boy. He was given his maternal grandmother's maiden name, Robertson, which had become a first name thanks to Mary's older brother. Shortly afterward Emma Wilkinson produced yet another girl, who was christened Mary James. The Wilkinsons were even with the Jameses now in this business of names, and it was time for Mary to recognize the formal symmetry with another letter, this one much softer than the last and all but flowing with mother's milk: "When I take my Wilkie and *yours* upon my knee, and think of you, pouring out your maternal tendernesses upon your little Mary and *mine*, I feel my dear friend that a new and most delightful sort of intercourse is established between us." With no daughters of her own, Mary was delighted to have a girl named for her and she let down her guard and wrote from her "mother's heart," revealing that she had weaned thirteen-month-old Wilkie in order to make room for Bob (as Robertson was familiarly known). "Shoved off," Wilkie had begun fending for himself more aggressively and making his grievances known. If his mother followed the advice she gave a daughter-in-law years later, she probably let the one-year-old cry. Her pity would have been "more strongly excited," she told Emma, "were he less able or ready to take his own part, but as his strength of arm or of will seldom fails him, he is too often left to fight his own battles." The strenuous combat that others were to note among the James boys had already established itself, both parents feeling they were best left alone to fight it out. One result of this regime was that Henry Jr. often found himself at a disadvantage. William was an expert at making his wants known and Wilkie had great "physical force," but Henry was good both day and night. Whatever might be said of the others, *he* was definitely not a beast of the forest.

In August 1845 New York's Court of Chancery ordered a partition of the now enormously valuable real-estate holdings in Syracuse. Five-eighths of these belonged to Jameses, two-eighths to the Townsends, and one-eighth to James McBride. The court appointed three commissioners to make surveys and assess values and then perform the final dismemberment, first dividing the whole into eight equal portions and then further dividing William of Albany's five-eighths into eleven equal parts, one of which would go to Henry. The allotments were labeled A, B, C, and so forth, and the drawing took place in Syracuse on November 13. Gus and Edward both went, as did two brothers-in-law, Robert E. Temple and Smith Thompson Van Buren. Gus drew for John Barber and Rev. William as well as for himself, but a commissioner drew for Henry, who got allotment G. Thanks to his substantial new holdings in rapidly growing Syracuse, he was now completely independent.

Decades later, after Henry Sr.'s death, Henry Jr. had to go to Syracuse on estate business. He inquired when was the last time his father had "taken personal cognisance" of his property there and was told (it came as no surprise) that he "had never in all his years of possession performed such an act."

A LECTURE ON THE STATE

Around the time of the Syracuse partition, James resolved to vanquish his old trepidation and step up to the lecture platform once again. Twelve years earlier a civic organization had been founded in Albany that Benjamin Franklin would have approved of, the Young Men's Association for Mutual Improvement. Open to any man who could fork up a $2 membership fee, the YMA offered a winter lecture series and a well-stocked reading room at a time when Albany was without a public library. Edward James signed up as a charter member, and a few years later he and Gus became life members by contributing $25. 1845–46 turned out to be a banner year for the YMA, thanks to an energetic new president, Franklin Townsend. The lecture season, running from November to February, was said to be the most successful ever. The speakers lined up by the lecture committee included the well-known—John C. Spencer, Horace Greeley, Eliphalet Nott—and the unknown Henry James.

It was James's practice to make generous donations to those organizations that gave him a forum, and on December 8, 1845, he bought a life membership in the YMA. Eight days later he took the platform in the association's "spacious lecture room." His topic was "What Constitutes the State?" Members attended free, non-members paid twenty-five cents. When Horace Greeley came up from New York to speak, his fellow newspaperman, Thurlow Weed of the *Albany Evening Journal*, summarized his remarks, noted that the room wasn't half big enough, and hoped the lecture would soon be published. When Henry James spoke, Weed did not attend and no notice was taken. A couple of months later, however, prompted by a local bookseller, Weed informed the public that the lecture had been published in New York by John Allen and was being sold locally by Mr. Little. Presently, the *New York Tribune* ran a notice that reprinted five paragraphs from James's peroration. Although the *Tribune* was a mere stripling compared to the New York *Evening Post* (which had given James a boost back in 1843), it was obvious to any Whig editor with an eye half open that Greeley's paper was the coming thing. If James had that kind of backing, there must be something in him. On March 10, three months after James had addressed the YMA, the *Albany Evening Journal* also printed a long section of his lecture.

The question with which the lecture began reflected the hard traveling of one who left his parents' church for a tiny band of Separatists, found himself increasingly isolated, went to pieces overseas, and then returned to the bosom of his family. That question was, what keeps humans from being selfish and separate and living in individual solitude? Why do we form aggregations rather than (as one might expect) remain apart? James's answer, definitely Transcendental, was that we come together because we are already essentially one, and that this underlying unity accounts for the sense of obligation we feel to one another. At the present time in particular, self-love is fading and love of others brightening. A glorious transformation of society is imminent, as indicated by many signs—the extension of commerce, the spread of education, the translation of the Bible into barbarian tongues, and even "the increasing spirit of pleasure-travel." Steamboats, railroads, telegraphs, these all herald "the descent of that divine and universal spirit, which even now yearns to embrace all earth's offspring."

As James concluded with the rapt augury that was standard in public addresses, a strange horror intruded:

> Let us not wonder that in the yet imperfect light and imperfect warmth of the early morning, many lowering phantoms and shapes of mist lift their lurid heads between us and the crimson dawn! Elaborately exhumed ghosts of departed superstitions do shriek and squeal along the twilight streets: but let none of these things move us! . . . That blissful day grows meanwhile, and ever grows; soon its meridian light and heat will dissipate the mists.

Six years earlier the lecturer had invoked the rapid approach of Judgment Day in a baleful letter to Marcia Ames James. Now, as was the case with many other lecturers in the 1840s, Emerson and Thoreau included, the great day had been transformed into a dawning considerably less doctrinal and threatening. But James still heard the night's shrieks and squeals.

This sermonlike lecture had some other peculiar features. By "state" James meant the "Social State," or rather, going back to the Latin root, "*that which stands*"—that which is fundamental and universal. Saying nothing about government or social contracts or the structures of civil order, James collapsed man and the state into a single glowing point that defied clear definition. Everything was rushing toward social unity, and the basis of this unity was profoundly religious. Wiping out the hard-won distinction between church and state that had been fought for in the Enlightenment and written into the American Constitution, James maintained that a universal moral and religious impulse was responsible for all social and political arrangements. This was an idea he never gave up, insisting many years later that "the State as a civil polity is wholly contingent upon the Church as an ecclesiasticism."

This theory, so characteristic of fundamentalist regimes, reflected James's troubled history and character. As he admitted a couple of years later, if he were to allow an independent will to any of God's creatures, "my future would present me with an utter blank, relieved only by the baleful struggles of infernal might against supernal weakness. For what assurance could I feel that I myself might not at some future time throw off my allegiance to the source of life, and proceed to live by the consumption of my own vitals?" James felt that his morbid, suicidal impulses were lying in wait. It was because they had to be kept down by a supreme power outside himself that he could not see the point of the liberal secular state, designed to carve out a space for private interests. Still fixated on absolute sovereignty, James could not sense the danger of exalting the authority of a state seen as divine.

There was an odd contradiction in James's lecture that closely matched his psychological situation. If everyone is essentially one, there is little point in urging self-love to give way to the love of others, for no boundaries between individuals means no discernible difference between love of others and love of oneself. One might as well assume that to love oneself *is* the supreme ethical act—a position James would in fact move toward over the next few years. "Why should another be inhibited from my outward injury," he asked in 1848, "save on the ground of his own inward unity with me?" James's lecture on the state shows how the idea of ultimate loving unity enabled a certain kind of self-aggrandizing temperament to see itself as selfless. Indeed, a lecture that spins out a universal religious/social/political order from the lecturer's fear of his own vitals not only argues for but enacts an oddly unconscious tyranny.

The pamphlet was noticed by the *Harbinger*, a small but influential weekly published from Brook Farm. In a long review, one of the magazine's frequent contributors, Charles A. Dana, praised James's emphasis on human unity but vigorously criticized his obscurity and the "want of an accurate analysis of the soul." The author had failed to appreciate "the universal principle of order." James at once whipped up a reply to Dana about the "bipolarity" of love and self-love, but Dana had the last word in the exchange. Across the ocean, Wilkinson read his friend's pamphlet and the resulting debate in the *Harbinger* and delicately called attention to Dana's "hardest hits."

This exchange had a significant impact on James. He seems to have realized he was poorly equipped as a social thinker, and that Swedenborg would not enable him to hold his own with Dana and other *Harbinger* writers. Two things happened: James began to read and take a serious interest in Charles Fourier, the French utopian socialist whose name was tantamount to social science for many advanced Americans in the mid-1840s, and he made productive contact with a group of social visionaries in New York who had begun as the social-activist wing of the Transcendental movement. In 1859 James recalled this moment as a major turning point in his life, equivalent to his first hearing the name of Swedenborg:

> I so felt the want of a knowledge of the true laws of nature, that I was on the point of despairing a second time . . . I felt that the social sentiment, that new feeling of equality or fellowship . . . was the true presence of God in nature: but how to organize that sentiment, how to give it expression or form worthy of its source: alas! alas! my way was again fearfully obstructed . . . Imagine my gratitude to God then, when about those days, I heard the name of Fourier.

As James began to read Fourier, he finally acquired a conceptual apparatus for thinking about the "Social State," and at the same time he linked up with an actual society of young New Yorkers whose minds and company he found tremendously energizing. In 1842, James had rebuffed Brisbane when he expounded Fourier to him and Emerson. Four years later, the seed fell on fertile ground.

BITTEN WITH FOURIER

Charles Fourier had died in 1837, his general bearing, a disciple remembered, "tinged with melancholy, and indifference to current notions and opinions." Convinced that the present state of civilization was evil and temporary, and that the development of mankind as a whole was analogous to the development of the individual, he worked out in great detail the form that human society would inevitably assume in the future. The basic social unit would be the phalanx, a "perfect, self-supporting organism" consisting of about sixteen hundred persons. Fourier conceived of the phalanx, or township, as a kind of human anthill, with all the necessary social functions being performed by specialized workers of various kinds. No compulsion would be necessary to keep a township running. Instead, its perpetual harmony would be guaranteed by the diversity and distribution of human desires and needs ("passions" in Fourier's terminology) and by the development of industrial specialization, which would allow each member to perform the functions that satisfied his or her ruling passion. There would be no more policing or Christian self-denial: "Antiquity, nearer to the true religious spirit than we are, deified the pleasures and made them objects of worship."

In his analysis of the passions, Fourier was relentlessly systematic, distinguishing between compound and bi-compound, "direct and inverse, major and minor, active and passive," and arranging the various combinations—hyperminors and compound majors and harmonic fifth degrees—in elaborate and exhaustive arrays. If his own ruling passions included a mania for pedantic classificatory analogues with grammatical systems and musical theory, this mania accompanied an admirably critical and comprehensive survey of French customs. At heart, as a recent biographer has argued, Fourier was a creative dreamer who tried to imagine a less repressive society than what he knew in France. He might be thought of as an early writer of science fiction. Of course any good utopian is inevitably a scathing critic of his times, and Fourier was one of the best:

> As long as the theories of good morals shall consist in depriving women of liberty in love, in making them slaves to the stronger sex which enjoys all the freedom that is refused to women,—while this endures, the female character will be and must be what it is in the present day,—obligatory hypocrisy.

Albert Brisbane had introduced Fourier's thought to American readers in *The Social Destiny of Man*, but it wasn't until 1843 that the Frenchman's thought really took hold in the United States, accompanied by a flurry of activity. James's old seminary friend Parke Godwin founded the *Pathfinder* in order to expound the new gospel. Brisbane, Greeley, and William Henry Channing gave group lectures in Albany on "Association and Social Re-Organization." At a time when there were only two small, struggling French phalanxes, twenty-four were started up in the Midwest and Northeast, the most successful being the North American Phalanx near Red Bank, New Jersey. Brook Farm reorganized itself in 1844 as a phalanx, devised a Fourierist constitution, and started building a large communal phalanstery. The commune sent out traveling speakers and began putting out a weekly paper designed to usher in the new age and also serve as a forum for America's widely scattered Fourierists. Back in the 1830s a group of Baptists had founded a paper called the *Millennial Harbinger*. The Brook Farm editors called their paper the *Harbinger*, a bilingual pun on *fourrier*, French for precursor. It had a high literary standard and for a time was the most important radical journal in America.

Of course, American Associationists came under bitter attack from various groups, and adding injury to insult, Brook Farm's half-built phalanstery burned to the ground in March 1846, shortly before the *Harbinger* reviewed James's lecture on the state. This particular phalanx was evidently doomed, and George Ripley, its founder and the main force behind its distinguished weekly, realized that American Fourierists would have to remobilize. In May a new umbrella organization was formed, the American Union of Associationists, created in part to issue "cheap tracts." New England's radicals were now working in alliance with New York's well-to-do sympathizers and backers, among them a banker named Edmund Tweedy, the new Union's treasurer, and before long New York was in charge. Ripley and the *Harbinger* moved to the city in the fall of 1847, Godwin came on board with his considerable experience in the metropolitan press, and the magazine became more secular, contestatory, and national. It continued to keep abolitionists at arm's length (supposedly because they were devoted to a single reform). But it grew more vulnerable to the kind of fanatic who vitiates radical causes from within—the uncompromising stickler for some special doctrine or revelation.

In the winter of 1845–46 James took a trip to New York, perhaps to arrange for the publication of his lecture, perhaps to meet the "excellent and agreeable" Tweedy, whom Wilkinson wanted him to know. Like James, this New Yorker had only recently returned from London, where he, too, had frequented Wilkinson's parlor. Ever since, the treasurer of the American Union of Associationists had been bombarding the Englishman with issues of the *Harbinger* and expositions of Fourier, and now Wilkinson wanted James, "*for our sakes*," to retaliate with Swedenborg. But the encounter did not go as Wilkinson hoped, and after reading James's report he wrote: "I am glad you have seen Tweedy. My object in wishing to bring about his acquaintance with you, was, not that he might bite you with Fourier, but rather that you . . . should instruct him in Swedenborg." The bite went deep, and the infection was soon passed on to Wilkinson, who confessed to James a year and a half later that "all you say of the Association movement, I echo from my heart. It is *the* morning brightness of the world's day, & has all my sympathies." Sympathies of another kind developed between James and Tweedy, who formed an easy, jocular friendship that lasted many years. These two well-to-do men not only shared a social cause but a social class as well: Tweedy married Mary Temple, the sister of one of James's brothers-in-law, adopted some of the James family orphans in the fifties, and saw much of James in Newport.

If Tweedy had not bitten James with Fourier, someone else would surely have done so. Godwin, always up-to-date, had informed readers of the *Pathfinder* that the Frenchman was the Isaac Newton of modern times: "Social science can hardly be said to have existed before" him. In 1844 Godwin brought out *A Popular View of the Doctrines of Charles Fourier*, a book James owned and marked. He also read the introduction to Fourierism that Sophia Chichester had translated from the French, *The Phalanstery; or, Attractive Industry and Moral Harmony*, by Madame Gatti de Gamond. This book painted a glowing picture of the perfect future, for which "the harmonic nature in man pants and sighs." At-traction was the fundamental law of human nature and the basis for association and universal harmony. There were three successive dispen-sations: first the family, then the nation, and finally universal unity. The book's focus was on the reorganization of labor and industry, but a good deal was said about future forms of education, household economy, and the position of woman. At present, woman's biggest problem is that she cannot survive except through marriage. In order to be emancipated, she must first be assured of the "*rights of labour.*" Also, she must be better educated and live in collective households. The author did not, however, want to give woman full political rights at the present time and "put her upon an equality with man." To do that "would be but a new source of disorder."

Mary's letter to Emma Wilkinson about "your little Mary and *mine*" was written precisely at the time she and Henry were reading Mrs. Chichester's translation. The letter is so exuberant about "the glorious plans and prospects which Fourier opens for the world" that it hardly seems characteristic of the writer. Except for her second son's stories, nothing Mary read for the remainder of her life elicited the sort of excitement this letter exhibits. Although one would like to attribute her response to Gatti de Gamond's vision of woman's potential, Mary's in-terest was probably an echo—a harmonic vibration—of her husband's enthusiasm. As her letter reveals, she was not reading the translation on her own but hearing it read by "my hopeful loving Henry," who convinced her that if this beautiful book was not true, then "something much better must be." It was Henry's infectious hopes that caused Mary to see the Frenchman's thought as the practical embodiment of Christian prophecy: "These are bright prospects for our suffering race, but does not the Word of God warrant us to look for just such a state of things upon the earth? and does not Fourier prove that it may be brought about by means the most simple and rational, by merely taking advantage of certain laws of our nature." The simple and rational laws of our nature were what Henry had been searching for since 1841 or 1842, and now that he had found them, Mary, too, was ecstatic, and rejoiced in "the advances we make together in truth." There is no evidence that Gatti de Gamond's remarks on the position of woman even registered. The wife who spoke of "my" Henry could not take in the notion of a collective household—even as she went into raptures over the idea of attractive association.

James had found the key to a new vision of redemption, one that connected individual regeneration with a scheme for the historic social progress of the human race as a whole. Salvation, it now appeared, was not something that happened to the individual. Instead, it involved mankind collectively, and had not yet fully arrived. With this insight, James at last found a way to distance himself from his guilt, religious manias, night terrors, and memories. These shrieking and squealing presences were not just produced by evil spirits from the Swedenborgian hells. They also reflected the current stage of social development.

It was becoming more and more clear to James that his troubles did *not* stem from his own history or psyche. He was not so much a man with private difficulties as the theater of action for a momentous, worldwide transformation. With this new perspective came a huge relief, and also a renewal of energy and ambition.

TRUE EDUCATION

Margaret Fuller was yet another American in London who got to know Wilkinson. They often talked about Henry James, and as often as they did so they "wondered," Wilkinson wrote, "when you would begin to work. She is quite indignant at you, & so shall I be very soon."

Heeding Wilkinson's advice to be up and doing, and also following his usual practice of at once going public with his last important discovery, James wrote another lecture, "A True Education," which he delivered to the Young Men's Association on December 11, 1846, and then repeated a week later at the Troy Athenaeum, just north of Albany. This time the *Albany Evening Journal* provided a long, respectful summary. Unlike James's talk of a year earlier, when his social vocabulary had been too impoverished for his subject, he now had a loosely Fourieristic scheme of the progressive stages of social development. The scheme begins (as in "What Constitutes the State?") with an original and instinctual self-fishness. First, man is softened by subjection to a patriarchal family bond. In time this is replaced by the "municipal bond," which gives way in turn to the "national bond." This represents the present state. The final step—the achievement of a supreme unity—is about to be taken.* This is the inner story of history, and as each individual grows up, he duplicates the movement from the isolated self to egalitarian identification with the whole. A true education, therefore, should not instruct us in some useless branch of learning, such as the "dead languages," but should prepare us to fill a position that will be of use to society. Although it is true that people in general cannot get a true education until society has been perfected, we see many signs of this impending consummation—a decline in aristocratic narrowness (exemplified by England's repeal of the Corn Laws earlier that year) and a new recognition that education should be adapted to the student's aptitudes and interests.

James did not name Fourier in his talk, or appear to realize that the Frenchman's embrace of the soul's passions was at odds with his own stress on disciplinary subjection. The depravity of the individual was still his starting point, and his chief doctrine still the necessity of beating down the self ("All history is only a record of the battle between individualism and society"). Nevertheless, the lecture, James's best work to date, went considerably beyond anything he had done. Thanks to Fourier, he now had a set of non-religious, non-ethical categories with which to articulate his thought. He was in contact with current political ideals and to that extent less isolated than in 1845, when Wilkinson sarcastically asked (before the checks started coming) whether James had "an intrinsic objection to form part of a larger unity than your own Society." The lecturer's tone had become less preachy, less intense, and when he drew on his private experience, it was not to castigate himself or others but to amuse, to illustrate—to show how he himself had inadvertently participated in prevailing trends. He was even relaxed enough to tell the hometown crowd that "we may some of us" feel a pride in our birth, "but we are ashamed to own it, ashamed to bring it out to the air." All

---

* Fourier's stages were more numerous: Edenism, Savageism, Patriarchalism, Barbarism, Civilization (the current stage), Guaranteeism, Socialism, and Harmonism.

in all, the lecture represented James's first successful integration of the secular and the religious, the urbane and the confessional.

James's new self-confidence shows up in his interesting reading of the story of Ishmael and Isaac. Ishmael, Abraham's son by his bondwoman Hagar, became the desert wanderer, whereas Isaac, Abraham's son by his wife, Sarah, inherited his father's land and flocks. James interpreted the difference between the two half brothers' destinies as follows: "Ishmael the *natural* son, shall be exceedingly blessed, only not with the blessing promised to Isaac, the son of marriage, the offspring of the social state." In this reading, Ishmael stands for man's natural state and Isaac for man's attained state—man as educated, as socialized. This distinction is a version of James's earlier contrast between the two Adams—man as created and man as he is remade (or remakes himself). But this later contrast is social as well as ontological, and what is more, the speaker assumes that he himself is at last fully socialized. *He* is Isaac, and it is because he knows he is that he speaks so assuredly about the rewards of the "social state." For some fifteen years he had been the Ishmaelitic wanderer, all but cut off by his father and then further detached when he abandoned Princeton and Presbyterianism. Now he is home, he has his full share of the paternal estate, he has recovered from his breakdown, he has worked out a higher-order Calvinism, and he is coming into his own intellectually and spiritually.

And who is Ishmael? When Henry returned from England to the United States, he hoped to proselytize his older half brother with his latest Swedenborgian discoveries.* Although Rev. William preached for other Presbyterian ministers on occasion and played an active role in Albany's Society for the Relief of the Poor (becoming president the same month that Henry delivered his lecture), he had no congregation of his own and remained isolated and professionless. By contrast, now that Henry was back in Albany, he was finding his "use" as prophetic teacher to the community at large. The older half brother might be "exceedingly blessed," but it was becoming evident he would get the smaller portion, like Ishmael. It was Henry, a product of the third and last marriage, who would inherit the father's powerful mantle—the ability to project himself, impose himself, on his countrymen.

New York State had recently expanded its public school system, and there was considerable interest in the proper goals and limits of public

---

* Henry may have given Rev. William's thinking a new impetus. "Sanctification," the latter once wrote, "is the identification of the social and the religious instincts; the religious being the culmination of the social. This is the thought which has been working in the upper or philosophical chamber of my soul since 1846."

education.* Now James's own flagrantly wasted education and his encounter with Bronson Alcott's theory of instruction in the pages of *The
Dial* and perhaps at Alcott House in England issued in a fresh vision of
the purpose of school—to call "forth in every one his distinctive faculty
or worth." Offering a splendid formulation of this goal, James told the
Young Men of Albany and Troy that education ought to "evoke [the]
living mind from its natural bed, to develop its assimilating and repro-
ductive energy to the highest pitch." Both the analogy with bodily functions and the faint suggestion of the speaker's long-ago and quite literal
confinement to his bed make this an eminently Jamesian proposition—
one that captures and celebrates a mental process precisely by undoing
the separation between mind and body.

James's own education, he made clear, had been too narrow and old-
fashioned, and he dwelt at some length on the pointless memorization
and discipline he had been forced to endure. Placing the blame not on
individual teachers but on the received ideas of the time (in accord with
his new social-historical framework), he went into fascinating detail on
his early school days:

> I do not think that a day ever passed when I was a school boy that I did
> not get at least one flogging from one or other of my teachers, not seldom
> one from each of them. I remember one old lady in particular, who
> inducted me into the mysteries of the spelling-book, and whose instru-
> ments of torture were a great black strap freely applicable to the body
> from the shoulders downward, and a huge stick of hickory held up at arms
> length till the whole body fairly ached with agony. I distinctly remember
> that I never rose to recite under her roof, without a silent ejaculation to
> God that he would preserve me from missing.

Albany Academy had no women teachers. All entering pupils were
expected to know how to read. James was recalling his primary schooling
at a "dame-school"—a place nowhere else referred to in his writing—
to which he had been sent before the age of eight. Happily, one memory
called up another:

> I am sure Columbus could scarcely have felt a thrill of deeper joy . . .
> than I did when one morning on going to school I learned that the huge
> black strap was missing and defied all efforts to reproduce it, and the
> feeling of mingled awe and admiration which filled my bosom toward the

---

* There is some slight evidence that James produced "An Address upon Education in the Common
Schools" in 1843. No trace of the lecture or pamphlet has been found.

intrepid little damsel who, it was whispered, had hid it, doubtless exceeded any homage I have paid to mortal heroism since.*

Memories like these help explain the writer's lifelong invocation of force, discipline, scourges, and prayerful supplication. His witty diction ("defied all efforts to reproduce it") hints that the huge black strap *wanted* to remain hidden and inactive. But the speaker's own vocabulary of punishment tells us that the strap managed to reproduce itself quite well from its hiding place in the dark.

Perhaps the chief reason schools were on James's mind was that he was now the father of boys whom it was his responsibility to educate. That this responsibility weighed on him we see from a passage in which the lecturer imagined himself as a rich man who is so careless in educating his son that he becomes a burden on society, a "spendthrift and vagabond." Was this a reference to some of the ne'er-do-wells in James's generation, perhaps even to his idle younger brothers, John Barber and Edward? Had he resolved to be a very different educator from what his own father had been? Whatever, the time had come to send first William and then Henry Jr. to *their* own dame-school.

The school was housed in one of the few yellow-brick, step-gabled structures that survived from Albany's homely Dutch period. This building, the old Vanderheyden mansion, was still there as late as the mid-1850s, by which time it was regarded as a familiar eyesore. "Everybody knows," wrote a sarcastic citizen, the "Dutch masterpiece a few doors north of the Female Academy." Henry Jr. saw it as simply the Dutch house. Frightened, perhaps, by its strange look, or by the stories Father told of his own early whippings at school, the three- or four-year-old boy could not be persuaded to enter. "Crying and kicking" on the threshold, he refused to be dragged inside even though he saw William "already seated at his task." Thirty-five years later, imagining the early life of *The Portrait of a Lady*'s Isabel Archer, who grows up in Albany, the novelist had her balk in just this way on the threshold of her education.

Unlike his heroine, Henry Jr. was eventually enticed into the school, probably in 1847. Sixty-five years later he vividly evoked the "small piping shuffling sound and suffered heat" along with the old Dutch-style windowpanes, which were "fitfully screened, though not to any revival of cheer, by a huge swaying, yet dominant object." This object, swaying

---

* In writing out his lectures, James used only one side of the page, probably to avoid confusion in the delivery. But his story about the stealing of the strap is found on the back of sheet 40, keyed to a passage on sheet 41. Evidently something prompted his memory after the lecture had been written.

in time with the drills she conducted, was the teacher, whose name, the novelist remembered, was "Miss Bayou or Bayhoo." It seems remarkable that he was able to retrieve this sound from a time when he did not yet know how to read and spell. But the preliterate memory can be amazingly accurate. According to *Hoffman's Albany Directory* for 1847–48, which would have appeared in the summer of 1847 (during the suffered heat), there was a Mrs. Bayeux, widow of Thomas, on North Pearl Street. She lived at no. 38, a few doors down from the Jameses at no. 50. Her husband had been a proprietor of a hotel on Market Street and then a "justice of justice's court" (justice of the peace?), and now she supported herself by running a dame-school in her house. Chances are, she had little learning and conceived of primary education as a standard repertoire of drills, chants, and exercises.

The next generation's education had begun, with a new set of pointless routines and whispered rumors and explanations never given.

THE BLACK STRAP FOUND

As James's new day dawned, he not only wrote and lectured but got involved in various organizational ways with Fourierists and Sweden-borgians. He made contact with the Reverends George Bush and Benjamin F. Barrett in New York, and together they talked about putting out a Swedenborgian monthly that would be less denominational than the Boston *New Jerusalem Magazine*. Barrett was the pastor of the Swedenborgian society that had been meeting at the New York Society Library. Bush, who had once been offered a position at Princeton Theological Seminary, was now Professor of Hebrew at New York University. He was also an old friend of Rev. William James. Highly suspicious of central ecclesiastical authority, Barrett and Bush were among the most liberal and articulate leaders of the New Church, and James was eager to inspire them with his vision of a loose fusion between Swedenborgian thought and the social ideals of Association. Not only did he have the money to back a new magazine, but he had a friend who could take charge of it, and during the spring and early summer of 1846 James tried to work out a deal with Barrett and Bush that would bring Wilkinson to New York to edit and contribute to the new venture. In pushing Wilkinson to take this plunge, James went so far as to offer him and his family living space in the Jameses' home. The Englishman declined the hospitality but found himself more and more intrigued by the idea of running a quality American magazine: "I presume something like the

Harbinger may be intended; or is it to be a statelier journal—an 8vo [octavo] Monthly?" He agreed with James that the journal must be "altogether extra-ecclesiastical," with nothing outside its scope and everything handled liberally: "we would review literature without at all ostensibly being pledged to render it up, a bound sacrifice . . . to the name of Swedenborg."

Not surprisingly, American Swedenborgians, "the Boston people" in particular, had serious reservations about this extra-ecclesiastical project, and the plan fell through by August 1846. On the whole Wilkinson was relieved and, in thanking James for his trouble, hoped "we shall never again hear of your . . . scheming in our behalf at three o'clock in the morning." One of the reasons for James's sleeplessness was that Wilkinson had let him know the transatlantic move must be completed before his wife's "accouchement" in September. Another was James's pressing need of an outlet for his newly expanded vision of the coming social state. He continued to scheme, and by the fall of 1846 he and Barrett were projecting a second journal, this one also designed to show the relevance of Swedenborg to "science and universal literature." Barrett, undoubtedly imagining the new venture in narrower terms than James, supposed it would be "for the New Church" in some way. Although Wilkinson would not be able to edit it, he would still contribute a regular London letter, with remuneration and assigned guidelines to come from James. The Englishman's job, James decided, would be to chronicle the progress of the "universal spirit, and the combined march of Providential events." Every two months he would have to exhibit the operation of Swedenborgian doctrines in the "every day world," most especially in "human society." The large, vague scope of this task made Wilkinson exceedingly nervous—"You have assigned to your friend both a delicate and a difficult occupation, and one which he cannot hope to succeed in to your satisfaction"—and before long he fell into "all sorts of depression" and began to miss deadlines. He also began to wonder why James insisted on *his* doing this work. "That one who can write such truly fascinating letters as you, should apply to me, quite puzzles me."

When this second journal also failed to see the light of day, Barrett went ahead and brought out the first number of what he hoped would be a continuing occasional publication, *The New Church Visitor*. He printed the first of the letters James had commissioned from Wilkinson, but the bulk of the issue consisted of two articles by Barrett dealing with touchy administrative issues within the New Church: should converts be rebaptized, and who should be allowed to take the Lord's Supper? Questions such as these, involving sacramental practice and institutional self-definition, were precisely what James wanted to avoid. His grand designs were not working out and he was beginning to feel constricted and angry. As the new year began, he turned his attention to two new projects, one grandiose, one punitive: a daily newspaper and a denunciation of the narrowness of Swedenborg's followers.

James had been associated with the Albany *Craftsman* when it became a daily in 1832, but he still had little idea how much capital and hard planning and ongoing supervision his latest pipedream would entail. From London, Wilkinson wrote that he was

> terribly alarmed for you in that project of the daily Paper! Of course I do not know . . . those possibilities which may lie embedded diamond wise in the deep strata of your genius, but looking at your transactions with *me*, I should say that you are such an unbusinesslike character & know so little of what is called the value of money . . . that I cannot help trembling for you.

Doing his best to kill the daily, Wilkinson proposed a more modest undertaking—a series of inexpensive pamphlets to be called "Tracts for the New Times."

With this suggestion, the frustrated James at last found an outlet for his grand dreams and growing wrath (and also for the sting of that sarcastic remark about his innocence in business). Two years earlier he had contemplated writing a "pamphlet about church errors," but then let the matter drop. Now, overriding Wilkinson's repeated advice to avoid controversy, he got to work on a philippic apparently aimed at Caleb Reed and the other Bostonians who ran the *New Jerusalem Magazine*. These men had not only obstructed James's efforts to proclaim the birth of a new mind and a new society; they had betrayed Swedenborg.

James's twenty-four-page *Letter to a Swedenborgian*, the first of the "Tracts for the New Times" (the second and third, much milder, were by Wilkinson), was organized as loosely as Sandeman's equally wrathful *Letters on Theron and Aspasio*, and as it trotted out its author's latest and greatest discoveries—the history of society, the errors of the Reformation, the perniciousness of evangelical Christianity—it let fly at one target after another. Tacitly repudiating his own extreme Calvinism of the later 1830s, James called justification by faith a "hideous dogma," which had destroyed charity throughout the Protestant world. His leading idea was that, far from intending to found another Christian denomination, Swedenborg's real message was that institutional religion had ended. The visible church had served its purpose, that was the whole point, and those who refused to let it merge with and transform the world were obstructing history. Swedenborg had disclosed the hidden ways in which the literal turns into the spiritual, and it was an outrage that those who claimed to follow him wouldn't understand that true religion was charity, a sense of equality with all, an abandonment of all sense of distinction. All the walls were falling down, but the only thing that interested official American Swedenborgians was keeping themselves intact and separate. James scourged them for their "puerility" and the "peculiarly odious aggravation" of their pretensions, which "repel the sympathy of every generous mind."

James might seem to be arguing that a religious era had given way to a secular one, that it was time to be liberal, but in fact he was saying something quite different—the church *has become* the world. He allowed that the American Constitution ruled out any establishment of religion, but he insisted that this apparent separation of church and state amounted, paradoxically, to the actual "consummation of the nominal Christian Church." Once again James was using his fist to enforce the spirit's unseen supremacy, in the process committing himself to a historical scheme as cranky, willful, and extreme as his 1845 lecture on the state, with its grand meltdown into universal love. And just as in 1838–40, when James insisted that the only righteous person is one who seems to be utterly foul, and who relies on God's grace alone, so now, in 1847, he proclaimed that the only true church is one that eagerly renounces the boundaries between itself and the world. From invisible saints James had progressed to an invisible church.

The *Liberator* reprinted large segments of the tract with approval, and so did the *Harbinger* (which mistakenly attributed it to Wilkinson). But the *New Jerusalem Magazine* stiffly repudiated it "as an unwarranted and unfounded attack." In their eyes, "the author belongs to the class of *destructives* who imagine that every positive institution is simply an impediment in the great path of modern progress." James sent the editors a rejoinder, insisting that he was a receiver of heavenly doctrine and disclaiming "all intention of provoking personal feelings," but they declined to print it on the grounds that he had no "claim to the use of our pages."

Their hearts are still dark, they are still given over to a separate self-love even as they proclaim their charity, they are overcome by their old narrowness in the very act of embracing a universal new spirit: one could easily turn these accusations back on the author of the intemperate 1847 tract. But the real point is the fatality, in both senses, of James's act. The man's inkwell was full of his dark unseen history, and he was driven to spend himself on tract after tract of merely parochial interest. The great irony of James's career is that he was undone by the sectarian narrowness he loved to attack. He could not let the quarrel with Caleb Reed or anyone else drop, and as the theological warfare continued to rage, he was moved to offer this justification for the punishment he loved to hand out: "Our love for all men constrains us to thwack any individual, who claims for himself a superior or different place in the divine regard to everybody else. But all the while is the tenderest pity shut up in our fist towards the subject!"

The big black strap was growing fiercer and more godlike in its hiding place.

Chapter 17

∎ ∎ ∎

ASSOCIATION IN NEW YORK:
1847–48

When James brought his family to New York in the summer of 1847, he headed for his mother-in-law's home on Washington Square and then rented all or part of a house at 11 Fifth Avenue, between Eighth and Ninth Streets. A few years later this and the adjoining houses were knocked down to make way for the Brevoort Hotel. But the Jameses' temporary perch was already shaky: the owner of record lived out of town, a complicated foreclosure suit was in process between successive leaseholders, and the building had been so neglected the rain had gotten in. Because of the carpenter's and mason's reports ordered by a court-appointed receiver, we know exactly what repairs were commissioned prior to the Jameses' arrival. The rain-soaked "stucco cornice in the tea room" had come loose and needed to be replaced; a marble mantelpiece was "tottering and unsafe & required to be reset"; the wooden "stoop" had to be rebuilt, as did the front balcony; the rear "piazza" was so rotten it needed a new floor; and because the back-yard privy had caved in, it was decided to have "the holes filled up." The house must have been in good order by the time Henry Sr. looked it over, but the unstable legal underpinnings would not have been evident. In February, near the end of the Jameses' occupancy, there was a sheriff's sale of the mortgage. The family moved out later that spring.

One of the reasons the Jameses were drawn to lower Fifth Avenue was that it was only a five-minute walk to 19 Waverley Place, where Mrs. Walsh was failing. Although the primary responsibility for easing her through the last few months of life fell on Catharine, the unmarried daughter, it must have been a convenience as well as a relief to have Mary close at hand, particularly in an era when personal nursing meant long hours of bedside watching. This ordeal finally came to an end three days before Christmas, 1847, when Elizabeth Walsh died. One of the tricky matters she had given close attention to in her last will and testament (drawn up eight years earlier) was the disposition of her silver. Mary, the older daughter, received "the best silver sugar dish and milk pot and small silver teapot and one dozen best tea spoons." Catharine got "the other silver tea set containing the same number of pieces and one dozen best tea spoons." All these "bests" show how hard Elizabeth tried to balance the claims of seniority with those of fair and equal treatment.

Also close at hand was Henry Jr.'s second dame-school, a small two-story house on the south side of Waverley Place where he was taught arithmetic and spelling by "a broad-bosomed, broad-based old lady" named Mrs. Daly. Perhaps the Walsh women's interest in formal tea service made an impression on the four-year-old boy, who remembered Mrs. Daly as "always having tea in a blue cup, with a saucer that didn't match." Unconventional as the Jameses were in some respects, they definitely did not make do in the way this teacher did. Thinking of her in his old age, the novelist was afraid she "must have been Irish."

One afternoon Henry Jr. was taken by his father to a row of houses on West Fourteenth Street, just east of Sixth Avenue. Walking up the steps of no. 58, the five-year-old boy saw a number of workmen, wearing folded newspapers as caps, casting plaster moldings and pasting a garish wallpaper from the floor up to the wainscot height. This was to be the family's new home. Henry Sr. had secured it by paying $5,000 for the remaining seven years of a long-term lease, and four years later he bought the property outright for an additional $4,000. It was assessed at $7,000, and there was a restrictive covenant preventing tenants from establishing "any stable slaughter house tallow chandlery smith shop forge furnace or brass foundry." No obnoxious trades or manufactures were allowed, but even so, the neighborhood was much less quiet, exclusive, and expensive than Washington Place, where the Jameses had bought in 1842. Fourteenth Street was broad and busy, empty lots abounded, and the new house was made not of brick but of brownstone, a material that encouraged architectural experimentation. The patterned wallpaper the James parents selected—"dragons and sphinxes and scrolls and other fine flourishes"—would seem to be in perfect keeping with their up-to-date location.

The Jameses moved in around May 1. Except for summers in Brooklyn and Staten Island and frequent visits up the Hudson to Albany, Rhine-beck, and elsewhere, their occupancy was uninterrupted for the next

seven years. This was both the most stable and perhaps the most stimulating period in the children's lives, and when they were taken to Europe
in 1855 for an extended residence in England, France, and Switzerland,
they looked back on the Fourteenth Street house and neighborhood as
home. Henry Jr. would always think of himself as originally a New Yorker.

Taking this house allowed the parents to consider a further enlargement of their family, and on August 7, 1848, almost nine months from
the date on the lease (November 15, 1847), Mary gave birth to her fifth
child—a girl, at last. She was called Alice, it is not known for whom.
Wilkinson grew quite giddy—"Ah, from the beginning to the end the
girls draw forth a new essence from the soul"—as he contemplated the
faery magic Alice would supposedly work on her nearly all-male family.
It might have been more apposite to wonder what the family would do
to Alice. How would she fit into the rough-and-tumble nursery established by four older brothers? What would she be taught by her coolly
judging and very superior mother? What sense would she make of her
ardent and confusing father?

ASSOCIATION IN NEW YORK

During the months in which James found and moved into a house of his
own and then completed his family, he showed a greatly increased interest
in the world outside his domestic circle. Familiar with New York for
many years, he was at last ready to engage with the city's stimulating
intellectual life. His failures of 1843 were behind him now, he knew
what men and movements he wanted to grapple with, and it wasn't long
before his manic energies were once again caught up in a strange, wild
crescendo.

One of James's first acts was to become a member of the New York
Society Library. A moderate user who checked books out once a month
or so, he began frequenting this private library the same winter Herman
Melville became a member. This fellow refugee from Albany had recently
made a name for himself with his first book, *Typee*, an adventure story
that offered readers a "peep" at the private life of Marquesas Islands
cannibals.

Manhattan's bookstores were another important literary venue for
James. A Swedenborgian he had met in Albany, William B. Hayden,
ran G. P. Putnam's main New York bookstore and later placed James
among the literary figures who visited the establishment "as often as once

a week." There was another bookstore that Henry Jr. recalled as the "fondest of my father's resorts." The small boy and his father visited its manager, an Englishman, in his office, and the Jameses had him and his wife over for dinner. Perhaps they were the Welfords, with a bookstore at 424 Grand Street.

The Jameses were in New York for a few weeks at most before they themselves dined with the Reverend Benjamin F. Barrett, one of the Swedenborgian ministers with whom James had tried to found a magazine. Another guest on this occasion was Anna Cora Mowatt, an actress with strong New Church connections. When Mowatt sailed to London two weeks later to seek a professional engagement, she carried a letter from James that introduced her to Emma Wilkinson and vouched for the actress as "unspoiled" and "perfectly feminine." The letter was not presented, and when the Wilkinsons saw Mrs. Mowatt onstage, they were not impressed. She was "better suited to genteel Comedy than to Tragedy," they felt.

In late October 1847 James read in the *New York Tribune* that there were letters waiting for him at the central post office. Going down at once to pick them up, he found a three-week-old invitation from James T. Fisher to attend an important Boston gathering of the American Union of Associationists. The meeting, already over and done with, had resulted in a decision to transfer the *Harbinger* to New York, and George Ripley with it. James immediately sent the Boston organizer an explanation of his absence and silence. He could not have attended even if he had got the invitation ("My affairs here give me a good deal of occupation just now") but he expressed his "complete sympathy" with the decision and made some remarks about the importance of avoiding all "petty wilfulness."

James concluded his letter with an amused yet somewhat ominous sketch of Ripley's siege of New York:

> I saw Mr. Ripley yesterday in busy, crowded Nassau St., taking a calm survey apparently of the force he is going to assail in the very citadel of its strength. When I saw him his countenance was still bright, and his voice full of cheer. But he had not yet reached Wall St, and of his state subsequent to that experience I am therefore unable to say anything. * A few moments before I had seen Godwin and Dana solacing themselves under the accumulated corruptions of that neighbourhood, by a lunch of a half-dozen oysters each in Downing's cellar.

* The next day Ripley wrote a friend he "hardly had time to look round or breathe."

Charles Dana had recently been promoted to city editor at the *Tribune*, and Godwin was prospering at the *Post*. Nassau Street was part of their beat, a stone's throw from Ripley's Spruce Street *Harbinger* office. James was representing himself as comfortably at home with the city's progressive newspapermen. He makes himself appear to know their haunts and the financial ropes a good deal better than Ripley, the hopeful struggling outsider.

James took this knowing tone partly because he was making his most sustained effort yet to float a radical monthly. He called his latest venture *The New Times* and conceived of it as "devoted to the new movement." On November 6, in the first issue of the *Harbinger* to be published in New York, he put out an announcement that his journal would appear "about" January 1. Instead of relying on someone like Wilkinson to run the thing, he boldly planned to be his own editor, with his editorial address at 9 Spruce Street—the *Harbinger* office. One of Ripley's letters confirms that James was given a "quiet desk" in a corner of the "inner shrine," and also that he jokingly referred to himself as "St James the Less."

James depended on Wilkinson to write for the new journal and line up contributors from overseas, and even to secure a British distributor. The Englishman dutifully approached several London prospects, but ran into difficulties on account of James's emphasis on "the political or practical side of the social question." John Chapman, the obvious choice for distributor, was distinctly lukewarm. "Movement" journals and newspapers were a dime a dozen, and most of them (like the *Harbinger*) were barely scraping by. James's advertisement for *The New Times* ran through December 4 and then ceased. As Hayden put it in a confidential note to George Bush, "Mr. James has concluded not to 'appear' at present."

Another brave new venture that engaged James's interest this winter was the North American Phalanx, a farming and milling commune in New Jersey. Now that Brook Farm was history, well-to-do Fourierists in New York and other cities needed a new outlet for their idealism and dollars. In February 1848 James joined Tweedy, Fisher, Greeley, Francis G. Shaw, Marcus Spring, and others in forming the Phalansterian Realization Fund Society, designed to underwrite capital improvements; like most of the others, he pledged $5,000. Also, with Tweedy and Shaw, he was elected to the Executive Committee. Full of enthusiasm, James sent Wilkinson a report on "the Phalanx" and perhaps urged his friend to move there with his family. But the cautious Wilkinson stayed put in Hampstead, and wisely so, for although the commune's wealthy backers dreamed of building a Grand Unitary Edifice, those who lived and worked at the North American Phalanx were chiefly interested in improving its productivity. In the end neither the workers' nor the capitalists' dreams were to be realized. The actual amount of money sunk in this venture was considerably less than what was pledged.

James had been drawn to New York by "the prospect of . . . preaching & lecturing," and one of the projects he joined during the winter of 1847–48 was a series of talks on Association. At first these were billed as a regular course of lectures by a varied roster of speakers—"Greeley, Ripley, James, Godwin, Macdaniel, Dana." Godwin opened the series with a talk on "The Tendencies of the Nineteenth Century in Art, Science, and Religion." He was followed by Dana on "The Progress of Society," Ripley on "The Problem of the Present Age," Greeley on "The Problem of Society." Whether it was because James's name was not felt to be much of a draw or for some other reason, the *Tribune* did not advertise him or his topic, "The religious grounds of Association." The meetings were held Friday evenings from November to March in a room at the Medical College. As the months wore on, those who came evolved into a sort of discussion club, the New-York Union of Associationists.

James's talk at once caught the attention of Boston's Associationists, whose weekly gatherings were more private and religious than those of the New Yorkers. The Boston group called itself the Religious Union of Associationists and included several former members or associates of Brook Farm—John S. Dwight, Anna Q.T. Parsons, Fanny Macdaniel. Half phalanx, half church, the group had a regular Sunday-evening "service" that included prayer and sacred music. At a certain moment members would form a circle, hold hands, and repeat a pledge to one another. They issued a call to William Henry Channing to be their "minister," and after accepting he persuaded them to celebrate the Lord's Supper. In effect, the Bostonians amalgamated Fourier's new order with the traditional forms of the Protestant worship service. If Mr. James had something to say about Fourier's "religious grounds," they wanted to hear about it. On March 26, 1848, Dwight read James's lecture at one of the regular weekly meetings, and when he was done (the secretary noted) there was "an animated conversation on Mr. James views & on the value of Swedenborgs writings." In Boston, animated conversation meant disagreement, debate. The argument was resumed the following week, when Channing led off with "some remarks respecting Mr. James late lecture before the Boston Union." Once again the un-Rev? Mr. James had proved a firebrand in the sanctuary.

By the beginning of 1848 most American phalanxes had collapsed, and it began to look as if Fourier's grand prophecies would produce little more than animated conversation among small groups of the earnest, the well-read, and the mostly respectable. Then, on March 18, the *Cambria* arrived from Europe with thrilling news: a revolution in France, troops firing on crowds, barricades thrown up, and King Louis Philippe fleeing the Tuileries for England. Gus and John Barber James brought the news in person to 11 Fifth Avenue, and little Henry Jr., still not quite five years old, never forgot "the apparent consternation of my elders" or the fateful words "fled to England." Gus may well have been alarmed, being a businessman who frowned on disruptions to the stability of commerce, but American Associationists were jubilant. The *Tribune* urged readers to waste no pity on the King, who had failed to work "in unison with the constructive tendencies of the epoch." Cannons were fired and flags hoisted, and when a public meeting was convened by New York's Fourierists, the roster of speakers was headed by James's new crowd—Godwin, Ripley, Dana. Several resolutions were approved, among them this: "We hail the Revolution of February with peculiar exultation, as an evidence of the progress of human affairs."

For the people who made up James's new intellectual circle, the upheaval in France was the most hopeful political event of their time. It confirmed their conviction that they were the harbingers of a new social era, that the New Times were truly on the way. Dana and Fisher left for Europe, Dana to cover political events in France for the *Tribune* and Fisher to attend a congress of Associationists. The latter, a publicist at heart, reported back to the Boston Religious Union that "wherever we may go in Paris the newsboy may be heard crying *voilà la Democratie Pacifique*." (This was the Fourierist newspaper Mrs. Chichester took.) Emerson, spending most of May in Paris, was tremendously impressed by the earnest political passions of the workers' clubs. Wilkinson was on the spot during the bloody June days and the summary executions of revolutionaries. Disturbed, he wrote Henry that the "visit is still engraven on me, and comes out in dream & reverie with singular vividness."

Curiously, the earliest evidence of James's support of the revolution dates from sixteen months after it had begun, at a time when Louis Napoleon had assumed the presidency and the conservative reaction had set in. On June 5, 1849, when the *Tribune* was anxiously awaiting the latest election returns from France, Greeley still bravely hoped for the best: "What though the vain, incompetent nephew of the great betrayer of European Liberty [Napoleon Bonaparte] sits in her Executive chair." Two days later, the featured headline on the *Tribune*'s first page announced the glad but misleading tidings: "The Socialists Triumph in All

France." On that day James scribbled a brief afterthought in a letter to Fisher: "The news from France is very significant of better things."

Was Henry Jr. right in supposing that his father felt consternation at the news of the French King's flight? The best answer seems to be that although Henry Sr. made common cause with New York's Association-ists, he harbored his own private agenda. He, too, spoke and wrote the words "equality" and "socialism," but always to construe them in a sense all his own.

WRITER FOR THE *HARBINGER*

In Albany city directories of the 1820s most people were identified by their occupation or business—merchant, attorney, hatter, hackman, cartman, waterman, hand in steamboat. A woman might be identified as "widow of George," unless she had to scramble for a living, as did "*Shely*, widow *Patience*, does all she can get to do, 5 Water." The ex-ceptions were those who stood below or above the whole system of specialized trades. If you were Stephen Van Rensselaer or William James, your name wasn't followed by anything except your address. Aristocratic titles having been abolished, the most that could be said of Rensselaer was that he was the former patroon. As for William James, what he was was William James.

The lives led by William James's sons show how difficult it can be for a king's sons living in a democracy to decide what they are going to be. Like their father, Gus and Henry never provided the compilers of city directories with an identifying profession after their names. In this and other ways the James boys exhibited the true royal stigmata. Rev. Wil-liam, for instance, the oldest surviving son, might have been "occasion-ally too brusque, and sometimes arrogant," in an admirer's eyes, but he had "a high and expansive forehead," and if he was occasionally rude, well, "he had to be frank by the regal type of his nature." But the crown never rests easily, and once, after Rev. William's feelings had been wounded, he complained: "How often have people said to me, 'If you had only been a poor man, and compelled to work'! Compelled to work indeed! . . . I did not need the stimulus of poverty; a far stronger stimulus was the disgrace which is attached, in this age and country, to a recluse or unofficial life."

Henry Sr. never came closer to having an official vocation than in 1848, the year of revolution. From November 1847 to February 1849 he functioned to all intents and purposes as a regular staff writer and assistant editor for the weekly *Harbinger*; he even got his mail there in the summer. It isn't known whether he accepted payment at the standard rate, $1 per page; perhaps not, since he was putting his "spare cash" into the magazine. Ripley described his role by telling a friend that "James is a saint & a host, & is up to any thing." He selected excerpts from the periodical press, noticed books and magazines, replied to critics, and edited various contributions including Wilkinson's letters from London. Although he wasn't asked to write the lead articles, hardly a week went by without something of his getting into the magazine, generally something on the belligerent side. Perhaps he was thought of as the polemics editor, the house bulldog. Without being one of the major contributors, he enjoyed their privilege of having his pieces identified by a pair of pseudonymous letters, Y.S. If these initials stood for Your Servant, as has been conjectured, they well exemplify the ambiguous humility with which he served the cause.

A shrewd contemporary critic of the *Harbinger* remarked that "while the *principles* to which the paper is professedly devoted are distinguished for favoring the common people, the *tone* of the paper itself seems to us quite aristocratic." A similar point could be made about Y.S.'s labors for the magazine: although he seemed to be putting his shoulder to the wheel along with Ripley and the others, he always propelled it in a direction all his own. A favorite novelist being G.P.R. James (owing, it seems, to the coincidental last name), Y.S. contributed brief notices of three of the popular Englishman's latest tales. Continuing his old quarrel with the Calvinists, he attacked the chief Presbyterian weekly, the *New York Observer*. He also attacked the *New Jerusalem Magazine* after it dared to question his understanding of Swedenborg, his essay spilling over into a second issue. In February 1848, after Bush had managed to launch the new Swedenborgian monthly that James had tried and failed to bring out, Y.S. responded with a hostile piece on the editor's opening statement. Over and over, James seemed to regard the chief Associationist weekly as the fitting vehicle for his own concerns, and if his animadversions on the two sects he had it in for most of all, the Presbyterians and the Swedenborgians, called up a reply, he would commandeer the *Harbinger*'s pages for a full and frank and often very personal rebuttal. "What possessed the man to prattle himself into such imbecility?" he would ask of his antagonist, and if the imbecile made any sort of noise in response, he got a second trouncing, and so on. No other *Harbinger* writer engaged in this sort of fisticuffs.

James's various contributions almost never spoke to the reorganization of labor and capital in industrial society. Instead—and in this he carried a basic American tendency to an extreme—his attention was held by certain tangential issues in theology, philosophy, and psychology. What particularly excited him was the prospect that the new psychic frontiers would effect a revolution in theology. He was even disposed, like many others in the late 1840s, to welcome the bizarre revelations of Andrew Jackson Davis, the mesmeric shoemaker from Poughkeepsie.

In 1845 Davis had been blindfolded by a "magnetic operator" and put into a clairvoyant state, the idea being to see whether an uneducated nineteen-year-old could discover the ultimate laws of nature. The experiment was pronounced a success and was then repeated in front of influential witnesses, including Bush and Edgar Allan Poe. Davis was illiterate and had a sunken chest and seemed blatantly effete (his father had been coarse and harsh), but the young man cherished a powerful private image of a magic staff, which he liked to lean on, mentally, during his trance-excursions. His insights were taken down by a trusted scribe, and when they were published in *The Principles of Nature, Her Divine Revelations, and a Voice to Mankind*, the book proved to be one of the sensations of 1847. The clairvoyant had discovered that the inhabitants of the planet Jupiter lived in an ideal state combining the best of Swedenborg and Fourier. They had a "peculiar prominence of the upper lip" that fully conveyed their inner thoughts; their "universal affection" was far greater than their self-love; and when they reached the end of their individual existence, instead of dying they "sink into repose by an expansion of their interiors which seek more agreeable spheres."

If Davis resembled Swedenborg and Fourier in being a gifted imaginer of alternative worlds, he was unlike them in his ability to put a greatly simplified form of their visions across to a modern mass audience. The *Harbinger*'s better educated but less successful publicists saw Davis as both a miracle and a miracle worker. Ripley called his book "the most surpassing prodigy of literary history." Godwin thought it displayed "an astonishing, almost prodigious power of generalization." Wilkinson was "mightily taken" and declared for its "absolute authenticity." But the official Swedenborgian guardians of visionary truth drew back warily. Bush wanted to believe that mesmerism heralded the arrival of a new age, bringing new psychic powers to mankind, and his initial reaction to Davis was unguarded and enthusiastic. But Bush changed his mind after seeing the young man's ravings in print and, together with Barrett, wrote a pamphlet discrediting them.

Ten years later, when Davis was no longer newsworthy and had become one more minor fringe American prophet, James dismissed him as a "mere sentimental sot." In 1847, however, James took the clairvoyant's side against Barrett and Bush, defending him with a very strange argument. We know, James premised, that man is both good and evil. But we also know from reading Swedenborg that God is essential man. Hence, it is clear that God embraces evil as well as good, and this being accepted, we see that "the attempt to crush Davis's book, by asserting its purely hellish genesis, in reality conveys a reproach to the Divine." Some of Davis's believers wanted to get a peep at Jovian social organization, but what James saw in the clairvoyant was a magic strap with which to belabor the Swedenborgian clergy.

James had come a long way from Rev. Campbell's solemn warning never to traffic in spirits, and he had also set aside his great obsession with regeneration. Suddenly he was much less concerned with the problem of transforming an evil man into a good man than with the very different problem of fully expressing both one's evil and one's good. For the first time in his life he was willing to heed whatever came out of the woodwork, even if it said dangerous things, even if it spoke the pedantic jargon of an uneducated mesmeric lecturer. The editors of the *New Jerusalem Magazine* were appalled by James's argument and quoted him at considerable length to show how misinformed he was, and also how bizarre was his argument "that to reject a thing on account of its purely hellish origin, is only casting reproach upon the Divine." Of course, James used the *Harbinger* to answer them at length.

The battle moved into a new phase when James got hold of an advance copy of a new book that seemed to tie everything together, *The True Organization of the New Church, as Indicated in the Writings of Emanuel Swedenborg, and Demonstrated by Charles Fourier.* The book's author, Charles J. Hempel, a German homeopathist practicing in New York, had come up with a formula that struck James and others as wonderfully illuminating: Fourier is to Swedenborg as science is to religion. In Hempel's words:

> Swedenborg leaves his disciples ignorant of the particular nature of Divine Order, or that Orderly Arrangement which exists from the Lord, in the Natural Man, and which must be realized first, in order that the conjunction of the External and the Internal Man may be effected. It is this Orderly Arrangement which Fourier has discovered, and which the disciples of Swedenborg require to know to organize their Church.

James welcomed the book in the *Harbinger* and gave long extracts from it. But the Swedenborgians, twice stung, would have nothing to do with the new synthesis. Caleb Reed pointed out that Swedenborg's "doctrine of regeneration" was not compatible with Fourier's hope that in the phalanx everyone "should freely act out his own natural inclinations," and Bush let Barrett have thirty pages of the *New Church Repository* for a detailed refutation. Responding immediately, James defended Hempel and scourged Reed and answered all earlier attacks on himself with unshrinking vigor and belligerence and fullness of expression.

By this time Rev. Barrett had left New York for a pulpit in Cincinnati, from which city he jealously followed whatever Y.S. was up to in the *Harbinger*. Barrett had his own ample stock of prickliness, and when he read James's latest squib in the July 8 issue, he dashed off a letter of protest to the magazine. James took the responsibility of answering his former associate. If he had followed the usual editorial practice, he would have printed the letter and then replied to it. Instead, he quoted a few brief passages, refuted each in turn and at length, and concluded with the claim that "the reader has now before him the whole pith of B.F.B.'s long communication, bating a few flippant personalities." It was a re-markably high-handed way of denying a critic a voice, and Barrett, far from New York, was helpless and outraged. When neither James nor Bush would print his splenetic rejoinder, he sent it to the Cincinnati *Daily Times*, whose readers were informed that the *Harbinger* had "opened its columns to false and railing accusations against the members of the New Church" from the pen of a writer "so mean, low and prejudiced, and so imbued with bitterness and scorn," that he deserved to be ignored. James's response was a further aggravation: he had the *Harbinger* print a reply to Barrett from "A New Churchman" that had appeared in a rival Cincinnati paper.

Barrett's postmortem on this minor fracas breathes with the resentment James stirred up in some of his contemporaries: "I have no idea that Mr. Godwin or Mr. Ripley, would willingly have acted so unjustly; but I suppose that Mr. J. on account of his wealth &c, is, very foolishly, allowed to have his own way entirely in that concern." This explanation of James's immunity is not far off. Ripley's and Godwin's need for ad-ditional capital persuaded them to take James's bailouts,* but the help did not come without strings. Having failed to found a magazine of his own, James eagerly seized the opportunity to merge his new social con-

---

* The *Harbinger* received $78.86 from James in February 1848, and in December Ripley acknowl-edged additional aid.

cerns with his private pipedreams and vendettas. Of course, he believed he was actuated by the collective good rather than by any "petty wilfulness," as he'd written Fisher. Refusing to allow his critics a hearing at the same time that he confidently proclaimed they surely must confess their doubts and errors, James was putting into practice the union of self-love and universal love. The boundaries between individuals had disappeared, love and science were in the ascendant, and James happily distributed his kingly thwacks to the many private interests that refused allegiance to the new times.

The consequences could have been foreseen. The thwacked drew the conclusion that James's "wealth &c" was the explanation of his royal absolutism, and the dream of equal association was discredited and corrupted.

THE DIVINE MAN

As James drove his pen week after week during 1848, he elaborated his basic philosophical position by taking on some of the standard topics of the day—duty, benevolence, freedom, necessity. Following a very different program from Emerson, who (at his best) teased out the most delicate organic growths from his reading and fugitive thoughts, James pounded out a number of major essays of startling originality. There was always a great show of logic, and the logic always carried him to a place nobody else had ever dreamed of going. He seemed to have an extraordinary sense of assurance, his sentences grew longer and more rhetorical and moved with a great rollicking staying power, and his diction crossed the line again and again between the refined and the colloquial. He stepped on toes right and left and snorted at those he offended—being "frightfully able to take care of himself," as Godwin wrote. Discerning readers sat up and took notice. Who was this American Carlyle? James was having his day, and as he did so, his handwriting changed significantly between 1847 and 1849. Formerly his written script had been tight and economical, with small letters and lines packed close together. Now his writing hand relaxed. His words were no less legible, but they expanded by two or three times, and there was a lot of empty space between them. He bought large quantities of paper, some of it (for his lectures) the finest vellum.

In July 1848 James had an essay in the *Harbinger*, "The Divine Life in Man," that expressed his new sense of coming into his own. This essay proved to be one of his boldest and most seminal productions. An amplified version appeared in Theodore Parker's *Massachusetts Quarterly Review* in December 1849 under the title "A Scientific Statement of the Doctrine of the Lord, or Divine Man." Soon after, James made this the opening lecture in his first real book, *Moralism and Christianity*. His revolutionary idea of the Divine Life played a pivotal role in his development: it marked the completion of his recovery from the disasters of 1843-44, and it finally established him as a controversial voice of great interest to a number of mid-century social/theological thinkers.

Not surprisingly, there was something flagrantly shameless in James's Divine Life writings. The opening lecture in *Moralism and Christianity* begins, safely enough, by exalting God as the only unconditioned being. But then the author allows that man is capable of participating in God's self-originating, self-satisfying power, and before long we are hearing about a remarkable being called the Divine Man. Contrary to what one might guess, this figure is not to be identified with Jesus, who was merely the harbinger, the foreshadowing type of one who is now arriving.

One of the breathtaking aspects of James's "Scientific Statement" is the completeness with which it reinvents the world. God is the one and only being, the universe is nothing but a huge theater of shadows and images of God, and nothing ever happens except for some further "imaging forth" of God. He alone is self-sufficient, self-generating, and spontaneous. Aside from him, all things exist only for "use." Unlike ordinary things, however, man has a "composite self-hood," being both person and thing, both internal and external, spiritual and natural. As James's essay proceeds, his purpose in setting up this system becomes clear: he wants to apotheosize a certain kind of human activity in which man's internal and external selves act in unison. At present, man still follows the law of nature and the law of duty: whatever he does is done to satisfy some material need or social obligation. In each respect, naturally and morally, man does not act spontaneously or "personally" but only in subjection to external laws. Only when he is released from all physical or social entanglements does he become godlike. Having made this point, James unveils his basic and outrageous idea: "He who has power to originate his own action is sufficient unto himself, and to be sufficient unto oneself is to be infinite or perfect."

The imperative duty that James had announced in "What Constitutes the State?"—submerging the self in others, subordinating self-love to universal love—had undergone a profound transformation. The self's expansive tendency, merely implicit in the earlier lecture, had come out into the open. James called his new ideal the "aesthetic man, or Artist," a term not restricted to the painter or poet but designating any person whose activity derives solely from "his own internal taste or attraction." The kicker here—it is one Thoreau would have hooted at—is that no poor man can be an Artist, nor can anyone with unsatisfied desires. Suppose I am wealthy, wrote James (asking his readers, rather oddly, to regard the actual as the hypothetical): only then can I become, like God, a true creator.

Originally, writing in the *Harbinger*, James did without the hypothetical pretense and actually cited his own, present, self-satisfying literary production as an instance of the divine superiority of "aesthetic activity":

> Take for example, my present employment. It does not spring from any necessity of the natural life, for I have bread for all my physical wants. Nor does it spring from any sense of obligation to my neighbor, for being addressed to the universal reason of man, it is not fitted to promote any specific or individual interests. It is exclusively the offspring of my own delight or attraction towards this kind of labor. I am happy in performing it . . .

James was freed from nature by his wealth and he had found a satisfying outlet. Acting just as he was, he constituted an authentic revelation of God, a "Lord of the new creation." And just as God was the one and only person who did not need to worry about his "use," so James had every right to command the pages of the Fourierists' weekly as he variously addressed the universal reason of man or caned the backsides of Barrett, Bush, and Reed. "It really passes patience," he sighed in a review, "that so utterly common place a set of men, distinguished neither for virtue nor intelligence . . . of a most mediocre culture in all respects . . . should have the face to parade themselves before the world as the fulfilment of all divine promise and all human hope."

One of the reasons James left his readers breathless in the latter 1840s was that few speculative thinkers had ever laid hold of Christian thought with such magnificent, unblushing arrogance. God being all-powerful, would it be correct to suppose that the Divine Man, the aesthetic man, the ideal Artist, the one and only personal man, should also make a grab for supreme power? It would, and James went so far as to declare that the only individual who can be considered good is one who makes himself the lord of all. He was quite explicit on the point. Imagine a merchant, Mr. A. or B., he said, who drives all his competitors out of business, "systematically strangling" them. This man's motive is nothing less than "an unmistakably divine aspiration after unlimited power." What will happen once this strangler achieves his goal? "The final and divine Mr.

A. or B.," James declares, "will have subjected both nature and society to himself, and will then exhibit, by virtue of that very force in him, which is now so destructively operative, a personality of unmixed be-nignity."

James's reflections from 1848 to 1850 on the Divine Life were an astonishingly open expression of a sense of absolute sovereignty. And precisely as one might have predicted, in the midst of his dazzling per-formance this daring, mercurial, and morbid man flashed a strange guilt-stricken abjection. The more he talked about the Divine Man, the more he seemed to return to the problem of criminality, murder in particular, for which he offered a single explanation—the murderer's need for money. James's chief point was that, because those who killed were merely satisfying this need (and thus obeying an external law), they were not to be considered guilty. James not only exonerated Professor Webster, the infamous murderer and dismemberer of his creditor, Dr. Parkman, but he chose to dramatize *himself* as murderer in an arresting hypothetical example:

> Let me precisely illustrate my meaning by a case in point. A certain man is murdered by me. You witness the deed and denounce me as the murderer. On my trial it is proved that the deceased stood in the way of a certain inheritance coming to me; that I had exhibited various marks of vexation at this circumstance, and had been heard to wish him out of the way, and even threaten to remove him myself.

The fictive example is elaborated for three or four pages, and as one reads it one has to wonder whether it emerged in some way from James's father's death and the troubled inheritance, especially when the hypo-thetical murderer, by now hardly distinguishable from the writer, pleads his essential innocence:

> I am not attempting to palliate the enormity of the act. It is perfectly detestable in itself, and will always be so. I merely deny that my spirit and my flesh were *one* in it, which unity is necessary in every act that is spiritually mine. I merely assert that my spirit was *overruled* by my flesh to do this evil thing.

Will always be so. There is a strange jumble of tenses here, alternating between the hypothetical present and the historical past, with just that one brief touch of the future and its eternity of blame. Was James once again disguising the actual as the hypothetical?

What James saw in the universe—a closed theater in which a single actor is reflected over and over in a complex system of images and correspondences—is an exact description of the little world of his lecture. We cannot know to what extent he was, or felt he was, guilty of his father's fatal apoplectic fit, or even how he regarded his part in the breaking of the will. But he was clearly sovereign in the world of his lecture, and this he constructed in such a way that he both made a hypothetical confession of murder and claimed a supreme self-authenticating spirituality. The lecture was a multilayered expression of James's new sense of legitimacy. The strangling man had achieved complete power and benignity. He was not a criminal but a divine rich man.

Or does divine *mean* rich? The striking contradiction in James's lecture is that while the poor man's desire for wealth is a sign of his "outward" or "natural" status, the wealthy man's successful greed only guarantees his perfect oneness with God.

Chapter 18

■ ■ ■

EROTIC LIBERTY:
1848–50

LOVE IN THE PHALANX

Antinomianism is the technical name for the religious enthusiasm that proclaims a new age of the spirit and the end of law. As the French Revolution of 1848 ran its course, James, like antinomians of many other times and places, became convinced that monogamy was obsolescent. This phase of his development, one of the most reckless, brought on a great deal of acrimonious and embarrassing controversy. He was accused of being a free lover, and there was such an air of scandal about his opinions that at his death more than one obituary writer considered it necessary to assure the public that, however "erratic in belief, he nevertheless led a pure and blameless life." His children threw a veil over his views on marriage and divorce, which in time dropped out of sight. In 1930, when Austin Warren was writing the pioneering biography of James, he assured the grandson who guarded the family papers that "I am trying to keep within properly modest bounds . . . his views on love and marriage, which ought neither to be omitted nor unduly 'played up.' " Henry III was reading certain parts of the manuscript, and Warren had to be careful.

Emanuel Swedenborg had declared in *Conjugial Love* that, although marriage was binding and sacred, it was permissible for a man to take a mistress in certain circumstances. Some Swedenborgians considered the seer's toleration of concubinage "a very *ticklish* thing," and in 1847, when George Bush came out with a brief reply to an attack on Swedenborg, James was reported to have said that the pamphlet was too apologetic and "hardly took ground bold enough on the scortatory doctrines." He and Wilkinson agreed that "the question of a particular man's alliance in concubinage must . . . be settled by himself." Not only that, but the Englishman considered James the ideal person to write about this dangerous topic: his "unexceptionable conjugality" would protect him.

Wilkinson also pushed James to get American Associationists to translate Fourier with less "Jesuitical timidity." But being candid about Fourier was an entirely different matter from being candid about Swedenborg. In 1843 Emerson and Bronson Alcott had talked about the Frenchman's "secret doctrines" on marriage and the "fury" anyone who advocated them would provoke. The following year, when Godwin wrote his little manual on Fourierism, he took a quick and nervous glance at the projected reorganization of the sexual passions. Because "the most irregular natures must be made to co-operate in the production of Harmonic Results," he rather opaquely informed his readers, those whom Fourier called Bacchantes and Bayadères would not be held to the same strict requirements as others. But all that, Godwin strenuously insisted, was strictly for the future. At present "freedom in matters of love, would lead to a frightful confusion—to the abandonment of children, to the degradation of women, and to the destruction of the family."

This combination of insinuation and piety might reassure willing believers (the quoted passages are all marked in James's copy of Godwin's book), but it could not ward off the fury of the suspicious. From March to September 1846—the very period when James was enrolling himself in the cause of Associationism—the Presbyterian *New York Observer* ran a series on Fourier's sexual teachings that was so aggressive the American Union of Associationists put out a statement disowning the master's teachings on the subject. Another powerful opponent was Henry J. Raymond, editor of the *New York Courier*, who set out to discredit Associationism as a whole by calling attention to Fourier's heterodox ideas on marriage. One result of Raymond's campaign was that Horace Greeley's *New York Tribune* distanced itself from the movement. "No aspect of Fourier's thought," writes Jonathan Beecher, "was more scrupulously avoided by his disciples than his reflections on love and sexuality." There was good reason for this avoidance, and by the time the *Harbinger* moved to New York, most of its editors and writers knew from bitter experience that the less they said about marriage the better.

On January 13, 1847, James T. Fisher began translating a pamphlet, *Les Amours au phalanstère*, by a French Fourierist named Victor Hennequin. Fisher's preface, possibly a translation from a French original, proclaimed the importance of candor and assailed the secret evils marriage promoted—adultery, abortion, infanticide, even "the conjugal use of arsenic." Beginning on May 29 of that year, Hennequin's *Love in the Phalanstery* was advertised in the *Harbinger* as being for sale at W. H. Graham's bookstore in the Tribune Buildings in New York. It is not known whether Fisher was responsible for this publication, or indeed whether it even existed, as no 1847 imprint has been found. Perhaps the booksellers were floating an untranslated or unpublished title to test the public's interest. In any case, it was not until the fall of 1848 that an English version of Hennequin's pamphlet went on the market, and was promptly reviewed with all the alarm and outrage Alcott had prophesied. Fisher may or may not have been involved in this publication, but it is certain that Henry James was. Taking full responsibility for the publication after the storm broke, James was the only prominent American Associationist of the time who had the courage, or the imprudence, or the fanatical excess, or the maddened self-destructiveness, or all of the above, to act on the belief that it was necessary to be frank and open about Fourier's vision of the erotic customs of the future.

According to Hennequin's pamphlet, all passions would be freely acted out in the harmonic phalanx. Anyone who wished to remain a virgin could do so. Anyone who preferred to take a single partner in marriage and remain faithful to this spouse would be able to have his or her way. Some people desire a series of sexual partners, or need more than one spouse at the same time. They will be accommodated, as will everyone else with a particular need (provided it is heterosexual). "God could not have given a small number of old men a tender interest in girls without having made a certain number of girls rather fond of old men." Fourier devised a series of technical categories—the *damoisellat*, the *faquirate*, the *pivotate*—for the various sexual passions, and Hennequin's tract explained each category in turn. *

The twenty-seven-page American translation ended with an exhortation: "Let us seek laws which accord with facts, and which are revealed to us by nature!" On the back cover the pamphlet was identified as one of a series sponsored by the American Union of Associationists, whose officers were named—Greeley, Ripley, Godwin, Tweedy. But the translator and author of the brief, defiant preface remained unnamed. This individual seemed to share the general aims of the Union—"the mastery and application of Fourier's industrial views"—but he avowed a "special interest in introducing the ensuing pamphlet to the public." His purpose,

---

* Emerson's response: "Will they, one of these days, at Fourierville, make boys & girls to order & pattern? I want, Mr Christmas office, a boy, between No 17 & No 134, half & half of both; or you might add a trace of 113. I want another girl like the one I took yesterday only you can put in a leetle more of the devil."

he said, was to refute the newspapers' "scurrilous falsities" and furnish an accurate account of Fourier's sexual teachings. He was confident that the pamphlet would succeed in "stopping the mouths of those who profess a great admiration of our present erotic institutions and manners, and charge Fourier with the design of corrupting them." It was time to revise "the present law of the sexual relations." This law is at fault because it gives each partner in a marriage "an absolute *property* in the affections" of the other, and thus "not only too commonly engenders a purely material relation among those who observe it, but directly instigates deception, adultery, domestic tyranny, and dissension throughout the land." The translator had curiously little to say about the content of Hennequin's essay, being chiefly concerned to argue that marriage, so far from being sacred, only encourages "our profuse prostitution and licentiousness."

The preface, terribly embattled, bristles with rage, sweeping condemnations, and a contestatory logic that wrenches the received sense of words. While the writer proclaims his lofty and pious "hope for the eventual extinction of the present adulterous and promiscuous commerce of the sexes," he seems to regard adultery and promiscuity as transgressive acts that take place *within* marriage rather than outside it:

> Where the husband does not inspire the highest affection of the wife, nor the wife that of the husband, then their intercourse is truly promiscuous, being the intercourse of consenting bodies merely, and dissentient souls. However much the law may declare these bodies united, their own souls pronounce the union adulterous, because destitute of all spiritual sanction.

Suppose the case were reversed and an *unmarried* couple happened to feel the highest affection for each other: would *their* union be promiscuous? The translator's answer shows that he was prepared to go all the way, so to speak: "Where this mutual preference for each other exists between the parties, there Love exists, and in a true social order every expression of it would be divinely beautiful and sacred." Of course, he issues the usual disclaimer that the reforms he speaks of are possible only in the future perfect.

Ripley stood behind the pamphlet to the extent that he quoted "the whole of the admirable preface" in the *Harbinger*. But the *Tribune*'s book reviewer made a laconic prediction of trouble to come: "We . . . presume the anti-Fourierites can find something in it which they might quote to great advantage." He was right, and one week later the *New York Observer* devoted two columns to a bare-knuckle attack on the pamphlet. The

reviewer was undoubtedly Samuel Irenæus Prime, who at this time conducted the *Observer* almost single-handedly. A product of Princeton
Theological Seminary and an admirer of Professors Samuel Miller and
Archibald Alexander, Prime was the nation's leading evangelical journalist. A co-religionist remembered him as "a great power in this land
. . . conservative by nature and education . . . When a principle was at
stake he set his face like a flint . . . If any impious hand touched the
ark of God his voice was a menace and his attitude martial at once.
Hands off! he cried." Prime began his review by pointing out that the
pamphlet was evidently an official publication of the American Union
of Associationists, which had up to now followed the "cowardly course"
of disowning Fourier's sexual libertinism. The translator, refreshingly,
showed "candor and courage." He "frankly avows the whole length of
Fourierism, and defends his most licentious views. We like such an
opponent. We know where to find him." Prime also knew how to wipe
the floor with him, and at the end of his review was able to conclude
that no one could read the pamphlet "without being convinced that
Fourierism is only another name for *promiscuity*, and the doctrines of
Association the most corrupt and corrupting that were ever promulgated
under the guise of virtue and reform."

James had brought precisely the kind of discredit on American Associationists that they had sought to avoid, and when he wrote his
rebuttal at his desk in the *Harbinger* office, he took sole responsibility
for translating and introducing Hennequin's tract. He claimed that it
was through a printer's error that "a chance advertisement of the *American
Union*" appeared on the cover, and in other ways he sought to limit the
damage. His purpose, he declared, was neither to endorse nor to deny
Fourier's detailed reorganization "of the love relations." All he wanted
was "to awaken public attention to the enormous evils which beset the
intercourse of the sexes at present." But sticking to his guns, he questioned whether "God has *absolutely* restricted the gratification of the
sexual passion to the conjugal relation" and he backed this position with
two very unorthodox arguments. First, since no man can act in opposition
to God, every sexual act must reflect *some* divine concurrence. Second,
the moral law, which forbids sex outside marriage, is only a stopgap until
the perfect society evolves and the law withers away and everyone attains
a perfect union of self-love and universal love. These arguments would
have had no effect on an Old School Presbyterian, as James perfectly
well knew. They represented a defensive tactic, an attempt to keep the
argument on his own turf and avoid an engagement on his fearsome
antagonist's terrain. Prime's editorial position gave him direct access to

James's family and old acquaintance. He could have tarnished an enemy's name once and for all. But while James reined in his invective, he pointed out that Prime and his backers belonged to a powerful conservative establishment: "The *Observer* and its friends, having for the most part secured a comfortable maintenance in this life, and a dazzling reversionary interest in that which is to come, are naturally disposed to justify the present." The debate between Hennequin's translator and the *Observer*'s editor was not just religious. It was a family quarrel between two sons —one bad, one good—of New York's Presbyterian aristocracy.

The publication of James's essay, signed Y.S., was one of his most consequential acts. He was now a standing target, and the confusions, contradictions, and dangerous implications of his thought were exposed to opponents and defenders alike. As it slowly became known who Y.S. was, the tiny band of radicals who dreamed of what would soon be called free love turned to him as a rich and powerful potential ally. Virtually everyone else, even among the Fourierists, considered him reckless and dangerous and at best exceedingly impolitic. James now began to learn how difficult it can be to defend a controversial position against the whole gamut of opinion.

One of his first and most tenacious opponents was the Reverend Alfred E. Ford, a Fourierist sympathizer who had recently entered the New Church ministry in Pennsylvania. Ford wrote to remind the *Harbinger* that Associationists would be well advised to abjure the master's views on marriage. This was the type of enemy—a liberal clergyman in favor of prudence and respectability—James loved to attack, and he handled his new antagonist much more insultingly than he had treated Prime. James became less inhibited in another way as well, arguing again and again that the only reason men are lustful and licentious is that sexual desire is under legal restraint:

> Why has sexual commerce among men ever worn a merely material or sensual character? The reason, in my view, is plain, and it is this: that *love* has not been left free. It has been confounded with marriage . . .
>
> When society binds two lovers in exclusive bodily intercourse for ever, all that freeness of reciprocity which before existed between them and which constituted the total divine charm of the relation disappears . . . The parties are . . . in reciprocal bondage . . .
>
> If society left its subject free to follow the divine afflatus of his passion whithersoever it carried him, we should never hear of such a thing as sexual promiscuity or fornication.
>
> I presume a day will come when the sexual relations will be regulated

in every case by the private will of the parties; when the reciprocal affection of a man and a woman will furnish the sole and sufficient sanction of their material converse . . . Thus, if a man's or woman's affections bind them to an exclusive alliance all their days, the law will approve. If, on the contrary, they lead the subject to a varied alliance, the law will equally approve.

FREE LOVERS

The organized followers of Swedenborg had found out it was a costly error to make a convert of Henry James. Now it was the Associationists' turn to learn this lesson. Where Godwin reminded the *Observer* that the American Union of Associationists drew a firm line "between the organization of Industry as such and the organization of the domestic and sexual relations," James made a point of endorsing Fourier's harmonies "in every sphere whether of . . . passions or active administration." Years later, looking back at these exciting days, he was certain he had been in the right: "They told me, Ripley and the rest, that [Fourier] was an enthusiast: I found him only wrong by defect in that particular." Once again it was James against the constituted group. He was not only more enthusiastic than "Ripley and the rest" but unswervingly devoted to the single issue they could not afford to ventilate. As the *Harbinger* struggled to stay afloat, James's replies to Ford became longer and more uncompromising and arcane. There were eight of them during the magazine's last three months, and if it hadn't expired with the February 10, 1849, issue, Y.S. would no doubt have continued to belabor Ford's "demonstrably small and fatuous" understanding of love and marriage.

Godwin, Fisher, and others at once went to work to revive the magazine as a monthly, but to no avail. Ripley might have had James in mind when he complained, "The whole movement is becoming more & more ambiguous. The theoretical, speculative, uncertain element has got too far ahead of the practical." Fanny Macdaniel, on the other hand, approved of James's "lucubrations," and when he thanked her for her support (enclosing a check as a "fraternal offering"), he was quite unrepentant. He knew that some thought he had been "too severe" with Ford, but James assured Macdaniel he had been quite "unconscious . . . of any feelings towards A.E.F. but those of the purest good will." Anyway, he had "a certain jocosity of nature which it would be useless to attempt restraining."

Another approving reader was the remarkable John Humphrey Noyes.

The same age as James, Noyes had attended conservative seminaries at Andover and Yale, and his turn from Calvinism to Perfectionism had a great deal in common with James's embrace of the Divine Life. Both men had total confidence in their reasoning powers as they went about extracting a radical new message from Scripture. Noyes concluded that "in a holy community, there is no more reason why sexual intercourse should be restrained by law, than why eating and drinking should be." This position, as Whitney R. Cross has shown, was undergirded by three doctrines:

> Those who are saved enjoy total security from sin.
> The Second Coming occurred about the time Jerusalem fell, in the year 70.
> Ever since, those who live "in the holiness of the resurrection" are allowed a complete communism in their sex relations.

One of the most practical utopians of all time, Noyes managed to domesticate the holiness of the resurrection at a commune in Oneida, New York. Here, all the members of each sex were married to all the members of the other, men practiced coitus interruptus to avoid undesired pregnancies, and exclusive attachments were severely reprobated and exposed in sessions known as Group Criticism. The Fourierists considered Noyes mistaken in thinking "that men can live Christianity perfectly, while in present society." Noyes, in turn, wished Fourier had not postponed the challenge of reinstitutionalizing human sexuality.

When Noyes read Y.S.'s arguments in the *Harbinger*, he was startled and delighted. At last, a Fourierist who was able and willing to reason dangerously! Writing in the Perfectionist paper that served as his mouthpiece, he provided an accurate summary of James's argument and then stamped it with his approval: " 'Y.S.' handled his weapons with great ability, and exhibited powers of logic and analysis which we have rarely seen surpassed." Noyes conjectured that it was because Y.S.'s essays had "proved to be too heavy 'freight' " that the *Harbinger* had gone under.

There is reason to think James went out of his way to get in touch with Noyes. In the late 1840s, for considerations similar to those that had brought the *Harbinger* from Brook Farm to New York, the Oneidans shifted their "printing or *propagandist*" operation to Brooklyn. James was drawn to oppositional journals and presses, and he went to Brooklyn several times to converse with some of the colony's "leading men." A few years later he recalled these visits in a letter to the *Tribune* referring

to the sect's leaders as "*ultra*—that is to say, consistent—Calvinists."
He characterized them as "fathers and husbands and brothers like myself,
disfigured to be sure by a morbid religious conscience, but no less capable
of suffering on that account whatever I suffered." This emphasis on shared
masculine experience and morbid conscientiousness suggests that even
though James eventually decided the men from Oneida had lost their
common sense, he still felt a special kind of sympathy with them, as if
they had gone where he had once been headed. He claimed he had
lectured them on their "disorderly lives."

Oneida's leader had a lucid memory, and when he read this retrospective account in the *Tribune*, he promptly set the record straight.
What James had really lectured them on, Noyes said, was "our narrow-
minded views of the value of the Bible; and also on the foolishness of
our slow way of propagating our sentiments, advising us to operate on
the public mind through such established journals as the *Tribune*." This
recollection rings true: James had not only saved himself from Calvinism
by learning how to construe the Bible allegorically rather than literally,
but in the late 1840s he was preoccupied with the work of getting radically
unpopular views before the public. Fresh from his *Harbinger* adventure,
he evidently urged Noyes to put his subversive ideas before the public
at large, regardless of the very real dangers. James wanted to push the
most extreme sex radical in the United States out into the mainstream.

Another sex radical who linked up with James about this time was
Dr. Marx Edgeworth Lazarus, one of the most eccentric and interesting
radical thinkers (and doers) of the time. A product of the wealthy Mor-
decai family of North Carolina (his mother had corresponded with Maria
Edgeworth), Lazarus wrote for the *Harbinger*, was given to a hermetic
sort of theorizing, and absolutely loved Melville's goofiest novel, *Mardi*.
He is Dr. Ellery, the gentle bohemian in Mary Nichols's 1855 novel,
Mary Lyndon.

Lazarus was a charter member of the Religious Union of Associationists
in Boston. One evening in 1847 he told the story of his life in the
presence of the Union's recording secretary:

> He said he was born & educated as a Jew . . . By the anguish which he
> witnessed endured by a near relative on the occasion of the death of her
> husband, he felt he said the terrible position in which woman was placed,
> having no resource for mental & bodily activity at all commensurate with
> her needs, & saw how much *some sphere* was needed where this *one* relation
> of Wife & Mother should not be considered her *only* prospect.

Lazarus studied homeopathy in Philadelphia and became a Christian convert. As a result of his new medical and religious faith, he saw the falsity of civilized society and began searching for

> some tangible means for reconstruction. While in N York he met with some writings of Mr Brisbane & this led him at once to Fourier. Here he found as he said *"the man for him"*— From that day he has had but one hope— The future was perfectly clear. He had no "if," nor "peradventure," as to the work he was called upon to do.

This narrative, the secretary noted, "excited a profound feeling of interest in all who listened . . . all agreeing that these relations of personal experience are what is most needed."

Like James, Lazarus sought greater public attention for the difficult social questions that had been shrouded in secrecy. He soon lost patience with Channing, who preached to the Religious Union for "nearly six months without unfolding the laws of the passional series." Somehow Channing lacked the "magnetism" of those who dare to live their beliefs: he was able to spiritualize and individualize, but he wouldn't socialize. When Lazarus's turn came to speak to the Bostonians, it was on the subject of "compound immortality," a high and difficult ideal pertaining to groups more than to individuals and that seemed to involve sexual expression. Compound immortality was equivalent to James's teaching that salvation must be social, not individual, and that there will be no legal restrictions on sexual expression once the Divine Life begins. And just as James had tried to draw out the social and practical implications of Swedenborgian thought, so Lazarus joined a committee in the summer of 1847 that aimed, rather vaguely, at "some Practical Associative Movement."

Did James understand himself in the later 1840s as laboring in a common cause with Lazarus? The question is important because this man was about to become the most explosive force in the mid-nineteenth-century free-love movement. All that can be said with certainty is that on June 6, 1849, the Jameses had Lazarus (and Dana) to dinner, and that three years later, when Lazarus brought out his scandalous but prescient book, *Love vs. Marriage*, he regarded his former host as a fellow traveler who was not yet fully self-conscious. Lazarus proved to be a very wild man indeed, and it would seem that while he and James shared a commitment to practical compound immortality, Lazarus was more interested in the practical part, in doing something now, than James was. He was also fonder of a spurious-sounding jargon. "Until the passional trinity is formed and the circuit of life restores itself by its own action," the doctor warned, "our effort must be at once inefficient and exhaustive."

Quite a few years later, when James was living in Newport, he jokingly alluded to "the very bad companionship I underwent in New York." After his death his son William recalled "all the men I used to see" at the old Fourteenth Street house, as did Henry Jr., and Bob named Dana, Ripley, and Godwin ("the homeliest countenance in America") as being among Henry Sr.'s many visitors. But the children were still too young in the late 1840s to gather an impression of their father's flirtations with Noyes and Lazarus.

THAT HEMORRHAGE

In March 1847 Emerson asked James to look after a Danish novelist visiting the United States. Later that year, when Emerson crossed the Atlantic, James put him on to Wilkinson as a great unrecognized genius whose career could use a gentle push. The ice was broken, the two Americans were once again in communication with each other, and in the spring or summer of 1849 they had a "score of conversations," probably in New York. James's letters no longer exhibited the intense highs and lows of 1842–43, but even so, he seemed to be singing the same old tune when he wrote his friend on the last day of August 1849. At the time the Jameses had occupied their Fourteenth Street house little over a year.

> My wife & I, are obliged—so numerous has waxed our family—to enlarge our house in town, and get a country house for the summer. These things look expensive and temporary to us, besides being an additional care; and so, looking upon our four stout boys, who have no play-room within doors, and import shocking bad-manners from the street, with much pity, we gravely ponder whether it would not be better to go abroad for a few years with them, allowing them to absorb French & German, and get a better sensuous education than they are likely to get here?* To be sure this is but a glimpse of our ground of proceeding—but perhaps you know some decisive word which shall dispense us from any further consideration of the subject.

* The novelist altered the latter phrase to "get such a sensuous education as they can't get here," in this way making America look more vacuous than vicious. This substitution would take on a life of its own in F. O. Matthiessen's *James Family* and later biographies.

Emerson had heard this before: we have too many cares, we're unhappy, we're thinking of Europe, there are languages to learn, can you dissuade us by suggesting an alternative? But this time there were some curious new discords. James flatly declares he and Mary have to enlarge their house and spend the summer in the country. But by the next sentence the plan already seems moot. Summer has all but flown, after all, and it appears that what he and his wife are *really* thinking of is a trip to Europe lasting several years. The question mark that ends this announcement may be technically incorrect (and Henry Jr. changed it to a period in editing the passage), but it does capture the writer's uncertain tone and mind. Would Emerson kindly save him from the bother of solving his domestic problems? Yet even as the writer asks for advice, he makes it clear he has provided no more than a "glimpse" of the relevant considerations. There is something else weighing on him besides the boys' bad manners and the need to economize, something he is not putting down on paper.

There is no doubt the boys, some of them, were not growing up the way their parents desired. William could be rude and bullying, and once, when Henry Jr. asked to join him at play, the older brother boasted, "*I* play with boys who curse and swear!" Henry Sr. had not forgotten his extreme sense of guilt after pelting a younger brother with snowballs to keep him at home. On balance, he felt, the North Pearl Street shoemakers had been "very harmful to us"; the independence of boyhood had grave perils. Yet he couldn't help wanting his own sons to be self-governing, and in fact Henry Jr. was allowed to dawdle by himself along New York's streets. The responsibility of bringing up and educating the boys had brought to the surface the father's troubled history and inner ambivalences.

In his letters to England, James fretted so much about his sons' educational expenses and the need to "retrench" that the Wilkinsons realized they would have to stop taking their friend's money. He gave them the impression he was actually on the point of sailing: "So you really think of visiting Europe again! And France too! And for a few years!" This constant talk about crossing the ocean gave young Henry Jr. a lasting sense of the Old World's advantages. In 1855 the family did in fact embark, but in 1849 and 1850 there was something factitious in the father's repeated threats to do so. "The solutional 'Europe' " was a half-serious evasion, an expression of his yearning for some final, sweeping answer to his domestic headaches. He was feeling the duties of fatherhood in a new way now, feeling them just as his career was finally taking off. (It was partly this new sense of pressure that impelled him to attack the constraints of married life with such astonishing energy.) But there was another and more serious domestic worry eating at James, and the reason he couldn't write about it to Emerson was that it involved Mary.

The nineteenth-century solution for the problem of excess human fertility was self-restraint, which in practice probably meant restraint initiated by the wife and agreed to by the husband. On a large scale the solution apparently worked, for even though there was no trustworthy method of contraception in nineteenth-century America, family size showed a steady decline. It would seem that the Victorian idea that sex was animal-like and must be curbed served a necessary repressive function. The idea provided the justification for the two most important birth-control practices within marriage, continence and total abstinence, both of which depended on the man's willingness to abide by the woman's prohibitory signals. Did some or many men insist on their conjugal rights anyway? Was this what James had in mind in his preface to Hennequin when he loudly condemned prostitution and promiscuity *within* marriage? An act of love threatening to become an act of force at the moment the wife realizes she wants no more children: perhaps this was what James saw as the real inner truth of marriage.

It is surely no accident that Henry and Mary's last child was born about the time James began to attack marriage as an institution. One of the curious aspects of his *Harbinger* letters is that at the same time they celebrate the joys of an ideal union between man and woman—where "each drinks in a plenary refreshment from every inmost and covert fountain of the other's spirit"—they also extol the superiority of abstinence. In a true marriage, according to James, "these lower and transient delights which are the very heaven of Love, sink into comparative insignificance, sink into comparative, if not complete, desuetude. [The couple's] union is henceforth a union of souls, and they . . . little regret the lapsed endearments of the body." Letting the body's endearments lapse is easier said than done, however, and judging from James's lubricious imagery and his raging attack elsewhere on the legal restrictions on erotic liberty, he himself felt more than a little regret.

Henry and Mary were cramped for room, they were feeling the pressure of increased expenses, and they finally had the girl they had no doubt been hoping for. Had erotic satisfaction become a thing of the past? Henry may have been facing the middle-aged Victorian husband's sternest duty—ceasing to impregnate his wife. If so, he may have seen his pre-Victorian father in a harsh new light, for where Mary had her fifth child at thirty-eight, Catharine Barber James had had her tenth child at forty-six. A suspicion that William of Albany had been some kind of matri-

monial brute would help explain the tone of Henry Sr.'s obscure
fulminations in the *Harbinger*. Once again, it would seem, the son was
being energized by his father.

There was someone else to resent, someone much closer. In 1860
James told a woman friend that a passionate interest in individuals was
a "foolish snare." He himself had done nothing, he confessed, "but
tumble in it from my boyhood up to my marriage, since which great
disillusioning* I feel that the only lovely person is one who will never
permit himself to be loved." Mary permitted her husband to love and
depend on her ("with the absolute whole of his weight," wrote Henry
Jr.), and her husband's letters often hint at her limitations. While he
liked to articulate the inexpressible, to push things to the limit, to expand
to the full capacity of his desires, she seems to have had a buttoned lip
and a very practical and dutiful mind-set. Her mentality was that of a
subordinate, with no enthusiasms that were not vicarious. If she ever
lost patience with her man, she did not leave behind a single document
that suggests as much. He, on the other hand, though praising her
effusively, made it clear he found her narrow, technical, and anxious.
Henry got a great deal from his marriage, but one thing he clearly missed
was equal companionship. This was another reason to yearn for Emerson—who in 1843 had not permitted himself to be loved by his admirer
in New York.

As if all this wasn't enough, Henry seems to have gotten Mary pregnant
for a sixth and last time, with the pregnancy ending badly. A week or
two after Henry alluded to certain nameless considerations in his letter
to Emerson, Mary became gravely ill, and when James informed Wilkinson (a doctor) of this latest trouble, the Englishman offered his prompt
sympathy:

> This steamer has brought us such heavy news of your dear wife's health,
> that I run to talk with you upon the subject, though time & space are
> long between us. Most ardently do we hope that the intelligence that the
> dear sufferer is quite safe, will be confirmed by another speedy arrival.
> Dana writes me that on the 19th [of September], she was pronounced by
> you to be out of danger! We feel for your heart under such terrible emer-
> gencies, knowing ourselves by experience what a time it is for the sound
> as well as the sick whilst that hemorrhage continues.

---

* When Henry Jr. excerpted this passage in *Notes of a Son and Brother*, he inserted a "yes!" between
dashes at this point. This minute but ingenious fraud implies that the father at once sensed and
sought to overcome the anticipated protest of his correspondent, unable to believe the Jameses'
marriage could be so flawed.

Judging from the sound of this, Mary had been pregnant at the time James wrote Emerson, her condition imposing some stern constraints on the question of a change of residence. Then she went into labor, and whether it was a miscarriage or a full-term birth, the fetus or baby died and a uteral hemorrhage resulted. James hadn't divulged his wife's pregnancy before Wilkie's birth, but this time there was fear for Mary's life and the crisis could not be concealed. Both Dana and Wilkinson were informed.

The upshot: a new and overpowering argument for complete sexual abstinence in the James household. The endearments of the body were forcibly proscribed even as Henry proclaimed to the world that love was too heavenly to be boxed up in marriage.

It was not going to be easy to end one's subjection to nature and society, to reenact God's perfect self-sufficiency, to become the Divine Man.

OUT OF HIS PARTICULAR POTATO PATCH

The late 1840s were James's best of times and worst of times. He wrote and lectured, tackled big questions head on, voiced some very dangerous opinions, and began to command public attention and get a reputation. Yet even as he attacked customary social and moral arrangements with rising vehemence, he gave no sign he was putting his free-love opinions into practice. Instead, as the gap between his bold self-projections and his frustrating actualities grew larger, he began to sound a maniacal note.

James was glad to hear that William Henry Channing had bought the *Univercoelum*, the weekly magazine published by Andrew Jackson Davis's handlers. Acquiring the *Harbinger*'s old subscription list as well, Channing inaugurated a socialist weekly he called *The Spirit of the Age*. The new editor was still leery of James, but he had a ready welcome for his less heretical contributions, and at the end of July he ran an essay by Y.S. called "Vanity Fair, or Rather Becky Sharp." James had sided on principle with the world's unblushing sinners ever since his Sandemanian phase. He liked and approved of Thackeray's keen-eyed cynic, feeling that her wickedness was an honest human response to her "inharmonic society," which denied "the orderly gratification of [her] passions." Wilkinson pronounced the essay "second to none of your writings for its geniality & comprehensiveness," and urged James to tackle Milton's Satan and Belial. Instead, James's next piece in *The Spirit of the Age* dealt

with a poem by a little-known author he'd learned about through
Wilkinson:

> Dear mother! dear mother! the church is cold,
> But the ale-house is healthy, and pleasant, and warm.

It was William Blake's "The Little Vagabond," and from it James drew
an anticlerical message dear to his heart: the body's needs must be met
before true worship becomes possible. This was James's last article to be
signed Y.S. Like his other attempts at literary criticism, it showed a
strong tendency to revert to theological disputation.

"*Your* mission," Wilkinson had advised James, "arises out of the grave
of *the Harbinger*: a theological descent into art and science." The reflections on Blake's and Thackeray's social outcasts represented one way of
carrying out this program. In the spring of 1849 James tried another way
by composing an ambitious series of lectures "on Art and the Artist."
He was thinking of braving the lecture hall once again, this time with
his daring Divine Man speculations. Apparently there was a question of
taking these new lectures to Boston, but when James sent the opening
talk to James T. Fisher, the response was that the subject was "imperfectly
sketched." Although Fisher issued some sort of invitation anyway, James
turned him down. He was nervous about speaking "to any but the most
indulgent auditors, and those too who had been somewhat familiar with
my train of thought." Clearly he missed his assured outlet at the
Harbinger.

Then, out of the blue, there came an invitation to speak at the Town
and Country Club in Boston, which held "conversations" every other
Thursday "on Subjects attractive to Philanthropists and to Men of Business and Letters." Normally, this club got its speakers from its own
membership, but Dwight had informed Emerson that James had an interesting paper and Emerson pushed for his friend so hard and so wittily
(Why are we content with Indian corn when we can have "grapes &
pomegranates?") that the New Yorker was unanimously invited to come
and speak that November.

The invitation "horrified" James. He had performed acceptably before
a hometown crowd in Albany or when speaking to committed Fourierists
in New York, but Boston was different. For a New Yorker to lecture in
Boston was like a Roman expounding philosophy in Athens, and to
address the Town and Country Club was to begin at the top. Emerson
made it clear he backed James all the way, and there was no way to say
no. But James dreaded the reception his special revelations were likely

to meet with from a group that was anything but a self-selected gathering of the converted. In his letter of acceptance, he defended himself by belittling the secularism of the authorial vocation:

There is nothing I dread so much as literary men, especially *our* literary men . . . You come to them with some grand secret that opens heaven to the lowest and and most excluded hut, that lifts your own life out of bottomless and stifling mud, where living is abject toil, and expect some involuntary token of human sympathy, even of natural curiosity, but no, a supercilious smile decks every visage.

The task of choosing a topic for such an audience drew forth James's riskiest humor. He expressed the wish that the Astor Library (later the New York Public Library) would go up in flames if literature did not become more earnest, and he informed his friend that if socialism, the topic James preferred, was deemed objectionable ("a stench in the nostrils of all the devout and honorable"), he had a beautiful paper in reserve —"on Sin"—which happened to "involve a practical social bearing."

It was agreed that socialism would be the topic. The lecture was scheduled for November 1, and Bronson Alcott, the club's corresponding secretary, had a formal announcement printed:

A Monthly Meeting of the Town and Country Club will be held at the Rooms, No. 15, Tremont Row, on Thursday, Nov. 1, at 9½ o'clock, A.M.
Henry James, Esq. of New York City, will read a Paper on that occasion; and a Conversation will follow the reading of the same, at 3, P.M.
A full attendance of members is respectfully requested.

James's disclosure of his domestic worries and his threat to leave for Europe had the desired effect on Emerson. Still uneasy about his part in James's 1843 transatlantic trip, the Sage of Concord went to work to drum up a full house, advising club members whose attendance could not be counted on that "Mr James is the best man in New York—that I know, and he is on the wing now with his family for Europe—for years to remain—I fear." When the great day arrived, Mary accompanied her husband to Boston, and although she may not have been permitted to join the men at the dinner that preceded the afternoon's discussion, she was present in the morning when he stood up, mastered his trepidation, and began reading.

The lecture opened quietly enough as an examination of the relative merits of socialism and civilization. It soon became clear, however, that, instead of conducting a dispassionate inquiry, the speaker was laying out his private understanding of God, man, nature, history, society, and many other topics, all in the most impassioned tones and with the conviction that no other point of view was possible. James devoted the first part of his lecture to a resumé of his Divine Man idea: God is the only self-sufficing actor; humans become divine only when they too begin to act "purely from delight or attraction"; this kind of action is possible only when we escape the constraints of nature and society. Socialism is a program to perfect society, and society will be perfect only if it stops limiting our individual selfhood and gives each of us full title to everything and everyone. In other words—and the paradox seems characteristic of the speaker—socialism is a consummate individualism.

The lecture's peculiar character lay in the openness with which it protested against all social constraints and duties. The man who gave money to Macdaniel and Wilkinson and probably many others complained that philanthropy was an "utter crucifixion of selfishness—such an incessant and immaculate [sic] deference to the will and even the whimsy of another, that I am worried and fretted into my grave." Even worse were one's paternal obligations: "The incessant action of society is to shut up all my time and thought to the . . . necessity of providing subsistence, education, and social respect for myself and my children." (Perhaps one of the reasons James relied on "incessant" and similar words—"incontinent," "immediate"—was that they did away with boundaries and intervals.) But nothing was quite so imprisoning as extended family ties—"the great tiresome dispensation of uncles and aunts and cousins and nieces. I have a "native and God-given appetency," James intoned, and nature and society "should have no power to identify me with a particular potato-patch and a particular family of mankind all my days." Of course the purity of his motives was beyond question:

> How should I . . . as pure in my inward parts as [God] himself, become a thief, unless society tempted me by giving some one else an exclusive property in that which every want of my nature makes equally appropriate to me? How should I become an adulterer unless society affirmed some one else to possess an exclusive property in some person, whom the very fact of the adultery proves to belong equally to me?

Adultery? How can there be adultery? When God "sends us wives, the statute against adultery will confess itself superfluous."

If the lecture was James's most remarkable high-wire act yet, he was not performing without a net. Not only had Emerson gone warrant for him, but the speaker's wife's reassuring presence proved there must be a saving equivocation in his outrageous claims. Wilkinson had supposed that James's "unexceptionable conjugality" would serve as his safe conduct, and James himself had told Emerson he would bring "certificates of good citizenship from my wife & family and neighbours, in case the worst comes to the worst." That was Mary's function: to certify the speaker's respectability, to prove he kept to his own potato patch, to let others see that his witty complaints about the unpleasantness of a husband-and-father's life weren't quite in earnest. She was the net above which the spangled ropedancer demonstrated his divine independence of social and natural restraint.

JAMES'S CRITICS

James was so uninterested in "low information" that he curtly dismissed Wilkinson's 1849 biography of Swedenborg. A narrative had value only when read symbolically, and this was particularly true of the Bible. In James's lecture on "Morality and the Divine [or Perfect] Life," which he delivered twice in December, he maintained that what all biblical narratives were really about was the final consummation of history. The life of Christ was not intended to be read as history but as a prophetic allegory for "the transcendent realities in which we now live and act." The present or imminent transformation of society: that is what revelation and history have been pointing towards. "These things," James advised his listeners, "have happened for our instruction, upon whom the ends of the world have truly come." The apocalypse had begun, cause and effect were done with, and all human passions would "assert their divine and imperishable freedom."

Also, authors would continue to try to catch the public's ear. On November 18 New Yorkers had a chance to hear the lecture on socialism that James had recently read in Boston. The "service," as the *Tribune* called it, was held on a Sunday evening at the Stuyvesant Institute, and among the listeners was Fredrika Bremer, a Swedish novelist who later published her impressions of America. Bremer was under the impression James spoke "extempore," and she had more regard for his "flashing vivacity" than for his theories, which she dismissed as pantheistic and antinomian; she had heard that sort of talk back in Sweden. For her, the high point of the evening came right after the speech, when Channing stood up and told his fellow auditors that

if the doctrine which we had just heard enunciated were Christian Socialism, then he did not agree with it; that the subject ought to be searched
to the bottom; that he considered the views of the speaker to be erroneous,
and that on the following Sunday he would take up the question in that
place.

When the time came for Channing to deliver his promised rebuttal,
Bremer was once again on the spot. In her opinion, he achieved a
complete triumph over James, being "carried along by a continued inspiration." Although he was not vindictive or personal, he did say at
one point, "in a somewhat sharper tone, that the 'person who did not
in his own breast become conscious of the duality of human nature, who
did not combat with a lower self, is either without humanity, or is deeply
to be pitied.' "

> The hall was quite full of people, and the profoundest attention prevailed.
> At the close of the oration a circle of congratulating friends gathered
> around Channing. I saw even the speaker of the former evening, Mr. H.
> James, go forward to Channing, lay his hand upon his shoulder, as if
> caressingly, as he said "You have done me an injustice; you have mis-
> understood me!" He seemed pale and agitated, but perfectly kind.

Later that evening Channing said to Bremer with "a half sigh," "I have
wounded Mr. James!"

There was something in James that mesmerized Channing even as it
stirred his fighting spirit. He reprinted another of James's heretical lectures in three issues of *The Spirit of the Age*, but when *Moralism and
Christianity* appeared, Channing severely criticized book and author in a
four-part essay in the same journal. James was an "EGO-PANTHEIST." He
was blind to the distinction between God and himself. He was under
the impression that the perfect man uses "all relations as means for the
aggrandizement of [his] supreme individuality." He couldn't conceive of
the idea of social reorganization. And he deified sensual instinct. In reply
James whipped off a heated, thirty-page letter that begins, "You scarcely
do your perspicacity justice in the treatment you give my innocent little
book."

At James's death in 1882 it was still remembered that he had "delivered
a course of lectures in [New York] during the winter of 1849–50, which
attracted great attention." He'd become, briefly, a major intellectual
presence in the city, doing so by developing a position so disturbing the
chief sages of the time had to try to answer him. Ripley didn't care for

his evident preference for "enlightened self-interest" over practical social cooperation, but even so, now that the former *Harbinger* editor had moved to the *Tribune*, he gave *Moralism and Christianity* a column of extracts and praised the author's "profound interior life" and "condensed force of expression." Another enthusiastic response came from the radical New York *Journal of Progress and Industrial Review*:

> [The lectures] lay bare the root of the whole evil of the times, and the lecturer wields upon it his intellectual axe with a superhuman power. He proves with the clearest logic, that man has outgrown the Social Institutions in which he now dwells; that they are no longer useful, but hurtful in the extreme, repressing, stultifying and preventing all the heaven-born aspirations of the soul.

In London the leading English Fourierist, Hugh Doherty, read James with great interest, thought his book open to serious misinterpretation, yet felt on balance that the author's "moral rectitude" could not be impugned. Wilkinson, on the other hand, considered *Moralism and Christianity* so impractical and vacuous he could no longer contain his vein of sarcasm, and he warned his American friend that his writing was in danger of becoming "a thing of most uninfluential words." To embrace self-sufficiency, as James was doing, was to neglect the "use of Society."

The critique James received from Emerson was as keen as it was unassuming:

> I am awed & distanced a little by this argumentative style: every technical *For* & *Suppose* and *Therefore* alarms & extrudes me and moreover I find or fancy . . . that you have not shed your last coat of presbyterianism, but that a certain catachetical & legendary Jove glares at me sometimes, in your page, which astonishes me in so sincere & successful a realist.

Emerson was making use of his friend's old metaphor of the succession of shed garments and recalling that old fear of the Calvinist deity's great searching eye. It staggered Emerson that a thinker as fresh and alive as James was could be so unaware of the old, dead self that continued to usurp his voice.

Hermetic, self-justifying, endlessly creating the world in his image, James clearly resembled the god he was imagining. But he was also a reincarnation of the stern, implacably reasoning Calvinist deity of his childhood, whose *therefores* clanged like chains. How to put oneself right with this glaring, reasoning monster was a problem that might well occupy a lifetime. What made James so interesting to his contemporaries was that he seemed determined to work this problem out in full view of the reading and lecture-attending public. *

One thing at least was certain. God Himself did not answer prayer more incontinently or incessantly than James answered criticism. Soon after getting Emerson's letter, James wrote back to express "downright rapture" at having engaged his friend's close attention. Solid criticism at last, and from such a mind! Unfortunately, the Sage of Concord had not explained exactly how James should "put [him]self right with [his] readers." "I really beg this boon of you," James pleaded. Just "one word more."

---

* Herman Melville had known James's family in Albany, and perhaps James himself (though there is no firm evidence proving their acquaintance). The Melvilles lived a couple of blocks from the Jameses, and Herman attended Albany Academy with two of James's brothers and clerked in the bank James's father had helped run. From April to October 1849, Melville was apparently living in New York. He returned early in 1850, following a short trip to Europe. Thus, while he could not have been present when James read his wildly speculative lectures, he was back in the city at the time the lectures came out in book form and were still being talked about. That was in February 1850—the same month *Moby-Dick* seems to have been started. Could the suddenly much-talked-about cork-legged man from the shadows of the novelist's past have shaped his conception of a mad, one-legged, metaphysical avenger who (like James) dreams of slamming a harpoon into the old god's side? The circumstances under which Captain Ahab lost his leg remain obscure, but they seem to have been as protracted as they were painful—like young James's ordeal. Melville had moved to Albany two years after this ordeal was concluded.

Chapter 19

■ ■ ■

FAMILY LIFE ON
FOURTEENTH STREET: 1848–55

The same year James began complaining about the narrow limits of his potato patch, he and Mary settled into the most permanent domicile their children were to know, 58 West Fourteenth Street, home base from 1848 until the move to Europe in 1855. Prior to this uprooting the James children—or rather, the James boys, for Alice wasn't granted their freedom to wander—turned into the indigenous inhabitants of a big-city neighborhood. Their boyhood had a very specific urban geography: Pinsent's sweet shop, the railing where William's friends liked to hang out, the sharply differentiated neighbors, the odd maternal relatives across Sixth Avenue to the west, the livery stable at University Place and Thirteenth, to which the boys were sent when a conveyance was needed, and dozens of other locations. The James boys played with other boys and got to know their upstairs and downstairs and even their attics, the choice location for the youthful theatricals in which William was not only the "constant comic star" but the scriptwriter, director, and costume designer, leaving Henry Jr. to stand around half undressed, "waiting alike for ideas and for breeches."

The Jameses' next-door neighbors to the east were the Edward C. Centers (or Senters), who a few years later would show up in Paris. Farther east, at number 48, lived the Bean family from New Hampshire. They formed a household of sixteen, with three girls roughly the same age as the James boys. The future novelist dimly remembered a children's Christmas party given by the "kindly Beans," but he and his brothers ran with boys, not girls, and got better acquainted with Charley, Freddy, and Johnny Ward, who lived across the street at number 45. The Wards, recently arrived from Connecticut, were the only children Henry Jr. knew who attended public school.

When a new brick and brownstone church began to go up on a vacant lot west of the Wards, the young Jameses joined the neighborhood boys in climbing the temporary scaffolding. Consecrated in 1853, this church belonged to the same Presbyterian congregation Mary had attended in her girlhood, and it seems likely that Henry Jr.'s caricature of the minister's pulpit manner—"tight-closed eyes, strange long-drawn accents and gaunt scraggy chin, squirming and swaying and cushion-thumping"— reflects his father's strong animus. The boys were allowed to visit other churches (or synagogues) as they pleased, but they made little use of this privilege. They were much more regular (their parents saw to that) in their attendance at the other new building on the block, Edward Ferrero's dance academy, which faced the Jameses' house.

Two doors west of the Jameses, at number 62, lived the highly respectable Van Winkles, whose household included four servants, three daughters, and a son named Edgar, one year older than Harry (as Henry Jr. was known at home and on the street). Harry looked up to Edgar as a "serious and judicious" lad who moved "in a regular maze of culture." In 1856, a year after being taken to Europe, Harry penned a note to this distant Fourteenth Street chum that was full of inarticulate yearning:

> Dear Eddy
> 　As I heard you were going to try to turn the club into a Theatre And as I was asked w'ether I wanted to belong here is my answer. I would like very much to belong.
>
> 　　　　　　　　　　　　　　　　　Yours Truly
> 　　　　　　　　　　　　　　　　　H. James

This is the novelist's first known letter. His second expresses strong resentment of William for writing to Edgar before Harry himself had a chance to do so, in this way "usurp[ing] my rights."

Beyond the Van Winkles, at number 64, lived the most colorful family on the block, the Frederick Norcoms. Henry Jr. remembered the father as "a large bald political-looking man, very loose and ungirt" and the mother as "a desiccated, depressed lady" who was always pregnant. To New York eyes and ears, the family seemed conspicuously Southern: their word for *stoop* was *porch*, and they used this public space to grind sausages and consume hot cakes and molasses. In the Jameses' home, by contrast, with its carefully demarcated zones, cooking was done in one part of the house and eating in another, and both activities were performed far from the street. What made the Norcoms really stand out were their slaves, turbanned "An'silvy" and her son, Davy, who show up in the 1850 census as forty-year-old Silvia, a "mulatto" born in North Carolina, and ten-year-old David. Mingling freely with the neighborhood boys, this young captive gave Harry the thrill of direct contact with the peculiar institution, made notorious by *Uncle Tom's Cabin*, the runaway bestseller of 1852. Then, all of a sudden, Silvia and David also ran away, to their owners' dismay.

Farther west, across Sixth Avenue at number 72, dwelled an odd assortment of Mary James's Wyckoff connections. The senior person in the group was her maternal aunt, Mary (Robertson) Wyckoff, known to the James children as Great-aunt Wyckoff. Born in 1778, she was their oldest living relative. With her lived her daughter and son-in-law, Helen and Leonard Perkins; her one surviving son, Henry A. Wyckoff; and her only grandchild, an orphan known to the James children as Cousin Albert. Much of the land hereabouts had once belonged to Albert's great-grandfather Alexander Robertson, and there was something shrunken and spectral in his huddled descendants, especially when looked at from the lively James household. The old woman, Henry Jr. recalled, spent her time sitting in a chair like an idol in a shrine, and her attendants, the "pious ministrants," would say "she had 'said' so and so when she hadn't spoken at all." Her daughter Helen, clearly a product of "the same nest" as Mary James, was busy, strenuously good, and full of anxious precautions. Her husband worked at the Custom House and when at home paced back and forth between the two big parlors. He was a polite nullity whom anyone could slight without causing Helen to take offense. The couple had no children.

The other adult household member, Henry A. Wyckoff, had a defective intelligence. He was the ward of his sister Helen, who managed his fortune, doled out an allowance of ten cents a day, and, fearful of his "passions," kept him under permanent guard. Years later, when this half-man made his one recorded speech—"Work works work"—Henry Sr. "didn't wholly catch his meaning" but pronounced "the form of the remark . . . nothing short of superb." Henry Jr., more protective, saw this unfortunate relative as a patient victim who had to wait half a century to show how inoffensive he really was.

The Wyckoff home was larger and emptier than the other neighborhood houses, and the James boys spent a lot of time there with Cousin Albert. Only three years older than Harry, this young man had achieved an impressive independence, already traveling on his own to the Beaverkill, to the tract of land in Sullivan County that had come down to

him from Alexander Robertson. When Albert invited William and Harry
to join him on a trip to this place, the James parents put their foot down,
partly, it seems, because they didn't approve of the boy. Family genealogies show that Albert was born seven months after his parents' marriage.
Nothing is known of his mother, Mary A. Russell, who apparently died
the year of his birth. The novelist remembered this cousin as the sort of
boy who was always winking, and in fact he seems to have vanished into
the obscurity of an unedifying life. His two wives were evidently on the
fast side, especially with his money. When the James parents worried
about the bad influence of their boys' New York acquaintance, it may
have been Albert Wyckoff they were thinking of.

Mary's sister Catharine was a steady though not a continuous member
of the Jameses' household. She moved out in 1846–47 in order to care
for her dying mother, and in 1851 to nurse her failing brother John. In
1853, soon after passing forty, she got engaged to a retired captain named
Charles H. Marshall. As she prepared to move out for good, James praised
her good-natured diplomacy with the servants: having Catharine around
was like doubling their wages. Also, she had "always been a most loving
and provident husband to Mary, a most considerate and devoted wife to
me, and an incomparable father and mother to our children." When the
marriage fell apart two years later, Catharine came back to her sister's
family, where once again her "cheery strenuousness of speech" kept the
domestic machinery well oiled. But there was friction between her and
the man of the house, a "sort of sub-antagonism," as William put it in
1870. "Unlike Mary," Jean Strouse has written, "Kate had political
opinions," which in her earlier years often proved more liberal than those
of her brother-in-law. If she was a second (nonsexual) wife, as Henry
Sr. claimed, she was also a rival theory-spouting husband.

One of the memorable events in the James family annals took place
in the summer of 1848, when Gus's oldest daughter married Robert
Emmet, Jr. This marriage, which united the grandchildren of William
of Albany and Thomas Addis Emmet, was the occasion for a famous
bash at the two clans' Hudson Valley estates. The knot was tied at the
Emmet place in Staatsburg, and then the huge wedding party sailed to
Gus's place, Linwood, already packed with "family and friends from
Albany." The Emmets brought an "old Irish fiddler," and the feasting
and dancing continued day and night. Gus had helped run the seasonal
dances in Albany (the "city assemblies"), and he must have been in his
element, unlike his one-legged younger brother. When a follow-up party
was held at an Emmet residence near Washington Square, Mary went
with five-year-old Harry but not her husband. The occasion made a

lasting impression on the boy, who nevertheless looked back with considerable haughtiness at these early New York festivities. He would remember the young bride—in fact, "all the female relatives on my father's side"—as intensely, "indescribably, *natural.*"

In the winter of 1849–50 (about the time James had to stop fathering children) a second Mary moved in with the family. This was Mary Temple, a sister of James's brother-in-law, Robert Emmet Temple. Unlike the first Mary, she was "quite exceedingly handsome," and before long Edmund Tweedy began to haunt the parlor. He and Mary were joined in matrimony in June 1850 and presently sailed for Lucca, Italy. Several years later, in a teasing letter to Edmund, James hinted that his "sentimental woes" might be explained by the "two splendid creatures" he had known—Anna (Barker) Ward and Mary Tweedy. When the birth of Mary's second child was announced, he teased Edmund for being a conscienceless old dog. He predicted that a mutual friend in New York who was staggered to think of Mary "as a mother at all" would "probably punch you badly when he sees you again," and added, "I hope he will."

The house was full of a number of other young unmarried women— the servants. Although these were rarely named in family correspondence, they played an indispensable role in the domestic regime, not only doing the cooking, cleaning, and child-tending, but taking care of Mary James's substantial investment in clothes. The amount she spent on her wardrobe in 1851 came to $300, equivalent to $5,000 or so today. She was warily alert to changes in fashion, being particularly "sorry to hear that round waists are coming in, they are so unbecoming to my figure." Given the endless refitting, repairing, spot cleaning, starching, and ironing, it comes as no surprise that, according to the 1850 census, the Jameses had five servants living with them, all born in Ireland and all between twenty and twenty-five years of age—Margaret, Margand [?], Catherine, Mary Ann, Mary. By the time the state census was taken five years later, there had been a complete turnover. Now the domestic staff consisted of Margaret Obrien, aged twenty-five; Ann Fool or Tool, twenty; and a thirteen-year-old girl named Mary Gallager. There was also a governess from the Lorraine named Annette Godefroi, who had come with Wilkinson's recommendation. Annette was satisfactory, but the Irish work crew probably took a heavy toll on Mary, who handled the hiring and firing. And her supervision and suspicion probably took a heavy toll on them. Nothing evokes the situation more vividly than Alice's early assumption that "servants lie because they are Catholics." It was almost a relief to learn, years later, that English servants also told lies.

Not to mention the Jameses themselves. One of the oddest facts to be gleaned from the census schedules is the family's chronic inaccuracy in declaring their ages. In 1850 William, then eight years old, was reported to be nine. He seemed to be turning the years faster than the calendar, and when the state census taker came by five years later, his age was padded by two years rather than one: only thirteen, he was now reported as being fifteen. If these errors were not caused by the marshal's carelessness (and the fact that Mary's age was lopped by exactly five years in each survey suggests the misinformation was deliberate), it would appear that age was not hard and fast in the James household. How old you were had something to do with the calendar, but it also reflected more subjective matters, such as your relation to the others. It may be that the tendency to exaggerate William's age reflects the supplemental boost he got from his parents. Thanks to them and his own great energies, he was able to pack more growing up into each year than his less favored brothers.

Certainly, in the eyes of the second-born son, William enjoyed an unbeatable head start. It was

> as if he had gained such an advance of me in his sixteen months' experience of the world before mine began that I never . . . caught up with him or overtook him. He was always round the corner and out of sight . . . We were never in the same schoolroom, in the same game, scarce even in step together or in the same phase at the same time; when our phases overlapped, that is, it was only for a moment—he was clean out before I had got well in.

One wonders whether the novelist ever understood exactly how he had been handicapped in the race with William.

SUCH A FEAST

All his life Henry Jr. remained extremely protective of his parents. He professed himself a "fond votary of the finest faith in the vivifying and characterising force of mothers," and he portrayed his father as a supremely unpretentious and energetic saint. His fictive mothers and fathers, on the other hand—Mrs. Light, Mrs. Gereth, Dr. Sloper, Gilbert Osmond, the Tarrants—are often distinctly crippling. The novelist felt himself to be the product of an exceptionally happy and stimulating family. But what reader goes to his fiction for a study of happy family life?

With Alice, the story is much the same. She was certain it had been a great privilege "to have grown up with" Father and William. Life at home had been so rich and warm, "such a feast" of "convulsive laughs." That, however, was the retrospective view. The few contemporary glimpses we have of Alice's childhood make it look constrained to the point of misery. A daguerreotype taken of her around the age of nine features a large, caped, wide-sleeved, armorlike dress topped by a small, plain, thin-lipped face. It is obvious that the stiff moment recorded by the camera fell painfully short of the elaborate preparation represented by the dress and studio props. The picture bears testimony to its subject's stricken inability to live up to her parents' punishing hopes. "No woman had a right to be plain," Father informed a crowded lecture hall; "her nature entitles her to be beautiful only." Alice worshipped Father for expecting so much and detested herself for returning so little.

Father's paradoxes, ambiguities, and contradictions were so deep-seated and intricate his children could not really grasp them. His leading ideas made sense chiefly in reference to the stages of his development. The ideas were a kind of therapy, serving to neutralize his early religious training or quiet his torments. Proclaimed daily, backed by the authority of perfect conviction, they were a collapsed sign system, a kind of short-hand, for the remedies, resolutions, evasions of his inner history. You couldn't reconstruct the history from the shorthand, yet the shorthand wouldn't parse unless you knew the history. The children couldn't catch on, couldn't see how their parent's domestic fatherliness was a performative version of himself—a statement, a demonstration, an expression not of a natural self but of a self-created self. It became flagrant that Father was wonderful. And he was—"wise, gentle, polished," as Emerson privately wrote, "with heroic manners, and a serenity like the sun." Affectionate and outgoing, he would give other men a warm pat on the back, almost "caressingly," as Fredrika Bremer and Emma Wilkinson both noted. He talked to, laughed with, embraced and kissed his children. He took them along on his errands, Harry in particular. Ardent and exuberant, he was the opposite of William of Albany and many other silent, reserved, and absent fathers. But he was also, as Bronson Alcott told him to his face, "damaged goods," and as he had been crippled, so he would cripple others.

His children were particularly nervous about his lack of a producible identity. What exactly was he when he wasn't home? Not only did Father not go to work, as did the other men on the block, but instead of his home being his refuge from the workaday world it became the theater of his activity and self-display. Mr. Bean went off to be a wine merchant. Mr. Norcom and Mr. Van Winkle went off to be lawyers. Even negligible Mr. Perkins intermitted his pacing and went off to be a Custom House officer. Mr. James went off to read lectures a few nights in the year and ran errands during the day, but (except in 1848) his real work took place in his private library, where he was at once domestic, professional, quite impenetrable, and furiously absorbed. When the census marshal asked him what his profession was in 1850, the answer was "None." Five years later, after James's labors in his library had resulted in three books, the answer became "Author." But the answer came unstuck. That same year, the twenty-fifth anniversary of his graduation from Union College, he was sent an alumni questionnaire that posed some difficult questions about his vocational identity. Asked what profession he had studied for, he answered "Theology." Asked where he had practiced this profession, he answered "Never graduated in the ministry." Asked what other oc-cupations he had followed, he wrote "Authorship," then crossed that out and wrote "Student." Typically, he communicated this uncertainty to his children when they asked him to supply the formula that could explain him to their friends. "Say I'm a philosopher," he advised, "say I'm a seeker for truth, say I'm a lover of my kind, say I'm an author of books if you like; or, best of all, just say I'm a Student." This waffling response did not prove satisfactory for the son whose friend proudly declared that *his* old man was a stevedore.

With his strong sense of the expected and the stylish, young Harry became much more self-conscious about his family's strangeness than did his siblings. He was nine years old when William Thackeray took his 1852 tour of the United States and, catching a glimpse of the shy child from the Jameses' Fourteenth Street library, said, "Come here, little boy, and show me your extraordinary jacket!" The jacket had a close row of buttons, and "Buttons," Thackeray said, was what Henry Jr. would be called if he wore it in England. "In a flash," the novelist later wrote, he realized "we were somehow *queer*." No doubt his father's physical de-formity and staggering gait aggravated the sense of queerness—a word the novelist used again and again in his memoirs, begun in 1911. Was queerness a stigma or a sign of rare privilege? The question pressed on Harry, who developed a fascination for children unencumbered with parents. He became convinced the life led by his orphaned cousins was "necessarily more delightful than our father'd and mother'd one." He also became profoundly curious about the real opinions of adults and loved to listen in on their talk.

Although the evidence is mixed, it appears that Henry Sr. tried to initiate his children into the "interior truths of the Scripture" as disclosed by Swedenborg. "I instruct my family in the knowledge of these truths," he wrote in 1854, "so far as their tender understandings are capable of receiving them." The instruction must have been forceful and graphic, for James wanted his children to share his hatred of the traditional God, "half-pedagogue, half-policeman." Against this bogey "I . . . raise my gleeful fist, I lift my scornful foot, I invoke the self-respect of my children, I arouse their generous indignation." Once, James tried to compose a catechism in which a child asks, and a father explains, what spirit means and why God cannot be seen with "bodily eyes." Formal religious indoctrination was an important part of the inner life of the James family. As Henry Jr. tersely admitted, he got "plenty" of religious instruction.

Convinced that the sacred was finally becoming identical with the secular, James believed it was vitally necessary to puncture established sanctities and ceremonies. He held Easter in such abhorrence that once, years after his death, when Alice sent someone a holiday card, she could almost hear how "Father must have groaned on high." Even at Christmas, when the family kept up a "merry pother," he always did the unthinkable, to his daughter's great confusion:

> [He] used to spoil our Christmasses so faithfully for us, by stealing in with us, when Mother was out, to the forbidden closet and giving us a peep the week or so before. I can't remember whether he used to confess to Mother after, or not, the dear, dear creature! What an ungrateful wretch I was, and how I used to wish he hadn't done it!!

Henry Jr., who also remembered this ritual desecration, had the impression Mother was kept in the dark:

> We saw those "surprises" in which he had conspired with our mother for our benefit converted by him in every case, under our shamelessly encouraged guesses, into common conspiracies against her—against her knowing, that is, how thoroughly we were all compromised.

In this way the children were not only persuaded to violate a ceremonial secret but forced to side with one parent against the other. They got their premature gratification—and with it a heavy dose of regret and complicity, not to mention a sense of dull inadequacy for failing to rise to Father's affectionate irrepressibility. He was a "chartered rebel against cold reserves": that was the going household line, and it was true enough.

Yet the charter of rebellion was not merely temperamental but had a history and an ideology. A program was being carried through. The children were to belong to the New Times. They were not to think of any custom, any person, any day as more sacred than any other. They were to learn to rend all veils, to let the light of day into forbidden closets.

No one knew ahead of time just when a closed door would blow wide open. In the fall of 1849 the tragedienne Charlotte Cushman returned to the States for a series of engagements. The following January the James parents went to the Park Theater to see her as Queen Katharine in *Henry VIII*. William and Harry stayed home, quietly doing their lessons by lamplight. Suddenly, into the room burst Father, who had left the play between acts so that he could snatch up eight-year-old William and hurry him off to see the celebrated performer. At a period when the theater was under such suspicion that even Barnum's dramatic hall had to disguise itself as a lecture room, James preached that plays had "very divine uses" and took his children to a number of productions, including a stage version of *Uncle Tom's Cabin* that had a "great and blood-curdling" Cassy. He also took them to *Jocko, or the Brazilian Ape*, in which a kindly and heroic monkey saves a small boy from drowning but is then killed by "some cruel bullet," to the unbearable agony of the small Jameses.

There was an even more memorable spectacle in store for the young theatergoers. One of the great steam packets of the day happened to be long overdue, having left Liverpool for New York on December 28, 1850. Day after day the *Tribune* ran a laconic announcement: "Nothing has yet been heard from the steamer *Atlantic*." Each arriving packet was mistaken for her, the city was swept by a series of false rumors, and gradually the presumption grew that the vessel had gone down. The passenger list was published without comment. On the night of February 15, 1851, a Saturday, when the ship was a month overdue, the James parents took their children out to see a double billing—the new farce *Betsey Baker* and "the Grand Romantic Spectacle, in three acts, entitled FAUSTUS, OR THE DEMON OF DRACHENFELS." Harry was much impressed by the farce, in which Mr. Mouser, whose wife operates a laundry with a bevy of female assistants, is pursued "round and round the premises by the troop of laundresses, shouting his name in chorus." More vivid yet was the moment afterward when Mr. Mouser stepped before the curtain and announced, "Ladies and gentlemen, I rejoice to be able to tell you that the good ship Atlantic is safe!" The house broke into a roar and the seven-year-old boy got his first taste of a "great immediate public emotion." The cries of the newsboys could still be heard at two in the morning.

When ether came into use, James was enormously relieved that his children would never have to suffer as he had suffered. He and Mary wanted to protect them in other respects as well from New York's raw onslaught. It was probably a mistake, they decided, to expose them to the agonizing exhibition of Jocko's tragic end. The future novelist was allowed to "dawdle and gape" through the city's streets, but all the same he was so well protected that when he composed his memoirs in old age he represented the city as a safe and homogeneous world. He did not seem to know about the hundreds of vendors of "obscene publications, and indecent pictures," about which *The New York Times* complained in 1855.

In 1853 the *New York Tribune* began a series of exposés of poverty and lowlife under titles like "Madalina: the Rag-Picker's Daughter." The sketches were a hit, and when the author, Solon Robinson, gathered them and a thick portfolio of unpublished pieces under the title *Hot Corn* (a street vendor's cry), the book sold well. It sold even better once buyers realized it was full of risqué stories, like that of the clergyman who thinks he is sleeping with the lovely Athalia but afterward uncovers the face "of a common street-walker." About the time *Hot Corn* was denounced as suitable only for "the vile and the vicious," eleven-year-old Harry got his hands on a copy at the *Tribune*'s headquarters. He was about to wade in when someone advised his father that the work "was not one that should be left accessible to an innocent child." The book was taken from him and a much safer read substituted—*The Lamplighter*, by Maria S. Cummins. Recalling his disappointment in old age, the memoirist doubted that Robinson's "novel" (as he mistakenly called it) could have been very improper, given the general "platitude of the bourgeois" in mid-century New York. But he was as mistaken about the book's salubrity as about its genre. One reason Henry James represented his native land as homogeneous and boring was that he had been shielded from its ranker extremes.

NO MORE INSANE THAN I AM

In his memoirs Henry Jr. recalled the family's "tremendously respectable" dentist, the venerable William H. Parkhurst, who had operated on Mary James's teeth when she was a girl and still occupied the same "torture chamber" down near Wall Street (97 Fulton, according to the directories). About the family's half-cracked physician James had nothing to say.

Dr. Joseph T. Curtis was a man of many achievements. He helped compile a manual of homeopathic procedures, invented an automatic triturator for grinding powders to the regulation fineness, and, practicing in New York from 1836 to 1857, gained a reputation as one of the city's most up-to-date, resourceful, and high-minded physicians. He also suffered from two major afflictions: he went blind from time to time, and he was hounded by voices from the spirit world. These beings, as he informed James, belonged to a "great society of illuminati" who guided human history and in every age selected a certain man "to be the Lord Christ of the time." Appointing Curtis as the Lord Christ of his generation, the spirit voices asked him to perform "certain fasts and austerities," which he resolutely attempted to carry out, and even told him to kill his children. In 1848 he was twice committed to an asylum for the insane. Although he was able to resume his medical practice, he remained agonizingly conscious of the "brooding presence" of the spirits. They seemed to be lying in wait for him until he should "become sleepless." In the fall of 1857, as Curtis labored to perfect an impossibly complicated mechanical sewing machine he had invented, he found he could no longer fall asleep. The spirits returned, this time in force, and it wasn't long before the frazzled man's distress became intolerable. He tossed on his bed for twenty-four hours, then "rushed out and bought a pistol" and shot himself in the heart.

James always required a great deal of homeopathic doctoring for his frequent complaints—"rheumatism" in the summer of 1847, "influenza" in March 1848, "bilious diarrhea for a whole summer" in 1849, and so on. The first consultation with Curtis may have taken place in 1844–45, when James was still recovering from the "vastation" he had suffered in England. By 1847, when Curtis himself went to England for a few months' rest and medical advice, the two men seem to have developed a close personal and professional relationship. It may well have been James himself who persuaded Curtis to seek help from Garth Wilkinson. The Englishman endorsed James's high opinion of the sufferer—"What a fine physician he is, & otherwise how generous a spirit & mind!"— but soon came to see him as a bizarre hothouse creature, self-enwrapped and supersubtle. Curtis's "long & painful relation of his miseries & illusions" repelled Wilkinson, who concluded the man's "noble but aberrating spirit" was probably beyond curing.

Strongly drawn to men with fanatical obsessions, James continued to believe in his physician. One of his more obscure friends, Temple Chapman, was subject to fits of "demoniacal possession." While they lasted, evil seemed to be "supreme and resistless in the universe." One visit to Dr. Curtis (James reported in 1852) and Chapman realized his trouble was "very curable." Indeed, the doctor's own infirmities only enhanced his powers: "shut up all winter with inflammation of the bronchia," he still somehow remained "first-rate in power," according to James. When Curtis left his wife in 1853 and immediately remarried following a questionable out-of-state divorce, James incurred the doctor's resentment by offering some unwanted advice, and the two men's friendship suffered a lasting breach. But again, although the doctor broke with James, James's respect and loyalty never wavered. Writing from Europe a couple of years later, he told a mutual friend he could "find no physician comparable with [Curtis] here. He is a born genius in that line." In 1867, ten years after the suicide, James was still insisting that Curtis had been "no more insane than I am at this moment." The voices he heard were dangerous, demonic, and real. In 1873, recounting Dr. Curtis's story in an *Atlantic Monthly* essay* (but without naming him), James praised him as "the most highly gifted man I have ever known." Coming from one who had been acquainted with Joseph Henry, Faraday, Emerson, Carlyle, Mill— the list could go on and on—this was and is a startling judgment.

An adept in the spirit world, a healer of obscure mental afflictions, a skilled pseudo-scientific homeopath, Curtis seems to have been poised on that peculiar nineteenth-century cusp that transformed demonology into psychology and psychiatry. One would like to know whether, and how, James's children were impacted by this strange healer who united science and shamanism. Decades later William became so interested in spirit possession he investigated cases for the American Society for Psychical Research and had numerous private sittings with a medium, Mrs. Leonora Piper, whose powers he more or less believed in. For his part, Henry Jr. wrote a celebrated ghost story, *The Turn of the Screw*, which tells of a young English governess who tries to stand off a malignant visitation of the dead. This woman, who seems to be as refined, idealistic, and noble as Henry Sr. believed Dr. Curtis to be, is certain that the two sinister visitants, Peter Quint and Miss Jessel, are in demonic pursuit of the children. The secondary narrator who reads the governess's first-person account to a group of listeners has been sitting on it, someone says, for forty years. This, as it happens, is the interval between Curtis's

---

* As James composed this essay, Mary and William each made a point of praising it in letters to Henry Jr. For Mary, it was "a most interesting paper—perhaps the best thing he ever did."

suicide in the fall of 1857 and Henry Jr.'s composition of the story in the fall of 1897.

Apparently the novelist intended the governess to be a lucid and trustworthy reporter. For modern readers of this tricky story, however, her reliability and psychology have become the very points at issue. This discrepancy in response is a product of the novelist's powerful need to dignify his childhood's disorderly beginnings. Could Dr. Curtis possibly have been a lunatic instead of the great and noble genius that Father proclaimed? No, no!—and so we get a narrative, an entire oeuvre in fact, that leaves *us* mesmerized by its ambiguity.

SCHOOLS

James's inability to decide whether he wanted to shield or expose his boys expressed itself most fully in the bizarre education he provided for them.

Anyone could see what was wrong with the Europeans' way of bringing up children:

> They will ensure a child born of one parentage, a good education, good manners, a graceful development in every respect, sumptuous lodging, sumptuous food, sumptuous clothing; and they will ensure another child, born of an opposite parentage, the complete want of all these things . . . Let them ensure all the children born among them a precisely equal social advantage.

James's own privileged education at Albany Academy and Princeton Theological Seminary had subjected him to the discipline of "dead languages" and the rigors of Calvinist theology. These subjects, he had decided, were useless and narrowing, fostering the proud, aloof superiority he passionately wished to undo. A true education must set in motion the living mind's assimilative capacities and inspire it with the highest social ideals.

But the father who sent his children to Ferrero's dance school was not about to deprive them of a graceful development. In practice if not in theory James was not all that far removed from James Buchanan, the British consul and his former "Elder," who had condemned New York's schools for setting a low standard of learning and encouraging insubordination. In this Tory's eyes, democratic education tended to overturn lawful authority and "canker youth." Perhaps James had similar tendencies in mind when he complained about the "shocking bad-manners" his boys were picking up.

While the children of dead Aunt Jannet attended New York's French-language boarding schools (Madame F. Reichard's boarding and day school for young ladies on Fifth Avenue and Professor E. Charlier's establishment on Bond Street), James's children were never placed in such institutions, perhaps because he saw them as elitist. Yet if James was determined to prevent his offspring from becoming snobs, he was equally set on their acquiring "the languages" (having himself failed to learn German or acquire much fluency in French). A series of French instructors were brought into the home. Some of them, like the large Russian lady Henry Jr. remembered as "rather rank," moved into 58 West Fourteenth Street for a time. Others, Mademoiselle Delavigne, for instance, dropped in at regular intervals to "converse in tongues." One of the oddest of these visiting teachers was the impecunious Polish émigré Count Adam Gurowski, who arrived in New York in November 1849. Gurowski had a huge head and belly, wore a veiled broad-brimmed hat (to protect his eyes), and was given to violent excesses of temper. His French, German, and Russian may have been impeccable and there is no doubt he was fearfully learned in European history, but his English had been acquired from books. Gurowski did not last long. As Henry Jr. put it, he was "invoked for facility and then relinquished for difficulty."

For their primary instruction, the James boys were sent to coeducational day schools run by women. Mrs. Bayeux of Albany and Mrs. Daly of New York were succeeded by the Sedgwick sisters, who operated a respectable boarding and day school in their father's home on Ninth Street, between Fifth and Sixth Avenues. Next came Lavinia D. Wright, whose boarding and day school, previously for girls only, had recently opened its doors to boys. The experiments conducted on the second floor for advanced pupils led young William to pronounce her a "very able woman."

It was probably in 1852, not long after Henry Sr. denounced the European system of privilege, that he enrolled William and Harry in Professor Vergnès's Institute for Young Gentlemen at 166 East Tenth Street. Most of the other boys had been sent from Cuba or Mexico to reap the benefits of what their parents no doubt hoped would be both a Yankee and a Gallic education. In its first year of operation, the institute advertised instruction in French, Spanish, English, Latin, and Greek, as well as commercial arithmetic and higher mathematics. But as time went on, the school promoted subjects like surveying and civil engineering. Conditions must have been grim, for according to Henry Jr.'s memoirs there was no playground, the rooms were poorly lit, and the instructors were in a constant rage. The pupils could not be thrashed, but the staff hurled books at them and in other ways made an open display of their contempt. Henry Jr. felt an "unmitigated horror" of the place.

For the 1853–54 school year, James transferred his two older boys from Vergnès's institute to the best school they were to know in New York. It was run by Richard Pulling Jenks, a Harvard graduate and a member of a once-wealthy Salem family. Jenks had no playground and he administered corporal punishment (being "the last of the whackers," the novelist supposed), but he offered a solid introduction to the classics and he respected his pupils. For the first time in his life, Harry had teachers he could look up to, particularly the drawing master, an enormous man named Benjamin H. Coe, who tossed off tiny, charming "drawing-cards"; the boy found this man "deeply attaching." Coe's main appointment was at New York University, where he taught the art of making "accurate copies" of paintings by Asher Durand, Frederick E. Church, and others and where William was enrolled in one of his classes.

James clearly wanted a classical education for his two older boys. Unfortunately, the future novelist does not seem to have done well at Jenks's academy, and when the school year ended he and Wilkie were remanded to the instructional care of a woman whose house adjoined the Jameses' summer lease on Staten Island. Harry was dismayed: not only was summer ruined but he found it humiliating to have a woman teacher at the advanced age of eleven. He suffered another demotion as well, being ranked now not with William but with Wilkie, the only member of the family who didn't care for reading. Like Bob, Wilkie was to be educated for a career in business.

For the 1854–55 school year, James pulled his boys out of Jenks's academy and sent them to yet another school, this one only a stone's throw from home, at Fourteenth Street and Sixth Avenue. The new school seemed plainer and more regimented than any of the others—in Henry Jr.'s words, the "prosiest" and "most sordid" of the lot. Looking back, the novelist tried to explain this latest jump by supposing that Jenks had moved to "the far upper reaches of the town." But in fact Jenks's new address (on Fourth Avenue between Twelfth and Thirteenth Streets) was much nearer the Jameses' home than his former one (689 Broadway, near Fourth Street). Distance was a pretext—the sort of explanation a parent could fob off on a child when it was hard to produce the true reason. Henry Sr. had decided his namesake had little aptitude for Latin and should be trained for what was called Industry and Usefulness, and he placed the boy under a dry old disciplinarian named William Forrest, who had taught Mary's brothers a generation earlier and may have been recommended by Robertson Walsh. William was also shifted to the new school, but he got to enter the "classical department" run by George P. Quackenbos, a much younger man than the fossil Harry was stuck with.

It isn't known how Forrest and Quackenbos affected the other boys, but for Harry the school was a disaster. He wilted under the "dreadful blight of arithmetic" and the feeling that he had been relegated to an inferior educational track. Double-entry accounting was what he was supposed to be learning, but while his classmates filled their copybooks with neat columns of figures and slanting lines and balanced sums, he wallowed in total noncomprehension, getting little help or sympathy from his elderly black-suited pedagogue. The boy was ill served by his scattered education, and his self-esteem suffered a grave injury, as did his capacity for learning technical matters and getting on with his age mates. (The only individual fellow pupil he remembered from the school was Simpson, whose lower lip protruded in "a crude complacency of power.") Looking back from old age at the numbing depression of Forest and Quackenboss (as Harry spelled the names in A Small Boy and Others), he decided he must have lost touch with "constituted reality" during his term at this institution.

Years later, writing to William, the novelist deplored their father's educative folly and hoped his nieces and nephews wouldn't be subjected to a similar kind of "moral and spiritual" instruction. In his memoirs, however, even as he confronted the damage done to him by his random schooling, he made an earnest attempt to defend the paternal theory he imagined lay behind it. Drawing on Father's most cherished ideas, the son argued that the most important part of education was learning how to refine waste experience into higher uses. The literal had little value in and of itself; it mattered not at all whether a child "breathed inconsistency and ate and drank contradictions." The real trick, as he and his older brother had shown through their later accomplishments, was to "convert" the contradictions into something higher. With this argument, Henry tried to rationalize the crazy quilt of schools, tutors, and governesses that had nearly smothered him. And indeed, even as he tried to find the cryptic inner order in the accidental, the unruly, the unbelievably snarled, he was once again applying his father's program.

But it was beyond even Henry Jr.'s powers to make sense of his erratic schooling or the paternal motives responsible for it. His father had not been able to settle on a single school or instructional system, he favored the firstborn William, and he badly misjudged the second-born's talents. When eleven-year-old Harry was taken from a classical school and placed in the hands of a superannuated teacher of double-entry accounting, the idea was not to stimulate the boy to be more creative, spontaneous, and social. The idea was to make him learn—for that year—certain technical skills.

The father's arcane theories and the son's mature narrative techniques have at least one thing in common: both were exercises in "conversion." The novelist's use of the point of view of a gifted outsider; his fantastically sensitive touch, as of one who feels his way in the dark toward some gross fact universally understood; the uncanny sense of airlessness and absence: all this was the converted, the redeemed form of an education so chaotic it was as numbing as Father's amputation.

SUMMERS

A letter Henry Sr. wrote years later, when he had moved his family to Cambridge, leaves us in no doubt about one point. It got hot in the Jameses' second-story parlors, the temperature sometimes climbing as high as 100 degrees Fahrenheit. This was one more reason to seek a periodical respite from the noise, smells, and other abominations of nineteenth-century New York.

During the family's seven years on Fourteenth Street, they generally passed their summers in large resort hotels by the sea. The children became hotel children for the season, and Mary, Catharine, and Henry Sr. sat or promenaded with fellow guests on breezy verandahs. The great bother of supervising the cook, the housemaids, and others could be forgotten, and at the same time a Fourierist who believed in communal living arrangements and saw the isolated family as a vanishing institution could feel that he was virtually putting his ideals into practice. For the brave new spirits of the 1850s, boardinghouses and family hotels were a harbinger of future harmony. An Oneidan saw the trend toward residential hotels as a sign that Americans were abandoning "old fashioned familism" for "a new world of social pleasure." What that meant was that you could install your wife and children in a comfortable suite of rented rooms by the sea and still believe you were contributing to social progress.

The Jameses spent several seasons at Hamilton House in Brooklyn, on the South Shore Narrows. Fort Lafayette, visible out in the channel, seems to have held a special attraction for young Harry, casting "a stronger spell upon the spirit of our childhood, William's and mine at least, than any scene presented to us up to our reaching our teens." Eighteen fifty was probably the Jameses' first year at Hamilton House. It was that fall, at any rate, that Wilkinson complained of James's "provokingly" idyllic account of the family's situation by the "blue waters." One August evening, having gone to Manhattan on an errand, the two Henrys, father and son, ran into Washington Irving on the ferry headed back to the hotel. The famous author gave them the latest news—the death of Margaret Fuller, drowned in the fierce storm that had hit New York a couple of days earlier. A quarter century later Henry Jr. ran into an older American woman in Paris who remembered passing the time with Henry Sr. on the Hamilton House verandah and being so impressed by his conversation she still considered him *"the best man in the world!"*

Another summer resort favored by the James family was New Brighton on the north shore of Staten Island. George Washington Curtis had a large, pleasant house here, as did a Boston couple, Sarah (Sturgis) and Francis G. Shaw. The Shaws were the neighborhood's social leaders and a good deal more: Francis translated George Sand, wrote for the *Harbinger*, and pushed hard for several reforms, and Sarah had an intense correspondence with Henry Sr. on social and religious topics. When the Shaws sailed for Europe in 1851, spending four years abroad for the sake of their children's education, they anticipated the Jameses' transatlantic move. The two families had much in common and were on easy terms, and when Henry Sr. and Jr. visited the Shaws during the Jameses' first summer on Staten Island (probably in 1848), the future novelist carried away a lasting impression of the scene. He saw the five Shaw youngsters as enjoying the amenities of civilization even while living in a state of nature: they seemed superlatively healthy and beautiful, ate their meals outside, and (most impressive of all) went "stockingless and shoeless."

Evidently the little Jameses were not allowed to go barefoot in summertime. One reason for this was that they were living at Blancard's Pavilion, New Brighton's largest and most luxurious hotel. Henry Jr. remembered its appearance as "that of a great Greek temple shining over blue waters in the splendour of a white colonnade and a great yellow pediment." Contemporary engravings confirm the accuracy of this: there was an impressive Greek-revival façade and a long columned gallery from which guests could study Manhattan's far-off spires and the masts that spiked the bay. Closer at hand was a swimming basin, where little Harry's "stout nurse" ducked him again and again. The hotel's suites of communicating rooms, along with the bureaus and "presses" provided by Mr. Blancard, made it a convenient summer residence for large families. The owner was especially proud of the large "dining and concert room . . . surrounded with columns representing green marble, and surmounted by a splendid dome." It was in this ornate setting that the Jameses ate their meals, next to the Southern plantation families that flocked to New Brighton for the hot months.

In 1854, when the Jameses returned for their second summer on Staten Island, they did not stay at the Pavilion but rented a house, or part of a house. This was the place, as the novelist remembered, that was next door to his remedial teacher, Mrs. Vredenburg (as he spelled her name). Going to an old map that names the principal proprietors, and then to Richmond County's archived deeds, one learns that Mrs. Narcissa J. Vredenburgh resided on the street that runs along the waterfront, Richmond Terrace. The map shows her spacious home as close to the ferry landing, some livery stables, and a row of small and tightly packed buildings. Not surprisingly, what the future novelist mainly remembered about the place was the "dust and glare and mosquitoes and pigs and shanties and rumshops." Perhaps his parents chose this location because it was within easy reach of the steam ferry to Manhattan. But they were definitely not in the desirable section, west New Brighton, where their friends lived. The Jameses had to drive a mile west in order to savor what a reporter called the "refinements and elegances of metropolitan life" in a pleasant "compound of town and country."

Luckily for Harry, a boy he had met at Jenks's, Louis De Coppet, was also summering on Staten Island's North Shore. Having grown up in Geneva, Louis had a French accent and the cultural authority that went with it, and he gave eleven-year-old Harry a sense of foreign vistas far more enchanting than Mrs. Vredenburgh's dusty neighborhood. Even better, Louis asked Harry if he wanted to collaborate on a romance and then get it published. Although their concoction never saw print, the two young authors giving less time to the task of writing than to their grand schemes for publication, Louis had offered the future novelist something his parents and teachers had withheld—"the very first . . . approval offered to the exercise of a gift."

In this way, Henry Jr. glimpsed an alternative to the incoherence and depression visited on him by his father. There really was a distinguished world elsewhere. It was not clear as yet just where this world was to be found, whether in transatlantic manners or works of fiction (the two did seem to be connected), but it was definitely proven that the bruising world he'd been thrown into by Henry Sr. was not the only one there was.

Chapter 20

■ ■ ■

PUBLIC PHILOSOPHER:
1850–53

When James wrote for the poorly capitalized *Harbinger* in 1848, he was on the fringe of thought and politics. Now, joining other 1840s socialists who had moved into the mainstream, he was able to attain a powerful but ambiguous position at the large metropolitan *New York Tribune*. Without being a member of the editorial staff (as he had been at the *Harbinger*), he operated as a contributor who had been granted special privileges. His two-column letters on unpromising topics were invariably printed, his books and lectures got long and respectful reviews, and even some of the lead editorials came from his pen. In the winter of 1850–51 James delivered his most ambitious lectures yet. The book in which they were collected, *Lectures and Miscellanies*, tackled some of the big questions of the time—democracy, private property, art, ghosts. His productive energy increased as his output expanded, and presently he began to look like one of those thinkers you had to grapple with if you claimed to be up-to-date. "You are so full of celestial animality," wrote Wilkinson from England, "writing, lecturing and fighting, all with keenest enjoyment. What a Man you are! Age, which dries others up, discloses in you new fountains & fertilities."

But the more active and involved the celestial animal became, the more a conservative reaction began setting in. In 1852–53 Marx Edgeworth Lazarus and the unsilenceable Stephen Pearl Andrews forced James to confront the implications of his theoretical free-love antinomianism. He began to downplay the individual's divine inner selfhood, there were fewer and less reckless encomiums of individualistic desire, and the need for social and psychic repression came to the fore. On the marriage question he dramatically reversed himself. Instead of being a prison awaiting demolition, a vestige of an obsolescent preharmonic state, marriage became a necessary penitential institution. Marriage compelled husbands to undergo their big transformation, passing under duress from the selfish to the social. And what made marriage work was the wife, or rather "woman," whom James now extolled as the redeemer and divine servant.

As before, James continued to regard monogamy as a form of slavery. The difference was, he now began to celebrate rather than seek to reform marriage. Submission became as crucial an aspect of his thought as it had been for the Presbyterian Calvinists who had formed him.

TRIBUNE OF THE PEOPLE

In April 1850, soon after *Moralism and Christianity* came off the press, a series of five articles advocating free divorce appeared in the *New York Tribune*. The first of them, conspicuously placed on page 1, column 1, set forth the same basic argument James had enunciated in the *Harbinger* a year and a half earlier. Every human passion should be freely expressed. Marriage must be an expressive release rather than a constraint. Whenever a wedded man and woman find they are no longer attracted to one another, they are already effectively divorced, and this divorce will at once be recognized in a state of true harmony.

Curiously, the first article in the series appeared the same day the *Tribune* ran a lengthy notice of a remarkable new novel about an adulterous woman—*The Scarlet Letter*. Hawthorne, too, it seemed, was absorbed in the marriage question. When his heroine, Hester Prynne, utters a fervent defense of her adultery with Arthur Dimmesdale—"What we did had a consecration of its own"—she employs the same argument as James, who insisted that "reciprocal affection" has its own self-justifying holiness. But where the conservative Hawthorne required his heroine to qualify her self-affirming and revolutionary antinomianism, James would not back down from an extreme position few Americans of the time were ready to accept. He did make one compromise, however. At the time he delivered the first letter in the series to the newspaper's offices, his self-incriminating initials were placed at the end. Someone at the paper, perhaps Horace Greeley, decided that if the author wasn't prudent enough to conceal his identity the editors would have to do it for him. Accordingly "H.J." was changed to "H.T." In his second letter James acceded to this sensible disguise: "Since your types have a will of their own, I will follow their behest as conveyed in the signature of my former paper, by now subscribing myself, as I did not then, H.T."

James's letters on divorce marked his debut as a writer for what was becoming the nation's most influential reform-oriented Whig newspaper. They also inaugurated a running argument with Greeley, who in addition to being editor-in-chief was one of the paper's two major stockholders. Always more aware of practical consequences than James, Greeley wrote in an editorial reply that in effect H.T. was redefining marriage as an agreement "to live together during pleasure." H.T. had blithely predicted that the abolition of all legal compulsion would inspire couples to take a spontaneous pledge of mutual fidelity, but Greeley pointed out the obvious—that free divorce would mean freer sexual activity. A scandalized subscriber threatened to cancel if the *Tribune* "printed any more such articles as H.T.'s—he could not consent to have the sacredness of Marriage discussed, pro and con, in any work which he allowed to be read in his family"—but Greeley continued to give H.T. a forum. The paper's policy was "to let every body know what every body else is thinking." But the paper was also careful to let everybody know that James's thinking was screwy: "If a man will persist in standing on his head, it is impossible that the rest of the world should not seem to him topsy-turvy."

James's turn to scoff at Greeley soon came around. In Rochester a couple of years earlier, Margaret Fox and her sisters had begun to hear some mysterious sounds in the walls of their house—knockings, rappings. They seemed to be caused by an intelligent agency, for when questions were posed the answering raps came back in an easily deciphered code. Moving to New York, the Fox sisters attracted hundreds of curious visitors, among them Greeley, who became their most influential backer. American spiritualism had begun its long, astounding run. Andrew Jackson Davis, the mesmeric lecturer, was no longer the only show in town. Like others who were troubled with loss of faith, Greeley wanted to believe that making contact with the world of spirits would demonstrate the fact of an afterlife. In December 1850 he reported a conversation with a dead friend (through the medium of a "clairvoyant"), who disclosed that the late Mr. Poe was presently residing in "the third society, second sphere." James at once cooked up a lively and amusing letter that made Greeley the butt of his own famous practicality. That there were spirits operating in the world and that it was possible to get in touch with them, James freely granted. But since all their messages had proved singularly useless, he would not heed them:

> Hands off, gentlemen! You may be very proper persons, but I insist upon seeing my company. You have uttered a great many elevated sentiments,

no doubt; but sentiment is cheap on this side of Jordan, where we chiefly value deeds. Now if you will only *do* something for us . . . we shall welcome you with all our hearts . . . Give us an invention like the electric telegraph, or the spinning jenny. Give us a solution to some of the great questions of the day—the questions of finance, of an increased agricultural production, of the abolition of poverty and crime. Give us an improved medication, say a cure for smallpox, scarlet fever, gout, or even tooth-ache.

James had another and better reason for urging the living not to get involved with the dead: spirits were likely to prove malignant. Somehow or other they enjoyed access to human memory (which they could read "like a book"), and whenever they managed to get hold of a subject's "criminal remembrance," they were disposed to "drive him almost frantic with remorse." In a follow-up letter, James made it clear he was thinking of himself—of the obsessive guilt he had not been able to master until he learned from Swedenborg that it was caused by "certain ghostly busybodies intent upon reducing the human mind to their subjection." James had survived this "infernal tampering," but others—and James may have been thinking of Dr. Joseph T. Curtis—had been wrecked by it:

> We have all heard of tender and devout persons, who having through some foolish asceticism, or other accidental cause, come under the influence of this attenuated despotism, have at last got back to their own firesides, so spent with suffering, so lacerated to the very core, as to be fit . . . only for the soothing shelter of the grave.

In May 1851 James informed a friend he had invested $10,000 in the *Tribune*. Although he was not able to explain "the exact process of the transaction," the expectation was that he would earn $1,500 a year and his friend Charles A. Dana would acquire five shares of the Tribune Company. Another result—one that James probably had his eye on throughout negotiations—was better access to his bulliest pulpit yet. Now he could propagate his message to the world in a large circulation daily, and he promptly whipped off a letter to one of his severest critics, Professor Tayler Lewis of Union College. When it appeared in the *Tribune*, it was headed by a revealing disclaimer: "Though we can ill afford the space for such discussions, we do not feel authorized to refuse the request."

In April, leaving for a short trip to England, Greeley placed the *Tribune* in the hands of his second-in-command, Dana. During this interregnum the newspaper printed three of James's essays as unsigned editorials. One of these replied to an approving French review of a stuffy book by Xavier Marmier, who had excoriated the unmannerly familiarity of Americans. Another, a survey of some recent religious and philosophical books from England, denounced the doctrine of a celibate priesthood as promulgated by the Oxford Tractarians. The kind of chastity that "springs from a constrained disuse of nature is spurious, is vicious," James argued, since whenever some bodily organ is made forcibly inactive, the eye, for instance, we quickly "become all eye." Curiously, James's novel-writing son not only created a series of protagonists who renounce sex—Guy Domville, Fleda Vetch, Lambert Strether—but he may have died celibate. In a way, his lifelong effort to become one on whom nothing was lost—to be "all eye"—bore out his father's warning.

James's third editorial, "Newspaper Personalities," dealt with a sensational contemporary scandal—James Watson Webb's accusation in the pages of *The Morning Courier and New York Enquirer* that Nathaniel P. Willis, editor, writer, and socialite, had seduced a young woman.* At the time Willis was the man of letters Americans most loved to hate (after Cooper). He defended his and the woman's honor by declaring he had never known "so wild, brilliant, and apparently lawless a creature, who inspired so universal a confidence in her virtue." In his comment on the unseemly fracas, James reminded the *Tribune*'s readers that Webb's accusation had been provoked by Willis's prior attack, but he refrained from expressing any "opinion as to the merits of the quarrel." His chief concern was to condemn the self-righteous spirit that vindicates itself by humiliating another. Privately, however, James admitted that his sympathies lay with the accused seducer, and also that one of Webb's friends had altered the editorial. And the girl *had* been reckless—"a natural *bayadère*, disposed to tempt the brink of the dizziest precipices."

The Willis and Webb affair, like Professor Webster's murder of Dr. Parkman a couple of years earlier, was one of many celebrated scandals in which James inserted himself. In every instance he protested the indecency of holding anyone, no matter how sinful or criminal, up to public contempt. Few things aroused his indignation as much as the pillorying of some private guilt or shame.

---

* Willis is best known as the brother of Fanny Fern, who gave a devastating portrait of him in her thinly veiled autobiographical novel, *Ruth Hall* (1854), and also as the employer and protector of Harriet Jacobs, the slave who hid in an attic for six years before making her way North.

LECTURING

In old age Henry Jr. recalled a pantomime he had observed some sixty years earlier from the parlor window on Fourteenth Street. Henry Sr., accompanied by Mary, was leaving home to deliver one of his lectures. They were standing "under the gusty street-lamp" preparing to enter a carriage and ride away. Abruptly, Father pulled some papers from his coattail pocket and shook them in Mother's face, proving to his anxious caretaker that the reading manuscript had not been left behind—as had once happened.

Perhaps it was in 1851 that this little scene played itself out before the watchful eyes of the young novelist-to-be. That, at any rate, was the year his father had his greatest success behind the podium, appearing at the Mechanics' Institute and giving six major lectures at the Stuyvesant Institute, both on Broadway. He attracted a number of influential listeners, including the writer Caroline Kirkland, and after each evening's talk George Ripley informed the *Tribune*'s readers exactly what the speaker had had to say. The talks were revised and published in James's most ambitious book to date, *Lectures and Miscellanies*, which was so well received the author briefly entertained hopes of a second edition. The lecture on property made such an impression on Octavius B. Frothingham that he quoted a page of it in his memoirs forty years later. In 1852, a group of impresarios planning the next season's lectures announced that, instead of inviting "Radicals who discuss debatable topics," they had secured "less flighty and more conservative essayists" such as James and Emerson. This announcement gave a writer at the *Tribune* a good laugh, seeing that the latter were "decidedly the two profoundest and most sweeping radicals of our time." James had come a long way in the last ten years. His name, easily yoked with Emerson's, would never be more famous.

In the lecture on "Democracy and Its Issues," James continued to work out the contrast between Europe and America and the meaning of popular self-rule. Europe had progressed from monarchy (the rule of one) to aristocracy (the rule of a minority), and America had gone one step further by establishing the rule of the majority. But true democracy had not yet arrived. True democracy, having nothing to do with politics or legislation or any particular form of government, was to be the culminating utopian state, one in which people exercise complete responsibility for their mutual relations. Under democracy, people will "spontaneously do the right thing," and the police and all other coercive institutions will wither away. At the same time, and most confusingly, James also

identified democracy with "the destructive legislation now in progress."
This notion of a temporarily destructive stage is not easily reconciled
with the idea of a final, apolitical heaven-on-earth. On balance, it seems
that James understood democracy as a necessarily chaotic and distressing
interregnum—a basically negative period that does away with worn-out
institutions. Democracy is what comes just *before* that structureless social
unity he had invoked in "What Constitutes the State?" It was not democracy he cared for but its "issues," its glorious sequel.

Another lecture, "Property as a Symbol," remains one of James's most
fascinating concoctions—a public attempt to reconcile his commitment
to social and economic equality with the unearned wealth he had demanded in New York's courts and now comfortably lived on. The lecture
began with the claim that possessive greed is what distinguishes humans
from all other animals, a point James illustrated with a domestic scene
of noisy competition among his "vociferous nurselings" (as he elsewhere
called them):

> Take home with you . . . a picture book or child's toy of any sort, and
> expose it to the gaze of your children: you all know how furious a storm
> of entreaty will greet you on every hand for the sole possession of the
> bauble. You may assure the little circle that each shall possess it in turn
> . . . But no, each must call it his own absolutely, each must have complete
> possession of it, and then of course he will do the generous thing towards
> the others . . . and you are glad to purchase final quiet for yourself by
> bestowing it out and out upon the noisiest lungs of the group, promising
> the others that their turns shall come next time.

With maturity, this possessiveness does not disappear but becomes more
subtle and shamefaced. Whatever people may claim to feel, they secretly
value property for its own sake rather than its exchange value. "I admit,"
James said,

> that I should be very much ashamed to be caught toadying a rich man,
> and that I could say things on the baseness of such conduct which would
> really stir your blood. But all this is dramatic. I am acting a part, the part
> assigned me by public opinion. For in private, I feel an instinctive respect
> for property. It does in some mysterious but infallible way embalm the
> possessor, so that while my theory bids me defy him, I never come into
> his presence but with 'bated breath, and differ from him with painful
> reluctance.

Was this how the lecturer had felt in William of Albany's presence? If so, he must have reached a partial accommodation with his father's ghost, for his big point was that we are only sentimentalizing when we refuse to recognize the great power property has on our imagination. Instead of denying this power or feeling ashamed of it, we should try to understand its spiritual meaning, its symbolism.

This said, the lecturer took a sudden but characteristic jump from psychoeconomics to the theological absolute. The reason we worship property, he announced, is that property symbolizes our eventual dominion over nature. It dimly prefigures our universal mastery and the coming Divine Man. The reason we are greedy, especially as children, is that that is how we express our desire for the approaching infinite. Thus, after insisting on a frankly iconoclastic approach to the question of property, James vanished once again into the arcane, the cosmic, the apocalyptic. Yet even as he did so, he was justifying the present unequal distribution of wealth. If some are richer than others, he explained, that is because they have a greater spiritual potential. Hierarchy will always be with us, for even when human society is finally made perfect, each man will enjoy "outward homage" in proportion to "his capacity of ideal action."

James was looking at the question of property through a rich man's eyes, a perspective that became apparent when he turned to a matter that weighed heavily on him—the poor man's envy of the rich. This envy could not help but prove troubling for a wealthy radical who believed Europe's privileged classes were destined to be "swept into oblivion." Characteristically, James resolved the problem by decreeing it out of existence. To suppose that anyone could possibly envy another for anything but "the social appreciation he enjoys" was a "simple absurdity." Anyway, when we finally have a true society and everyone has the power to develop his own genius, even this mild social envy will vanish.

Of course, among the extremes of rich and poor were certain degenerates, the "scum and froth," who took pride in their own wealth or envied that of others. But these malignant populations were certain to be eliminated: "In any decisive uprising of the people, both sides alike would instantly unite to rid themselves of this factitious and disorderly element." James found this rosy scenario confirmed by what had happened in Paris in 1848, during the so-called bloody June days, when military force was brought against rebellious workers and radicals, with considerable loss of life. James defended this repressive moment in remarkably absolutist language: "The thief, or the destructionist of whatever sort, when refractory to counsel, was instantly shot down to show that the will of the people when freely expressed is the will of God, and tolerates no lower righteousness." It would seem that James's harmonic fantasies easily lent themselves to mass violence. Coercive institutions would definitely pass away—but first there would probably have to be one last cleansing and coercive exercise.

The huge black strap was getting bigger. In his last three lectures, James turned away from democracy and property and other mundane topics in order to renew the attack on the "old theology." For him, the heart of this theology was the belief that God was a being entirely separate from man and infinitely superior to him. Thrashing this bogus sovereign with tireless zeal, James declared that there is only one feeling we can have for such a being—"hatred of the intensest sort." James also took a swing at the priests who serve this god, calling them a parasitical class and recommending that they be allowed "an actual minimum of meat, drink, and sleep, until they do their duty." Only if we punish and defrock the false priests will we "stand a chance at last of getting a capable or real priesthood, the priesthood of men of science."

Among James's listeners sat some liberal-minded members of the class whose food and sleep he proposed rationing, the Reverend Henry W. Bellows, the Reverend Edwin Chapin, and others. Not only did these clergymen seem to enjoy their public whipping, but James preened himself on their applause most of all. Bellows, New York's leading Unitarian minister, told the lecturer he "had *never* heard anything in his life that interested him so much," and, urging James to read his talks in Boston without delay, all but guaranteed good audiences in that city. The Reverend Orville Dewey, an occasional preacher and lecturer, ran into John Barber James on Fifth Avenue and told him his brother's "ideas were making a decided impression on the community." Each day brought fresh raves, and as the series came to an end James was certain he had finally resolved an old and nagging problem. "Of one thing at all events no doubt remains," he wrote Tweedy; "my business is lecturing. All parties unite in telling me that I must do nothing else for a living, but disseminate the gospel of the divine humanity now henceforth and forever."

But how would the gospel of the divine humanity play in Boston, "the focus of Lecturing," with the coolest, most critical audiences in America? James was nervous about Boston, and it wasn't until the following November that, following Bellows's advice, he felt ready to take the plunge. Hoping to avoid a humiliating reception, he urged Emerson to be present—"seeing thus an hundred empty seats obliterated." Also, just as on the eve of his 1849 address to the Town and Country Club, the anxious speaker defied his expected auditors by threatening to say something outrageous: he would convert himself "into an army of Goths and Huns, to overrun and destroy our existing sanctities." But this was bravado, and when James made one last pass through his lectures before leaving New York, he was horrified by their "loud-mouthed imbecility." Stricken with fear, he doubted it was possible to communicate "vital truth."

James and Mary made a flying visit to Albany and then took the train to Boston one day before his November 5 opening at the Masonic Temple. Arrangements had been made by James T. Fisher. There would be two or three lectures a week, and tickets for all six nights, costing $1, could be purchased at Boston's two premier bookstores—Crosby and Nichols, high-minded and radical, and Ticknor, Reed, and Fields, high-minded and literary. Emerson bought two tickets and assured friends who might not otherwise show up that the lectures (which he hadn't heard or read) were "really brilliant." On the fifth the Jameses dined with the Wards, Anna afterward noting in her diary that "Henry is an extraordinary talker." But that same day it was announced that the opening night had been pushed back to November 7, and when that day's *Advertiser* came out, it appeared the series had been called off, "owing to sudden and severe illness." The Jameses fled back to New York, where their arrival must have been quite a surprise. Perhaps this was one of those never-to-be-forgotten moments when Father poured out, "as he alone could, the agonies of desolation thro' which he had come," his concerned children pressed close around him.

The letter of apology and explanation that James sent his disappointed Boston impresario a few days later hints at the ambiguity of his sudden illness. "My health has improved," he wrote, "though I am not utterly well; and I am going on vigorously in the improvement of my lectures." This curious sentence says that the writer is not well but is feeling vigorous, and it joins two apparently unrelated matters—the state of the writer's health, the quality of his lectures—in order to suggest that the improvement of the latter accounts for the melioration of the former. Then, dropping all reference to his physical complaint, James sought to justify his abrupt withdrawal by claiming the newly revised lectures would "do [his] thought so much more justice," would "be *perfectly* apprehended" and "give *permanent* pleasure." "The fact is," he wrote (hinting that the illness was not quite a fact), "my visit to Boston, the sort of shuddering contact I felt with its fast-anchored orthodoxy, was greatly serviceable to me in throwing me more and more upon the everlasting gospel of God's humanity." Next time, he promised, "there need be no fear of my backing out." He wanted Emerson to be informed that the lectures were being improved.

Emerson put his own construction on the fiasco. Alluding to Christ's doubting disciple, he confessed he had only a "Thomasian faith in the acute disease which drove you from Boston." Something other than a physical indisposition had destroyed the lecturer's resolution. Whatever it was—disappointing ticket sales, some critical remark from Emerson or Fisher, some hint of Boston's keen-eyed intellectual hauteur—James hadn't been able to face it. Like Verena Tarrant in his son's novel *The Bostonians* (though for very different reasons), he had to cancel at the last minute.

Boston never got to hear James's six lectures. Even in New York he never again attempted a comparably ambitious series. Lecturing was not his business after all.

LOVE VERSUS MARRIAGE

By now, most of those in James's revolutionary generation had slowly and painfully realized that something was wrong with their glorious prophecies. In the summer of 1848, reporting from Paris, Charles A. Dana had seen for himself how irrelevant the Fourierists were in French political life. Wilkinson had decided in 1850 that, however faulty the present institution of marriage might be, it was "better not to discuss the matter at all." That same year, done with Fourier and quite "wearied out," Hugh Doherty came back to England from France. "He seems to have come here to rest," Wilkinson told James—to take refuge in "the manifold truths of green lanes and successive seasons." Doherty favored "practical men" now, and so did Wilkinson, who hinted to James that the time had come to "drop all notion that the righting of the universe is [our] business."

But James wasn't ready to let it drop. As late as August 1852, he was still issuing loud complaints about the encumbrances married men have to bear in the present state of society:

How poorly does one now play the part of father, pestered and oppressed as he is by the entire physical and social responsibility of his child! . . . How poorly also does one now play the part of lover, seeing that his recognition of his mistress's spotless infinitude is made an occasion by society for saddling him with the whole burden of her finiteness, for reducing him to the life-long servitude of her material interests!

Also, James was showing an unusually relaxed interest in others' sexual escapades. "Our married women were never so *fast* as this winter," he informed Tweedy early in 1851. Everyone was talking about Mrs. Haight's ball, the grand feature of which was "a dark room . . . in the center of all the other rooms, a bed-room with all the appurtenances of a bed-room, through which the guests circulated . . . going into closets, and cuddling up in the most unprecedented corners." George G. Foster, author of *New York by Gas-Light*, had recently left his wife and children and become a "copartner" with a Madame de Marguerittes. Mary "re-mains with me still," James joked.

James's letters to Tweedy frequently brought up the topic of marital infidelity, especially during Edwin Forrest's messy divorce suit, one of the great scandals of the time. After the actor's English wife walked out on him in 1849, she made her home with the Parke Godwins, in whose parlor James and Tweedy evidently got to know her. Catherine Forrest's enemies would accuse her of adopting "the freer, harmonic theories of Fourierism." James followed the trial closely, and when the verdict came down in the wife's favor, he was surprised at the size of the alimony she was awarded, particularly in the light of her indiscretion in "sending for gentlemen to her bedroom at midnight." Forrest had made wild accu-sations of adultery against some of his wife's friends, and James banteringly congratulated Tweedy—"You old villain, you!"—for having "got off most surprisingly." He also warned Tweedy not to read this part of the letter to his wife.

But a frightening quantity of "scum and froth" was rising to the surface. A New York abortionist was caught advertising his services as a "Professor of Diseases of Women and Children." A grand jury looked into a wax anatomical museum of disease and deformity. Two water-cure physicians, Thomas and Mary Gove Nichols (the latter another acquaintance of Tweedy), started a school for young ladies in Port Chester that offered instruction "in the truths of physiology." One of the textbooks, *Esoteric Anthropology*, written by Thomas Nichols and purchasable only through the mail, explained the function, appearance, average dimensions, and proper care of the sexual organs. Nichols provided his readers with a picture of a detached penis lying horizontally across the bottom of a page and looking rather slug-like, but his illustration of the female genitalia was as explicit as something chalked on the wall of a male privy. The book was meant to demystify sex, but without taking a sterile clinical approach. It was made clear that the sexual act brought "exquisite plea-sure." Nichols had high praise for Swedenborg's treatment of conjugal love and "Fourier on Social Relations." Without naming James, Nichols recommended some recent books on marriage reform that either reprinted James's writings or cited them with approval.

One of the books the author of *Esoteric Anthropology* most admired, Marx Edgeworth Lazarus's *Love vs. Marriage*, mentioned James by name and claimed him as a fellow traveler. Published in the summer of 1852, this was the book that crystallized the free-love movement and at the same time drove James out of it, forcing him to rethink the radical libertarianism that had up to then been a major element in his social thought. Lazarus drew on a large body of writing—Bernardin de Saint-Pierre's *Harmonies of Nature*, Nichols's *Woman in All Ages and Nations*, Emerson's poem "Give All to Love," the works of Swedenborg and Fourier—to argue that the principle of "self-sovereignty" was "totally incompatible with the fixed and arbitrary forms of the civilized marriage." Lazarus summed up his message in an epigraph that mischievously jux-taposed two New Testament verses:

> For in heaven they neither marry nor are given in marriage, but are as the angels of God.
> Thy kingdom come, thy will be done, on earth as it is done in heaven.

Love vs. Marriage, like James's *Love in the Phalanstery*, gave an exposition of Fourier's passional series. Unlike James, Lazarus pushed for complete and immediate erotic freedom on the principle that humans were pro-miscuous by nature. "Monotony, monogamy, or exclusive constancy" was the death of love, which required "for its vigor and permanence in action, the charm of variety, the alternation of its objects."

All along, however complicated his motives may have been, James had maintained that his purpose was to purify marriage in a perfect harmonic future. Lazarus, by contrast, offered his readers up-to-date information on the formation of semen and the ovulation cycle and explained how to avoid pregnancy. What was most alarming was that he included *Love in the Phalanstery*, *Moralism and Christianity*, and *Lectures and Miscellanies* in his selective bibliography and praised the tendency of James's thinking. A first-class mischief maker, Lazarus aspired

> to clear away that confusion of opinions and of action which has hitherto compromised the efficiency of our propagandism and of our practical ef-forts; to reveal men to themselves and to each other . . . I take pleasure

in acknowledging the substantial integrity of the writings of Henry James,
of John S. Dwight, of Albert Brisbane, and Dr. C. J. Hempel among our
American friends, although considerations entirely personal may prevent
them from taking openly the same ground as myself.

The following year Nichols's *Esoteric Anthropology* praised *Love vs. Marriage* as "the most recent presentation" of the divorce question. Contemporary readers could hardly be blamed for thinking of this Henry James as some sort of libertine.

One wonders who proposed this very person as the *Tribune's* reviewer of Lazarus's incendiary book. James himself, eager to clear his name? Greeley, hoping to shock him into taking a more conservative position on the divorce issue? Ripley, as the editor in charge of the *Tribune's* literary department? Whatever the exact train of events, James not only found himself face-to-face with a frighteningly down-to-earth expression of his own antinomianism, but he saw himself blazoned before the world as one of the begetters of the free-love movement. At the time there was a widespread feeling among Americans that a male seducer could legitimately be killed or horsewhipped by his victim's menfolk. James was in little danger of a whipping, but his respectability was definitely in jeopardy. The long, three-column essay he wrote in response to Lazarus was a hard-pressed effort to reconstruct his views on marriage and rehabilitate himself in the public mind.

Of course, James did not admit to any such purposes in his review. In fact, the review did not much look like a review, even though it appeared in the "New Publications" department and was preceded by the usual information on the author, title, and publisher of the book under notice. Lazarus was not once named within the review, and his book remained unmentioned until the final paragraph, where James haughtily dismissed it as "mere childishness, mere imbecility"—not a book, properly speaking, but a "needless affront to public decorum." Speaking for himself, the reviewer could not imagine a society of men each "trotting around like an insatiate ape, after the varied gratification of his passions." A month earlier, James had written about erotic desire as if it had its own divine rights. Now, in a complete reversal (and alliterating rather wildly), he denounced "this odious slang and slaver of personal adulation now called love." (Around the time he wrote this review, he confessed to Wilkinson that he had a "horror of pen and ink.")

James was fighting for his name, fighting Lazarus's effort to reveal him to himself, and fighting to reestablish a basis for social stability and control and the superiority of the spiritual over the apelike. Without admitting that he was overhauling his previous doctrines, he devoted almost the whole of his review to a fervent defense of marriage, which was now seen not as some "merely voluntary" arrangement but as an exclusive union for life. It is the civil magistracy that defines, authorizes, and regulates marriage. Anyone who chooses to enter the institution must conform to it, as it has a stringent social function—to guarantee the "unitary paternity" of each woman's children and in that way make sure their father will assume the responsibility of bringing them up. Formerly, James had talked about marriage as an intolerable burden for the husband, a lifelong disciplinary ordeal that derives from civilization's incomplete state of development. Now the husband's ordeal has become obligatory and unavoidable, something not to be ameliorated but, rather, accepted and even welcomed, in fact apotheosized.

What is a man really doing when he falls in love? He is catching a glimpse, James declared, of his own divine selfhood. The woman he desires is no more than a symbol of his own divinity. Of course, since the man does not understand this symbolism—and also since no wife fulfills "the promise which the unappropriated woman held out"—he is inevitably disappointed after wedding and bedding her. But if he then abandons her for some other woman, he is not being faithful to his own high spiritual quest. The task before him is to find an "exhaustless ideal charm" in "the wife of his bosom," and in no one else. The only way he can transcend his brutal materiality is by finding a radiant glory in the "downcast eyes" of the woman he has subjected and bound to himself for life.

A new ideal, transformation through servitude, had moved to the center of James's social thought, displacing his reckless antinomianism and dulling his interest in liberal social reform. This ideal had two components—the doctrine that everything in nature and society has a spiritual meaning and the claim that woman is subservient, secondary, and inferior to man. Bringing these two ideas together, James concluded that man is a symbol of the general or the universal and woman a symbol of the "proper or individual." Just as selfhood is given to human beings only as a starting point for social development, so woman is given to man for the sake of *his* development. She is not an independent being, with natural or separate rights, but bears "a strictly subsidiary or depen-dent relation toward man." He is "her pole star and glory, and her highest dignity and pleasure must be found in being the mother of his children." In the early stages of history, woman was not even human, being man's "patient and unrepining drudge, his beast of burden, his toilsome ox, his dejected ass." The reason she has slowly risen over the ages from "the lowest mire of contempt and degradation" is that the institution of marriage has given her certain guarantees. To do away with marriage would be to let woman, and hence man, sink back into the horrors of the abyssal past.

One of the salient features of James's new gospel of marriage was its startling emphasis on antediluvian brutality. Force was at the root of things, physical desire was a kind of slaver, a decent self-respect was not to be thought of. James was finding a way to reassert the Calvinism he had tried to leave behind. He was also giving a doctrinal meaning to his private life—his strong egotism, his unhappy restlessness in his early married years, his necessary acceptance of domestic constraint. Energized by Lazarus's provocation, he had achieved a major recrystallization of his ideas. Yet the new configuration still contained his old and funda-mental paradoxes and contradictions. Although he claimed, as earlier, that the male must painfully outgrow his selfish individuality, this very doctrine was calculated with only male needs in mind. He defined woman as the symbol of (man's) selfhood, yet insisted she lacked a functioning self of her own and could not help but devote herself to others. So what were the James women to make of themselves? What were they to make of their husband and father, who reduced them to the bestial only to install them in a glorified private shrine?

The father's expectation of social revolution had resolved itself into a claustral allegory justifying the status quo. The mother's eager partic-ipation in his apparently radical ideas had shifted to an intense cultivation of domestic life. Within the respectable brick and brownstone walls of 58 West Fourteenth Street, huge energies had been unleashed and then painfully recorralled.

CONTROVERSY

Few things can be more maddening than to be raked over the coals for a heresy one wants credit for having given up. In 1856 a major five-column essay in *The New York Times* on the rise of the free-love move-ment glanced in passing at "HENRY JAMES, a literary gentleman of great ability," who had "denounced and ridiculed the legal bond" of matri-mony. When the article was picked up by the *Boston Daily Advertiser*, a Swedenborgian wrote in to say that whatever this literary gentleman "may have said or done . . . —either in public or private—we do not consider ourselves accountable" for him. This insinuating letter was in turn reprinted by *The New York Times*. The widespread suspicion that James was unsound on marriage was not about to go away.

Of all those who refused to let James forget his reckless assaults on marriage and orthodoxy, the *New-York Observer* was probably the most persistent and damaging. In November 1852 one of the editors of this conservative Presbyterian weekly brought out a hard-hitting essay attacking social reformers for always "bring[ing] up . . . against the seventh commandment" (which forbids adultery). The writer, probably Samuel Irenæus Prime, cast himself as the two-fisted defender of common sense and stable arrangements: "Whilst marriage stands safe and strong the State will stand, the church will stand, society will be a fountain of law-abiding or conservative influences." He singled out three groups who were plainly bent on destroying the family—the fanatical perfectionists at Oneida who had abolished monogamy; the women's-rights people as exemplified by Elizabeth Oakes Smith, a lecturer then in the news; and the Fourierists as exemplified by Henry James, who had tried to throw a "spiritual atmosphere" over the Frenchman's sensual antimatrimonialism. Suspecting perhaps that James's recent repudiation of his free-love tendencies was less than sincere, the writer accused him of a consistent evasiveness and, worse, quoted the reckless complaint James had dashed off three months earlier: that as soon as a man recognizes "his mistress's spotless infinitude," society "reduc[es] him to the life-long servitude of her material interests!"

In *Adventures of Huckleberry Finn*, the *Presbyterian Observer* seems to be the only periodical subscribed to by the pious, genteel, and murderous Grangerford family. Prime's editorial voice had great carrying power, reaching all the way to the Mississippi River and down to the 1880s (when Mark Twain's novel appeared). The same day James read the attack on himself, he drafted a long and angry reply. When Prime refused to print it, James sent or hand-delivered it to Horace Greeley, who obligingly published it in the *Tribune*. The letter excoriated the "dishonest instincts" that led the *Observer*'s editors to overlook James's recent defense of marriage (which they had previously mentioned). He accused the paper of wishing to "prejudice me before the community" and, saying nothing about his special status at Greeley's newspaper, claimed to be "a humble individual, without any influence to commend my ideas to public acceptance, apart from their intrinsic truth." His antagonists, on the other hand, were moved by their resentment of the "criticism which I have occasionally brought to bear upon that fossil and fatiguing Christianity," that "stagnant slipslop which your weekly ladle deals out." This was the first of James's long *Tribune* letters to carry his name printed in full.

This belligerent answer saw print the same day the famous author of *Vanity Fair*, William Thackeray, arrived in New York City. His visit was a signal event for James, who looked up to the novelist as the leading contemporary "critic of manners and society" and puffed him in a long unsigned editorial in the *Tribune*. Unlike Charles Dickens, who was "a mere adipose tumor of sympathy, running pailfuls at every puncture," Thackeray refused to cater to the cheap and easy virtues or duck "his manly head to the strident inanities which claim to regulate the popular intelligence." The great man spent some time in James's library and was probably given a dinner as well. Sometime later James had his portrait done by Eyre Crowe, the novelist's secretary, illustrator, and traveling companion; the portrait's whereabouts isn't known. Was Thackeray aware of his host's strange roaring contest in the *Tribune*'s pages, and if so, what did he think? It was around this time that his comment on Henry Jr.'s buttons confirmed the boy's suspicion that "we were somehow *queer*."

A week later, in the middle of Thackeray's lecture series on Augustan humorists, the *Observer* struck back at James with an attack even more personal, slashing, and contemptuous than the first one. This time the writer seemed to know a great deal about James's past: "You and I have been students of the same school in theology, subscribed to the same articles [of belief], and panted for the honor and joy of ministering at the same altars." Not surprisingly this panting fellow aspirant saw James as an apostate who had gone whoring after strange gods: "In different periods in your history you have held to systems of religious faith that are widely variant from those in which you sojourn at present." He scornfully predicted that before the end of the decade James would adopt "some as yet unimagined scheme of religionism," and he tried to imagine the new projects James would presently "have on foot for the relief of distressed husbands." Whatever James's present view of divorce might be, he would no doubt abandon it "a week after printing it over [his] own name." To this sarcastic conservative, James looked as scandalous and crazy as Lazarus looked to James. Indeed, the editor may have been thinking of Lazarus when he blamed James's inability to maintain an "elevated and decent style of argument" on his present "associations."

James replied immediately in a second letter printed in the *Tribune*. He defended his strong language and argued that the states' laws on marriage and divorce derived from the will of the people rather than the Bible. He condemned the *Observer*'s "unmannerly allusions to my private history" and nobly refused to retaliate in kind or indulge in his opponent's sarcastic sniping. Instead, he issued one of his most dignified repudiations: he wanted it "distinctly understood" that he felt an "unmeasured contempt" for the orthodox creed. Anyone capable of worshipping a God who condemns the creatures he himself creates—a God "prone to take cruel vengeance" against the helpless—must be excused for regarding "every manly or magnanimous instinct as a sheer affront to the divine infirmity."

As the exchange of hostilities continued, new antagonists joined the fray and James found himself attacked from all sides. He insisted his interest in divorce was "purely philosophic" and did not reflect any socially destructive inclinations. He also proclaimed "a huge personal proclivity to your 'old fogy,' whether in politics or religion," and a strong aversion to "your lank and angular Reformer." But Greeley was not about to admit James into the ranks of the old fogies. He still suspected that James's position amounted to nothing more than free love, and that divorce on demand would play into the hands of "licentious and fickle" men, who would go through the form of marriage in order to seduce innocent maidens. The men who ran the *Observer* were delighted to see the *Tribune*'s editor weigh in against the heretic. In times past, they had pilloried Greeley as a destructive "Fourierite." Now they praised his "strong healthy common sense" and slyly remanded James to his "tender mercies."

Greeley's opposition was so troubling to James he issued a half-joking ultimatum. Either the editor must cease distorting James's position or James would haunt him "as no dining-table or bedstead in town is haunted, until you consent to give my wronged spirit rest, by a really intelligent and thoughtful criticism." With this allusion to New York's hordes of rapping spirits, James was threatening to be more tenacious than any mere ghost—to come back again and again with lengthy communications. Greeley surely understood that the threat was real. James was the kind who answered every criticism. He had the true esoteric doctrine, and he held the newspaper's column inches in a very tight grip. It would take a painful editorial effort to pry this demon writer loose.

What James did not know was that he was about to be haunted by an even more tenacious controversialist, Stephen Pearl Andrews. Unlike James, whose social views emerged from a vision of divine order and social harmony and the inherent differences of the sexes, Andrews based his criticism of contemporary marriage laws on a principle he called individual sovereignty. An early libertarian, his strong sense of the oppressiveness of the existing social/political order led him to support women's rights: for him, feminism and free love went hand in hand. He approved of Lazarus's *Love vs. Marriage* and was angered by James's "saucy and superficial" review, and as the controversy on marriage and divorce heated up in the *Tribune*, he realized that the time had come to expose James's radical pretensions, and in the process make the case for free love in a large-circulation newspaper.

On December 18, Andrews politely addressed some embarrassing questions to James in the *Tribune*'s pages. James tried to give his latest assailant the brush-off—"I do not see that Mr. Andrews's queries need detain us"—but Andrews persisted, and before long James found himself besieged from the left as well as the right. Andrews showed that when James argued for the right to terminate an unhappy marriage he was arguing for the rights of love and individual happiness—in effect, free love, even though he noisily disavowed this consequence. Greeley quite agreed: Andrews's detestable libertinism was the obvious consequence of James's own position. The wily editor pointed his moral by inserting the story of Henry Schriver, who had "eloped . . . with the wife of a neighbor, leaving behind a wife and several children."

James was trapped, the practical consequences of his thinking were out in the open and his respectability was once again on the line. Losing his temper, he wildly flailed away at the "lurid and damnable" lie that his proposals sanctioned "license," and then he resumed the high *a priori*, philosophic road, announcing that humans lived under a "threefold subjection, first to nature, then to society, and finally to God." Until recently he had been maintaining that the only way for men to enter the divine life was to escape the constraints of nature and society. Now subjection, submission, had become the one true path to deliverance: "It constitutes the express and inscrutable perfection of the Divine life, that he who yields himself with least reserve to that, most realizes life in himself." Choice and individual satisfaction were both moot now, and as for the "foolish notion of 'the Sovereignty of the Individual,' " that belonged to "the purely disorganizing ministries of democracy."

Shocked at what looked to him like a complete about-face, Andrews accused James of lacking "the *pluck* to stand by" his earlier critique of marriage. John Humphrey Noyes, who had been following the controversy from Oneida (and relishing it), let it be known that he preferred Andrews's "clearness, consistency, and precision" to James's "metaphysical and transcendental ambiguities." There was "a straightforward Yankee meaning" in the principle of individual sovereignty, which addressed "the practical understanding of our people, much better than the imported speculations of Fourier or Swedenborg."

The time had come for James to show the public he was not a resident of cloud-cuckoo-land. He needed to dissociate himself from plain-speaking radicals and extremists and at the same time to display the "masterly ease of execution" he had praised in Thackeray. The previous summer the Young Men's Association of Albany had invited James for the winter 1852–53 lecture season. He had accepted, offering to speak on " 'woman' or something similar which will easily carry off a defective treatment." The lecture committee put him down for early January 1853. By the time the day arrived, he was so notorious for what the *Albany Evening Atlas* called "his somewhat peculiar views on the question of Divorce" that he had "an entirely full house." His talk lasted an hour and a quarter and was pronounced "the most brilliant, finished and witty" of the season so far. A reviewer for the *Albany Atlas* praised its "light and unconstrained humor" and "great descriptive power." The speaker had been so consummately "natural and genial" in extolling woman's "higher and better qualities" and satirizing "the 'women's rights conventions' " that it was quite uncalled for to disparage his "peculiar views."

The *Observer* would have had many subscribers in Albany. Even so, tarred as he was by the paper's editors, James had redeemed his reputation in front of a critical hometown audience. He had also managed to distill one of his most polished and entertaining compositions. When *Putnam's Magazine* was started up that same winter and James was solicited for a contribution, he submitted the Albany lecture, which appeared in the March issue, anonymously, as "Woman and the 'Woman's Movement.' " One of James's key productions, this essay shows the extent to which he reconstructed his thinking on the basis of women's civic and intellectual inferiority. From his opening sentence—" 'The Woman's Movement,' as it is called, does not, in our opinion, presage any directly valuable results"—James made it clear that he stood with the old fogies rather than the lean and lank reformers. He conceded there were women who should have been men and men who should have been women, and he predicted that in the next world these unconscious transsexuals would openly assume their latent gender: "Many a woman who has unmisgivingly laid down on this side Jordan in short-gown and petticoat, will wake up by sheer spiritual gravitation on the other side in corduroys and top-boots, and many a man who has laid down in coat and pantaloons, will similarly come to true self-consciousness in petticoat and curl-papers." But these wrongly sexed individuals were the exception, and the ladies who ran the suffrage movement misconstrued their own nature by seeking to imitate men. The truth is, James announced, woman does not care for abstract causes but only for what is close to her—husband,

children, home. Her genius is for the visible, the concrete, the practical.
She is so much more impulsive and less reflective than man that she is
not capable of entering the learned professions or the political arena.
With her many inborn disabilities, she is man's "inferior in passion, his
inferior in intellect, and his inferior in physical strength." Woman has
risen from her original debasement not through her own direct efforts
but because "her natural *inequality*" has an irresistible appeal to man.
"Every man knows this experimentally," James confided. "Every man
knows that any great development of passion or intellect in woman is
sure to prejudice his devotion."

Henry Sr.'s emphatic opposition to women's rights* found an echo
thirty years later in Basil Ransom, the Southern reactionary in Henry
Jr.'s *The Bostonians*. When Wilkinson read "Woman and the 'Woman's
Movement' " in London, he judged it the best thing James had done for
some time—"one of your happiest efforts, full of the splendid courtesy
& vigour of a Man & a husband." The Englishman supposed that Mary
had surprised him some night, after he had donned his nightcap, with
a warmly approving "curtain apotheosis."

But "Woman and the 'Woman's Movement' " also came in for heavy
criticism. A woman who identified herself only as "one of the 'Strong
Minded' " replied to James and others in a witty putdown titled "The
Proper Sphere of Men." What was perhaps the most direct and bitter
rebuke, "Man and Woman," appeared on the *Tribune*'s editorial page.
The unknown author allowed that James (not identified by name) was
"the most liberal and candid of any we have read on the conservative
side" of the women's-rights question, but took offense at his assumption
that the chief point at issue was "how Woman shall render herself most
bewitching and serviceable to Man." Replying with some heat, this critic
staged a brief debate between "Man" and "Woman," the former voicing
James's words and arguments and the latter expressing a feminist coun-
terstatement. Thus, to James's claim that women are not suited to the
learned professions, Woman asks, "Why enact laws at Albany and Washington to fortify Nature's resistless fiat?" To James's praise of woman's
"delicious weaknesses and softnesses . . . which constitute the arms of
her omnipotence to the imagination of Man," Woman points out that
those of her sex who lack these attractions still need to earn a living.

---

* Not all contemporary men were as hard-nosed on women's issues as James was. In 1853 Theodore
Parker agreed that women were naturally disadvantaged but urged that the learned professions be
opened to them anyway. Emerson's 1855 lecture on "Woman" began by endorsing the going opinions
but ended by supporting female suffrage.

As for James's exclusion of women from the better-paying professions, this, Woman declares, has an ulterior economic motive—the wish to ensure an abundant supply of cheap labor. The sharp exchange ends when Woman administers a stinging rebuff of Man's "greasy gallantry and sterile flattery." Once again, James had called up the kind of antagonist who means to draw blood. This was one of the few controversies in which he did not identify himself as author and defend himself on the printed page.

Meanwhile, Andrews was boiling. Not only had James jeered at his "small insolences and puerile affectations," but he had pulled strings at the *Tribune* to get advance copies of Andrews's contributions to the debate. On top of that, Greeley suppressed the letter by Andrews that James was permitted to read and publicly refute. In revenge, the silenced reformer gathered James's, Greeley's, and his own letters and published them in a little book titled *Love, Marriage, and Divorce*. (The Nicholses planned to make this one of the textbooks at their physiological school for girls in Port Chester.) Taking the last word for himself, Andrews argued that women would be seriously disadvantaged as long as their civil rights were not equal to men's. He also proposed to explain why James had fizzled as a reformer and social thinker. Obviously the man was brilliant, being "terribly searching and merciless" in his social critique. But he tended so "powerfully toward metaphysical subtleties and spiritual entities" that he lost sight of practical matters. He belonged to "the class of purely ideal reformers, men who will lounge at their ease upon damask sofas, and dream of a harmonic and beautiful world to be created hereafter." Unlike Greeley, who would have been improved if he had gotten a classical or mathematical education, James should have been enrolled in "a workshop or a counting-house." Of course, to speak of Greeley and James in the same breath was to liken Hyperion to a satyr, as Greeley had, after all, "done something."

Although it isn't known what impression this assessment of James's defects made on him, it is suggestive that in 1854, the year after *Love, Marriage, and Divorce* came out, he turned his namesake over to old Mr. Forrest to learn the mysteries of business arithmetic. This ill-conceived move was not well explained to the future novelist, but he still got the idea that "some rank predominance of the theory and practice of bookkeeping" was behind it. He even saw the school as a sort of workroom or countinghouse—"a shop of long standing, of numerous clients, of lively bustle and traffic."

Was the father making sure his quiet, bookish second son would not incur his own educational deficits? Did the ghost of old Billy James of Albany (who knew all about countinghouses and had definitely "done something") rap his approval? In devious and painful ways, the sins and virtues of the fathers seem to have been unloaded on the scarcely comprehending son.

Chapter 21

■ ■ ■

THE LAST DAYS
OF NEW YORK:
1853–55

In an 1857 book contrasting American and European culture, Count Adam Gurowski, once a tutor in the Jameses' house, named three American men who had developed "independent philosophical minds" after breaking away from their early theological training—Emerson, Ripley, and "James, the brilliant rhetorician."

From 1853 to 1855 James continued to express his many strong opinions on the topics of the day, and his ripe, commanding, full-voiced eloquence became widely admired or detested. You have "renewed your youth like the eagles," Wilkinson enviously wrote. Yet there were signs that James's career as civic rhetor and philosopher had reached its zenith. The lecturing ceased, and turning away from the secular themes and audiences he had recently addressed, he once again got absorbed in religious controversy. In the space of about a year he produced two theological works, a tract opposing the institutionalized New Church and an ambitious treatise on evil and redemption.

Simultaneously, an obscure New York journalist was putting the finishing touches on a strange little book called *Leaves of Grass*. Both Walt Whitman and James were fired by the dream of a new democratic society unlike anything seen in the Old World. But where Whitman made himself the mouthpiece of both ordinary and forbidden voices, James grew increasingly alienated by New York's filth, disorder, and corruption. He'd become a family man, with authority and responsibility, and the energy he formerly put into promoting an enlarged sexual candor now went into resolving the problem of evil. In his one abortive attempt to resolve the problem of Whitman, he allowed that *Leaves of Grass* was "vastly less poisonous" than its "French & English & Italian prototypes" (these mysterious volumes had been "hawked about in our college days"), and also that the new poet clearly stood for progress insofar as he seemed less prurient than his (supposed) European predecessors. But Whitman was too carnal to be "savoury," he was not attractive from a literary point of view, and his school of writing had a detectable "stercoracious" odor. The word comes from *stercus*, Latin for shit.

Eighteen fifty-five was a significant watershed in American literature. That was the year a rough kosmos of Manhattan brought out the great poem of New York and an oddball theologian took his family to Europe to defecate himself, and to get his children to defecate themselves, of the barbaric new city.

RELIGIOUS CONTROVERSY

James went to church from time to time in spite of his disapproval of the institution. One fall Sunday in 1853 he attended a regular worship service of the city's Swedenborgian Society, which at that time met at the Stuyvesant Institute. The officiating minister was Alfred E. Ford, the same man with whom James had enjoyed an acrimonious sparring match in the *Harbinger* several years earlier, when both were ardent converts to Associationism. Perhaps James had got wind of what Ford was going to preach on and went to hear him with an antagonistic motive, for the sermon, aimed at "the young," was a sober exhortation to honor the church as one honors one's mother. By church, Ford meant a particular and visible institution, the "external body of Christians professing the doctrines of the New Church."

Doctrines like this went against everything James believed about mothers, churches, and honorific distinctions, and he quickly whipped up a rebuttal and sent it off to a Swedenborgian journal:

> I heard a sermon the other day from a gentleman whose private character I much esteem, the burden of which was, to teach children to obey not merely their parents—who, in all conscience, should be their main teachers—but *the church* also; and this church was—what do you think? *the outward and visible body of persons worshiping in any particular place* without regard necessarily to their regenerate character.

What a grotesque error, James exclaimed, this substitution of a "sensuous" institution for a spiritual brotherhood! The true church was nothing but the aggregate of the regenerate—those who devote themselves to their vocation, their society, and in other ways lead good lives. Certainly the regenerate may wish to gather together for worship. But these gatherings do not have a special dignity and do not call for solemn allegiance. Instead, they should be thought of as "sacred delights or sports," comparable to the kisses the writer lavished on his children—kisses expressing "the exuberance of my love, the joyful and sportive running-over of a life already there in its fulness."

This sportive reply to Ford's sober sermon did not exhaust James's impulse, and before long his feisty exuberance took the form of a 72-page tract, *The Church of Christ Not an Ecclesiasticism*. Like his earlier tracts, this one was a "letter of remonstrance" addressed to an unnamed antagonist. The pamphlet maintained that it was as fallacious to honor any particular sect as it was to exalt one man's righteousness above another's. The New Church, so far from being a visible body, represented the final disappearance of distinct ecclesiastical institutions. It was not by insisting on her proper honors that "*Mother* Church" fulfills herself but rather by forgetting "herself and her own interests utterly in zeal for the welfare of her children. She finds her best happiness in . . . being totally spent for them, instead of binding them to her service." James had first worked out these teachings in his belligerent *Letter to a Swedenborgian*, seven years earlier. What was new was the way he brought in his recently developed notion of woman's essential selflessness. The tone was also new—mellow, confident, steady, not so strident. "Life seems to me a greatly more real and blessed thing than it seemed a few years ago," James informed a friend. The true saint was he "who cheerfully abounds in social uses, who diligently pursues his lawful calling, who trains his children to noble and patient labors, who dodges no juries and shirks no political responsibility."

One of the by-products of James's anti-ecclesiastical crusade was the diffused civic responsibility he tried to instill in his children. They were to become what he now aspired to be—an energetic participant in society as a whole rather than a member of some exclusive sect or class. Not surprisingly, this program of serving the universal by avoiding entrapment in the particular involved a great deal of wasted effort. The children were encouraged to establish themselves in particular schools, circles, cities, languages, and occupational paths; then the ties were ruptured. How to get from means to ends was always a problem in the James family. Launching yet another assault on the New Church was perhaps not the best way to get enlightened readers to do their jury duty. James might claim that "the controversial form of discussion is always the most favorable to the evolution of truth," but what he mostly ended up evolving was more controversy. Certainly the fervency of his assault on a tiny Christian sect effectively sabotaged his proclaimed purpose of appealing to a "larger audience."

James sent his tract to a couple of old friends, Sam and Anna Ward. Sam, a Boston banker now, responded by praising Swedenborg as well as James—Swedenborg for being "as positive & real as the Hebrews," James for taking him "out of the hands of Sectarians," both for avoiding the mistake of "liberal religion," which dug the ground out from under itself. Anna bought out Ticknor and Fields's entire stock of the pamphlet and scattered the copies among her friends, including the singer Jenny Lind. James at once sent Anna a dozen more copies to distribute. Another of his devotees in Boston was Mary Bullard Dwight, whose husband once said of her that "James has a church of one member, and I am the unbelieving sexton."

In the *New York Tribune* there was a two-column notice of James's tract by George Ripley, who gave generous extracts and commended the author's "beauty of diction" and "profound and significant ideas." But the only reviewers who paid much attention to these ideas were committed New Churchmen, who resented James's persistent effort to scatter their fold. George Bush ran a two-part refutation in the *New Church Repository* (to which James replied before the second part appeared), and the Reverend Richard De Charms (now of Philadelphia) assailed his "fallacies" in the printed version of a sermon originally preached before New York's Swedenborgians. De Charms had taken over the troubled New York Society for a few months in 1852. No doubt he had more than one run-in with James at the time. Now, pointedly answering the "distinguished man" who wondered why Swedenborg hadn't founded a church, De Charms warned against the destructiveness of "converts from the solifidian sects" (sects believing in faith alone). He also rebuked those "enthusiastic spirits" who were puffed up by "the pride of self-derived intelligence." Quoting James's tract, the angry minister asked, "What must we think of those intellectual peacocks, who strut, spread their tails . . . and make us mistake declamation for logic?" The answer was a vehement anathema: "Out upon such spiritual coxcombs, or intellectual dandies! The sphere of their vapid conceit and flippant vanity is very brimstone in our nostrils!" The Philadelphian had some strong advice for the New York group. You must stop meeting in this rented hall. You must get some land and "erect a temple of holy worship." Most of all (his sermon implies), you must shut your ears to Henry James.

De Charms's diatribe against James's intellectual vanity seems to have touched a nerve, judging from his response to an ambitious new book that now commanded his attention, Edward Beecher's *The Conflict of Ages*. Beecher was pastor of the Salem Street Church in Boston and editor of the *Congregationalist*. He was also a son of the old Congregational patriarch, Rev. Lyman Beecher. In *The Conflict of Ages*, he set out to reconcile the age-old conflict between Augustinian or Calvinistic thought, which stressed divine sovereignty, human depravity, eternal damnation, and the more benevolent and liberal schemes, which expected God to live up to certain minimal standards of human decency. The book was partial to the Calvinists, being particularly anxious to dispose of the question their enemies were always bringing up: How can God be just and honorable if He condemns to hell those helpless sinners He Himself created? The answer, Beecher brightly proposed, was that souls existed *before* being born and were *already* bad. By permitting them to be born on earth, God was in effect offering them a grand opportunity to repent. If they chose not to do so, God was well within his rights in incinerating them for all eternity. The doctrine of preexistence had been the missing link in Augustinian theology for eighteen hundred years. Now that Beecher had discovered it, honorable and progressive men could no longer accuse Jehovah of being a tyrant. The conflict of ages had been resolved.

Unfortunately, Beecher did not realize that regeneration and evil were topics about which one of his readers was prepared to argue till kingdom come. James's huge energies were fully aroused, and the letter of remonstrance he sat down to write ballooned into a 348-page book—*The Nature of Evil Considered in a Letter to the Rev. Edward Beecher, D.D., Author of "The Conflict of Ages."* Published in January 1855, this was one of James's least disciplined productions, an extended monologue that wandered from topic to topic without the convenience of chapter divisions or subject headings. There was a blow-by-blow account of how the author had once confounded a professor of philosophy in an argument over the meaning of choice, and there were endless replays of matters that had been previously explained: "Let me try to put my finger still more nearly upon the very centre and heart of our ecclesiastical corruption." There seemed to be a festering wound James couldn't keep his hands off. His pen wouldn't rest, and his antagonist couldn't be let go. (James's Sandemanian resentment of the honorific letters his title called attention to surely had something to do with this animus.) At one point the writer offered a glimpse of the dynamic that drove him on and on: "But I must be drawing to a close. Let me get back therefore to the fundamental idea of my Letter, to see if I can make it still more plain to you by new illustrations." That is to say, because I can feel you are still unconvinced and wish to get away from me, I am going to begin all over from the beginning. James wrote this passage on page 225. He then went on for 120 more pages, and if he hadn't been "obliged to crowd out much matter" when he gave his manuscript to the printer, the "Letter" would have been even longer.

All the same, this repetitious and disorderly work was James's most important production, for it was here that he first assembled the unique cluster of doctrines from Calvin and Swedenborg that formed his message, his burden, and his stigma for the rest of his life. God as the only being in the universe; Christ as the divine self-humbler who somehow effected a permanent alteration in human nature; creation as a spiritual process that has nothing to do with the origin of things; human existence as an illusion that makes it possible for us to will our conjunction with God (this very act of choice being the most dangerous illusion of all): these hard teachings represented James's grand bid to unite the one and the many, the spiritual and the natural, timeless being and historical progress. All philosophers had gone astray by flattering the human sense of an independent being. Except for Swedenborg, all theologians had been "blind" to the real meaning of the Scriptures. Did Edward Beecher, D.D., presume to think he had solved the riddle of the ages? Let him now know that Henry James, divinity school dropout, has solved all the riddles of all the ages. "This is a remarkable book by a remarkable man," wrote James Freeman Clarke, a leading Unitarian minister and editor, aptly characterizing the author as a modern Goliath striding "up and down before the camp of our theological Israel" and "defying all our armies."

Paradoxically, the theme of this loudly defiant book was humiliation —that of God, Christ, all human beings, and the author most of all. With his about-face on marriage and his realization of what he called the "poorness of [his] past thought & life," James had once again attained a new level of insight into himself. In one of his rare confessions of error, he introduced *The Nature of Evil* by disowning his previous books, whose understanding of Swedenborgian truth was "extremely partial and in- firm." James did not name the books or elucidate the nature of their infirmity, but he was undoubtedly referring to the way he had praised human "selfhood, proprium, individuality" in *Moralism and Christianity* and *Lectures and Miscellanies*. These works dated from his radical Fourierist phase, before his controversies with Marx Edgeworth Lazarus and Stephen Pearl Andrews convinced him that the ideal of individual self-realization was in flagrant contradiction with his basic sentiments and convictions.

What James did in *The Nature of Evil* was to make his recent rejection of self-sovereignty the basis of spirituality itself. The one great evil in the universe, he announced, was "the principle of selfhood, the principle of independence in man." Utterly dependent on God, man is at best a passive receptacle for the divine. The moment he imagines he is self-sufficient and thus feels proud or guilty, he becomes wicked beyond expression—wicked because in taking credit for his own being he denies God and the possibility of union with Him. James was categorical: "The sentiment of independent selfhood: the conviction of being the source of one's own good and evil: such is the sole ground of every evil known to the spiritual universe."

Clarke was struck by the discrepancy between James's humbling message and the "entire complacency" with which he corrected all previous thinkers. There was something ridiculous in the way he patronized his opponent, standing "Dr. Beecher before his chair, as a well-meaning little boy, who deserves to have his somewhat gross errors explained to him." But James had made the discovery that gave his life meaning and simultaneously solved the universe, and for his remaining twenty-five years, like a self-taught inventor of a perpetual-motion machine, he tinkered and adjusted and endlessly reformulated, trying to make the thing go for more skeptical eyes.

The problem was, the ingenious device that should have kept James's universe-machine humming had a fiendish inner twist: the sense of selfhood that ruins creation happens to be the very thing that makes creation possible. James's contraption was designed to run as follows: The end of human life is union with God; this union cannot be attained unless man approaches God (for if God takes the initiative man will be swallowed up); yet God cannot create an independent power of action in man, for to do so would be to create *another* god or godling—a manifest impossibility; therefore, man must be endowed with an *apparent* selfhood only, an individuality that James variously speaks of as quasi or illusory or simulated or phenomenal. It is this unreal independence that somehow makes possible a voluntary conjunction with God. At the same time, the one great Luciferan evil is to take this apparent power of choice at face value—to feel that we deserve credit or blame for what we do. Spiritual evil thus becomes an inevitable aspect of things, and yet, since this evil amounts to our mistaken presumption of our own substantial selfhood, God is in no way responsible for it.

Evil could now be attributed wholly to man without calling God's infinite power and goodness into question. However, a new problem appeared, an appalling contradiction really, since the one thing that made spiritual life possible, the sense of selfhood, also happened to be so unspeakably vile it had to be repudiated. God was cleared, but at the cost of rendering human self-consciousness too unstable to be tolerable. Thus, the wobble in James's patented universe-machine was shifted to a new region—man's now wildly rocking conception of his own powers and responsibility. Jamesian man was expected to exercise his will without being able to. He had to move toward God without having the power to set himself in motion, and then he had to repent for the delusion that he had acted in and of himself. One reason *The Nature of Evil* ran on and on and on was that with each new adjustment James made in his invention, some other part at once began to grind. This was the secret of his endless explaining. He, not his universe-machine, was in perpetual motion.

One of the many questions that popped up for James led to a rather ugly line of thought about Jews. The question was: Since God is no respecter of persons, why did He incarnate Himself among the proudest and most legalistic of peoples? James answered it by deciding that the Jews' "external or carnal" understanding of the religious life rendered them the "lowest" of races. "To this very day," he confided, "you will find the most of their descendants . . . willing to believe that God does really esteem one people and one day [the Sabbath] above other people and other days." To save man, God had to feel the temptation of, and then reject, this literal-minded self-righteousness. That is, He had to undergo the ultimate degradation of being born "a Jew of the Jews." (As for Jesus' mother, she was "in all probability . . . one of the basest of her kind.")

For the rest of his life James would be obsessed with the closet drama of Jesus' pained repudiation of his Jewishness. In 1863 he gave the drama a typically elaborate development:

> Christ was born subject to the most diabolic fanaticism ever enkindled on earth; the fanaticism of the Jew in behalf of a kingdom of God which should put all nations under the Jewish feet. Of course like every child he believed his natural traditions with unsuspecting confidence; listened devoutly to the recorded promises of God to bless Israel and Judah with unheard of blessing; and saw himself with childish pleasure pointed to by all about him as the person through whom these long-waiting promises were to be at last fulfilled. Put yourself, reader, in that tender child's place. Would it have been easy, think you, to have resisted what he resisted?

No doubt this claim to know the inner truth of Jesus' private feelings was to be expected of a man with James's messianic tendencies. The reason why this passionate identification first showed up in *The Nature of Evil* was that this was the book in which James relinquished his fantasy that unlimited greed would prove to be "divine." Looking back, this son of William of Albany could see that he had been singled out for great "external or carnal" privileges even while inheriting a desiccated religion. He, too, had been asked to meet and overcome the temptations of earthly power, self-righteousness, individual self-sufficiency. Just by living his own hard life he had discovered what made God tick. The upshot was, like many Christians before and after him, James made the Jew the symbol of the part of himself he wanted to abandon. (In his last and most confessional book, he referred to Jews as a "filthy race" and spoke of Jesus as overcoming "the devil of his secret thoughts, the devil born with his Jewish blood." In the same book James declared that "my inherited personality is full of stain or frailty derived from some or other of my progenitors.")

By 1855 James's Presbyterianism had undergone a racking metamorphosis that resulted in the restoration of his progenitors' belief in divine chastisement. All humans necessarily incur correction from their heavenly father. If there are times when the discipline seems "arbitrary and cruel," that is because we are "unaware of the benignant aspect." And just as God allows us to suffer for our own eventual good, so a human father punishes *his* child in order "to free him . . . from the bondage of his nature." Some ten years earlier James had been deeply troubled by his offspring's inevitable encounter with suffering and evil. Now he claimed to "see without terror in my child, the dawn of evils which may overshadow the heaven of his inward innocence . . . Suffering is invariably sanatory, and ends in peace."

In spite of the apparent comprehensiveness of James's new theory of evil, it had nothing to say about what might be called relational evil, or the damage one person can do to another—as when a parent, even without ill intentions, injures his or her offspring. In the 1860s Alice began to realize that, contrary to what Father said, suffering was not invariably sanatory. There were times, as she sat beside him in his library trying to read, when she felt like "throwing [her]self out of the window, or knocking off the head of the benignant pater as he sat with his silver locks, writing at his table." The daughter's very muscles seemed to be invaded by "waves of violent inclination." She dared not "let [her]self go for a moment." There was nothing to do but sit "immovable." It seemed that "the only difference between me and the insane was that I had not only all the horrors and suffering of insanity but the duties of doctor, nurse, and strait-jacket imposed upon me, too."

"Benignant," one of the family's favorite epithets for Henry Sr., was one of *his* favored epithets for the god of pain and discipline. Alice worshipped Father and of course did nothing violent to his large-browed pate, only resolving once again to live out her life in the straitjacket. With this word she was not referring to what her father and others had taught her to believe about herself. Instead, she was thinking of the imperatives forced on her by her unlucky "temperament," which required intense, unending suppression. There was no doubt in Alice's mind that the benignant father was all-wise and that she alone was chargeable for the peculiar and personal evil that filled her, the bondage of her nature.

But she still wanted to knock his head off as he sat there writing, writing, writing.

CIVIC CHAOS

One of the causes contributing to James's conservative turn in the first half of the 1850s was the frightening increase in social disorder and political strife. New York's growing Irish Catholic population, the source of the Jameses' domestic help, was becoming a rowdier presence on the streets and a dominant force in city politics. Except for the presidential elections of 1840 and 1848, the Democratic Irish were on the winning side in every contest from 1828 to 1856. The Whig Party, meanwhile, which James had joined two decades earlier, was being destroyed by the unmanageable disputes leading to civil war. Southern Whig gentlemen wanted to be able to carry their slaves into the Western territories. Northern Whigs wanted slavery kept out of the West, and a few insisted that it be abolished. Daniel Webster tried to preserve national unity by stitching the Great Compromise of 1850, which gave the South the Fugitive Slave Act and the North *Uncle Tom's Cabin*. But while the Union held for the time being, the Whig Party that Webster led suffered a fatal split. There was a third party now for disgusted Northerners— Free Soil.

One of the reasons James didn't join Free Soil was that his stand against the principle of self-sovereignty disposed him to feel rather cool toward any cause that assumed individual freedom as an unquestioned good. To his mind, it was not the slave but the slaveholder who was chiefly vulnerable to "spiritual injury." Anyway, the real need was not for some partial reform but for a total social and spiritual renovation. Also, unlike Northern abolitionists, he favored the annexation of Cuba, on the grounds that the island was "so horribly misgoverned at present."

As the presidential campaign of 1852 got under way, James remained

a staunch anti-Webster Whig. He was pleased by a report that an early
Webster nomination meeting in New York "was a sad failure," with the
hall one-third empty and "not a mechanic or labourer" present. This
poor turnout indicated that Webster would not be able to siphon labor
votes from the Democrats. By contrast, the candidate James favored,
General Winfield Scott, was supposed to have wide popular appeal. It
was thought that, as a hero of the Mexican war, he would attract the
working class, while as a Virginian who owned no slaves, he would carry
a few Southern states. What happened was that Scott antagonized the
Irish by praising their "brogue," the Cotton Whigs feared he was a secret
abolitionist, and the Conscience Whigs voted Free Soil. The election
campaign was closely followed in the James household. Young Henry Jr.
never forgot the evening in November when his father came home with
the news that Scott had been defeated. That put an end to the Whigs.

With the White House occupied by Franklin Pierce, the most mediocre
President yet, disillusionment was rampant. In Walt Whitman's eyes,
the Pierce and Fillmore Administrations were the nation's "topmost
warning and shame." Parke Godwin, a typical Democrat in some ways,
suspicious of abolitionists and in favor of expansion toward the South-
west, decided in 1854 that "the golden hour for narrow intellects and
base hearts has arrived . . . Toads crawl into the seats of the eagles.
Public policy fluctuates between the awkwardness of conscious incom-
petence and the blustering arrogance of bullyism." Reversing himself on
abolition, Godwin became a key player in the maneuvers that gave rise
to the Republican Party: it was he who drew up its first national platform
in 1856. James, too, had a vigorous contempt for the nation's pro-slavery
leaders during the decade preceding Lincoln's election. But while Godwin
and other old Fourierists became movers and shakers on the national
level, James's disillusionment with "the Democracy" turned him into a
cheerleader for a municipal anti-vice campaign and then, when that
failed, for vigilante justice.

Five years earlier James was quite certain that Christ had "opposed
the best virtue of his time" and "never failed on any occasion to justify
the criminal." Now he felt a growing fear that democratic chaos might
not prove to be the seedtime of harmony after all. Vice, crime, corruption, and the insolent Irish all seemed to be on the increase, and partyless
Whigs began to suspect it would be wiser to curtail individual liberties
than to enlarge them. In 1853 a former Italian priest named Father
Gavazzi warned New Yorkers that "the Catholics, in a great measure,
ruled the press and politics of America." The ex-priest's lectures drew
audiences of thousands, and when he characterized the "Popish church

in Italy as an organization of police," his spellbound listeners felt their "blood curdle." It isn't known whether James heard these grim disclosures, but several months later he gave voice to the widespread Protestant fear that the Pope had dispatched his "swarming legions" to America. As long as these operatives merely placed their "foolish and aggressive prayers in the public newspapers for the 'conversion of the United States' to Popery," James believed that no harm would be done. But the minute the Catholics sought "ever so covertly any political ratification of their ecclesiastical supremacy," he rumbled, "their very existence as a church will be instantly jeoparded."

Maine had a statute prohibiting the sale of alcohol. When New York passed a similar (and short-lived) law in 1855, it got James's strong support:

> It is very much the fashion [in London] to denounce the Maine Law as an interference with private rights; but I, for my part, believe in the supremacy of society—that is, in its unquestionable right to interfere in the most summary manner with every form of private indulgence which impairs the public prosperity.

One sign of the world's approaching regeneration was precisely "the gathering determination of society to put away its own evils, to crush the business of the rum seller, to extinguish the hell of the gambler, to shut up the brothel, to stifle rowdyism." James still believed that democratic America would "exhibit a deeper bond among men than has hitherto come to the surface—the bond of an exact and rigid fellowship or equality." But there was a whiff of Robespierre in his adjectives— *exact, rigid*—and also in his apparent sanctioning of extra-legal modes of social enforcement. "It has long been my conviction," he wrote in 1856, "that our social salvation would yet be due to the incorruptible Judge Lynch, and I have time and again disserted upon the subject in The Tribune." When the news reached James that summer that San Francisco's municipal government had been taken over by a vigilance committee, he rejoiced in "the altogether delicious tidings . . . of the establishment of Judge Lynch's benignant sway."

Popular despotism did not establish itself in New York, but there was a moment when James hoped and believed it was about to do so. In November 1854 Fernando Wood, a badly tarnished Democrat who had come up through Tammany Hall, was elected to a two-year term as mayor. Although some of Wood's corrupt financial practices had been exposed shortly before the election, the German and Irish vote held steady and the new mayor squeaked into office with a 34 percent plurality. Those who favored a crackdown on vice expected nothing from him. But Wood had a daring and ingenious plan for enlarging his power base. Assuming he could survive a short-term betrayal of his natural constituency, he cast himself as a progressive reformer following his inauguration on January 1. Thus it came about that during the same month James read proof for *The Nature of Evil*, he also read the cheering news that Wood was forcing the city's taverns to close on Sunday (the one day laborers could patronize them) and ordering police raids on whorehouses and gambling halls. On January 27 James sent an ecstatic letter to the *Tribune* lauding hizzoner's transformation: "A mere dunghill cock, craven to all noble enterprises, has turned out a lordly falcon." The lesson to be drawn was that immediatism worked: there was "no *outward form of evil* known to society . . . *which society is not perfectly competent to cure,* IF SHE HAVE THE WILL TO DO SO."

Judging from this letter, the social evil that bothered James the most was professional gambling. He sketched a grim picture of the domestic heartache and ruin caused by professional gamblers, who were "fed and fattened and pampered on the tears of broken-hearted fathers and mothers, on the anguish of wives, on the sighs of kindred, on the desolation of all the virtues and pleasant charities that sweeten home." He also told readers where the chief gaming establishments were located (Broadway between Houston and Spring Streets), stigmatized their proprietors as "social vermin," and even gave the full name of one of them, "Patrick Hearn."

In March the *Tribune* ran a follow-up:

Pat. Hearn, one of the most celebrated gamblers in New-York, was apprehended and taken to the Eighth Ward Station-House, where he was detained for the night. Hearn has kept a gambling-house . . . for many years, and, according to rumor, has made as high as $15,000 or $20,000 a night. Pat. is an Irishman . . .

James must have sat down at his writing desk the moment he read this, as it took only two days for his approving comment to appear as an unsigned editorial. In general he refrained from naming his enemies in print, but once again he went for Hearne (the correct spelling) and another gambler the way a ferret goes for a rat. He told readers exactly where the malefactor was to be found—"at No. 587 Broadway, in the house next north of John Jacob Astor's old residence"—and he tried to imagine how his father's old acquaintance would feel if he knew that a "social pest-house" sat next to his "honest mansion." The old-time high-wayman had been bad enough, but the professional gambler was infinitely worse, and it was time to take steps toward his "extermination." Once again James offered a lurid sketch of the gambler's depredations:

> He knows that the poor fool whose senses he has debauched, whose blood he has maddened, whose thousands he has pocketed over night, has, perhaps, a wife and children dependent upon him. He knows that he has a father and mother, brother and sister, kinsman and friend, intimately linked with him by every cleanly tie of natural and social affinity; and yet he can see wife and children degraded to the street—can see the poor wretch he has poisoned stripped of every title to the respect and affection of relative and friend.

This portrait of the respectable dupe who distresses his relatives by losing thousands in a night was based on Henry Sr.'s next younger brother and one of the family favorites. Since the death of his wife in 1846, John Barber James and his two children had been living with his mother in Albany. He was the only son who carried Catharine's maiden name. She also made him the executor of her will. Others seem to have shared the view that he was trustworthy and responsible, for in 1850 he became a director of a newly organized railroad, and in 1853 was appointed to the board of inspectors at Sing Sing. In Albany he was a generous supporter of the Young Men's Association and the Gallery of the Fine Arts, and in New York City he was a bondholder in, and probably a member of, the Union Club. A handsome, easygoing charmer, John was "the brightest of the Albany uncles" in young Henry Jr.'s eyes. Once, when there were tableaux vivants at a fashionable New York party, John did a memorable impersonation of Richard III (with a Mrs. Schermerhorn as Lady Anne). All the same, he was dangerously out of control—drinking too much, having an affair with a Mrs. Little, and taking enormous plunges at New York's gaming tables. He evidently knew he was in trouble, for when he drew up his will in the summer of 1855, he asked his executor not simply to pay his debts (the usual provision) but to pay them "as soon after my decease and burial as may be." John died owing a great deal to Patrick Hearne, and also to Charles H. Hileman, who had a gambling house on Spring Street and a clever system for drawing in customers. Hileman agreed to "compromise" for $1,450, but Hearne insisted on getting his last two cents' worth—$2,481.32. In order to settle the Hileman obligation, John's hard-pressed trustee had to dip into another man's account to the tune of $1,000 (later repaid).

A lawsuit brought against this younger brother offers vivid testimony of his helpless profligacy in New York's gambling establishments. On May 15, 1854 (according to the stiff and crumbling judgment roll), John sat down to a game of faro with a cardplayer named William M. Foster. When they were done playing, John wrote a draft on his bank in Albany for $2,975 and gave it to Foster, who endorsed it and turned it over to William C. Burdick. Burdick showed up in Albany the next day and presented the check to the New York State Bank. Payment was refused.

John also returned to Albany, to the family home on North Pearl Street. Eleven days before Burdick's attorney initiated legal action, a member of the James clan living elsewhere was discreetly informed that "poor Uncle John is down again—but better last night." *Down* is subject to various interpretations—sick, depressed, drunk. All three seem likely, particularly the last, drink being John's refuge from his folly as well as one of the leading causes of it. Drunkenness, however, would have been a lame defense in *Burdick vs. James*, and the only argument John's attorney could muster was that, gambling being illegal in New York, nothing of value had been exchanged between his client and the faro dealer, and therefore no money was owed. Burdick won the case.

Foster and Burdick remain obscure, but Hearne was for a time New York's most notorious professional gambler. He was never without "white or yellow kid gloves," and when a census marshal inquired as to his profession, the answer was "gentleman." After this spectacularly successful Irish immigrant suffered the indignity of a police raid and a night in the Eighth Ward Station House, he retained as his attorney the hardball Democratic politician and soon-to-be congressman from Tammany Hall, Daniel Sickles, who got his client off scot-free.

Hearne surely resented the vitriolic personal attacks on him in the *Tribune* by a debtor's loudmouth brother. William of Albany, with his powerful friends up and down the Hudson River, might have known how to handle this Hearne problem. Not his descendants. They had not inherited the patriarch's muscle and sound judgment, and anyway, the old days were gone. On balance, it seems likely that Henry's rash public letters, which virtually invited a mob attack on Hearne's opulent Broadway house, only aggravated John Barber's predicament.

Henry Sr.'s children probably became aware of little more than the outlines of John Barber's story. Half a century later, when Henry Jr. composed his memoirs, *A Small Boy and Others*, he dropped an occasional hint of tragedy but for the most part portrayed John Barber and his other uncles as charmingly improvidential and "tipsy." But there is one particularly tantalizing sequence where the aged novelist struggles to make sense of a vignette his young self had not been able to interpret.

At 9 Waverly Place, on the corner of Mercer Street, there lived a respectable businesswoman named Anne Cannon who made her living off the silk stocking trade. According to New York City directories, she sold "made linen" and offered "boarding." According to Henry Jr., she purveyed "pockethandkerchiefs, neckties, collars, umbrellas" and rented "furnished apartments" to high-toned gentlemen. One August afternoon in 1854, after the two Henrys, Junior and Senior, had had their daguerreotype taken at Mathew Brady's studio (the boy still wearing the close-buttoned tunic Thackeray had snickered at a year and a half earlier), they dropped in at Mrs. Cannon's. The boy was impressed by the air of distinguished service and the absence of a "vulgar till." Two employees were present, Miss Maggie and Miss Susie, stitching in their rocking chairs and very polite.

As was customary, the talk turned to "Mr. John and Mr. Edward and Mr. Howard." These Albany uncles "were somehow always under discussion" at Mrs. Cannon's, and the discussion always involved "where they at the moment might be, or . . . when they were expected, or above all . . . how (the 'how' was the great matter and the fine emphasis) they had last appeared and might be conceived as carrying themselves." Eleven-year-old Harry clearly understood that his father was anxious about how the uncles were holding their liquor. But there was something else in the air that eluded the boy:

> If I didn't understand, however, the beauty was that Mrs. Cannon understood . . . and my father understood, and each understood that the other did, Miss Maggie and Miss Susie being no whit behind. It was only I who didn't understand—save in so far as I understood *that*, which was a kind of pale joy; and meanwhile there would be more to come from uncles so attachingly, so almost portentously, discussable.

What the boy didn't know was that two months earlier Mr. John had played an unlucky game of faro and written a huge rubber check. The reason Henry Sr. had to find out whether Mrs. Cannon's steady customer was in town and drunk or sober was that if he came down from Albany and drank more than he could carry, he would be mercilessly skinned by Patrick Hearne or Charles H. Hileman or William M. Foster.

"There would be more to come." There was a good deal of hindsight in this innocuous phrase about John Barber and the other Albany uncles. There *was* no more to come for Henry Jr.'s readers, however, as his memoir neither explains the mysterious scene at Mrs. Cannon's nor reveals what happened to the three uncles. In effect, Henry Jr. passed on to his readers the "unfathomed silences and significant headshakes" he often met with as a child when he asked about his vanishing relatives. He concluded his sketch of his father's anxious visit to Mrs. Cannon's establishment by evoking its Old World "amenity," as if that was the chief lesson to be learned there.

For a quiet and well-behaved boy growing up in a family exposed to the chaos of New York, European manners held out the promise of a safe and dignified alternative. The future novelist can be said to have founded his life on this promise. But there was an illusion involved. Seen in perspective, Patrick Hearne's despoilment of Uncle John was only another phase of the Old World's troubles—an act of retribution in which a Celtic arrivist made up for age-old injustices by taking a self-destructive Protestant gentleman to the cleaners. The Irish problem had come to New York in a way old Billy James hadn't anticipated. The patriarch's helpless ghost was being bled whiter and whiter.

FAMILY RESPONSIBILITIES

Henry Sr. was not the only one of his generation who had to look out for the family's alcoholics. Early in 1854, on a trip to New York, Rev. William became worried enough about Edward that he asked one of his daughters back in Albany for a confidential favor:

> NB☞ I wish, when you have read this you would step up to Grandmothers, & ask *Libby Gourlay privately* where Uncle Edward is & if in N York where he stays & send me word immediately—If he is at home, *when* he may be expected to be in NY.

Rev. William lived in Albany and was a good deal older and quieter than Edward and the others, and was thus mostly out of the picture. Inevitably, the burden of guarding the less responsible brothers and sisters fell on Henry Sr. He was the success among his siblings, the one who seemed to know the world and where power came from and how to exercise authority. As Henry Jr. put it, he was "the person in all his family most justly appealed and most anxiously listened to." Henry Sr.'s one surviving letter to Edward tactfully recommends that he "economize" on his gout, so as "not to feel all its force at once," and also urges him (less gently) to exercise "a little manful self-control and circumspection as to your speech" with their mother.

In the summer of 1854 a brother-in-law, Robert Emmet Temple, lay dying of tuberculosis at 50 North Pearl Street in Albany (the same house Henry Sr. and his growing family had occupied eight years earlier). The question was, what should be done with Catharine, Temple's wife and Henry Sr.'s sister, who had herself reached an advanced stage of the disease? For her own safety, she had been persuaded to leave her husband's side and go to Linwood, the Rhinebeck estate that was now in Gus's hands. Then Catharine decided against this prudent separation. She "cared no scrap" for her own health and passionately demanded to be allowed to nurse her husband (who, incidentally, was dying intestate). There was a painful dilemma here, for if wife and husband both died, there would be six orphan children to care for. So a message went out to Henry Sr. at his summer rental on Staten Island (next to Mrs. Vredenburgh's) to come up and deal with his only living sister.

The father took the future novelist on this hard errand. When they arrived, the boy couldn't help feeling "abashed and irrelevant" and wishing he hadn't come. He stayed outside while his father climbed the steps of Linwood's broad verandah and went indoors to persuade or compel Catharine to accede to the family consensus. It was a hot, still day. The boy waited. Then, from far within the house came a "wail" of protest and grief, a cry the grown-up listener said he could still hear seventy years later. It scared the boy, but it also gave him unmistakable testimony of his father's authority, his "resources of high control." It was tender and necessary control, surely, and as Henry Jr. stole away to the vista point where the land dropped and the great Hudson River Valley unfolded, with mountains beyond, he felt a "proud assurance" at being involved in great and tragic doings. A version of this moment, including the fear of fatal illness, appears in *The Wings of the Dove*.

Another person who called on James's authority that summer was Catharine (Kitty) James, Rev. William's third and most fragile daughter. Kitty was nineteen years old and, like many girls and women of that time, an aspiring writer. She wanted Uncle Henry to forward to the editor of *Putnam's* a poem written (she said) by a friend of hers. Instead of doing so, Uncle Henry sent her an improvised lecture. The vanity of authorship, he assured her, was "as sad and vulgar a sight as to see the kitchen-maid exalted to the parlor, and diffusing the aroma of her culinary presence over the sacred precinct." If he were to explain matters to Kitty's friend, he would say:

Dear Anastasia, or dear Lucy, (as the case may be) the disease of every
man and every woman . . . is, that he thinks entirely too much of himself
. . . Why therefore will you strive by this literary tintinnabulation of yours
to deepen the public sense of your importance . . . ? Vastly better is it
for the truly manly or womanly sort, to be unknown to the public . . .
Feed your sheep, milk your cows, support your aged mother, teach the
village school . . . do all these and every other mean thing that need be,
not like a foolish tragedy queen unjustly debarred her throne . . . but
sincerely.

Carried away by his sarcasm, James seems to have forgotten that whatever
was published in *Putnam's* was unsigned and could to that extent draw
down no public laurels on an author's brow. Kitty's temerity had called
up his disdain for the "damned mob of scribbling women" (as Hawthorne
called them) whose fiction dominated the market in the 1850s. All
authorship was inherently presumptuous and pretentious, but female authorship was the vainest of all, and James wanted it back in the kitchen
with the cooking odors and the Irish help.

This letter reached Kitty in Lenox, Massachusetts, where she and her
sister Anna and their father, Rev. William, were boarding for the summer. In the letter's margin, opposite the *faux*-polite address to Anastasia
or Lucy, is a passionate invocation in someone else's handwriting—
"Darling one Darling one." These words seem to have been added that
fall, at a time when Kitty's father had gone back to Lenox to retrieve
his corkscrew and blacking brush and other personal effects and was
feeling an "awful loneliness." As he picked up Anna's "night clothes,"
out tumbled the letter. Reading it, he realized that Kitty had confided
in Henry Sr. and in Anna but not in him. He was keenly disappointed.
The alternative invocation may have been a way of letting his daughter
see that he had found the letter after all. Maybe he wanted to point out
the contrast between Uncle Henry's style of authority and his own.
Maybe, wishing to shield his daughter from Uncle Henry, he saw that
it was already too late to do so.

Protecting the younger generation had by now become a major concern
in the James clan. Catharine Temple having died of tuberculosis after
all, Bob, her oldest, soon defined himself as a classic reprobate, heavy-
drinking, wildly unpredictable, sardonic to the bone. The only remedy
seemed to be to pack him off to a noted boys' school in Fochabers,
Scotland, Milne's Free School, after which he spent two years, 1857–
59, at the University of Aberdeen. When he returned to the United
States, it was found that he had converted to Roman Catholicism and

acquired an "oddly *civilised* perversity." But he was the same old "wanton, impossible" Bob.

Another tough case was John Vanderburgh James, or Johnny. His father, John Barber, only too well aware that he had "no gift for control or for edification" (as Henry Jr. delicately put it), had gone to Switzerland in 1851 to place his son in the kind of private school that was thought to be best for "cases of recognised wildness"—the Pension Sillig in Vevey. Johnny was then sixteen years old. His father returned to New York, quite pleased by the "judicious course" he had taken with his unmanageable boy. The combination of M. Sillig's "rich *bonhomie*" and "celebrated firmness" would be just the thing. But Johnny was, like his father, on a downward path, and a few years later he succumbed to what Henry Jr. would only speak of as "monstrous early trouble." What the trouble was is dimly visible in the leather-bound books kept by his father's trustee, who, on October 11, 1856, and again on April 15, 1857, paid $130 to Johnny's maternal grandfather, a homeopathic physician, for "board at the Asylum at Bloomingdale." In 1858, one day after his twenty-third birthday, Johnny died. No contemporary document reveals how his life ended, but twenty-four years later, dining in Washington, D.C., Henry Jr. was informed by President Chester A. Arthur no less that he had been present at Johnny's "suicidal death-bed." The novelist remembered this cousin as a tragic and "very charming boy," interested in music. How William remembered him may be surmised from the future psychologist's vigilance for signs of latent insanity in himself and other family members.

In Henry Sr.'s opinion the chief threat to the younger generation was not psychological but social. What the children needed was "a virtuous and well-ordered community, which shall diligently foster all that is noble and gentle and manly in them, and rebuke and correct whatever is opposite to these things." Instead of disciplining their offspring and thus instilling the power of self-rule, the better classes of New York City recklessly encouraged habits of indulgence and ostentatious luxury. "Premature exposure . . . to the contact of a vicious and rotten civilization" was ruining a whole generation of young men. The same was true for young women, who even in the best society were recklessly abandoned "to all the casualties of a promiscuous acquaintanceship."

Since 1849, when James worried about the "shocking bad-manners" his boys were picking up in New York, he had been talking about getting an Old World education for them. When John Barber left for Vevey with Johnny in tow, James eagerly awaited his brother's report on "schooling, and expenses of living." Tweedy, too, was asked to be on the lookout for news of "the Geneva schools." The information must have been encouraging, for, as Henry Jr. remembered in old age, "there was an hour when we invoked, to intensity," a European schooling. That was in the fall and winter of 1851–52, when James and Wilkinson were comparing notes on the cost of education in London and New York. Nothing was decided at the time, but the Swiss schools continued to beckon, and three years later James announced to Wilkinson that the family would leave for Europe "next year." Having heard this before, Aunt Kate advised the Wilkinsons not to take her brother-in-law at his word. But this time Aunt Kate was wrong.

Back in 1851, James's career as writer and lecturer was still in the ascendant, his democratic hopes had not yet been put to the test, and he believed that vice and crime were merely the expression of man's impatience "to actualize his ideal and essential infinitude." Four years later the lecturing had ended, the books James was writing were increasingly parochial, and vice and crime had turned out to be grave social evils that needed to be repressed by a stern collective will. The uncontrollability of Bob Temple and John Barber and Johnny could be read as vivid warnings of the effects of the New World's disorders. American society had begun to look sinister as well as disorganized. The fantasy of an imminent municipal clean-up was fading, and Mayor Fernando Wood was lapsing back into a dunghill cock. He had already reneged on the Sunday closings. His vice-squad raids had become bafflingly erratic. And each day's *Tribune* ratcheted up the bad feeling between North and South.

The Tweedys were not the only American Fourierists among James's acquaintance who had fled to Europe. Osborne and Fanny Macdaniel had gone to England for a time, and William Henry Channing had moved there for good. Francis and Sarah Shaw of Staten Island had spent several years on the Continent for their children's education. Mary's relatives, the Kings, were in Europe, as were Henry Sr.'s, the Masons. It was painfully clear that a true education was not to be had in New York. Even a father who talked revolution and classlessness and the rising glory of America and the benignant extermination of vice and crime might decide that at least his own children need not be sacrificed.

When James sailed from New York in 1837, his international banking had been handled by James McBride. Now that McBride was dead and James had grown away from his father's Scots-Irish connections, he arranged for a $10,000 letter of credit on London's Baring Brothers through his Boston friend Sam Ward. In 1843 James had unloaded his fine house on Washington Place before leaving for Europe. This time, intending to be away for some time, he leased the Fourteenth Street property to

William Brenton Greene, merchant (for five years, it seems). One thing
had not changed. As before, James wrote a last, loving farewell to Emerson, "the best and most memorable man to me here, whether the com-
putation begin from my heart or my head." Awarding his friend the
highest praise possible—"You are an inspired poet"—James ranked himself as "only an inveterate *doctrinaire*" and "unordained preacher of the
gospel."

Although the Jameses may have planned an eventual return to New
York, they never again made the city their home. The easy give-and-
take of Fourteenth Street, the ferry trips to Staten Island and Brooklyn,
the train trips up the Hudson to Rhinebeck and Albany, the memories
of the big house on North Pearl Street full of "charming creatures of the
growing girl sort"—all this receded into the past as the ship departed
New York Harbor on June 27 and steamed eastward. Henry Sr.'s children's lives were cut in two by this journey to the Old World, just as
his own childhood had once been severed. Now they, too, were detached
from their experience, forced to stand to one side of the lives they had
taken for granted. Of course, their break was a good deal less traumatic
than his had been. They didn't lose a leg, and whereas he had been kept
home for a period of years, they were given an unparalleled opportunity
to escape the confines of a provincial world. Still, it was a kind of death,
and not without pain. If things worked out, the children would be forced
to reinvent themselves, as their father had, and thus achieve a degree
of mastery over their native endowment. Yet the kind of isolation the
Jameses fell into in Europe was not good for all of them. Alice was not
benefited, and neither was her suddenly disconnected father. It is not
too much to say that in 1855 Henry Sr.'s intellectual growth came to
an end.

The Jameses' steamer, the *Atlantic*, one of the flagships of the Collins
Line, was almost three hundred feet long with a capacity for 200 passengers. Its public rooms were strewn with mirrors, carvings, and luxurious sofas, and the first-class cabins were built with communicating doors
for the convenience of large families. Henry Sr. ate at the captain's table
along with other notables, Professor James Renwick and Sir Allan
McNab, Premier of the Canadas. They formed a congenial group, with
the exception of one young married woman who struck James as belonging
"to 'the lower classes' in manners and deportment."

Captain West's course took the ship farther north than was customary,
supposedly to avoid icebergs (of which two or three were seen). "Cold
weather and stormy seas" oppressed the passengers "for nearly all the
voyage." As the Jameses plunged and tossed, it would have been hard

not to think about the *Arctic*, which had gone down the previous year. The *Arctic* was a sister ship of the *Atlantic*, and the *Atlantic*—which they were on—was the identical vessel that had been given up for lost in 1851, when the Jameses stepped out to see *Betsey Baker*.

Afterward, on solid ground, James praised the captain's skill in quieting the passengers' sense of "menace."

Chapter 22

■ ■ ■

EUROPE BY ZIGZAG: 1855–58

GENEVA

The entourage that disembarked at Liverpool included Aunt Kate and a French maid. This was the second time in eight months Mary's sister had landed here. On her previous arrival, in October 1854, she was accompanied by the elderly widower she had recently married, Captain Charles Marshall. They spent six months in Europe, and then, immediately following their return to New York in May 1855, she walked out on him. Her husband had been petty and cold, James explained to a friend, with "a spiritual isolation and iciness which left no green thing alive in his presence." From then on Mrs. Walsh, as she called herself, would throw in her fortune with her sister's itinerant household.

The maid, Annette Godefroi, originally from Metz, was also a recent addition. She was the children's *au pair* nanny, their *bonne Lorraine*, hired for the same double chore she had performed in the Wilkinson home from 1850 to 1854—serving the children "as much French with their bread & butter as possible." Henry Jr. remembered her as "fresh-coloured, broad-faced and fair-braided."

When the Jameses reached London, they added a courier to their party, Jean Nadali, his job being to handle travel arrangements from England to Switzerland. Then it was found that twelve-year-old Harry had come down with malaria—the same illness Daisy Miller would die of in Rome in his best-known story. It was thought he'd caught the "seed" on Staten Island the summer before. On his bad days he had to stay in bed in the Euston Hotel, whose "fusty" old four-poster and ancient heavy smell he never forgot; this was a lastingly English odor for him.

The boy's intermittent fever and chills did not prevent the family from pushing on to Paris, where they checked into the Hotel Westminster—"in no respect a capital house," Henry Sr. warned readers of the New York Tribune. His children, however, were entranced by the view of the rue de la Paix from their hotel balcony, and Harry was positively awed by his first visit to the Louvre. Of course, the Jameses had tons of art in their Fourteenth Street house—a bust of a scantily covered Bacchante, a view of Florence by Thomas Cole that covered half the parlor wall,* a large French treatment of rural Tuscany. Also, there had been trips to the galleries along Broadway, including an after-dinner excursion to the Stuyvesant Institute to view Washington Crossing the Delaware and gape at the commanding general's heroic nose. But young Henry's first view of the Louvre's early-nineteenth-century warhorses—Géricault's gigantic Raft of the Medusa, David's Oath of the Horatii, Prud'hon's Psyche Sleeping—left him with a fevered sense of a culture far more alluring and crushing than anything seen in New York. Then it was on to Lyons by train, and from there by carriage to Geneva, the sick boy resting on a cushioned plank that bridged two seats.

In Geneva the Jameses quickly settled into what was probably their most pleasant rural or suburban retreat since Frogmore Cottage in 1844. For $10 a week, they had a five- or six-room apartment in the Campagne (that is, Villa) Gerebsoff. This was a spacious and elegant mansion located a mile and a half from the center of the city and surrounded by twenty acres of private grounds. The owner, Count Gerebsoff, was a retired Russian cavalry officer; his wife was the former Marie Hofrichter. For Henry Jr., still malarial and often necessarily indoors, the thick-walled house was an intimation of age and solidity—of hushed "depth, depth upon depth." He remembered Madame Gerebsoff as a distant invalid reclining on a chaise longue in a private part of the garden. The boy's father, on the other hand, described her as "motherly and human," graciously attending to her guests' needs by day and entertaining them in the evening with "the most exquisite morceaux to be culled from the musical repertories of Italy and Germany."

James sent this florid description in the first of a series of travel letters to the Tribune, "An American in Europe." He was even more ebullient in describing the school he found for William, Wilkie, and Bob. The conventional choice would have been Dr. Haccius's large institution, but James was afraid the many American pupils there would keep his

---

* James acquired this painting from his brother Edward. Today View of Florence, from San Miniato is owned by the Cleveland Museum of Art.

boys from becoming fluent in French or German. The school he selected, recently established by a German pedagogue and political exile named Achilles Heinrich Roediger, had forty pupils from France and Germany and only five from the United States. At last the boys would have an opportunity to absorb the languages their father had not been able to master. Another reason James approved of Roediger's school was that it deemphasized the academic in favor of the social, the recreational, and even the rehabilitative. The playground was almost as large as New York's Washington Square, and there was gymnastic equipment and a bowling alley and an occasional swim in the nearby Rhône. The atmosphere was wholesome and homelike, like that at the Campagne. There was none of the "tyranny and oppression" of English schools, and the schoolboys were so polite they never gave one another so much as "a sly punch in the ribs." Indeed, Geneva as a whole was quite free of the rudeness and "ribaldry" that marred the open-air scene in New York and London.

In fact, Switzerland was the James father's Forest of Arden. One of the family's most adored books on Fourteenth Street had been Rodolphe Töpffer's *Voyages en Zigzags*, an account of a Swiss schoolmaster's summer excursions with his pupils. Now, bragging in the *Tribune* about the summer tours Roediger would conduct, James gave his readers the impression his own boys had already enjoyed their own zigzag through paradise: "They invade the fastnesses of the Jura; they ride on mules and donkeys; they pluck the wild strawberries; they drink at the wayside fountains; they eat the bread and honey of the mountaineers as they pause to avoid the noon-day sun." James was dreaming of the golden age, and as the days passed at the quiet Campagne Gerebsoff he and Mary were perpetually exclaiming over the wonderful "relation" between the master and his schoolboys. The institution was a standing demonstration of what could be achieved by a man of "enormous practical power," James told his mother, using a word he could not stop repeating. Roediger had the "power of ruling refractory boys." He had a "powerful personal magnetism," such that "you feel that you could confide in him very thoroughly." Two decades earlier James had implored Rev. William for the closest "drilling and disciplining," and in the intervening years he had searched for an authority, a deity, who would be wholly in charge and yet allow his creatures the illusion of self-direction. Roediger, whom Henry Jr. remembered as big and bearded, would be the ideal giant. He would know how to form the young without resorting to huge black straps. This is the man, Henry Sr. wrote Albany (offering the ultimate testimonial), to whom bad Bob Temple should be consigned.

The wise pedagogue had even solved the old problem of how to honor the Sabbath, and James devoted his second *Tribune* letter to the benign social festivities the scholars enjoyed on Sunday. Everything seemed perfect. Still, James admitted to his mother, he didn't look forward to a winter in Geneva and was thinking of spending a month in Paris by himself. By late August he was feeling so rusty and disconnected his newspaper letters had deteriorated into sermons. He took a perfunctory swipe at local events—a dull gathering of Swiss clergymen, the death of General George Napier—but the bulk of his third and fourth dispatches consisted of an energetic attack on the theorists of socialism. Fourier had "glibly" run on about social reorganization without understanding what it was that constituted society. Auguste Comte (glowingly reviewed in the *Tribune* in 1854) had gone astray by discarding the revealed truths of man's fall and ultimate redemption. The big Comtean mistake was to exalt the material, the natural, and vacate the spiritual. James allowed that the founder of the religion of humanity had a correct understanding of "the strictly progressive nature of science," but he felt sure—and the prediction has come true—that in the end Comte's reputation would be "very modest." In retrospect, this distrust of the hubris of socialist rationalism looks shrewd and prophetic. One notes a resemblance between James and Alexander Solzhenitsyn—whose sweeping judgments have also been entangled with an archaic religious dogmatism.

James's attack on socialism marked the end of his endeavors with New York's well-to-do radicals. As if prompted by his own detachment, he informed the *Tribune* that people do not "*naturally* tend to fellowship." "No man ever performed an act of love to his brother" unless compelled by "some superior obligation to that of his nature." These proclamations proved too much for Arthur Young, a rich English philanthropist who was trying to reorganize the recently dissolved North American Phalanx in New Jersey and who now drafted an angry rebuke for publication in the *Tribune*. "I have been told," he began, "that the initials H.J. signify one, who ought to know something of Fourier, and ought to be capable of gathering the true sense of Comte." The rest of the letter was a blistering exposé of H.J.'s "profound ignorance" of "Sociology." Who H.J. was could have been no mystery to Young. James had owned over one hundred shares of the commune's capital stock, worth $10 each.

James still paid lip service to equality and even offered a perfunctory defense of America's distressing rowdyism, which signified "the *social* recognition of the masses." Yet it was precisely to escape the rough democratic masses that he had brought his boys to Geneva and laid out large sums of money on a special educational program. How to reconcile theory and practice? At the end of his fourth letter to the *Tribune* he introduced a cloudy biblical allegory that makes a case for inherited privilege and caste distinction. The passage involves a contrast similar to the one James had worked out nine years earlier between Ishmael and Isaac. This time the dyad consists of Esau, "son of the bondmaid," and Jacob, "son of the freewoman." The descendants of Esau are the earthy elder race, the precursors. They have never been allowed to claim a share in the inheritance of the descendants of Jacob. Instead, they have been required from time immemorial—and rightly so—"to serve the younger race and promote its subtler necessities." Only after the children of Jacob have "attained [their] desires" will the elder and inferior race enjoy "an earthly dominion of endless peace and order."

The following spring, when James incorporated this sibylline prophecy in an expanded version of *The Church of Christ Not an Ecclesiasticism*, he disconnected it from his critique of socialism. Now Esau stood for the "external natural man in whom self-love rules" and Jacob for the "internal or spiritual man in whom brotherly love rules." But in its original context the passage bore a different message. It implied that the sons of Jacob must be allowed their privileges, and that the crudely materialistic socialists, descendants of the race of Esau, must not forget their place. The Jameses' idyllic sojourn in Geneva was justified by their subtle spiritual necessities. The children of Esau would have to wait their turn.

In addition, James was saying something about his position in his own family: his mother, Catharine, was William of Albany's true wife, while the mother of his older half brother Rev. William was only a handmaid after all.

OCTOBER IN PARIS

At some point Annette Godefroi left and was replaced by a young Swiss woman, Amélie Cusin, who acted as governess for Henry Jr. and Alice. By September 8, when James wrote his fourth *Tribune* letter, the family had left the paradisal Campagne Gerebsoff and moved into the Hôtel de l'Écu, on the Place du Rhône. Installed in the rooms recently vacated by the Henry Stones of New York, the Jameses were in the center of town now and within reach of other foreigners in residence. But as James admitted to his mother, Geneva had become "very dull for one who has no active pursuits."

The next zigzag loomed. When the Jameses applied to the Genevan authorities for a *permis de séjour* in September, it was for no more than a month's duration. A couple of weeks after moving into the Hôtel de l'Ecu, James decided to ask Roediger for a refund (annual fees being $350 per pupil). The school was "greatly overrated" after all—in William's opinion "all humbug." Also, it was too hard on Wilkie and Bob, who hadn't been to boarding school before. Mary was sure her youngest boys needed a mother's care, and she was probably right about Bob, barely nine years old, who had been "bumped and thumped" in the gym. Henceforth, the new governess would have to take on Bob and Wilkie as well as Harry and Alice, with certain subjects taught by the father. But home instruction would not suffice for William. A new school had to be found for him, possibly in Paris, possibly in England's West Country, which had so impressed James in 1837. When he broached these alternatives to Wilkinson, however, he was frankly advised to forget his "fantasies about Devonshire." Instead of looking for some instructional Arcadia, he should put his family up in a good hotel in Paris and then come to London for a week to hash out the great school question. In Wilkinson's opinion, London was the only place for solid education. But James wasn't convinced.

In October, having persuaded the new governess to share their peregrinations, the Jameses left Geneva. This time there was no courier, and travel arrangements were less assured. The party of nine covered the first leg of their trip in a mail coach rather than a private carriage, and when they reached Paris the city was so packed with tourists (drawn there by the Universal Exposition) that suitable accommodations were not to be had. Uncertain where to turn, the Jameses pulled up in front of the hotel where Howard James was staying.

Howard, still single, was Henry Sr.'s youngest brother and an object of Henry Jr.'s admiration. In general, the future novelist tried to overlook or palliate his father's improvidence, but he couldn't help wondering whether this uncle "really liked us, and . . . whether I should have liked us had I been in his place." There was an anxious wait, and then Howard appeared and cheerfully helped his brother locate vacant rooms for his large family. Soon after, visiting the art show at the Palais de l'Industrie, the two Henrys, father and son, made a long, restorative stop in front of John Everett Millais's *The Order of Release* (now at the Tate). This painting, rich in domestic sentiment, stages the moment of reunion between a wounded Highlander rebel of 1745 and his sturdy wife. Perhaps Henry Sr. expounded on the picture's artistry and meaning, for his twelve-year-old son never forgot the treatment of the "baby's bare legs, pendent from its mother's arms." There was a lesson here about family unity under trying circumstances.

James wanted to spend the winter in Paris, but when he and Mary tried to find a suitable apartment, the only one that seemed large enough went for the unheard-of rent of $2,200 a year. This was $800 more than the Jameses were getting for their house in New York, so it was on to London, as Wilkinson had advised.

WINTER AND SPRING IN LONDON

James quickly found a small, expensive house on Berkeley Square that was close to the family's hotel (and also to the Piccadilly addresses where he had spent the unsettled winter of 1843–44). He rented the house for a month and then set about finding a proper day school for "the boys." With his usual precipitation, he at once announced he would send them either to the London University Grammar School or Rev. Markby's school in St. John's Wood, both of which were "first rate." Then, just as quickly, both institutions were ruled out. From now on he would have "absolutely none of" the London private schools that Wilkinson thought so highly of. Their social exclusiveness disgusted him, and when a girls' school in St. John's Wood turned away a draper's otherwise qualified daughter, he was filled with outrage. Back in Albany, Rev. William tried to assist by tossing out a suggestion relating in some way to Schenectady. Perhaps the idea was that William attend Union College. If so, Henry Sr.'s transatlantic "Ugh!"—a word that shows up nowhere else in his correspondence—trenchantly summed up his feelings about his alma mater.

Reverting to the plan he had announced in Geneva—"home tuition"—James placed a want ad in *The Times*:

> To teachers.—The advertiser wishes to ENGAGE a TUTOR, by the month, for three or four hours a day, who is competent to give his boys instruction in Latin, and the ordinary branches of an English education. None but well qualified persons need apply. Address H.J., 3, Berkeley-square, between 5 and 7 in the evening.

At the appointed hour a mob of applicants materialized. Henry Jr. never forgot how "they hung about the door, cumbered the hall, choked the staircase and sat grimly individual in odd corners." The lucky candidate was a Scotsman, Robert Thomson, who would be responsible for William, Henry Jr., and Wilkie. Unlike the Scottish ministers preferred by the previous generation of Jameses in New York, Thomson didn't whack. His harshest command was "Come now, be getting on!" Kind, modest, formal, and awkward, he always wore a dress coat and often tripped over his feet. There were occasional field trips to places like the Tower, the tutor rubbing in his lessons on English history from what the novelist remembered as "a fine old conservative and monarchical point of view."

On December 1, the Jameses moved into a furnished house at 10 Marlborough Place in St. John's Wood, one of London's most pleasant suburbs. Their new home had plenty of rooms and a large yard and was situated on a quiet residential street a short walk from the Wilkinsons, who had lived for the last four years on busy Finchley Road. Although the tutor didn't reside with the Jameses, he moved when they did, taking a room above a nearby baker's shop. The Jameses had gained another dependent. There was something typically erratic in hiring a Scottish tutor after coming abroad for "the languages," but the important thing was that the boys were now on track for becoming "well educated and polished." Better yet, as James informed his mother, they were being "sweet and good, all of them"—the added phrase probably being a veiled reference to William.

What William and Henry Jr. mainly remembered about their half year in St. John's Wood was feeling isolated, inactive, and bored. Their chief pastime was to stroll up and down Baker Street or walk to a certain purveyor of art supplies. Outfitted with top hat and gloves on these excursions, they had to brave the cold "head-to-foot" stares of insular Britons and the catcalls and other aggressions of rude boys—"rude with a kind of mediaeval rudeness," wrote Harry. Withdrawn as he was, even Harry had known something about boyish street life back in New York. Now he and William were learning that coming of age as gentlemen necessarily involved a rupture with the ancient and honorable order of boys.

Accustomed as he was to being teased, Harry didn't mind the social distance as much as his older brother did. One of William's favorite writers was Captain Mayne Reid, whose adventure novels had a wide readership in the 1850s. Reid glorified the outdoor life of hunters and trappers and Indians and ridiculed those who got their nature lore sec- ondhand, the "closet-naturalists." One of the lessons William picked up from Reid was that "a closet-naturalist must be the vilest type of wretch under the sun." Now, miserably, he himself was trapped in an artificial and unedifying life. For him, London was "a great huge unwieldy awkward colorless metropolis with a little brown river crawling through it." Years later, he told his brother that the scattered education they had gotten in London and Paris had been "poor and arid and lamentable."

The novelist didn't see it that way. More of a spectator than his active

older brother, he found London's streets a confirmation of what he had
read in Dickens and Thackeray and seen in Cruikshank (Dickens's illustrator). The extremes of class, the shocking low-life "horrors," the
"stale servility" of menials, the liveried footmen clinging to aristocratic
coaches, the hints of a protected private sphere: all this had a profound
appeal to him. He was learning how to see a constituted social order,
and what he saw fed back into his own developing social and aesthetic
orientation. For him, London meant a deeper acceptance of his own
spectatorial relation to the world, a further saturation in form, artifice,
caste distinction, and the powers of language. He was taking his first
steps toward his mature narrative art, which would articulate the observer's, the traveler's, peculiar social powerlessness. William was
the opposite sort of traveler and thinker, restlessly seeking new intellectual worlds to conquer. He couldn't stand the exile's sense of remoteness.

While William and Harry could always count on one another's companionship away from home, Alice seems to have been utterly without
playmates. The three memories the precocious seven-year-old retained
from her winter in London were of going to a bonnet maker with Mademoiselle Cusin and seeing *Henry VIII* and *Still Waters Run Deep* in
company with her family. "Shall I ever forget Wolsey going to execution,
or [a tag line from *Still Waters*], 'My sister is a most remarkable woman!' "
Harry also remembered these plays, which were probably talked over at
home. But what stuck in Alice's mind was how her enjoyment of *Henry
VIII* had been spoiled by Aunt Kate's "anguish" at not being able to go.
Similarly, what the girl remembered about the bonnet was the governess's
dissatisfaction with it. It was the regrets felt by her grown-up female
guardians that the isolated girl noticed and recorded. Her own regrets
faded away, so that when she herself was grown up she could get no
closer to them than by staring at "a bit of brown wall that always brings
up St. John's Wood."

Henry Sr. had many more social resources in London than did his
wife and children. One of his first acts was to arrange for a letter of
introduction from Martin Van Buren to James Buchanan, at that time
the American minister to England. He saw his old friend Fanny Macdaniel, and he must have seen Thackeray, as Bob remembered being
carried on his shoulders. As for new acquaintances, James informed his
mother he had met some "very nice" people, some of them "literary."
He wrote Emerson, who may have provided the usual introductions, that
he planned to look up Arthur Hugh Clough, and that after meeting

Arthur Helps he wouldn't approach him again except to ask his advice for "a hatter or bootmaker."

Then there was Thomas Carlyle, whom James inimitably summed up to Emerson as "the same old sausage, fizzing and sputtering in his own grease." Carlyle spoke only for "picturesque effect" nowadays and had grown crankier than ever. When James's old friend from Buffalo, James McKaye (formerly McKay), an early and avid Transcendentalist, showed up in London, he wanted to meet the great Chelsea seer. McKaye had done well for himself in the last fifteen years, having organized the parent companies of American Express and Western Union, and he wanted to tell Carlyle how much his books had helped him. James prudently cleared the path by getting the Scotsman to promise to treat McKaye kindly and not "altogether pulverize" him. The next day the two Americans walked into the parlor at Cheyne Walk. Carlyle was standing on a chair adjusting a shutter. Without interrupting what he was doing or even turning around, he called out an unceremonious greeting: "Is that you, J[ames], and have you brought your friend McK[aye] with you?" McKaye made his little speech about the "aid and comfort" he had drawn from Carlyle's early books, whereupon the writer ungraciously declared he didn't believe a word of it. No man had ever helped another, and the only sincere praise he himself had ever received was from a ship captain who wrote to say he had named a vessel the *Thomas Carlyle*. McKaye felt mocked, and when James wrote to Emerson about the encounter, he complained about Carlyle's lack of "conventional culture." The man should have been a "Cameronian preacher" and stayed far away from the "circle of London's amenities."

In the eleven years since James and Wilkinson had last seen each other, their friendship had become strained and insincere. In 1849 Wilkinson called him "the most genial and unctuous of bullies," a phrase neither man dared unpack. The next year, when James showed little interest in the Englishman's magnum opus, *The Human Body and Its Connexion with Man*, the author was aggrieved and indignant: "You are a little painful about my book & its forthcoming dedication. It is *you*, Sirrah, who have kept me working in Literature for these five years, & I have done nothing for you, if not this book. The book craves to have its parentage acknowledged." James took his cue and coughed up some extravagant praise: "If you were well recognized, recognized at your worth as a writer, you would so dwarf all our existing celebrities as to have the whole field of literature to yourself." All the same, he had to confess he couldn't see the point of Wilkinson's ornate "correspondential lore." He didn't finish the book,* and neither did Emerson, who granted the writer's "prodigious genius" but admitted that no one in England seemed to believe in him. The one thing Wilkinson's book proved was that he wasn't going to be an author after all, in spite of all the genius and hard work and American financial support. There was resentment on both sides, and the following year, when Osborne Macdaniel told Wilkinson of a nasty crack James had made about him, an explanation was demanded. James was sugary, evasive, and unapologetic: "What could the man have meant by such a tale, and of my being offended moreover of all men with you, you darling old soul!" Two years later it was James's turn to be insulted by something Wilkinson had reportedly said about him. Wilkinson was abject, not only spanking himself for his "impertinence," his "so very stupid & inapposite a smartness," but humbly renouncing any pretension to "equality" with his correspondent. That was in the fall of 1854. When the two men met in London several months later, the Englishman was so tense he was in knots—like "a dumb man," he afterward wrote. He was intimidated by his American friend's wealth and social eminence and "frightened" by his own inability to "entertain you as you dearly deserved." Worse, "the knowing you so much better in heart & mind than in body, made me feel that I had a stone wall to get through, before I could get at you."

Although James and Wilkinson were virtual neighbors in St. John's Wood and apparently saw each other often and casually, the stone wall did not come down. Reporting on his friend to Emerson, James was almost entirely critical. Wilkinson's goodness and wisdom were not up to the "enormous power" of his imagination. He was too caught up in the rage for spirit communication. He was too intolerant of philosophy. His sarcasm was "awful." "This is it," James summarized, "he is now finding his youth." James saw himself as having entered a more mature and mellow phase.

One of Wilkinson's worst failures was his inability to rule Emma, his wife, "a dear little goose of a thing." A wise husband would have stopped her from becoming so "egotistical," but as things were, her "enormous domestic inflation" made visitors feel "crowded . . . into the most inconsiderable of corners." (Years later Henry Jr. reported that Emma spoke in "a stream of mingled sentimental & practical utterances which are redeemed from the common-place only by . . . [her] immense fund of energy & shrewdness.") Henry Sr. was accustomed to being heard, and

---

* For his part Wilkinson did not do much better. The copy of *Lectures and Miscellanies* that James presented "with the Authors most affectionate regards," and that is now owned by the Swedenborg Society in London, is otherwise unmarked.

he resented being overpowered by a friend's garrulous wife. In his own household, where the husband was clearly in charge of the talking, there was none of this troubling domestic competition. When Mary pounced on Emma's "egotism," she was echoing Henry Sr.'s view that a good wife holds her tongue.

The following winter James penned twenty formal letters to Wilkinson and then gathered them into a book, *Christianity the Logic of Creation*. Each letter forms a segment of a continuous disquisition in which every point is explained with painstaking clarity and considerable repetition. The writer is professedly eager to meet his correspondent's doubts: "But here you may ask, 'What is the necessity of any revelation at all?' " "I have no doubt that I shall be able to satisfy your reasonable demands in some sort, if I am only sustained by your cheerful attention and goodwill." But this conspicuous rhetorical courtesy turns out to be misleading. It gradually becomes clear that the writer takes no interest in what his correspondent thinks or feels. No messages ever get back to him that alter the current of his exposition. All the words are on his side, all the attention and goodwill on the other. Of course, the book's formal conventions do not coincide with the give and take of James and Wilkinson's "real" correspondence. But the book helps explain why this friendship had gone stale.

A London acquaintance James probably met through Wilkinson was Dr. William B. Carpenter, an all-around naturalist and author of an influential essay, "The Microscope and Its Revelations." Carpenter assisted James in selecting a microscope as a Christmas gift for William. Another friend was William White, a publisher of Swedenborgian and spiritualist books and journals. Years later Henry Jr. described White as a "shrewd little North British vulgarian," a view that has much to recommend it if one ignores the regional slur. On one occasion the enterprising publisher tried to take over the London-based Swedenborg Society by bringing in 125 new members at a stroke—a putsch the society foiled by getting an injunction from the Court of Chancery. White seems to have been more successful in dealing with Wilkinson's rich American friend, for in the spring of 1856 he brought out a considerably enlarged edition of James's tract *The Church of Christ Not an Ecclesiasticism*. Although James often talked of second editions, this was to be his only one during his lifetime. Oddly enough, a third edition of the tract was also projected, the idea being to reprint the *unrevised* text and supplement it with a pair of James's lectures and an introduction by Wilkinson. James's part of this little book was set up in type and the sheets run off, but then, for some unexplained reason, publication was held up for seven years. When the imprint finally came out in 1861, it was introduced by an unknown editor. Wilkinson had backed out. James continued to trust White, however, allowing him in 1857 to bring out the English edition of *Christianity the Logic of Creation.*

The letters James dispatched to the *Tribune* while living in London record his varying responses to the news, books, and topics of the day. He belittled Kossuth's and Mazzini's struggles for national unity in Hungary and Italy, on the grounds that nationalism, like sectarianism, was yielding to the sentiment of universal humanity. For his Christmas letter[*] he composed a weird sermon on redemption, which he interpreted as a divine cure for the world's constipation. What Christ had done was to salvage and recycle the "excrementitious product of human history" and thus counteract the devil's tendency to "suck in the universe, and lie . . . gorged, swollen and immovable." In his letter on George Henry Lewes's life of Goethe, James attacked the German writer as "little better than a sensualist" and accused his biographer of wishing "to ventilate . . . some new theory of marriage"—to suggest that "adultery is the privilege of genius." Given that Lewes was known to be living with George Eliot, this was recklessly insinuating.[†] In January James was full of enthusiasm for a theory propounded by Henry C. Carey, the leading American political economist, to the effect that over the long run the value of labor tends to rise and the value of capital tends to fall. For James, this was proof positive that society has an evolutionary tendency to "equalize the extremes" and thus usher in universal brotherhood.

These letters give an impression of a mind eager to assimilate whatever London had to offer and always ready to jump the gap between the mundane and the eternal. James crossed established boundaries, he made connections no one else would ever think of, his diction constantly transgressed the line between the correct and the vulgar. At the same time, he was parochial, obsessed, hermetic, invariably seeking to confirm and disseminate his special doctrines. His energetic thought and expression helped form the minds of his children, detaching them from the usual pieties and pushing them to make their own high-level syntheses. After hearing George Dawson, James informed the *Tribune* that "the bother" with this popular and liberal lecturer was that, "being a second-

---

[*] One sentence of the essay glances at the children's holiday play, in which the father seems not to have participated: "From the bobbery which the children have been making for several hours past up stairs, I conclude that St. Nicholas, the merry old elf, crossed the water to us last night, and that we are in for at least five stockings full of overflowing jollification."

[†] Over two decades later, when someone pushed some volumes of Henry Jr.'s fiction on Lewes, he returned the loan, saying, "Ah those books—take them away, please, away, away!" Did he associate the novelist with the author of the *New York Tribune* review?

rate or third-rate man, he insists upon giving himself the airs . . . of a first-rate one." If the children, the boys, were going to be first-rate men, they had to learn to live with paradox, to convert the literal into the symbolic, to turn themselves inside out. In the relative isolation of exile, these lessons were pressed home day and night. Father's fizzing mind pervaded 10 Marlborough Place as it had never pervaded 58 West Fourteenth Street, where the boys had lives of their own. But was Father a first-rate or a third-rate man? Was he some sort of Christ, always redeeming and recirculating the world's refuse, or was he the devil, so puffed and swollen with himself that he was unable to move?

Just as James's children had to develop their own mechanisms for holding this man at a distance, so he, too, as if to escape himself, often gave way to fatigue, disillusionment, open self-contradiction. Whenever he let his grand manias drop, he was likely to turn slack, scattered, unfocused. By the time he was ready to leave London, he'd become "sick of pen and ink & paper" once again. Particularly troublesome was the problem of summing up the English. He had friends among them and greatly admired the solid qualities of "brother Bull" and "sister C[ow]." But then again Carlyle and Wilkinson and many others were trapped in a sterile sort of contempt for the country's institutions and government. British society was so rigid and "fossilized" that James vowed he "would not move a finger to save the established Government or the established Church from popular overthrow"; he wanted to cry when he thought of all the goodness in the poorer, more crowded sections of London. But then again he shrank from lower-class brutality, which would make an English revolution "unspeakably indecorous." Finally, reading and then reacting against Emerson's *English Traits*, James decided that the British were "not worth studying." They were "intensely vulgar." They were "abject slaves of routine." They loved whoever wears "their own livery," but they couldn't "even *see* any one" else.

Certainly, as James recalled a few years later, they often couldn't or wouldn't see him:

I lived . . . nearly a year in St. John's Wood in London, and was daily in the habit of riding down to the city in the omnibus along with my immediate neighbors, men of business and professional men . . . After eight months' assiduous bosom solicitation of their hardened stolid visages, I never was favored with the slightest overture to human intercourse from one of them. I never once caught the eye of one of them. If ever I came nigh doing so, an instant film would surge up.

Much later, when William recollected the "monotony" of St. John's Wood, he saw his parents as stuck at home and without society.

PARIS

On June 3, leaving Robert Thomson in London and also Amélie Cusin (who had found a new and richer employer), the Jameses departed for Paris, where they intended to spend the next two years. James and Aunt Kate had gone there ahead of time to scout up a suitable apartment, but they had to settle for a small, expensive house, which they took for a couple of months.

The Jameses' new address was 44, Avenue des Champs-Élysées, on the north side. Their landlord was Martial Sorrel of Attakapas, Louisiana—the largest planter in St. Mary Parish, with 364 slaves and 3,050 horses, mules, oxen, and cattle (and whom the novelist pitied fifty years later as a "poor unadmonished gentleman of the eve of the Revolution"). With its alarmingly steep staircase, "glassy" floor, and abundant mirrors, clocks, vases, and stiff brocaded chairs, Sorrel's charming Paris pied-à-terre struck young Henry as an "odd relic." William was impressed by the "naked gilt babies all over the ceiling." Outside, there was a pump in a private cobbled courtyard, which formed a terrace overlooking the broad avenue.

In the two decades before 1856 the nearby triangle formed by the Rond Point, the Tuileries, and the Seine had been transformed into a well-managed Gallic paradise unlike anything in London or New York. This had been the site of the previous year's exposition, and there were wide sidewalks, gaily decorated pavilions, neoclassical cafés-concerts, and throngs of strollers enjoying Europe's most up-to-date suburban playground for elegant leisure and amusement. The Jameses' section of the Champs-Élysées, two blocks to the west, was more scattered and irregular, with occasional woodyards or brasseries or coupé-rental agencies. Frontage alignments were not yet uniform, but the area was undergoing rapid redevelopment and regularization. Across the avenue from number 44 stood the Jardin d'Hiver, a glassed-in tropical space that had light afternoon and evening concerts, with M. Sax at his newly invented saxophone. Close by was the elegant town house of Émile de Girardin, a big-time newspaperman and political insider. A row of cast-iron streetlamps—a recent innovation—stretched all the way to the Arc de Triomphe. Omnibuses were not allowed here, carriages and horsemen and strollers had the avenue to themselves, and the afternoon promenade became extremely popular. The Emperor, Louis-Napoleon, whose coup d'état five years earlier had by now been ruthlessly consolidated, liked to take a leisurely ride on the Champs-Élysées with the Empress and the infant Prince Imperial. Indeed, this street was one of the locations in which a new conception of state power—orderly, non-democratic, spectacularly modern—tried to legitimate itself through a typically grandiose display of power and glory. The scene made a deep impression on the James children as they watched from behind Sorrel's iron railing. Henry Jr. kept a particular lookout for the imperial carriage. Because of an attempted assassination in 1855, it was attended by a crack cavalry guard who rode with pistols out and cocked.

If these were the modern Elysian fields, the pleasure they gave the Jameses must have been very mixed. A letter bomb had arrived at number 44 soon after they moved in, with a deadly piece of news. On May 22, at Chicago's elegant Tremont House Hotel, corner of Lake and Dearborn, John Barber James had killed himself. Why Chicago? The best guess is that he was desperate to raise cash for his gambling debts and that he had traveled to this city to try to unload the Illinois lands inherited from his father. He evidently disposed of some of them, but there must have been a hitch, since the first payments didn't reach his estate attorney until over a year after his death. Not to mention John's enormous gambling debts, he left behind a hotel bill of $193.92.

As usual, the survivors had abundant cause for guilt. It was probably John Barber whom James had pelted with snowballs in boyhood, an act for which he had once shed scalding tears of contrition. A few months before the suicide, James reproached John for breaking "his promise" to furnish some information about an audit of the lawyer in charge of the family's Syracuse properties. There was also the awkward fact that while John had been desperately short of money, James's own fortune was still intact.

Earlier that year, while the Jameses were still living in St. John's Wood, a prominent Irishman had killed himself under conditions that captured public attention. John Sadleir had plundered a bank of which he was a director, and when the institution's insolvency was disclosed he apparently poisoned himself on Hampstead Heath. Other frauds quickly came to light, *The Times* pronounced the swindler a "national calamity," and Dickens made him the model for *Little Dorrit*'s Mr. Merdle. In a letter to the *Tribune*, James took an astonishingly sympathetic view of Sadleir's life and death, blaming his various crimes on "our corrupt social methods" and offering a sentimental picture of his last hours as he wrote his "frenzied letters, and wandered out all alone under the silent heavens to die." What particularly struck James was that his own home was "nearly in a line" between Sadleir's house and the "bleak heath" where he took his life. Thinking about this, James couldn't "but fancy him going past my door steps on that dismal errand." Once again, James was projecting himself on a criminal about to be unmasked.

Ordinarily, it took two or three weeks for information to cross the ocean. The bad news probably reached James as he was settling into 44, Champs-Élysées. No extant letter expresses his immediate response to the suicide. No letter by anyone else in the extended James family so much as mentions it. * Not until the early twentieth century did a member of the family commit to paper the information that John Barber James had "killed himself." Henry Jr.'s one reference in his memoirs is so heavily veiled as to be impenetrable: "J.J. the elder, most loved, most beautiful, most sacrificed of the Albany uncles." Through the hushed, funereal tone of this, we catch a faint echo of the boy's intense, adolescent brooding. John had been "the handsome man of the family," the most charming and attractive of the Albany uncles. He was the one with the social gifts that impressed his quiet nephew. Why did *he* kill himself? What did his suicide say about America's crude and disorderly civilization? Was there no place in America for the leisured gentleman? Troubling questions for the novelist in embryo, as he stood at Sorrel's iron grille and looked at the fashionable promenaders on the Champs-Élysées and waited for the Emperor's carriage.

A couple of months later Henry Sr. got a letter of condolence from the Tweedys that revived his grief and inspired an impassioned reply. (One reason this letter wasn't burned is that its recipient was outside the family.)

> I don't think I had ever such a shock as the news of his death. I had been used too to say he will soon die unless he stops; but I always supposed that he *would* stop. And when at last I heard that he had actually been hurried away into that distant and dishonoured grave, when I thought of his youth and his beauty and his wit and his generosity and his genial feeling for all that was noble or manly under the sun, I felt as if my heart must break within me, or that madness would be a relief. He was inexpressibly dear to me.

In James's opinion, John's drinking and gambling were merely symptoms. His real trouble was a liaison with a married woman. Having once probed

---

* Edward's death on December 20 of this same year, at the age of thirty-eight, remains a complete mystery. Not one surviving family letter of the time throws any light on it.

his brother about this affair when he was drunk or hung over ("prostrated by debauch"), James was convinced that what bothered John most of all was the conflict between his love for the woman and his affectionate esteem for her husband: "John had an enormous *social* instinct . . . Though he loved Mrs. Little . . . he could not bear that any other human being should be disparaged by it . . . And this it was literally that killed him."

James sealed the envelope. Then he broke it open, having more to say about this vexing question of extramarital love. In an affair like John's, he added, everything depends on "the nature of the affection between the parties." Love is divine and always seeks to marry. But if John truly loved, why did he feel shamed and degraded? Why didn't he blame "the corrupt administration of marriage in society"? Did his feeling for Mrs. Little merely reflect the present-day "compression to which the natural passions are subject"? James was struggling to regularize the muddled complexities of the tragic episode, and by the time he resealed the envelope he had managed to reconfirm his teachings and forget some of the facts—his brother's idleness, irresponsibility, and fecklessness with money. He had also exorcised the specter of his own guilt.

It is hard to believe that the writer of this letter could have done an adequate job of telling his children why their uncle had done away with himself. The theory that John was torn between an erotic and a "social" motive would not have been an easy one to set forth. The children, Henry Jr. in particular, were probably left mystified and disturbed. They knew Uncle John gambled and imbibed, but the rest was mostly silence.

Curiously, John happened to kill himself the same day an enraged congressman from South Carolina walked onto the Senate floor and gave Senator Charles Sumner of Massachusetts a severe caning on the head. News of the outrage reached Paris on a pleasant June morning, and the Jameses discussed it with some of their American friends on the terrace of 44, Champs-Élysées, far from Sorrel's gangs of slaves in Attakapas. Everyone, including "a passionate lady in tears," was indignant. In Henry Sr.'s opinion, Sumner's assailant was a "cowardly ruffian." It was this attack and not the cannonade at Fort Sumter, Henry Jr. later wrote, that constituted the *real* opening provocation of the Civil War. One of the senator's head wounds became infected, and the following spring he went to Paris to recuperate. His journal shows that on April 16, 1857, he had dinner "with Mr. Henry James, who is here with his family." Young Henry Jr. was present, watching (just as he'd been doing on the terrace). The boy saw Sumner as the perfect type of "the statesman and the patriot." He looked closely at the great head, but the wounds were "disappointingly healed."

This dinner took place not on the Champs-Élysées but at 19, rue d'Angoulême (today rue la Boëtie), in the large second-floor apartment the Jameses had taken in August 1856. The apartment was not unfamiliar: Henry and Mary had seen it the previous October, on their rebound from Geneva to London. At the time they felt they couldn't afford it. Now they could, perhaps because it seemed cheap in comparison with the Louisianan's house. There were six bedrooms, and the furnishings included a piano. "It's a queer way of living, this," wrote William to a friend on Fourteenth Street, "all huddled up together on one floor." Mary, who spoke little French, was anxious about the dishonest cook, who insisted on doing the marketing and thus doubling her wages. (In New York, Bob remembered, Mary had done much of the daily market shopping herself, "with a basket on her arm.") The other servants were careless, dirty, and insolent, and their manners were much too demo-cratic, with "the spirit of 'Liberty, Fraternity, & Equality' show[ing] itself in most unhandsome forms." France was a "degenerate land" as far as Mary was concerned.

The people the Jameses saw in Paris consisted mainly of Americans and an occasional visitor from Great Britain. Thackeray showed up in September and again the following spring and, just as in New York, dropped an embarrassing and never-to-be-forgotten remark on the chil-dren's attire. "Crinoline?"—turning to eight-year-old Alice with mock horror—"So young and so depraved!" James's cousin Lydia Mason was in Paris with her husband and daughters, and the two families saw a great deal of one another. Lydia was rich, relaxed, and quite unspoiled: in Mary's eyes, "the same imperturbable placid creature"; in Harry's, "the gentlest of mammas." Her oldest daughter, a great belle, had been pre-sented to the Empress. Caroline (Sturgis) Tappan, an old friend of Emer-son and Margaret Fuller, was living in Paris with her husband and daughters. She had not shared Fuller's commitment to "such outward things" as women's rights. "A picturesque, gipsy-like person," Tappan shared a good many ideas, interests, and social references with James, and by the time he eventually left Paris there was even more history in common. "How sweet & pleasant & long to be remembered you were in all those Paris days," he later wrote. Another woman he often saw was Elizabeth (De Windt) Cranch, a granddaughter of John Adams. She and her husband, Christopher Pearse Cranch (who had started out in the pulpit and was now behind an easel), resided in Paris for most of the 1850s. The painter remembered James and "his clever and attractive family," but surviving letters show that the real friendship was between Mrs. Cranch and James. A new pattern was emerging: his closest friendships were not with men interested in socialism but with women interested in his theology.

Some of his most intense moments were with Anna Ward, who went to Europe for the summer of 1856 to visit her son at a Swiss school, and also to recover from what she told others was "neuralgia" or "the headache." While in Paris, she seems to have stayed with the Jameses. When she was about to sail back to Boston in early October, James sent "darling Anna" a saccharine goodbye. Home had become "sweeter" because of her visit. Both his "good wify" and Aunt Kate remembered her with the greatest warmth (a message he insisted on). Twice he made the point that he was not expressing his "private feelings": "I leave unsaid only what many letters would not be adequate to say, and what I must trust to more liberal skies to bring forth." The part of the letter where he came the closest to speaking his mind defies exact interpretation: "Though I feel only joy and exultation in your behalf, I at the same time feel a certain softening towards myself which makes it good to be reminded of their [his wife's and sister-in-law's] sympathy." A concluding apostrophe addresses her as "my chaste and noble Anna." Soon after this, writing to her husband, Sam (who had stayed behind in Boston), James referred to Anna as Sam's "angel-wife."

Upstairs from the Jameses' apartment on rue d'Angoulême lived another woman friend with her second husband, a British "half-pay officer." Henry Sr. often "mounted to their apartment" and passed the evening with them, socializing with their visitors or trying to calm the woman's religious anxieties. Years later he recalled one such evening when his story (culled from Swedenborg) of an executed criminal's posthumous experience caused the woman's husband to put down the book he was generally reading when James was present. The evidence is not conclusive, but it appears the woman was the former Mary (Osborne) Macdaniel. Originally of English birth, she had been an early member of the Swedenborgian Society in Washington, D.C., until her husband's death. Her unmarried daughter, Fanny, four years younger than James and one of his best friends, lived with her in Paris. It was Fanny who had approved of James's "lucubrations" on phalansteric love in the *Harbinger*. The tone he took with her (once calling her "my dear Fanny-panny") suggests she was the one he liked to talk to when he made his way upstairs. In 1858, on the eve of returning to America, he wrote that he "didn't know how much I loved you, till I came to leave you behind in Paris." He would always preserve her "gentle and womanly memory as one cherishes the image of a sister," thus putting on record the gallantly sublimated affection he enjoyed in his friendships with women. James was faithful to Mary, but he loved courting his sisters of the spirit, his angel-wives. Once he tried to protect a young lady in Paris who seemed to him to be "in danger" by counseling her as if he were "her father, or rather her lover," thus negotiating (in words) that mystifyingly easy nineteenth-century glide from the paternal to the erotic.

Fanny's sister, Eunice, was the wife of Charles Dana, who helped run the strongly antislavery *New York Tribune* (all three being old Brook Farmers). During the presidential campaign of 1856, one of the paper's European correspondents reported that America was where the "battle of Freedom" was being fought and that "every steamer from the United States is now as eagerly expected as European news was in America in 1848–49." Unhappily, it was the pro-slavery candidate, James Buchanan, who won the election, leaving free-state Republicans more embattled than ever. Following Buchanan's inauguration in 1857, Fanny dropped in on her downstairs neighbors with a transatlantic challenge from Eunice: "I want to know when their high mightinesses the Jameses intend to return, to resume the duties they have so long unworthily neglected in their own country." The question was jocular in tone but not in substance.

James's answer, composed immediately, wobbled between evasive blarney, boasting self-justification, and self-mockery:

> Dear, darling, dutiful, and beautiful *you*. Well, I never knew such an unreasonable person as *you* is! [punning on *Eunice*]. Do you suppose my dear friend that I don't fulfil all my American duties, simply because I am now a European citizen? Why this is to make time and space real, or put shadows above substance . . . It is a great pleasure to love you, whenever you are pleasant and appreciative and don't look anxious . . . but I should like to know whether you have not heard that all duties which do not willingly become pleasures, are going henceforth to be thrown overboard . . . ? Such are the orders lately received from the great admiral of the fleet, and it is excessively agreeable I must say to those old salts whose grinders have hitherto seen some hard service.

Dramatizing himself as a veteran who had earned his retirement, James looked forward to spending the evening of his days in "peace and jollity." The prospects for this well-deserved rest were much better "under a strong government like that of which we are at present the happy subjects, than under an unsettled administration like that of Buchanan, to which every mornings Tribune has power to give a fit of the colic." As James described the pleasures of life in a stable dictatorship, his tone became curiously ambivalent:

> We saw the Empress yesterday promenading en voiture, and shortly after the Emperor driving his American waggon. Certainly it is a high compliment to our country that he should thus adopt one of its most distinctive institutions. We see the infant hope of the Empire every bright day . . . Certainly the skies smile upon this paternal government, let who will scowl . . . Seated here as we are, Mother [i.e., the former Mrs. Macdaniel], Fanny & I, above the hum of mundane politics, listening only to tidings from interior and upper worlds, we naturally look down a little upon you poor slaves of the actual.

A slave, here, is someone who does not live under an absolute tyrant, and who must therefore engage in the contention of democratic politics. The paradox is outrageous, particularly as being addressed to an abolitionist in the 1850s. But it is not simply *blague*. James had been seduced by the Second Empire, which simulated the harmonious, post-political social order he had been dreaming of. He had to marshal all his rhetorical resources to charm Eunice out of her justifiable suspicion.

After Louis-Napoleon assumed dictatorial powers in 1851, the French press was forbidden to air political questions, Tocqueville and other liberals were thrown in prison, and there were executions. For the *Tribune*, the Emperor was a betrayer of the revolution of 1848, a "perjured assassin" who had "manacled and enslaved" his country. Several years later James himself denounced "the sombre sanguinary mime, who has been Providentially allowed to vault for a day upon the throne of France" (still insisting, notably, on providential legitimacy). But in 1856–58 James's public and private comment on the regime was startlingly sympathetic. When the Emperor's crony Émile de Girardin devised a grandiose universal insurance scheme, James praised it as "philosophically conceived," "a very practical and practicable Socialism." In his eyes, Louis-Napoleon was somehow revolutionary, at one with Mazzini "and all the rest." He was "irresistibly precious and sweet to my heart," as a rat-hunting weasel is to the heart of a farmer.

"Vast numbers of people here," James informed the *Tribune*, regard the Emperor as a consummately clever socialist who seized power because the regular French socialists were too faction-ridden to govern. The Emperor realized that "the political evolution of mankind is ended, and that it only remains to inaugurate their social evolution in an orderly manner." In other words, the politicians had to be removed and silenced. Although James did not openly endorse this enlightened-despot inter- pretation, he thought it had an "*a priori* probability." Two years later, he suggested in another *Tribune* letter that the government's refusal to censor the socialist *La Presse* revealed the Emperor's cryptic benevolence. Proudhon might be thrown in prison for a dangerous book, but "Louis Napoleon, I'll warrant, chuckles over it!" Few liberals took this view. When Sumner arrived in Paris, Tocqueville gave him to understand that "the intelligence of the country is against the emperor." Further con- versations with other prominent Frenchmen, such as Guizot, Laugel, and Lamartine, led the senator to conclude that "nobody believes in the present dynasty." One of the reasons James fell for it was that it seemed to confirm his theory that the "merely national or political" mentality was giving way to a "*social* one."

James's muffled sympathy with the second Napoleonic regime un- doubtedly played into the political and intellectual formation of his children. Fourteen-year-old William decided that Paris had been "won- derfully improved by the 'emperor' " in spite of his obvious inauthentic- ity. Harry, far more impressed, picked up a lifelong awe of "the shining second Empire." He was thrilled by the heroic display, the armed guard, the "archangels of the sword." The little Prince Imperial was "sublime, divine," the Empress "all-wonderful," "ineffable." The boy was aware the regime was "new and queer and perhaps even wrong," but for all that, it was so radiant with style and glory it flooded his inner life. His most memorable dream was set in the Louvre's Galerie d'Apollon. In his later years he acquired several then-unfashionable First Empire pieces of furniture. In old age, the dictation he gave after suffering a series of strokes assumes the voice of the original Napoleon and addresses the James siblings as if they were Bonapartes.

In 1849 Henry Sr. had projected an invincible figure he called the Divine Man, someone who would "cleave down every thing that stands in the way of his inheritance" in order to satisfy his instinct for "unlimited power"—and who would then pour out a "measureless and universal benediction." Louis-Napoleon was probably not on Henry Sr.'s mind at the time he wrote these words, but seven years later he couldn't resist seeing the ersatz Emperor as the incarnation of this wise and ruthless tyrant. Somehow or other, the future novelist absorbed a version of this half-secret paternal fantasy. For both Henrys, the Napoleonic dynasty became the vehicle of a cherished dream of power and glory.

Strangest of all, the parallel between the Jameses and the Bonapartes was no mere fantasy. William of Albany *had* belonged to the same revolutionary generation as the first Napoleon. Both men yoked republican ideals to an astonishingly successful grab for personal power. Their individual fortunes became part and parcel of their grand schemes of nation building—the development of a New World Syracuse, the opening of the Erie Canal, the integration of "fiscal or physical resources." Of course, William did not operate on Napoleon's scale, and his dynastic ambitions were frustrated by his sons' refusal to follow him in business and by the family's shredding of his will. Also the Bonapartes (as Karl Marx saw) regressed from tragedy to farce in their foolishly literal reassertion of power, whereas the generations of Jameses underwent a series of creative metamorphoses, transforming the "fiscal or physical" into the spiritual and then turning that (with William and Henry Jr.) into the philosophical and the literary.

EDUCATION IN PARIS AND BOULOGNE

Meanwhile, there was the usual chaotic sequence of tutors and schools. Soon after moving to Paris, Mary reported to her mother-in-law that she and Henry had found "good teachers" for the children, especially Alice and Bob, whose new governess, Augustine Danse, was not only sensible and ladylike but "really quite an acquisition to the family circle." She seemed expert and knowing, and her "salient smiling eyes" and "flexible *taille*" (figure) lastingly impressed Henry Jr. She liked Bob, *l'ingenieux petit Robertson*, as she called him, but William she regarded as an *ours* —a bear. Then, after a year's employment, it was discovered that Mademoiselle Danse was quite luridly unsuitable. "A cloud of revelations," never specified, followed her departure. Harry decided she was an irregular character, an adventuress, but brilliant and genial for all that.

By contrast, the tutor retained for the older boys, Monsieur Lerambert, was stiffly respectable. He was an author (Henry Sr. spotting "one of his books in a shop window") and was remembered as "spare and tightly black-coated, spectacled, pale and prominently intellectual." Coming for two-hour sessions four days a week, he taught the boys French, German, Latin, and arithmetic. (Their lessons in history and geography—the "social" subjects—were conducted by Henry Sr.) In Lerambert's opinion, Henry Jr.'s general "aptitude show[ed] for nil." This "fell judgment" was communicated to the father, who then passed it on to the boy without mitigating its "cold finality." Years later the novelist happened to remember that his tutor lived on rue Jacob with his mother and sister. Going to a Paris directory of the 1850s, one finds an entry

for "Lerambert, anc. [former] notaire, Jacob, 28." Lerambert's father had
been a notary, and thus a member of the small and select group of powerful
French officials who had (still have) the exclusive privilege of drawing
up and recording conveyances of real property. In other words, the tutor
felt he had the right to be haughty, and when the time came for him
to be sacked after four or five months' employment, he was so surprised
he made a scene. He let these barbarous Americans understand he had
made "sacrifices" for them.

Maybe it was because James abominated prigs that he got rid of Lerambert. Or maybe it was because he had found a school in the neighborhood, the loosely organized Institution Fezandié at 6, rue Balzac, to
which he now sent three of his boys. In A Small Boy and Others, Henry
Jr. characterized this establishment as a bold experiment in Fourierist
idealism. Unwary biographers have taken him at his word, not noticing
his telltale equivocations—"I like to think of the Institution as all but
phalansteric." The truth turns out to be somewhat prosaic. From 1850
on, there had been a French-language school at the rue Balzac location
that catered to the British ("établissement anglo-français"). Because of the
area's rapid development and rising rents, the enterprise became unprofitable, and in 1856, when the lease came up for renewal, the institution was taken over by Fezandié. Raising tuition, he advertised the
shrunken language school, quite misleadingly, as an "institut polyglotte et
polytechnique." He had one good instructor, an aging republican with a
high standard of correct enunciation. The school appealed to Henry Sr.
because it was close to the family's apartment, the language instruction
was pitched to foreigners, and there was none of Lerambert's stuffiness
and discipline.

Hoping to put the children in school in Germany, Henry Sr. and
Mary made two trips there to look for a suitable educational establishment. The first of these may have taken place in the fall of 1856, when
the couple passed through Geneva once again and registered as foreigners.
The second trip took them to Frankfurt (where James was displeased by
the hot and dusty riverside park). Heidelberg, Wiesbaden, and Bonn
were also sampled and rejected, and the dream of a German education
given up for the time being.

In the summer of 1857, the family left Paris for the port city of
Boulogne-sur-Mer, where they took a spacious apartment on rue Neuve
Chaussée. Boulogne was an agreeable resort on what was then the usual
cross-Channel route between Paris and London, and there were lots of
semipermanent British residents. A governess named Marie Bonningue
was hired for Alice, and the boys were enrolled in the Collège Imperial,

still in session through the first half of summer. The student body consisted of two hundred boys, a fourth of them English. Although this was the first public school the James boys had attended, Gallic method and regularity gave it a higher standard than any of the private schools they had gone to in New York. In mathematics, William told a friend, "nothing is learned by rote here, but a reason is given for every thing." "As for the inflated, pompous, pedantic literary Professors," he wrote later, "the less said of them the better." During August and September, the summer vacation, William and perhaps the others got daily home tutoring.

On August 23 Harry came down with a case of typhus (which is spread by lice). His temperature shot up and he was "for several days delirious." His father confided him to the care of a local Irish homeopathist, who prescribed rest, a shaved head, and little or nothing to eat. The illness was severe and protracted, and it was almost a month before the boy began "to cost something again in the way of chickens & peaches." The future novelist's life was in question at times, and when he finally tottered out of his room he had grown "excessively thin" and "a half-head taller." He himself looked back on this near-fatal illness as marking the end of his boyhood, the strangely timed spurt of growth having turned him into a youth.

During the same month Harry left his sickbed, Anna Ward, also gravely ill, passed through Boulogne on her way to the South of France. She didn't see the Jameses, perhaps on purpose, as she was suffering from "nervous depression," "overaction of the brain," and "violent attacks of Hemorrhage"; one of her drugs was an anti-bleeding agent, ergot. After reaching Nice, Anna sent James a letter that vibrated between depression and ecstasy. "You know how I grew up!" she exclaimed, thinking of the change from her untroubled early years to the sorrows of maturity. She had "gone thro' very dark places" (her journal reveals that a miscarriage had resulted in an "unceasing flowing" that lasted for months), but there was this consolation, that she "could never have become conjoined to the Lord, but thro' suffering." The letter suggests Anna had taken to heart the brief sermon James had recently sent her on the necessity of suffering. (The "breaking down of nature," he had written, is divinely ordained, so as to force us to give up our "vanity & ostentatious indulgence.") James was flattered to see his hard-won wisdom prove so serviceable, and a couple of months later he wrote Anna that "the true friend is the intimate one who partakes your thought and helps your sacredest aspiration, without making you justify yourself every moment by long argumentation." He very much wanted to talk to her about "*the veritable Christian hope, which is that of a perfectly innocent life for man upon the earth.*" It was a bad shock when her next letter revealed that she'd become a Roman Catholic. James refused to accept this unwelcome news, "on the grounds that only they who were born and reared in spiritual penury could be capable of such nonsense."

The James parents had their own ailments, Mary a "derangement of the liver" and Henry Sr. a nausea attack every morning "and a great sense of debility." He knew he was too sedentary, but walking could not be the remedy for a man whose gait involved some dramatic contortions. Edward Emerson, Ralph Waldo's son, remembered how James "limped along on his wooden leg with some activity," and for Jane Carlyle he remained a lasting example of how not to use an artificial leg. The lurch and twist of walking seem to have brought on some painful orthopedic side effects—"a weakness in his back," as Mary put it. Lameness also induced a vivid and justifiable fear of the loss of balance. There could be no more "odiously repulsive experience," James once wrote, than "falling from a building." He is known to have taken at least one "bad fall," which laid him up for several days.

In October the Jameses moved from Boulogne back to Paris and took an expensive sublet at 26, rue Montaigne (now J. Mermoz) for eight months. The severity of the Panic of 1857 was just then becoming apparent, and around the first of November James got word from Robertson Walsh, his business agent, that he had "lost some of [his] income." Badly frightened, James confessed to a friend that he didn't know "where another year may find us." He was "anxious for the future," as he had never yet been, and he turned to his mother and brothers and implored them "to contribute as large a sum" as they could manage: surely "the warm hearts at home . . . [would] not suffer us to lack any thing which their necessities may spare." Writing to Rev. William, he promised to return to the United States as soon as he could "command the means." For the time being, however, "present obligations"—not specified— would detain him in Paris. He went on to advise the brother whose help he needed that the Panic had been caused by "the lack of the sentiment of brotherhood," and that it was high time for ministers of the Gospel to preach social salvation and stop "overworking" individual salvation. This letter, the only known document in which Henry Sr. asks for money, is one of his most characteristic productions. Forced to queue up at the family's bottomless money drawer, he bristles with spiritual wisdom. He begs, but makes it pointedly clear that there will be no bending.

Before long, James bowed to necessity. As much as he wanted to spend the winter in Paris, there was no choice but to return to Boulogne and its lower cost of living. On Christmas Eve Mary wrote her mother-in-law: "I cannot begin to tell you dear Ma how great an effort this resolution to remain here until the spring has cost us— With Henry it is still a daily battle, so strongly does he feel home pulling at his heart." Henry added: "We had half a mind to go over by the next trip of the *Adriatic*, but Mary ciphers out such enormous impediments to our comfort in America, on our reduced income, that we are content to remain where we are." (Their New York home, having been leased, wasn't available.) They rented a comfortable house on the Grande Rue, in the busiest part of the city, and cut down on expenses by hiring only two servants. Their cook was English, chosen less for her culinary skill, one imagines, than for Mary's convenience in supervising the shopping.

This second period of residence in Boulogne lasted till the end of May 1858. Harry remembered the interval as "too endlessly and blightingly prolonged," and Mary complained about the lack of "congenial" people. William, however, reported that "we had a very nice time in Boulogne, and got to have a real home feeling there." In fact, as far as education was concerned, returning to the seaport for another six months was the Jameses' most sensible zigzag yet. William, Wilkie, and Bob not only got better schooling at the Collège Imperial than anything their father had been able to find in Paris, London, or Geneva, but there were opportunities for friendship with other students. Thanks to Boulogne, James could at last feel he had done the right thing in removing the boys "from New York, where, having no place to amuse themselves but the street, they were sure to be degraded in manners and character by the contact of vicious associates."

Two years of France had rid William for the time being of his (and his mother's) "miserable prejudice against the French." He seems to have flourished in Boulogne, collecting and experimenting and looking through his microscope. The problem of choosing a profession had begun to "torment" him; he felt he ought to be an engineer or inventor. But given his choice, he would be a farmer and study natural history—"get a microscope and go out into the country, into the dear old woods and fields and ponds . . . [and] try to make as many discoveries as possible." One of his professors considered him an "admirable student," and urged that "all the advantages of a first-rate scientific education which Paris affords ought to be accorded him." The recommendation pleased the father, who was even more pleased to report that William was "perfectly generous and conciliatory" toward the younger boys, "always disposed to help them and never to oppress." The same could not have been said of him back home. Another change for the better was that William had begun to echo Father's ideas. "All the evil in the world," the boy informed a friend, "comes from the law and the priests and the sooner these two things are abolished the better."

However, the other children "might just as well have staid at home" (in William's opinion). Although Wilkie had shown a "talent for languages" and acquired a "perfect accent" (unlike William, who still couldn't speak French with ease), he hadn't learned much. Summing up the boy's attainments, the father could come up with little more than that he had "more heart than head." A similar picture emerges from Henry Jr.'s memoirs, which represent Wilkie as sociable and easygoing to the point of laziness. Given the father's commitment to the social, one would expect Wilkie to have come in for some strong paternal pats on the back. But to be social in Henry Sr.'s high-strung sense involved a tricky balance between the high and the low, and Wilkie was too relaxed for that.

Bob had proved "particularly forward" in learning French and, in addition, his father reported, was "clever and promising" and showed "ten times the go-ahead of all the rest." But Bob wasn't able to profit from this parental supportiveness. What he remembered from the Collège was looking on with envy as the happy, prize-winning schoolboys would "ascend the steps of [the mayor's] throne, kneel at his feet, and receive crown or rosettes, or some symbol of merit which *we* did not get. The luck had begun to break early." "We," in this self-pitying retrospect, meant Bob and Wilkie as opposed to Willy and Harry. Bob was convinced his potential had been unfairly balked at an early age.

Harry had as much reason as Bob to feel sorry for himself, being so languid from his bout with typhus that instead of returning to the Collège with his brothers he was given private instruction at home. His tutor (who probably came cheap) was a pathetic old man named Ansiot, who smelled so strong the boy wanted to open the windows after their sessions together. But the novelist-in-training had a refuge, Merridew's English Library, where he read so much fiction his parents began to worry. Harry was "not so fond of study, properly so-called," his father complained, "as of reading." The boy's long and lonely recuperation increased his fondness for fiction, making him the kind of reader who grabs hold of narrative as if it is something primary and life-originating. In a way, the theory the father had set forth to the other invalid, Anna Ward—that nature must break down before spirit can take its place—was being worked out within the future novelist. William went in for natural history, but Harry, compelled to seek an alternative to the natural, became "a devourer of libraries, and an immense writer of novels and dramas."

His father saw that he had "considerable talent as a writer" but questioned "whether he will ever accomplish much." This, 'the earliest-surviving record of Henry Jr.'s literary passion and talent, is also the earliest expression of Henry Sr.'s baffled sense of his second son's vocation.

Alice had a governess three hours a day and went to dancing school. What stuck in her memory was a tedious excursion to the country to visit her teacher's family and the brilliant thing suddenly uttered by Harry in the midst of a typically boring and unremunerative day: "This might certainly be called pleasure under difficulties." Alice never forgot how her whole being stirred in response to "the substance and exquisite, *original* form of this remark."

Making a life out of the ruins of life, making it out of words, was starting to become Alice's brother's business. Henry Jr. had glimpsed his imperial vocation and was already hard at work carving it out.

THE HIDDEN BRAND

As for Henry Sr., the results of his extended stay in France are to be seen in the nine long letters he sent the *New York Tribune* during the Boulogne period. These strongly opinionated communications convey a vivid idea of the impassioned monologues his children grew up with, and in fact the letters would find numerous echoes in William's and Harry's mature thought and writing. Henry Sr.'s favorable response to the American revivals of the spring of 1858 would reappear in William's sympathetic investigations of the psychology of conversion. The father's view of the French, which highlighted "the vivacity of [their] *social* sentiment, and the comparative inactivity of the *moral* sentiment," would show up in Henry Jr.'s similarly divided assessments of many French writers. We find Henry Sr. offering extravagant praise of the *Revue des Deux Mondes*, the same periodical that exercised a potent spell on the novelist's early reading. One of the sights the father particularly enjoyed—the "remarkable fisherwomen" who waded into the surf with their skirts hitched a good deal higher than was seen in Anglo-Saxon lands —would show up forty years later in the Boulogne segment of *What Maisie Knew*, where Sir Claude's roving eye catches "the fine stride and shining limbs of a young fishwife who had just waded out of the sea."

The one thing Europe always did for James was to restore his always-lapsing faith in America's world-historical democratic mission. More convinced than ever that New World "rowdyism is only the instinctual and uncouth play of the new life in man," he made fun of those who were offended by "Walt. Whitman, Captain Rynders, General Walker," in this way yoking the poet with a notoriously dirty Tammany Hall ward heeler and a murderous "filibusterer" who invaded Nicaragua. Weary of Gallic uniformity, James even expressed a genial appreciation of two "disorderly" Americans he otherwise had little use for, "my friend Bronson Alcot[t]" and "my friend Thoreau."

What upset James most of all was a French newspaperman's observations on suicide in the United States. According to Frederic Gaillardet, it was not the social outcasts who killed themselves in America but "the rich and respected." That was because Americans were so devoted to the pursuit of wealth that "the heart is always left out of American compacts." This was an early version of the view often expressed by European observers, that there is an emotional vacuum in American society. James was offended to the quick by Gaillardet's theory, which implied that John Barber had been an ordinary two-bit speculator and that America was not a perfect society in the making but a place of terrifying social isolation. Devoting two full columns to his rebuttal, James insisted that it is those with the warmest hearts, the highest hopes, who kill themselves in America—those who are "above all things disposed to unity with their kind, being used to associate their joys and sorrows with those of their fellow man."

If that is the kind of man who kills himself in America, what kind of man kills himself in France? On March 7, 1858, James devoted a long letter to an indignant account of an aged and respected paterfamilias who committed suicide in the most fearsome way possible, by jumping from a high window. In his youth the man had been inveigled by a predatory woman into an act of forgery. He was convicted and sentenced to the galleys. Released, he moved to England, got married, and had a long and irreproachable career, eventually returning to France. His past had been expiated and apparently forgotten, and his son made plans to marry. Then, on the eve of the nuptials, the father received a letter calling off the marriage on account of his own long-ago crime. The next thing his family heard was "the sound of his bleeding body upon the pavement beneath."

This, James heatedly explained, was "the European spirit from top to bottom." All that counted was respectability, and if a man went temporarily astray in his youth, the Old World idea was to cut off all hope by "heating its murderous irons . . . and burning in upon the naked shoulder of the culprit the letter F (*faux*), so [that] his ignominy might forever attach to him and exclude him from social forgiveness!"

Chapter 23

■ ■ ■

ANOTHER RIDICULOUS ZIGZAG:
1858–60

The Jameses concluded their European sojourn by spending three weeks in London in a large modern stucco house on Porteus Road, near Paddington Station, and then crossed the ocean on the *Persia*, reaching New York on June 22, 1858. Henry Sr. looked up his old Fourierist pals, Dana and Ripley, both still in harness at the *Tribune*, and found that the latter had become a complete professional, "as smooth and uninteresting as a gentleman's coach-horse." (This judgment may have been prompted by Ripley's bored notice of *Christianity the Logic of Creation*.) To William, who had European eyes now, New York looked "rather disorderly." Only one of the old Fourteenth Street gang was still around. The house was leased, there didn't seem to be much point in lingering, and the family soon took off for Albany and 43 North Pearl Street.

Seventy-six years old, Ma was accustomed to long naps in the house she had occupied for forty years. There may have been a few last orphaned grandchildren, and the four Gourlay nieces, now middle-aged, probably lived with her, but all her daughters were dead, and so were two of the three sons who, until recently, had lived at home (John Barber and Edward). Howard, twenty-nine years old, had just gotten married—but after his wife's death the following year he would move back in with his mother. Gus lived at Rhinebeck in premature retirement. And Henry and Mary were once again between residences. Of all Catharine Barber James's children and stepchildren, only Rev. William had established a household in Albany. But instead of pursuing a career, he spent his days on an ambitious theological opus that would never see print. In 1832 Catharine's husband had been the wealthiest and perhaps the most energetic man in town. A list of Albany's twenty richest men in 1863 didn't have a single James on it, and the few James sons who were still alive had no occupation. Everything William of Albany had been afraid of, had tried to fend off with his canny will, had come to pass.

What disasters lay in wait for the next generation? At some point in the later 1850s while the Tweedys were living in Europe, their two or three children all died of diphtheria. Returning to America, the bereft couple tried to make a new life for themselves by adopting the difficult Temple orphans and taking a summer house in Newport, Rhode Island. Henry couldn't tear his thoughts away from the unfortunate parents, who clung "so tenaciously" to his imagination he hardly felt "free to write about anything else." He was afraid Mary Tweedy was so "lonesome" she would "sink . . . under this burden." One apparent result: a fresh resolve to give the *James* children the closest supervision.

James McKaye was another old friend who spent his summers in Newport, in a Gothic cottage-cum-tower. The becalmed port had begun to look like the latest answer to the long-standing problem of where to go and what to do during the sweltering months. With Tweedy, McKaye, and other kindred spirits to talk to, and at, James might reasonably hope to elude the boredom and depression always lying in wait for him. No sooner were he and Mary back in Albany than they took off to have a look at Newport, taking Bob and Alice and leaving the three older boys with their grandmother.

Although the Newport directory for 1858 listed sixteen boat builders, the town was no longer a shipping and commercial center. But the summer climate was still mild and breezy, you could walk or ride everywhere in the open countryside, and there was wonderful sailing. Rich Southerners liked to come here for the hot months, and in the 1850s, Newport's so-called Bostonian period, Bay State Brahmins began buying or building summer cottages. (The palatial mansions built by vast New York fortunes didn't appear until after the Civil War.) There were large hotels—the Ocean House, the Atlantic House—and some pleasant homes to be rented for the season; Tweedy lined up three of them for the Jameses to look at. Transportation was convenient: to get to Boston you caught the New York steamboat to Fall River, and then it was fifty-three miles by rail. The Jameses were pleased with what they saw, and when the next Newport directory came out on August 14, it had this entry:

JAMES HENRY, (New York) h Beach c Tew's ct

"H" was house, "c" corner, "ct" court. That James identified himself as a New Yorker suggests he hadn't yet realized he would never again reside in that city.

The rented house was spacious and semirural, on a four-acre lot. With all that pasture, a pony for the boys was not out of the question, and in the middle of August James ran up to Boston to see whether Dudley H. Bayley's Carriage Bazaar had anything suitable. James knew horses and, as his namesake remembered, prided himself on being a good whip. Unlike Mary, who was city-bred, he had grown up enjoying country sports. She might worry about "ink-spots in childrens shirts and rents in their trousers," but he pronounced his boys "as good as good can be, inside of their shirts and trousers." They were "utterly abandoned to the enjoyment of their recovered liberty, boating & fishing and riding to their hearts content." They spent so much time in the water a friend remembered them as "veritable Sandwich Islanders."

One July day, Duncan Campbell Pell, lieutenant governor of Rhode Island, told his son and another boy that the recently arrived James boys might appreciate a visit. The other boy was Thomas Sergeant Perry, the offspring of a well-rooted Newport family and the grandson of the hero of Lake Erie. A half century later Perry still remembered his first impression of the newcomers. William had been "full of merriment and we were soon playing a simple and childish game," while Harry sat on a window seat reading the memoirs of the painter John Constable "with a certain air of remoteness."

In spite of this stiff beginning, Harry and "Sargy" became fast friends. They took daily afternoon walks, sometimes to the cliffs just east of town, sometimes through the mostly empty countryside to the Point or Paradise Rocks. Once, on a walk to Lily Pond, Harry earnestly talked up "Fourier's plan for regenerating the world." Perhaps the boy's father's ideal socialism had revived now that New York's disorders were a fading memory. Harry was fond of recalling these jaunts after being taken to Geneva the following year. "You've no idea," he would write Sargy, "what pleasure I have in thinking about the old place. I remember every little detail about it as well as if I'd only seen it yesterday." Geneva had "no such fields and meadows and groves . . . where you can halt and lie out on the flat of your back and loll and loaf and reverise (Don't you remember?)."

Newport also meant the dignified Redwood Library and long hours reading and discussing the exciting new writers from England and France.

Browning and Balzac became household names, but the Jameses also read America's leading mass-market story paper, the *New York Ledger*. One of Henry Sr.'s letters mentions the issue that carried the first installment of Mrs. E.D.E.N. Southworth's novel *The Hidden Hand*. This seems to have been the happiest period of Harry's boyhood—even if some of William's friends did call him "Sissy."

William assumed that when fall came he would do as Father had done thirty years earlier and enroll in Union College. While still in Albany, the two older boys had taken a day trip to Schenectady to look the school over and see Edgar Van Winkle, formerly of Fourteenth Street, now class of 1860. But Father abruptly put his foot down, declaring (as William complained to Van Winkle) "that he would not hear of my going to any college whatsoever. He says that Colleges are hotbeds of corruption where it [is] impossible to learn anything." One reason their "moral atmosphere . . . was very debasing" was that they taught young minds to define themselves in professional terms; another (one guesses) was that they stimulated youthful depravities. Henry Jr. was struck by Father's "great revulsion of spirit" and rightly supposed it was caused by sore memories of his own student days at Union. But neither son seems to have been aware of the more recent history that lay behind their parent's intransigence. In 1851 James had had an acrimonious public debate with Tayler Lewis, Union's eminent humanities professor. Lewis had charged James with undermining "the very foundations of all moral and religious truth," and James had accused Lewis of "malignancy and meanness." It was unthinkable that William's aspiring mind could be entrusted to this venomous professor.

By the time summer ended, James had decided to spend the winter in Newport, and presently the family moved to another rented house, it's not known just where. Perhaps it was in the neighborhood of the McKayes, whose Kay Street address became William's "second home." Once again, the children were to be educated near their parents. Alice was sent to the little school on Church Street that was run by Miss Rebecca Hunter and her mother, and about which little is known except that another girl recalled it as "certainly a school of great refinement." Harry, Wilkie, and Bob attended the Berkeley Institute at 10 Washington Square, billed as a "classical and commercial school of the highest grade." The principal was William C. Leverett, an assistant Episcopal minister and a recent product of Harvard Divinity School. Bob and Wilkie were probably enrolled in the commercial department, but Harry studied Latin with his friend Sargy, gave a declamation once a week out of Epes Sargent's *Standard Speaker*, snorted at the tepid praise the literary manual accorded Robert Browning ("himself no mean poet"), and read with pleasure *The Vicar of Wakefield*. Apparently, Leverett did not inspire much respect in his students. Sargy remembered him as "a little suit of clothes, stuffed out: a small Napoleon, in miniature." He would announce, " 'The class may lay aside their books,' and then . . . proceed to 'show off' his own oratory." William described him as "the prettiest little picture of a man you ever saw," with a "beaming little smile," but Henry Jr. remained detached and unresponsive, an "uninterested scholar." As for Henry Sr., it is hard to imagine a father who admired the large and powerful Roediger taking much satisfaction in the tiny, pompous Leverett.

But it was William who posed the real problem, not having a school to go to.* When he remarked that the summer had been very pleasant but very idle, his father said, ominously, that he and the other children couldn't "have been so idle had we been abroad." The sixteen-year-old boy tried to keep "busy teaching [him]self Mathematics and so forth," and he also studied German with "a governess resident in the house," a person otherwise unknown. He took lessons from a local artist, William Morris Hunt, and there was talk of his eventually going to the Lawrence Scientific School at Harvard, but for the time being the boy was trapped in a strange educational limbo. Van Winkle was studying to be an engineer. James McKaye's son Steele had gone to Paris to study art with Thomas Couture. What would Father allow William to be?

The problem of William's education seems to have precipitated a major domestic crisis. September 7 marked the beginning of the Berkeley Institute's fall term, which was to last fourteen weeks. Suddenly, at the end of the second week, using language reminiscent of his father's testamentary determination "to discourage prodigality and vice," James sent this announcement to his friend and banker, Samuel Gray Ward:

> I have grown so discouraged about the education of my children here, and dread so those inevitable habits of extravagance and insubordination which appear to be the characteristics of American youth, that I have come to the conclusion to retrace my steps to Europe, and keep them there a few years longer. My wife is completely of the same mind, and though we feel on many accounts that we are making personal sacrifices in this step, the advantages to the children are so clear that we cannot conscientiously hesitate.

* Following Ralph Barton Perry, all James family biographers who comment on William's education in Newport in 1858–59 mistakenly enroll him in the Berkeley Institute.

Proclaiming that his main purpose in life was "to do justice to my children," he booked passage on the earliest steamship possible, the *Persia*, scheduled to leave September 29. The abrupt change of plan was unwelcome news to William, who sent a sarcastic complaint to a friend: "Father took it into his head the other day that it was absolutely necessary for our moral and intellectual welfare to return immediately to Europe."

In Emerson's shrewd opinion, one of the reasons for James's frequent threats to leave for Europe was that he wanted to be "forbidden" by his friends. Taking a similar view, perhaps, Sam Ward got him and Mary to come up to Boston to thrash out an alternative. Apparently there was talk of moving to Cambridge and enrolling William in Harvard. Although these plans fell through, as James's next letter to Ward reveals —"Behold us fast anchored in Newport for the winter at all events, and those fine Cambridge dreams dispersed in air"—Ward had succeeded in getting the Jameses to postpone Europe till the spring.

But the complex tensions between the restless father and his restless firstborn son were still unresolved, and before long they expressed themselves in a striking fashion. At the end of October Wilkie purchased a young greyhound and brought it home. For some reason the care and training of the dog devolved on William. Whenever it misbehaved, there were cries from other members of the family: " 'Willy, that wretched dog is on the bed again,' or 'Willy, the dog is tearing the buttons off the sofa again.' " When Henry Sr. scolded Willy for "the 'ineffectual & pusillanimous' way" in which he applied the rod, the boy made up his mind to do the thing thoroughly. "I rush with savage frenzy," he told his friend at Union (adopting the hyperbolic language he often amused himself with),

> fury flashing from my eyes, and ~~belabor him with~~ apply a strap with passionate energy across his back till his mournful howlings make the welkin ring. Notwithstanding . . . Father said the other day with tears in his eyes: "Never, never before did I so clearly see the utter & lamentable inefficiency & worthlessness of your character; never before have I been so struck with your perfect inability to do anything manly or . . . a . . . good.

There are many hints of discipline and punishment in the Jameses' family papers, but this is the strongest and the strangest of Henry Sr.'s paternal tongue-lashings to be recorded. The obvious signs of pained feeling in the father must have made his proclamation of his son's worthlessness all the more wounding. The huge black strap was reconstituting itself, leaping from the hand of one generation to that of the next, and even entering the son's choice of words.

From the father's point of view, it looked as if the hellish interior wastes he had observed in himself and his brothers and nephews were sapping the character of the boy from whom he hoped so much. Perhaps some such despairing paternal outburst lay behind the abrupt decision a few weeks earlier to yank William and the others back across the Atlantic for more "education."

When James lay dying in 1882, one of his last messages for William was "not to punish Harry [William's first child] for his little naughtinesses but reason with him and it would be all as it should be—only not punish him."

CONTROVERSIES IN ARCADIA

James regretted giving up the "advantages of society" in Boston and Cambridge, but fortunately there were several agreeable people in Newport with whom to pass the winter. One of them was George Henry Calvert, a descendant of Maryland's Lord Baltimore, who lived on his inheritance and followed literary pursuits. Educated in Germany, Calvert was a dignified man of the old school. * He and his wife "lived very simply," as a friend put it, "but they had great charm & hosts of friends, in fact you might say [they] had a 'salon.' " All the same, Calvert was as odd a mixture as James, being a committed Fourierist and a practicing spiritualist in rapport with John Jay, Guy Fawkes, and Dr. Gall (a ghostly spread that nicely represents the man's varied interests). James was amused by Calvert's spirit-rapping and presently began writing some lectures on spiritualism, which never materialized.

Depending as always on the despised clergy for stimulating conversation, James sought out the Reverend Charles T. Brooks, the Unitarian minister and an active poet and translator of German literature. With the Reverend A. G. Mercer, pastor of Trinity Episcopal Church, James did "not hesitate to avow [his] deepest convictions." He also enjoyed their wives' company, Mrs. Brooks having "a certain ragged remnant of womanly tenderness and beauty in her expression now and then which makes it worth one's while to walk down there." All in all, as James

---

* When Henry Jr. reviewed Calvert's essays in 1875, he considered the attack on certain "vulgarisms" of usage unnecessarily restrictive. He found the essays an amateurish case "of that union, so rare in this country, of taste and leisure."

told a friend, "one is not absolutely without one's kind here." Like other well-heeled radicals of his generation, he was settling into a life of comfortably gregarious alienation. Newport was the ideal place for that kind of life in the later 1850s.

Fifteen years had passed since James had been magnetized by Emerson, yet in spite of the continuing fascination—"No man I think of oftener than you, and of none with greater affection"—it was not till the fall of 1858 that James traveled to Concord and visited his friend at home. During this visit Alcott tried to give one of his famous philosophical impromptus, which were known as "conversations" even though he did all the talking. In James's opinion Alcott was vapid and egotistical and objectionably intimate with Emerson. But Emerson believed in Alcott and his transcendental improvisations, which lifted him to such heights he had been known to reach down "a plume from an archangel." Emerson wanted others to see this Daedalian man fly, and he convened a select gathering in his parlor. Besides James, the guests included Thoreau, Sam Ward from Boston, and Mary Moody Emerson, the host's aged, astringent, and still vigorous aunt.

The white-haired speaker began by invoking his listeners' consent ("We find,—do we not?"), but before he was able to launch himself on their respectful attention James interposed some queries and objections. He seemed to be under the impression (probably knowing better) that Alcott meant to get a discussion started. The speaker tried to ignore the interruptions, but James persisted and before long Alcott fell silent, leaving the talking to James alone, who went on to fulminate against religion and morality in his usual fashion. Emerson's aunt had never heard such talk and was scandalized. "Let me confront the monster," she finally broke out and, moving to a chair on the other side of the fire from James, strenuously upbraided him. Ellen Emerson remembered the encounter as "a glorious occasion for those who love a battle of words." It soon became a part of James's growing legend in sedate New England, and part of Aunt Mary Moody's legend, too.

Not long after this Concord fight, James had an engagement with another doughty antagonist, Horace Bushnell, widely regarded as America's premier theologian. Bushnell had just brought out his major work, *Nature and the Supernatural*, which sought to reconcile science and religion and expose the fallacies of modern intellectual fashions. At one point, arguing that licentiousness had gone so far it had developed its own "feeble perversities" of theory, he directed his withering glare at a book he scorned to name:

Thus we have seen a volume recently issued from the American press, the formal purpose of which is to show, even as a christian fact, the blamelessness of sin; nay more, that the main object of Jesus Christ in his mission of love, is to disabuse the world of the imposture, deliver it of the terrible nightmare of sin. Not to deliver it of sin itself—that is a mistake—but to deliver it of the conviction of sin, as an illusive and baleful mistake.

On February 10, 1859, James struck back in the first of a series of letters sent to the *New York Tribune*. What Bushnell had failed to grasp was that "the great problem of philosophy, since the beginning of history, has been to reconcile HUMAN FREEDOM with HUMAN DEPENDENCE." Becoming more abusive as he wrote, James raked the eminent theologian over the coals for his "petty insolence," "ineffable puerilities," and "undeniably trashy" thinking. At the end of his second long epistle, he found he hadn't finished. "Still one letter, and I shall have done," he promised Greeley. The promise was broken, and it was not till letter number four that James finally mentioned the attack on his own "licentious" book: "It pleases Dr. Bushnell to denounce, not in a manly, honest way either, some of my writings, for their criticism of the moralistic or pharisaic attitude of the Church toward the Gospel of the grace of God." By the time James finished his fifth and last letter, dated March 1, he had filled eleven columns of small type. * No other *Tribune* letter writer was indulged to that extent.

The previous August, James had come across a supercilious British reaction to a recent "Free Convention" of advanced American thinkers, one of whom, Julia Branch, had proclaimed woman's "*right to bear children when she will, and by whom she will.*" The generally anti-American *Saturday Review* pronounced Mrs. Branch's speech "the very pemmican of insolence and nastiness" and advised her to take up prostitution, and even got in a wholly gratuitous dig at Garth Wilkinson. Stung in more ways than one by this sneering Toryism, James quickly drafted a long letter to the *Tribune* defending free speech and the right of privacy:

The law utterly disdains to punish any strictly private iniquity . . . Two persons may agree to live together as man and wife without invoking any legal sanction to their agreement. Society simply ignores the bond, and

---

* As usual, James brought up the metaphor of fecal waste. Bushnell interpreted creation as "not a Divine operation at all, but at best a Divine defecation, intended to work off in Satanic or diabolic form certain peccant humors, which eternally disturbed the Divine repose, and might eventually —but I imitate Dr. B.'s discretion, and go no further."

never thinks of punishing it. Two or more persons may agree to gamble
together till one or the other is 'cleaned out' . . . Society takes no notice.

With New York a fading memory, James was ready to repudiate his
position of a few years earlier—that society had a "right to interfere"
with private vices. But he could not get access to his preferred forum for
his new and dangerous (and temporary) libertarianism. Greeley refused
to print the letter, in spite of various cuts and alterations in the manuscript. Instead, he ran "A Metropolitan Free Lover," a story about a
policeman who deserted his wife and daughter for a young, single woman.

Five months later a spectacular murder presented James with an opportunity to strike back at Greeley. In February 1859 Daniel Sickles,
formerly counsel for Patrick Hearne and now a member of the House of
Representatives, shot and killed his wife's lover, Philip Barton Key, son
of the author of the national anthem. It was a deliberate "crime of honor,"
committed in full public view, and several lawyers rushed to the murderer's defense. (Sickles had been Secretary of Legation in London when
James Buchanan, now President, was there as American minister.) The
Tribune's position was that private vengeance must not be sanctioned.
Sickles must be convicted or the criminal code would become a "wretched
farce." Reading this, James reached for his pen. In his long counter-
statement, he argued that Sickles's vengeance was quite in keeping with
the Tribune's legal view of marriage. To be consistent, the newspaper
ought to side with Sickles rather than against him, for as long as the
law gives a husband legal possession of his wife's body, he is surely within
his rights in defending his property.* The only way to avoid future
murders is to abolish legal marriage and make divorce free for the asking.

With this argument, James rebounded to his old critique of marriage.
Greeley, meanwhile, had dug in his heels against liberalized divorce,
partly because he blamed "this unclean spirit of Free Love" for scattering
and destroying the cause of Associationism. His editorial reply cited a
recent dispatch from Cap-Haïtien by James Redpath, which stated that
in Haiti free love was the law of the land and that the women had been
degraded by it. "When a man here wants to leave a woman," Redpath
reported, "there is never any difficulty about it . . . Men change about a
great deal." Does anyone know of some other country, Greeley ingen-
uously asked, where free love has different and better results? If not, he

---

* The jury, which found for the accused, evidently saw things the same way. In 1863, after Sickles
became famous for his heroism at Gettysburg, William sent his picture to Alice with the remark
"Isn't he a bully boy?" This act suggests the children knew of their father's involvement in the
earlier murder case.

TWO CONTENDERS FOR FREE LOVE WHO
WANTED TO CLAIM JAMES FOR THE CAUSE

Marx Edgeworth Lazarus. "I take pleasure in acknowledging the substantial integrity of the writings of Henry James . . . although considerations entirely personal may prevent [him] from taking openly the same ground as myself " (*Labadie Collection, University of Michigan Library*)

Stephen Pearl Andrews, who assigned James to "the class of purely ideal reformers" (*Labadie Collection, University of Michigan Library*)

Mary James
(*Houghton Library, Harvard University*)

Anna Hazard (Barker) Ward. "Henry is an extraordinary talker." Portrait by William Morris Hunt, 1861 (*Mrs. Benjamin Warder Thoron; photo, courtesy Museum of Fine Arts, Boston*)

Alice James, age 4?
(*Houghton Library, Harvard University*)

Alice James in Paris, c. 1857 (*Houghton Library, Harvard University*)

Henry James, Jr., in Geneva, 1859 or 1860 (*Houghton Library, Harvard University*)

William James (*Houghton Library, Harvard University*)

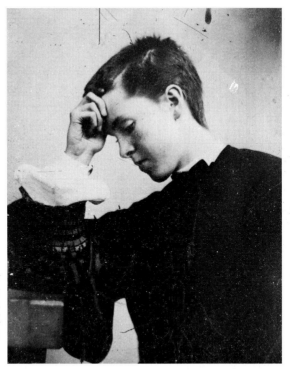

Minny Temple, 1861, her
hair cropped, apparently
because of an illness
(*Houghton Library, Harvard
University*)

Henry James, Sr., mid-1870s
(*Houghton Library, Harvard University*)

Mary James (*Houghton Library, Harvard University*)

Henry James, Sr., and grand-child (*Schaffer Library, Union College*)

Garth Wilkinson James in
Milwaukee (*Houghton Library,
Harvard University*)

Henry James, Jr., early 1880s?
(*Houghton Library, Harvard
University*)

Henry James, Sr. Portrait by Frank Duveneck, 1882, now
displayed in a conference room in William James Hall at
Harvard (*Portrait Collection, Harvard University Art
Museums*)

said in thunder, any man who defends "Free Love, or Free Divorce, or whatever name may be given it," should be regarded as "a corrupter and destroyer of human bodies and souls."

Once again James was in it up to his eyes. All his native pugnacity —what in a more conciliatory mood he admitted to be his "spirit of pride and domineering"—was at once aroused and rampant. Why wouldn't Greeley see that he was fighting "not for the *lesser* but the *greater* sanctity of Marriage"? How could anyone smear a nobly disinterested philosopher such as himself? "You are by no means a stupid man," James permitted himself to say, "and yet at times how very stupidly you talk!" Up to this point, neither man's name had appeared in print in the debate. Now James crossed the line. "Are you not ashamed, Horace Greeley, to have paraded in your columns the unwomanly confession of guilt wrung from that poor creature's [Mrs. Sickles's] abject terror!" In saying this, James was playing the sentimental card, his own previous letter having assumed that Mrs. Sickles was unfaithful to her husband.

Taking off his gloves, the *Tribune*'s powerful editor addressed his reply not to "H.J." or "H.T." (as in 1850) but directly to "Henry James," who now found, as had others before him, that no one punched harder from the shoulder than Greeley. You have no right, he told James, to sneer at the Free Lovers, as they "are as sincere and honest as you ever were." You say you believe in marriage, but that "is a deceitful evasion, if not a conscious fraud." You are living in a "world of paradox and moonshine." "There was never a brass watch palmed off for gold by a Chatham-street stuffer more utterly and palpably bogus" than your claim to be contending for "sanctity of Marriage." We have been willing to print "even your" speculations, but now we "have had about enough of it." If you wish to reply "at reasonable length" (recalling the never-ending Bushnell letters), we will oblige you. But that will end the controversy.

James must have known he was finished as a correspondent of the *Tribune*. In his reply he played the dignity card, announcing his "cordial indifference" to Greeley's opinions. He played the John Stuart Mill card, quoting what the philosopher had said in favor of divorce. He declared his gratitude for having been allowed to state his convictions in the paper's "widely-circulated columns," and he took the opportunity to offer one last lengthy exposition of "the secret of human history" (this may have been what really annoyed Greeley). Then, with a flourish, he threw down what was left of his odd hand:

> My socialism, in short, proceeds upon the frankest possible acknowledge-
> ment of Christianity, which is the doctrine of God's intimate alliance

with man alone; while yours proceeds upon the most frigid and feeble and respectable Deism, which is the doctrine of His equally intimate alliance with dogs and cats, owls and bats.

In their replies, Redpath and Greeley made James out to be a pretentious and ill-mannered crank, and not without reason. In his second letter he had announced that in Haiti there was "no hatred between man and wife," no prostitution, and very little masturbation. Redpath soberly corrected the first two divinations and laughed at the letter as a whole as "the Second Epistle of James to the Tribune." Greeley (who had worked his way up in the world) bitterly raked James over the coals for parading his "transcendent superiority in every moral and intellectual quality, courage and honesty included":

> If you have, in this discussion, evinced more courtesy, suavity, good breeding, &c, than I, our readers will perceive it, and credit you accordingly—but none the more because you tell them, almost in so many words, that you are a very superior being to myself, and that your plane of thought is inconceivably higher than mine.

James stood accused of what he detested in the clergy—"Pharisaic assumptions" of superior virtue and insight.

This rancorous blow-up was widely noticed, and a few days after it ended, James got a letter from an old classmate at Princeton Theological Seminary, the Reverend Edward D. Bryan, who remembered James "as a gay young student with an ardent temperament—sparkling social qualities & a free use of money." Bryan had dutifully completed his studies and been ordained, and for the last twenty years had been serving as minister of a Presbyterian church in Rye, New York. He was "sorry that a person like [you] should be reproved by such persons as Redpath and Greeley," and he couldn't help wondering, rather insultingly, whether James was still "pure in character—correct in morals & upright in practical, daily living." It seemed a shame that "the rich inheritance which God has caused to entail upon you in the forms of *mental, physical, educational,* and *spiritual* nobility, should be so recklessly wasted, as I judge it has been from your published performances." Although James's reply is not extant, he was clearly outraged by this offensive sympathy from a man of the "professional" class, for a later letter of Bryan's begins:

> Take a walk on the beach & let the sea breezes cool down your "hot brow" then give my note another reading if you can gather up the torn

fragments. I think you will discover that your simple minded correspondent has less of "strategy" & "disingenuousness" & "audacity" than you give him credit for. And be not concerned I pray you about your "good name" & your standing with the public from anything you have written to me.

James was also corresponding with his old friend Sarah Shaw during the summer of 1859. She did not agree with James that suffering was an illusion (when she was eight, a brother near her in age broke through the ice while skating and died), and she also failed to understand how a truly "scientific" society could get started. James was happy to oblige her with long letters of explanation, of which he had his sister-in-law make copies. He also explained how his doctrines had developed, in the process composing his first surviving account of the breakdown in Windsor in 1844.

No big-circulation newspaper or magazine was open to James now that he had made himself *persona non grata* at the *Tribune*. For the time being, he could disseminate his revealed truths only through private correspondence. Once again he was balked and isolated. Put another way, Europe beckoned.

ARTISTS

Two painters, William Morris Hunt and John La Farge, gave James the decisive push that sent him back across the Atlantic.

Hunt had recently returned from Paris after studying with Thomas Couture and Jean-François Millet. He painted in what was thought of as the French style, with large swashes of color and soft edges and shadings and none of the detail the English school loved. In September 1858 he had a studio built in the back yard of his home on Touro Street.

On October 18 William started taking lessons from Hunt. By now the boy had been given a good deal of instruction in art, having drawn for Benjamin Coe in New York and Léon Cogniet in Paris in the winter of 1857. The Boulogne dream of going out into the fields and making discoveries with a microscope had faded, the boy was increasingly anxious about choosing a vocation, and Hunt was a great inspirer of the young. He had persuaded Steele McKaye to forget Harvard and apprentice himself to Couture (a pseudo-classical French artist very popular with Americans), and he drew the talented John La Farge away from his law studies in New York. Hunt was a devoted artist, but he taught with what the future novelist remembered as "an easy lightness, a friendliness of tact, a neglect of conclusion." His style of teaching was altogether different from Henry Sr.'s (or Leverett's), and it bestowed a special authority on the painter, who became in Harry's admiring eyes "from top to toe and in every accent and motion, the living and communicating Artist."

The boys' education had reached a stage where their father could feel his control challenged. He believed that youngsters were "under the dominion of sense" and thus rightly responsive to "mere sensuous forms," but a grown man must learn to dwell among true spiritual substances like "goodness and truth, love and wisdom." Hunt posed an insidious challenge to the power of the abstract, allegorized Word. "His speech is broken and too exclusively professional for me," James confided, identifying the two aspects of the painter's talk that proved so attractive to his boys, who liked, precisely, that "broken form of discourse." At home there was the constant pressure to articulate and rationalize and "convert," and at the Berkeley Institute one was stuffed with stilted oratory. In such contexts Hunt's gestural and pictorial language created the subversive margin of freedom the adolescent mind seeks out.

The studio's intoxicating air can still be sensed in an anecdote dating from the summer of 1859, when the painter's star pupil came to town. As Steele McKaye later recalled, Harry, Sargy, and some other boys happened to be on one of their frequent walks when William ran up in great excitement. "There's a new fellow come to Hunt's class. He knows everything. He has read everything. He has seen everything—paints everything." The new fellow was John La Farge, the product of a family of aristocratic French *émigrés* who had found a home in New York City. La Farge had studied under Couture and claimed acquaintance with some French writers. He seemed incredibly informed, wore black velvet jackets or "cool white" suits (depending on the season), and bowed in a way that advertised his refined fastidiousness. For Annie Fields, he was the "mediaeval type," but for young Harry he was simply "the 'European' "—someone whose mannered self-exhibition marked him as a consummate man of the world. The boy felt an intense admiration for La Farge's serene assumption of independent superiority, for the "settled sovereign self" that never seemed to yield "the first inch of any ground." La Farge had Father's defiant hermeticism, but without being at all theological or abstruse. The lesson the future novelist learned was that the parent's absolutism could be imported into the world of art and literature. A painter, a writer, could *also* be haughtily self-sustaining, austere, worldly, and professional all at the same time. Thus, while William took lessons in drawing and painting, Harry learned how to craft himself. This was the art of self-creation, and for a boy whose father scorned the

professional world of writers, it was also the art of self-defense. One day
La Farge proposed to Harry that they drive out into the country and find
breakfast somewhere and then paint—"*we* paint." Mary did not at all
care for La Farge's influence on her son. "I know no man," she warned
him, "who strikes one so disagreeably—he is *so* selfish and filled with
pretention and conceit." A few years later, when the painter came for
a "visit of *two weeks*," she was relieved to see that he "exacts very little
of Harry in the way of long talks."

There was a moment in the spring of 1859 when Henry Sr. was so
pleased with William's "capital progress in drawing with Wm Hunt" that
he contemplated another year in Newport. But the moment passed, and
afterward, reconstructing the decision to return to Europe, the father
said that he and Mary had been afraid William felt

> a little too much attraction to painting—as I supposed from the contiguity
> to Mr Hunt: let us break that up[,] we said . . . I hoped that his career
> would be a scientific one, as I thought and still think that the true bent
> of his genius was towards the acquisition of knowledge: and to give up
> this hope without a struggle, and allow him to tumble down into a mere
> painter, was impossible.

The clear choice for William would have been the Lawrence Scientific
School at Harvard, which would initiate him into the mysteries of science
without the stultification of the usual "college course." But Henry Sr.
and Mary were not about to let their seventeen-year-old son live away
from home without parental surveillance. If William roomed with other
youths, as his father had at Union, he would be tempted, corrupted,
depraved. Only if he continued living with his parents would it be safe
for him to enter Harvard. Once again the Jameses went up to Boston to
look for a furnished house. And once again they couldn't find one that
was suitably large and comfortable.

Years earlier, writing Emma Wilkinson, Mary had sent a "double share"
of kisses for her namesake, little Mary James Wilkinson. No doubt the
parents' preferential distinctions felt completely natural and inevitable.
There appeared to be no other choice. The whole family would have to
go to Geneva so that William could enter the academy, as the fledgling
university was then known. They booked passage on the *Vanderbilt*,
which was scheduled to leave New York for Le Havre on October 8.
Sargy was "in depths of a boyish despair" when he got the news, and he
never forgot the evening he and Steele McKaye (who was back from
Paris and Couture) saw the James boys off on the New York ferry. Harry,

too, was torn, writing Sargy on the day of embarkation that he was "thinking much more of what I leave behind than what I expect to find." The family probably occupied one of the finest first-class cabins, as the passenger list begins with their names—"Henry James, lady and 5 children, Mrs. Walsh."

Ma had died that summer, spending her last week in "painless quiet, sleeping most of the time." A couple of months previously, the ball of Henry Sr.'s left thumb developed a strange growth resembling "baked-apple." Diagnosed as a "tumour," it was removed by Dr. Henry J. Bigelow of Boston. This, the patient's second experience of surgery, proved infinitely less painful than the first. The doctor administered the anesthetic as James talked, and when he came to, still talking, he didn't realize that the operation was over and done with. As the truth dawned, the man of words felt his "dignity seriously wounded." Then it came over him how beneficent the "gift of ether" was, and he felt a tremendous relief. From now on, his children would be rescued "from pain whenever pain becomes a terror."

GENEVA AND BONN

At the Geneva Academy William took a class in anatomy and dissected a cadaver. He studied osteology, a subject that wasn't offered, by reading an up-to-date manual on his own and getting permission "to visit the Museum and there examine the human skeleton by himself." He received advanced, systematic instruction, but he was also indulged, and the lesson he had drawn from his earlier education was reinforced: you are free to follow each and every respectable interest, you will not have to choose.

For Harry, there was painful discipline followed by complete freedom. Having decided he was too interested in light literature, his parents sent him as a day student to the Institution Rochette, a cram school for polytechnic aspirants. The building was grim and black and faced a prison where "none but the most harmless and meekest of men" were incarcerated. Harry took science and math and studied hard and wrote bravely to Sargy about catching up, but it was only in his memoirs that the truth came out: he did as badly as he'd done a few years earlier in New York in Forrest's class in business arithmetic. He couldn't catch on, felt humiliated at the blackboard, and in the end knew himself to be "an obscure, a deeply hushed failure." After five months or so of this penitential ordeal, it was conceded the boy might just as well amuse himself with French, German, and Latin literature and audit whatever he liked at the academy.

Alice became a day student in a girls' school. If her fellow pupils were as cliquish as the Genevese boys her brothers couldn't approach, she must have had a miserable time of it. At the end of the year, her father tersely admitted she had not done well: "Our chief disappointment . . . has been in regard to Alice, who intellectually, socially, and physically has been at a great disadvantage compared with home." Nothing more, but it looks as if Geneva was a disaster for Alice.

The younger brothers, Wilkie and Bob, now irrevocably grouped together, were (as William put it) "destined for commerce." As this glib formula indicates, their future was much less open and ambiguous than William's or Harry's, and little anxiety was expended on their educational needs. Back in Newport, "it was not thought desirable" to send them off to boarding school, but here in Geneva they were quickly dispatched to the Pensionnat Maquelin out in the country, where they probably followed the curriculum then considered suitable for future businessmen. The following summer, when the Jameses moved to Bonn, Wilkie's tutor had him write "a commercial letter every day in German." Characteristically, all this dull, laborious preparation was fatally undermined at home, or so one gathers from Wilkie's assuming in a letter to his parents that no "decent person" could put himself "on the same par with the merchant."

On Sundays Bob and Wilkie joined the others in their suite of apartments at the Hôtel de l'Écu, on the south side of the Rhône. There, parents and children grew more closely intertwined than ever. The letters written by Alice, Wilkie, and William convey a sense of a close, animated life at home driven by the children's energies, mainly William's. *Adam Bede* came out that winter, and when the Jameses learned that an English hotel family could take no interest in George Eliot's "village carpenters and Methodists," they "quivered as with the monstrosity." Altogether, there were only about a half dozen American families living in Geneva, none of them as stimulating as the Jameses' friends back in Newport. The quiet regularity is evident from one of Alice's letters, which notes as an event worth mentioning that Mrs. Thomas was "not down to dinner yesterday." (The girl was still scrutinizing women's lives for signs of trouble.) There was no possible entrée into good Genevan society. In the spring the Jameses moved to another hotel, just across the Rhône.

In May James complained to Sarah Shaw of having "been cut off from human intercourse this winter." The letter gives the impression he had stuck it out in boring Geneva, but in fact he had left his family behind and traveled to London and Paris. James liked to describe himself as wholly devoted to his children (this being a kind of vocation), and the myth that he was unhappy apart from them was well established in the family. Once, when Alice was trying to write to him but didn't know what to say, someone else got her started by invoking the usual formula in a dictated first sentence: "We have had two dear letters from you, and find you are the same dear old good-for-nothing home-sick papa as ever." Homesick or not, Papa seems to have been absent a matter of months, long enough to seek out "comfortable apartments" in London. Where he stayed and what he did can only be conjectured. He returned home near the end of March. The inspired letter he at once got off to Elizabeth Cranch, whom he'd failed to see in Paris before catching the night train to Lyons, vividly conveys the gallant energies his home life could not contain:

> The night was clean and cold and brilliant with stars. Every time I woke up and gazed at the superb canopy, I thought of my Paris friends, until at last I christened one dazzling orb Lizzy Cranch, another Carry Tappan, another Fanny MacDaniel, and set myself to watch which would first descend below the horizon & prove anew the frailty of man's dependence upon woman. Who could have thought it! But I forbear to state particulars . . .

Late in May James again left Geneva to travel the short distance to Neuchâtel. He wished to check up on Bob Temple, who was spending a year in disciplinary rustication with the Guillaumes, a family in modest circumstances. Afterward he sent a detailed report to Edmund Tweedy, the Temple orphans' guardian. Bob didn't seem altogether hopeless. His "Roman contempt for luxuries" boded well for his capacity for discipline. But he was shockingly indolent, and his mobile grin suggested that "vive la bagatelle" was his philosophy of life. The writer gave a vivid sketch of the young man lying "gathered upon the hill-side under the shade of a magnificent beech." James was the kind of father who brought his impressions home, and Henry Jr. the kind of son who listened with a responsive imagination. In *Roderick Hudson*, his first important novel (with a number of open-air scenes in Switzerland), he would recount the downfall of a self-indulgent painter who bears a strong resemblance to Bob Temple. This work draws on a number of family stories about the *Hudson* Valley Jameses and seems premised on the great James fear that unfocused energies may provoke a sudden and complete collapse of the will.

The family's European program entered its second phase in July. Leaving his youngest son at the Maquelin school, Henry Sr. and the rest took off for Bonn so that the three older boys could study German. Harry and Wilkie were placed in the tutorial household of Herr Professor Humpert and William moved in with the younger and more worldly Herr Stromberg. The lodgings taken by the rest of the family were so ample that Mary had her own sitting room.

In August Henry Sr. and his womenfolk departed for Paris, leaving the three older boys in Germany. Aside from William's two months at Roediger's in 1855, this was the first time the eighteen-year-old youth had been allowed to live away from home. One of his father's last acts was to impress him and his brothers with the importance of keeping themselves chaste in thought and deed. The advice was taken seriously, William replying, "In regard to our self respect and purity, I hope the day may never come when your wishes will be disappointed. I am sure that *I* should as deeply deplore any loss of them in myself as as [sic] you possibly could for me." No doubt Henry Sr. had warned him against the grim practice he had darkly alluded to in the Second Epistle of James to the Tribune—"that horrible self-pollution . . . which is fast turning our young people into puling hypochondriacs." Perhaps he also touched on the youthful depravities that turned colleges into "hotbeds of corruption."*

The original plan, following the summer in Bonn, was to give the boys a full year of schooling or tutoring in Dresden, Frankfurt, or Berlin. That way, the parents would spend two years abroad, William would gain access to one of the chief languages of modern scientific thought, and the other children would surely find a use for whatever they happened to pick up ("convert, convert"). But soon after the family got settled at Bonn, the favored son made the momentous announcement that he

---

* A generation later, when one of William's own sons left home for boarding school, the boy was given this paternal counsel:

Now that you are at Brown and Nicholses, exposed to all sorts of bad boys older than yourself, I ought to give you a word of moral advice. You'll hear a lot of dirt and smut talked, and if you have a taste that way, you can talk it yourself as much as you please, and no one will prevent you, and some boys will grin to hear you. Nevertheless, they won't respect you or care for you as much as they care for a clean-mouthed boy. They mostly outgrow their smut. I know how it was when I was a boy, and you probably know it is the same now. So be clean mouthed; and tell the truth; and shame the devil, though you needn't preach to the other boys about it if you have no wish to . . . You must grow up as straight as any member of the family. It is a straight clean family.

If any boys try to make you *do* anything dirty, though, either to your own person, or to their persons, it is another matter, and you must both preach and smite them. For that leads to an awful habit, and a terrible disease when one is older.

would rather be a painter than a scientist. The decision, he told his
father, was influenced "by my strong *inclination* towards Art, & by the
fact that my life would be embittered if I were kept from it. That is the
way I feel *at present*. Of course I may change."

In spite of having his heart set on a scientific career for William, Henry
Sr. altered course with surprisingly little fuss, perhaps because of a private
conviction that the changeable young man would eventually come
around. He warned him that artists and writers and aesthetic natures in
general tend to neglect their spiritual potential, but he also made sure
his son got the latest issues of a new art magazine, *Gazette des Beaux-
Arts*, and in other ways offered the fullest practical support. Suddenly
everything recrystallized. Steamship schedules were looked into. Plans
were made to return to Newport, where the aspiring artist could again
study with Hunt, this time in earnest. Various considerations were
brought forward to justify the new move, the father admitting that the
family's stay in Europe had been determined chiefly by the "imagined
needs" of William's education, and that it could do no harm to jerk the
other children back to America, since "none of them [was] cut out for
intellectual labors" anyway. This bleak assessment of the four younger
children included the future novelist.

This newly altered course chimed with the father's own inclinations.
Isolated and unproductive, he "had gradually ceased to 'like' Europe,"
as Henry Jr. recalled. He shared the Genevan attitude toward the "degradation" of Louis-Napoleon's annexation of the Savoy and had grown
disillusioned with the Second Empire. When William tried to picture
his three parents in their Paris sitting room, he saw "Mother and Aunt
in armchairs, their hands crossed in front of them, listening to Father,
who walks up and down talking of the superiority of America to these
countries after all." A decade later James summed up his growing disgust
with the Old World: "The historical consciousness rules to such a dis-
torted excess in Europe that I have always been restless there and ended
by pining for the land of the future exclusively."

There is a time to bind and a time to set loose, and sometimes the
looser the better. James supposed that once Harry and Wilkie were back
in Newport they would find friends "among their own sex, and sweet-
hearts in the other," and he hoped the two boys would " 'go it strong'
in both lines." "Early marriages are thought very bad as a prudential step
here in Europe," he added, quite carried away, "but an immense deal of
imprudence may yet be transacted in America with the happiest social
and individual consequences." This passage apparently says that a bad

early marriage might be a very good thing for his second and third sons (but not the first?). Several years later Mary reminded Harry how "Father used to say to you, that if you could only fall in love it would be the making of you."

Henry Jr. was not about to fall in love. Growing up in his tightly indrawn and reverberating family and exposed to the kind of paternal supervision that was both careless and intrusive, the future novelist had learned to guard his privacy and meditate his own purposes and strategies. In Geneva he often spent his free time shut up in his room. Unlike William, who sought public validation for everything he wrote, Harry kept his early compositions to himself. He'd been given an illustrated Tennyson in 1858, and this spurred the boy into producing an imitation of "Dora" and a labored elegy in the In Memoriam stanza and style; both were confided to Sargy's eyes alone. Not surprisingly, the parental act Harry resented most of all was having his mail inspected. Only after Father had left Bonn for Paris could Harry "soften" toward him and accept the "opening of Perry's letter." Apparently the children's mail was still being opened as late as 1863. "I hope such a thing . . . will not occur again," wrote William after finding out that a letter to him from Kitty Prince had been unsealed.

Shortly before the family's scheduled sailing, the three older brothers joined their parents in Paris. Harry was deeply embarrassed by the need to explain the abrupt change of plans, and also by his family's appearance of being grossly uninformed. Leaving Paris for Rhode Island to learn to paint? The future novelist hated to look gauche or provincial and seems to have felt some grave doubts as to his father's judgment. When the time came to compose his memoirs, he completely wiped out the year the family had spent in Newport in 1858–59, leaving the reader to infer that the Jameses had remained in Europe straight through from 1855 to 1860. Judging from an early biographical sketch by W. D. Howells, the novelist began concealing this giant transatlantic zigzag as early as 1882. Around the same time, characterizing the foolish theories of the heroine of The Portrait of a Lady, he wrote that her mind took "a thousand ridiculous zigzags." Alice was greatly struck by her brother's absolutely "physical repulsion from all personal disorder."

When Oliver Wendell Holmes asked James whether his sons "despised" him, the answer was no, "he was not oppressed in that way." One reason he was not was that his children developed complicated strategies for living with his intimate aggressions. William chose art at the end of the family's year abroad partly because art was not in Father's plans: art meant distance, and distance safety. It was after the three older boys had been left behind in Bonn that William noted the paradox: "At home I only see [Father's] faults and here he seems all perfection."

Half a century later, revising this sentence for his memoirs (Henry Jr. revised everything, even if someone else had written it), he made "faults" more emphatic by replacing the word with "striking defects." In general, the aged novelist tried to present an ennobling portrait of his crazed old man. Why did that protective impulse not operate at just this point? Perhaps the answer is to be found a few pages earlier, where we are given an excerpt from the two July 1860 letters to Tweedy in which Henry Sr. justified the family's abrupt return to Newport. The excerpt shows the writer must have read the letters in which his father expressed the view that William alone was "cut out for intellectual labors" and that the other children's educational needs didn't really matter.

At the time Henry Jr. confronted those invidious words, his beloved parents had been dead for thirty years. It was 1913, his three brothers and his sister were dead, and he himself had completed his last work of fiction. Now that it was all over, in other words, it was given to him to see how much had been done for William's sake and how little had been done for his own and the other children's sakes. William's mind had been carefully tended, and his own mind had been alternately neglected and straitjacketed. That treatment was what had brought his strange imagination into being.

Chapter 24

■ ■ ■

NEWPORT AND THE
CIVIL WAR:
1860–64

All along, the military had been a strong and persistent feature in the James family annals. Catharine Barber's father and uncles had helped officer the Revolutionary War, and her future husband had enthusiastically followed its course from distant Ireland. One of their daughters married a West Point graduate who fought the Seminoles in Florida, served on the Rio Grande frontier against the Mexicans, and headed the New York State militia. In the war against secession and slavery, five grandsons volunteered.

Henry Sr., the most aggressive of his brothers, had been in many hard fights over the last quarter century and often talked about manliness and manhood. But he fought with words, his teenage dismemberment having deflected him from action to thought. Also, he held that national independence was a dying superstition, he was alienated from the practical aspects of democratic government, and for all his talk about society he always seemed to assail whatever group he joined.

The Civil War raised troubling questions for the uprooted and privileged Jameses. Did the boys owe it to society to enlist? Should someone with William's intellectual promise imperil his future? What if he or Harry was traumatized by the same horrors—pain, mutilation, the threat of death—that had thrown a pall over Henry Sr.'s youth? The Jameses dealt with such questions in complex and ambiguous ways. Two sons joined the battle against slavery. Two did not. One of those who did flamed out in a great burst of democratic idealism. The two who did not join were evasive, convinced they were inwardly unsound, and all the more anxious to define a public vocation and throw themselves into it.

In retrospect, it looks as if the family chose to sacrifice the expendable sons to action so that the favored sons could be dedicated to thought.

THE JAMESES OF NEWPORT

Back in his native land, James quickly made arrangements to rent McKaye's house at 13 Kay Street, Newport, taking possession on October 1, 1860. That same day he wrote Tweedy in London and asked him to pick up a special dissecting microscope: "Willy needs it & will be much obliged." Already, it would seem, Willy was hedging his wager on art, with his father's encouragement. The next day, thinking of the two younger sons, James sent off for information on an innovative boarding school in Concord.

Newport had become more animated and brilliant, especially in summertime. Anna and Sam Ward had a place at Ocean Point now, and at Lawton's Valley, a short drive north, there was a congenial and stimulating group of seasonal residents that included Julia Ward Howe, author of "The Battle Hymn of the Republic." When young Leslie Stephen arrived in the summer of 1863 to sample Newport's touted charms, "the amusements, as far as I could see, consisted in sitting on a verandah listening to a band of music, the men smoking." But the large tourist hotels were a very different scene from the cottages, and the Englishman lacked an entrée to the private yachting and picnicking, the afternoon drives and calls, the dining out with friends, the entertaining of visitors for a week or two. With their five teenage children, the Jameses were not only in the thick of these activities but helped give them a tone at once high-spirited and intellectual. It was in the early 1860s that the spectacle of their lively domestic life began to attract fascinated comment.

One reason for the fascination was Henry Sr.'s unusual line of talk. He was playful or flirtatious with his children's friends, and when he took on the obligatory note writing other husbands left to their wives, he would whip up the most ingenious concoctions. When Katy Rodgers, one of Mary's distant New York connections, came for a visit and sent a bread-and-butter note afterward, it was Henry Sr. who replied with a cleverly flattering lament: "I think I *could* be a good man if I had any domestic encouragement. I have a susceptible bosom, and an appreciative word now and then from those around me could hardly fail to find a good soil, and bring forth goodly fruit. But an unamiable family is a hard trial to a well-disposed mind." The writer trusted the charming visitor would lay the blame for his defects in character in the proper quarter.

After the Tweedys came back to Newport, their wards, the Temple girls, spent a great deal of time with the James children. At first William got on best with Kitty, the oldest, to whom he sent what is probably his single most effervescent letter: "Thereout fell the Photograph. Wheeeew! oohoo! aha! la-la! [*Marks representing musical flourish*] boisteroso triumphissimmo, chassez to the right, cross over, forward two, hornpipe and turn summerset!" Toward Minny, on the other hand, William was so prickly she wondered whether he had "rather *renounced* [her], in the depths of his heart, as a *bad* thing." That was in the spring of 1863, after she had caused trouble at her boarding school and the headmistress had sent a complaint to Henry Sr. Minny was an unusually outspoken and unflinching girl, the kind who inspires powerful resentments and loyalties. Her bosom friend, Helena de Kay, was warned by her mother not to let Minny "become an engrossing passion." Henry Jr. also became engrossed, so much so that many jumped to the conclusion he was in love with her. But it wasn't love so much as heroine worship: he liked to get close and show sympathy and be petted a little. "Harry is as *lovely* as ever," she wrote Helena from the Jameses' Newport parlor; "verily the *goodness* of that boy passeth human comprehension." William, by contrast, stalked back and forth like a madman, "the same strange youth as ever," Minny wrote, "stranger if possible."

The Emerson and James children became friends, though not the closest of friends. In the spring of 1861, when Edward Emerson was preparing for the entrance exams at Harvard, he came to stay with the Jameses in Newport. The young man spent two hours studying each morning. This was a mistake, in Henry Sr.'s opinion, and he sent a warning to Emerson not to let his "beautiful boy [be] so imprisoned by these baneful books." It was a "shame to starve the physical life out of any deference to the intellectual." Forgetting the educational regimes he had forced on his own children (for the moment the idea was to keep Willy and Harry out of college, not to get them in), James inveighed against "the snubbing of [children's] innocent natural delights." He clinched his point by recalling a macabre Swedenborgian vision—"a woman combing the hair of a child (hair corresponding to the sensual life): and every time she drew the comb through its hair, *blood followed the comb*." This was the inward truth about the imposition of "moral discipline."

Still, James was not about to let his own children go uncombed. The following spring, when Wilkie wanted to join Edward on an expedition to Yosemite's giant redwoods, James said no. His excuse was that Wilkie wasn't serious enough, being less interested in the pursuit of science than in having a grand adventure with a friend. James defended this stern prohibition in a verbose letter in which the words "fear" and "afraid" and "apprehensive" keep resounding like an ominous background rumble. The writer was afraid Wilkie would get into trouble so far away from home. He suspected that the son he persistently underrated would only squander special opportunities.

James complimented Emerson on his boy's equable temperament, a sign that "a new race is getting born, clean, sweet, innocent, without misgivings or distrust such as has palsied us in the past." Next to his own boys, Edward was a "muskmelon among . . . pumpkins." All the same, James couldn't quite believe in Edward, being convinced that a true spiritual life was rooted in a strong physical endowment and great inner torment. For his part, Emerson's son saw the James gang as rather wild. At dinner they became so loud and robustly argumentative and gesticulated so freely with their knives that Mary was moved to reassure their guest: "Don't be disturbed, Edward; they won't stab each other. This is usual when the boys come home."

In the summer of 1862 Edward's sisters, Ellen and Edith, came to Newport for a three-week visit, almost half of which was spent with the Jameses. The two sisters couldn't stop laughing, "what with Mr James and all the four boys." Wilkie and Bob had a sailboat (called the *Alice*), and plans were made for an expedition. Ellen assumed the children's father wouldn't join them, "knowing by experience that he 'liked to make his little plans,' " and Wilkie "hooted at the idea of his . . . going on a sail." During the excursion the twenty-three-year-old woman was allowed to take the helm. Instantly fifteen-year-old Bob, the family's "honest Jack Tar," was at her side with his vigilant advice.

"Envy me, Miss Waterman!" Ellen wrote her favorite teacher,

> I have seen the James Family at home. And it was a sight beyond my anticipations. Every day was Carnival . . . When there were many at the table Mrs James would put all five children on one side that they might crowd no one but each other, and Edith and I contemplated that vivacious row with rapture. "Oh!" cried Robby, beside his Mother as he looked up the long line to Alice beside his father, "Look at the five potatoes!" And it did look very funny to see the row of plates with a great round potato on each.

William was the leader of the revels. With him in the house, wrote Ellen, "one is sure of as much noise, conversation and fun as will keep one laughing from sunrise to sunset. His room was right over ours, and the chronic earthquake that he kept up there would make me roar even alone." Summing up for another correspondent, Ellen reported herself

> perfectly delighted all day with the whole family. Willy is the happiest, queerest boy in the world. Harry the most lovely, gentle and good, Wilky you already know is equally queer and equally good but very different, and Robby, dear child, by his piquant silence and dancing eyes kept us in a chronic fever of curiosity.

Delighted with the whole family? Although Ellen Emerson was no-toriously fair-minded, for some reason she failed to include the boys' sister in these thumbnail sketches. Within the James family, Alice was the object of a relentless flow of ironic, superheated gallantry—"You lovely babe," "Charmante Jeune Fille," "Perfidious child." In Geneva William had gone so far as to write a burlesque lament about her refusal to become his "wife." Outside the family, however, few people spoke of Alice as attractive, amusing, or even particularly likable.

When the time came for Ellen to return hospitalities, she invited the James daughter to Concord for the December holidays. With his usual precipitation, Henry Sr. "gave the palpitating Alice *carte blanche* to go at any expense of health, and got her expectations so exalted, that her more affectionate and truly long-suffering Mama found it one of the trials of her life to reduce her to the ordinary domestic routine." After what must have been an unpleasant scene between mother and daughter, the father tried to console the girl by blithely explaining the relationship between the phenomenal world and heaven:

> [I] say that the Emerson house is only a foretaste of that festivity [heaven], the Emerson girls being what they are only by an interior most unconscious and unsuspected contact with benignities and generosities and sincerities that she shall there see one day, poor child, in beautiful human form. I think however the tears still trickle in solitude.

He could have said, the blood still followed the mother's comb.

This is the first family letter to speak of Alice's health as an ongoing problem. Is it a surprise that the charmante jeune fille turned out to be both pathologically sensitive and tough as nails? "Oh, Alice, how hard you are!" her father exclaimed one day in Newport, leaving her with a lasting sense of the "repulsion" she inspired in his "human benignancy." Alice was scornful of "great Men unable to have a tooth out without gas," and she sneered at George Eliot for fretting over her headaches: "What an abject coward she seems to have been about physical pain." But if Alice drove her nails deep into others, she spiked them all the way into herself. Once she expressed the wish that she would be awake when she died so as "to watch the rags and tatters of one's Vanity in its insolent struggle with the Absolute." John Walker would have liked that.

SHELTER

When James wrote off for a prospectus for Sanborn's school in the fall of 1860, he freely admitted that Wilkie and Bob were "not exceptionally studious." As a rule, the father of a dull boy would "put him in a store, or send him on a cruise" rather than continue to educate him, but James had a reason for keeping his youngest boys in school: school would be the "best shelter." The one possible hitch was that Concord seemed "a little further off than their mother likes." As for their father, what he wished to have explained were Sanborn's "peculiarities of method" in instructing his less talented pupils. Judging from James's disapproval of Edward Emerson's excessive studying, he didn't want Bob and Wilkie subjected to a rigid curriculum or disciplinary system. But neither did he want their idle habits encouraged.

Sanborn's school, a late Transcendental offshoot, was an experiment in coeducation and lofty idealism. Emerson was the school's leading sponsor, and for a time his two girls were enrolled as students. The principal, F. B. Sanborn, a militant abolitionist, had been so deeply implicated in John Brown's raid on the federal armory at Harpers Ferry that he'd been forced to seek temporary asylum in Quebec. All this had taken place during the Jameses' quiet year in Geneva.

The day after the James parents left their two younger boys in Sanborn's care, Henry Sr. sent an exuberant letter to his good friend Caroline Tappan, then on the point of moving from Europe to Newport. Mrs. Tappan's Transcendental credentials were as solid as Emerson's, and like Henry Sr., she went in for "play of mind," especially of the "incurably ironic or mocking order." Some of the more ardent letters Henry Sr. sent her careen so wildly they are easily misinterpreted. Now, although he claimed to be "heartbroken" at having "buried" Bob and Wilkie in Concord, his euphoric tone told a different story:

Out into the field beside his house Sanborn incontinently took us to show how his girls and boys perform together their worship of Hygeia. It was a glimpse into that new world wherein dwelleth righteousness and which is full surely fast coming upon our children and our children's children; and I could hardly keep myself, as I saw my children's eyes drink in the mingled work and play of the inspiring scene, from shouting out a joyful Nunc Dimittis.

Seeing one of John Brown's daughters, he "kissed her (inwardly) between the eyes, and inwardly heard the martyred Johannes chuckle over the fat inheritance of love and tenderness he had after all bequeathed to his children in all good men's minds." There isn't much of John Brown one can recognize in this mellow image, but James was going it strong. Coeducation was new to him and others, and he could not see how his boys would be able to concentrate on their lessons while surrounded by fellow pupils like "arch little Miss Plumley . . . with eyes full of laughter and a mouth like a bed of lilies bordered with roses." He wanted to ask Miss Waterman to "put out any too lively spark" that might be kindled in Wilkie and Bob (playing with the teacher's liquid name), but she

> proved of so siliceous a quality on inspection—with round tender eyes, young, fair and womanly—that I saw in her only new danger and no promise of safety. My present conviction is that a general conflagration is inevitable, ending in the total combustion of all that I hold dear on that spot.

Another erotic apocalypse loomed on the horizon.

At the end of the school year, when the time came to pay Sanborn's bill, James sent a brief note with his check. Now he sounded as if his boys had been given too much freedom and come home rather too often: "It seems to me that you have a good many vacations. I suppose you have good reasons for them." The school had not been wholly satisfactory. The James boys had been much liked (in young Julian Hawthorne's eyes they were as "simple and hearty as sailors on leave"), but they were also bored and restless. Bob wouldn't go back for a second year. Wilkie did, but time dragged heavily. He was too old for school, his future was as unsettled as ever, and many of his friends were enlisting. Some, like Edward, tried to sign up but couldn't get past the physical examination.

The war Wilkie's headmaster had done his part to stir up was raging now. If the father really meant to shelter his robust and restless boy, he would have been wise to let him quit school and join Edward Emerson on that 1862 expedition to California.

IN THE LORD'S HANDS AT LAST

James had praised the *Tribune* for saying "a manful word, ever and anon, upon the crying abominations of negro-slavery," but contrary to what is often said he was not an abolitionist. A subscriber to the *Liberator*, he hinted at his position in a letter he sent this crusading weekly in 1859. He allowed that many current reforms—"anti-slavery, temperance, the woman's movement"—were driven by a belief in human equality. But these causes were only "harbingers" of the new day, James said, seizing the occasion to "whisper" a word of advice to the editor: "If all these specific reforms of yours claimed the authentication of some more universal doctrine . . . they would be greatly enhanced in importance to the popular conscience."

One of the hardest things to understand about James is that he did not feel much sympathy for oppressed groups. In the summer of 1863, when the Civil War was at its apogee and the Emancipation Proclamation had been issued (thus making abolition a thing of the past), he set forth some of his peculiar views on the matter:

> Though I have a great respect for the "Abolitionists" personally, based upon their thorough truth and manliness as contrasted with the sordid and skulking crew who have always formed the bulk of their assailants, I yet have never been able to justify philosophically their attitude towards slavery. They attack slavery as an institution rather than as a principle; that is, on moral grounds rather than spiritual; making it primarily a wrong done the slave rather than one done the master . . . *The practical working of the institution has been on the whole, I doubt not, favorable to the slave in a moral point of view*; it is only the master who from recent developments seems to have been degraded by it, spiritually, out of every lineament of manhood.

Normally, one would not expect to hear a Northern supporter of the war voice the widely held Southern argument that blacks had been improved by slavery. Of course, James did not arrive at this position by any of the usual Southern routes. For him all experience, including whatever was done to the slave, was phenomenal and illusory, a mere adumbration of eternal things. What really counted was how a man saw himself. Slavery was harmful to the slaveholder because it led him to exaggerate his power, to see his selfhood as real and substantial. Yet even James could not always be explaining this disagreeable line of thought, which must have landed him in some nasty arguments before and during the war. Forty years later, recalling the discomfort felt by Northern conservatives, Henry Jr. vividly evoked his father's—and most of the family's—odd position: "It is thus impossible, in looking back on the 'quiet' people of that time, not to see them as rather pitifully ground between the two millstones of the crudity of the 'peculiar institution' on the one side and the crudity of impatient agitation against it on the other."

After Lincoln was elected and the Southern tier of states withdrew from the Union, James got to work on the "universal doctrine" the abolitionists had neglected. By the end of March 1861, he was nearly ready to set forth a "Philosophic view of the crisis" to a Newport lecture audience. This was probably the same oration he delivered a few months later at the town's Fourth of July celebration. Well received locally, the speech was published in Boston by Ticknor and Fields and excerpted in the New York *Evening Post.* Full as it is of wartime bombast and severe reflections on England (which favored the Confederacy), the speech is vintage James, setting forth his long-meditated scheme of the historic development of the sentiment of human equality. Europe stands for the triumph of Protestantism and political liberty, but America's "inward significance" is a new conception of social equality. The idea of "numerous cunning constitutional checks and balances" is European, but the New World idea is that government should be "a grandly social force, reflecting every honest human want." If America has failed to realize itself as history's culminating phase, that is accounted for by the foreign "poison" or "virus" of slavery. But the time has now come for this corrupting residue to be finally and forcibly expelled. The speech makes it clear that James saw the Civil War as an Armageddon in which a newly emerging social order fights one last battle against Europe's cunning political divisions. The real parties to the conflict were not North and South but America and Europe.

Although James's millenarian expectations were extreme even for the time, his undeviating faith served to comfort those who didn't quite fathom his point of view. In the fall of 1862, when the Federals suffered several defeats and many Northerners lost heart for the conflict, one of the Shaws' militant daughters was cheered by the good, strong confidence expressed [by] Mr. Henry James . . . in the people's "coming to self-consciousness," as he called it. When I asked him if he thought it would take long to make them feel that they were the one and only power, and that they must save their native land, he said: "No, perhaps a day might do it. Some manly act on the part of a leader might crystallize the men near him."

James's faith in an imminent and instantaneous transformation scene was stronger than ever, and he was quoted as saying, "When the people do wake up and know themselves, we shall have blessed happy peace forever." As he put it in his Newport oration, "We know not when the hour of this great salvation shall strike." To Wilkinson (who had Northern sympathies), he declared that "the world at last has got fairly into the Lord's hands, and that He is going to have His own eternal way with it." The great transfiguration was going to happen.

James's stress on God's "own eternal way" had a lot to do with his curiously absolutist notion of freedom. The American ideal of liberty, he insisted, "does not flow from any man-made constitution under heaven, but is one on the contrary which all such constitutions are bound under fatal penalties simply and servilely to reflect, being the liberty which is identical with the God-made constitution of the human mind itself." Liberty, this nearly impenetrable sentence says, is neither of nor by the people, nor does it allow separate self-governing spheres or satellites. Instead, liberty imposes a centralized uniformity, a point James makes by means of that strange and quite unpejorative adverb, "servilely." The sentence goes on to praise individual freedom, but not before the diction has flashed a startlingly contradictory signal.

Under the surface, James's idea of liberty was tangled up with something other people thought of as slavery. Liberty, he was hinting, is the good kind of slavery.

VOLUNTEERS

At the time Fort Sumter was fired upon, William had been studying with Hunt for half a year. He did life drawing (his cousin Gus Barker serving as a nude model), and then he went on to paint an oil portrait of Kitty Temple that shows her in profile, looking down demurely at her needlework over a spectacularly rounded bosom. William's talent, John La Farge said many years later, with the generosity of retrospect, was "extraordinary." The young man had shown "promise of being a remarkable, perhaps a great, painter."

Then he gave it up, "with much reasoning and many sophisms, all charming," as La Farge put it. The comment nicely touches off the young aspirant's tendency to lose himself in verbose, self-conscious explanation. Unfortunately, La Farge didn't bother to specify the "sophisms," and a considerable debate has blown up over William's real reasons for quitting. The dominant view, that his father coerced him into giving up art for science, has little to recommend it. The supporting evidence is slender and ambiguous, more obvious motives are available, and the abrupt change of plan is eminently in character. Gifted and indulged, William often found himself torn between competing alternatives. His original decision to become a painter was not the single burning arrow of his being but the expression of many conflicting needs, among them the need for commitment. There had been an ulterior hesitation in his original choice of art over science. "I shall know in a year or two whether I am made to be [an artist]," he had written, leaving an opening for a future change of mind; "there's nothing in the world so despicable as a bad artist." Years later he told one of his two sons who went in for painting that when he asked Hunt whether he should continue, he was told, discouragingly, that America didn't sufficiently value its artists. He said substantially the same thing to his other painter-son: "The year I spent in a studio completely quencht in me all artistic ambition." Finally, there was the question of art's social utility: could an idealistic youth hope to do as much for mankind with a brush and palette as he could with a dissecting microscope?

On top of everything else came the great national crisis of the spring of 1861. Northerners rose in indignation against the South, and there were many public meetings and much drumbeating and volunteering. On April 26, two weeks after Fort Sumter, William signed up as a ninety-day volunteer in the Newport Artillery Company, a state militia unit. He ended up not serving, and the following month, when a much more serious three-year enlistment program began, he did not step forward or seek a transfer. There are many unanswered questions about the episode, but it seems likely that the onset of war played into his growing disillusionment with art and prompted the idealistic and now uncommitted young man to make a token enlistment.

The one point that is clear in this obscure episode is that William's father took energetic steps to keep him out of military service. Writing shortly before Virginia voted to secede (April 17), James described the war fever sweeping the North:

Affectionate old papas like me are scudding all over the country to ap-
prehend their patriotic offspring, and restore them to the harmless embraces of their mamas. I have had a firm grasp for three days past upon
the coat tails of my Willy & Harry, who both vituperate me beyond
measure because I won't let them go. The coats are a very staunch material, or the tails must have been off two days ago, the scamps pull so
hard. The Virginia news is reassuring however, and I hope I may sleep
to-night without putting their pantaloons under my pillow. The way I
excuse my paternal interference to them is, to tell them, first, that no
existing government, nor indeed any now possible government, is worth
an honest human life and a clean one like theirs, especially if that government is like ours in danger of bringing back slavery again under one
banner: than which consummation I would rather see chaos itself come
again. Secondly, I tell them that no young American should put himself
in the way of death, until he has realized something of the good of life:
until he has found some charming conjugal Elizabeth or other to whisper
his devotion to, and assume the task if need be of keeping his memory
green. *

The second reason is in line with James's views on marriage and "manly"
development. But the overwrought attack on slavery, coming from one
who had kept his distance from abolitionism, is not to be taken at face
value. There would be more loud talk in the peroration of James's Fourth
of July speech, where he hoped to see "our boasted political house itself
laid low in the dust forever" if Lincoln or Seward should make any
compromise with slavery. (At the time the administration's policy was
to keep the border states in the Union.) James's rhetoric was a cover for
two powerful feelings—an anxious wish to protect his sons and a per-
sisting contempt for the makeshifts of democratic rule.

The telling statement in James's letter was his repudiation of "any now
possible government." He was fully persuaded that the present political
order was about to be swept away by a new "social" dispensation. As he
told Wilkinson, his prayer was that God would "put every where an end
to the government of man by man, since every such government must
be misgovernment, sheer and simple." The prayer was sincere, but for
a father eager to keep his boys out of the military it was also very
convenient. Why should they risk their lives for a federal state that was
about to wither away?

---

* The one surviving page of this letter lacks the date and addressee. It was probably written to
Christopher or Elizabeth Cranch (thus the "conjugal Elizabeth") in Paris. Like most of James's other
Cranch letters, this fragment has come to rest in the Vaux collection.

The striking fact revealed by James's letter is that even Henry Jr. had been swept up by war fever and was threatening to volunteer. The future novelist wasn't "manly" in the usual way and showed little interest in strenuous physical activity. On April 17 a volunteer militia unit marched from the Newport armory down to the harbor to sail for Providence. Two students from the Berkeley Institute were among them, and William was there to cheer them off. In the middle of the night a fire broke out in an empty house and threatened to spread. Young Henry joined the volunteer crew at an old and wheezing pump. Fire pumping was hard, dangerous work, and the young man suffered an injury he would only describe, in his memoirs, as "a horrid even if an obscure hurt." This vaguely insinuating language left a suspicion after his death that he had sustained an incapacitating genital injury. The pain did not let up, and after eventually speaking of it to his father, the sufferer was taken to Boston for an examination. The surgeon, perhaps the same one who had operated on Henry Sr.'s thumb, only pooh-poohed the young man's complaint. Leon Edel's solution of the mystery—that Henry Jr. had sustained a typically elusive back injury—has won widespread acceptance. In September 1863 the young man was exempted from the draft because of "physical disability."

Henry Jr.'s back problem provided him with a definitive reason not to enlist even while leaving him in the embarrassing predicament of not having much to show. He would be able to relax and read to his heart's content, just as when he was recovering from typhus in Boulogne, but he would also know that others would inevitably put their own construction on his failure to volunteer. Under these circumstances, he took comfort in the fact that he had hurt himself while acting as a volunteer in a quasi-military effort. Fire brigades were seen as a sort of militia, and firefighting had a romantic mystique: "Mose the b'hoy," the New York equivalent of Mike Fink or Davy Crockett, performed his most heroic deeds at fires. The isolated young man was not without a pretext for thinking of himself as one with the young soldiers of the time. If this sense of "tragic fellowship" was mostly imaginary—the novelist's memoirs speak of it as a "queer fusion or confusion"*—it still enabled the young man to feel he wasn't a shirker. At home, the announcement that

---

* In his influential biography, Edel, apparently unaware of the April fire (which accords with Henry Jr.'s "shabby conflagration"), claims he was injured in a much larger fire six months afterward. All later family biographers follow this mistake, which in effect denies the novelist's ability to remember what he was doing at the time of a national calamity as impressive as a presidential assassination. Edel's error in dating nullifies James's point about his youthful imaginative "fusion" of Newport fire and Fort Sumter firing. Charles and Tess Hoffmann have set the record straight.

he was hurt met with instant "sympathies, supports and reassurances." Perhaps his parents saw the accident as a way to keep him from signing up.

While William and Henry were kept out of the war, Bob got a strong paternal assist in joining it. In May 1861, near the end of his year at Sanborn's, the Naval Academy moved from Annapolis into temporary wartime quarters at Newport. The family sailor paid close attention to this exciting development: when William wanted to know "whether any of the mids. [midshipmen] are to be or have been detached to the Charlestown Navy Yard," he directed the question to Bob. Perhaps the academy had something to do with his refusal to go back to inland Concord. At the end of September, soon after the boy's fifteenth birthday, his father took a step that seems flagrantly inconsistent with his tight grip on Willy's and Harry's coattails: he asked Thurlow Weed to use his influence to get one of James's sons admitted to the "Naval School." James didn't say which son, but his description of "a fine boy whose heart has been set for years upon the navy" points to Bob, who had probably coaxed his father into writing some such note. As Henry Jr. recalled, Bob "had strained much at every tether" during the war.

James knew Weed as someone who had run an influential Albany newspaper thirty years earlier and played a key backroom role in state and national politics. Weed had whipped up Antimasonry and then helped organize the Whigs, and now the cagey old pol had an inside track in the first Republican administration. He was a crony of William H. Seward, the Secretary of State, and he got on well with Lincoln, controlling much of New York's patronage during the war. Weed was not obnoxiously corrupt, and James, regardless of the hard language he threw at the government, was not obnoxiously pure. He would have preferred to go directly to the President, he wrote Weed, but of course

the President has no knowledge of me, and my chance is small to succeed, unless some friend endorse me . . . I have just that sort of feeling of your great good nature, which leads me in a desperate strait to apply to you to give me that needful endorsement, and to confide, in case of your not being able to grant it, in your pardoning the application.

The only surviving official reply is dated the following year, on October 11. It was scribbled by none other than Seward himself, with hurried wartime corrections (not noted here):

Washington

My dear Sir:

Your note of the 30th ult has been received & I have with pleasure made the recommendation which you requested.

Yours very truly
W. H. S.

The Hon. Henry James
    Newport R.I.

Inquiring at the Naval Academy, one finds an old file on nominees that still contains a card for Robertson James. It reads:

BORN: 16 IN AUG. 1862
B.6–P. 13—J56

What the second line means is anybody's guess. If it could be deciphered, it might clarify the obscure anticlimax of this little episode—the fact that Bob never became a "mid." All that is known is that the following year his father was still "a little sorry that he was disappointed in his naval aspirations."

KNOWING AT LAST WHAT THEY ARE ABOUT

William began his studies at Harvard in September, the same month Henry Sr. got his note off to Weed. That was in 1861, the year two of William's first cousins *left* Harvard in order to enlist. Willy Temple, of the Temple orphans, was universally seen as a paragon of youth, a brilliant foil to his loutish brother Bob; he got killed two years later at Chancellorsville. Gus Barker was the handsome youth who stood on a pedestal for Hunt's life-drawing group. In October he was commissioned second lieutenant in the 5th Regiment New York Cavalry, and by the time he was twenty-one, he'd made captain. He was routed by Stonewall Jackson's cavalry, nearly died of typhoid fever, got well, was captured by Mosby's guerrillas, and went to Libby Prison. After being exchanged, he rejoined his regiment, "fought all day" at Gettysburg and lived, and was afterward picked off in the woods of Virginia by sharpshooters. One ball caught him in the right side, another in the left. They carried him to a church near Kelly's Ford, on the Rappahannock, and he died in the middle of the night.

Living in Cambridge now, William felt "turned out of doors." At first

he "did not know what to do with [him]self or how to fill [his] time."
He missed his family and, following his parents' wishes—and his own
—made a point of informing them whenever a suitable house became
available. It was taken for granted that the family would join him in
Cambridge or Boston when the opportunity arose, that they would all
live there together, and that this would be the ideal arrangement. Money
was an issue, and there were occasional exhortations from Newport not
to be extravagant. Once he found a note on his table from Wilkie, who
had walked the fifteen miles from Concord for some brotherly companionship: "Father will send money to morrow! He is going to break your
head for spending so much!"

William's letters home often echoed Henry Sr.'s opinions, as when
he reported that a funeral sermon was a "prolonged moan"—"a whine
consciously *put on* as if from a sense of duty." Even when he had to
correct Father's scientific ignorance, he did so in a way that showed
where his loyalties lay: "The fact is, 'quantitative' [analysis] is a higher
branch than 'qualitative' among chemists, and they often as in this case
confound other affairs with their science." The latter pronoun is symptomatic. William may have decided for the time being to study chemistry,
but it was not and never would be *his* science. But what science was?
Only once do his first year's letters show any real enthusiasm for the
scientific disciplines then taught at Harvard. After a long talk one night
with a student of Louis Agassiz, William wrote, he finally saw "how a
naturalist could feel about his trade in the same way that an artist does
about his." Once again the versatile youth was swept away with an excited
vision of a course of study other than the one he was following. Years
later his chemistry teacher still remembered William's fondness for "excursions into other sciences and realms of thought," and also that he
was "irregular in attendance at laboratory." His grade in organic chemistry was 85, definitely so-so.

One of William's first purchases in Cambridge was his father's recent
book, *Christianity the Logic of Creation*. If William read the slender volume, he would have found a saccharine quotation from Thackeray on
King George III's madness, followed by Henry Sr.'s reflection that anyone
could be overtaken at any moment by "some hideous calamity." The
possibility of a sudden attack of insanity or worse came up again and
again in William's letters. In one of them, he imagined his future course
of study with Harvard's leading biologists spinning out of control in a
terminal crash: "One year study chemistry, then spend one term at home,
then one year with Wyman, then a medical education, then five or
six years with Agassiz, then probably death, death, death with inflation

and plethora of knowledge. This you had better seriously consider."

Although William's actual course of study in the years ahead roughly followed this program, he had no way of knowing as yet that biology and medicine would enable him to specialize in a field just being born, "mental science," or psychology. Neither could he have realized that his own erratic mental state would last for twelve years and more. Seeking to explain William's weak performance in chemistry, his first professor supposed he was troubled by "ill-health, or rather by something which I imagined to be a delicacy of nervous constitution."

Why was William studying something he didn't find congenial while Willy Temple and Gus Barker and other young men his age were fighting in the great crusade? The question must have been agonizing. Seventy years later, his oldest son explained William's failure to sign up by his obvious "physical and nervous frailty," and then briskly dismissed the subject. * At the time William no doubt realized that his nervous troubles fully justified his remaining a civilian. All the same, there was little comfort in such a reflection, especially for someone so indecisive and erratic he couldn't help wondering whether his will was diseased.

Was it any consolation to learn that Father was also as unpredictable as ever? Henry Sr. had passed two winters in McKaye's comfortable house when a Newport realtor named Alfred Smith tried to interest him in an attractive property on the edge of town—a large stone house with six bedrooms and enough land for a stable. Smith would become legendary as the man who marketed Newport's Bellevue Avenue to big New York money. He was a wizard at matching men and land and houses, and he knew exactly what James was looking for, having gotten a letter of inquiry from him in 1860 from Bonn. James told the realtor he wasn't interested, as he still intended to move to Cambridge, but Smith smelled a deal and kept pushing. The reason his clever sales pitch is known is that James told a fellow passenger all about it on the Providence ferry, and she communicated the story to her husband, and the Newport Historical Society now holds her letter. The realtor persuaded James to at least have a look at the house, and then,

> says friend Alfred, "suppose you make an *offer*, you can get it cheap," "but I don't want it," "well but say what you would give for it," so more to stop the conversation than anything else, Mr. James says, "I'd give $6,000 for house & furniture," & went home thinking that sum perfectly

---

* In 1918 this son enlisted as a private at the age of thirty-nine, refusing officers' school; he seemed determined to see combat, as if he hoped to make up for his father's failure to enlist during the Civil War.

absurd, what was his surprise, when the next day, up comes Alfred, with
the necessary documents, to inform him that Mrs. Breeze accepts his offer.

I do think Smith is a remarkable man, with wonderful talents for his
business—he no doubt ascertained that Mr James was looking for a house
elsewhere, and he determined to make him live in Newport.

The writer of this gossipy letter was right on the money: $6,000 is the
price on the recorded contract, with the furniture included. The dwelling, on the corner of Spring and Lee, had two full stories and was built
of cut, uneven stone. Apparently the attic was too cramped to allow for
servants' quarters and extra sleeping rooms, since the first thing the
Jameses did with their new property was to have the roof raised six feet.
The house still stands, and although it has been turned into a funeral
home, there is a visible line high on the south wall topped by a few last
courses of more finely cut stone—meaning the stone cutters also succeeded in lightening James's pockets. The remodeling was pushed through
by summer, in plenty of time for Ellen Emerson's gales of laughter as
William turned his capers in the renovated top floor. Ellen's word for
the house was "beautiful." One of its features, an impressive staircase,
was ripped out decades later to make room for the funeral parlors, with
nothing to show for it except a mortician's story of his Auntie May
walking in afterward and shrieking, "You've ruined this beautiful house!"

While Mary went out to supervise the remodeling, Henry Sr. stayed
home and passed the time composing a serendipitous comic riff for his
youngest brother, Howard:

> I have established my financial reputation afresh: by buying a house at
> half its worth. I shiver to think how soon I may be elected a director,
> and next President, of the Newport Bank; and how sure an elevation of
> that sort is, to lead to my being called to one of the great cities to preside
> over financial circles there. I shan't go. People who would like their
> interests presided over by me, may come to Newport. I think it altogether
> probable they will. But it is absolutely certain that I shall not go away
> . . . The ocean breeze shall fan my fevered brow and lift my flowing hair
> (or rather my flown hair) while I live . . . So you see I know what I am
> about at last.

How would Henry's father have reacted to the spectacle of his idle,
middle-aged son preening himself on a shrewd business deal, burlesquing
the old ideal of the respected sharp-dealing banker-businessman, and
simultaneously allowing friend Alfred to dip into the family's money
drawer?

On the other hand, William of Albany couldn't have written a letter as good as Henry's in a million years. And Henry had the last laugh in another way as well, for when he and Mary sold the house and its furniture the following year to a woman from Philadelphia, they got $8,000 for it.

SHRINKING BACK FROM BEING RECOGNIZED

In September 1862 Henry Sr. gave stark expression to the emerging differences between his second and third sons. He sent nineteen-year-old Henry Jr. off to Harvard, and on the twelfth of the month he "witnessed the enrollment" of seventeen-year-old Wilkie at the Newport recruiting station. The following May, when Bob enlisted at the age of sixteen, the father laid claim to "heart-break"—but rejoiced nonetheless that his most troublesome son had been lifted "out of indolence and vanity."

Henry Jr. had wanted to go to Harvard in 1861, when William did, but Father said no, "deprecat[ing] the 'college course' with such emphasis" that the question seemed closed. One year later, however, the young man was becoming increasingly restless. "Just staying at home when everyone was on the move" was humiliating, especially during wartime, and so he once again brought the matter up. This time Henry Sr. told him "in the most offhand and liberal manner" that Cambridge "wouldn't be wholly unpracticable." The son was glad to have his father's consent but resented the bland inconsistency and wondered why he had been kept home for a year.

Avoiding the regular "college course," Henry Jr. entered the law school, of all places. He vaguely supposed it would be an introduction to a cultivated sort of life, but the performances of his fellow students soon disillusioned him. Taking no more interest in the law than his father had thirty years earlier, the young man spent a lot of time in his room writing short fiction—"mainly of a romantic kind," as his friend Sargy remembered. Romantic meant sensational and melodramatic, "dripping with lurid crimes," in line with the French fiction Henry had been reading. Romantic also reflected his and his father's alert interest in shocking murders. In 1857, for example, when Madeleine Smith was tried for her ex-lover's death by arsenic, the future novelist seems to have gotten an unforgettable shock when she was found innocent. Now, quietly pushing his pen in his room in Cambridge, he was becoming what he " 'wanted to want' to be . . . just *literary*." Presently he began submitting his work to the magazines.

At the time Henry Sr. accompanied Wilkie to the recruiting station, the preliminary Emancipation Proclamation was still ten days away. Years later, this son gave a heavily regularized account of his and his parents' motives: "To me, in my boyish fancy, to go to the war seemed glorious indeed, to my parents it seemed a stern duty, a sacrifice worth any cost." But Wilkie tended to project his youthful antislavery enthusiasm on his father, whose ideas were more tangled and ambiguous than the younger sons quite realized. When Bob left for service in July 1863, his mission, in Henry Sr.'s mind, was to promote "that Divine spirit of liberty which is at last renewing all things in its own image." The one thing that was communicated was the spirit of zealotry.

What had happened to James's unwillingness to see his sons risk their lives for "any now possible government"? Part of the answer lies in the distinction he drew between volunteer state units and the regular Army or Navy. When Wilkie enlisted, it was with a nine-month volunteer unit, the Massachusetts 44th. Bob signed up with a similar group, the 45th. After the young man had taken this step, his father defended it as vastly better than joining the regular Navy:

> All liveries are bad, I suppose, viewed absolutely; but a volunteer livery, inasmuch as it is imposed less by the government and more by the people, or reflects a social rather than a political obligation, seems very much inferior in prestige to the other, and consequently much more favorable to the manhood of the wearer.

That is to say, Bob and Wilkie were doing the more manly thing because they weren't backed by the full power and authority of the federal government. Instead, they were participating in the spontaneous action of the people. They were out in the open, spearheading the great leap forward from the political to the social. Implicit in this strange interpretation was a willing embrace of a higher degree of risk as being more manly.

After seeing some confused combat in North Carolina, Wilkie began to look forward to the end of his brief term of enlistment. Afraid that the government would ask the volunteer militia to re-enlist for three-year terms, he wrote home to say that he could do so if the country asked him to, "but it would come hard I assure you." Statements like this could not have made William and Harry feel particularly satisfied with themselves. When Edward Emerson learned that some friends had been wounded in action, he broke out: "Oh don't you envy them? Don't you envy them? Wounded for their country! They can feel that it has cost them something." In January 1863, when the two older James boys were home for Christmas vacation, their father informed Wilkinson they thought of "going down to labour among the contrabands, or now, thank God, the *freed* blacks. They have applied for places, but have as yet not heard of the success of their application." He was referring to the Boston Educational Commission, which had begun sending volunteers to the liberated tidewater areas of South Carolina to promote "the industrial, social, intellectual, moral and religious elevation" of former slaves. William's and Harry's applications were turned down, it seems, but at least they had tried to do *something*.

Soon after Wilkie's enrollment, it was decided to form the nation's first black regiment, the 54th Massachusetts. If this radical venture was going to succeed—and many thought, hoped, it would not—it had to be officered by white "gentlemen of the highest tone and honor," who believed "in the capacity of colored men for military service." The man the governor of Massachusetts sought as commander of the regiment was Robert Gould Shaw, son of Henry Sr.'s old friends Sarah and Francis G. Shaw. It had been Sarah (ironically enough) whose fears for the future well-being of her one boy and four girls had elicited James's darkest confessions about his own early years as a parent, and also his blithest assurances.

Once Robert Gould Shaw agreed, reluctantly, to head this dangerous experiment, the next problem was to identify able and willing subordinates. Most white officers would have felt degraded serving in a "nigger" outfit, and there was a Confederate statute that any white man in command of blacks "shall, if captured, be put to death." Wilkie James was one of the select number asked to volunteer. He consented to do so and was transferred from the white 44th to the black 54th, in the process incurring "many sharp rebukes" from his fellow soldiers. When another black regiment was formed soon afterward, Bob volunteered for that. It isn't supposable that either son would have taken on these scorned and perilous assignments without paternal backing. And so it came about that the father whose relationship to slavery and abolitionism was so conflicted, and who had been so extremely protective of his children, sent his two youngest boys, teenagers, up against the deadliest American form of social inequality.

While the 54th was in training at Readville, Henry Jr. made a single visit from nearby Cambridge. In his memoirs half a century later, he supposed the scene must have been sinister and sad—perhaps simply through the fact that, though our sympathies, our own as a family's, were, in the current phrase, all enlisted on behalf of the race that had sat in bondage, it was impossible for the mustered presence of more specimens of it, and of stranger, than I had ever seen together, not to make the young men who were about to lead them appear sacrificed.

This was the view of a fairly conservative white man living in an age of reaction and looking back at an era he now judged to be somewhat unrealistic. In fact, the family's sympathies had not been "all enlisted" (the phrase merits a double take) on the side of black slaves. At the time William had this to say about his and others' lack of fervor: "[Wilkie] is the best abolitionist you ever saw, and makes a common one, as we are, feel very small and shabby."

The day the 54th marched through Boston bound for the coast of South Carolina was like the day a century later when civil rights marchers tried to cross the Pettus Bridge in Selma, Alabama—one of those sublime moments in which the people stage the never resolved struggle between their heroic idealism and their savagery. As the country's first black foot soldiers threaded the city's streets, they were greeted by applause and jeers and catcalls and hurrahs, and also by barely suppressed threats of physical outrage. When they marched past the house of Oliver Wendell Holmes, out he came supporting Henry James, Sr., who was there (in Bob's words) "to say Godspeed to his boy." William Lloyd Garrison, founder and editor of the *Liberator*, was stationed at another house, and as Shaw saluted him and then rode on, tears ran down the old abolitionist's—and pacifist's—face.

Shaw's nineteen-year-old sister, Josephine, was a passionate believer in the war, a well-educated young aristocrat, and a "fine horsewoman." Riding beside her fiancé, Charles Russell Lowell, Jr. (who would also not come back from battle), this Massachusetts Valkyrie "came whirling up on horseback" as her brother's regiment marched by. She happened to rein in just behind where William James was standing in the crowd. "I looked back and saw their faces and figures against the evening sky," he was able to admit decades later, "and they looked so young and victorious, that I, much gnawed by questions as to my own duty of enlisting or not, shrank back—they had not seen me—from being recognized. I shall never forget the impression they made."

Henry Jr., whose relation to the war was also "a sore and troubled, a mixed and oppressive thing," wasn't present. In his 1914 memoirs he implied, twice, that it was not his fault he was "helplessly absent." But he never made clear exactly why he hadn't come over from Cambridge to see Wilkie go.

SO MUCH MANHOOD SO SUDDENLY ACHIEVED

That was on May 28, 1863. Three days earlier Willy Temple had been buried in Albany Rural Cemetery. Because the ground on which he'd been killed was held at day's end by Secessionist forces, weeks had passed before the body was recovered and shipped North. A correspondent with the initials T.W. (Thurlow Weed?) noticed a box with the dead officer's name on it in a Hudson River baggage car. The box must have been pried open, but all T.W. would say was that the young friend he scarcely recognized was " 'smear'd in dirt and blood.' " The James clan was desperate to find the bright side. Henry Sr. told Minny that continued life would have been fatal for Willy's soul, as "no human-being can stand for a life time without almost superhuman strength the spontaneous *worship*" he had attracted. Howard wrote to express the sanctimonious hope that Willy's death would shame bad brother Bob out of "his troublesome habits." No such luck. Bob served in the Army for the duration, never got scratched, never stopped drinking, and couldn't get promoted to second lieutenant because of "bad habits."

On July 17, Wilkie's regiment was ordered to lead an assault on Fort Wagner, South Carolina. This attack, as pointless and poorly thought out as the charge of the Light Brigade, has become one of the best known events of the Civil War. In the last century Augustus Saint-Gaudens commemorated it in a stirring bas-relief that stands opposite the Massachusetts State House, and in the 1960s Robert Lowell, a World War II pacifist, wrote a poem about it that is too shattered to be beautiful, and all the more beautiful for that. In order to approach the fort, Shaw, Wilkie, and the rest of the regiment had to run for a mile or so over exposed sand straight into punishing fire. Shaw was one of many who never came back. "He is buried with his niggers," a Southern officer was reputed to have said. "When it was suggested, after the war," Jane Maher writes, "that Shaw's body be exhumed and buried in a place of honor in New England, his parents insisted that it was already buried in the most honorable place possible: with the black men whom their son had led into battle."

Wilkie got shot in his foot and side and was barely able to crawl away. One of the stretcher-bearers who helped rescue him had his head shot off. If the father of a fellow officer, Cabot Russel, hadn't shown up

looking for his son (never found), Wilkie probably would have died; it
was Mr. Russel who escorted him back to the Jameses' home in Newport.
A trip to South Carolina would have been difficult at best for Wilkie's
one-legged father, and Bob couldn't have gone because he was in service
by this time, but why didn't William or Henry go down? "Vivid to me
still is one's almost ashamed sense . . ." wrote the novelist a half century
later (referring, it is true, to something other than his helpless inactivity).
Even while Wilkie was still en route, Henry Sr. confessed that "I seem
to myself to be far more interested in the fate of Bob Shaw and poor
missing Cabot Russell [sic], than in Wilky. Cabot was lovely to my eyes."

When the wounded son was finally carried into the house at the corner
of Spring and Lee, he was so weak he couldn't be moved off the stretcher,
which remained just inside the door: the war's blood, dirt, and pus had
come to the foot of the Jameses' beautiful staircase. Henry Sr. kept his
friends—Sam Ward, Caroline Tappan, Elizabeth Peabody—informed of
his son's condition and state of mind. As Wilkie recovered, his chief
desire was to rejoin his unit. He bitterly resented the fact that his men
received less pay than white soldiers. His father was surprised at the
strength of his attachment to his outfit and hinted more than once that
it was somewhat excessive. "I rather suspect him of deeming the negro
superior in all qualities to the white, except command," he told Ward.
To Tappan, who always invited a note of slight mockery, he reported
that Wilkie was "vastly attached to the negro-soldier cause; believes (I
think) that the world has existed for it; and is sure that enormous results
to civilisation are coming out of it."

What particularly impressed Henry Sr. was the sight of "so much
manhood so suddenly achieved." How could a thoughtless, idle boy have
managed this great achievement? The point that interested Ward was
the manhood of the blacks. Were they as brave under fire as whites would
have been? Would Henry Sr. ask? The question reflected back on the
proud mystique of Anglo-Saxon masculinity. But it was hard to bring
the matter up with Wilkie, who struck his father as overly "sensitive
about the colored troops." Then a letter came from Bob declaring that
the 54th had "fought like devils, but to no purpose," and with this as
an opening Henry Sr. presented the question: had the men "wavered,
or fallen into confusion," so as to make one question "their pluck and
endurance"? Wilkie's answer was categorical. There was no wavering,
the confusion was temporary and resulted from an accidental mix-up,
and the charge was then renewed "with a yell of enthusiasm never
surpassed." Henry Sr. wasn't entirely satisfied with this response and
asked his boy a few more questions, delicately, without "awakening his

suspicions of my object." Afterward, James cautiously informed Ward that if the blacks had shown any "hesitancy," the boy seemed to be "perfectly ignorant and unsuspicious of it." He was equally unsuspicious of the depth of his father's private reservations.

One Sunday the young man said, " 'Come now, father, sit down here & take my hand in yours, and preach me a sermon.' " Taking his text from the Twenty-third Psalm ("The Lord is my shepherd, I shall not want"), Henry Sr. proceeded to develop the idea that God looks after all of us alike and that we should have faith in His care. Then he was interrupted by his son, who had a story to tell. After he had been carried unconscious to a field hospital, he came to in the night lying on sand under a tent. Next to him he heard a groan, "a poor Ohio man with his jaw shot away." James's letter recounting the story continues:

> "Finding that I was . . . unable to move, [the jawless man] crept over on me and deluged me with his blood. At that moment I felt"—here [Wilkie] stopped too full to proceed, and I suppose he was going to say, that then he felt how hard it was to hope in God. But the story made me realize some of the horrors of this dreadful war.

It isn't known whether James went back to his sermon after this vivid account. Henceforward, Wilkie walked with a pronounced limp.

THE LITERARY LIFE

In November 1863, as the Jameses made plans to leave Newport, a flattering notice appeared in the *Newport Daily News*:

> The removal of Mr. James will be deeply regretted by our community, as he is a gentleman of rare endowments and of the highest literary position, and is one of those gentlemen of refinement and culture, who, by settling among us, are fast reviving the Augustan age of "old Newport."

James's principal wartime project, *Substance and Shadow*, was designed to settle "the internecine contest between Religion & Science." Settling a contest did not mean peace negotiations, as far as James was concerned, but, rather, the scorched-earth policy and no prisoners. The chief enemy this time was none other than Immanuel Kant, whom James seems to have been reading with measureless outrage. Hadn't Kant realized that to say that the world and God were unknowable in themselves was to disturb the "foundations of human belief"? The man had exhibited a "fatuity unpardonable in a philosopher," and James put him in his place by professing a "hearty conviction that he was consummately wrong, wrong from top to bottom, wrong through and through, in short all wrong." Near the end of the book, James announced, "I might indeed stop short here, because I have already answered as I went along, either directly or by implication, every question my reader will probably feel prompted to put to me." It was said that William designed a picture of a man beating a dead horse for the title page.

Substance and Shadow cannot be taken seriously as philosophy, but it offers some fascinating glimpses of its author's subterranean processes. "The tap-root of every one's spiritual character," he says at one point, "is the conception he entertains of God." At another, speaking of his own natural feelings for God, James writes:

> I hate Him with a cordial hatred . . . for His alleged incommunicable infinitude, for that cold and solitary grandeur . . . For all this difference between God and me as affirmed by my natural deism,—which is my reason unillumined by revelation,—my crushed and outraged affections writhe with unspeakable animosity towards Him.

Juxtaposing these two passages, one gets a sense of the seismic instabilities deep within this thinker.

Emerson read James's book and appreciated its "pure & absolute theism:—there is but one Actor in the Universe,—there is no self but devil;—all must be surrendered to ecstasy of the present Deity." But why was this serene doctrine set forth in a tone of "perpetual contemptuous chiding"? There was surely "some deduction from pure truth to generate all this wrath."

Substance and Shadow was published between Wilkie's departure for South Carolina and the attack on Fort Wagner. James's letters from this interval indicate that the book's reception weighed more heavily on him than his son's danger. He believed he had finally captured "the inner force of the Xn truth," and he was dying to know what Emerson would say and how the reviewers would jump. He sent "thanks, many thanks," to Elizabeth Peabody for her praise of the book, adding, "I wish you would say a word to your friends about it, to give it currency." He bragged about an expected review in *The Atlantic Monthly*, impatiently awaited Godwin's notice in the New York *Evening Post*, and complained of Ripley's delay in bringing out his notice. This was the summer of Gettysburg, the New York Draft Riots, and so much more. On August 7 Ripley gave

James almost two full columns in the *Tribune*. No other book the news-paper reviewed that summer got comparable treatment.

Back in 1861, when James discovered that Parke Godwin had bought into the *Evening Post*, he sent a note to his old friend, and an extended correspondence followed. For the first time since 1859, James had a potential outlet in the large-circulation New York press, and he promptly asked for and got a notice of his Fourth of July speech. Three years later, as the 1864 election approached, he happened to read an essay in the Paris *Journal des Débats* contrasting the Southern policy of McClellan, the Democratic nominee, with that of Lincoln and the Republicans. The essayist, Prevost-Paradol, who favored the Republicans, warned that a premature armistice would result in an independent Confederacy and a greatly weakened North. The Frenchman hoped the North would persevere and demand the South's unconditional surrender. The argu-ment so impressed James he urged Godwin to have the piece translated for the *Post*. (He also reported that an abandoned baby boy had been found in the Jameses' front entry—they were living in Boston now—with "a suspicion of Tweedy in his features.")

After the war, when it appeared that the extirpation of the virus of slavery had not brought in a perfected social order, James looked forward to the election of General Grant, who would see that the South would at last be "properly looked after." Southerners were "the most absurd people on the face of the earth: very little above the negro in intellect, and below him in heart." He bombarded Godwin with a series of ex-tremely long letters evidently intended for publication in the *Post*. Some of these, judging from a reference to the Strong divorce case, were written in the winter of 1865–66. Had they appeared, they would have seriously damaged their author's reputation. Explicitly rejecting individual rights, he questioned the assumption that the state should distinguish between "public and private interests." "This democratization of government," he wrote, is the "*reductio ad absurdum* of the popular superstition under which the intellect has been so long stifled." James's latest shocking message to the world was that "democracy is the crowning invention of human stupidity." This was not exactly what he had proclaimed to the citizens of Newport in his Fourth of July oration during the first year of the war.

Chapter 25

■ ■ ■

NEW ENGLAND SAGE:
1864–74

At the end of 1863 James found a buyer for his recently acquired Newport property and resumed his frustrating hunt for a large furnished house in Cambridge or Boston. A friend reported him as still looking in February. He and Mary were in their early fifties now. When they found what they wanted, at 13 Ashburton Place, it was their first home in a large American city since 1855. We have "settled down here for the remainder of our lives," James announced, somewhat rashly.

Being settled in Boston meant it was time to get rid of the house in New York. By now it was clear the family would never move back, and the sons were making heavy drains on the parents' capital. On November 28, 1865, Henry Sr. and Mary deeded their Fourteenth Street property to Eliza Harriet Greene, the surviving member of the couple that had leased it ten years earlier. She paid $24,000.

The family had virtually reconstituted itself in Boston. Wilkie was home recovering from his foot wound for much of 1864, and William and Harry gave up their lodgings in Cambridge and moved back in with their parents. (The two older brothers were listed as boarders in the city directory that came out in mid-1865.) Bob finished the war with his regiment, sending his parents a string of complaints from the South and clearly wishing he, too, could rejoin the family circle. His parents told him to stay where he was and do his duty.

At war's end, Wilkie went off to a risky cotton-growing venture in Florida using free black labor and $5,000 and more of family money. Technically, the investment was Henry Sr.'s, but morally and emotionally the son was held responsible for the outcome. Wilkie was resolute, hopeful, and quite unprepared for the troubles to come—illness, insect pests, plunging markets, shifty business partners, and a surge in violence from vengeful Southern whites determined to keep former slaves from becoming citizens and Yankee carpetbaggers from making any money.

Although none of the other children took equivalent risks, they all made tentative excursions away from home with varying degrees of success. William joined Louis Agassiz's collecting trip up the Amazon in 1865 and discovered he was not cut out to be a naturalist after all. In 1867, troubled and unwell, he left for a year and a half in Germany for study and health, as the formula went. Two years later Henry Jr. enjoyed a wonderfully stimulating and restorative European tour, meeting the leading English writers and getting his first ecstatic taste of Florence and Rome. His and William's extended trips abroad were paid for by their parents. Bob, bouncing back and forth between Northern railroad jobs and the Florida plantation, got nothing comparable.

Alice's first lengthy move away from home occurred when she and Aunt Kate went to New York for the winter of 1866–67. There, at 1303 Broadway, the young woman became a live-in patient in the home of Dr. Charles Fayette Taylor, a pioneering orthopedist and specialist in women's complaints. James spoke of this doctor as a friend and praised his office as "one of the most interesting places in New York to visit," owing to the display of mechanical contrivances for curing "spinal & hip-joint" deformities. It may well be, as Jean Strouse has suggested, that Alice's treatment involved physical exercise. It also seems probable, given her doctor's views on women's health, that she was given a heavy dose of ideological restraint. One of Taylor's papers, "Emotional Prodigality," recounts the case history of a girl who was languid and irritable and gave "evidence of curvature of the spine." The doctor determined that the source of these problems lay in the girl's occasional visits to her grandmother, a "very intellectual woman" whom the girl looked forward to seeing "with great anticipations." He ordered the visits stopped, and in no time at all the girl cheered up and her back became perfectly straight. Taylor had a withering contempt for "so-called 'higher education' for women."

A couple of years before subjecting his daughter to this spine straightener, James had a lively correspondence with Gail Hamilton, an inspirational and very popular essayist. (It began when she nailed him as the perpetrator of an anonymous letter.) Hamilton agreed with James that women should be "distinct and different from man" but scolded him for insisting that women (in her words) "be kept away from the tree of knowledge."

Alice wasn't kept from books, but unlike some of her female cousins she was never sent away to school. Minny Temple boarded at an academy for girls that was run by a pair of Robertson sisters. Kitty James, high-strung and often unwell, went to a school in Orange, New Jersey, and then to the Sedgwicks' excellent school in Lenox. Alice went to a day school in Boston taught by a Miss Clapp, and during the winter of 1865–66 she seems to have joined a class taught by a Miss Brown.

CAMBRIDGE

The Jameses didn't own their residence at Ashburton Place, and when the landlord raised the rent to $2,500 in the spring of 1866 and demanded a two-year lease, they decided such a commitment would be too risky in view of the outlays the children were likely to require. They secured a large and comfortable perch in Swampscott, which got them through the summer, and all the while they kept up their interminable search for a permanent dwelling place. Finally, they found one in Cambridge for $2,000 a year, located on Quincy Street, the eastern boundary of Harvard Yard. Their new landlord, Louis Thies, was a curator in the library. Across the street was the home of William's former chemistry professor, Charles W. Eliot, from 1869 the college president. A few doors north were the large and imposing homes of Professors Agassiz and Wyman.

The house proved satisfactory, and for the next fifteen years, the longest time by far the Jameses had ever lived in one place, 20 Quincy Street was home. James was able to buy the property in 1870, after which he and Mary were householders once again, with upkeep and taxes to think of. One year they had the rooms repapered; another, they successfully petitioned to have a streetlamp installed. The lot ran through to Prescott Street in the rear and had a lawn to be mowed and a wisteria vine to trim. In the 1872 tax rolls the house and stables were appraised at $22,500.

Of the eleven houses on the block, the Jameses' was the only one that had a simple foundation plan, without any of the fancy excrescences then in vogue. It was a large, rectangular building, three stories high and standing on a slight rise, with a driveway curving up to the front porch. Judging by a photograph taken soon after it was sold (the Harvard Faculty Club now stands on the site), it was a very solid-looking, dignified building. There were four large rooms on the first floor, each with its own fireplace; perhaps Henry Sr.'s library was here, his desk facing the window he liked to gaze through in the intervals of writing. There were five bedrooms on the second floor. The servants' rooms were up on the "mansard story" and the kitchen in the basement, thus keeping the sounds and smells of cooking remote from the parlors, dining room, and library.

When the census marshal stopped by on July 2, 1870, he found three Irish-born servants sharing the Jameses' quarters—Eliza W. Smith, twenty-two; Elizabeth Newton, twenty-nine; and Catherine Black, forty-two. As always, there was a good deal of friction between the domestic staff and the woman of the house, with frequent turnovers. Eliza in particular required the closest watching. "In your provision of fruit for the table," Mary warned her careless husband, "do not be too lavish, for she always serves for herself a double share."* Once, when Eliza got sick and James sent his absent wife a pathetic sketch of himself holding the girl's head up, Mary was indignant ("Where *was* Lizzy?") that he hadn't been shielded from this sorry trouble. The Jameses' most dependable servant was someone named Ellen. After she left, Henry Jr. felt "a real pang" and tried to believe she would return to the family, being "the very keystone of the arch."

Under "occupation" the census taker penciled in some of the usual categories:

James	Henry [Sr.]	author
	Mary R.	keeping house
	William	physician
	Henry Jr.	author
	Alice	no occupation
Walsh	Catherine	no occupation

William had taken his medical degree and was to that extent a physician, but instead of going into practice he had sunk into a mysterious and ongoing malaise. Somehow the son whose growth had been accelerated in boyhood was stalled on the threshold of adulthood. What he would be and do in life seemed completely unsettled. How to choose was part of the problem. For the time being he read, voraciously, in all fields.

Author, meanwhile, was exactly the right label for the two Henrys. The elder's essays and reviews and the younger's short stories, reviews, and profiles were appearing in the best American magazines of the

* Mary kept a jealous proprietary eye on her pantry. When Tom Perry dropped in for breakfast at a time when she was peeved at him and then asked for eggs, he was told there were none in the house. "Whopper," commented Henry Sr., who had heard his wife mutter that Tom "shant have a single one of my eggs."

time—*North American Review, The Atlantic Monthly, The Nation*. Henry Sr.'s literary career was on the rise again, but his appeal was no match for that of his son and namesake, whose magazine fiction, polished and smart and with no apparent doctrine for ballast, was "much more generally read" than the father's work. Writing rapidly and steadily, bad back notwithstanding, Harry had surged ahead of the other men in the family. For the first time in two generations, the Jameses had a professional worker with the discipline and canniness to make his way in his chosen field. The young author became friends with William Dean Howells, second-in-command at *The Atlantic*, and they had long talks about the direction American fiction ought to be taking.

As shrewd as he was energetic, Henry Jr. built his career with a deliberation Henry Sr. hadn't been capable of. Where the father was always overwriting, the son had a masterly and tantalizing line of understatement. His hope was to become a "(sufficiently) great man." His aim in his first novel was to compass a "certain form." There was a certain facelessness in the young man's work, so that you wondered about his feelings and opinions, especially when he wrote about people who were overlooked. But he didn't write about the downtrodden and he avoided local color like the plague, preferring to refract the world through the lens of high formality. He had a high regard for quiet good behavior, announcing in an early story that "we can imagine no figure more bewitching than that of the perfect young lady" under trying circumstances. He drew on family history (in his first serial novel a man who resembles a gambler and is desperately short of money shoots himself in a hotel), but he gave nothing away. When Henry Sr. pressed him to bring out a collection of his early work in 1873, even offering to pay for the stereotyping, Henry Jr. wisely turned him down. That first novel hadn't made it from serial to book, and the early stories would require extensive revision. He knew his slightly later international fiction was much stronger, and he wanted that to define him with the public. Also, Father's career had made it painfully obvious that paying a publisher to bring out whatever was on your mind was not how it was done.

All the same, there was a great deal of the father in the son. Henry Jr. didn't beat the drum the way the old man did, but he was exceptionally high-minded and severe in his judgments of current literature, and in his reviews he assumed the mantle of authority with an aggressive twitch. His solemn denunciation of *Our Mutual Friend* was a restatement of his father's case against Dickensian grotesquerie: "Let us boldly declare it, there is no humanity here . . . [Humanity] is in what men have in common with each other, and not in what they have in distinction . . .

[A novelist] must know *man* as well as *men*, and to know man is to be a philosopher." The young reviewer had an embattled anti-modern note and came out strongly against the modish, the fleshy, the deterministic; he was absolute death on moral and aesthetic vagaries. He rather sneered at Flaubert's "realistic *chique*," and he was offended to the quick by Whitman's *Drum-Taps*. The poet was pretentious, egotistical, and vastly uninformed, and he was given a condescending lecture on the nature of art, which "requires, above all things, a suppression of one's self." "You must also be serious," Henry advised the bard, "you must forget yourself in your ideas."

Whitman's working-class family was radically democratic and full of scorn for official authority. When his mother saw Henry Jr.'s unsigned review of *Drum-Taps* in 1865, she called it "a long piece with flourishes." Forty years later, the novelist was so ashamed of the "little atrocity," which he blamed on "the gross impudence of youth," that he wouldn't tell an inquirer where it had been published. But the impudence of youth was only part of the story. Henry had been brought up to say no in thunder to everything Whitman represented. Only twenty-two years old, the young writer was already an excruciatingly disciplined professional, with dozens of screens between the blank page and his own feelings and experiences. "Suppression of one's self" was exactly what writing was all about for him. Self-expression would have to wait some thirty years, until after he had survived his early success and his punishing mid-career and suddenly unfurled his strange late manner. Until then, what Whitman said about American literary culture in "Song of the Open Road" would apply particularly well to Henry James the novelist:

> *Keeping fair with the customs, speaking not a syllable of itself,*
> *Speaking of any thing else but never of itself.*

CONVERSATIONS IN CAMBRIDGE AND BOSTON

The senior author continued to take a lively interest in current affairs. When Andrew Johnson showed up drunk for his inauguration in 1865, there was a long and angry letter from Henry Sr. in the New York *Evening Post* defending the President against the English journals that trumpeted his shame. When there was intense public interest in 1873 in two convicted murderers who were not given stays of execution, he sent a long letter to the *Boston Daily Advertiser* suggesting that chloroform be substituted for hanging, or better yet, that the death penalty be abolished

—not for the criminals' sake but to stop all the "sentimental sympathy" for them. When war broke out between France and Germany in 1870, he and Mary rooted for Prussia, which stood for the "highest civilization." He quarreled with Swedenborgians, wrote long letters to correspondents who wished a fuller understanding of his teachings, and delivered occasional lectures. Summers, he and Mary tried one inviting locality after another—Pomfret in northeastern Connecticut, Scarborough Beach in Maine, Bread Loaf Inn in Ripton, Vermont. Ideally their vacation would be spent close to friends—Francis Boott, E. L. Godkin of *The Nation*. How Godkin "roared over [Father's] jokes," Alice remembered. Failing good companions, there would be a receptive audience for James's monologues, with Mary informing the children that "Father seems happy & is an immense favorite among the ladies." At worst, if the hotel turned out to be noisy and dull and full of "respectable common people," the Jameses could go back home and sweat it out on Quincy Street.

Literary society in Massachusetts was much better organized than in New York, and a man who knew how to visit and be visited and speak his mind and use the language was likely to be a prized acquisition. Definitely not a native, James was the kind of colorful outlander who would fill a want anywhere, especially in Boston and Cambridge. He was brilliant and necessary in small, private, intellectual gatherings, being in James Russell Lowell's opinion "the best talker in America." His talk moved like no one else's, flowing on its own juices, rich in anecdote, vigorous, critical, comprehensive, unusually genial but with dangerous undertows. The novelty of his views together with his good faith and enthusiasm gave him a sort of license, an exemption from the usual prudential considerations. The intemperance and extremism often came out looking like a special sort of wit. His social and intellectual peers were able to relish his conversation without getting anxious about his ideas. The anxiety was for "disciples," or the poor Swedenborgians still warding off his tireless assaults.

James brought a kind of intellectual glamour to Boston and, fully conscious of his role, knew there was no need to kowtow to the serried Bay State gods (as young Howells, an Ohioan, had to). He met and measured the local great as an equal, and inasmuch as he often took William, Henry Jr., and Alice on his forays, they inherited the entrée he commanded and assumed his habit of easy, superior judgment. New England was settling into a kind of Indian summer, but the James children were not oppressed by the veneration that proved so deadly to the local younger generation. Henry Jr. in particular, just setting out as a writer, was able to profit from his father's superb connections, but without compromising his own sense of professional artistry. Also, his early European experience gave him a considerable advantage in a culture still secretly afraid of being colonial; the young writer got a lot of mileage from this.

The Brahmin who ranked first with Henry Sr. (leaving Emerson and the Wards out of the picture) was the man from whose house he had watched Wilkie's regiment marching off to war—Oliver Wendell Holmes, doctor, poet, witty autocrat of the breakfast table, and writer of psychological novels. When a controversy blew up over Harriet Beecher Stowe's shocking revelations on Lord Byron's sex life and Holmes took her side, he was "backed very heartily on one occasion" by James. Annie Fields reported that James placed Holmes "very high, above almost all other men of our time perhaps at the head."

Somewhere near the foot was Henry Wadsworth Longfellow, for whom James had very little use, "the good inoffensive comforting" poet having dissipated all his "human substance." At a time when Longfellow was the center of a group that was zealously translating Dante, Godwin came to dine with the Jameses. Henry Sr. took him into his room and shut the door and anxiously inquired whether he read Italian. The next question was "Did you ever read Dante?" This time the answer was "No." "Ah," said James with relief, "then I have a brother yet." The "dear dismal old" poet belonged to the past, being of no interest except to "those 'd——d literary fellows' who are all memory, being shut up to it as a miser is to his money bags." James was for burying Dante "six fathoms deep out of human memory."

Another man of the past who was definitely not James's brother was the art historian Charles Eliot Norton. The son of the man who had blasted Emerson's Divinity School address as the latest form of infidelity, Norton had been a precocious child, so earnest and studious the other boys called him "Pope Charles." In the early 1850s he had written an anonymous attack on the radical ferment of the time in which he stated that the new "schemes for social reorganization . . . have repelled sound-thinking men by the mystical and affected method of their declarations and formulas." In James's eyes, this conservative social critic seemed "attenuated" and "spectral," a smiling, mothlike zombie. Norton wasn't fully incarnate, and when he encountered someone solid and real, like Hawthorne, he would extend "his long antennae" and stroke the man. How Norton viewed James may be inferred from an incident of 1873, when James took a carriage to Shady Hill to make a polite call. Norton had just returned from Europe but was too busy "arranging his books" to see his visitor. He wasn't even "civil," sniffed Mary, who blamed his ungracious behavior on his "very strong antagonism to Father's views."

Mary's account of this rebuff was sent to Henry Jr., who had got a great deal of advice from Norton on how to look at certain paintings and churches in northern Italy and also how to regard the vulgarities of American culture. It was Norton who opened the *North American Review* to the young novelist's first reviews of contemporary fiction. So even as Henry Sr. taught his son how not to take Cambridge at its own evaluation, Cambridge pointed out a certain path away from Henry Sr. This worried Mary.

Annie Fields, wife of James T. Fields, Boston's top-drawer publisher, made her Charles Street parlor a salon for writers and talkers and kept a journal that noted their comings and goings. James being one of the regulars, Annie noticed he wore his moods quite openly, often being animated, occasionally depressed, and always exceedingly severe in his judgments. Carried away, he would come out with the most shocking and offensive opinions, which he would afterward retract with abject contrition. Once, in accepting an invitation, he vowed with mock solemnity "not to perplex the lovely atmosphere which always reigns in your [home] by risking a syllable of the incongruous polemics your husband wots of."

James's ardent manner caught the fancy of Bostonians and gave rise to many stories about him. On one of his trips to Staten Island to see the Shaws, it was said,

> he found them just taking tea preparatory to going to Brooklyn to hear Mr [Henry Ward] Beecher preach. They tried to persuade Mr James to go but it was hard work—at last Mrs Minturn prevailed—After the service was over Mrs M. asked him how he liked it. "I was so much moved by it" he said "that if your husband had been there I should have kissed your hand!"

The anecdotes that circulated about James often involved his enthusiastic response to female charms. After meeting a certain Miss Palfrey at dinner, he exclaimed to Annie Fields (the hostess): "What a perfect Art her conversation is. I never heard anything like it! I hated her at first but I admired her before I left. It is exquisite, the perfection of sex." Regular Bostonians didn't talk like that.

Once, making a morning call on Mariana P. Mott, who was visiting from Pennsylvania, Annie Fields found James already on the premises and recorded what he said:

He observed that circumstances had placed him above want and inheritance had given him a position in the world which precluded his having any knowledge of the temptations which beset many men. His virtues were the result of his position rather than of character—an affair of temperament. He said society was to blame for much of the crime in it and as for that poor young man who committed the murder at Malden* it was a mere fact of temperament or inheritance. He soon broke off his talk saying it was "pretty well to be caught in the middle of such weighty topics in the presence of two ladies at 10 o'clk in the morning."

When Mrs. Mott died after "a good deal of suffering," James told a mutual friend (with his usual challenging bluntness) that she had lacked "truth in the inward parts." On the other hand, she definitely had the perfection of sex: "How *thoroughly* womanly she could appear! No mother half so generous, no sister half so credulous! no wife half so confiding. She made one feel . . . what a lovely thing the marriage of man and woman will be when it becomes lifted out of animal into human dimensions." Mrs. Mott's great virtue was a "faculty for intimacy," which allowed James to "explore one's thought to her . . . with unparalleled frankness."

Caroline Dall's diaries offer a frank and vivid record of how James explored his thought with confidential women friends. Dall was a writer and book reviewer and an activist in the women's movement; she was separated from her husband at the time James first met her. She made a strong impression on him, and in a later meeting he tried to describe—*to her*—his initial reaction. Her journal entry recording this meeting is technically a quote within a quote—a narration of what James had originally told his wife about Dall and now repeated for the diarist's ears alone. " 'I have had a curious experience,' " he'd said to Mary (and now to Dall); " 'we had a little talk—I think *she* [Dall] was on her guard.' " ("I *know* I was," Dall at this point confided—to her diary.) " 'She said little, did not assert herself, but I *felt* her *predominance*, wanted her approval, found myself growing diplomatic in order to obtain it. I was conscious of a sort of dread, wh. I never feel for a man.' " Then, ceasing to quote himself, he added, "So I am now"—meaning he was conscious of the same feeling as he spoke. It was a kind of confession, one that not only revealed a private conjugal scene to a relative stranger but made a dizzily self-referential display of the speaker's inner life. And even as James turned himself inside out, as it were, he addressed his new

* Edward W. Green, heavily in debt, had killed a man while stealing $5,000 from the Malden Bank director's office.

acquaintance in the third person. Dall thought it was "the funniest thing I ever knew. It never seemed to me for a moment that he was talking about me." She repeated the conversation to a friend and "he fairly rolled on the floor in convulsions of laughter."

After the Jameses had Dall to dinner, there was an argument between Henry Sr. and his sons about the gender of this forceful woman's mind, the sons judging it to be masculine but the father pronouncing it "remarkably feminine." To Dall's consternation, he then sought by letter and in person her "*own judgment* on the subject!!" This obsessive interest in the question reminded her of a friend's (a man's) jaundiced opinion of Henry Sr.'s "fussy & futile distinction of sex." The friend's private name for Henry Sr. was "Absolute James."

The following year, when Elizabeth Peabody accused Dall of an unknown but apparently grave offense, James promptly became Dall's champion, not only offering sympathy but questioning Peabody's "goodbreeding" and personally reproaching her; the episode marked the end of James's friendship with the well-known reformer. Dall felt depressed during this difficult time and was troubled by other uncertainties. Most of all, she "wanted a fuller richer life." It happened to be the spring of 1866, when the Jameses were leaving Ashburton Place for Swampscott. Dall came to bid them goodbye, and since Mary was busy packing, the visitor saw Henry Sr. alone. As the visit came to an end and Dall stood up to take her leave, "a dreary tremor passed over" her. Looking down at James, who kept his seat (because of his amputation), she held his hand "with a light farewell clasp." Then (according to her diary) he "drew my head down with a gaze—as compulsory as a blow—and kissed me on the mouth." It was like "an electric shock." It was "prolonged, steadfast—and compelling," and while the kiss lasted, the serious woman conducted a "keen intellectual inquisition into its purpose." Afterward, "a divine Pity—seemed to stream from his eyes—but I felt as if the kiss sealed a compact." Then it was back to mundane life, with James once again taking it upon himself to be her champion and Dall nervously trying to regain her composure:

> "People shall not talk about you in this style—I will not let them"— he said as I rose & said coolly "thank you"—and then I laughed—as if any handful of dust could check the current of this world's petty hate!

When the year ended and it was time to make an abstract of its signal events, Dall wrote, "Henry James—April 25, 1866—Kiss."

For a biographer, the question is whether this unhappy and indiscreet diarist may have blown the cover on the games James liked to play with the ladies of New York, London, Paris, Newport, Boston, and Cambridge. Not adultery, not the bedroom, but a rarefied and involuted though still intimate conversational expression of sensual desire, culminating on at least one occasion in a passionate and forceful kiss. The scene with Dall seems to re-enact James's idea of human sexuality—two utterly distinct sexes drawn together by generic attraction but unable to find satisfaction until the final, phalansteric moment of history. One thinks of James's harping on gender difference, his constant anticipation of what marriage will be when it is "lifted out of animal into human dimensions," his endless romancing of women, and wonders whether he was a strange one-of-a-kind sex specialist, practicing an arcane Victorian talking cure.

As for Dall, she, too, was left with a keen but unresolved "inquisition." There was no second kiss to clarify matters, and the friendship seems to have petered out. The best commentary may be her own nervous snort of a laugh.

NOT CLUBBABLE

On the last Saturday of the month Boston's select literary society, the Saturday Club, gathered at the Parker House for dinner, cigars, and high-toned conviviality. Hawthorne was a member in spite of being what Anna Ward called "painfully shy," and in 1861, when James went up from Newport as an invited guest, he saw the aging and elusive author for the first and probably last time. James was seated at such a distance he could scarcely see and hear him, and even so had to strain out the chatter of Frederic Hedge, a great clubman. Rustic and mannerless, Hawthorne "buried his eyes in his plate, and ate with such a voracity that no person should dare to ask him a question!" He looked like "a rogue who suddenly finds himself in a company of detectives." But he was obviously the real thing, a man, and not a mere member of society—and how thrilling it was "to see him persist in ignoring Charles Norton."*

James was elected a member of the Saturday Club late in 1863, when he was on the point of moving to Boston. Senator Charles Sumner had

* The original letter lacks the comment on Norton's engagement that Henry Jr. tacked onto the version in *Notes of a Son and Brother*. In this comment, the novelist has his father referring to Norton as his young fiancée's "snuffers"—the same strikingly repellent image appropriated by Gilbert Osmond in *The Portrait of a Lady*.

been admitted the previous year. Other members included Emerson, Sam Ward, Lowell, Longfellow, and Holmes. James attended from time to time—in 1873, for instance, when there was a grand turnout to welcome Emerson back from a trip to Egypt—but his name does not show up very often in Annie Fields's attendance records. At home James would declare that Holmes "was worth all the men in the Club put together" and heatedly object to "Lowell's manner of snubbing" him.

Once, after James walked out of a meeting of the Saturday Club and James T. Fields wondered why, the answer was that "Hedge was so impolite, so personal and unkind in his remarks, always bringing up Swedenborg against [James]." This teasing may have masked a perse-cutorial or even vindictive attitude; the seating chart for the Emerson dinner shows Hedge squeezed in at the last minute next to James, as if in pursuit. If so, there was a reason for Hedge's animus. He was a "Rev-erend Doctor," a member of the class James loved to trounce. After hearing one of James's lectures, Annie Fields noted that he hadn't failed "to whip the 'pusillanimous' clergy, and as the room was overstocked with them, it was odd to watch the effect. Mr. James is perfectly brave, almost inapprehensive, of the storm of opinion he raises." Hedge's un-kindness blew from out of that storm.

The Radical Club was another circle that sought, with mixed success, to pull James in. Founded in the spring of 1867 and lasting until 1880, this club consisted of Boston's most prominent "freethinkers"—religious liberals no longer comfortably Unitarian. They met in the home of Mary and John T. Sargent, 17 Chestnut Street, where they would listen to and then discuss a paper. Unlike the Saturday Club and the earlier Town and Country Club, the Radical Club was open to women as well as men. It was seen as Boston's brainiest and most advanced discussion group and was sometimes made fun of.

James attended several meetings of the Radical Club and read a few papers to it. One of them was solicited in order to get a new fall season off to a "brilliant" start. In accepting this flattering invitation, James predicted his paper would be of particular interest to those "concerned with the problems of the future." He hoped "some serious people" (nam-ing James Freeman Clarke) would be there. "But probably they will have other engagements," he at once added, "so dont give yourself any con-cern." Mary Sargent was not one to ignore a hint as broad as that, and when James began reading his paper on "Nature and Person" at eleven o'clock on a fall morning, four heavyweights had been lined up as dis-cussants, Holmes among them. The paper seems to have been somewhat mystifying, judging by the secretary's diligent but not always comprehensible summary of the proceedings. Evidently James set forth his basic idea that selfhood is both necessary and evil: "Personality is the dense mask behind which the Supreme Artist securely operates the enlargement of our nature in giving it gradual social form." The speaker proved more accessible in his provocative applications, as when he "affirmed that the rage for multiplying schools and colleges in our country was a real insanity" or announced that the spiritual world was "fast becoming a complete nuisance to human thought." The reactions of the first three respondents weren't recorded, but when Holmes's turn came, he gracefully compared his feelings to those he would have if a chemistry lecturer asked him for an opinion of a test-tube precipitate that had been passed from hand to hand until it became "turbid." Holmes would prefer "to take the essay home, slowly assimilate it, and not talk about it until it had become a part of himself. This closed the discussion," the secretary noted, "but many of the members lingered to talk over the essay socially."

Another circle that drew James in for a time was the Examiner Club, founded in 1863 and affiliated with the liberal *Christian Examiner*. Meetings consisted of monthly suppers at the Parker House with a paper "no more than ½ hour in length," followed by discussion. Topics were to be in "Theology, Philosophy, and General Literature, including Political and Social Ethics." James became a regular member on April 3, 1866. Few meetings drew more than fifteen members, and as usual James skipped much more often than he attended. Yet thanks to one particular secretary, J. P. Quincy, who tried to record comments "verbatim, or very nearly so," the Examiner Club ledgers provide the closest thing to a tape recording of James's philosophic talk we are likely to get. They document the part he played in Boston's intense symposia, showing where he chose to remain silent and what provoked him into speaking and how rarely anyone agreed with or expanded on his ideas.

On January 3, 1870, James read a lecture on "Revelation" to his fellow Examiners. When he was done, someone wished to know whether "create" was being used in its etymological sense. James doubted it was "but claimed a 'logical instinct' for his use of the word." Hedge declared he did "not see the distinction between 'create' and 'make.' " James replied, "You *make* out of another thing, but *create* out of your own personality." When his nemesis noted, skeptically, "It is after all a question whether there is any such thing as Creation," James answered according to a strictly Swedenborgian formula: "As we are only forms of life ourselves, we can only conceive of forms." Presently, a man who had not yet had a go spoke up:

> Mr Wasson: You have said that the natural involves the realm of our identity; but I cannot agree that the identity of man and mineral is the same.
> Mr James thought that a mineral had an identity and a distinctive self.
> Mr Wasson: Then you have a singular way of using the word "identity."
> Mr James: I should feel abashed if I felt identity with the Holy Ghost. I do not claim to possess individuality of character, but my identity is very strong. [Meant to illustrate his use of "identity."]

Mr. Wasson drew back and another contender entered the ring:

> Mr Whipple: Why do you call angels phenomenal . . . ?
> Mr James: Because the angel is involved in the man. This is the temporary manifest[at]ion. Angels see their true being in God, not in themselves. They see that He is the only Individuality.

Mr. Whipple fell silent, but near the end he renewed the attack with a suave question that made James bristle:

> Mr Whipple: I should like to ask you, Mr James, what you have to say to those who maintain that it is utterly impossible for man to think or speak on such subjects as you have introduced tonight.
> Mr James: Say, well, I dont know—perhaps I should ask them, where they lived!
> Mr Whipple: I refer of course to the prevailing scientific belief of the period.
> Mr James: It can be no man's belief; it is only put forward as a defence against theological criticism.

This was the voice of Absolute James, disallowing that others could believe what he knew they didn't. But the last word was reserved by the ironic recording secretary:

> After this satisfactory disposition of the modern sceptical spirit, the Secretary's notes show no general conversation. The members of the club went out one by one, physically and mentally—full.

The next month (James being absent) the minutes were read and "a murmur of appreciation [was] elicited by the remark with which Mr Whipple brought the conversation to a conclusion." But Mr. Whipple wished the minutes had been more complete:

Mr Secretary, you have omitted the best thing I said. I explained to Mr Frothingham the difference between *make* and *create* thus: So long as you make money we will receive you with all honor, but if you attempt to create it, we shall put you in prison.

James stayed away for more than a year, not returning until April 3, 1871. On this day Mr. Chaney read a paper proposing that Thomas Huxley's two arguments for the existence of a self, "the trustworthiness of memory and the constancy of Nature," could form a generalized argument for a rational belief in the existence of God. Hedge, who was always present and always talked, opened the discussion by flatly disagreeing. If this application of Huxley's argument were sustainable, anyone who believed he had a self would be a monotheist. But such is not the case, and hence the argument is fallacious. Others joined a very vigorous argument on atheism, the relationship between conceptions of deity and degrees of civilization, and the problem of self-consciousness. The talk (as reported by Quincy) was exceptionally crisp, with many keen inferences and questions and a continual invoking of the opinions of famous men. What would be the precise difference, someone wondered, between two equally cultivated men if one was an atheist? At this point a very different sort of voice made itself heard:

> *Mr James:* Is not this discussion going astray because we do not take into consideration the difference between knowledge and belief? We say we believe in the existence of God, because we are ashamed to say we know it.

Following this comment there is the one and only hiatus in the minutes—a row of x's—implying that the secretary did not bother to record what Mr. James went on to say. Evidently his line of thought was judged to be irrelevant or tiresomely familiar. When the other men spoke, it was to participate in a collective and urbane canvassing of certain open questions. When James spoke, it was to state on his own authority what everyone knew but had somehow failed to recognize. The next comment, by Hedge, reads like a sly judgment of James's way of talking: "Every time the idea of self occurs it is a creation,—a production from within."

Later, as the discussion focused on the sensation of personal identity, Dr. E. H. Clarke brought up "the influence of India hemp" (which makes one "conscious of what goes on in his organism") and cited a published case of multiple personality: "For three months she was Maria, and for three months Julia, but she took up Maria's thoughts and memories just where that lady had left them." James now spoke up for the second time: "I once knew a lady who was subject to these singular changes. If the change found her at needle-work, she resumed the motions of sewing when it left her, though no work was in her hands." Again, unlike the other men, the speaker was drawing on personal experience—perhaps referring to Rev. William's wife, Marcia.

When James quit the Examiner Club in 1873 or 1874, he gave an acquaintance to understand that he had found the meetings "barren." The minutes show that he took little interest in practical social or political matters, mainly spoke up when there was an opening for one of his pet ideas, and positioned himself outside the other members' joint play of thought. One senses why James preferred the company of women.

Dr. Clarke and Mr. Wasson and Mr. Whipple and the Rev. Dr. Hedge all have entries in the *National Cyclopaedia of American Biography*. They talked the same language as one another and ran the culture of their time and made many contributions. But it was the man who was obsessive and half-cracked, always on the lookout for an opportunity to expound his obscure private vision of the self and the cosmos, who raised up genius.

MEMORIES OF PERSONALITIES

In 1861 James had gone up from Newport to Boston to preach at James Freeman Clarke's Church of the Disciples "on the urgent necessity there is for our religion to give way to life." James would always belong to the party of the future rather than the party of memory, yet even he could not wholly resist the retrospective mood that fell on Boston. With his bald head and full white beard, he was seen as one who had consorted with the giants from before the war. People wanted to hear about the old names now. They wanted facts and memories, not prophecies.

It was probably in 1864 that James composed the single most successful lecture of his career, on Thomas Carlyle. The Sage of Chelsea posed a vexing problem for the North, as he was a vocal defender of the Confederacy and an outspoken enemy of industrial democracy. James's lecture, a salvage operation, discarded Carlyle's ideas as of little value and made a compelling exhibition of his personality and lively talk, focusing on the ferocity of his spontaneous diatribes. "He is an artist, a willful artist, and no reasoner," James advised Annie Fields; "he has only genius." James read the lecture in New York in the fall of 1864, arranging ahead of time with Godwin for a favorable reception: "Would it be necessary to take on my own bowie-knife or do the Association guarantee life to their speakers?" He read it at the Concord Lyceum on December 28 (for $15), and in Albany on January 5. When Caroline Dall heard him give it in Boston on January 19, she praised it as "the finest *lecture* I ever heard." Holmes got "so many thrills of pleasure" from it. Reading it at a benefit for the Homeopathic Hospital Fund, James told an admirer his motive was to put his listeners' ears "into an hour's bondage to my idle tongue." The admission shows he was well aware the talk's appeal lay in its on-the-spot record of a famous man's crankiness. However, James T. Fields thought the lecture took unfair advantage of Carlyle's hospitality. It was compromising in another way as well, for it implicitly conceded the weakness of James's usual gospel that the social self was everything and individual personality nothing.

The past came up in another way in 1868, when Emerson gave his lecture on Brook Farm. He had long felt that Hawthorne's *Blithedale Romance* offered a "ghastly and untrue account" of the socialist community, and he wanted to correct the record. On October 27, before a large audience, Emerson read a genial reminiscence that included sympathetic character sketches of Alcott and Thoreau. Putting much of the blame for the commune's failure on its conversion to Fourier, he blasted the Frenchman's "false and coarse view of marriage." James, an enthusiastic backer of Fourier's matrimonial reforms during the period Emerson was recalling, was sitting in the audience, and the next day he got off a peevish note to Caroline Tappan objecting to all the "eulogy" in the lecture and the "unprincipled (because ignorant) denunciation of Fourier." The talk was "intellectual slip-slop of the poorest kind," and the speaker was "full of affectation and coquetry" and "dreadfully seedy."

The next month the Boston correspondent of the *Springfield Daily Republican* ran a titillating report that "Henry James, somebody says, 'is very mad about Emerson's criticism on Fourier, and has confessed to him that he never read his works, but only knows of them from extracts which Mrs. Emerson read to him while he was shaving.' " Eleven days later the *Republican* printed a stiff letter from James denying that Emerson had made any such confession but insisting all the same that he didn't understand Fourier. The letter vigorously complained about "that witless rage of gossip which seems to be organizing the correspondence of so many of our papers." More letters followed, and the controversy was picked up for Boston readers by the weekly *Commonwealth*. James was embarrassed and angry at having his loose private language broadcast in public, and he sent Emerson a frank account of the "scandal," along with a complaint about the "scurrilous liberty taken with my name." That the American press was intrusive and focused on personalities was becoming one of the James family's most forcefully held doctrines.

A few years later James was asked to present "a short appreciation" of Emerson at one of the Fieldses' Friday-night salons. Given this opportunity to repair the earlier slight, James quickly produced a warmly confessional paper on the seer's "evangelic significance"; this was the talk that stressed James's first passionate attraction to the "feminine" Emerson. As with Carlyle, the focus was on personality, the subject's ideas being curtly dismissed. James read the lecture on February 16, 1872, to a "brilliant company" of thirty-three people in the Fieldses' parlors. Four days later he went to Concord to read it to Lidian Emerson, having been prompted, as he explained to her husband, by an uneasy feeling "that I owe it to her to say nothing of you, which her heart does n't also say." From the sound of this, James wanted Mrs. Emerson to confirm the authenticity or legitimacy of his own early passion for her husband. It is interesting that Emerson's private opinion of the piece isn't known, and also that it wasn't printed until 1904, even though it was read at the New England Women's Club and the Examiner Club and probably several other venues. One recording secretary thought it would do "injustice" to the paper to try to summarize it, but noted "the literary workmanship & the flavor of personality which made a large part of its interest." Annie Fields said nothing about its content. All in all, James's New England auditors seem to have been fascinated and moved and obscurely embarrassed by the exhibition of his strange ardor for Emerson. They heard the speaker with profound respect, then covered him with silence.

FATHER ON WOMEN AND MARRIAGE

At any moment James's unimaginable past was apt to revive and breathe upon his children. In 1873 he wrote, and some of them read, an essay recalling the spirit communications and suicide of Joseph T. Curtis. He also wrote Henry Jr. about a long-ago acquaintance in Albany, Matthew Henry Webster, who was rejected by his fiancée following a bank failure yet never lost his graceful aplomb. The father remembered Webster as a noble fellow and urged his equally well-mannered son to write him up. The narrative that resulted, "Crawford's Consistency," is one of Henry Jr.'s most gentlemanly and dullest stories.

What were William and Henry to make of their father now that they were grown up? How had this man come to be, and how did he come to think the way he did, holding his strange ideas with such total and intimidating conviction? The enormous gaps in the children's knowledge of his past, gaps of which they were mostly unconscious, made the task of understanding and assessing his thought all that much more difficult. Still, if the two older sons hoped to become men of intellect in their own right, they had to reach an accommodation of sorts with Father's ideas. What made this task so challenging was that his ideas had played a decisive role in forming their *own* identities. In a powerful sense, the children were their father's waste product—*thinking* waste product—leaving them as their own Augean stables waiting to be cleaned. This was the Herculean labor assigned them.

When William systematically read Henry Sr.'s books in 1869, he was struck by their hermetic absolutism: Father's "ignorance of the way of thinking of other men, and his cool neglect of their difficulties is fabulous in a writer on such subjects." William acknowledged his father's depth and originality in his early *Moralism and Christianity* and *Lectures and Miscellanies*, but struggled with a sense of cryptic obstruction:

> Father is a genius certainly—a religious genius. I feel it continually to be unfortunate that his discordance fm. me on other points in wh. I think the fault is really his—his want or indeed absence of *intellectual* sympathies of any sort—makes it so hard for me to make him feel how warmly I respond to the positive sides of him.

Henry Sr.'s refusal to enter into others' ideas forced his oldest son to develop his superb capacity for grasping diverse points of view and mental states. That there is a great variety of minds and ways of thinking was to become one of William's basic ideas. The torment was, with all his suppleness the son still couldn't get through to Father.

Henry Jr. positioned himself very differently vis-à-vis Henry Sr. Without reading his parent's contentious philosophical and religious works, let alone wrestling with them as William did, he tried to assume that Father had things right. "Father saw," and the reflection that "he might be 'wrong,' wrong as a thinker-out, in his own way, of the great mysteries," was kept down: it wasn't thinkable that this tremendously authoritative parent could be living in a fool's paradise. His great achievement was that, unlike ordinary optimists, he sympathized without sentimentalizing. Henry Jr. took over many of his parent's views on social, moral, and literary matters. Assessing Carlyle, he dismissed the ideas and the brutality but held the artist in high esteem: "What a genius,

painter, humourist, what a literary figure, what a faculty of expression."
The novelist's condescending view of Emerson—that he was provincial
and innocent and didn't show enough "contempt"—reproduced the long-
standing paternal complaint that Emerson was too tolerant of Alcott and
Thoreau and other mediocre Concord folk.

Still, Henry Jr. often escaped his father's horizons, taking a signally
unpaternal pleasure in the Catholic and Mediterranean cultures of Europe. One of the son's most moving and memorable experiences was his
first sight of Rome. He wrote home about it, whereupon his father
promptly replied that if *he* were on the scene he would be revolted by
the "historical picturesque." All he would hear would be "the pent-up
moaning and groaning soul of the race, struggling to be free." Henry Sr.
never got to Rome, but when William visited it in 1873 he had his
father's anticipated experience, amusingly enough. St. Peter's proved to
be a "monument of human pride," and the Colosseum was so "inhuman
and horrible" William could think of nothing but "that damned blood-
soaked soil." Such judgments were pathetically incomplete as far as Henry
Jr. was concerned.

Henry Sr. had a huge impact on his children's thinking about gender
differences, sex and marriage, and women's rights. At the time he originally worked out his views on such matters, the late 1840s and early
1850s, Willy and Harry were too young to grasp them. When he had
his ugly 1859 fight over the Sickles murder and sex in Haiti, they may
or may not have noticed (William did, one guesses). But after the Civil
War it was impossible for the boys not to be aware of Father's persistent
involvement in the ongoing public debate over the proper social role of
"woman."

By 1868, when the New England Women's Club was founded, the
women's-rights movement had grown respectable. This club admitted
men as members, and during its first year of operation Henry Sr. and
Mary joined and paid their dues. The following year they withdrew, thus
terminating Mary's affiliation with the one society she is known to have
entered in adulthood. The reason they had originally signed up was that
James had been invited to speak at the organization's first monthly "literary entertainment" on December 7, 1868. His lecture, on "Woman"
bravely explained that man's "distinctive activity is physical and moral,
being more particularly identified with the civic consciousness of the
race. Woman's action is of a higher or more spiritual scope." James was
willing to see woman's legal disabilities done away with. He could accept
her taking any public role she wanted. But the point of his talk was that
women who sought to enlarge their civic scope were disregarding their

real calling, which was domestic and spiritual. He lightly predicted (in a summary corrected by himself) that men would "continue to claim the highest place in the synagogue . . . and that women would continue to accept the lowest seats." The reason why this inequality would persist was that "what is high [woman spiritually considered] always gives precedence to what is low."

The lecture was successful, James being asked to read it at least five times during the 1868–69 season. But Boston's moderate feminists did not care for it, and neither did the lecturer's old friend Fanny Macdaniel, now back from Europe. She discerned James's "antagonism to woman's entering upon a political & professional career" and realized that he dismissed her "to a deeper *home* sphere than any she has yet realized," doing so "with a compliment which might turn her head." Annie Fields had the opposite reaction. She found the lecture deeply moving and felt that it took "the highest, the most natural, and the most religious point of view." She agreed with James when "he spoke with unmingled disgust of the idea of woman . . . forsaking the sanctity and privacy of her home to battle and unsex herself in the hot and dusty arena of the world." In a way, the lecture acted as a saving exorcism for Annie, helping "to lay that dreadful phantom of yourself which appears now and then conjured up by the W.[omen's] rights people, haranguing the crowd and endeavoring to be something for which you were clearly never intended by heaven." The one point on which Macdaniel and Fields were in agreement was that James was an effective enemy of women's rights.

The following winter James was asked to write an essay for *The Atlantic* on several recent publications that concerned the women's movement, including John Stuart Mill's *Subjection of Women* and Horace Bushnell's *Women's Suffrage: The Reform against Nature*. James's forbidding title, " 'The Woman Thou Gavest with Me,' " taken from the excuse Adam gives God for eating the forbidden fruit, hinted at the degree to which his root understanding of the issues continued to be governed by an allegorical reading of Genesis. Mill's mistake, he argued, was to favor individual liberty over the "interests of order." Also, Mill was too wrapped up in the cause of freedom to acknowledge the inherent "rational or moral" differences between the sexes. But James had little to say about Mill's or the other authors' positions and arguments, instead using the occasion to set forth his own revealed teachings on women and marriage.

By January 1870, when James's essay appeared in *The Atlantic*, he had succeeded in alienating the editors of *The Nation* with his proprietary assumption that the magazine's columns would always be open to his diatribes against Swedenborgians. ("I have sent a paper to the Nation," he told a friend, "which they ought in fairness to me to have printed last week, but will no doubt this.") The literary editor, John Richard Dennett, got so fed up he dashed off a wicked lampoon of Absolute James for a survey of recent magazine articles:

> "The Woman Thou gavest with me," by Mr. Henry James . . . proves that both parties to the woman's rights dispute are all wrong . . . Mr. Mill, and Dr. Bushnell . . . and the women of the *Revolution*—none of them has the rights of the matter; and none of them will, nor any more will any of the rest of us, till he or she comes to look on man and woman as "two contrasted terms of a great creative allegory in which man stands for what we call the World, meaning thereby human nature in moral or voluntary revolt from God; and woman, for what we call the Church, meaning thereby human nature in spiritual or spontaneous accord with its divine source."

Henry Jr. read his father's essay while enjoying his first independent trip to Europe. His response was prompt, emphatic, and unreserved: "Your *Atlantic* article I decidedly like—I mean for matter. I am very glad to see some one not Dr. Bushnell & all that genus insist upon the distinction of sexes. As a mere piece of writing moreover I enjoyed it immensely." William, who had no doubt seen Dennett's sarcastic jeer, had some doubts about Father's promulgations: "I can't think he shows himself to most advantage in this kind of speculation," he wrote Henry. Henry ignored this cool assessment and, referring to a scandalous divorce case then in the news, asked Alice a month later to "tell father I read his article with real pleasure. It's a good thing. All England just now is engrossed with the Mordaunt trial—a hideous tissue of [misery?]. It strengthens the ground under father's feet." A week later, writing William, he endorsed the paternal doctrine yet again: "Among the things I have recently read is father's *Marriage* paper in the *Atlantic*—with great enjoyment of its manner & approval of its matter." When Henry Jr. read *The Nation*'s insinuation that Henry Sr. had become a public nuisance on the woman question, he reaffirmed his filial loyalty yet again. "The notice of your *Marriage* paper seemed to me [?] rather flippant," he wrote his father. "I heard some time since that the great Dennet [sic] had left the Nation . . . but I still detect his hand." Nothing the father ever wrote evoked such strong but nervous raves from the novelist as the essay defending "the distinction of sexes."

When William compiled a bibliography of Henry Sr.'s writings a couple of years after his death, " 'The Woman Thou Gavest with Me' " was left out. But in the summer of 1869, when he was asked to review the same books by Mill and Bushnell that his father had commented on, William worked out a position very close to that of his father. The problem with Mill, wrote the son, was that his "hot vehemence," his "fervid passion for . . . 'justice,' " had run away with him. Mill sounded rational, but there was a "sentimental kernel" in his argument—namely, an inflated ideal of equal friendship between man and woman. But the fact of the matter is that the "representative American" man has an opposite ideal: "The wife his heart more or less subtly craves is at bottom a dependent being." As for Bushnell, the reviewer quoted the claim that "the woman's law" requires her to submit to man, and that if man "has no sway-force in him" he is not "what Nature means when she makes a man," and then expressed his approval: "So far so good. If Dr. Bushnell is contented to urge this as an ideal, a matter of inexplicable sentiment, he remains in a strong position." Unfortunately, Bushnell's arguments were weak. In summary, Mill was the better thinker—and Bushnell had the superior ideal.

The "distinction of sexes" was deeply entrenched in the Jameses' family heritage. It can be traced back to William of Albany's relationship to Catharine Barber, it governed the formation of character, it enlisted the most fundamental loyalties, and it fermented and percolated in William and Henry Jr. all their lives. Generally they endorsed it, though sometimes they struggled against it from within. Each of them had his own private reservations, and Henry Jr. in particular knew that marriage was not for him. Still, both sons carried strongly felt and thought-out versions of their father's—and mother's, not to mention the dominant culture's—antifeminism.*

In 1872, when people were starting to talk about the Reverend Henry Ward Beecher's alleged seduction of a member of his congregation, an inquirer named Harvey Y. Russell asked James for his take on adultery. Sending a long letter in reply, Henry Sr. rehearsed the argument he had worked out twenty years earlier in response to Marx Edgeworth Lazarus—that marriage stimulates man's spiritual growth by confining his sexual desire to one woman. He took himself as an example:

---

* William in 1902: "The woman loves the man the more admiringly the stormier he shows himself . . . But the woman in turn subjugates the man by the mystery of gentleness in beauty." Henry in 1906-7: " 'Don't let us have women like that,' I couldn't help quite piteously and all sincerely breaking out; 'in the name of our homes, of our children, of our future, of our national honor, don't let us have women like that!' "

I marry my wife under the impression that she is literally perfect, and is going to exhaust my capacity of desire ever after. Ere long I discover my mistake . . . My good habits, my good breeding, my hearty respect for my wife . . . prevent my ever letting her suspect the conflict going on in my bosom; but there it is nevertheless, a ceaseless conflict between law and liberty, between conscience and inclination.

Others may get divorced, "but as for me I will abide in my chains."

James may not have known that Russell was the printer of a Twin Cities newspaper and a believer in free love. The letter collected dust until 1874, when Rev. Beecher was accused of adultery in a divorce suit and minutely detailed transcripts of the trial began showing up in respectable newspapers. Suddenly the opinions of the famous and not-so-famous on sex and marriage were found to be tremendously newsworthy. On February 19, a long extract from James's letter was published in the *St. Paul Daily Press*. Russell clipped and mailed it to *Woodhull & Claflin's Weekly* in New York City, a magazine dedicated to free love and socialism and widely regarded as the nation's most scandalous sheet—and edited by none other than Stephen Pearl Andrews, James's antagonist of 1852–53. For the last two decades Andrews had been laboring for a number of radical causes. He had been tireless and enterprising and hadn't accomplished much. He also hadn't forgotten how the *New York Tribune* had killed his last letter in that old controversy with James. On April 18 the letter to Russell appeared in *Woodhull & Claflin's*, enabling everyone to read James's infatuated confession that his wife hadn't afforded him complete sexual satisfaction and that only his good breeding and strong principles kept him from informing her of the fact and breaking free. He at once replied and there was the usual exchange of published rejoinders, Andrews bearing down on the resemblances between James's idea of marriage and the antebellum idea of slavery.

Several months later James tried to get up a public letter to Emerson denouncing the press's exploitation ("hideous," "hell-broth") of the Beecher story. The time had come to "record judgment against our existing civilization." The document James had in mind would have been the culmination of his long campaign against those who humiliate sinners in public. Emerson wouldn't touch it. In what may be his single most forceful letter to James (or anyone), the mild Sage of Concord began, "No, once & forever No . . ."

There is no firm evidence that James's children were aware of his letter to Russell in *Woodhull & Claflin's*. But the family's correspondence for

1874 seems to have been preserved in a highly selective way, and a letter to Bob suggests the father may have mailed him the pertinent issues of Andrews's rag: "I will send you the magazines you require—though they are generally pretty trashy." Chances are, given Henry Sr.'s brazenness and his sons' alertness to his teachings on marriage, they found out about his latest and messiest controversy.

The intriguing question is what the novelist made of the whole business. In later years Henry Jr. wrote a number of stories and novels about intrusive journalists and publishing scoundrels and interesting private papers that ought to be burned. It is likely that the public and private embarrassments of 1874 irritated a sense of privacy that was already extremely tender. Put another way, the father's strange exhibitionism helped create the novelist's hatred of the democratic press.

Late in the year, in one of those curious loops with which the Jameses' history is replete, Henry Jr. was asked to review a book that dealt with the communitarian era his father had observed and been involved in twenty-five years earlier—Charles Nordhoff's well-informed survey, *The Communistic Societies of the United States*. What caught the reviewer's eye was the section on the Oneida Colony, particularly a report of a meeting in which a young man was criticized for falling in love with his temporary sexual partner and thus disobeying the community rule against exclusive attachments. Henry Jr. heatedly condemned this "attempt to organize and glorify the detestable tendency toward the complete effacement of privacy in life and thought everywhere so rampant with us nowadays," and he urged readers to go directly to Nordhoff and read the story of "young man Henry" for themselves. The reader who takes this advice is in for a surprise. The name of the young man who was criticized for letting a particular attachment override his communal affections was Charles. It was the reviewer who named him Henry.

Was the reviewer aware his father had translated *Love in the Phalanstery* and vigorously argued that monogamy was about to be replaced by new forms of marriage? The inadvertent substitution of *Henry* for *Charles* is too insubstantial a piece of evidence to justify an assured answer. But it seems right to conclude that the novelist had a vague and anxious sense of his father's sexual past, and that he wanted to hear no more disturbing rumors. In the long shelf of fiction he went on to produce, he would often contrast investigative candor with a high and noble sort of mystification. When he was making plans for what he called his "very American tale," *The Bostonians*, he wrote himself a confidential note: "There must, indispensably, be a type of newspaper man—the man whose ideal is the energetic reporter. I should like to *bafouer* [scoff at] the vulgarity and hideousness of this—the impudent invasion of privacy—the extinction of all conception of privacy."

The novelist wrote this vehement passage a few months after his father's death. One of the wild old man's legacies to his prudent and loyal namesake was a steely determination to keep the lid on.

FAMILY TROUBLES

The members of the James household felt themselves as part of an extended family and saw that family's ongoing troubles as confirming some powerful lessons in emotional discipline. With each fresh disaster, there were renewed exhortations to have a strong and prudent will; yet there were also renewed anxieties as to whether the family will was sound or not. The will . . . an aspect of the mind, a problem in theology and philosophy, a recurring family name, an ambiguous legal document. For the Jameses, the will was the central and infinitely proliferating family pun. It was their salvation, but also their disease.

Howard, the youngest of Henry Sr.'s three living brothers, had become a recurring headache for his more responsible relatives. In 1861 a niece reported he was "drinking again—Josephine [his second wife] is sick. I do not know exactly what will be done." Eight years later Mary informed Henry Jr. that Howard had shown up in Albany "far from sober," intending to go to the Binghampton Asylum and "get some occupation there that will pay his board!" During the war Howard decided to take up carpentry and painting. Several years later, writing on cheap lined paper in a large and sloppy hand, he informed the niece he credited with introducing him to "litterature" that he was going to begin "writting a novel." It was when Howard talked about getting his life in order that he sounded most feckless. In 1874 his lawyer appealed to Henry Sr. to bail him out of a Baltimore asylum by discharging his bill there. Henry did so, and then helped commit his brother to an inebriate asylum in New York: "I will pay for his board & treatment . . . *but for no extra expenses whatever* either in the way of necessary clothing, or of luxuries, such as segars, pocket money, or what not." It was time for discipline again in the endless cycle.

There was another appeal for help when Gus suffered financial trouble and a stroke. Going at once to Rhinebeck, Henry found his older brother in a terminal state of depression. He had taken off his wig, looked thin and white, and was subject to fits of crying. He hoped God would take

him soon and even talked of suicide. According to Mary, he had spec-
ulated* and lost heavily, and then it became a question of bluffing. A
couple of years earlier, when a daughter married, Gus had given her a
beautiful Kashmir shawl that set him back $1,000. "The trouble with
him," Mary wrote, voicing her and her husband's sternly trenchant judgment, "has been an utter lack of courage and manliness in his character.
He had not pluck enough even with ruin staring him in the face, to
confess his losses to his children and the world, and to change in time
his manner of living . . . What a wretched failure he has made of life."
Gus's obituary mentioned "a long and painful illness," and also that the
deceased had "formerly" owned much property in Syracuse.

Gus dead, the only member of the family older than Henry was Rev.
William, the half brother who had been his spiritual counselor following
the conversion of 1834–35. For decades now Henry's letters to this
brother had been stiffly didactic and armed to the teeth. "I have observed
in you a certain set purpose of piety for its own sake," wrote the superior
younger brother. The hostile tone seems to have troubled William, and
in 1860, having suffered "a *sensible* injury in my head," he sent his brother
a letter that tried to place their dispute in a larger intellectual context.
Their basic disagreement, he said, was that in his view "the consciousness
both of freedom & of moral obligation which belongs to us reflects our
true nature," while in Henry's view the consciousness of selfhood was a
passing illusion. William conceded that his arguments, "were they ever
so well elaborated," would not persuade his brother, and he promised
not to try to "change" his views. The letter was a gesture of accommodation. In his reply, Henry apparently took no notice of his brother's
physical distress. After William commented on this omission, Henry
offered a diagnosis of his own, a blithe prediction of continued good
health, and a restatement of his usual teachings. Soon afterward, the
ministerial brother went to Clifton Springs for rest, exercise, and the
water cure. Bushnell happened to be there, and the two men were soon
absorbed in theological talk. "We perfectly agree in *feeling*," William
wrote his daughter, "which is the great difference between my relations
to him & to brother Henry."

Rev. William died in 1868 of a "very painful disease," all the while
maintaining "the most cheerful submission to the divine will." One of
his last letters conveys the severe and correct Calvinism of this former
mentor of Henry's:

---

* Gus may have damaged himself by trying to hold his father's empire together. In 1845, for
example, he and John Townsend had bought the Syracuse House and the mill for $73,200.

I wish also to correct the impression . . . that my peace springs from some deep consciousness of Xn character . . . Nothing can be further from the fact— All my *Evidences* of a . . . sanctified state are no more to me now than the driftwood upon which the drowning mariner would rest for a moment amid the surges of the ocean— They have all been thrust out of my mind long ago by the vast overshadowing view of *sin* particularly my own sin.

The document was composed with a trembling hand.

After his death, when there was a plan afoot to publish a collection of his letters and a daughter asked Henry Sr. whether he had any, the answer was that William had shown a "decided epistolary gift" but that Henry had burned all his letters, not having "foreseen this posthumous demand" for them. William "had the best heart in the world," Henry added, with his usual downright authority, "but his head on matters of speculation disowned [the heart's] control." However, in spite of this "pusillanimous" habit, Henry claimed he always felt an "immense personal respect and affection" for his brother.

Minny Temple put in a week with the Jameses in late 1869, a time when she had grown very thin and had a bad cough. One of the events still fresh in everyone's memory was the wedding of her eighteen-year-old sister to a man twenty-eight years her senior. This had been the second Temple orphan who chose to marry a much older man, and Minny made it clear to everyone that *she* would break the pattern established by her sisters. Minny was an extraordinarily alert young woman, bold, direct, plain-speaking, but also charming and attractive, and with strong independent opinions on the literary and intellectual issues of the time; her theory was that one should never settle for second best in anything. William had gotten over his old disapproval of her, and Henry Jr. admired her more than ever. In their different ways, the two brothers had grown deeply and complicatedly attached to this cousin whose natural eminence was so striking.

Minny posed a very tall order for William and Henry. Orphaned at the age of eight, she was not only loose in the world in a way the well-fathered and -mothered James children could never be, but she had somehow acquired the "sway-force" men alone were supposed to wield: she was a standing refutation of the family's deeply ingrained sense of ideal womanhood. Mary explained her as one whose fine capacities had not been disciplined and cultivated. Alice chose to see her as full of feminine wiles, informing a friend that Minny was "not nearly as interesting as she used to be, she is so much influenced by the last person she has been with and taken a fancy to that one never knows where to find her. She was looking very pretty and her manner is certainly perfectly fascinating." By 1869 the James daughter's nasty defensiveness had become an old story with Minny, and when she arrived in Cambridge in November and Alice began to "snub" her as usual, the visitor immediately "asked her to stop, wh. she consented to do."

There was another bad moment when Minny showed her disdain for Uncle Henry's philosophic "talk," which she judged to be "neither reasonable nor consoling." This talk, she told a friend,

> so far disgusted me, that I fear I manifested plainly unto him that it seemed to me not only highly unpractical, but ignoble & shirking—& knew all the time that he ~~hate~~ disliked me for what he called my *pride* & *conceit* —& I have felt that his views didn't touch my case a bit—didn't give me the least comfort or practical help & seemed to me wanting in earnestness & strength.

This was an astute judgment of the man who preached that everyone, women especially, must extinguish their consciousness of self. In another letter to her friend (a lawyer), Minny wrote, "I agree with you perfectly about Uncle Henry. I should think he would be very irritating to the legal mind— He is not at all satisfactory even to mine." In Minny's eyes, Henry Sr. looked as evasive and unmanly as Gus had appeared in Mary's.

Minny's religious faith remained unsettled, and in the weeks that followed her visit to Cambridge the twenty-four-year-old woman had such trouble breathing she couldn't sleep. During a restless night in January, she had a sudden insight into the kind of repose offered by Christian belief. Suddenly it seemed possible to join "intellectually . . . the long line of Christians" who had found comfort in "unconsciousness of self, love & trust," and she wondered whether Uncle Henry "had all along got hold of the higher truth, the purer spirituality." Was he right in teaching that the self's strife was only illusory and that she ought to renounce her strength? "We see the proud old Pagan ideal of moral virtue . . . giving place to the humble and harmless Christian ideal," James had written several years earlier, as if anticipating his niece's dark night of the soul.

Two days later Minny realized she wanted nothing to do with Uncle Henry's spirituality. The "vision of Redemption from thinking & striving" had evaporated, and in its place she sketched a moving tribute to a kind of natural religion:

So back swings the universe to the old place—Paganism—natural Religion, or whatever you call the belief whose watch word is "God and our own Soul"— And who shall say there is not comfort in it— One at least feels that here one breathes one's native air—welcome back the old *human* feeling, with its beautiful pride, and its striving—its despair, its mystery, and its faith.

At the time she wrote this she had a month and a half left to live.

Meanwhile, William was still wallowing in his personal morass. His future was unmapped, the complaint that had troubled Harry since the first year of the war had somehow "descended on the small of *my* back," and he was sunk in a depression he could neither understand nor master. He read Francis Anstie on stimulants and narcotics and Jacques Moreau on hashish and madness and experimented on himself with chloral. He needed a woman and, after his marriage several years later, would recall "those old dead dull stagnancies of despondency that filled so much of my time when I was a bachellor." In February there was an intense but poorly documented efflorescence of his relationship with Minny, and then, on March 8, 1870, she died.

Two weeks later, writing in his notebook, William addressed a passionate invocation to his dead cousin and then to himself:

By that big part of me that's in the tomb with you, may I realize and believe in the immediacy of death! . . . Acts & examples stay. Time is long. One human life is an instant. Is our patience so short-winded, our curiosity so dead or our grit so loose, that that one instant snatched out of the endless age should not be cheerfully sat out[?] Minny, your death makes me feel the nothingness of all our egotistic fury. The inevitable release is sure; wherefore take our turn kindly whatever it contain. Ascend to some sort of partnership with fate, & since tragedy is at the heart of us, go to meet it, work it in to our ends, instead of dodging it all our days, and being run down by it at last.

William was reaffirming what Minny had swung back to—the value of the individual's striving. But instead of finding comfort in our "beautiful pride," his tormented and very Jamesian sermon strains to redeem our "egotistic fury." Although William went through life with a page of his cousin's last letter to him folded up behind her photograph, he was never comfortable with her basic orientation. When he argued in *The Variety of Religious Experience* that the healthy-minded person has a thinner sense of ultimate reality than the sin-sick person, he was saying that Minny's assured self-reliance was inferior to his and his father's guilt-ridden and self-punishing mentality.

Henry Jr. treasured yet betrayed Minny's image in a remarkably similar way. The twenty-six-year-old writer was abroad at the time of her death, which he hadn't expected, and the two long letters he composed to William and his mother not only convey his grief but exhibit the energetic imaginative activity she inspired in him. Yes, Minny had been too restless to live, he thought he saw that now, pronouncing her "the helpless victim & toy of her own intelligence." But he was certain she would live on in others, and he got "positive relief in thinking of her being removed from her own heroic treatment & placed in kinder hands." It was his own hands he was thinking of—which is partly why this strange passage speaks of Minny not as one who lived and died but as the author of herself, writer and heroine together. Already the young writer was turning her into a character. Ten years later Minny's image became the basis of Henry Jr.'s Isabel Archer, the heroine of *The Portrait of a Lady*, his first novel with a claim to greatness. Isabel's central act is the one Minny repudiated—marrying a man twice her age. After realizing that he is a fussy and vindictive aesthete, Isabel does what Henry Sr. had prescribed. Accepting her chains, she changes from a callowly independent girl into a quiet lady who behaves extremely well under difficult circumstances. In effect, the novelist had altered his cousin to fit his father's prescriptions. Minny's posthumous fictive self is made to give up the "pride & conceit" the novelist's father had ~~hate~~ disliked.

On August 7, 1869, Alice's twenty-first birthday, there was a solar eclipse. Something had gone very wrong in the life of the one James daughter. "Nervous hyperaesthesia"—excessive sensitivity—was one of the names the doctors applied to her trouble. Give her the wrong "stimulus" and she would behave in a way she called "going off." One of the doctors brought in after Charles Fayette Taylor tried to straighten her out thought the trouble lay in her stomach, and since her death and the publication of her diary, various other explanations have been proposed. One of the best, by Strouse, is that Alice was confused by the contradiction between the love and the denigration she got from her father. When a nephew was born, she was "glad that it is a boy and not a miserable girl brought into existence." Selfhood was bad enough, but female selfhood was utterly contemptible, made even worse by the constant flattery. To be a girl and a James was a contradiction in terms, your will and your intellect turning on you with unimaginable fury.

In 1890, two years before her death, Alice wrote a diary entry that hints at her self-undoing nature. In her brother's novel, Isabel is shown to be greatly improved by learning to suppress herself; here, the benefits are not so evident.

> I had to peg away pretty hard between 12 and 24, "killing myself," as some one calls it—absorbing into the bone that the better part is to clothe oneself in neutral tints, walk by still waters, and possess one's soul in silence. How I recall the low grey Newport sky in that winter of 62–3 as I used to wander about over the cliffs, my young soul struggling out of its swaddling-clothes as the knowledge crystallized within me of what Life meant for me.

Alice's father's message was that man can find redemption only in the act of turning against himself, "a long, toilsome, most bitter, and vexatious conflict . . . with his own puny, crooked, insincere and ineffectual ways." The first two sons, William and Henry, learned how to articulate this teaching in indirect and creative ways—one developing his remarkable mind by ascending to some sort of partnership with tragedy, the other transforming the strong orphan cousin who rejected the teaching into her fictive opposite. Deprived of her brothers' professional resources and opportunities, Alice applied the paternal wisdom with lethal directness on what her family would have called her organism. *

---

* One mustn't forget Mary's (and other mothers') rigid sense of decorum. Once Alice dreamed that a girl friend's mother "came into the room & said, with wrath and indignation in her face and voice, that you [Alice's friend] must not write to me again until I had answered your letters that my conduct was past forgiveness." What the dream-mother says is that close same-sex friendships must give way to grown-up propriety and distance.

Chapter 26

■   ■   ■

SACRED OLD FATHER:
1875–82

George Ripley, the *New York Tribune*'s genial literary critic, made a great deal of money from his publishing ventures and became a prominent member of New York society. Parke Godwin did so well as editor of the *Evening Post* that his income soared to $70,000. Charles Dana, thought by many to be a total cynic, ran the popular and tasteless New York *Sun*.

For Ripley, Dana, and Godwin the radical crusades of the 1840s had led directly to big-time metropolitan journalism. For Rev. Alfred E. Ford, who had tangled with James on the marriage question in the now-forgotten *Harbinger*, the road led to Italy—Sunday-morning services for American artists and expatriates in a "spacious drawing room" in Florence. Edmund and Mary Tweedy subsided into well-cushioned international drifters, and when they turned up in Rome in 1873, Henry Jr. described them as living in fabulously overheated rooms, Edmund complaining about his health and Mary complaining about an English butler. The writer pitied the aging couple's "want of a central influence or guiding principle. (Such as their children would have been.) They don't know where to go, what to do, or why to do it." After Henry Sr. reportedly said something insulting about Tweedy, the latter sent his old friend an incensed letter. "It is one of those accidents that all friendships are liable to," reflected Henry Sr., adding, "They are generally poor enough to justify a sudden ending."

The generation of world renewers was dispersed, no one more so than James's old provoker, Marx Edgeworth Lazarus, the Jewish Transcendentalist. Having abandoned free love, Lazarus joined the Rebel side in the Civil War and then turned his energies to the rights of the working class. But the articles he wrote for the *Palladium of Labor* failed to toe the line on platform issues and either got rejected or caused trouble. His last years he spent in isolation and poverty in the small northern Alabama town of Guntersville. Why, he wondered, did those in the "vanguard of sociology" end up living in the sticks or doing menial work? Finally, suffering from paralysis and "deserted" by his goats, he resolved to store his papers in a certain box for a distant Northern admirer and fellow radical named George Schumm. He made arrangements for the box to be shipped north after his death. But all Schumm ended up getting was a childishly rounded scrawl:

> Dear Sir I received your note in reguard To Doctor Lazroues Death And allso in regard to a Box of papers . . . poor old man he was so absent minded he must hav forgot to fix them up he Becom like a Child he would forget nearly ever thing . . . I looked after him two year and nursed him thrugh his sickness he died the 20 day of may he was put away nicly.
>
> verespectfuly
Mary miller

James turned sixty-nine the day the 1880 census enumerator climbed the porch at 20 Quincy Street. Alice, thirty-one, was the only child still living at home, and there were only two servants, Margaret McLean of Scotland and Mary Crowley of Ireland. The parents no longer spent the summer in the country or by the seashore, and it was five years since James had seen New York. But he continued to take the horsecar into Boston to visit Williams' Bookstore in School Street, showing up so dependably that parcels were left for him there. He circulated in other ways as well, for when Walt Whitman took a trip to Boston in 1881, one of those he ran into was "old Mr. James." He evidently looked his age: Frank Duveneck's portrait of him from 1882 shows a bewildered patriarch staring into the present from the days of the ancients.

Mentally, the old man was as energetic as ever, "keep[ing] remarkably well," Mary assured the children, "and more intensely absorbed in working out his ideas than ever." But she was able to admit what none of her husband's letters mentions, the discouragement he felt after giving a lecture: "All that he has to say, seems so good and glorious, and easily understood to him, but it falls so dead upon the dull, or skeptical ears who come to hear him." Decades later, Henry Jr. composed a tribute to his father's tireless expository zeal: "No more admirable case of apostolic energy combined with philosophic patience, of constancy of conviction and solitary singleness of production unperturbed, can I well conceive."

James had a penchant for beginning a letter by saying he was too ill to write and then writing anyway, in this way parading his weaknesses but also his great reserve power. Amused by the habit, Francis Boott couldn't resist twitting his old friend: "You begin your letter with the expression of fear that you will not be able to write one! Hereby showing a power of *mental* self-diagnosis much inferior to that of physical one." The preface of James's last book, *Society the Redeemed Form of Man* (1879), opens in the same way as many of his letters: "My dear friend:—You know that I am not in good health. Ever since my illness of last May, now more than a year ago, my nerves are easily unstrung by protracted labor." Maybe so, but the book was James's second longest.

James may have seen himself as old and infirm, but his powers of invective were green and flourishing. "There is no more diabolic state of mind," he vociferated, attacking the popular evangelist of the time, "than the feeling of joy and gratitude which parson Moody's converts express, that their own dirty little souls have been divinely rescued from hell-fire, while other souls . . . are left there, by the infamous scoundrel who rescues *them*, to sizzle in eternal agony." Modern religious liberals were dismissed as a "thin scum." Any modern textual scholar who questioned the Bible's historic accuracy was a "cold-blooded prig or pedant," an "ambitious scavenger." Any scientist who discredited the creation story was "conceited," wrote in "crass ignorance," spouted "absolute drivel," and was "a noodle" rather than a philosopher.

This intemperate abuse was part and parcel of James's system. There was only one creative force. Its sole reason for existing was to perpetuate itself in others, bringing others into existence through their illusion of separate, conscious selfhood. There had to be consciousness in order to make possible an intelligent union with God, yet it was consciousness, precisely, that stood as the supreme distraction and impediment to that union. First conscious egos had to be—and then they had to be beaten to smithereens, being absolutely hellish. Swedenborg alone had seen how the Bible lobbed the truth at the vain human mind in a fashion that bypassed its ordinary way of working. But the great seer's visions would never penetrate human consciousness unless some devoted apologist, someone like James, pounded the hell out of it.

James believed as strongly as ever what he had written in *Substance and Shadow*: "Infinite Love and Wisdom create us every moment physically as well as psychically." There were no separate beings, and nothing could possibly work on its own. The universe was an expression of divine creativity racing ahead at full throttle at every instant at every point, and what was true for God was true for James's talk about God. Each point, each idea, had to be redemonstrated in every book, every article, every paragraph. The tireless repetitiousness of his writing was an integral part of the philosophy it set forth, being the formal expression of his doctrine that nature could not exist if God were not incessantly, incontinently, rigidly pumping it up. James's universe system would at once collapse if James weren't there pushing, yelling, insisting, proving, abusing. But how does a man slow down if he is committed by every sinew of his mind to this way of living and thinking? How does he get ready to die?

When *Society the Redeemed Form of Man* was given a critical review by W. H. Galbraith in the *New Church Independent*, James wrote a long reply, which the editor rashly consented to publish, and from then on for the next two years nearly every issue of this non-official Swedenborgian monthly had a long, tough, Jamesian essay on the Divine Method in Creation, or on God's Spiritual Incarnation in Human Nature, or on the Only Conceivable Method of Spiritual Creation. Each article required a sequel, as had always been the case with James, and the ensemble gradually took the shape of yet another comprehensive book-long explanation; as it appeared, chapters were sent to Godwin. These formidable monthly installments were sandwiched between the usual puerile effusions of lower-order minds—"The Holy Child Jesus," "Personal Preaching," "The Immortality of Youth," "The Moonbeam's Mission," "Only an 'Outsider.' " The last of these, a moral tale by T. S. Arthur (creator of the immortal *Ten Nights in a Bar-Room*), ended on a grace note of personal reform: " 'Again, my friend, a thousand and a thousand thanks for the great deliverance to which you have helped me!' " What could readers who swallowed this kindly pap make of James's austere misanthropy? Thanking the pustules of smallpox that "come to preach their little gospel of redemption to me"! Praising physical disease as "a miraculous Divine *sewerage* adjusted with infinite art to bear away into the ocean of God's oblivion the hideous unknown evils and corruptions which stifle—and in truth *are*—that unconscious natural life of mine"! James was saying what he had always said—"This formidable evil is named SELFHOOD—but saying it louder and with more emphatic typography than ever.

The distance between T. S. Arthur's voice and James's was as unbridgeable as that between Mary Miller's and Marx Edgeworth Lazarus's. Where Ripley, Dana, and Godwin had made themselves the voices of New York City, and prospered accordingly, James and Lazarus had become voices in the wilderness.

Of the two troublemakers, James was the more insistent on being heard, and it wasn't long before the *Independent*'s editor, a Mr. Weller, made the same two melancholy discoveries the editors of the *Harbinger*, the *New York Tribune*, and *The Nation* had made—that James bored most readers, and that he wouldn't stop boring them until the periodical that printed his lengthy communications either refused them or ceased publication. At the conclusion of the twelfth issue for 1880, Weller addressed his subscribers "with fear and trembling." The year had not been a prosperous one. The generous space given to certain subjects "too deep and abstract for general comprehension" had alienated many readers. He promised more variety for the coming year and vented his resentment of those contributors who took "advantage of . . . our columns by crowding upon us long, exhaustive papers." He asked for money. In response, James sent Weller a note to the effect that he would discontinue his articles if the magazine's readers had had enough. Advising him to go ahead and post the remaining essays, Weller rashly informed subscribers they might expect "one or two more." What they got in 1881 was seven more.

Still, in spite of all his difficulties and obscurities, James attracted a scattering of admirers. "Mr. James has one of the best articles I have read for a long time," wrote one of Weller's subscribers. "Henry James is wonderful, but he is hard to bear," wrote another. William and Henry Jr. were mistaken in supposing that he met with no response whatever. In England two unorthodox religious seekers named Edward Welch and Horace Field became avid followers. In Chicago a Nora Perry wrote a long letter to that city's *Tribune* gratefully citing James's attacks on popular evangelists. In St. Louis, the Reverend Samuel C. Eby read and collected James's writings around 1880, and Lydia Fuller Dickinson had a correspondence with him on the question of miracles. It was said that she would rarely get together with her friends "that the conversation did not center on Henry James." Horace Field had such thoughts as he read *Substance and Shadow* that "the very door of heaven . . . seemed to be opening."

Of all James's disciples, the most faithful and scrupulous was Julia A. Kellogg. Born in 1830, she, too, had started her religious odyssey as a Presbyterian. The brother with whom she was closest had been a member of the North American Phalanx, a sister taught Southern freedmen, and Kellogg herself tried to enlist as a nurse during the Civil War. She met James during a temporary residence in Cambridge and had a lengthy correspondence with him after she moved elsewhere. He apparently "regarded her as the one among his disciples who most fully grasped his views." The many letters in which he explained matters to Kellogg convey a vivid idea of his didactic authority. "There! Enough for one day," he would write. "Think well before you answer, unless your answer be one of sweet spontaneous accord, which will require no delay." When Kellogg became concerned about her guru's stand on women's issues and brought up his old essay "Woman and the 'Woman's Movement,' " he explained the distinction of sexes and then ended the discussion by declaring his disciple's position and his own "hopelessly at one." When she became critical, he became wrathful and peremptory:

> You may go on to entertain what opinions of me you conceive to be congruous with the facts of the case; but please withhold the knowledge of them from me . . . I can't permit you to impose any of your specific judgments of my conduct upon my own understanding, under the menace of a forfeiture of your friendship unless I acknowledge its truth.

REALIZING HIMSELF IN HIS CHILDREN

At the heart of James's system was the notion that God could be God only by undergoing a thorough process of disintegration or dissemination. People had God backward: instead of being self-sustaining, His "insufficiency to Himself" is "so abject that He is incapable *of realizing Himself except in others.*"

This notion throws considerable light on James's sense of himself in relation to others, as when he pronounced the crowded American horse-car the symbol of a perfect society:

> Whenever I get my stupid sconce above water for a half an hour, some of the reigning idols, Plato or Emerson or Washington, is sure to plump himself down upon it and submerge me . . . The people in the horse-cars never do this . . . They talk so heartily of household expenses and weather & raising chickens that it is sweet to be near them.

One reason James could embrace the weather- and chicken-people in this fashion was that he was so distant from them. It was by projecting itself on others that the one huge self lived. The abjectness expressed the total sovereignty, and vice versa. According to William, one of his father's friends was so impressed with his "divine rage with *himself*" that he (or she) sensed "away down at bottom of the man, so sheer a humility and self-abasement as to give me an idea of infinity."

This peculiar theism helps explain how a monomaniacal theoretician could also be a loving and devoted father, sincerely regarding his offspring as his life's work. James was determined to be immanent in his children's lives rather than the remote and all-powerful deity his own father had been, operating through obedient intermediaries like Archibald Mc-Intyre. All the same, Henry Sr.'s intense participation in his children's lives brought special pressures, both for them and for him. For them there was the difficulty of establishing, in fact of realizing, their sepa-rateness. For him the devotion to family was maddeningly inconsistent with the divine imperative to play no favorites, and also with a lingering commitment to the Fourierist critique of the isolated household. "Shall I continue to thank [God]," he asked in 1879, "for giving me wife, and child, and neighbor, when the fatal sweetness of these gifts does but enhance their final capacity to make me suffer?"

As James's children tried to establish independent adult lives, he con-tinued to live and suffer through all of them except Wilkie. One of the reasons Henry Jr. proved less troublesome than the others was that this son had the wisdom to put an ocean between himself and his father, and also to cultivate the kinds of writing—light essays, stories, novels—Henry Sr. didn't approach with high seriousness. Not surprisingly, Henry Jr. became the kind of writer who could function well only when situated at a considerable distance from his raw materials and readers. Private space and wide margins were his conditions of productivity. Living and writing in Europe, he could take his own direction and still pay respectful lip service to the father's transatlantic sermons. He could also take ad-vantage of the father's excellent social and literary connections and his eagerness to help his son along. The father was not allowed to negotiate with publishers, but he proved extremely helpful as banker, adviser, critic, professional secretary, and vigilant clipping service.

On the whole, the novelist was glad to avail himself of his father's strategic help. When Henry Sr. assumed the task of reading proof for one of Henry Jr.'s *Atlantic* stories, the latter professed to be "very com-fortable" with his parent's handling of the matter. When Howells wanted "The Madonna of the Future" cut and altered and Henry Sr. gave the necessary authorization, the son once again approved. When another editor, "spectral" Charles Eliot Norton, had a query for Henry Jr., the father not only dispatched the business ("I will gladly serve your need with respect to Harry, and adjust the matter finally according to the merits of the case") but laid some vague but useful flattery onto a man he didn't like (the Norton household "abounds so in better types of our nature, that I cannot help regarding them as prophetic of a more universal result"). Addressing another influential Brahmin he didn't personally care for, James Russell Lowell, Henry Sr. was grateful for a " 'munificent' notice" of his son's work.

During the winter of 1875–76, when Henry Jr. was living in France, the New York *World* ran a long, detailed, discriminating review of *Roderick Hudson* that judged it to be "the best romance . . . since [Hawthorne's] 'Marble Faun.' " It was the kind of review a beginning novelist dreams of, and Henry Sr. promptly wrote the editor, Manton Marble:

> My dear Sir:
>   If the question be not indiscreet will you kindly tell me who wrote the flattering criticism . . . ? I should like to communicate the name to my son, and at the same time express to the writer my own high appreciation of his critical acumen. I have seen nothing half so good in the way of a discrimination of my son's merits and demerits, and I am sure he himself will be very thankful for it.

The unknown critic judged Hudson to be superior to Hawthorne's Donatello as a "portrayal of a man with exquisite sensibilities and without moral sense," considered the secondary characters "a trifle wooden or a trifle shadowy," and noted the author's inability "to take a deep, wide and human interest in the lesser and more trivial men and things of the world." These were the merits and demerits Henry Sr. wanted his son to become aware of.

Apparently Henry Sr. did not send his son's hostile reviewers the angry ripostes he got off to his own, but he once "talked pretty squarely" to James T. Fields "about a certain critic of his son's work, and thinking he had said too much wrote to ask forgetfulness and forgiveness." Annie Fields found the apology "quite touching from its exhibition of home love and conscientious endeavor." There is no doubt the younger Henry understood the importance of keeping his work separate from his father's work in the public mind. What is interesting is that the father also understood this. Often critical of his son's writing, he nevertheless showed a great deal of tact in public. In this way also, the father embodied the god he had conceived. *

All the same, Henry Sr. was genuinely baffled by his son. When Godwin wrote to say how impressive the boy was looking, the father replied:

---

* At the end of Henry Jr.'s first independent European tour, Mary wrote Alice: "Such a burden has been taken off my heart, by Henry's decision to come home. And Father confesses to the same feeling very strongly, although he has said nothing about it; not wishing to add to my anxiety, and wishing to leave ~~you~~ H. free."

I am greatly touched by your appreciation of Harrys labours . . . The youth
is so much more to us here at home for his domestic worth, that we cant
help wishing him success in every field to be sure; but he has so little push
about him, that we fear his merit such as it is will not [be] recognized for
a good while.

At the time the "youth" was thirty-one years old, with a kind of force
his father couldn't recognize. Instead of stepping forward and manfully
duking it out whenever provocation arose, as Father had so often done,
Henry Jr. preferred to meditate his work in private and shrug off the
opinions he judged beneath him. He was aiming higher than Henry Sr.
or anyone else (Howells excepted) was able to guess. Unlike his father
and his father's brothers, Henry Jr. knew what he was about. There was
no hurry. Nothing would be wasted. But for the time being it was good
to have Father in Cambridge looking after the business side.

Aunt Kate once confided that James's affection for William "was very
deep, a peculiar thing in its expression, but something unlike his feeling
for his other children." Continuing to live at home until the age of
thirty-six, William lacked his brother's margin of freedom. He took an
intense interest in philosophical questions involving the will, the self,
the nature of consciousness, always feeling the intimate pressure of Father's mind. In his later life he declared that "the intellect's most cherished ideal" is "to find an escape from obscure and wayward personal
persuasion to truth objectively valid for all thinking men." But how can
the intellect pursue this ideal with Father always on, always establishing,
the premises? After Father's death, it dawned on William that "the
thought of his comment on my experiences has hitherto formed an
integral part of my daily consciousness, without my having realized it at
all."

Then there was the question of marriage. As William kept his eyes
open for the right woman, his parents vigilantly protected him from the
legions of the unfeminine, the overdelicate, and the excessively reflective. The boy needed quality care and should obviously marry a stalwart
mother-woman, as his father had. Once, when Henry Sr. and Mary were
planning a trip to Milwaukee to see the younger boys, it was decided at
the last minute, William being unwell, that Mary would have to remain
behind in Cambridge. It would be too risky to leave the boy "alone with
no one but Chauncey Wright & Juliet Goodwin to look after him. Juliet
[was] very desirous to read to him." The fragile bachelor was thirty at
the time.

William's debility began to subside when he was offered a temporary instructorship in physiology at Harvard. His lectures began January 1873, and he threw himself into the work with characteristic vigor. One after-noon in March he announced to his father that his mind was "cleared up and restored to sanity." The change was owing (his father reported) to his reading of Wordsworth and Charles Renouvier and, even more, to

> his having given up the notion that all mental disorder required to have a physical basis. This had become perfectly untrue to him. He saw that the mind did act irrespectively of material coercion, and could be dealt with therefore at first-hand, and this was health to his bones. It was a splendid confession, and though I knew the change had taken place, from unerring signs, I never was more delighted than to hear it from his own lips so unreservedly.

William had at last found a way to reconcile the materialism and mech-anism of science with his father's spirituality, and also his father's denial of individuality with Renouvier's freedom of the individual will. This new accommodation constituted a decisive moment in the son's matur-ation. By adopting a qualified version of his father's religion, William could be loyal and loving without abandoning the modern critical and scientific spirit. The solution was to take the creative power his father ascribed to God alone and parcel it out to each thinking individual. Each mind, starting with William's, thus became a first-order reality. This compromise denied Henry Sr.'s paralyzing claim that selfhood was merely "phenomenal" yet reaffirmed his actual practice of trusting to the mind's resourcefulness in finding what will work best for it. The notion of the human mind's godlike sovereignty came to be one of William's central ideas even as it released his own great energies. At the same time it introduced an element of religious mystery into his psychology and compromised his science.

The next year William was offered a permanent appointment at Har-vard in physiology and anatomy, and he gradually parlayed this into the specialty he preferred—"mental science." But the most decisive change in his life was owing to his father. One evening in 1876, Henry Sr. attended a gathering of the Radical Club in Mary Sargent's home and met a plain twenty-seven-year-old woman named Alice Howe Gibbens. She supported herself and helped support her mother by teaching at a private girls' school in Boston. The opposite of William, she had had to assume family responsibilities at an early age. Henry Sr. talked with her a little, and when he returned home announced that he had met his son's future wife.

Intrigued, William attended the next session of the club and met the woman. He wasn't sure he had the right to inflict himself on this second Alice, but Henry Sr., promising financial help, urged him to marry her at once. The courtship was stormy and protracted. William arrogantly, manfully, insisted that Alice Gibbens belonged to him: "You and I are [in some] . . . degree one, in the heart of being . . . You can't escape me there, nor I you." But once she had agreed to an engagement, he interposed the most dithering confessions and postponements. Now he was "simply shocked at the thought of a being like you countenancing one like me. You *ought* not to be willing to do it . . . until it becomes certain that every other fuller path is closed upon you." Not surprisingly, she put a stop to proceedings for a time. When they started up again, William came on like a constipated Lord Byron: "O friend of my soul how could you write the note which has thrown me into such a frenzy? . . . Here in the dead bowels of the night, I concentrate myself afresh. I will not abdicate." By the date of their marriage, in 1878, Alice Gibbens must have been fully aware that this edgy, willful, mercurial man would require huge amounts of patient support. In 1911, a year after his death, she told a friend that her mission had been "to make my life serve his, to stand between him and all harmful things." It is uncanny how successful the father was in finding the same kind of wife for his oldest son that he had found for himself. Henry Sr. had been certain that he would have been lost if he "were not able when the celestial powers . . . were in *flight* to run to the bosom of your mother." Now William had the identical refuge.

But if William gained a lifelong mate and protector, the old Alice lost the brother who had flattered and courted her. There seems to have been bad blood between the two Alices at the time the engagement was announced. That was in May, and the following months proved to be a season in hell for the sister. A decade later she recalled this time as "that hideous summer of '78, when I went down to the deep sea, its dark waters closed over me and I knew neither hope nor peace." After getting back on her feet, the painfully dependent young woman described her trouble as a form of "moral prostration":

I was pretty wretched through the summer & gave my poor family an immense amount of trouble, but for the last couple of months I have been learning to behave myself better & better all the time. My physical suf-

ferings would have given me no concern, but my patience, courage &
self-control all seemed to leave me like a flash & I was left high and dry.

It is odd that Alice's two accounts of this crisis employ the same metaphor
in opposite ways, the contemporary account leaving her stranded above
the waterline and the retrospect speaking of total immersion. Perhaps
one of the things William's marriage revealed to the thirty-year-old spin-
ster was that she was simultaneously swallowed up in her family and
devoid of a life of her own. Worse, she was afraid to strike out for a life
of her own. How could she ever forget the misery of those nights when
she succumbed to her "attacks" and "Mother and Father would watch
by me" and she would "cry out to them to know what would become of
me when I lost them"? Alice suffered the abjectness of those who fear
they can't grow up, and who feel such contempt for their own unworthy
dependence that the self-pity balloons into a huge and hopelessly delicious vice. Had she become the parasite of herself as well as of her family?
This was one of the questions William's marriage pressed on her. One
of the answers was to be harder and tougher than ever.

In September Henry Sr. received a complaint from Bob about his
occupational and domestic troubles. In reply the beleaguered father declared that he and Mary were "so wholly immersed in Alice's terrible
malady" they wouldn't be able to offer any help at present. "Half the
time, indeed much more than half," she was "on the verge of insanity
and suicide." The father's nerves (not surprisingly) "could bear no stouter
tension." He had instructed Alice that she was the object of a malignant
spiritual "influx," and the teaching seemed to have taken effect, Alice
having "perfectly understood for a long time past that her frightful ner-
vousness was a part of our trouble as a race, struggling to get free; that
there was nothing in it peculiar to herself." Although this diagnosis was
of little value in explaining the particular sources of Alice's troubles, it
did allow her the relief of seeing herself as victim. To that extent at
least, she could ease up on the guilt and anxious introspection.

There was another and more drastic remedy. "One day a long time
ago," James told Bob, Alice asked him whether he thought that "suicide,
to which at times she felt very strongly tempted, was a sin." His answer:

It was absurd to think it sinful when one was driven to it in order to
escape bitter suffering, from spiritual influx, as in her case, or from some
loathsome form of disease, as in others. I told her that so far as I was
concerned she had my full permission to end her life whenever she pleased;
only I hoped that if ever she felt like doing that sort of justice to her

circumstances, she would do it in a perfectly gentle way in order not to distress her friends. *

Alice thanked him for his permission but declared that

> now she could perceive it to be her *right* to dispose of her own body when life had become intolerable, she could never do it . . . When she had felt tempted to it, it was with a view to break bonds, or assert her freedom, but that now I had given her freedom to do . . . what she pleased, she was more than content to stay by my side, and battle in concert with me against the evil that is in the world.

Alice's response (as reported) is saturated with Father's ideas: her struggle with madness is a version of his battle with evil, a higher-order mind never takes advantage of a mere right, and so forth. In fact, her desire to kill herself was not permanently removed by his granting her the "freedom" to do so. As James admitted, she continued to be "strongly tempted."

Alice needed a caretaker outside the family. This she found in the person of Katharine Loring, on whom she became extremely dependent. She also established a home of her own by borrowing $2,500 from her father and having a cottage built in Manchester, Massachusetts, not far from Loring. Discovering the women's movement, she began voicing some caustic opinions about men and women. But there was to be no real revolution within.

The two youngest boys were not doing much better. In 1867, when Wilkie revisited Cambridge, taking a much-needed break from the Florida plantation, he looked "altered, very thin and sallow, and his mind evidently shaken." A few years later the investment was abandoned, resulting in the loss of a great deal of money and the end of the young man's idealism. Wilkinson was shocked to learn that after all the struggles his godson had gone through, he could "hope no better for his coloured brother than that he may die out."

Moving to Wisconsin, Wilkie and Bob both went into railroads—as employees, not capitalists. Perhaps they were anxious to maintain their social eminence, as they each married into well-to-do though not particularly cultivated families. Wilkie described his father-in-law as having "no occupation save of sitting on his piazza & reading the papers &

---

* A London doctor consulted in 1909–10 by William and Henry later revealed that the brothers had "discussed the question of suicide & William told Henry that if he felt life was no longer bearable, he was justified in putting an end to it, & they discussed the question as to how this should be done, & they decided in favour of chloroform or opium."

looking at the thermometer & opening & closing the window-blinds."
His bride he characterized as never betraying "an emotion of feeling on
any subject scarcely." When she came to Cambridge for her first visit,
she made a poor impression. "I can't for the life of me imagine," Henry
Sr. admitted to his other children, "why Wilky fell in love with her."
When Bob brought *his* wife to Cambridge to be inspected, Mary reported
that at least she was "not too Western in her manners." Alice couldn't
"make a companion of her, [but] found she could make a pet." The
parents' reactions to their Wisconsin daughters-in-law moved in a narrow
range between the haughty and the nasty. These wives were not to be
compared to Mrs. Alice.

Bob continued to be unsettled and dependent on his parents. He
philandered, had drinking binges, and complained that his wife threatened his manhood by not siding with him against her father. Henry Sr.'s
prescription:

> It is simply indispensable in my opinion that you fix yourself within the
> bounds of civilized & cultivated life, where you can have intercourse with
> home once a year at all events, and oftener if need be. This thing is
> necessary to my happiness. I cant stand this tremendous separation from
> you.

Although Wilkie's marital life was happier, he admitted to a friend in
Boston that "every year of this western life becomes more & more intolerable." It was "the dreary commonplaceness of its social life" that he
found he couldn't stand.

Farther West, in various army forts in Washington Territory, Bob
Temple continued his steady decline. He drank, re-enlisted under an
assumed name, went to prison for some unknown offense, lost a finger.
Whenever he wrote his Eastern relatives for money, he was the person-
ification of dignity and contrition. He still dreamed, as he went down
and down, of returning to his "proper and rightful social status." His
one desire was "to mingle once more with that class in which I was born
& educated."

"MÈRE (MARE) DE FAMILLE"

Mary died one evening in 1882, in the middle of a winter in which she
was troubled by lung congestion and asthma. She had been seen by
everyone, herself included, as the family's one robustly healthy person,

always "strong in the back, strong in the nerves." Gail Hamilton had pronounced her "a fine woman, physically and morally, healthy and happy"—which was what she had to be, considering how the entire household depended on her. For Mary, there was never the slightest vocational uncertainty. Yet looking past her domestic role and the family myths, one notices occasional mentions of her sicknesses in her husband's correspondence. Once she was "so miserably racked by cough & headache" she was "incapable of acknowledging" a note from Annie Fields. In 1850, a year after the apparent miscarriage and its complications, the Wilkinsons offered her (but not her husband) rest and refuge in their Hampstead home.

When the novelist returned from England three months before his mother's death, he was surprised at how "worn and shrunken" she was. Harry was the son who never caused trouble in the nursery, who always entered into his mother's domestic anxieties. The father thought she loved him "more than all her other progeny," and she herself once addressed him in a letter as "the dearest" of her absent boys—though at once adding, "because the farthest away, perhaps." Another time, as if seeing herself in him, she exclaimed: "You dear reasonable over-conscientious soul!" He was her and Alice's "absent 'angel.' " After spending some time in Cambridge, Henry Jr. went to Washington, D.C., where he was visiting friends when a telegram arrived: "Your mother exceedingly ill. Come at once." He tried to do so, but by the time he reached home she was laid out under a shroud in the unheated north room. He was "very much shocked," noted Bob, impressed by Harry's "passionate childlike devotion to her."

A couple of weeks later Harry announced his mother's death to her English goddaughter, Mary James (Wilkinson) Mathews: "She was the perfection of a mother—the sweetest, gentlest, most beneficent human being I have ever known." Reading this in London, Wilkinson at once wrote Henry Sr.: "I know you are consoled, for such a man & wife cannot be far from each other, and she who is better off will comfort her dear old man to the end." These vigorously affirmative Victorian sentiments—that Mary was the perfect mother and wife, that death had transformed her into a comforting spiritualized presence—show up in everything that was said about her. "Ever since the night that Mother died," Alice wrote in her diary, "and the depth of filial tenderness was revealed to me, all personal claim upon her vanished, and she has dwelt in my mind a beautiful illumined memory, the essence of divine maternity." Henry Jr. developed the same idea in a memorial eulogy confided to his notebooks:

> She was patience, she was wisdom, she was exquisite maternity . . . It was a perfect mother's life—the life of a perfect wife. To bring her children into the world—to expend herself, for years, for their happiness and welfare—then, when they had reached a full maturity . . . to lay herself down in her ebbing strength and yield up her pure soul to the celestial power that had given her this divine commission.

This mellow idealization does not even hint at the shock Bob had observed in his brother. Perhaps that is because the novelist was not expressing his private feelings about his mother but summing up the official family sentiment. "She was our life, she was the house, she was the keystone of the arch," he wrote, putting into service the same metaphor he had used twelve years earlier, when he praised a dependable former servant as "the very keystone of the arch."

Leon Edel has argued that the novelist concealed his true feelings about Mary James even from himself, only to express them in his fictional portraits of stifling mothers. The problem with such explanations is that they impose a twentieth-century psychic model on a nineteenth-century mind. Henry Jr. was not speaking for himself in his tribute to his mother but for "us," the family, and he was not expressing what we call "feeling" but what they called "sentiment"—feeling supported, structured, disciplined by doctrine. The doctrine had been worked out three decades earlier by Henry Sr. when he set forth the theory that would shape the children's sentiments about Mary:

> The word "mother" suggests to the imagination all that is most unselfish, most uncomplaining, and most beneficent, in human nature. The mother forgets herself and her own interests utterly in zeal for the welfare of her children. She finds her best happiness in developing their affections and nascent sensibility, in being totally spent for them . . . She willingly leaves their discipline and correction and their intellectual growth to the father.

Henry Jr.'s tribute to his mother was an inadvertent tribute to the intellectual and emotional discipline he (and she) had gotten from Henry Sr.

Was a loving wife and mother no more than an idealized servant? William was deeply impressed by the representation of a peasant woman in Jules Bastien-Lepage's *The Hay-Makers*. He was convinced he saw a "childlike virginity under her shapeless body" and "a look of infinite unawakenedness" in her face. The patient, hardworking women of Germany, "dragging their carts or lugging their baskets," made him want to cry. As he told his wife,

> All the mystery of womanhood seems incarnated in their ugly being—the Mothers! the Mothers! Ye are all one! Yes, Alice dear, what I love in you is only what these blessed old creatures have; and I'm glad and proud, when I think of my own dear Mother with tears running down my face, to know that she is one with these.

This, too, like Henry Jr.'s eulogy, was a highly seasoned version of the paternal teaching. All women participate in Woman, and what Woman does is to serve (quoting Henry Sr.'s typically emphatic language) as man's "patient and unrepining drudge, his beast of burden, his toilsome ox, his dejected ass." Astonishingly, Mary herself would speak of her domestic role in such terms, as when she gaily adopted her favorite son's punning phrase for her—"mère (mare) de famille."

In their final decade together, Henry Sr.'s relationship with Mary had grown more stable than ever. Ideally, he had written, a couple "of an interior quality" outgrows the sexual bond and develops "a sacreder communion" based on "gentleness, forbearance, peace, and innocence." What this meant in practice is suggested by a letter in which Henry Sr. describes a comfortable scene at home, with his wife reading *The Eustace Diamonds* (by Trollope) and giving her attention now and then to her husband's philosophizing. "She is altogether lovely, I would have you to know," he admonished Henry Jr., asking this son to "tell Alice I hope *she* may always enjoy her husband's approbation to the same extent her mother does mine." Immediately following this passage, the husband and father reported his reaction to *Francia*, a novel by George Sand: "I dont think I ever read any thing that reflects a viler light on her personal history. How bestial a woman must have been born, or become, to grovel spontaneously in such filth."

Henry Sr. saw Mary as the one great exception to the rule that people who aim no higher than an anxious satisfaction of the ethical code cannot enter the spiritual realm. As he put it in a letter to one of his female disciples, "I never saw any technically *good* person but my wife, capable of living with me in spiritual intimacy." With all her myopic virtue about small things, Mary was still capable of operating on her husband's superior plane. Which is to say, she believed in him, listened to him, and nodded appropriately at his monologues.

The death of this devoted wife was the ultimate catastrophe for Henry Sr. In the letters he wrote afterward, his handwriting shrank to what it had been in the early 1840s, and his headlong jocularity vanished. It was obvious to his children he would never again be the man he was. A week after the funeral Henry Jr. described him as "rather seriously unwell" and planned to "remain near him for the present." Near him meant renting rooms in Boston, writing in privacy several hours a day, and taking daily walks across the bridge to Cambridge. Bob, untempered and without a daily routine or a profession, grandly declared that he "had not much else in life to live for now but [to] keep very close to father." "I sleep beside him in mother's empty bed," he told his wife (from whom he was estranged), "and we have quite happy talks at night about Mother's nearness and about our pride in her." This infantile closeness was too suffocating to last, however, and after two months of it Bob took off for the Azores without warning.

It was Alice, inevitably, who took the place of the deceased mother and became her father's mainstay. For years, he had relied on his daughter's nearness—her "studious companionship"—as he worked in his library. She got him to sell the emptied family home on Quincy Street (for $20,000) and to rent a much smaller house in Boston, at 131 Mount Vernon Street. In July the two of them moved for the summer to her new house in Manchester.

Father was taken care of—meaning his second son could go back to London and resume his social and literary life there. Henry Sr. urged him to do so, packing him off in May with a last loving farewell. All the children, he declared, trying not to discriminate, had "been very good and sweet from their infancy," but it was Henry Jr. who had "cost us the least trouble, and given us always the most delight." Henry Sr. appreciated his son's "perfect sweetness" to Mary in her last months. "That blessed mother," the widower broke out, "what a link her memory is to us all henceforth!" He praised "her sleepless sense of justice" as a much finer thing than Aunt Kate's "eminently *partisan*" attitude. Where the latter had been "so *loquacious* . . . as to provoke constant contention," Mary had carried out her steady, selfless, lifelong, domestic activity "altogether unconsciously." How he would prefer to "rejoin her in her modesty . . . than have the gift of a noisy delirious world!"

To Godwin, the bereaved husband confessed that Mary's death "was such an unexpected calamity that I was fairly prostrate under it. For four or five months I didn't see how I was going to live without her." The solution was to undertake one last effort (with Alice nearby) to impress his ideas on the noisy world. All summer he rose soon after five and wrote until one in the afternoon. The new book would be called *Spiritual Creation*. It would be brought out by Osgood in the fall. James felt such "huge delight in doing [his] work carefully and thoroughly" that he ceased writing his children and friends. He wondered (in a letter to Henry Jr.) why it was such a satisfaction to write for the public when he felt "a most robust and preternatural dislike" for writing friends and family, and then answered the question (rather unconvincingly) by saying that age expands the circle of one's sympathies. When Henry Jr. showed the letter to his older brother, who was taking a sabbatical in Europe, William came up with a different answer. This aversion "to 'private' writing" was a token of old age. Father had begun to turn away.

CONSUMMATING HIS LIFE'S WORK

Father and daughter moved back to Boston around the first of October, Alice writing, "We are all well, Father unusually so." When Wilkie came East for a visit, looking dreadful, a doctor found that his heart was enlarged and pronounced him "unfit for work." The bad news didn't seem to register with Henry Sr., who had the impression his thirty-seven-year-old son was "in capital spirits to resume his work" in Wisconsin and predicted that diet and exercise would get him through "a good many years of life." In fact, Wilkie was depressed, mired in debt, and in such bad physical condition he had only a year to live. Before he left Boston, his father tried to sound him out on the touchy question of how he should be treated in the will. On this point, too, Henry Sr. blithely misread his luckless son's mind.

Aunt Kate wanted Henry Sr. to leave everything to Alice, who had no livelihood, but the daughter threatened to "break" the will if it didn't include her brothers; she also refused to be executor. A compromise was reached and the will drawn up and signed on November 21. Alice was to get one full share of the estate, all the household effects, and Duveneck's portrait of Henry Sr., the $2,500 loan being forgiven. William got his full share plus his father's library and papers and the portraits of William of Albany and Catharine Barber James. Henry Jr. got his share and nothing more. Bob had his share reduced by $7,000, the amount he had borrowed. As for Wilkie, the testator declared he was "not unmindful" of his love for him, "but I have omitted him at his own request and in justice to my other children, he having received during my life his full share of my property, but I give to him full release and acquittance from any debt." Alice "objected strongly" to this treatment of Wilkie, but James "insisted that he would put on record what he considered justice to the children." Like his father before him, James was determined to make his will an instrument of final judgment.

For executor, the choice was between the two sons who had achieved financial independence, William and Henry Jr., both of whom were on the other side of the Atlantic. Henry Jr. was chosen, probably so that William would not have to sail home to settle the estate. Henry Sr. returned to this point again and again over the next few weeks. William's sabbatical was not to be interrupted.

Suddenly everyone was struck by Henry Sr.'s growing "indifferen[ce] to things and people," and how he had even ceased to worry about Alice, now wholly "off his mind." At the end of November he had a serious "attack of nausea and faintness" that left him greatly weakened. The physician, a homeopath by the name of Ahlborn, took the position that the seventy-one-year-old patient could live a year longer if he wanted to, but James was convinced he was dying, and he was right.

During the next two and a half weeks they got him to swallow something from time to time—a brandy and Apollinaris, a baked potato, an orange, bread and butter, quail, baked apples—but for the most part he refused to eat or drink, as if bent on dying as soon as possible. The year before he had called Socrates' death "signally beautiful," denying at the same time that it was any more heroic than that of "our ordinary un-annealed suicides." (One of the heroic suicides James had in mind was that of Isaac Edwards, a niece's husband, who killed himself in 1879. In his note of condolence, James said his esteem for Edwards had been greatly increased by his violent manner of death, which showed "how much he must have suffered before resorting to it.") James's own death, however, was not precisely an act of suicide. He was old, he may have had a fatal condition in his alimentary system, and those who knew him were agreed that "the force of the whole system [was] spent." Ten days before the end, he briefly decided it "was wrong to want to die; that he must wait till Providence appoints." All the same, he managed to die as he had lived, maintaining control by exerting his extraordinary strength of purpose. As one who had survived a botched amputation, who pronounced alcoholism a disease of the will and then cured himself, and who asserted his improbable ideas in hundreds of hard-fought controversies, James was not about to leave the hard work of dying to his body alone. Alice put it well when she said that "by the manner of his death his life's work was consummated." William and others made the same reflection.

But watching oneself go out in a willed, responsible way is not particularly easy. Good days alternated with bad. Sometimes he lay there peacefully, looking out the window or imagining a group of "kind old men sitting along the wall" or quietly saying to himself, "It is weary work this dying." At other times he exploded in wrath. He was indignant with those who urged food on him, insisting that "life is sustained by 'God Almighty,' and needs not bread and meat, and any difference from him irritates him extremely." When Aunt Kate read him a letter from William and came to Mrs. McKaye's name, he refused to "listen to another word." Even after he lost control of his fingers, he would grip his cane excitedly and pound the floor. Taking a drink of water, he spluttered, "What vile-tasting stuff, and what a vile world!"

A professional nurse was hired, but it seems to have been Aunt Kate who sat by James's bedside, often holding his hand. A patient and experienced caretaker, she was always "ready *not to do* or *to do*," as the dying man required; what he chiefly required was her presence. Early on, after one of Dr. Ahlborn's visits, James asked his sister-in-law about the prognosis. When she said the doctor thought he would get well, James said "Ridiculous!" but then fell asleep, "repeating to himself the word *delicious*." When he awakened, Aunt Kate "rubb[ed] his chest and he said 'It is exquisite—the rubbing, and what you have just repeated from the doctor.' " Later he announced he "didn't want Aunt Kate near him, she was 'such a sentimentalist.' " Now he was glad to have the doctor's word that he was dying, and he proclaimed that "he had already begun the immortal life." He wanted everyone to know he had "passed through death and that it has no sting." Dr. Ahlborn, unaware of James's notion that selfhood must be got rid of, decided the patient was suffering from mental aberration or "anaemia of the brain."

For James's daughter, the task of managing the dying man was flat-out intolerable. Years later she remembered being "haunted by the terror that I should fail him as I watched the poor old man fade." The question of her own responsibility caused her to go to pieces, as when some well-meaning person urged her to tell Father "he must eat for *my sake!!*" The most agonizing decision of all was when to cable for Henry in London. This Alice mishandled, waiting far too long before admitting that her father was dying. She retreated to her room, to complain about her feet and suffer "attacks of pain in her stomach" and be tended by her friend. Hostile and remote, she was so averse to being "broken in upon when Miss Loring [was] with her" that William's wife was afraid to stop by. It came out later that Miss Loring was allowing Alice to take "a good deal" of opium, "contrary to the doctor's wishes." Alice loved opium, finding "the quiet languor . . . the most blissful thing imaginable."

When the end came and Henry Sr. had trouble breathing, he was given morphine. In his last speeches, carefully noted down, he failed to mention Alice. "I am going with great joy." "Oh, I have such good boys—*such* good boys!" "There is my Mary." He died December 18, 1882, in the afternoon.

If the guilty son, intent on extinguishing himself, had lived a few hours longer, it would have been fifty years to the day since the death of his father, William of Albany, on December 19, 1832.

HENRY SR.'S BOX

The daughter who had once wanted to knock the head off her "benignant pater" decided to have it dissected in order to determine whether anemia (softening) of the brain had been the cause of death (as Dr. Ahlborn and Aunt Kate believed and some obituaries announced). Alice was persuaded to drop the idea, but her "imperativeness of speech and manner" grew more aggressive and she "turned against Aunt Kate again, worse than before." So did Miss Loring, who "happened" to catch Alice's aunt burning some packets of letters that had been kept in a chest of drawers. If this relative's motive was a wish to protect her past, she probably had good reason to be anxious about her late brother-in-law's epistolary indiscretions: in 1847 James had given Wilkinson the impression Aunt Kate was "in hot water" with some sect. If her idea was to protect her sister, she seems to have been devastatingly effective, wiping out every trace of Mary's courtship.

Henry Jr. left England on December 12, a few days after Alice telegraphed. In his latest novel he had lavished all his narrative arts on some tender bedside scenes between Ralph Touchett and his dying father, and Isabel and the dying Ralph. Isabel travels all night from Florence to London to be with Ralph, but when the creator of this touching last moment disembarked in New York, he found a letter announcing that his father had just been buried. The novelist pulled into Boston late that night and took to his bed with "the worst headache he ever had." He kept to his room for several days, and when he finally came downstairs, he "looked very ill and was sitting in an attitude of despondency." Alice's future weighed on him, and also the "extraordinary tie" between her and Loring (the quoted words being Mrs. Alice's). And he had to make some decisions about that punitive will he was supposed to execute.

Henry's letters to William register a keener sense of loss than anything he is known to have written about his mother's death the previous winter. At that time he had waxed solemn and rhetorical: "She is with us, she is of us—the eternal stillness is but a form of her love. One can hear her voice in it." Now, straining to catch Father's "remarkable voice," Henry was less affirmative:

> I sit here at his table, I sleep in his bed, I am surrounded with everything that belonged to him in life, and it seems to me that I still hear his voice, and that if I go downstairs, I shall find him. But he is already a memory, & every hour makes him more so—he is tremendously & unspeakably absent. It doesn't seem so much, however, that he is dead, as that a strange deadness has fallen upon *us*.

And upon the writer's own idealizations. Not long afterward, he confessed that up to now his best fiction had had "too damnably much" of "a certain 'gloss.' " He began making plans for a new novel, *The Bostonians*, his most confrontational and controversial work, and suddenly his career took an abrupt swerve. Setting out to defend his father's views on the "Woman business" and American democracy and many other matters, the anxiously filial novelist ended up questioning them. For the rest of the decade, he would be in trouble with readers and publishers. His voice was changing, from the depersonalized professionalism of his earlier writing to his late and highly idiosyncratic manner.

The deceased's estate was inventoried at $95,000, consisting chiefly of three Syracuse buildings appraised at $75,000 and $19,000 worth of railroad stocks and bonds. When Wilkie learned he had been excluded from any share of this, he was outraged and vowed to take legal action. In a letter to Bob, he condemned the will's exclusions in the strongest language possible—"a base cowardly act of father's, a death stab." Why punish those sons who "dared fight through the war for the defense of the family" and "attempted while very young to earn their own living"? Wilkie's letter brought into the open the resentments generated by a history of favoritism. After being humiliated by William of Albany's invidious will, Henry Sr. had spent half a century denouncing legal and moral discrimination, yet when the time came he, too, made his will the occasion for some harshly drawn lines, chiefly between those "destined for commerce" and those who had been given a chance at Harvard and a Grand Tour of Europe and years of enabling leisure. The former would have to repay what had been given them; the latter (and Alice) would have their debts canceled. As executor, Henry Jr. wisely elected to ignore the will and arrange for an equal division across the board. William balked at this, preferring to defend his father's sense of justice and his own financial interests, but an amicable compromise was worked out.

For William, it was a "bitter thought" that neither he nor Henry was able to bid their father goodbye. Doing the best he could under the circumstances, he sat down on December 14, four days before Henry Sr.'s death, and composed a justly famous farewell letter. He wanted to say, not just that he loved his father, but that he had understood him and would transmit his teachings to his own children and others—that the torch would be passed on. "All my intellectual life I derive from you," he testified, "and though we have often seemed at odds in the expression thereof, I'm sure there's a harmony somewhere." He promised to bring out his parent's unpublished papers, and he mentioned a couple of European thinkers who professed to admire him, and then it was time to say the last words: "It comes strangely over me in bidding you good-bye how a life is but a day and expresses mainly but a single note. It is so much like the act of bidding an ordinary good-night. Good-night, my sacred old Father!" When the letter reached Boston, the younger brother saw "Henry James" on the envelope and, thinking it was meant for himself, opened and read William's moving expression of filial love and loyalty. Then he took it to the cemetery and read it aloud to the fresh grave.

The two older sons had been shaped by their father in a thousand ways: *they* were his box of carefully selected papers. James's belief that the dissolution of compulsory morality would usher in a new and spontaneous virtue reappears in the novelist's many exalted protagonists, who often adhere to a high, fine, and even self-punishing ideal of conduct in spite of the other characters' selfish and deceptive practices. But Henry did not commit himself to his father's vision to the degree that William did. It was the favored son who continued to feel Father's breath long after his heart stopped and who assumed the task of preservation, of public mediation. In January 1883 he wrote of his determination to

> make amends for my rather hard non-receptivity of his doctrines . . . by trying to get a little more public justice done them now . . . Father's cry was the single one that religion is real. The thing is so to "voice" it that other ears shall hear,—no easy task, but a worthy one, which in some shape I shall attempt.

William was to be astonishingly successful as a revoicer of certain aspects of his parent's thought—the tormenting primacy of our "unconscious natural life," the importance of heroic manliness, the stultifying effect of the official and the sectarian. For thirty years and more Henry Sr. had attempted to capture the meaning of American democracy, but it was left to William to articulate what has become the loose national philosophy of relativized and energetic openness. One of the reasons William appropriated pragmatism from Charles Sanders Peirce was to dignify religious belief in general, and in particular his father's lifelong practice of adopting certain philosophical positions because of their psychic payoffs. Jamesian pragmatism may well be linked to the New World's grand aspirations, but it has also proved useful in authorizing the freakish, the obscure, and the obscurely embattled. Like Henry Sr. before him, William may be judged as more fertile than lucid. When Leslie Stephen read his "denunciation of the wicked determinists" in 1884, he judged William to be "a clever fellow, but, I think, rather flighty," adding: "I stick to Spinoza and Jonathan Edwards and Hume and all really clear-headed people."

For some thinkers, particularly in the United States, pragmatism has become a sacred intellectual Americanism, a way of resisting the evils of "essentialism" and rational force. But just as Henry Sr.'s views on democracy in America often issued in an appeal for an exacting and even violent millennial resolution, so pragmatism has lent itself to powerfully anti-democratic forces. One early self-described pragmatist, Giovanni Papini, enthusiastically adopted William's belief in sentiment as a lever for action and a muscular will-to-believe as a force for world renewal. Papini edited a Florentine review, *Leonardo*, whose emblem was a man thrusting a lance through the neck of a peacock-like dragon. William warmly appreciated this energetic disciple and in 1906 wrote a laudatory article about him. The American had some reservations about the Italian's penchant for carrying philosophy into politics, but he found in Papini's writings "a way in which our English views might be developed farther with consistency" and also a tone "well fitted to rally devotees and to make of pragmatism a new militant form of religious or quasi-religious philosophy." Benito Mussolini considered Papini's first intellectual autobiography, *Un Uomo finito* (translated as *The Failure*), "extraordinary and admirable." In 1926 Il Duce told the foreign editor of the Madrid *A.B.Z.* that the writings of William James had inspired his "faith in action and that ardent will to live and fight to which Fascism owes a great part of its success." One can't help but be reminded of Henry Sr.'s anticipation of "Judge Lynch's benevolent sway" in New York City in the mid-1850s. Of course, it must be understood that William opposed militarism, nationalistic adventures, and the glorification of collective force in the state.

One of the ways in which William tried to get a hearing for Henry Sr.'s ideas was to bring out an edition of his unpublished papers that featured a long interpretive introduction. As William worked on *The Literary Remains of the Late Henry James* during the summer of 1884, he "seemed to sink into an intimacy with Father." He also sank into a fever, and when his wife rejoined him at summer's end she found him "rather used up." The volume was poorly calculated to keep Henry Sr.'s thought alive. It ignored his lively essays of the late 1840s and paid no attention to the development of his thought, focusing instead on his latest and most tedious restatements. In London, Henry praised the volume and tried to believe Father "was yet a great writer" and felt a "pious melancholy" at his failure with the public. But he didn't read beyond the introduction and fictional autobiography, and he admitted his parent's "manner" of writing often displeased him.

Copies of *The Literary Remains* were dutifully distributed. Holmes replied that the book would be by him for a long time, "not so much to be read page by page as to be consulted as an oracle, often to be believed and always to be listened to." He warmly recalled his old friend's "sincerity and strong manhood," "his searching intelligence and outspoken honesty." Most of those who were given copies of the volume did not acknowledge it. The only important review was in *The Nation*, which trenchantly dismissed James's thought as of no value to the modern thinker.

The disciples James attracted during his life were not discouraged by his death. In 1883 Julia A. Kellogg brought out a meticulously paraphrased digest of his philosophy. In 1895 the Reverend E. Payson Walton tried to launch something called the Ontological Society, the purpose of which would be to republish the writings of the late Henry James. In 1928 Samuel Marshall Ilsley, who had come to James's books through Wilkie, tried to find a publisher for a selection of his writings. Simultaneously, he informed readers of *The New Republic* that James "was a mystic of profounder mind than Emerson." The next year Alice Spiers Sechrist discerned signs of "a real revival of interest" in James from the fact that "somebody in Washington [D.C.] besides myself and one or two personal friends is interested—and I wish I could find out who it is." One of the many ironies of James's career is that the man who campaigned for the universal and against the sectarian became the focus of a tiny cultlike following.

But who can trace the eddies into which a powerful writer diffuses himself? One of James's most fervent adepts was Caroline (Eliot) Lackland, a member of Lydia Fuller Dickinson's circle in St. Louis. Mrs.

Lackland had been an enthusiast for spirit-rapping in the 1850s, and the Civil War so intoxicated her she felt a "sense of disappointment" when a friend came out of battle unhurt. "That which was once called politics, has become principle, religion!" she exclaimed. In 1866 she sued her first husband, John Kasson, for divorce on grounds of adultery, and three years later married a banker, Rufus J. Lackland. Soon after having "begun the study of the writings of Mr. James," she wrote an ecstatic article, "Henry James, the Seer," that was published in the *Journal of Speculative Philosophy*. That was in 1885, shortly before her great-nephew T. S. Eliot was born.

Henry Sr.'s descendants hold him in very high regard. One, a great-grandson, recalls what he was told about him at the age of eight, some sixty years ago. The scene took place in the room where the Duveneck portrait hung above the fireplace, in the house where William the philosopher lived and died, in Cambridge, Massachusetts. The ancient bearded man in the picture, the boy was told, had taught that God was in everything, in all human beings and in all things. Even in this pillow? the boy asked. Yes, even in that pillow, and the boy looked down, delighted to think he was sitting on God.

Acknowledgments

∎ ∎ ∎

The author is indebted to the following libraries, societies, churches, and individuals for permission to quote unpublished materials. Papers and Collections are identified as specified by the libraries holding them: Abernethy Library, Middlebury College; Albany Public Library; Alexander R. James; Julius Hawley Seeley Papers, Amherst College Archives; Family Papers and Sermons of Rev. William James, Amherst College Library; Burton Historical Collection, Detroit Public Library; Special Collections, Colby College Library; Drew University Library; Special Collections Library, Duke University; First Congregational Church, Canandaigua, NY; First Presbyterian Church, Albany, NY; Henry J. Vaux; Houghton Library, Harvard University; The Huntington Library, San Marino, CA; Henry Borneman Papers, Illinois Historical Survey, University of Illinois Library; Margaret A. James; Annie Adams Fields Papers, Caroline Healey Dall Papers, Examiner Club Papers, Horace Mann III, James T. Fisher Papers, Religious Union of Associationists, Theodore Dwight Papers, Massachusetts Historical Society; Newport Historical Society; New-York Historical Society Library; New York Public Library, Astor, Lenox and Tilden Foundations, Henry W. and Albert A. Berg Collection, and Rare Books and Manuscripts Division: Miscellaneous Papers (William James, Sr.), Account Books (James McBride), DeWitt Clinton Papers, Bryant Godwin Collection (Henry James, Sr.); New York State Library, Albany, NY; Onondaga Historical Association, Syracuse, NY; Ontario County Historical Society, Canandaigua, NY; Hodge Papers, Princeton University Libraries; Schaffer Library, Union College, Schenectady, NY; Schenectady County Historical Society; Seymour Library, Knox College, Galesburg, IL; Smithsonian Institution Archives; Speer Library, Princeton Theological Seminary; Henry James Collection, George Bush Letterbooks, Swedenborg School of Religion, 48 Sargent Street, Newton, MA 02158; Swedenborg Society, Swedenborg House, London; United States Naval Academy Archives; Special Collections, University of Kentucky Library; Labadie Collection, Special Collections, University of Michigan Library; Rare Books and Special Collections, University of Rochester.

I wish to express my gratitude to the following libraries and record centers for their indispensable help in running down leads, sources, and facts, singling out a few librarians for their exceptional helpfulness and resourcefulness: Albany County Hall of Records; Albany County Surrogates Court; Albany Institute of History & Art; Albert Barkas Room, Richmond Library, England; Appellate Division Law Library, Rochester, NY (Ian Woodward); Archives de Paris; Archives Nationales, Paris; Archives d'Etat, Geneva; Beinecke Library, Yale; Berkshire Athenaeum, Pittsfield, MA (Ruth T. Degenhardt); Bibliothèque historique de la ville de Paris; Boston Public Library; Buffalo and Erie County Historical Society, Buffalo, NY; Centre d'iconographie genevoise, Geneva; Chicago Public Library (Galen R. Wilson); Cincinnati Historical Society; Concord Free Public Library, Concord, MA (Marcia E. Moss); Delaware County Clerk's Office, Delhi, NY (Debra K. Lambrecht); Evangelical Library, London; Grampian Regional Archives, Scotland; Guildhall Library, London; Hamilton College Library Special Collections, Clinton, NY; Historic New Orleans Collection; Historical Society of Princeton (Phil Hayden); Library of Congress; Madison County Historical Society, Edwardsville, IL; Missouri Historical Society, St. Louis; Monmouth County Historical Association, Freehold, NJ; Newport City Hall; New York County Clerk Archives (Bruce Abrams); New York Genealogical and Biographical Society; New York Hall of Records; New York Municipal Archives; New York Public Library (Microfilm Division and Local History and Genealogy Division); New York Society Library; New York State Archives, Albany (James D. Folts, William A. Evans); Onondaga County Public Library, Syracuse, NY (Patricia Finley); Pierpont Morgan Library, New York; Presbyterian Church Office of History, Philadelphia; Rochester Historical Society; Smith College Library; Staten Island Institute of Arts & Sciences (Hugh Powell); Surrey County Archivist's Office, England (Mrs. E. A. Stazicker); Swedenborg Library, Bryn Athyn, PA (Carroll Odhner);

Troy Public Library, Troy, NY (Robert B. Hudson); Union Theological Seminary Library, New York; University of Aberdeen Archives, Scotland; University of Kansas Libraries (innumerable staff members in Reference, Special Collections, and Interlibrary Services).

Other librarians and archivists who have gone well beyond the usual line of duty in handling my difficult and seemingly endless queries: Betty Allen, Denison Beach, Lisa Browar, James Corsaro, Nancy S. Dawson, Ellen H. Fladger, Susan Halpert, William O. Harris, Jean S. Hilliard, R. Shawn Johnstone, John Lancaster, Patience-Anne W. Lenk, Jonathan Mitchell, Jane H. Price, Jennie Rathbun, Mariam Touba, Emily Walhout, Judith Wilson, Melanie Wisner, and Louise Woofenden.

Among the many others who furnished invaluable leads, sources, information, advice, or stimulating questions and suggestions, and without whose help my research on various matters would have languished indefinitely, I wish to single out Dorothea Abbott, Roger Asselineau, Jonathan Beecher, Donna Campbell, Jennifer Dean, Silvia D. Greenwood, Carl Guarneri, Dorothy Harkness, Rev. Earl Holt, Floyd Horowitz, Margaret A. James, Michael James, Steve Jobe, Fred Kaplan, Dr. Jacqueline E. M. Latham, Jane Maher, Heather L. Nadelman, Suzi Naiburg, Paul Nielsen, Clyde de L. Ryals, Rev. Norman Ryder, R. A. Sheehan, Ph.D., David E. E. Sloan, Henry J. Vaux, Bill Veeder, and Pierre A. Walker.

Jan Martin Moreno was the graduate assistant who transcribed the Wilkinson letters and other documents. James Olney found a place in the *Southern Review* for an early version of John Barber James's story, Dan Fogel offered repeated opportunities to present my findings at conferences, and Linda Smith Rhoads showed me how to tell the story of Henry Sr.'s Princeton years for the *New England Quarterly*. Warder Cadbury, Donna Campbell, and Fred Kaplan offered the most welcome and gracious hospitality on my research trips, and Myrtle Wulff of Flora, Oregon, provided the space and electrical hook-up that enabled me to compose the book, and also kept me sane with her lunchtime companionship.

I shrink from the thought of the errors I would have made and the questions that would have stayed in the shadows if parts of the biography had not been scrutinized by Carol Holly, Dr. Jacqueline E. M. Latham, Suzi Naiburg, Sheldon M. Novick, Joel Porte, R. A. Sheehan, and Eugene Taylor. Leon Edel generously advised me to attempt this biography in spite of his disagreement with some of my contentions in a previous book. I am immeasurably indebted to him, Fred Kaplan, Jean Strouse, Howard M. Feinstein, Jane Maher, and the many others who have investigated the Jameses, not forgetting the scholarly pioneers from an earlier era—Katharine Hastings, Austin Warren, Ralph Barton Perry, Harold A. Larrabee, Robert C. Le Clair.

Producing a fully investigated biography is a costly undertaking. This one could not have been completed in the six years it consumed if it hadn't been for a fellowship from the National Endowment for the Humanities, a grant from the American Council of Learned Societies, a sabbatical semester from the University of Kansas, fellowships and travel grants from the Hall Center for the Humanities, and summer awards from the University of Kansas General Research Fund.

Thanks to Lynn Warshow, copy editor, and Paul Elie, assistant editor. For essential help that includes but goes far beyond the tangible, I'm particularly grateful to Nat Sobel, my agent, and Jonathan Galassi, my editor.

Notes

■ ■ ■

ABBREVIATIONS OF SELECTED LIBRARIES AND PRIVATE COLLECTIONS

A	Amherst College Library
APL	Albany Public Library
C	Miller Library, Colby College
H	Houghton Library, Harvard University
IHS	Illinois Historical Survey, University of Illinois Library
LC	Library of Congress
MHS	Massachusetts Historical Society, Boston
N-YHS	New-York Historical Society
NYMA	New York Municipal Archives, 31 Chambers Street
NYPL	New York Public Library, Astor, Lenox, and Tilden Foundations
NYSL	New York State Library, Albany
OCPL	Onondaga County Public Library, Syracuse
OHA	Onondaga Historical Association, Syracuse
PTS	Speer Library, Princeton Theological Seminary
SIIAS	Staten Island Institute of Arts and Sciences
SL	Swedenborg Library, London
SSR	Swedenborg School of Religion Library, Newton, MA
UC	Schaffer Library, Union College
V	Henry J. Vaux

ABBREVIATIONS OF SELECTED INDIVIDUAL NAMES

ABW	Anna (Barker) Ward
AF	Annie Fields
AHJ	Alice Howe (Gibbens) James
AM	Archibald McIntyre
CBJ	Catharine (Barber) James (1782–1859)
CD	Caroline Dall
CH	Charles Hodge
CT	Caroline (Sturgis) Tappan
CW	Catharine Walsh ("Aunt Kate")

EC	Elizabeth Cranch
EN	Eliphalet Nott
EP	Elizabeth Peabody
ET	Edmund Tweedy
EVW	Edgar Van Winkle
EW	Emma Wilkinson
FM	Frances Macdaniel ("Fanny")
GB	George Bush
Gus	Augustus James (1807–66)
GWC	George W. Clinton
GWJ	Garth Wilkinson James ("Wilkie") (1845–83)
HJ	Henry James ("Henry Jr.," "Harry") (1843–1916)
HJSr	Henry James, Sr. (1811–82)
IJ	Isaac W. Jackson
JAK	Julia A. Kellogg
JBJ	John Barber James (1816–56)
JCG	John Chipman Gray
JH	Joseph Henry
JJ	Jannet (or Jeannette) James (1814–42)
JJGW	James John Garth Wilkinson
JM	James McBride
JTF	James T. Fisher
Kitty	Catharine (James) Prince ("Kitty") 1834–90
MAJ	Marcia (Ames) James
MJ	Mary Robertson (Walsh) James (1810–82)
MT	Mary Temple ("Minny," "Minnie") (1845–70)
PG	Parke Godwin
Rev. WJ	Reverend William James (1797–1868)
RJ	Robertson James ("Bob") (1846–1910)
RWE	Ralph Waldo Emerson
SGW	Samuel Gray Ward
SSS	Sarah (Sturgis) Shaw
TC	Thomas Carlyle
WJ	William James ("Willy") (1842–1910)
WJ of Alb.	William James of Albany ("Billy") (1771–1832)

ABBREVIATIONS OF SELECTED
PUBLISHED AND UNPUBLISHED SOURCES

AA	*Albany Argus*
AEJ	*Albany Evening Journal*
AH	Alexander, Henry Carrington. *The Life of Joseph Addison Alexander.* New York: Scribner's, Armstrong, 1875
AJ1	Alexander, James Waddel. *Forty Years' Familiar Letters.* John Hall, ed. 2 vols. New York: Scribner's, 1860
AJ2	———. *The Life of Archibald Alexander.* New York: Scribner's, 1854.
AL	Allen, Gay Wilson. *William James: A Biography.* New York: Viking, 1967.

AN   *Annals of Albany*. Joel Munsell, ed. Vols. 1–10 (1850–59). Vols. 1–4 (1869–71)

AT   *Atlantic Monthly*

BE   Beecher, Jonathan. *Charles Fourier*. Berkeley: University of California Press, 1986

BEN   Benson, Lee. *The Concept of Jacksonian Democracy*. Princeton, NJ: Princeton University Press, 1961

BLA   Blayney, J. McClusky. *History of the First Presbyterian Church of Albany*. Albany, NY: Jenkins & Johnston, 1877

BLO   Block, Marguerite Beck. *The New Church in the New World*. New York: Swedenborg Publishing Association, 1984

BO   *Boston Daily Advertiser*

BR   Bremer, Fredrika. *The Homes of the New World*. Mary Howitt, trans. 2 vols. New York: Harper, 1868

BRF   *A Brief History of the Theological Seminary . . . at Princeton*. Princeton, NJ: Bogart, 1838

BU   Buchanan, James. *The Order to be Observed in a Church of God*. London: Jones/Dublin: Carson, 1845. Only known U.S. copy at Union Theological Seminary

BUR   Burr, Anna Robeson, ed. *Alice James: Her Brothers—Her Journal*. New York: Dodd, Mead, 1934

CAR   Carlyle, Thomas, and Jane Welsh Carlyle. *Collected Letters*. 21 vols. to date. Durham, NC: Duke University Press, 1990

CEL   *Celebration of the Semi-Centennial Anniversary of the Albany Academy*. Albany, NY: Munsell, 1863

CHE   Chester, Alden. *Courts and Lawyers of New York*. 3 vols. New York: American Historical Society, 1925

CIR   *The Circular*. Published in Brooklyn by the Oneida Community from 1851

CO1   Cooke, George Willis. *John Sullivan Dwight*. New York: Da Capo, 1969

CO2   ———. *An Historical and Biographical Introduction to . . . The Dial*. 2 vols. New York: Russell & Russell, 1961

CRA   *The Craftsman* (Albany)

CRO   Cross, Whitney R. *The Burned-over District*. Ithaca, NY: Cornell University Press, 1950

DAL   Dall, Caroline. Journals. Caroline Healey Dall Papers. MHS

DNB   *Dictionary of National Biography*

DO   Dodge, H. Augusta, ed. *Gail Hamilton's Life in Letters*. 2 vols. Boston, MA: Lee & Shepard, 1901

ED   Edel, Leon. *Henry James*. 5 vols. Philadelphia: Lippincott, 1953–72

EM1   Emerson, Ralph Waldo. *Journals and Miscellaneous Notebooks*. 16 vols. Cambridge, MA: Harvard University Press, 1960–82

EM2   ———. *Letters*. Ralph L. Rusk and Eleanor M. Tilton, eds. 9 vols. to date. New York: Columbia University Press, 1939, 1990–

EMD   Emerson, Edward Waldo. *The Early Years of the Saturday Club 1855–1870*. Boston, MA: Houghton Mifflin, 1918

EML   Emerson, Ellen Tucker. *Letters*. Edith E. W. Gregg, ed. 2 vols. Kent, OH: Kent State University Press, 1982

FEI   Feinstein, Howard M. *Becoming William James*. Ithaca, NY: Cornell University Press, 1984

FLD   Fields, Annie. Journals. Annie Adams Fields Papers. MHS

FOX   Fox, Dixon Ryan. *The Decline of Aristocracy in the Politics of New York*. New York: Columbia University Press, 1919

GUA   Guarneri, Carl J. *The Utopian Alternative: Fourierism in Nineteenth-Century America*. Ithaca, NY: Cornell University Press, 1991

HAB   Habegger, Alfred. *Henry James and the "Woman Business."* New York: Cambridge University Press, 1989

HAG   Hageman, John Frelinghuysen. *History of Princeton*. 2 vols. Philadelphia, PA: Lippincott, 1879

HAM   Hammond, Jabez D. *The History of Political Parties in the State of New-York*. 2 vols. Cooperstown, NY: Phinney, 1846

HAR   *Harbinger*

HARL   Harlow, Virginia. *Thomas Sergeant Perry*. Durham, NC: Duke University Press, 1950

HAS1   Hastings, Katharine B. "The Barbers of Orange and Albany Counties, N.Y.," *New York Genealogical and Biographical Record* 62 (January, April, July 1931)

HAS2   ———. "William James (1771–1832) of Albany, N.Y., and His Descendants," *New York Genealogical and Biographical Record* 55 (April, July, October 1924)

HE   Henry, Joseph. *Papers*. Nathan Reingold et al., eds. 6 vols. to date. Washington, D.C.: Smithsonian Institution Press, 1972–

HEN   "Henry James, Sr./The Foremost Metaphysician and Philosopher in America./ Successive Steps in His Development of Opinions," *Boston Herald*, April 17, 1881, p. 3

HI   Hill, John J. *Reminiscences of Albany*. New York: Medole, 1884

HIS   Hislop, Codman. *Eliphalet Nott*. Middletown, CT: Wesleyan University Press, 1971

HIST   *Historical Sketch of the New York New Church Society*. New York: Prall, [1860?]. Copy at SSR

HOF   Hoffmann, Charles & Tess. "Henry James and the Civil War," *New England Quarterly* 62 (December 1989) pp. 529–52

HOW   Howell, George R., and Jonathan Tenney. *Bi-Centennial History of Albany*. New York: Munsell, 1886

HU   [Hun, Henry.] "A Survey of the Activity of the Albany Academy: The Ancestry and Achievements of Its Students." 5 vols. NYSL

IN   *In Chancery, before the Chancellor. John Townsend and Abba his wife, and Augustus James . . . vs. James McBride and others. Final Decree in Partition*. Albany, NY: Van Benthuysen, 1846

JA   James, Alice. *Diary*. Harmondsworth, England: Penguin, 1982

JH1   James, Henry, Sr. *Christianity the Logic of Creation*. London: White, 1857

JH2   ———. *The Church of Christ Not an Ecclesiasticism: A Letter to a Sectarian*. New York: Redfield, 1854. 1st edition

JH3   ———. *The Church of Christ Not an Ecclesiasticism*. London: White, 1856. 2nd edition

JH4   [———.] *The Gospel Good News to Sinners*. New York: Scatcherd & Adams,
           1838. Only known copy at N-YHS

JH5   ———. *Lectures and Miscellanies*. New York: Redfield, 1852. Facsimile reprint:
           New York: AMS, 1983

JH6   ———. *The Literary Remains of the Late Henry James*. William James, ed.
           Boston, MA: Houghton Mifflin, 1884

JH7   ———, Horace Greeley & Stephen Pearl Andrews. *Love, Marriage, and
           Divorce*. New York: Source Books, 1972. Reprints first edition: New York:
           Stringer & Townsend, 1853

JH8   ———. *Moralism and Christianity; or Man's Experience and Destiny*. New York:
           Redfield, 1850. Facsimile reprint: New York: AMS, 1983

JH9   ———. *The Nature of Evil Considered in a Letter to the Rev. Edward Beecher,
           D.D. Author of "The Conflict of Ages."* New York: Appleton, 1855. Fac-
           simile reprint: New York: AMS, 1983

JH10   ———, ed. Robert Sandeman. *Letters on Theron and Aspasio*. New York:
           Taylor/Boston, MA: Weeks, Jordan, 1838

JH11   ———. *The Secret of Swedenborg*. Boston, MA: Houghton Mifflin, 1869

JH12   ———. ["Seminary Days"]. Houghton Library [bMS Am 1094.8 (5)]

JH13   ———. *The Social Significance of Our Institutions: An Oration Delivered by
           Request of the Citizens of Newport, R.I., July 4th, 1861*. Boston, MA:
           Ticknor & Fields, 1861. Facsimile reprint: Pottstown, PA: Americanist
           Press, 1966

JH14   ———. *Society the Redeemed Form of Man, and the Earnest of God's Omnipotence
           in Human Nature: Affirmed in Letters to a Friend*. Boston, MA: Houghton,
           Osgood, 1879

JH15   ———. *Substance and Shadow*. Boston: Ticknor and Fields, 1863

JR1   James, Henry, Jr. *The Complete Notebooks*. Leon Edel and Lyall H. Powers,
           eds. New York: Oxford University Press, 1987

JR2   ———. *Letters*. Leon Edel, ed. 4 vols. Cambridge, MA: Harvard University
           Press, 1974–84

JR3   ———. *Letters*. Percy Lubbock, ed. 2 vols. London: Macmillan, 1920

JR4   ———. *Literary Criticism*. Leon Edel, ed. 2 vols. New York: Library of Amer-
           ica, 1984

NSB   ———. *Notes of a Son and Brother*. New York: Scribner's, 1914

SBO   ———. *A Small Boy and Others*. New York: Scribner's, 1913

JR7   ———. *William Wetmore Story and His Friends*. 2 vols. Boston, MA: Houghton
           Mifflin, 1904

JW1   James, William. *Correspondence*. Ignas K. Skrupskelis and Elizabeth M. Berke-
           ley, eds. 1 vol. to date. Charlottesville: University Press of Virginia, 1992–

JW2   ———. *Letters*. Henry James III, ed. 2 vols. Boston, MA: Atlantic Monthly
           Press, 1920

JW3   ———. *The Varieties of Religious Experience*. Cambridge, MA: Harvard Uni-
           versity Press, 1985

JWR   James, William, Rev. *The Marriage of the King's Son*. New York: Randolph,
           1869

KA   Kaplan, Fred. *Henry James*. New York: Morrow, 1992

L1   Larrabee, Harold A. "The Fourth William James," *Colby Library Quarterly*
           Series 9 (March 1970) pp. 1–34

L2 ———. "William James of Albany as Syracuse Salt Merchant." UC

LEC LeClair, Robert C. *Young Henry James 1843–1870.* New York: Bookman Associates, 1955

LEW Lewis, R.W.B. *The Jameses.* New York: Farrar, Straus & Giroux, 1991

LEY Leyda, Jay. *The Melville Log.* 2 vols. New York: Gordian, 1969

MA MacKaye, Percy. *Epoch: The Life of Steele MacKaye.* 2 vols. New York: Boni & Liveright, 1927

MAC Maclean, John. *History of the College of New Jersey.* 2 vols. New York: Arno, 1969

MAH Maher, Jane. *Biography of Broken Fortunes: Wilkie and Bob, Brothers of William, Henry, and Alice James.* Hamden, CT: Archon, 1986

MAI Maitland, Frederick William. *The Life and Letters of Leslie Stephen.* London: Duckworth, 1907

MAT Matthiessen, F. O. *The James Family.* New York: Knopf, 1948

MCD McDowell, R. B. *Ireland in the Age of Imperialism and Revolution 1760–1801.* Oxford: Clarendon, 1979

MIL Miller, Kerby A. *Emigrants and Exiles: Ireland and the Irish Exodus to North America.* New York: Oxford University Press, 1985

MIN Minutes of the Board of Directors of Princeton Theological Seminary. PTS

MYE Myerson, Joel. "New Light on George Ripley and the *Harbinger's* New York Years," *Harvard Library Bulletin* 33 (1985), pp. 313–36

NCI *New Church Independent and Monthly Review*

NJM *New Jerusalem Magazine*

NSB *Notes of a Son and Brother.* See James, Henry, Jr.

NX See Niven, John

NYM *New-York Medical and Physical Journal*

NYT *New York Times*

NYTr *New York Tribune*

NX Niven, John. *Martin Van Buren.* New York: Oxford UP, 1983

PE Perry, Ralph Barton. *The Thought and Character of William James.* 2 vols. Boston, MA: Little, Brown, 1935

PR Pruyn, John V. L. *Remarks on the Life and Character of the Late Gideon Hawley.* Copy at NYSL

RE Religious Union of Associationists. Records, 1847–1850. MHS

ROS Rose, Anne C. *Transcendentalism as a Social Movement.* New Haven, CT: Yale University Press, 1981

ROW Rowley, William Esmond. "Albany: A Tale of Two Cities 1820–1880." Diss: Harvard University, 1967

SBO *A Small Boy and Others.* See James, Henry, Jr.

SC Scott, Leonora Cranch. *The Life and Letters of Christopher Pearse Cranch.* Boston, MA: Houghton Mifflin, 1917

SI Silver, Ednah C. *Sketches of the New Church in America.* Boston, MA: Massachusetts New Church Union, 1920

SL Slater, Joseph, ed. *The Correspondence of Emerson and Carlyle.* New York: Columbia University Press, 1964

SM Smith, J.E.A. *The History of Pittsfield.* 2 vols. Springfield, MA: Bryan, 1876

SP Sprague, William B. *An Address Delivered on Occasion of the Funeral of the Rev. William James.* Albany, NY: Munsell, 1868

SPR   *Springfield Daily Republican*

SPU   Spurlock, John C. *Free Love: Marriage and Middle-Class Radicalism in America, 1825–1860.* New York: New York University Press, 1988

ST   Sterling, John, and Ralph Waldo Emerson. *A Correspondence between John Sterling and Ralph Waldo Emerson.* Boston, MA: Houghton, Mifflin, 1897

STO   Stokes, I. N. Phelps. *The Iconography of Manhattan Island.* 6 vols. New York: Dodd, 1926

STR   Strouse, Jean. *Alice James: A Biography.* Boston, MA: Houghton Mifflin, 1980

TH   Thoreau, Henry David. *Correspondence.* Walter Harding and Carl Bode, eds. New York: New York University Press, 1958

TO   Townsend, John, et al. complainants. *John Townsend and Abba His Wife.* Albany, NY: Van Benthuysen, 1844. Copy at NYSL

UN   Union College Student Records/3rd Term 1828–1829 to 3rd Term 1834–1835 [ledger]. UC

VA   Van Deusen, Glyndon G. *Thurlow Weed.* Boston, MA: Little, Brown, 1947

WA   [Walker, John.] *Essays and Correspondence.* 2 vols. London: Longman et al., 1838

WAL   Walsh, William. *A Record and Sketch of Hugh Walsh's Family.* Newburgh, NY: Newburgh Journal, 1903. Copy at H

WAR   Warren, Austin. *The Elder Henry James.* New York: Macmillan, 1934

WE   Weed, Thurlow. *Autobiography.* Boston, MA: Houghton, Mifflin, 1884

WLK   Wilkinson, Clement John. *James John Garth Wilkinson.* London: Kegan Paul, Trench, Trübner, 1911

WO   Worth, Gorham A. *Random Recollections of Albany.* Albany, NY: Munsell, 1866

YE   Yeazell, Ruth Bernard. *The Death and Letters of Alice James.* Berkeley: University of California Press, 1981

MISCELLANEOUS BIBLIOGRAPHICAL INFORMATION

For nineteenth-century federal censuses, see the *Population Schedules* as published by National Archives Microfilm Publications. The microfilmed 1855 New York State Census is available at various locations in the state; the New York Public Library has an unpublished index of Ward 15 of New York City. City directories will be found at local libraries or historical societies. New York City real-estate conveyances are at the Hall of Records and tax rolls are at the Municipal Archives, both housed at 31 Chambers Street. For New York City will libers, I have gone to the New York Genealogical and Historical Society.

Most of J.J.G. Wilkinson's letters to HJSr are in the possession of the Swedenborg Library, London. The Swedenborg School of Religion, Newton, MA, has a set of photocopies.

The bulk of the James family papers are at the Houghton Library, Harvard. For most of those materials that are inadequately or misleadingly catalogued and thus hard to find, I supply the shelf marks in the appropriate endnotes.

An adequate bibliography of Henry James, Sr.'s published writings does not exist. The author has one in the works.

CHAPTER 1

3 "Mind well": *JH14* 94.

4 "in *feeling*": Rev. WJ to Kitty, 1–25–1861, C.

4 "great indelicacy," etc.: HJSr to JAK, 9–8–[1869], H.

4 Emerson: HJSr to CT, 10–20–1868, H; *SPR* 11–21–1868, p. 2; (Boston) *Commonwealth*, 12–12–1868, pp. 1–2.

5 "I presume": Y.S. [HJSr], "Remarks," *HAR* 8:37.

5 "I marry my wife": HJSr, "Morality vs. Brute Instinct," *Woodhull & Claflin's*, 4–18–1874, p. 5.

6 biographers: See *WAR, ED, FEI, STR*.

7 "little iliad": *JH12*, folder 9, p. 140.

7 compose his story: See *JH6* 123–91.

7 "envy, hatred": HJSr to RJ, 12–10–[n.y.], V.

7 "temperamentally": HJIII to Robert James (b. 1840), 2–10–1922, H.

8 "How perfectly": HJSr to SSS (CW's hand), 5–10–1859, H.

8 "If by any one act": *JH15* 201.

CHAPTER 2

9 first epitaph: AN (1871) 3:188.

10 The flaked-off year: Samuel Lewis, *Topographical Dictionary of Ireland* (London, 1850), 1:96; *LEW* 3–7; *MIL* 48; *HAS2* 103; HJIII, narrative of visit, 6–7–1931, by permission of Margaret James.

10 William's older brother: Marie E. James to HJIII, 3–2–1922, H; Obit. of HJSr, *Boston Evening Transcript* 12–20–1882; *JW2* 1:1–2; HJIII to Robert James, 2–10–1922, H; typed notes from James H. Manning, ed., *New York State Men* (Albany, NY: Albany Argus Art Press, 1916), UC.

10 footnote: *SP* 11; A.B., "For the Evening Journal," *AEJ*, 12–20–1832, p. 2.

10 William must have spoken: *MIL* 169–71, 180; *MCD* 14; *JW2* 1:2.

11 There is no doubt: *FEI* 25–27; Lewis, *Topographical Dictionary* 1:96; *MCD* 167–68; *HAS2* 103.

11 The fierce: *HAS2* 104; Thomas Addis Emmet, M.D., *Memoir of Thomas Addis and Robert Emmet* (New York, 1915), 1:79; *MIL* 42, 86–87.

12 One of the most important: A.B., "For the Evening Journal"; Emmet, *Memoir* 1:500, 506–9, 465, 551–52; "The Astor Claim," *AA* 5–30–1827; "William James, appellant, *against* Davenport Morey, impleaded with Caleb Johnson, respondent," *Reports of Cases . . . in the Supreme Court; and in the Court for . . . the Correction of Errors . . . of New York* (New York: Banks, 1883), 2:254, 265, 322.

12 Robert Emmet: *JH6* 191; W. H. Maxwell, *History of the Irish Rebellion in 1798* (London, 1887) 432; *SBO* 40.

12 James McBride, Henry Eckford: Account Books (James McBride), Rare Books and Manuscript Div., NYPL; *L2* 5.

13 emigration of brother and nephews: *FEI* 28.

13 citizenship: Certificate of Naturalization, 8–3–1802, H.

13 De Witt Clinton: *FOX* 76, 346; Dorothie Bobbé, *De Witt Clinton* (New York, 1933), 124, 213.

13 "spoke of": *ROW* 69.

13 The key fact: AA 4–28–1818; printed circular, Misc. Clinton, DeWitt, N-YHS; HAM 1:527, 2:98; David Hosack, *Memoir of DeWitt Clinton* (New York, 1829), 467–68.

14 Edward Livingston and Martin Van Buren: *NX* 169–70.

14 funeral: Hosack, 524–25; A.B., "For the Evening Journal."

15 "Albany is one": *AN* (1859) 10:222.

15 "Being nearly at the head": William Sampson to Grace Sampson, 8–17–1806, William Sampson Papers, LC.

15 On arriving: Obit., *AEJ* 12–19–1832; memorandum of agreement, April 1795, between Gerrit W. Van Schaik and WJ of Alb. and David Horner, Misc. Mss. Van Schaik, G. W., N-YHS; *HAS2* 101–2; *AN* (1854) 5:72.

15 sale of spirits and other products: *Albany Gazette* ad, UC; *ROW* 100; typed statement quoting William Le Roy Emmet, HJSr's file, UC.

16 nephews in business: John James to parents, 10–9–1816, 8–15–1817, H.

16 1818 ad: AA 7–17–1818.

17 assigned mortgage: "William James, appellant," 253, 283.

17 Court of Errors: *CHE* 2:791–97.

17 miscellaneous investments: Goldsbrow Banyar Papers, box 6, folder 4, NYSL; Franklin H. Chase, *Syracuse and Its Environs* (New York, 1924), 1:103, 306; ads in *AEJ* 3–22–1830, p. 1, and 8–3–1831, p. 2; "Notice," *AEJ* 3–26–1831, p. 2.

18 "the wilful destruction": Quoted from *L2* 8. Facts from *L2* and Dwight H. Bruce, *Memorial History of Syracuse* (Syracuse, NY, 1891), 93–103.

18 Syracuse Salt Co.: Syracuse Salt Co. Minutes, pp. 1–2, OHA; Henry Eckford to Joshua Forman, 12–19–1823, acc. 14760, NYSL.

18 Meanwhile: D. A. O[rcutt], "Major M. D. Burnet's Early Experience in Syracuse," *Syracuse Sunday Courier* 7–22–1879, p. 4; Recorded Deeds, Onondaga Co., Book M.M., p. 411; Daybooks for 1820–54, p. 94, Account Books (James McBride), Rare Books and Manuscripts Div., NYPL; Syracuse Salt Co. Minutes, pp. 4–9, OHA; *L2*.

18 William now: Joshua Forman to WJ of Alb., 11–3–1824, Misc. Papers (Wm. James, Sr.), Rare Books and Manuscripts Div., NYPL; William M. Beauchamp, *Past and Present of Syracuse and Onondaga County* (New York, 1908), 1:445; Bruce, *Memorial History* 112, 93, 103.

19 Unfortunately: Orcutt, "Major Burnet"; *L2* 7, 9.

19 HJSr's Syracuse holdings: *IN*; 1850 census, roll 552, ward 15, dwelling 991, p. 117; Clipping of Robert McN. Barker, "The Non-Resident Property Owners of Syracuse," *Syracuse Sunday Herald*, 5–20–1900, OHA.

20 Two years after: *L2* 9; ad in AA 1–2–1826, p. 3; *The Tourist, or Pocket Manual for Travellers* (New York, 1835), 56; Lewis C. Beck, "An Account of the Salt Springs," *NYM* 5:196–97.

20 In developing: *HE* 1:73; *CEL* 23.

21 "less convenient": *AEJ* 9–17–1831, p. 2.

21 William James of Albany and John R. Williams: *L2* 9–11; mortgage papers and WJ of Alb. to Williams, 7–22–1825, 8–20–1825, courtesy of Burton Historical Coll., Detroit Pub. Lib.

22 Back in Ireland: *MCD* 19; AA 5–27–1825, 2–11–1825; *ROW* 61: James Stuart, *Three Years in North America* (Edinburgh, 1833), 1:51.

22 Albany Basin: *AA* 4–11–1823, 4–15–1823, 7–26–1825, 7–29–1825; *HOW* 611.
23 canal celebration: *AA* 9–16–1825, 10–4–1825, 11–7–1825; *JH6* 191; Martin Van Buren, *Autobiography* (Washington, D.C., 1920), 84, 157.
24 footnote: Paul E. Johnson, *A Shopkeeper's Millennium* (New York: Hill & Wang, 1978), 67.
24 second footnote: *JH6* 146.
25 portrait: Theodore Bolton and Irwin F. Cortelyou, *Ezra Ames of Albany* (New York: N-YHS, 1955), 241.
25 James King and William James of Albany: *WE* 67–69; *NX* 78. King's *Argus* squib has not been found.
26 William James of Albany's letter from Syracuse: WJ of Alb. to James King, "Syracuse Saturday morning," Misc. James Family, N-YHS.
27 Henry Seymour, David Colvin, John Wilkinson, Thomas Davis: *HAM* 1:455, 497; WPA card file (Burnet in "Persons—Prominent"), OCPL; Chase, *Syracuse and Its Environs*, 1:39, 212.
27 case lost: "In Chancery Before the Chancellor[.] William James, Isaiah Townsend, John Townsend and James McBride vs. Henry Seymour and David S. Colvin," 11–12–1832, Misc. James Family, N-YHS; *IN* 10–13.
28 philanthropies: *JH6* 147–48; *AA* 1–20–1824, 12–16–1823, 1–30–1827; *AEJ* 8–21–1832, 7–25–1832.
28 "Tell me": Misc. Papers (Wm. James, Sr.), Rare Books and Manuscripts Div., NYPL.

CHAPTER 3

30 epigraph: *JH15* 495.
30 "Ma": HJSr to CBJ, 2–4–[1856], 8–25–[1856], H.
30 "I confess": HJSr to CBJ, 5–1–1844, H.
30 "maternity itself," etc.: *JH6* 147–49.
31 John Barber: *JH6* 148; *HAS1* 8, 120–22.
31 Jennett Rea: *JH6* 149–51; William James (d. 1855) to parents, 7–28–1817, H.
32 Francis Barber: *Portrait Gallery of Distinguished Americans* (New York, 1835), Vol. 2; *HAS1* 10–11, 14–22.
32 William Barber: *JH6* 149; *HAS1* 122–24.
33 "she seemed someway ashamed": *JH6* 149.
33 "saw a lady": *JW2* 1:3.
33 William James of Albany's marriages and offspring: *HAS2* 104–6.
34 "Ma says": JJ to MAJ, 11–16–1827, H.
34 Janette Barber Gourlay: *HAS1* 131–32.
35 "attack," "a fixed persuasion": HJSr to CBJ, 7–23–1857, H.
35 "dear old nursery," "They tell a story": Ts., Katharine Van Buren Wilson to HJIII, 7–3–1920, H [bMS Am 1092.9 (4600) folder 15].
35 HJ's memories of Catharine: *SBO* 4–5, 14, 177.
36 Catharine Barber James's will: Typescript, 1, 3, 4, 7, H.
36 furniture and china: Wilson to HJIII, 7–3–1920, H.
37 William James of Albany's will: Typescript, 1, H.
38 "In the present case": *James v. James*, 4 Paige 114. Decision dated July 1833.

38 "tuition and custody": Typescript of will, 8, H.

38 "For example": *NCI* 28:162.

39 HJ on Jameses and "business": *SBO* 189–90.

39 Gus: HJIII, sheet headed "*Augustus James*," H [bMS AM 1092.9 (4600) folder 14]; Gus to John Townsend, 12–31–1844, 1–8–1844 [1845], Acc. 13277, NYSL.

39 footnote: Gus to John Townsend, 1–10–1843, 2–28–1851, 1–8–1844 [1845], Acc. 13277, NYSL; *SBO* 180.

39 cemetery plot: "Albany Cemetery," *AEJ* 8–1–1845, p. 1.

41 "She represented": *SBO* 5–6.

41 Scot's Quarters: *HAS1* 4.

CHAPTER 4

42 The heroine: HJ, *The Wings of the Dove* (New York: Scribner's, 1922), 1:111; *JR4* 2:1290.

42 quotes from *Small Boy*: *SBO* 14, 42.

43 life expectancy: *Christian Examiner* (1829), 7:243.

44 In 1810: *HAS2* 103, 107; 54 State Street in Albany tax rolls, 1817–1819; *JH6* 188–89; National Archives, *Population Schedules of the Third Census*, roll 26; *CHE* 2:663.

46 "tiresome," "that tag": *JR3* 2:326.

46 "It is rumored": *AEJ* 9–22–1831, p. 2.

46 "As Father": JJ to William H. Barker, [1832], Acc. 6020, NYSL.

47 William of Albany's early years: *AN* (1856), 7:137; *Albany Gazette & Daily Advertiser* 3–25–1820, p. 1; *HAS2* 106; John James to his mother, 2–4–1824, H; *AA* 11–2–1824, p. 3.

48 Curiously: *JH6* 146–47, 188, 170, 151, 169.

49 "honour of your family": EN to Rev. WJ, 4–5–1821, UC.

49 cash drawer: *JH6* 165–69.

49 Did William: Academy bills for 1824, Misc. Albany Academy, N-YHS; Daybooks for 1820–54, pp. 243, 250, Account Books (James McBride), Rare Books and Manuscripts Div., NYPL.

50 "As to what": HJSr to Rev. WJ, 12–21–[1860], C.

50 "This precisely": Ts., HJSr to RJ, [1872 or 1873], V.

51 If individual: *BLA* 54; "Pew Book 1805 to 1843," 223, congregation archives.

51 In 1829: *ROW* 67, 97; *HI* 15; *JH6* 155.

51 Reverend Weed: *BLA* 30.

51 Reverend Campbell: *BLA* 31; *WE* 365.

52 Both these ministers: *AN* (1850) 1:131; HJIII in *JW2* 1:4; *MCD* 172; *JH6* 173; *HEN*.

52 church membership: *BLA* 92, 105, 107.

52 1830–31 revival: *Albany Telegraph & Christian Register*, 6–18–1831, p. 1; JJ to Rev. WJ, 3–4–1830, A.

52 enlargement of edifice: *BLA* 85; Silas, "The Old Brick," *AEJ* 6–1–1831.

52 Henry always remembered: *JH6* 152–53.

53 Sabbatarian rules: *JH6* 154; Silas M. Andrews, *The Sabbath at Home* (Philadelphia, PA: Presbyterian Board of Publication, 1836), 8, 15.

53 memories of Sunday morning: *JH6* 155–57; Albany directories, 1820–25.

54 "who used to make": *BUR* 39. The passage, supposedly from HJSr's *Autobiography*, is not in *JH6*.

54 Henry was: Recorded deeds, bk. 24, p. 196, and bk. 45, p. 25; Albany tax rolls, 1818, 1819, 1833; Munsell, ed., *Collections on the History of Albany* (1865), 1:487.

54 The family now occupied: Albany tax rolls, 1823; J. Silk Buckingham in *AN* (1869) 1:291; "For the Evening Journal," *AEJ* 3–23–1831, p. 2; *CEL* 37.

55 HJSr and siblings: *JH6* 151, 172; HJSr, "More Criticism on 'Spirits,'" *NYTr* 1–13–1851, p. 5.

55 "I was never so happy, etc.": *JH6* 188, 145, 173, 183.

56 Although Henry spoke: *JH6* 188, 162–63, 190–91; Jesse W. Hatch, "The Old-Time Shoemaker and Shoemaking," *Publications of the Rochester Historical Society* (1926), 5:82.

56 Among the boys: *JH6* 162–64; Obit. of Maria Clinton, *AA* 8–4–1818; Dorothie Bobbé, *De Witt Clinton* (New York, 1933), 227.

57 "When I was," "The demon": HJSr to RJ, [c. 1875–77], V.

57 stopped drinking: JJGW to HJSr, 7–13–1849, 8–3–1849, SL; HJSr, "Intemperance," *NYTr* 8–26–1851, p. 6.

CHAPTER 5

58 "Piano Fort": *AEJ* 1–19–1832, p. 1.

58 Catharine: E. D. Bryan to HJSr, 6–22–[1859], H.

58 Jannet: Gus to Rev. WJ, 5–6–1828, A; Longworth's NY directory (1829), 523; JJ to Rev. WJ, 3–4–1830, A.

59 Albany Female Academy: Charles W. Blessing, *Albany Schools and Colleges* (Albany, [c. 1936]), 36.

59 For his sons' education: *BLA* 18; *SP* 11–12; William B. Sprague, *Annals of the American . . . Presbyterian Pulpit* (New York, 1869), 52–56; William S. Young, "Some Reminiscences of Dr. Banks," *Evangelical Repository, and United Presbyterian Review* O.S.41:218–28.

59 William was fourteen: *SP* 12–13.

60 Berkshire Gymnasium: JBJ to Rev. WJ, 2–20–1828, A; Adelbert M. Dewey, ed., *Life of George Dewey* (Westfield, MA, 1898), 943; Calvin Durfee, *Williams Biographical Annals* (Boston, MA, 1871), 140–41; *SM* 2:677; Chester Dewey to GWC, 9–17–1828, George W. Clinton Letterbook, Acc. CZ10407, NYSL.

60 The best school: *HOW* 684; *HE* 1:248; *HU* 3:[J]4–6; *LEY* 1:45–64; death notice for Allan Melville, *CRA* 1–30–1832, p. 2. Bank: *AN* (1854), 5:51; *AA* 6–6–1827, p. 2, 6–6–1828, p. 2, 6–3–1829, p. 2; *AEJ* 6–2–1830, p. 2.

60 William James became: *HE* 1:19, 132, 162–63; Child's Albany Directory for 1832–3, lx; *CEL* 83; *HAM* 1:569.

61 building the academy: *HOW* 684; *Historical and Financial Summary of the Albany Academy* (Albany, NY, 1913), 18; *AA* 5–18–1824, p. 3.

62 records destroyed by fire: *HU* preface.

62 curriculum: *HE* 1:47; *Statutes of the Albany Academy* (Albany, NY, 1819), 5, 12, 14–15.

63 "a huge pleasure": *JH6* 191.

63 Since Henry: *CEL* 84, 21, 20, 46; 1820 tuition bill, Misc. Albany Academy, N-YHS.

63 Discipline was not confined: *CEL* 46–47; *Statutes* 8, 16; tuition bills, N-YHS; *Historical and Financial Summary* 29.

64 rules for faculty: *Statutes* 8–9, 15–16; *HE* 1:129–30.

64 population statistics: *AEJ* 12–24–1832, p. 2.

64 Albany Institute, Rosetta Stone: James M. Hobbins, "Shaping a Provincial Learned Society," *The Pursuit of Knowledge in the Early American Republic* (Baltimore, MD: Johns Hopkins University Press, 1976), 117–50; *HE* 4:105.

64 Joseph Henry: *HE* 1:118, 4:115; *JR7* 2:269.

65 "some commoner method": HJSr to RWE, [Feb 2, 9, or 16, 1843], H. Mistakenly dated 1842 by H.

CHAPTER 6

66 "good Cork leg": *HE* 3:380, 429.

67 If his stoic dignity: *NSB* 192; William C. Gannett, *Ezra Stiles Gannett* (Boston, MA, 1893), 207; *JR4* 1:278–79.

67 "He was certainly": *JH6* 147.

68 "At the age of thirteen": *JH6* 147.

68 Caroline Dall: *DAL* 6–25–1866.

69 bookstore first opened: *HOW* 702.

69 "On a summer afternoon": *JW2* 1:7–8. Original letter not found.

70 Woolsey Hopkins: *New York Genealogical and Biographical Record* 40:206–7; Klinck's Albany directory for 1822; Cuyler's Albany directory for 1824, p. 95; *HU* 2:[H]133.

70 Joseph Henry still a tutor: Harold A. Larrabee, "Henry James, Sr., '30 at Union," *Union Alumni Monthly* (1926), 15:242.

70 treatment of burns: Richard K. Hoffman, "Remarks on Burns," *NYM* (1829–30): N.S.2:85, 260, 261.

70 It has generally been assumed: *JW2* 1:221; WJ, *Essays in Psychology* (Cambridge, MA: Harvard University Press, 1983), 205; HJSr to RJ, [c. 1875–77], V.

71 The worst was: HJSr to RJ, [c. 1875–77], V; alumni questionnaire, 6–4–1855, UC.

71 Several months: *L1* 10; MAJ to JJ, 1–1–1825, A.

71 miss three meetings: *HE* 1:128, 129, 162.

71 Dr. James McNaughton: "Associate Contributors," *NYM* (1829) N.S.2:iv.

71 Dr. William Bay: *AA* 1–14–1825, p. 3; *WE* 62–63.

72 Dr. John James: *HOW* 209; Sylvester D. Willard, *Annals of the Medical Society of the County of Albany* (Albany, NY, 1864), 281–86; Wilbur T. Norton, comp., *Centennial History of Madison County, Illinois* (Chicago, IL, 1912), 389; William E. Aikin to GWC, 3–15–1828, 5–19–1829, George W. Clinton Letterbook, Acc. CZ10407, NYSL.

72 "*Visit, consult*": This and later quotes are from Dr. John James's account book, Acc. 10991, NYSL.

72 Strang's execution: *AA* 5–9–1827, p. 2, and 8–25–1827, p. 2.

73 "It was with": HJSr to Rev. WJ, 11–3–1827, C.

73 "and bailed water": *AN* (1858), 9:161; *AA* 11–12–1827, p. 2.

74 "Henry's leg": JJ to MAJ, 11–16–1827, H.

74 "Since you left us," etc.: HJSr to Rev. WJ, 12–14–1827, H.

74 John Yates: WO 66–67.

76 HJSr and Thomas Chalmers: DNB; James McCosh, *The Life of James McCosh* (New York, 1897), 40; Chalmers to HJSr, 12–26–1827, Drew U. Lib.

77 Often the limb: Nathan Smith, "Remarks on Amputation," NYM (1825), 4:313–21.

77 Around the middle of April: Gus to Rev. WJ, 5–6–1828, A.

78 Clinton monument meeting: *Albany Gazette* 5–9–1828, p. 1.

78 Augustus's letter: Gus to Rev. WJ, 5–6–1828, A.

79 "After my religious life": HJSr, "More Criticism on 'Spirits,' " NYTr 1–13–1851, p. 5.

79 "The dark silent night," etc.: JH6 159, 172.

80 Swedenborg volume: *On the New Jerusalem, and Its Heavenly Doctrine* (London: Hodson, 1841), 100. HJSr's copy, at SSR, is bound with Swedenborg's *A Brief Exposition of the Doctrine of the New Church* (London: Hodson, 1840).

81 "[God] cannot weakly sympathize": JH9 271.

81 "morbid self-portraiture," "I remember": JH12, folder 9, pp. 140–41.

82 "process of brutal surgery," etc. HJSr, "The Decay and Petrifaction of European Society," NYTr 4–3–1858, p. 6.

CHAPTER 7

Unless otherwise noted, the sources for HJSr's grades and college bills are the various "Merit Rolls" and quarterly bill books for the Class of 1830, kept in Schaffer Library, UC.

83 dormitory residence: HEN; HIS 176; *Perseverance Conquers Much* (Schenectady: Union College, 1990), 45.

84 "was to make men," "a mechanist": WO 76–77.

84 As "mechanist": HIS 210–13.

84 1830 enrollment: HIS 218, 230.

85 As a money-raiser: HIS 89, 162; HAM 2:92–93, 1:514; obit. of AM, NYT 5–8–1858, p. 2; Jonathan Pearson diaries, 4–11–1859, UC; lottery ad, AA 3–7–1823, p. 1.

85 Nott's gambles: HIS; AA 3–22–1825, p. 3; [Joseph C. Yates?] to WJ of Alb., 1–31–1826, Schenectady Co. Hist. Soc.; Codman Hislop, "High Finance at Union 1814–1833," 89, alumni file (HJSr), UC.

85 By the time: HIS 302; "Papers delivered by Mr James to Mr Yates Dec. 4, 1832," UC; AEJ 12–17–1832, p. 2. It's unlikely that HJSr's 1829 flight put UC's "future" (FEI 53) at risk.

86 President Nott's second tactic: *Catalogus Senatus Academici* (Schenectady, NY, 1828) 22; Harold A. Larrabee, "The Jameses," *American Scholar* 1:409; HIS 180.

86 Vermont student: A. B. Smith to EN, 3–12–1832, UC.

86 Union discipline: *Catalogus* 26; UC catalogue, 1824, p. 4.

87 paying their off-campus bills: UC catalogue, 1824, p. 3.

87 rhetoric, Latin: *Catalogus* 23.

88 Fisk's weekly charge: Bill book entry, 12–15–1829, UC.

88 Isaac Jackson: Eliphalet Nott Potter, *Discourses Commemorative of . . . Jackson* (Albany, 1878), 44–45; obit., *NYTr* 7–30–1877, p. 2; HJSr to IJ, 1–13–1830, H.

88 fraternity: *HIS* 389–90; *The Centennial Celebration of the Sigma Phi Society* (1927), 12; *Catalogue of the Members of the Sigma Phi* (Troy, NY, 1838), 3–4; Somers in *Perseverance* 47–52.

88 second-term grades: [Larrabee?], notes headed "Henry James Sr at Union," UC.

89 third-term grades: In addition to the Merit Roll, see *UN*.

89 "garrulous," "insufferable": HJSr, "The Decay and Petrifaction of European Society," *NYTr* 4–3–1858, p. 6.

89 "Dynamics, Hydros.": UC catalogue, 1833–34, p. 16.

90 Nott's lectures on Kames: *HIS* 235–36, 240, 244, 238.

90 fall 1829 grades: *UN*.

91 Richard Cooke, Leonard Sprague: *The Traveller's Pocket Directory and Stranger's Guide* (1831), UC; *Schenectady Directory and City Register* (1841–42), UC.

91 George Eaton: Union University, *Centennial Catalog* (Troy, NY, 1895), xii; HJSr to IJ, 1–13–1830, H.

91 "Were I not," "I have heard": AM to HJSr, 11–12–1829, H.

92 "quite definitely 'wild' ": *NSB* 189.

92 "*exposé*," etc.: HJSr to RJ, [c. 1875–77], V.

92 intemperance essay: *JH5* 428, 426–27, 431.

93 "our first men," "the ultimate improvement": HJSr to Rev. WJ, 12–14–1827 (H), 11–3–1827 (C).

93 But Henry's rebellion: *NSB* 189; HJ to WJ, 3–2–1899, H; HJSr to Rev. WJ, 12–14–1827, H.

93 "Let your studies": AM to HJSr, 11–12–1829, H.

94 "[He] has," "Deception": WJ of Alb. to AM, 12–2–1829, H.

94 footnote: *DAL* 6–25–1866.

94 Henry *had* gone: EN to AM, 12–8–1829; AM to EN, 12–22–1829; EN to AM, 12–25–1829; all UC.

95 The latest news: WJ of Alb. to AM, 12–2–1829, H; *FEI* 52.

96 The chief organ: *Christian Examiner* 7:129, 136, 42–43, 279.

96 Francis Jenks: *General Catalogue of the Divinity School* (Cambridge, MA: Harvard University, 1915), 26.

96 "neat recess," etc. HJSr to IJ, 1–13–1830, H.

97 Sarah Maria Nott: *HIS* 177, 300.

97 pacifying Nott: *FEI* 54–55.

97 Elizabeth Pomeroy: File on Jackson's Gardens, UC; *SM* 2:81.

98 "I have just heard": EN to AM, 1–2–1829 [1830], UC.

98 "two or three months": *NSB* 188.

99 "Duncan for board": Bill book, class of 1830, Sept.–Dec. 1829.

99 German, Blackstone, Kent: "No. 9 Merit Roll for 3 Term of Collegiate year 1829–30" and "Merit Roll for 3d Term of Collegiate year 1829–30," UN.

100 graduation: Trustees' Minutes, 7–27–1830, UC; *HIS* 230.

CHAPTER 8

102 "Each contemporary": *SBO* 47; Brad S. Born, "Henry James's *Roderick Hudson*," *Henry James Review* 12:199–211.
102 These tales: *WE* 447; *HE* 4:222.
102 "studied law": *HEN*; *HU* 3:[J]4.
102 *The Craftsman*: Albany directory for 1831–32; *WAR* 21, 231; *CRA* 1–12–1832, p. 2. Extant issues with DeWitt Clinton newspapers, NYSL.
103 "brief ventures": Unattributed quote in *L1* 30.
103 Back in 1826: *WE* 273, 302–3; *BEN* 22; John C. Spencer to Martin Van Buren (copy), 6–22–1829, Ontario Co. Hist. Soc.; *AEJ* 8–12–1830, p. 2; *Syracuse Gazette & Daily Advertiser* 2–25–1829, p. 2.
103 Masons liked to think: Peter Ross, *A Standard History of Freemasonry in the State of New York* (New York, 1901) 207, 296; Dorothie Bobbé, *De Witt Clinton* (New York, 1933), 285; *BEN* 11; Caleb Atwater to GWC, 4–19–1828, George W. Clinton Letterbook, Acc. CZ10407, NYSL.
104 U.S. Bank branch in Albany: *AEJ* 12–13–1830, p. 2; Nicholas Biddle to WJ of Alb., 12–27–1831, Misc. Papers (Wm. James, Sr.), Rare Books and Manuscripts Div., NYPL.
104 Jackson's anti-bank policy: Ivor D. Spencer, *The Victor and the Spoils* (Providence, RI: Brown University Press, 1959), 56.
104 Albany newspapers: *HAS2* 101; William L. Mackenzie, *The Life and Times of Martin Van Buren* (Boston, MA, 1846), 74, 190; *WE* 8, 361–63.
104 Meanwhile: *AEJ* 2–25–1831, p. 2, 7–14–1831, p. 2; *CRA* 1–16–1832, p. 2, 1–7–1832, p. 4.
105 The evidence: *CRA* 1–19–1832, p. 3, 1–31–1832, p. 2; *AEJ* 9–8–1831, p. 2; *AA* 1–14–1832, p. 2.
105 Tellingly: *AEJ* 1–6–1832, p. 2; *CRA* 1–6–1832, Feb. 6, 13, 14, 1832.
105 footnote: JJGW to HJSr, 2–28–1847, SL.
105 While Henry James: *VA* 68; *AEJ* 9–18–1832, 10–9–1832, 9–20–1832, 11–1–1832.
106 footnote: *AEJ* 6–14–1831, p. 2.
106 Clintonians turning into Whigs: *FOX* 351.
106 orphan asylum: *AEJ* 7–14–1831, p. 2; *AN* (1871) 3:165.
106 cholera epidemic: *AEJ* 9–3–1832, 7–10–1832, 7–27–1832, 9–1–1832.
107 William James of Albany's will: Typescript, H; Exemplification, N-YHS.
107 Charlotte James's marriage: *AEJ* 7–26–1832, p. 2. *HAS2* 313 probably errs in placing the wedding in Cazenovia.
107 5 percent: *Hawley v. James*, 5 Paige 485.
109 "In preparing his will": *FEI* 60.
109 Revised Statutes: *Hawley, King v. James*, 16 Wend. 123; *PR* 9.
109 Rev. William James: *L1* 18–19; Jonathan Pearson Diaries, 5–24–1835, UC; GB to Rev. WJ, 2–13–1826, C; *SP* 13–14, 19; George R. Howell and John H. Munsell, *History of the County of Schenectady* (New York, 1886), 103.
110 footnote: *HAS1* 4.
111 Sir Walter Scott: *AEJ* 11–29–1832, p. 1; *JH6* 191.
111 "We regret," etc.: *AEJ* 12–17–1832, p. 2.
112 "Mr James['s] death": *AEJ* 12–19–1832, p. 2.
112 actual net worth: *Hawley, King v. James*, 16 Wend. 82.

112 The next day: A.B., "For the Evening Journal," *AEJ* 12–20–1832; *AEJ* 12–19–1832, p. 2; *AN* (1871), 3:165; *LEY* 54; William M. Beauchamp, *Past and Present of Syracuse* (New York, 1908), 1:448; *HE* 2:35; W.P.A. file, "Persons-Prominent," OCPL.

113 "a few days before": *JW2* 1:4.

113 footnote: *AEJ* 12–15–1832, p. 2; HJSr, "Further Remarks," *HAR* 8:53.

114 After the funeral: *Hawley v. James*, 5 Paige 319; John V.L. Pruyn (Gus's attorney), copy of statement to Chancellor 5–11–1833, Misc. James Family, N-YHS; *James v. James*, 4 Paige 117–19.

114 On other points: Claim by Gus to Hawley and King, 5–6–1833, Misc. James Family, N-YHS.

114 HJSr's provisional income: *L1* 21.

115 "I left Albany": HJSr to RJ, [c. 1875–77], V.

115 He did not go: Alumni file (HJSr), UC; HJSr to RJ, [c. 1875–77], V.

115 In old age: HJSr to RJ, [c. 1875–77], V; *HEN*; Mary E. Bleecker, Clinton genealogy, Acc. CZ10407, NYSL; *Ontario Repository* April 3 and 24, 1833, and 6–26–1833.

115 Yet it had not been easy: DeWitt Clinton to [?], 5–2–1826, DeWitt Clinton Papers, Rare Books and Manuscripts Div., NYPL; "Class of 1825," *Hamilton Literary Monthly* 20:159–60; *JH5* 432; *Ontario Repository* 3–5–1834.

116 Another reason: Timothy Dwight, *Travels in New England and New York* (Cambridge, MA: Harvard University Press, 1969), 4:31; *History of Ontario Co.* (Philadelphia, PA, 1876), 103, 107; James Stuart, *Three Years in North America* (Edinburgh, 1833); *The Tourist, or Pocket Manual for Travellers* (New York, 1835), 104; Canandaigua Village Minutes, June 1833 and 1834; *WE* 140; Alexis de Tocqueville, *Democracy in America* (New York: Langley, 1843), vi.

116 When President Jackson: *Ontario Repository* 3–12–1834; *Ontario Freeman* 7–23–1834, 7–30–1834.

117 voting percentages: *BEN* 167, 171.

117 "decline was rapid": HJSr to RJ, [c. 1875–77], V.

117 card playing: Ann Fabian, *Card Sharps, Dream Books, & Bucket Shops: Gambling in 19th-Century America* (Ithaca, NY: Cornell University Press, 1990), 41, 21.

118 Perhaps Henry's drinking: Matthew Henry Webster to GWC, 10–14–1833, George W. Clinton Letterbook, NYSL; *HU*, entry for Franklin Clinton; Clinton family chart, New York Genealogical and Biographical Society; *SBO* 48.

118 It was in Buffalo: H. Perry Smith, ed., *History of the City of Buffalo* (Syracuse, NY, 1884), 1:211; 2:135, 311, 329; 2[B]: 53–54; Buffalo directories for 1832 and 1835; *Buffalo Whig*, June 18 and 25, 1834, and 7–9–1834; Dorothy H. Dehn, "Records: First Presbyterian Church of Buffalo," Buffalo and Erie Co. Hist. Soc.; *MA* 1:22; *JH6* 446; HJSr to RWE, [1856], H.

119 Eagle Tavern: "A Glimpse of Old Buffalo," clipping at Buffalo and Erie Co. Hist. Soc.; Buffalo directory for 1837; *Catalogue of the Sigma Phi* (1846), UC; alumni file (Hudson), UC; *Diary of Philip Hone* (New York, 1927), 1:165; HJSr to RJ, [c. 1875–77], V; Samuel Welch, *Home History* (Buffalo, 1891), 76.

119 During the winter: Letter from "C," *Buffalo Whig* 2–11–1835, p. 3; HJSr to RJ, [c. 1875–77], V; *CRO* ch. 13.

120 HJSr's letter: HJSr to Rev. WJ, 2–3–1835, A.

120 Gilbert Morgan: Rochester directory for 1834; Albany Presbytery, *Report of the Board for Domestic Missions* (Albany, NY, 1826); *Necrological Report*, PTS, 1876.

120 Thomas Beals: Caroline Cowles Richards, *Village Life in America* (New York, 1913), 167–69; *History of Ontario Co.* 104; "TEMPERANCE" [Franklin House ad], *Ontario Repository* 5–15–1833, p. 3.

CHAPTER 9

122 Ansel Eddy: *The One Hundredth Anniversary of the First Congregational Church* (Canandaigua, NY, 1899), 11, 27; "Records of the First Congregational Church of Canandaigua," 393, congregation archives.
122 Charles Finney: *LI* 18–19; Paul E. Johnson, *A Shopkeeper's Millennium* (New York: Hill & Wang, 1978), 92–94; CRO 75, 202, 155; *One Hundredth* 80–81; "Records" 393.
123 New Measures: CRO 178, 196.
123 Perfectionism: "Information for New Readers," *The Perfectionist and Theocratic Watchman* 4:95; Noyes, as quoted in William Hepworth Dixon, *Spiritual Wives* (London, 1868), 2:36; CRO 240.
124 Annesley sisters: *BLA* 100–4; Dixon, *Spiritual Wives* 2:20–21; JH11 240.
124 Although there is no reason: HJSr to Rev. WJ, 2–3–1835, A; JH5 378.
124 Rev. William James: *SP* 15–16; William B. Sprague to CH, 2–16–1868, box 18, folder 86, Hodge Papers, Rare Books and Spec. Coll., Princeton U. Lib.; Rev. WJ, *Grace for Grace* (New York, 1874), 212.
125 "I vowed": JH5 378.
125 trustees' meeting: *MIN* 3:267, 285.
125 It seems unlikely: *SP* 18, 14; *AN* (1855), 6:237.
126 HJSr's church membership: "Session. Rough Notes. 1822 to 1845" and "Session Records 1826 to 1852," 163, congregation archives; Albany tax rolls for 1834 and city directories for 1834 and 1835.
126 "sacred obligation," "felt insecure": JH5 377.
126 John Campbell: *BLA* 31; *HI* 15.
127 Eaton controversy: *The Autobiography of Peggy Eaton* (New York: Arno, 1980); *Memorial of the Rev. John N. Campbell* (Albany, NY, 1864), 21, 50.
127 salary of $1,600: Cuyler Reynolds, *Albany Chronicles* (New York, 1906), 486.
127 Campbell on Catholicism: J. N. Campbell, *Papal Rome Identified with the Great Apostasy . . . Discourses Addressed to the First Presbyterian Church in Albany, January, 1838* (Albany, NY, 1838), 3, 7, 25, 46–48, 90.
128 In any case: JH5 378–79.
128 course of studies, procedures, rules: *BRF*, 11–12, 17–22, 33.
129 dates of B.A.'s: Seminary catalogue for 1835–36, 9–10.
130 lodging: Seminary catalogues for 1835–36 and 1836–37; 1840 census, Mercer Co., NJ, p. 35, Hist. Soc. of Princeton.
130 James W. Alexander: Charles Hodge and John Hall, *Sermons Preached before the Congregation* (New York, 1859); "Hints for a Lecture on Style," Alexander family papers, PTS; [James W. Alexander and A. B. Dod], *Two Articles from the Princeton Review* (Cambridge, MA, 1840); *AJ1* 1:274.
130 Archibald Alexander: Warner M. Van Norden, *The Fatness of Thy House* (New York, 1953), 58; *AH* 364–65; HAG; *AJ2* 420–21.
131 Samuel Miller: *HAG* 2:352; *AJ2* 381, 421; JH9 314–15.

131 Alexander and Miller were strong: *JH12*, ch. IV, sheets 62–63; *JH9* 315, 126.

131 Joseph Addison Alexander: *AH* 404, 251, 493–94.

132 Breckenridges: *HAG* 2:332–33; *JH12*, ch. IV, note to sheet 63, H.

132 Charles Hodge: *HAG* 2:356; A. A. Hodge, *The Life of Charles Hodge* (New York, 1880), 234; *Cambridge History of American Literature* (New York, 1921), 3:202; *Proceedings Connected with the Semi-Centennial . . . of Rev. Charles Hodge* (New York, 1872), 52.

133 "all of our teachers," etc.: *JH12*, ch. I, sheets 1–2, and ch. IV, note to sheet 63, H.

133 "I should have run": *HE* 5:367.

133 "means and measures," "a *cant*": *AJ2* 511–12.

134 schism: Robert Ellis Thompson, *A History of the Presbyterian Churches* (New York, 1895), chs. 10–11.

134 "sometimes demanded," "the course": *AJ2* 480.

134 Archibald Alexander was an old hand: *Proceedings* 52; *HEN*.

135 There was another: Seminary catalogues for 1835–36 and 1836–37; *HE* 3:498.

CHAPTER 10

137 "*causes célèbres*": *PR* 9.

137 The two lawyers: *TO* 9; *Hawley v. James*, 5 Paige 323.

138 In learning: *CHE* 2:872–73; *Ontario Freeman*, 7–23–1834, p. 3; *Hawley v. James*, 5 Paige 410, 362, 349, 358, 423; *AA* 4–17–1827, 4–26–1827.

138 Talcott argued: Ts., WJ of Alb.'s will, H; *Hawley v. James*, 5 Paige 347.

139 John Duer, attorney: *Hawley v. James*, 5 Paige 388.

139 Spencer's arguments: *Hawley v. James*, 5 Paige 416–20.

140 Walworth's decree: *Hawley, King v. James*, 16 Wend. 184; *Hawley v. James*, 5 Paige 461, 483, 486; *TO* 9.

140 Only one interested party: *Hawley, King v. James*, 16 Wend. 93; *HAS2* 114; *SL* 509; *ROS* 182; HJSr to ABW, 10–8–[1856] and envelope dated 4–17–1835, H [bMS Am 1465 (717, 720)].

141 Court of Errors decree: *Hawley, King v. James*, 16 Wend. 114, 182, 277; *TO* 9.

142 $17,000: Harold A. Larrabee's notes, UC, of Gideon Hawley, Executor, *Report of Master Rhoades upon the Accounts of the Executors under the Last Will . . . of William James . . . from December 19, 1832 to July 31, 1837* (Albany, NY, 1837).

142 Illinois land: *Hawley v. James*, 7 Paige 214, 220.

142 $18,800: Augustus James, *Augustus James and Elizabeth his wife, vs. William James and others. In Partition. Further Supplemental Bill* (Albany, NY, 1840), 14, 19, NYSL.

142 division of $500,000: Indenture, 10–10–1839, Misc. James Family, N-YHS.

142 footnote: Assignments of mortgage, Misc. James family, N-YHS.

CHAPTER 11

143 "had some idea": *HE* 3:340.

143 literary purchases: HJSr to JH, 3–7–1837, Spec. Coll. and Archives, Knox College Lib., Galesburg, IL; *MAC* 2:295.

143 £250 loan: *HE* 3:346.

144 footnote: *LEY* 1:64–71.

144 This economic collapse: *MAC* 2:362–63, 311; "American Affairs," *Times* 7–10–1837, p. 3; CH to Hugh Lenox Hodge, 5–13–1837, box 10, folder 3, Hodge Papers, Rare Books and Spec. Coll., Princeton U. Lib.

144 In trying to explain: *HE* 3:381, 379.

144 leave of absence: *HEN*.

144 On April 20: NY *Herald* 4–20–1837, p. 3; "Ship News," *Times* 5–15–1837, p. 7; *HE* 3:344; *NSB* 270.

145 But Joseph Henry: *HE* 3:186, 366–67, 497, 379, 378. 65 Albany St. isn't listed in the Guildhall Library's 1837 street directories. The 1838 Robson's London Directory shows S. T. Hughes, painter, at that address.

146 Taking for granted: *HE* 3:345, 380; typed fragment, HJSr to HJ, 12–26–1869 (original probably destroyed by HJIII), H.

147 Cork leg: *HE* 3:380, 429.

147 But James had: HJSr to IJ, 1–13–1830, H; *HE* 3:380, 428–29, 418.

147 Perhaps the long confinement: *SP* 13; MJ to AJ, 7–18–[1872?], H.

148 "strong disposition," etc.: *AEJ* 8–14–1837, p. 2.

148 donated books: *MIN* 3:348–49. *Tahiti* and *India* are credited to HJSr in an 1852 PTS book catalogue; the four other titles are shelved at PTS.

148 missionary support: *JH5* 378; Albany Presbytery, *Report of the Board for Domestic Missions* (Albany, NY, 1826) 11; *BRF* 12.

149 The most startling: *Protestant Penny Magazine* 1:3. The marked article is in an August 1835 issue.

149 Reading, reflecting: *HE* 3:379–80; HJSr to JH, 3–7–1837, Spec. Coll. and Archives, Knox College Lib., Galesburg, IL.

149 "went to the roots": *HEN*.

149 On July 21: *HE* 3:413, 419, 4:102.

150 In early August: *HE* 3:429; *AEJ* 8–16–1837, p. 2.

150 parliamentary election: *Times*, Aug. 3, 9, 14, 21, and Sept. 1, 1837.

150 "conjoined hospitality," etc.: *NSB* 266–69.

151 The one detail: Robert James (b. 1840) to HJIII, 3–2–1922, H; Marie E. James to Katharine Hastings, 3–9–1922, H.

151 " 'Billy Taylor,' " etc.: *NSB* 266, 269–70.

151 "[James] brought with him": *HE* 3:429.

152 All these memories: *HE* 3:497; "American Affairs," *Times* 8–7–1837 (p. 5), 8–22–1837 (p. 3); *HE* 4:353.

153 Back in London: *HE* 3:497–99; "Ship News," *Times* 9–20–1837, p. 7; "Ship News," NY *Morning Herald* 10–24–1837.

CHAPTER 12

154 "doubts about the viability": *ROS* 103.

155 "Had the tender": Bryan to HJSr, 7–28–1859, H.

155 James Platt: *Necrological Reports . . . of the Alumni Association of Princeton Theological Seminary* 3:269; *MIN* 3:371; Platt to Edward North, 6–8–1881, Hamilton College.

155 Hugh Walsh: James A. Platt to W. E. Schenck, 1–21–1882, Alumni Sequence

#1069, PTS; Milton Halsey Thomas, *Columbia University Officers and Alumni* (New York, 1936); MJ to CBJ, 12–24–[1857], H.

155 There are two conflicting versions: *HEN; HU* 3:[J]4.

156 "failed to answer," etc.: *MIN* 3:329–30.

156 The newspaper interviewer: *HE* 3:498; *MIN* 3:348–49; *HE* 4:14; *TO* lxi–lxiv; *HEN*.

156 Van Buren dinner: Ts., Katharine Van Buren Wilson to HJIII, 7–16–1920, H [bMS Am 1092.9 (4600) folder 15].

157 "at his own expense": Platt to Schenck, 1–21–1882, PTS.

157 Robert Sandeman: Samuel Miller, "[Lecture Notes on] Ecclesiastical History, 1814–1841," package 2, notebook titled "Sandemanians. Bereans," sheets 3, 6–7, PTS; Alfred Habegger, "Henry James, Sr., in the 1830s," *New England Quarterly* 64:56–61.

158 "straining hard," etc.: *JH10* 34, 33, 73, 76.

159 "probably no two sentiments," etc.: *JH10* viii.

159 David Russell was the Scottish minister: *AJ1* 1:214–15; *HE* 5:18.

159 Russell cast his book: David Russell, *Letters, Practical and Consolatory* (Philadelphia, PA, 1836), 2:73, 316, 82.

160 When an American edition: *Encyclopedia of the Presbyterian Church* (Philadelphia, PA, 1884), 83; John Angell James, *The Anxious Enquirer* (New York, 1844), ch. 2; Russell, *Letters* 1:xxvii.

160 "severity of censure," "DR. RUSSELL holds": *JH10* vii, viii.

161 footnote: John Hall, *History of the Presbyterian Church in Trenton* (1912), 250; Henry W. Jessup, *History of the Fifth Avenue Presbyterian Church of New York City* (1909), 42; Charles Hodge and John Hall, *Sermons Preached before the Congregation* (New York, 1859), 21.

161 "Father's cry": *JW1* 1:344.

161 "subliminal regions": *JW3* 192.

162 "only *feelings*": HJSr to CBJ, 5–1–1844, H.

CHAPTER 13

163 "Henry James has re-gone": *AJ1* 1:273.

164 John Walker: Harold H. Rowdon, "Secession from the Established Church in the Early Nineteenth Century," *Vox Evangelica* 3:77–78; [Walker], *Seven Tracts on Scriptural Subjects* (New York: Ludwig, 1839), 16, 48, 20, 11. The *National Union Catalog*'s author entry attributes the book to Walsh on the basis of a copy at Yale (missing). The only known extant copy is at Union Theological Seminary.

165 HJSr's tract: *JH4* 3, [51], 9 (my italics), 28–30.

166 Alexander's tract: Archibald Alexander, *A Treatise on Justification by Faith* (Philadelphia, PA: Presbyterian Board of Publication, 1837).

166 "explain," "thought he saw": *HEN*.

166 "a certain form," etc.: *JH4* 39–46.

167 WJ on prayer: *JW3* 365ff.

167 "glorious": HJSr to Rev. WJ, 2–3–1835, A.

168 "depends wholly," etc.: *JH4* 24, 23.

169 James Buchanan: Harold H. Rowdon, *The Origins of the Brethren* (London, 1967), 23–25; Buchanan, *The Religious Belief of James Buchanan* (Belfast, 1955); *BU* 255,

256, 125; [Buchanan], *Report and Observations, on the Banks* (New York, 1828); Buchanan, *Facts and Observations* (New York, 1834), 51, 52.

170 "subjects mentioned," etc.: BU 71–77.

170 *New-York As It is* (New York: Colton & Disturnell, 1839), 114–15, 120.

171 "to the Church of God," etc.: BU 143, 148.

172 Walsh family: WAL; STO 3:702; Assessors Book for 1838, ward 15, Waverley Place, NYMA.

172 Rev. William James: SP 13; Record Book of Murray Street Church, 1823–48, BV NYC-Churches, N-YHS.

172 Murray Street Church: SBO 232–33, 128; Record Book, p. 12, N-YHS; Gardiner Spring, et al., *Discourses Delivered in Murray Street Church* (New York, 1830); STO 5:1278.

173 Alexander Robertson: Mary Darden Rodgers Griffiths, "Reminiscences," H [bMS Am 1092.9 (4600) folder 4]; STO 4:795; NYC wills, Liber 53, pp. 59–61.

173 "old-fashioned," etc.: WAL 9–10, 19.

174 HJ on his mother's marriage: SBO 233.

175 yoking with non-Separatists: WA 2:321.

175 MJ's age: JJGW to HJSr, 2–11–1848, SL; 1850 federal census, roll 552, ward 15, dwelling 991, p. 117; 1855 state census, ward 15, elect. dist. 5, dwelling 50.

175 Anna Barker's age: Barker Newhall, *The Barker Family of Plymouth* (Cleveland, [n.y.]).

175 "to run to": HJSr to RJ, 12–10–[n.y.], V.

175 Elizabeth Walsh's will: NYC wills, liber 95, pp. 235–42.

176 A trip to Europe: HE 4:118; NY *Morning Herald*, 10–13–1838, p. 3.

176 In 1827: HE 4:115–16; draft of JH to Faraday, 10–9–1838, Smithsonian Institution Archives, Record Unit 7001, Joseph Henry Coll., 1808, 1825–78, and related papers to c. 1903, box 7; HE 4:215.

177 An American interviewer: [John Dix], "From the Boston Atlas . . . Pen and Ink Sketches . . . Abernethy & Faraday," *Newark Daily Advertiser*, 9–1–1845, p. 2; Geoffrey Cantor, *Michael Faraday* (New York: St. Martin's, 1991), 43, 58, 60.

177 Several months later: HE 4:209; White to HJSr, 8–29–1867, 1–12–1868, H.

178 Leaving his inflated hopes: Ellen King James to Edward James, 1–31–1839, Acc. 6021, NYSL; HE 3:405, 4:209.

178 "We shared": [HJSr], "Democracy and Its Critics," *NYTr* 5–2–1851, p. 4 [Attribution: HJSr to ET, 5–30–1851, H].

178 As often happens: HU 3:[H]169; HE 4:210.

179 "the most important": HE 4:209.

179 "I beg of you": HE 4:210.

180 "I send herewith": AJ1 1:295.

180 *Remarks on the Apostolic Gospel: NYTr* 12–20–1882, p. 5; *Boston Evening Transcript*, 12–20–1882; JH4 27; WA 2:232.

180 gift of Walker's *Essays*: Trustees' minutes (5–8–1840), 1:220, 223, PTS; Habegger, "Henry James, Sr.," 76.

181 The fervency: [Alexander Haldane], *Eclectic Review* N.S.4:520, 524; WA 1:471, 559.

181 James's new master: WA 1:362, 66, 374; Walker, *An Expostulatory Address to . . . the Methodist Society* (Edinburgh, 1807), 39; [Haldane], 520, 521.

181 Walker's corrosive intelligence: *WA* 1:198; *JH3* 5; *JH12*, ch. II, sheets 39, 42; HJSr, "Knowledge and Science Contrasted," *Index* (1876), 7:172.

182 A faculty wife: MAJ to Angelo Ames, 1–6–1831, Misc. James Family, N-YHS; *A Memorial of Mrs. Margaret Breckenridge* (Philadelphia, PA, 1839).

182 "most highly," etc.: HJSr to MAJ, 9–30–[1839], H [bMS Am 1093.1].

182 desk in Albany: *HE* 4:209.

183 Marcia's nervous trouble: Rev. WJ to Ezra Ames, 12–2–1825, A; GB to Rev. WJ, 2–13–1826, C; [HJIII], typed sheets headed "*Rev. William James,*" H [bMS AM 1092.9 (4600) folder 14].

183 "drilling and disciplining": HJSr to Rev. WJ, 2–3–1835, A.

184 *"absolutely inconsistent,"* etc.: *WA* 2:309.

184 travel to Scotland: John Walker and R. L. Chance to William Smith, M.P., 6–18–1822, Spec. Coll., U. of Kansas Lib.

184 "being married by a justice of the peace": *NYTr* 6–3–1853, p. 4.

184 James wedding: *WE* 405; "Married," *AEJ* 7–30–1840, p. 2; *SBO* 233.

185 James family Bible: Photostat in album assembled in 1937 by Katharine Hastings, H [MS Am 1092.9 (4599)].

185 "undiluted masculine": MJ to EW, 11–29–1846, H.

CHAPTER 14

186 "really did arouse my heart": HJSr to HJ, 5–9–[1882], H.

187 When the Astor House opened: John W. Barber, *Historical Collections of the State of New York* (New York, 1851), 203.

187 Looking back from 1912: *SBO* 7; "Arrivals at the Principal Hotels," NY *Herald*, 2–15–1841, p. 2; *HE* 5:17.

188 "Occupt.": Assessors book, 1841, ward 15, NYMA.

188 "I want to see you": *HE* 5:17.

188 Henry and Mary's first child: MJ to HJ, 12–8–1873, H; *SBO* 8; *JH6* 145.

188 According to Henry Jr.'s: *SBO* 8; HJSr to RWE, 3–[3–1842], H.

189 21 Washington Place: Conveyances dated 1–8–1842 and 7–6–1840, NY Hall of Records; "WASHINGTON PLACE," *New-York Commercial Advertiser*, 7–18–1843, p. 4.

189 planting fancy roses: JBJ to IJ, 5–1–1842, UC.

189 "finished attics," etc.: "WASHINGTON PLACE."

190 J.J.G. Wilkinson: *WLK* 40–41.

190 William Henry Channing: Octavius Brooks Frothingham, *Memoir of William Henry Channing* (Boston, MA, 1886), 185, 192; *SC* 88; *TH* 111.

191 James's opinion: Frothingham, *Memoir*, 185; HJSr to RWE, 5–11–[1843], H.

191 social historian Anne C. Rose: See *ROS* ch. 2.

191 George Ripley: Charles Crowe, *George Ripley* (Athens: University of Georgia Press, 1967), 60; *ROS* 51.

192 "fully and intelligibly": *ROS* 66.

192 "was a pilgrimage": *The American Transcendentalists*, Perry Miller, ed. (Garden City, NY: Doubleday, 1957), 37.

192 "hostile to the teachings": *ROS* 93.

193 "ensure a more natural union": *ROS* 105.

193 "a little desire": *BR* 1:175.

193 "What sentences!" "It is Emerson lecturing!": JJGW to HJSr, 2–8–1850, H.

193 On March 3, 1842: EM2 3:23; EM1 8:202; [Mary Nichols], *Mary Lyndon* (New York, 1855), 343.

194 "I listened," etc." HJSr to RWE, "March—Thursday eveng" 3–[3–1842], H.

194 footnote: NSB 183.

194 The two men: EM2 3:23, 26, 30.

195 " 'taken upstairs,' " "his blessing": SBO 8.

196 "intemperate fondness," "misery to himself": Evelyn Barish, *Emerson: The Roots of Prophecy* (Princeton, NJ: Princeton University Press, 1989), 94.

196 On that date: NY *Evening Post*, 1–23–1843, p. 2; 1–26–1843, p. 2.

196 from "The peculiar doctrine" to "course of lectures": AEJ 1–31–1843, p. 2.

197 from "INWARD REASON" to "The Two Adams": NY *Evening Post*, 1–30–1843, p. 2; 2–6–1843, p. 2; 2–14–1843, p. 2.

198 "important discovery," etc.: JH14 43.

198 "the *super*natural constitution," etc.: HJSr to RWE, 10–3–1843, H.

199 "good audiences": JH14 44.

199 "I came to night," etc.: HJSr to RWE, [Feb. 2, 9, or 16, 1843—HJSr's lecture dates], H. Erroneously dated 1842 by Ralph Barton Perry (PE 1:41), who didn't realize that HJSr's age (thirty-one) allows a date as late as 6–2–1843.

200 footnote: NSB 181.

200 Emerson had been warned: EM2 7:526; 3:144.

200 At the end of February: "Mr. Emerson's Lectures," *Pathfinder*, 3–4–1843, pp. 19–20, NYPL; HJSr to RWE, [Feb. 2, 9, or 16, 1843], H.

201 Still, the friendship deepened: EM2 7:542. Letter dated 5–6–1843.

201 James was never very good: HJSr to RWE, 5–11–[1843], H.

202 "heart leaped up": Crowe, *George Ripley*, 68.

202 "aid and comfort": JH6 446.

202 from "the very best interpreter" to "heaped": HJSr to RWE, 5–11–[1843], H.

202 "Oh you man," "shall one": HJSr to RWE, 10–3–1843, H.

203 "some grand event": CRO 321.

203 H. D. Thoreau: HJSr to Thoreau, 5–12–1843, Pierpont Morgan Lib.; *TH* 110, 113; EM2 7:552.

203 Bronson Alcott: HJSr to RWE, 5–11–[1843], H.

204 Margaret Fuller: Rev. WJ to MAJ, 7–26–1850, C; HJSr to RWE, 10–3–1843, H; *Letters of Margaret Fuller* (Ithaca, NY: Cornell University Press, 1984), 3:151; JJGW to HJSr, #87 [11–2–1846], SL; HJSr to ET, 2–24–[1852], H.

204 Joseph Henry and HJSr: HE 5:367–69, 387–88; JH5 298.

205 "But I must stop": HJSr to RWE, 5–11–[1843], H.

206 But instead: TH 133; HE 5:368; HJSr to RWE, 10–3–1843, H.

206 "I have advertised": HJSr to RWE, 5–11–[1843], H.

206 "I hear of your plans," etc.: EM2 7:553. Letter dated 7–21–1843.

206 In advertising his house: "WASHINGTON PLACE"; Conveyance, NY Hall of Records; assessors book, 1842, ward 15, 9 Washington Place.

207 passenger list: NY *Evening Post*, 10–20–1843, p. 2.

207 One of James's last acts: HJSr to RWE, 10–3–1843, H.

208 "But truly": EM2 7:566–67. Letter written 10–11–1843.

208 "with heavy squalls": "Ship News," *Times* 11–4–1843, p. 7.

209 "I have written": SL 372.

209 not until 1847: *EM2* 3:381–82.

209 1872 lecture: HJSr, "Emerson," lecture mss. "A" & "B," H.

CHAPTER 15

211 "Occasionally the machinery": HJSr, "Dr. Bushnell's Book," *NYTr* 3–2–1859, p. 3.

211 "One day": *JH14* 44–45, *JH6* 58–71.

212 There is no doubt: *FEI* 73; *NSB* 173.

213 "proposing": *EM2* 7:565.

213 The manliness: HJSr to RWE, 10–3–1843, H; *SL* 347; *CAR* 17:182.

213 When the *Great Western*: *CAR* 17:180–81.

214 For his part: *JH6* 427; *SI* 22–23; Samuel C. Eby to Austin Warren, 11–8–1929, H.

214 James thought: *JH6* 428; JJGW to HJSr, 2–8–1850, H.

215 Jane Carlyle: *CAR* 17:190, 235–36.

215 Having the entrée: *CAR* 17:169; *Dial* 3:231.

215 The year before: *HEN*.

216 footnote: *NSB* 187; *CAR* 17:164.

216 James met Sterling: *ST* 70; Karl Baedeker, *Great Britain* (Leipzig, 1887), 61; *CAR* 17:199.

216 But Ventnor: Carlyle, *The Life of John Sterling* (London, 1897), 256; *ST* 85, 87; *CAR* 18:226; *SL* 372.

217 John Stuart Mill: *JH15* 322–23; HJSr to SGW, 4–1–1859, H; *HEN*.

217 The Isle of Wight: JJGW to HJSr, 2–24–1882, H; *BUR* 41; *SBO* 82; *JH14* 71; JJGW to HJSr, 2–3–1846, SL.

217 In this revealing vignette: MJ to EW, 11–29–1846, H; *SBO* 82.

218 "screamed incessantly": HJSr to CBJ, 5–1–1844, H.

218 By now some members: Harriet Langdon Pruyn Rice, *Harmanus Bleecker* (Albany, NY, 1924), 138, 152, 176, 229–30; HJSr to CBJ, 5–1–1844, H.

218 Recrossing the Channel: HJSr to CBJ, 5–1–1844, H; *Post Office Directory of Berkshire*, 1847–48; Pamela Clark, Royal Archives, to author.

219 from "luxuriant hedge" to "some principle": HJSr to CBJ, 5–1–1844, H.

219 Gideon Hawley: *PR* 11; [Hawley], *Essays on Truth and Knowledge* (Albany, NY: Munsell, 1856), 3, NYSL.

220 farm at Albany: WJ of Alb. to Jonas Holland, 9–6–1832, UC; William Kennedy, *O Albany!* (New York: Viking, 1983), 88.

220 from "further promise" to "I confess": HJSr to CBJ, 5–1–1844, H.

221 A revealing feature: Ts., Katharine Van Buren Wilson to HJIII, 7–3–1920, 7–16–1920, H [bMS Am 1092.9 (4600) folder 15]; Albany directory for 1915.

222 "come to my bedside": *JH6* 148.

223 "I . . . sought": *JH15* 126.

223 "How perfectly I recall," "What troubled me": HJSr to SSS (CW's hand), 5–10–1859, H.

224 "interference": HJSr to RWE, 10–3–1843, H.

224 The great transition: *JH14* 45, 71.

225 letter to *Times*: 5–13–1844, p. 7.

225 "doubtless," "time, and patience": *JH14* 46.

225 Eighteen forty-four: Richard Metcalfe, *The Rise and Progress of Hydropathy in England and Scotland* (London, 1906), 45–50; Weiss's ad, *Times*, 5–18–1844, p. 10 (found by Jacqueline E.M. Latham); H. M. Cundall, *Sudbrook and Its Occupants* (London, 1912), 88–89.

226 The probability: Back cover of *Gentleman's Magazine* (May 1850), Albert Barkas Room, Richmond Lib.; *SBO* 82; *NSB* 173.

226 At the time: Cundall, *Sudbrook*, 89; Marshall Scott Legan, "Hydropathy, or the Water-Cure," in Arthur Wrobel, ed., *Pseudo-Science and Society in Nineteenth-Century America* (Lexington: University Press of Kentucky, 1987), 84; *JH14* 47.

226 Fortunately: C. L. Collenette, *A History of Richmond Park* (Yorkshire, Eng., 1971), 22; *Gentleman's Magazine*; *JH14* 47; *JR2* 1:104.

227 Also close at hand: *Dial* 3:227–55, 281–96; Joel Myerson, "William Harry Harland's 'Bronson Alcott's English Friends,' " *Resources for American Literary Study* 8:24–60; Jacqueline E.M. Latham, "Henry James Senior's Mrs. Chichester," *Henry James Review* 14:132–40; communications from Latham and Silvia D. Greenwood; Kelly's directory for 1845; HJSr to SSS, 5–10–1859, H; MJ to EW, 11–29–1846, H; Chichester to editor of *Démocratie Pacifique*, 2–25–1845, Archives Nationales (found by Pierre A. Walker).

227 "to question me": HJSr to SSS, 5–10–1859, H.

228 from "You are undergoing" to "into rational relief": *JH14* 49–51.

228 Swedenborg's life: *BLO* 3–4, 11; JJGW, *Emanuel Swedenborg: A Biography* (London, 1849), 75; [Charles J. Hempel], *True Organization of the New Church* (New York, 1848), 20.

228 Among Presbyterians: John Hall, *The Only Rule* (Philadelphia, PA: Presbyterian Board of Publication, 1842), 69; Miller's bound notebook, "History of the Secession . . . & the Swedenborgians," 30–36, PTS.

229 "fatally narrowed": RWE, *Collected Works* (Cambridge, MA: Belknap Press, 1987), 4:68.

229 Most of Swedenborg's followers: GB to Rev. WJ, 7–25–1844, 7–17–1834, C; "Professor Bush's Lectures," *AEJ* Oct. 14, 18, 19, 1843; George B. Arnold to GB, 5–9–1847, GB Letterbooks, SSR.

230 "from a state": *JH14* 45.

230 Eagerly obeying: *JH14* 51–52; *EM1* 16:329; Raymond H. Deck, Jr., "The 'Vastation' of Henry James, Sr," *Bulletin of Research in the Humanities* 83:226–27.

230 Newbery's bookstore: Deck, " 'Vastation,' " 230; JJGW to HJSr, 2–24–1882 (H), 2–1–1844 [1845] (SL); *WLK* 144, passim.

231 Swedenborg quotes and HJSr comments: HJSr's copy of ES, *The Heavenly Arcana Which Are Contained in The Holy Scriptures* (London: Hodson, 1837), 1:112, 8, endpapers, and of ES, *Angelic Wisdom concerning the Divine Providence* (London: Newbery, 1844), both SSR.

233 selfhood the principle of evil: *JH9* 258.

CHAPTER 16

234 On October 12: "Marine List," NY *Evening Post*, 10–28–1844, p. 3; "Passengers Arrived," *New York Herald*, 10–27–1844, p. 3; *JH14* 46.

235 "cheering voice": JJGW to HJSR, 12–1–1844, SL.

235 address: envelopes for 5–2–1845, 5–17–1845, 7–2–1845, SL.

235 Alexander Robertson Walsh: SBO 131; NSB 68; Doggett's NY directories from 1842–43 to 1845–46; assessors books (personal property section), 1845–50, ward 15, "82 8th Street," NYMA.

235 "It was here": HJ, *Washington Square*, ch. 3.

235 There is only: TH 161.

236 Chiefly occupied: JJGW to HJSr, 2–1–1844 [1845], 5–17–1845, SL.

236 That James cherished: JJGW to HJSr, 12–1–1844, 5–2–1845, SL; *JH14* 48, 43.

237 Once James began: JJGW to HJSr, 2–3–1846, 6–17–1847, 7–28–1848, 7–13–1849, all SL.

237 One impediment: JJGW to HJSr, 2–3–1846, SL; JJGW to his father, 12–2–1850, K/124, SL.

238 footnote: JJGW to EW, 1–25–1849, SL.

238 Unlike his English friend: CRO 82; JJGW to HJSr, 2–1–1844 [1845], 5–17–1845, SL.

238 The next summer: JJGW to HJSr, 8–2–1846, 8–18–1846, SL; HJSr to C.[J.]P. Stuart, 10–25–1863, H. On Stuart, see NCI 30:355.

239 On family matters: JJGW to HJSr, 7–2–1845, 9–2–1845, SL.

239 Mary James was a good deal less: JJGW to HJSr, 2–1–1844 [1845], 7–2–1845, 4–18–1846; EW to MJ, #2 [9–2–1845]; all SL.

239 Mary's thank-you note: MJ to EW, 5–28–[1846], SL.

240 "the flattest": MJ to HJ, 12–8–1873, H [bMS Am 1093.1 (52)].

240 "Mrs. W.": HJ to MJ, 3–2–1869, H.

241 James family addresses: Albany directories, 1845 to 1848, and tax rolls, 1829, 1833, 1841, 1845, 1846.

241 Before long: SBO 11; 1846 tax roll.

241 Perhaps: MJ to EW, 5–28–[1846], SL; SBO 12.

242 On August 29: JJGW to HJSr, #87 [11–2–1846], SL; MJ to EW, 11–29–1846, H; EW to MJ, #20, 4–3–1847, SL; STR 24.

242 Syracuse partition: IN.

243 "taken personal cognisance," "had never": SBO 73.

243 Around the time: Cash book, 1–6–1834, and 1849 *Annual Report*, 16, YMA records, APL; AEJ 11–3–1845, 12–1–1845, 2–5–1846.

243 It was James's practice: "Minutes of the Executive Committee," 12–8–1845, YMA records, APL; AEJ 5–6–1843, 12–16–1845, Jan. 7 and 12, 1846, 2–26–1846, 3–10–1846.

244 lecture: HJSr, *What Constitutes the State?* (New York: Allen, 1846), 44–45, 5, 17.

245 "the State as a civil polity": JH13 42.

245 "my future": HJSr, "Further," HAR 8:54.

245 "Why should another": HJSr, "Remarks," HAR 8:36.

245 HJSr and Dana: HAR 2:314, 378–79; JJGW to HJSr, 6–17–1846, SL.

246 "I so felt the want": HJSr to SSS (CW's hand), 5–10–1859, H.

246 Charles Fourier had died: Fourier, *The Passions of the Human Soul*, intro. Hugh Doherty (London, 1851), 1:v, xxiii–xxiv, 247.

247 In his analysis: Fourier, *Passions*, 1:9, 361; BE.

247 Albert Brisbane had introduced: AEJ May 4 and 6, 1843, 8–24–1843; GUA 23–24, 153; ROS 143 ff.

248 "cheap tracts": HAR 4:268.

248 In the winter of 1845–46: JJGW to HJSr, 11–29–1845, H; JJGW to HJSr, 2–3–1846, 7–17–1847, SL.

249 If Tweedy: *Pathfinder*, 3–18–1843, p. 52; Godwin, *Popular View* (New York, 1844) [HJSr's copy at SSR]; Gatti de Gamond, *The Phalanstery* (London, 1841), xi, 127–28.

249 "your little Mary," etc.: MJ to EW, 11–29–1846, H.

250 "wondered": JJGW to HJSr, 10–17–1846, H.

250 readings of "True Education": Troy *Northern Budget*, 12–19–1846; AEJ 12–14–1846.

251 quotes from ms. of "True Education," H.

251 footnote: Fourier, *Passions*, xix.

251 "an intrinsic objection": JJGW to HJSr, 7–2–1845, SL.

252 proselytize Rev. WJ: JJGW to HJSr, 2–1–1844 [1845], SL.

252 footnote: *JWR* 22.

252 Rev. WJ and Poor Society: AEJ 12–21–1846, p. 2.

253 footnote: MS Am 1092.9 (4588), xv, H.

254 The school was housed: Letter from "Dutch Brick," AEJ 6–8–1831, p. 2: AN (1854) 5:241; SBO 9.

254 Unlike his heroine: SBO 10; Albany directories from 1842–43 to 1847–48.

255 As James's new day: HIST 14; BLO 295–98; JJGW to HJSr, 8–2–1846, 7–2–1846, 7–17–1846, SL.

256 Not surprisingly: JJGW to HJSr, 8–18–1846, 8–29–1846, 6–17–1846, all SL; *New Church Visitor* (1847), 1:54, 49, 50, 60, SSR; JJGW to HJSr, 12–1–1846, #87 [11–2–1846], SL.

257 "terribly alarmed": JJGW to HJSr, 2–28–1847, SL.

257 With this suggestion: JJGW to HJSr, 5–2–1845, 4–2–1847, SL.

257 from "hideous dogma" to "consummation": HJSr, *Letter to a Swedenborgian* (New York: Allen, 1847), 6, 14–15, 11.

258 The *Liberator* reprinted: *Liberator* 17:76, 80; HAR 4:329–31; NJM 20:419, 553.

259 "Our love": HAR 7:79.

CHAPTER 17

260 When James brought: JJGW to HJSr, 7–2–1847, 8–2–1847 (envelope), H, from 9–18–1847 to 4–21–1848 (envelopes), SL; *Bayard Clarke v. Henry H. Elliott and Robert Edmeston*, D CH. 536–C, NY County Clerk Archives; Conveyances of lease from Robert Campbell to Edmeston (3–21–1837) and from Clarke to Nathaniel G. Carnes (12–31–1850), and sheriff's sale to Clarke (2–4–1848), NY Hall of Records.

260 Elizabeth Walsh: EW to MJ, #20, 4–3–1847, SL; NYC wills, liber 95, pp. 235–42.

261 Mrs. Daly: HJ, *The American Scene* (New York: Harper, 1907), 87–88; HJ, *Washington Square*, ch. 3; SBO 17.

261 58 West Fourteenth Street: Conveyance of lease from Joel Stevens to HJSr (11–15–1847), conveyance from George P. Rogers to HJSr (4–30–1851), lease between Edward G. Ludlow and Rogers (4–6–1833), NY Hall of Records; assessors books, 1846–54, ward 15, West Fourteenth St., south side, lot 1453, NYMA; SBO 98.

261 The Jameses moved in: JJGW to HJSr, 5–19–1848, SL.

262 "Ah, from the beginning": JJGW to HJSr, 8–31–1848, SL.

262 New York Society Library: "Charging Records, 1847—," "A Journal of Entries of Books returned and taken out . . . commencing . . . 1848," NY Society Lib.; *LEY* 1:269.

262 bookstores: Hayden obit., Portland *Transcript*, 3–1–1893; Hayden to GB, May 10 and 27, 1847, GB letterbooks, SSR; *SBO* 81; *EM2* 8:217; JJGW to HJSr, 2–11–1848, SL; *JR2* 1:92.

263 The Jameses were in New York: Barrett to GB, 10–9–1847, GB letterbooks, SSR; HJSr to EW, 10–27–1847, H; JJGW to HJSr, 2–11–1848, SL.

263 HJSr to Fisher: "List of Letters Remaining in the N.Y. Post Office," *NYTr* 10–25–1847, p. 4; *HAR* 5:316–17; HJSr to JTF, 10–26–1847, JTF Papers, MHS; *RE* 10–16–1847.

263 footnote: *MYE* 317.

264 "devoted": HJSr to JTF, 10–26–1847, JTF Papers, MHS.

264 "quiet desk," etc.: *MYE* 318 (letter dated 11–4–1847).

264 failure of *The New Times*: JJGW to HJSr, 12–2–1847, SL; Hayden to GB, 2–8–1848, GB letterbooks, SSR.

264 North American Phalanx: Herman J. Belz, "The North American Phalanx," *Proceedings of the New Jersey Historical Society* 81:232–35; Record of the PRF Society, H [Soc.1070.1*]; JJGW to HJSr, 1–23–1848, SL.

265 New York lecture series: JJGW to HJSr, 8–17–1847, H; *HAR* 6:37; *NYTr* Nov. 26, 1847; Dec. 3, 9, 24, 31, 1847; Jan. 14, 1848; Feb. 11, 18, 1848; Mar. 3, 16, 1848. JJGW to HJSr, 2–25–1848, H, implies HJSr gave more than one lecture.

265 James's talk: *RE* 1–3–1847, 3–7–1847, 8–22–1847, 3–26–1848, 4–2–1848.

265 By the beginning of 1848: *SBO* 53–54; *NYTr* 3–20–1848, p. 2; George Ripley to John S. Dwight, 4–2–[1848], Borneman Papers, IHS; *NYTr* 4–3–1848, p. 2.

266 For the people: *RE* 11–12–1848; Larry J. Reynolds, *European Revolutions* (New Haven, CT: Yale University Press, 1988), 32–36; JJGW to HJSr, 7–28–1848, SL.

266 Curiously: *NYTr* June 5 and 7, 1849; HJSr to JTF, 6–7–1849, JTF Papers, MHS.

267 "Shely": 1820 Albany directory, p. 57.

267 Rev. WJ: *JWR* 51, 50, 46.

268 HJSr at *Harbinger*: JJGW to HJSr, 8–25–1848, 9–29–1848 (envelopes), SL; PG to [JTF?], 3–29–1849, JTF Papers, MHS; JJGW to HJSr, 12–18–1847, H; *MYE* 325.

268 A shrewd contemporary critic: [John Humphrey Noyes?], *The Perfectionist, and Theocratic Watchman* 5:79; *NSB* 193; *HAR* 6:39, 111; 7:150–51; 6:12, 28, 54–55, 61, 126–27; 8:20 [HJSr's authorship of last item acknowledged in 8:29].

269 In 1845: Davis, *The Magic Staff* (New York, 1857), 299–306; *HAR* 5:177–84.

269 If Davis: *HAR* 5:184, 262; JJGW to HJSr, 10–18–1847 (envelope flap), 10–1–1847, SL; Bush, *Mesmer and Swedenborg* (New York, 1847), x, 170; Bush and Barrett, *"Davis' Revelations" Revealed* (New York, 1847).

269 Ten years later: HJSr to [SSS], 12–22–[1860?], H; *HAR* 6:15.

270 "that to reject": *NJM* 21:114.

270 HJSr and Hempel: Hempel's obit., *NCI* 27:536; *BLO* 155; *HAR* 6:132, 140–41; C[aleb] R[eed], *NJM* 21:299; B. F. B[arrett], *New Church Repository* 1:529–43, 596–610; *HAR* 7:78–79.

271 By this time: *HAR* 7:117; Barrett to Bush, 9–22–1848, GB letterbooks, SSR; Cincinnati *Daily Times*, 8–19–1848; *HAR* 7:140.

271 "I have no idea": Barrett to GB, 8–18–1848, GB letterbooks, SSR.

271 footnote: *HAR* 6:134; *MYE* 334.

272 "frightfully able": *HAR* 7:196.

273 quotes from *Moralism: JH8* 7, 13, 20, 25, 31–32.

274 Originally: *HAR* 7:69, 78.

274 quotes from HJSr: *JH8* 33–34, 176, 14–15, 17.

CHAPTER 18

277 Antinomianism: *Necrological Report . . . of Princeton Theological Seminary* (Philadelphia, PA, 1883), 37; Warren to HJIII, 12–8–1930, 8–10–1929, 7–8–1932, H.

277 Emanuel Swedenborg had declared: JJGW to HJSr, 6–1–1847, SL; William B. Hayden to GB, 6–28–1847, GB letterbooks, SSR.

278 Wilkinson also: JJGW to HJSr, 10–18–1847, SL; *EM1* 9:50; PG, *A Popular View of the Doctrines of Charles Fourier* (New York, 1844), 86–89, HJSr's copy at SSR.

278 This combination: Raymond Lee Muncy, *Sex and Marriage in Utopian Communities* (Bloomington: Indiana University Press, 1973), 70–71; BE 297.

278 "the conjugal use": JTF, "Les Amours," H [Soc 860.35*].

279 advertised . . . as being for sale: *HAR* 4:400.

279 "God could not have given": Victor Hennequin, *Les Amours au phalanstère* (Paris, 1847), 40–41, my translation.

279 footnote: *EM1* 10:359.

279 [HJSr], Preface, *Love in the Phalanstery* (New York: Dewitt & Davenport, 1849 [1848]).

280 Ripley stood behind: *HAR* 7:167; *NYTr* 9–28–1848; Prime, *Autobiography and Memorials* (New York, 1888), 194–95; J. R. Paxton in Prime, *Irenæus Letters* (New York, 1885), 14–15; *New-York Observer* (10–7–1848), 162.

281 James had brought: *HAR* 7:197–98, clipping at H.

282 Alfred Ford: *HAR* 8:12–13, 36; *Journal of the General Convention of the New Church* (July 1847), 460.

282 HJSr quotes: *HAR* 8:68, 37.

283 The organized followers: *HAR* 7:196; HJSr to SSS (CW's hand), 5–10–1859, H; *HAR* 8:13.

283 Godwin, Fisher, and others: *MYE* 335; HJSr to FM, 3–10–1849, H.

283 Another approving reader: Muncy, *Sex and Marriage*, 165; CRO 246–48; *HAR* 2:206; *Spiritual Magazine* 1:5.

284 When Noyes read: *Spiritual Magazine* 2:232.

284 There is reason: *CIR* 2:396; *NYTr* 11–16–1852, p. 5.

285 "our narrow-minded views": *CIR* 2:210.

285 Another sex radical: *SPU* 266–67; Taylor Stoehr, *Free Love in America* (New York: AMS, 1979), 13; Lazarus to GB, 7–14–1849, GB letterbooks, SSR; [Mary Nichols], *Mary Lyndon* (New York, 1855), chs. 9, 11–13.

285 Marx Edgeworth Lazarus: *RE* 3–7–1847.

286 Like James: Lazarus to JTF, June 1847, JTF Papers, MHS; *RE* 3–12–1848; *HAR* 5:144.

286 Lazarus dinner: HJSr to JTF, 6–7–1849, JTF Papers, MHS.

286 "Until the passional trinity": Lazarus to JTF, June 1847, JTF Papers, MHS.

287 Quite a few years later: HJSr to PG, 12–25–1861, Bryant Godwin Coll. (HJSr), Rare Books and Manuscripts Div., NYPL; *JW2* 1:221; *SBO* 59; *PE* 1:75.

287 In March 1847: *EM2* 3:382, 8:222, 218; JJGW to HJSr, 11–18–1847, SL; HJSr to RWE, 8–31–1849, H.

287 footnote: *NSB* 196.

288 There is no doubt: *SBO* 259; *JH6* 190.

288 In his letters: JJGW to his father, 12–2–1850, to HJSr, 8–30–1850, 10–16–1849, EW to MJ, 8–29–[1850], SL; *NSB* 195.

289 birth control: Harold Aspiz, "Sexuality and the Pseudo-Sciences," Arthur Wrobel, ed., *Pseudo-Science and Society in Nineteenth-Century America* (Lexington: University Press of Kentucky, 1987), 147.

289 "each drinks," etc.: *HAR* 8:61.

290 There was someone else: HJSr to CT, 6–22–[1860], H; *NSB* 177.

290 footnote: *NSB* 240.

290 "This steamer": JJGW to HJSr, 10–3–1849, SL.

291 James was glad: HJSr to JTF, 6–7–1849, JTF Papers, MHS; *Spirit of the Age* 1:50, 113–14; JJGW to HJSr, 8–6–1849, SL.

292 "*Your* mission," Wilkinson had advised: JJGW to HJSr, #89, #88 [early 1849], SL; HJSr to FM, 3–10–1849, H; HJSr to JTF, 6–7–1849, JTF Papers, MHS.

292 Then: Lecture announcement, 10–30–1849, JTF Papers, MHS; Kenneth Cameron, "Emerson, Thoreau, and the Town and Country Club," *ESQ* 8.3:2–17; *EM2* 8:222.

292 The invitation "horrified James": HJSr to RWE, 8–31–1849, H.

293 It was agreed: Lecture announcement; *EM2* 4:169, 8:226; JJGW to HJSr, 11–29–1849, SL.

294 lecture quotes: *JH8* 57, 52, 61–62, 68, 74, 67, 73, 70.

295 "certificates": HJSr to RWE, 8–31–1849, H.

295 James was so uninterested: JJGW to HJSr, 3–22–1850, SL; "Religious Items," *NYTr* 12–8–1849, p. 3; "Religious Notices," *NYTr* 12–29–1849, p. 3; *JH8* 133, 131, 124–25.

295 Also, authors would: "City Items," *NYTr* 11–17–1849, p. 2; *BR* 1:102–5.

296 There was something: *Spirit of the Age* 2:4–5, 19–21, 50–51, 186, 185; HJSr to [W. H.] Channing [mistakenly catalogued as W. E. Channing], 4–3–1850, H.

296 At James's death: HJSr obit., NY *Post*, 12–19–1882; Ripley to John [S. Dwight], 4–10–1849, Borneman Papers, IHS; *NYTr* 2–21–1850, p. 1; *Journal of Progress* quoted from *Daily Chronotype*, 1–7–1850, p. 1; Doherty to HJSr, #68B, 6–28–1850, SL; JJGW to HJSr, 10–16–1849, SL, and 2–8–1850, H.

297 Emerson and HJSr: *EM2* 8:238–39; HJSr to RWE, 3–1–[1850], H.

298 footnote: Melville facts from *LEY*.

CHAPTER 19

Undocumented quotations and facts in section 1 are from *SBO*, chapters 17–18; 1850 federal census, rolls 543 and 552; 1855 New York State census, ward 15, election district 5; New York City assessors' books, ward 15, 1850–54; and New York City directories.

299 Pinsent, railing: WJ to EVW, 7–1–1856, 9–4–1857, H; *SBO* 228.

299 Centers/Senters: WJ to EVW, 9–4–1857, 1–4–1858, H; *PE* 1:75.

299 "kindly Beans": *SBO* 60.

300 church: *Our Jubilee: The 150th Anniversary of the Scotch Presbyterian Church, New York* (New York, 1906), 17.

300 HJ letters: *JR2* 1:5; WJ to EVW, 1–4–1858, H.

301 Wyckoff family: *SBO* 122, 126, 145; HJSr to AJ, "Tuesday," H; "Descendants of Alexander Robertson," 3, 6, H [bMS Am 1092.9 (4600) folder 13]; M. B. Streeter, ed., *The Wyckoff Family in America* (Rutland, VT, 1934); JA 105; MJ to AJ, [1–16–1867?], H; *SBO* 124, 125. Cf. Delaware County [NY] Clerk, liber 48, p. 387.

302 Aunt Kate: MJ to EW, 5–28–[1846], SL; HJSr to ET, 9–19–1851 and fragment [prob. 1853], H; *WAL* 11; Peter G. Beidler, *Ghosts, Demons, and Henry James* (Columbia: University of Missouri Press, 1989), 157; *STR* 32.

302 One of the memorable events: Thomas Addis Emmet, M.D., *Incidents of My Life* (New York, 1911), 116–18; *AEJ* 11–24–1830, p. 2; *AN* (1859), 10:236; *SBO* 39–41.

303 Mary (Temple) Tweedy: *SBO* 273; "Married," *NYTr* 6–14–1850, p. 8; HJSr to ET, 5–23–1856, 9–5–1852, H.

303 MJ's clothes: HJSr to ET, 9–5–1852, H; *MAT* 271.

303 Godefroi: JJGW to HJSr, 9–30–1854, SL.

303 "servants lie": *BUR* 136.

304 "as if he had gained": *SBO* 9.

304 "fond votary": *SBO* 6.

305 Alice: *BUR* 101; *JH5* 74.

305 "wise, gentle": *EM1* 11:248.

305 backpatting: *BR* 1:105; EW to MJ, #20, 4–3–1847, SL.

305 "damaged goods": *FLD*, 7–28–[1864].

306 profession: 1854–55 NYC directories; 1850 federal and 1855 state censuses; alumni file, UC; *NSB* 69.

306 With his strong sense: *SBO* 87–88, 120–21.

307 Although the evidence: *JH2* 26; *JH1* 218; HJSr, "Dialogue between a Parent and Child," H; *SBO* 234.

307 Convinced that the sacred: *BUR* 205, 213, 125; JJGW to HJSr, 1–11–1850, H; *SBO* 86.

308 No one knew: George C.D. Odell, *Annals of the New York Stage* (New York: Columbia University Press, 1927–49), 5:518; *JR7* 1:259; *JH8* 144; *SBO* 162, 167.

308 *Atlantic*: *SBO* 277–78; *NYTr* Jan 17, 18, 20, 22, 24, 30, and Feb. 17, 1851; Broadway Theater ad, *NYTr* 2–15–1851, p. 1.

309 When ether: *SBO* 167, 25; *NYT* 9–28–1855, p. 2.

309 In 1853: *NYTr* 9–1–1853, p. 6; Robinson, *Hot Corn: Life Scenes in New York* (New York, 1854), 237; " 'Hot Corn' Sketches," *CIR* 3:130; *SBO* 75–78.

309 dentist: *SBO* 64.

310 Dr. Joseph T. Curtis was a man: *NYT* 11–14–1857, p. 4; Henry M. Smith, "Homoeopathic Directory," *New England Medical Gazette* 6:142–43; HJSr, " 'Modern Diabolism,' " *AT* 32:223; *FLD* 10–6–1867; H[?].T.C. [Temple Chapman?], "The Late Dr. Curtis," *NYTr* 11–17–1857, p. 3; *Adeline M. Curtis v. Joseph T. Curtis*, p. 10, Equity Judgments, 1857 GA 148, NY County Clerk Archives.

310 James always required: JJGW to HJSr, 7–17–1847, 4–21–1848, 8–6–1849, 6–17–1847 (SL), 7–2–1847 (H), 9–2–1847 (SL).

310 Strongly drawn: "Late Dr. Curtis"; HJSr to ET, 2–24–[1852], H; [R. Burnham Moffat], *A Moffat Family Record* (1982), NY Genealogical and Biographical Society; *Curtis v. Curtis*; marriage license, Curtis and Frances O. Howard, 11–30–1853, Hamilton Co., OH; *FLD* 10–6–1867; HJSr to Eunice (Macdaniel) Dana, 3–26–[1857], H; HJSr, " 'Modern Diabolism,' " 22.

311 footnote: MJ to HJ, 4–1–[1873], H; *JW1* 1:197.

311 Mrs. Piper: WJ, *William James on Psychical Research* (New York: Viking, 1969), 41.

311 *The Turn of the Screw*: (New York: Norton, 1966), 111, 112, 120–22.

312 "They will ensure": *JH5* 22.

312 "dead languages": ms. of "A True Education," H.

312 But the father: Buchanan, *Facts and Observations* (New York, 1834), 45–46; HJSr to RWE, 8–31–1849, H.

313 While the children: Ads, *NYTr* 9–1–1852 (p. 2), Sept. 1 and 2, 1853, p. 2; *SBO* 187, 172, 15–19, 195–96; Robert Carter, "Gurowski," *AT* 18:625–33.

313 Sedgwick sisters: Ads, *NYTr* 9–4–1848 (p. 4), 9–1–1849 (p. 4), 9–5–1850 (p. 7), 9–10–1851 (p. 3), 9–5–1853 (p. 2); 1855 NY State census, ward 15, elect. dist. 4, dwelling 494; NYC directories; *SBO* 18.

313 Lavinia D. Wright: Ads, *NYTr* 9–7–1849 (p. 3), 9–2–1850 (p. 7); *SBO* 18, 22.

313 Professor Vergnès: Ads, *NYTr* 9–2–1851 (p. 2), 9–1–1852 (p. 2), 9–2–1853 (p. 2); *SBO* 195–201.

314 Richard Jenks: *SBO* 32, 201–10; NYC directories for 1852–53, 1854–55; Harvard alumni records; *Memoirs of the Class of 1830* (Boston, MA, 1886), 71; Coe's ad, *NYTr* 9–3–1853, p. 2.

314 James clearly wanted: *SBO* 21.

314 For the 1854–55 school year: NYC directories for 1854–55, 1855–56; *SBO* 132, 85, 208, 212.

315 It isn't known: *SBO* 222, 223, 225, 213.

315 Years later: *MAT* 72; *SBO* 214–22.

316 100 degrees: HJSr to AJ, 7–5–[1872?], H.

316 "old fashioned familism": "Family Hotels," *CIR* 1:130.

316 Hamilton House: *SBO* 30, 61; JJGW to HJSr, 10–24–1850, H; *JR2* 2:21.

317 New Brighton: Mabel Abbott, "Some Faded Pages of Local History," *The New Bulletin* (Nov. 1965), 15:29; Charles Gilbert Hine & William T. Davis, *Legends, Stories and Folklore of Old Staten Island. Part I—The North Shore* (Staten Island Historical Society, 1925), 50–51; Richard M. Bayles, ed., *History of Richmond County* (New York, 1887), 572–74.

317 "stockingless": *SBO* 29.

317 Blancard's Pavilion: *SBO* 28; Ts. of "Blancard's Hotel," *Richmond County Gazette*, 5–4–1859, SIIAS; Hine, *Legends*, 23–24.

318 Narcissa Vredenburgh: 1874 map of New Brighton, SIIAS; Recorded deeds, Staten Island, liber 20, p. 122; *SBO* 21, 27, 31; 1862 clipping from NY *Evening Post*, SIIAS.

318 Luckily for Harry: *SBO* 32–35.

CHAPTER 20

319 "You are so full": JJGW to HJSr, 5–8–1851, SL.

320 "reciprocal affection": *NYTr* 4–1–1850, p. 1. Authorship acknowledged in *NYTr* 11–16–1852, p. 5.

320 "Since your types": *NYTr* 4–10–1850, p. 6.

321 James's letters on divorce: "Tribune Establishment," *CIR* 2:227; *NYTr* 4–1–1850 (p. 1), 4–17–1850 (p. 6); *JH7* 14; *NYTr* 4–19–1850, p. 6.

321 James's turn: *NYTr* 12–20–1850, p. 4; 12–26–1850, p. 3.

322 James had another: *NYTr* 12–26–1850 (p. 3), 1–13–1851 (p. 5); *JH5* 418.

322 "the exact process": Ts., HJSr to ET, 5–30–1851, H.

322 "Though we can": *NYTr* 3–18–1851, p. 6.

322 In April: L. D. Ingersoll, *The Life of Horace Greeley* (Chicago, IL, 1873), ch. 14; Rev. by Cuvillier-Fleury of Marmier's *Lettres sur L'Amérique*, *Journal des Débats*, 4–6–1851, pp. 1–3; *NYTr* 5–2–1851, p. 4; 5–10–1851, p. 4.

323 Willis and Webb controversy: Henry A. Beers, *Nathaniel Parker Willis* (Boston, MA, 1885), 306; *NYTr* 5–17–1851 (p. 5), 5–20–1851 (p. 4); HJSr to ET, 5–30–1851, H [this letter discloses HJSr's authorship of the three editorials].

324 "under the gusty street-lamp": *NSB* 199.

324 Perhaps it was in 1851: "Lecture Notices," *NYTr* Jan. 13 and 18, 1851, 2–1–1851; HJSr to ET, [Feb. or Mar. 1851], 9–5–1852, H; HJSr to JJGW, 9–6–1852, H; Octavius B. Frothingham, *Recollections and Impressions* (New York, 1891), 155; *NYTr* 11–24–1852, p. 5.

324 Quotes from "Democracy and Its Issues": *JH5* 11, 45.

325 "vociferous nurselings": HJSr to RWE, 1–12–1850, H.

325 Quotes from "Property as a Symbol": *JH5* 54, 56, 84, 39, 86, 92.

327 "old theology," etc.: *JH5* 240, 312, 314.

327 Among James's listeners: HJSr to ET, [Feb. or Mar. 1851], 5–30–1851, H; Henry Fowler, *The American Pulpit* (New York, 1856).

327 But how would: *NYTr* 11–24–1852, p. 5; HJSr to RWE, 10–30–[1851] [mistakenly dated 1852 in *NSB* 200], H.

328 James and Mary: *BO* 11–1–1851, p. 3; *EM2* 8:290, 4:263; diary of ABW, 11–5–1851, H [bMS Am 1465 (1340)]; *BO* 11–5–1851, 11–7–1851 (p. 2); JTF to RWE, 11–5–1851, H; *JA* 58; *SBO* 72.

328 "My health," etc.: HJSr to JTF, 11–14–1851, JTF Papers, MHS.

329 "Thomasian faith": *EM2* 8:302.

329 By now: *GUA* 337–38; JJGW to HJSr, 5–3–1850, 6–14–1850, 5–17–1850, H.

329 But James wasn't ready: *NYTr* 8–18–1852, p. 7; HJSr to ET, [Feb. or Mar. 1851], 9–19–[1851], H.

330 Forrest divorce: Beer, *N. P. Willis*, 309, 314; "The Forrest Verdict," *CIR* 1:50; HJSr to ET, 2–24–[1852], H.

330 But a frightening quantity: *NYTr* 2–15–1850 (p. 2), 3–12–1850 (p. 1), 7–21–1853 (p. 5); HJSr to ET, 9–19–[1851], H; Nichols, *Esoteric Anthropology* (Port Chester, NY, 1853), iv, 51, 56, 215.

331 [Lazarus], *Love vs. Marriage* (New York: Fowlers & Wells, 1852), 45, 250–51, 326.

332 "the most recent": Nichols, *Esoteric*, 216.

332 punishment of seducers: *NYTr* 6–20–1853, p. 4.

332 HJSr's review of Lazarus: *NYTr* 9–18–1852, p. 6.

332 "horror of pen": HJSr to JJGW, 9–6–1852, H.

334 free-love article: *NYT* 9–8–1855 (p. 2), 9–28–1855 (p. 2).

335 Of all those: *New-York Observer* 30:366.

335 "In *Adventures*": *NYTr* 11–16–1852, p. 5.

336 This belligerent answer: "Thackeray," *NYTr* 11–13–1852, p. 4 [clipping at H];
     NYTr 11–16–1852, p. 4; SBO 88.

336 A week later: *New-York Observer* 30:382.

336 James replied: *NYTr* 12–1–1852, p. 5.

337 As the exchange: *NYTr* 12–16–1852, p. 5; JH7 56; *New-York Observer* 30:402, 422.

337 "as no dining-table": *NYTr* 12–24–1852, p. 6.

337 Andrews vs. HJSr: JH7 24, 54, 74, 80–83, 59; CIR 2:86.

339 The time had come: *NYTr* 11–13–1852, p. 4; "Register of the Lecture Commit-
     tee . . . Commencing 1849," 113, 128–29, YMA records, APL.

339 *Putnam's*: HJSr to G. P. Putnam, 11–5–[1852], UC; "Woman and the 'Woman's
     Movement,' " *Putnam's* 1:279–88.

340 "one of your happiest efforts," etc.: JJGW to HJSr, 5–19–1853, SL.

340 critical response: *Putnam's* 4:305–10; *NYTr* 3–7–1853, p. 4.

341 Meanwhile: JH7 78–79, 24, 19–21; *NYTr* 7–21–1853, p. 5.

341 "some rank predominance," etc.: SBO 211.

CHAPTER 21

343 Gurowski's book: *America and Europe* (New York, 1857), 329.

343 "renewed your youth": JJGW to HJSr, 11–14–1852, SL.

343 HJSr on Whitman: Untitled, undated fragment, H [bMS Am 1094.8 (77) folder
     35].

344 James went to church: HIST 16–17; *New Church Repository* 6:536.

344 Doctrines like this: *New Church Repository* 6:573, 572.

345 This sportive reply: JH2 7, 64, 71; Ts., HJSr to SGW, 3–9–1854, H [bMS Am
     1237.18].

345 "the controversial form," "larger audience": JH2 3–4.

346 James sent his tract: SGW to HJSr, 1–23–1854, H; ABW to HJSr, 1–29–1854, H;
     HJSr to ABW, 2–4–1854, H; CO1 167.

346 In the *New York Tribune*: *NYTr* 1–14–1854, pp. 6–7; *New Church Repository* 7:184–
     87; De Charms, ed., *A Defence of Homeopathy* (Philadelphia, PA, 1854), 2:back
     cover; *Journal of the General Convention of the New Church* (June 1853), 25; HIST
     16–17; De Charms, *An Extended Dissertation on . . . an External Church* (Philadelphia,
     PA, 1854), 25, 21, 44, 76–77, 52, 141.

347 Unfortunately: JH9 273–82, 198, 225; Ts., HJSr to SGW, 3–16–1855, H [bMS
     Am 1237.18].

348 All the same: JH9 252; *Christian Examiner* 59:116, 118.

348 Paradoxically: JJGW to HJSr, 8–18–1853, H; JH9 7; JH5 234.

348 What James did: JH9 258, 143.

349 "entire complacency," etc.: *Christian Examiner* 59:118.

350 One of the many questions: JH9 333, 335, 339, 184.

350 For the rest of his life: JH15 232; JH14 375–76, 7.

351 By 1855: JH9 102, 99–100, 215–16.

351 Alice: JA 149.

352 events leading to civil war: James M. McPherson, *Battle Cry of Freedom* (Oxford: Oxford University Press, 1988), 71–73, passim.

352 One of the reasons: JH9 94; JJGW to HJSr, 9–9–1851, H.

353 1852 election: HJSr to RWE, 3–8–1852, H; McPherson, *Battle Cry*, 117–19; SBO 51.

353 With the White House: Whitman, *The Eighteenth Presidency!* (Lawrence, University of Kansas Press, 1956), 23; *Putnam's* 4:239; Edward K. Spann, *Ideals & Politics* (Albany: SUNY Press, 1972).

353 Five years earlier: JH8 135; NYTr 7–1–1853, p. 4; Catharine M. Sedgwick, *Life and Letters* (New York, 1871), 348; JH2 61–62.

354 Maine had a statute: NYTr 12–3–1855, p. 6; JH9 331; clipping of [HJSr], "Our Best and Worst Society," NYTr 3–12–1855, p. 4, H; NYTr, 8–26–1856, p. 5; NYT 6–14–1856, p. 1.

354 Popular despotism: Jerome Mushkat, *Fernando Wood* (Kent, OH: Kent State University Press, 1990), 35–44; MJ to CBJ, 1–14–[1855], H [dated by McBride obit., NY *Evening Post*, 1–12–1855, p. 3]; NYTr 2–1–1855, p. 5.

355 Judging from this letter: NYTr 2–1–1855, pp. 5–6.

355 In March: NYTr 3–21–1855, p. 7; Clipping of [HJSr], "Mayor Wood and the Gamblers," NYTr 3–23–1855, p. 4, H.

356 This portrait: Albany directories; Ts., CBJ's will, H; AN (1870) 2:337 and (1854) 5:335; *Annual Report*, 1851, 1852, YMA records, APL; Albany Gallery of the Fine Arts, *Catalogue of the Third Exhibition* (Albany, NY, 1848), 5; NSB 42; HJSr to ET, [Feb. or Mar. 1851], 9–14–1856, H; JBJ's will, Surrogates Court, Albany Co.; NYTr 2–6–1858, p. 3; Estate of JBJ, cash book, 17, 54, 55, 60, 66, Acc. 16640, NYSL.

357 lawsuit: *Burdick vs. James*, County Clerk index # LJ 1858 D–936, NY County Clerk Archives.

357 "poor Uncle John": Rev. WJ to Elizabeth T.J. Seelye, 1–12–1855, C.

357 Patrick Hearne: NYTr 2–4–1858, p. 5; 1855 NY State census, NYC, ward 8, elect. dist. 1, dwelling 213; NYTr 2–12–1856, p. 8.

358 "tipsy": SBO 49.

358 Cannon episode: Recorded deeds, 548–70, liber 573, p. 440, Hall of Records; NYC directories, 1851–56; SBO 86, 92–95, 42.

359 "NB": Rev. WJ to Kitty, 2–13–1854, C.

359 Rev. William lived: SBO 183; HJSr to Edward James, 11–2–[1855], H.

360 Catharine Temple: Albany directory, 1854–55; Rev. WJ to Anna McBride James, 10–15–1853, C; Robert E. Temple, Letter of Administration, proved 8–24–1854, Surrogates Court, Albany Co.; [HJIII], typed sheet headed "*Catherine Margaret James (Temple)*," H [bMS Am 1092.9 (4600) folder 14]; SBO 182–84.

360 Kitty: HJSr to Kitty, 7–24–1854, H; Rev. WJ to Anna McBride James, 9–20–1854, C.

361 Bob Temple: *Aberdeen Almanac, and Northern Register, for 1857*, 300; Francis H. Groome, *Ordnance Gazetteer of Scotland* (1883), 3:32–33; P. J. Anderson, ed., *Fasti Academiae Mariscallanae Aberdonensis* (Aberdeen, 1898), 2:579; NSB 144–45.

362 Johnny: SBO 192, 189; Estate of JBJ, cash book, 8, 24, NYSL; JR2 2:371 (Johnny misidentified by editor); [HJIII], typed sheet headed "*John B. James*," H [bMS Am 1092.9 (4600) folder 14].

362 "a virtuous," etc.: "Our Best," NYTr 3–12–1855, p. 4.

362 Since 1849: HJSr to RWE, 8–31–1849, H; HJSr to ET, 9–19–[1851], H; SBO 192; HJSr to JJGW, 9–9–1851, H; JJGW to HJSr, 12–28–1851, 9–29–1854, SL; EW to MJ, #62 [11–2–1854?], SL.

363 "to actualize his ideal": JH5 349.

363 When James sailed: McBride obit., NY Evening Post, 1–12–1855, p. 3; Ts., HJSr to SGW, June 19 and 26, 1855, H [bMS Am 1237.18]; JJGW to HJSr, 6–11–1855, SL; Trow's 1856 NYC directory (Greene); WJ to EVW, 7–1–1858, H; Greene to HJSr, 7–10–1863, H; HJSr to RWE, 6–18–1855, H.

364 "charming creatures": SBO 45.

364 crossing: "Marine Journal," "Passengers Sailed," NYTr 6–28–1855, p. 8; "The Collins Line of Steamships," NYTr 4–22–1850, p. 1; steamship ad, NYTr 6–11–1855, p. 3; Donald R. Beer, Sir Allan Napier MacNab (Hamilton, Ont., 1984), 356; HJSr to CBJ, 7–11–1855, H; NYTr 9–3–1855, p. 3; NYTr 10–11–1854; SBO 278.

CHAPTER 22

366 The entourage: "Passengers Sailed," NYTr 10–16–1854, p. 8; "Passengers Arrived," NYTr 5–5–1855, p. 8; EW to MJ, #62 [11–2–1854?], SL; JJGW to HJSr, 6–11–1855, SL; HJSr to RWE, 6–18–1855, H.

366 The maid: JJGW to HJSr, 8–2–1850, 9–30–1854, SL; SBO 283.

366 When the Jameses: SBO 283, 278–79; HJSr to CBJ, 7–11–1855, H.

367 The boy's intermittent fever: NYTr 9–3–1855, p. 3; SBO 267–71, 280–81, 350; LEC 246.

367 footnote: David Steinberg, Cleveland Museum of Art.

367 In Geneva: Leila El Wakil, Bâtir à la campagne, Genève 1800–1860 (Geneva, 1989), 2:79; Edmond Barde, Anciennes maisons de campagne genevoises (Geneva, 1937), 66; SBO 289, 286; NYTr 9–3–1855, p. 3.

367 James sent: LEC 159; SBO 292; HJSr to CBJ, 8–13–[1855], H; NYTr 9–3–1855, p. 3.

368 In fact: SBO 291–93; NYTr 9–3–1855, p. 3; HJSr to CBJ, 8–13–[1855], H.

368 The wise pedagogue: NYTr 9–8–1855, p. 6; HJSr to CBJ, 8–13–[1855], H; NYTr 9–22–1855, pp. 5–6; 10–9–1855, p. 6; 10–24–1854, p. 6.

369 James's attack on socialism: NYTr 9–22–1855, pp. 5–6; GUA 327; Arthur Young, "To Mistaken Friends and Declared Foes," NYTr 1–11–1856, p. 3; unsold share and "List of Voters," NAP Papers, Monmouth County Hist. Asso., Freehold, NJ.

369 James still paid lip service: NYTr 9–3–1855, p. 3; 10–9–1855, p. 6.

370 "external natural man," etc.: JH3 114.

370 At some point: HJSr to Edward James, 11–2–[1855], H; SBO 306; HJSr to CBJ, 9–25–1855, H.

370 The next zigzag: Fichier des étrangers, Dg 4, fol. 137, (Geneva) Archives d'État; NYTr 9–3–1855, p. 3; HJSr to CBJ, 9–25–1855, 8–13–[1855], H; WJ to EVW, 1–4–1858, H; JJGW to HJSr, 10–13–1855, H.

371 to and in Paris: SBO 294–97; HJSr to Edward James, 11–2–[1855], H; MJ to CBJ, 8–25–[1856], H.

372 James quickly found: HJSr to Edward James, 11–2–[1855], H; SBO 298, 312; NYTr 2–7–1856, p. 6; HJSr to CBJ, 11–30–[1855], H.

372 Reverting to the plan: HJSr to CBJ, 9–25–1855, H; *ED* 1:125; *SBO* 300, 305, 345.

373 On December 1: *SBO* 302, 304; HJSr to CBJ, 11–30–[1855], H.

373 What William and Henry Jr.: *SBO* 301, 308.

373 Accustomed as he was: *JW3* 352; WJ to EVW, 7–1–1856, H; *SBO* 301.

373 The novelist: *SBO* 309–10.

374 Alice: *JA* 45–46.

374 Henry Sr. had many: HJSr to Edward James, 11–2–[1855], H; *LEC* 205; HJSr to CBJ, 11–30–[1855], H; HJSr to RWE, [1856], H.

375 Carlyle: HJSr to RWE, [1856], H; *MA* 1:45, 101, 111; *JH6* 446–48.

375 In the eleven years: JJGW to HJSr, 6–28–1849 (SL), 12–17–1850 (H); HJSr to JJGW, 9–9–1851, H; *EM2* 4:255; HJSr to JJGW, 9–6–1852, H; JJGW to HJSr, 11–2–1854 (SL), 9–29–1854 (SL), 10–13–1855 (H).

376 Although James and Wilkinson: HJSr to RWE, [1856], H.

376 Emma Wilkinson: HJSr to RWE, [1856], H; HJ to MJ, 3–2–[1869], H; MJ to HJ, 12–8–1873, H.

377 "But here," etc.: *JH1* 154–55.

377 William B. Carpenter: JJGW to HJSr, 2–11–1848, SL; *DNB*; marginalia in HJIII's copy of *JW2* 1:21, H.

377 William White: *JR2* 1:92; "Swedenborg Society," "Miscellanea," *Monthly Observer and New Church Record* 4:end of vol., and 5:35–36; JJGW to HJSr, 8–12–1854, SL; HJSr, *The Old and New Theology* (London: Longman et al., 1861), v; *WAR* 242.

378 The letters: *NYTr* 12–3–1855 (p. 6), 1–16–1856 (p. 3), 1–15–1856 (p. 6), 2–7–1856 (p. 6).

378 second footnote: HJ, *The Middle Years* (New York: Scribner's, 1917), 83.

378 "the bother," etc.: *NYTr* 3–17–1856, p. 6.

379 Just as James's children: HJSr to ET, 5–23–1856, H; *NYTr* 2–7–1856 (p. 6), 3–17–1856 (p. 6); HJSr to RWE, [1856], H; HJSr to ET, 9–14–1856, H.

379 Certainly: *JH13* 14–15; *BUR* 41.

380 On June 3: *SBO* 328–29; HJSr to ET, 5–23–1856, H; WJ to EVW, 7–1–1856, H.

380 The Jameses' new address: *Sommier foncier* D. Q¹⁸ Art. 2, fol. 197, Archives de Paris; Joseph Karl Menn, *The Large Slaveholders of Louisiana* (New Orleans, LA, 1964), 388–89; Jewell Lynn de Grummond, "A Social History of St. Mary Parish," *Louisiana Historical Quarterly* 32:24; *SBO* 326–27; WJ to EVW, 7–1–1856, H; Mary A. Tappan to HJIII, 1–11–1921, H.

380 In the two decades: Thomas von Joest, "Hittorff et les embellissements des Champs-Élysées," in *Hittorff: un architecte du XIXème* (Paris, 1986–87); Paul d'Ariste and Maurice Arrivetz, *Les Champs-Élysées* (Paris, 1913), 248–50; La Délégation à l'Action Artistique de la Ville de Paris, *Les Champs-Élysées et leur quartier* (Paris, 1988); Étienne Eggis, *Voyage aux Champs-Élysées* (Paris, 1855), 41; *Galignani's New Paris Guide* (Paris, 1855), 199; Maurice Quentin-Bauchart, *Paris—les anciens quartiers* (Paris, n.d.), 27; *JR7* 2:30; *SBO* 331–32, 386.

381 If these were: JBJ obit., *Syracuse Journal*, 5–24–1856, p. 3, OHA; portfolio of views of Chicago (Jevne and Almini, 1866), Chicago Pub. Lib.; Estate of JBJ, cash book, 6–19–1857, 7–1–1856, Acc. 16640, NYSL.

381 "his promise": HJSr to CBJ, 2–4–1856, H.

381 John Sadleir: *DNB* 17:591–92; *NYTr* 3–17–1856, p. 6.

382 family memory of JBJ: [HJIII], typed sheet headed "*John B. James*," bMS AM 1092.9 (4600), folder 14, H; *SBO* 193.

382 "I don't think," etc.: HJSr to ET, 9–14–1856, H.

383 Charles Sumner: *SBO* 50; *JH15* 238; David Donald, *Charles Sumner* (New York, 1960); Edward L. Pierce, *Memoir and Letters of Charles Sumner* (Boston, MA, 1894), 3:536; *JR7* 2:31.

384 This dinner: *SBO* 334–35; WJ to EVW, 7–1–1856 [addition dated Aug. 2], H; *PE* 1:76; MJ to CBJ, 8–25–[1856], H.

384 The people: HJSr to ET, 9–14–1856, H; *SBO* 88–89, 381; MJ to CBJ, 8–25–[1856], H; *HAS2* 222, 231; *NSB* 213; *ROS* 183; *CO2* 2:59; HJSr to CT, 6–22–[1860], H; *SC* 201.

385 Anna Ward: *SL* 508–10; HJSr to ABW, 10–8–[1856], H; "Ship News," *Times* 10–13–1856, p. 9; *BO* 10–25–1856, p. 1; HJSr to SGW, 10–20–1856, H.

385 Upstairs: *JH14* 369–72; Alexander Gardner, "Contributions towards the early History of the New Church in Washington," 4–5, congregation records (from Dorothea Abbott); "Constitution and Minutes," p. 136, Brook Farm Papers, MHS; HJSr to FM, 5–13–1858, 6–10–[1858], 8–15–1858, H.

386 "battle of Freedom," "every steamer": "The State of Europe," *NYTr* 9–29–1856, p. 6.

386 from "I want to know" to "We saw the Empress": HJSr to Eunice (Macdaniel) Dana, 3–26–[1857], H.

387 After Louis-Napoleon: "Louis-Napoleon," *NYTr* 1–12–1854, p. 4; *JH15* 472; *NYTr* 8–26–1856, p. 5; *JH1* 182.

387 "Vast numbers": *NYTr* 8–26–1856 (p. 5), 6–24–1858 (p. 6); Pierce, *Memoir* 3:532, 536; HJSr, "The Order in American Disorder," (London) *Leader* (1856), 7:904.

388 James's muffled sympathy: WJ to EVW, 7–1–1856, H; *NSB* 59; *JR7* 2:30; *SBO* 381, 347; *JR1* 583–84.

388 "cleave down," etc.: *JH8* 33–34.

389 "fiscal or physical resources": *AA* 11–7–1825.

389 Meanwhile: MJ to CBJ, 8–25–[1856], H; *SBO* 307–8, 328, 334.

389 M. Lerambert: WJ to EVW, 7–1–1856, H; *SBO* 324–28, 335; *Annuaire et Almanach du Commerce* (Paris, 1858), 304.

390 Institution Fezandié: Pierre A. Walker and Alfred Habegger, "Young Henry James and the Institution Fezandié," forthcoming in *Henry James Review*.

390 trips to Germany: WJ to EVW, 9–4–1857, H; Fichier des étrangers, Dg 6, fol. 249, 10–1–1856, (Geneva) Archives d'État; *NYTr* 9–19–1857, p. 6.

390 In the summer of 1857: *LEC* 250; *SBO* 405, 306; *JA* 128; WJ to EVW, 9–4–1857, 1–4–1858, 5–26–1858, H.

391 typhus: WJ to EVW, 9–4–1857, 1–4–1858, H; HJSr to EC, [Sept. 1857], 9–24–[1857], V; HJSr to CBJ, 10–15–[1857], H; *SBO* 398.

391 Anna Ward: Diary of ABW, 1–6–1851, H [bMS Am 1465 (1340)], ABW to HJSr, 12–16–1857, H; HJSr to ABW, 11–2–1857, 3–12–[1858], H; HJSr to Christopher Pearse Cranch, 5–7–1858, V; *EM2* 8:563.

392 The James parents: HJSr to CBJ, 10–15–[1857], 7–23–1857, H; *EMD* 327; *Letters and Memorials of Jane Welsh Carlyle* (London, 1883), 3:279; MJ to CBJ, 8–25–[1856], H; [HJSr], "Works of Sir William Hamilton," *Putnam's* 2:476; HJSr to SGW, 10–5–[1859], H.

392 In October: *SBO* 397; WJ to EVW, 1–4–1858, H; HJSr to ABW, 12–25–1857, H; HJSr to Rev. WJ, 10–28–[1857], H.

392 Before long: *LEC* 264–65.

393 This second period: *SBO* 397; *LEC* 264; WJ to EVW, 5–26–1858, H; HJSr to CBJ, 10–15–[1857], H.

393 William: WJ to EVW, 3–1–1858, 1–4–1858, H; HJSr to CBJ, 10–15–[1857], H.

394 "might just as well": WJ to EVW, 5–26–1858, H.

394 "talent for languages," etc.: HJSr to CBJ, 10–15–[1857], H.

394 Bob: HJSr to CBJ, 10–15–[1857], H; *MAH* 6.

394 Harry: *SBO* 416–18, 413; HJSr to CBJ, 10–15–[1857], H.

395 Alice: *LEC* 264; *JA* 128–29.

395 As for Henry Sr.: *NYTr* 5–1–1858 (p. 6), 8–6–1857 (p. 6), 10–16–1857 (p. 3); HJSr to ABW, 11–2–1857, H; HJ, *What Maisie Knew*, ch. 22.

395 The one thing: *NYTr* 4–20–1858, p. 6; 9–19–1857, p. 6.

396 on suicide: *NYTr* 9–19–1857, p. 6; 4–3–1858, p. 6.

CHAPTER 23

397 The Jameses concluded their European sojourn: WJ to EVW, 5–26–1858, H; "Passengers Arrived," *NYTr* 6–23–1858, p. 8; HJSr to FM, 8–15–1858, H; *NYTr* 6–19–1858, p. 3; WJ to EVW, 7–1–1858, H.

397 Seventy-six years old: *LEC* 293; 1859 Albany directory; *L1* 25; *ROW* 490–92.

398 Tweedys' children: Anna F. Hunter, "Kay Street during my Life," *Bulletin of the Newport Historical Society* (April 1932), 4; HJSr to SSS, 6–1–[1859?], 5–26–1860, H.

398 James McKaye was another: *MA* 1:53; 1858 Newport directory; *LEC* 293.

398 Although the Newport directory: Maud Howe Elliott, *This Was My Newport* (New York: Arno, 1975), 85–90; WJ to EVW, 7–1–1858, H; *NSB* 72; 1858 Newport directory; Newport *Mercury*, 8–14–1858.

399 The rented house: WJ to EVW, 8–12–1858, H; HJSr to FM, 8–15–1858, H; HJSr to SGW, 9–18–1858, 9–27–[1858], H; 1858 Boston directory, p. 32; *MA* 1:76.

399 from "full of merriment" to "Fourier's plan": *JR3* 1:6–7.

399 "You've no idea," etc.: *HARL* 244, 248.

400 *New York Ledger*: HJSr to SGW, 1–26–[1859], H; Edward Everett, "The Mount Vernon Papers," *New York Ledger* 14 (2–5–1859), 5.

400 "Sissy": *MA* 1:70–71.

400 Union College: *NSB* 112–14; EVW's alumni file, UC; WJ to EVW, 8–12–1858, 9–18–[1858], H; Tayler Lewis, "The Higher Law," NY *Literary World* 8:209; *NYTr* 3–18–1851, p. 6; Harold W. Blodgett, *Union Worthies*, #11.

400 winter quarters: WJ to EVW, 11–12–1858, H; *MA* 1:70.

400 Alice's school: *STR* 61–62.

400 Berkeley Institute: Newport *Mercury*, 1–1–1859; 1858 Newport directory; *NSB* 81–82; *LEC* 283; *JR3* 1:7–8; *MA* 1:76–77; WJ to EVW, 11–12–1858, H.

401 But it was William: WJ to EVW, 9–18–[1858], 11–12–1858, H; *MA* 1:65.

401 The problem of William's education: Newport *Mercury*, 9–4–1858; HJSr to SGW,

9–8–1858 [not 1859, as claimed], H; HJSr to EC, 10–18–1858, V; steamship ad, *NYTr* 9–8–1858, p. 3; WJ to EVW, 9–18–[1858], H.

402 In Emerson's shrewd opinion: *EM2* 8:226; HJSr to SGW, 9–27–[1858], H.

402 " 'Willy'," etc.: WJ to EVW, 11–12–1858, H.

403 "not to punish Harry": AHJ to WJ, 12–18–1882, H.

403 James regretted: HJSr to SGW, 9–27–[1858], H; Ida Gertrude Everson, *George Henry Calvert* (New York: Columbia University Press, 1944), 283; HJSr to FM, 8–15–1858, H; HJSr to EC, 10–18–1858, V.

403 footnote: *JR4* 1:208–9.

403 "Depending as always": Joel Myerson, ed., *The Transcendentalists* (New York: MLA, 1984), 100–1; HJSr to SSS, 6–5–[1859], H; *NSB* 81–82; HJSr to EC, 10–18–1858, V.

404 "No man": HJSr to RWE, 4–24–[1855], H.

404 Alcott: *EM2* 8:588–89; *EMD* 329; AF, "Glimpses of Emerson," *Harper's Monthly* 68:459; Ellen Emerson to AF, 2–12–1884, FI 1394, quoted by permission of Huntington Lib., San Marino, CA; *TH* 537. Cf. HJSr to Mrs. Curtis, 1–27–1862, Knox College Archives.

404 Horace Bushnell: *Nature and the Supernatural* (New York, 1877), 148; *NYTr* 2–22–1859 (p. 3), 3–2–1859 (p. 3), 4–5–1859 (p. 6), 3–18–1859 (p. 3).

405 footnote: *NYTr* 3–18–1859, p. 3.

405 The previous August: *SPU* 145; London *Saturday Review* 6:78–79; HJSr, ms. fragment, bMS Am 1094.8 (30), H; *NYTr* 12–3–1855 (p. 6), 9–13–1858 (p. 6).

406 Five months later: *NYTr* 2–28–1859; 4–2–1859, p. 5; 4–16–1859, p. 9.

406 footnote: *JW2* 1:51.

406 With this argument: *NYTr* 5–4–1859, p. 6; 4–18–1859, p. 4.

407 Once again: *NYTr* 4–16–1859, p. 9; 4–23–1859, p. 5.

407 Taking off his gloves: *NYTr* 4–23–1859, p. 5.

407 James must have known and In their replies: *NYTr* 5–4–1859, p. 6; 4–23–1859, p. 5.

408 Edward Bryan: Bryan to HJSr, 7–19, 7–28, 8–1, all 1859, H; alumni files, PTS; HJSr to Bryan, 5–12–[1859] (CW's hand), H.

409 Sarah Shaw: Roger Faxton Sturgis, *Edward Sturgis of Yarmouth* (Boston, MA, 1914), 50; HJSr to SSS, fragment [1859?], 6–5–[1859?], 5–10–1859 (CW's hand), H.

409 Hunt had recently returned: Sally Webster, *William Morris Hunt* (Cambridge, Eng.: Cambridge University Press, 1991); Newport *Mercury* 9–11–1858.

409 On October 18: HJSr to EC, 10–18–1858, V; *SBO* 316; *JW2* 1:23; *NSB* 83.

410 The boys' education: *JH15* 71; HJSr to EC, 10–18–1858, V; *NSB* 83.

410 The studio's intoxicating air: *MA* 1:76; *LEC* 285; *FLD* 9–29–[1864]; *NSB* 92, 88, 90, 99, 102; MJ to HJ, 3–21–[1873], H; MJ to WJ, 5–27–[1867], 6–10–[1867], H.

411 "capital progress": HJSr to SGW, 4–1–[1859], H.

411 "a little too much attraction": HJSr to ET, July 24–30, [1860], H.

411 Years earlier: MJ to EW, 11–29–1846, SL; *MA* 1:75–76; *HARL* 239; "Passengers Sailed," *NYTr* 10–10–1859, p. 8.

412 Ma had died: AHJ to WJ, 12–3–1882, H; HJSr to SSS, 7–22–[1859], H; *PE* 1:186.

412 At the Geneva Academy: *JW2* 1:21; *NSB* 12.

412 For Harry: *LEC* 300; *HARL* 242; *NSB* 2–8.

413 Alice became a day student: WJ to EVW, 12–18–1859, H; HJSr to ET, July 24–30, [1860], H.

413 The younger brothers: WJ to EVW, 12–18–1859, H; *NSB* 2; GWJ to parents, [summer 1860], H; *MAH* 10.

413 On Sundays: HJ to WJ, 10–29–1888, H; *NSB* 19, 237; WJ to EVW, 12–18–1859, H; AJ to HJSr, 3–11–[1860], H.

413 In May: HJ to SSS, 5–26–1860, H; *NSB* 232; AJ to HJSr, 3–11–[1860], H; *STR* 56; GWJ to HJSr [1860], H [The date assigned by another hand, "(Dec. 1859)," is probably wrong, the letter apparently being written the same day as William's "matrimonial bond" letter, "1860 Sunday morning"]; HJSr to EC, 3–25[?]– 1860, V.

414 Late in May: HJSr to SSS, 5–26–1860, H; HJSr to ET, 7–18–[1860], H; *NSB* 147, 143.

415 The family's European program: *NSB* 24, 39; *HARL* 259.

415 In August: WJ to HJSr, [8–19–1860], H; *NYTr* 4–23–1859, p. 5; WJ to EVW, 8–12–1858, H.

415 footnote: WJ to Alexander Robertson James (b. 1890), [c. 1902–6], photocopy from Michael James, quoted by permission of Alexander R. James.

415 The original plan: WJ to EVW, 12–18–1859, H; HJSr to ET, 7–18–[1860], H; WJ to HJSr, [8–24–1860], H.

416 In spite of: WJ to HJSr, [8–24–1860], H; HJSr to ET, 7–18–[1860], H.

416 This newly altered course: *NSB* 61, 43; HJSr to SSS, 5–26–1860, H; Ts. frag., HJSr to HJ, 12–26–1869, H.

416 There is a time: HJSr to ET, 7–18–[1860], H; MJ to HJ, 7–24–[1869], H.

417 Henry Jr. was not about: *HARL* 249; HJ's copy of Tennyson, *Poems* (London: Moxon, 1857), H; *JR3* 1:8; Richard Cary, "Henry James Juvenilia," *Colby Library Quarterly* (March 1970), 58–63; WJ to parents, [8]–30–[1860], H; WJ to AJ, 9– 13–[1863], H [passage silently deleted in *JW2* 1:51].

417 Shortly before: *NSB* 62–63; *Century Magazine* 25:25; HJ, *The Portrait of a Lady*, ch. 6; *JA* 192.

417 When Oliver Wendell Holmes: *JA* 69; WJ to parents, [8–19–1860], H.

418 Half a century later: *NSB* 46 [revision noticed by Jennifer Dean], 41.

CHAPTER 24

419 West Point graduate (Robert E. Temple): George W. Cullum, *Biographical Regis- ter . . . West Point* (Boston, MA, 1891), 1:407.

420 Back in his native land: *MA* 1:75; HJSr to ET, 10–1–[1860], H; HJSr to F. B. Sanborn, 10–2–[1860, not 1858, as catalogued], Abernethy Lib., Middlebury College.

420 Newport had become: *EM2* 5:285; *MAI* 116.

420 "I think I *could* be": HJSr to Katherine O. Rodgers, 12–9–[1858?], H. For year, see WJ to EVW, 8–12–1858, H.

421 Temple girls: *JW2* 1:37; *HAB* 138, 162–63, 133, 169–70.

421 The Emerson and James children: HJSr to RWE, 3–26–[1861], H; *EM2* 9:41.

421 Still, James was not: HJSr to RWE, 4–9–[1862], H.

422 James complimented Emerson: HJSr to RWE, 3–26–[1862], H; *EMD* 328.

422 In the summer of 1862: *EML* 1:291, 287; WJ to parents, "Sunday eve," H.

422 "Envy me": *EML* 295, 297.

423 gallantry toward Alice: *STR* 52–53.

423 When the time came: HJSr to RWE, 12–22–[1862?], H. That HJSr was copying *JH15* (1863) for the printer argues against the 1861 date given this letter by RWE and H.

423 This is the first family letter: *STR* 68; *JA* 192, 129, 41, 135.

424 When James wrote: HJSr to Sanborn, 10–2–[1860], Middlebury College.

424 The day after: *NSB* 213, 221–24. "Siliceous" may be HJ's misreading of HJSr's script (not found).

425 At the end of the school year: HJSr to Sanborn, 5–6–1861, U. of Kentucky Lib.; *MAH* 19; GWJ to Thomas W. Ward, 5–24–1861, H; WJ to family, 9–16–1861, H.

426 James had praised: *NYTr* 5–4–1859, p. 6; HJSr to R. F. Wallcut, 6–1–[n.y.], Smith College; HJSr, "Physical and Moral Maladies," *Liberator* 29:116.

426 One of the hardest things: *JH15* 536, italics mine; *JR7* 1:63.

427 After Lincoln was elected: HJSr to RWE, 3–26–[1861], H; *Newport Daily News*, 7–5–1861; NY *Evening Post* 8–14–1861; *JH13* 29, 27, 38, 32.

427 Although James's millenarian expectations: William Rhinelander Stewart, *The Philanthropic Work of Josephine Shaw Lowell* (New York, 1911), 35–36; *JH13* 38; HJSr to JJGW, 1–20–1863, bMS Am 1237.18 (folder 2), H.

428 "does not flow": *JH13* 27.

428 portrait of Kitty Temple: *NSB*, facing 96.

429 La Farge's opinion: *NYT* 9–2–1910, p. 8.

429 WJ gives up painting: *FEI* ch. 8; James William Anderson, "Why Did William James Abandon Art?" *Psychoanalytic Studies of Biography* (Madison, WI: International Universities Press, 1987), 279–303; *JW2* 1:23; *AL* 70; WJ to Alexander James (b. 1890), 3–7–1909, copy from R. A. Sheehan, quoted by permission of Alexander R. James.

429 WJ's enlistment: *HOF* 535–36.

430 "Affectionate old papas": HJSr to [Cranch?], [Mar.–Apr. 1861], V.

430 "our boasted political house": *JH13* 40.

430 "put every where": HJSr to JJGW, 1–20–1863, H.

431 fire and HJ's obscure hurt: *HOF* 532–35, 529; *HARL* 13; *NSB* 296–301; George C. Foster, *New York by Gas-Light* (Berkeley: University of California Press, 1990), 172–73; *FEI* 198–99; *ED* 1:173–83.

431 footnote: *NSB* 298; *ED* 1:176–79.

432 Bob and the Naval Academy: WJ to family, 9–16–1861, H; *NSB* 375; *VA* 274; HJSr to Weed, 9–28–[1861], and Seward to HJSr, 10–11–1862, both U. of Rochester Lib.; microfilm copy of card file concerning nominees, Naval Academy Archives; HJSr to JH, 7–2–1863, Smithsonian Inst. Archives, Record Unit 26, Off. of the Secretary, Incoming Corr., 1863–79, box 2.

433 Gus Barker: Rufus W. Clark, *The Heroes of Albany* (Albany, NY, 1866), 410–19.

433 Living in Cambridge: WJ to family, 9–16–1861, 12–25–[1861], [3–9–1862], 12–15–[1861], all H.

434 William's letters home: WJ to family, [3–9–1862], 12–15–[1861], 12–25–[1861], all H; *JW2* 1:32.

434 One of William's first purchases: WJ to HJSr, [fall 1861], H [WJ's references to HJ as living at home and to Kitty James (*Prince* after fall 1861) invalidate H's conjectured date, 1863]; *JH1* 133; WJ to parents, 3–2–[1862?], H; *JW2* 1:42; *FEI* 155–59.

435 "ill-health": *JW2* 1:32.

435 "physical and nervous frailty": *JW2* 1:47.

435 footnote: *LEW* 596–97.

435 Was it any consolation: *MA* 1:70; *HARL* 260; Mary Rotch Hunter to Charles Hunter, 3–20–1862, Box 35, #221, Newport Hist. Soc.

436 The writer of this gossipy letter: Deed, vol. 36, p. 473 (3–24–1862), Newport City Hall; *EML* 1:286; Auntie May story from John Hayes, O'Neill-Hayes Funeral Home.

436 "I have established": HJSr to Howard James, 4–12–[1862] [misdated 1861 by H], H.

437 $8,000: Contract announced in *Newport Daily News*, 11–30–1863, p. 2, and signed 4–15–1864, deed, Newport City Hall.

437 In September 1862: *MAH* 25, 33, 58; HJSr to EP, 7–22–1863, Horace Mann III, MHS.

437 Henry Jr. had wanted: *NSB* 292–93.

437 Avoiding the regular: *JR3* 1:8, 2:387; *NYT* 7–25–1857, p. 2; *NSB* 290, 294, 342, 358.

437 At the time: *MAH* 25; HJSr to EP, 7–22–1863, Horace Mann III, MHS.

438 "All liveries are bad": HJSr to JH, 7–2–1863, Smithsonian Inst. Archives.

438 After seeing: *MAH* 35; *EML* 1:262; HJSr to JJGW, 1–20–1863, H; *HOF* 543.

439 Soon after Wilkie's enrollment: *MAH* 31; Russell Duncan, ed., *Blue-Eyed Child of Fortune* (Athens: University of Georgia Press, 1992).

439 Once Robert Gould Shaw: *MAH* 32, 35.

439 While the 54th: *NSB* 374; *JW2* 1:44.

440 The day the 54th: *MAH* 37–38.

440 Shaw's nineteen-year-old sister: Ferris Greenslet, *The Lowells and Their Seven Worlds* (Boston, MA: Houghton Mifflin, 1946), 288–89.

440 HJ's absence: *NSB* 244, 312, 374.

441 Willy Temple: Clark, *Heroes of Albany*, 411, 413; *HAB* 135; Howard James to Elizabeth T.J. Seelye, 5–12–1863, C; Bob Temple to Julius Hawley Seelye, 6–22–1876, Amherst College Archives.

441 "He is buried," "When it was suggested": *MAH* 47.

441 Wilkie got shot: *NSB* 245; HJSr to EP, 7–30–1863, Horace Mann III, MHS.

442 When the wounded son: HJSr to SGW, 8–1–[1863], H; *NSB* 242.

442 What particularly impressed: HJSr to SGW, 8–1–[1863], 8–15–[1863], H.

443 One Sunday: HJSr to EP, 8–11–[1863], Horace Mann III, MHS; *NSB* 392.

443 "The removal of Mr. James": *Newport Daily News*, 11–30–1863, p. 2.

443 "the internecine contest": HJSr to Rev. WJ, 12–21–[1860], C.

443 "foundations," etc.: *JH15* 285, 339–40, 345, 485, 207, 20.

444 flogging a dead horse: *JR3* 1:9.

444 RWE's opinion of book: *EM1* 15:354, 350.

444 *Substance and Shadow* was published: HJSr to EP, 6–20–[1863], 7–22–1863, Horace Mann III, MHS.

444 Back in 1861: HJSr to PG, 2–16–1861, 7–11–[1861], 10–5–1864, Bryant Godwin Coll. (HJSr), Rare Books and Manuscripts Div., NYPL; *Journal des Débats*, 9–16–1864.

445 After the war: HJSr to JJGW, 9–29–1868, H; *JH12*, folder 15, part 1, H.

CHAPTER 25

446 At the end of 1863: *FLD* 2–19–1864; HJSr to PG, 9–15–1864, Bryant Godwin Coll. (HJSr), Rare Books and Manuscripts Div., NYPL.

446 sale of house: NY Hall of Records.

446 The family: *MAH* 51; *Boston Directory* (1865) 222; Ts., HJSr to RJ, 8–29–1864, 8–31–1864, V.

446 Wilkie in Florida: Ts., HJSr to GWJ, 8–2–1866, V; *MAH* ch. 4.

447 Alice's first lengthy move: *STR* 106–9; Ts., MJ to GWJ, 10–28–[1866], V; HJSr to JJGW, 4–3–1867, H; Taylor, "Emotional Prodigality," *Dental Cosmos* 21:359, 361, 366.

447 A couple of years: *DO* 1:382, 433.

447 Alice wasn't kept: *HAB* 162; Rev. WJ to Kitty, 11–14–1850, C; Rev. WJ to [Catharine] Sedgwick, 9–10–1855, A; *STR* 91; HJSr to CD, [Jan 1866?], Caroline Healey Dall Papers, MHS.

448 The Jameses didn't own: Ts., MJ to GWJ, Mar 13 and 27, [1866], V; *KA* 72; Mrs. William G. Farlow, "Quincy Street in the Fifties," *Proceedings of the Cambridge Historical Society* (1926), 39–40.

448 The house: *STR* 97; MJ to AJ, [Aug 1874?], H; *YE* 58; MJ to HJ and another son, "Sunday morning" [7–10–1870], H; Cambridge tax rolls, ward 1, 1872.

448 Of the eleven houses: *Atlas of the City of Cambridge* (Philadelphia, PA, 1873); Ts., "The New Cambridge Club," *Cambridge Chronicle*, 11–23–1889, p. 1; *NSB* 227.

449 servants: 1870 census, Middlesex Co., Cambridge, ward 1, dwelling 180; MJ to HJSr, [1869?], and to HJ, 9–21–[1869], H; *JR2* 1:170.

449 footnote: HJSr to AJ, 8–27–[1872?], H.

450 "much more generally read": *SPR* 12–16–1868, p. 2.

450 As shrewd: *JW1* 1:295; *JR2* 1:262; "A Day of Days," *Galaxy* 1:308; "Watch and Ward," *Atlantic* 28:232–46; HJSr to HJ, 3–4–[1873], H; *JR2* 1:357.

450 All the same: *JR4* 1:855, 857, 827, 633–34.

451 Whitman's working-class family: Gay Wilson Allen, *The Solitary Singer* (New York, 1955), 361; *Henry James: Selected Letters*, ed. Leon Edel (Cambridge, MA: Harvard University Press, 1987), 348.

451 HJSr on current affairs: "The English Journals and President Johnson," NY *Evening Post*, 5–18–1865, p. 1; "The Death Penalty," *BO*, 3–25–1873; MJ to Mary James (Wilkinson) Mathews, 8–30–[n.y.], H.

452 summer quarters: MJ to HJ, 8–8–[1869], H; *LEW* 264; HJSr to A. V. De Witt, 7–31–1874, UC; *JA* 52; MJ to HJ and another son, "Sunday morning," H; MJ to AJ, 7–18–[1872?], H.

452 "the best talker in America": *NYT* 9–2–1910, p. 8.

453 The Brahmin: John T. Morse, Jr., *Life and Letters of . . . Holmes* (Boston, MA, 1896), 2:228; *FLD* 2–19–1864.

453 Somewhere near the foot: HJSr to RWE, "Sunday night" [1–27–1861], H; *FLD* 10–4–1867; HJSr to Mary Elizabeth (Fiske) Sargent, 4–14–[n.y.], Spec. Coll., Duke U.

453 Charles Eliot Norton: Kermit Vanderbilt, *Charles Eliot Norton* (Cambridge, MA: Harvard University Press, 1959), 22; [Norton], *Considerations on Some Recent Social Theories* (Boston, MA, 1853), 57; HJSr to RWE, [1–27–1861], H; *EM2*

9:42; MJ to HJ, 12–8–1873, bMS Am 1093.1 (52), H; HJ to MJ, 9–10–1869, H.

454 Annie Fields, wife of James T. Fields: *FLD* May 2 or 3, 1868; HJSr to John W. Field, 10–17–[n.y.], Pierpont Morgan Lib.; HJSr to AF, 2–13–[n.y.], H.

454 Minturn, Palfrey stories: *FLD* 5–18–1868, 11–2–1865.

454 Once, making a morning call: *FLD* 2–19–1864; HJSr to AJ, 7–22–[1872], H; Mott's death notice, *BO* 7–23–1872; HJSr to Juliet Goodwin, "Sunday 28th" [7–28–1872], H.

455 footnote: *BO* 2–9–1864, p. 1.

455 HJSr and Caroline Dall: *DAL* 1–13–1865, 4–25–1866, "contents" of vol. 27; HJSr to CD, 1–13–1865, Caroline Healey Dall Papers, MHS; *HAB* 213.

457 "lifted out of animal": HJSr to Juliet Goodwin, [7–28–1872], H.

457 On the last Saturday: *CO1* 247; ABW's diary, 10–26–1849, H; HJSr to RWE, [1–27–1861], H; *PE* 1:88–90.

457 footnote: *NSB* 209; *Portrait*, ch. 48.

457 James was elected: *EMD* 330–31; *CO1* 247, 239, 254; *JA* 68. *FLD* 10–28–1865 gives this as the date of HJSr's election.

458 Once: *FLD* 2–25–1866, 3–13–1869; *CO1* 239.

458 Radical Club: *SC* 291; Mary Elizabeth (Fiske) Sargent, ed., *Sketches and Reminiscences of the Radical Club* (Boston, MA, 1880), 37–40, 55–56, 208–11; HJSr to Sargent, 10–10–[n.y.], Spec. Coll., Duke U.

459 Another circle: Ledger, 1863–69; card, folder "Papers removed from vol. 2, 1863–1898"; constitution and by-laws; account book; "Records of the Examiner Club . . . 1869–1878," 112. Examiner Club Papers, MHS.

459 recorded conversations: "Records of the Examiner Club . . . 1869–1878," 37–38, 40–44, 103, 109–10, MHS.

462 "barren": J. E[lliot] Cabot to HJSr, 5–8–[1874?], H.

462 In 1861: HJSr to RWE, 10–10–1861, H; Julia Ward Howe, *Reminiscences* (Boston, MA, 1899) 324.

462 Carlyle: *FLD* 9–23–1863; HJSr to PG, 9–15–1864, Bryant Godwin Coll. (HJSr), Rare Books and Manuscripts Div., NYPL; "Concord Lyceum 1859–1881" and "Cash Book," Concord Free Public Lib.; *DAL* 1–19–1865; *PE* 1:126; HJSr to Mrs. Perkins, 3–17–[n.y.], UC; *FLD* 3–15–1869.

463 The past came up: *FLD* 9–6–1868; *SPR* 10–28–1868, pp. 4–5; HJSr to CT, 10–28–1868, H.

463 The next month: *SPR* 11–21–1868 (p. 2), 12–2–1868 (p. 2); HJSr to RWE, 12–7–[1868], H.

464 A few years later: HJSr to AF, 1–27–[1872], Huntington; HJSr to RWE, 2–13–[1872], H; HJSr, "Emerson," lecture MS "B," H; *FLD* 2–16–1872; HJSr to Mrs. [John?] Andrew, 2–19–[1872], Berg Coll., NYPL; "Records of the Examiner Club . . . 1869–1878," 132, MHS; *EM2* 6:208; HJSr to HJ, 3–4–[1873], H; *AT* 94:740–45.

464 At any moment: *AT* 32:219–24; HJSr to HJ, 3–4–[1873], H.

465 When William systematically read: *JW1* 1:102, 120.

465 Henry Jr. positioned himself: *NSB* 228–29; *JR2* 3:55; *JR4* 1:243; *DO* 1:429–32.

466 Still: *JR2* 1:160; Ts. frag., HJSr to HJ, 12–26–1869, H; *PE* 1:163.

466 By 1868: Papers of the New England Women's Club, Radcliffe College; *SPR* 11–30–1868, p. 2; Kate Field, "The New England Women's Club," *Woman's Advocate* 1:30–33; HJSr to Kate Field, 12–9–[1868], Boston Pub. Lib.; HJSr, ["Mar-

riage"], bMS Am 1094.8 (15), H; HJSr to W. A. Baker, 5–9–1869, Quaker Coll., Haverford College Lib.

467 The lecture was successful: HJSr to Theodore F. Dwight, 3–16–1869, MHS; FM to William Aspinwall Tappan, 1–23–1869, H; *FLD* 3–13–1869.

467 The following winter: *AT* 25:68–69.

467 By January 1870: HJSr to JAK, 6–5–[n.y.]; *HAB* 246–47; *Nation* 9:589.

468 Henry Jr. read: HJ to HJSr, 1–14–1870, H; *JW1* 1:141, 152; HJ to AJ, 2–27–1870, H; HJ to HJSr, 3–19–1870, H. Edel's "Drouet" (*JR2* 1:217–18; *HAB* 247) never existed.

468 When William compiled: *JH6* 470; *North American Review* 109:556–65.

469 footnote: *JW3* 296; HJ, *French Writers and American Women*, ed. Peter Buitenhuis (Branford, CT: Compass, 1960), 49.

470 "I marry my wife," etc.: *St. Paul Daily Press*, 2–19–1874, p. 2.

470 James may not have known: *Woodhull & Claflin's*, Apr. 18, May 9 and 16, June 20, 1874.

470 Several months later: draft of HJSr to RWE, n.d., bMS Am 1094.8 (77), folders 6, 29, H; RWE to HJSr, 11–3–[1874], H [bMS Am 1092.9 (4018)].

470 There is no firm evidence: HJSr to RJ, 1–19–[1874], V; *HAB* 57.

471 Late in the year: *JR4* 1:567; Nordhoff, *Communistic Societies* (New York: Schocken, 1965), 293.

471 "very *American* tale," etc.: *JR1* 19–20.

472 Howard: Kitty to Elizabeth T.J. Seelye, 11–14–1861, C; MJ to HJ, 8–8–[1869], H; HJSr to Howard, 4–12–[1862], H; Howard to Kitty, 1–2–[n.y.], C; HJSr to A. V. De Witt, 4–28–[1874], UC.

472 Gus: Kaplan's notes of ts. of MJ to GWJ, 9–3–[1866?], V; Obit. of Gus, folder "James, William & Henry," OHA; shawl and accession documents, Albany Institute of History & Art.

473 footnote: "Syracuse Partition Suit," bMS Am 1092.9 (4600), H.

473 Gus dead: HJSr to Rev. WJ, 5–1–1855, H; Rev. WJ to HJSr, 11–30–1860, A; HJSr to Rev. WJ, 12–21–[1860], C; *FEI* 141; Rev. WJ to Kitty, 1–25–1861, C. Cf. Mary Bushnell Cheney, *Life and Letters of Horace Bushnell* (New York: Arno, 1969), 445–46.

473 Rev. William died: Joel Munsell, *Collections on the History of Albany* (Albany, NY, 1871), 10; Rev. WJ to Elizabeth T.J. Seelye, 7–8–1867, C.

474 After his death: HJSr to Elizabeth T.J. Seelye, 12–16–[1873?], C; Sarah Humphrey to Elizabeth T.J. Seelye, 12–9–1873, UC.

474 Minny Temple: *HAB* ch. 6; *STR* 115; MT to JCG (copy), 11–19–1869, bMS Am 1092.12, H; Alfred Habegger, "Henry James's Rewriting of Minny Temple's Letters," *American Literature* 58:159–80.

475 There was another: MT to JCG (copies), 1–25–1870, 1–7–1869, H.

475 Minny's religious faith: MT to JCG (copy), 1–25–1870, H; *JH15* 13–14.

475 Two days later: MT to JCG (copy), 1–25–1870, H.

476 Meanwhile: WJ to ET, 12–18–1867, H; WJ's 1868–70 diary, H; frag. of WJ to AHJ, "early winter of '82," pasted in HJIII's copy of *JW2*, 1:198, H; Alfred Habegger, "New Light on William James and Minny Temple," *New England Quarterly* 60:28–53.

476 Two weeks later: *AL* 167–68; Habegger, "New Light."

477 Henry Jr. treasured: *JW1* 1:153; *JR2* 1:218–22.
477 On August 7: MJ to HJ, 8–8–[1869], H; *JA* 207, 176; *STR* 46–47; *YE* 67.
478 "I had to peg away": *JA* 95.
478 "a long, toilsome": *JH14* 172.
478 footnote: *YE* 83.

CHAPTER 26

479 George Ripley, Parke Godwin, Charles Dana: *ROS* 210; *CO2* 2:134–35; *YE* 54.
479 Alfred Ford: *Journal of the General Convention of the New Church* (July 1867) 13; *SI* 193.
479 Tweedys: *JR2* 1:328, 355, 367; HJSr to John S. Dwight, 4–15–[n.y.], H.
479 Lazarus: Lazarus's untitled autobiography; Lazarus to J. A. Labadie, 3–2–[n.y.], Labadie Papers; Lazarus to George Schumm, 8–1–1895, and Mary Miller to Schumm, 7–1–[n.y.], Schumm Papers. Labadie Coll., U. of Michigan Lib.
480 James turned sixty-nine: Census, Cambridge, Middlesex Co., enumeration district 428, dwelling 93; *JR1* 230; HJSr to RJ, "Sunday Oct 10" [1880], V; M. A. DeWolfe Howe, *Memories of a Hostess* (Boston, MA, 1922), 82; Whitman, *Correspondence* (New York: New York University Press, 1964), 3:246; *The American Tradition Exhibition of Paintings* (New York: National Academy of Design, 1951), 8.
480 Mentally: MJ to WJ, 1–23–[1874], H; MJ to HJ, 3–17–1874, H; *NSB* 62.
481 James had a penchant: Boott to HJSr, 3–23–[1877?], H; *JH14* 3.
481 James may have seen himself: *NCI* 29:224; *JH14* 175, 300, 296, 238, 241, 245, 244.
481 "Infinite Love": *JH15* 493.
482 When *Society*: *NCI* 27:229–35, 298–304; 28:307, 311–12; HJSr to PG, 10–1–[1882] and n.d. [refers to HJSr's May 1880 *NCI* essay], Bryant Godwin Coll. (HJSr), Rare Books and Manuscripts Div., NYPL.
482 Of the two troublemakers: *NCI* 28:531–32; 29:45–46.
483 Still: *NCI* 29:286; 28:387; 27:225–26; Eby to Austin Warren, 11–8–1929, H; Caroline Eliot Lackland, "Henry James, the Seer," *Journal of Speculative Philosophy* 19:54–55; Field to HJSr, 8–24–1867, H. Welch's letters to HJSr are at H.
483 Julia Kellogg: Alice Thacher Post, "Julia A. Kellogg," *The Public* 18:79; HJSr to Kellogg, 1–25–1864, 1–7–[n.y.], 9–17–[n.y.], H.
484 "insufficiency to Himself," etc.: *JH14* 334.
484 "Whenever I get": HJSr to Kellogg, n.d., bMS Am 1092.9 (4248), H.
484 "divine rage," etc.: *JH6* 76.
485 "Shall I continue," etc.: *NCI* 27:472.
485 On the whole: HJSr to HJ, 3–18–[1873], H; *JR2* 1:302, 333–34; HJSr to Norton, 3–5–[1876?], UC; HJSr to Lowell, "Sunday, June 27," [1869 or 1875], H.
486 During the winter of 1875–76: HJSr to Manton Marble, 12–4–[1875], vol. 91, Marble Papers, MS Div., LC; "Henry James's New Novel," NY *World*, 11–29–1875, p. 2.
486 Apparently Henry Sr.: *FLD*, May 2 or 3, 1868.
486 footnote: MJ to AJ, [1–14–1870?], H.
487 "I am greatly touched": HJSr to PG, 2–27–1875, NYPL.
487 Aunt Kate once confided: AHJ to WJ, 12–21–1882, H; *JW3* 341; *JW2* 1:222.

487 "alone with no one": HJSr to AJ, 5–21–[1872?], H.

487 William's debility: *AL* 175, 179–80.

488 Alice Howe Gibbens: *AL* 214–223; *LEW* 270–85.

489 Intrigued: WJ to AHJ, 10–6–1876, 4–30–[1877], H; *LEW* 283; AHJ to Frances Rollins Morse, 2–4–1911, H; HJSr to RJ, 12–10–[n.y.], V.

489 But if William gained: *AL* 221; *JA* 230, 201; *YE* 78.

490 from "so wholly immersed" to "strongly tempted": HJSr to RJ, 9–14–[1878], V.

491 footnote: Dr. James Mackenzie to Dr. Harold Rypins, 1–12–1925, Acc. 12094, NYSL.

491 The two youngest boys: MJ to WJ, 11–21–[1867], H; *WLK* 110.

491 Moving to Wisconsin: GWJ to MJ, 8–7–1872, H; *MAH* 125; MJ to HJ, 12–15–[1872], H.

492 Bob continued: HJSr to RJ, 12–10–[n.y.], V; GWJ to JCG, 1–20–[1882?], H.

492 Bob Temple: Temple to Julius Hawley Seelye, 6–22–1876, Amherst College Archives.

492 Mary died: RJ to Mary (Holton) James, 1–31–[1882], V; MJ to WJ, 6–10–1867, H; *DO* 1:528; HJSr to AF, 2–13–[c. 1870], H; EW to MJ, #71a, 8–29–1850, and JJGW to HJSr, 8–30–1850, SL.

493 When the novelist returned: *JR1* 228–29; HJSr to HJ, 8–8–1873, H; MJ to HJ, 9–6–[1869], 7–24–[1869], 4–27–[1873], H; *MAH* 142.

493 A couple of weeks later: *JR2* 2:379; JJGW to HJSr, 2–24–1882, H; *JA* 221; *JR1* 229–30; *JR2* 1:170.

494 Leon Edel has argued: *ED* 3:36–38; *JH2* 64.

494 Was a loving wife: *JW2* 1:210–11; HJSr, "Marriage Question," *NYTr* 9–18–1852, p. 6; MJ to RJ, 6–28–[n.y.], V.

495 In their final decade: *JH15* 510; HJSr to HJ, July 1872, H.

495 "I never saw": HJSr to Julia A. Kellogg, 9–17–[n.y.], H.

495 The death: HJ to CD, 2–10–1882, Caroline Healey Dall Papers, MHS; *MAH* 142.

496 It was Alice: HJSr to AJ, 8–27–[1872?], H; *Cambridge Chronicle* 37 (4–15–1882), 1; *STR* 204.

496 Father was taken care of: HJSr to HJ, 5–9–[1882], H.

496 To Godwin: HJSr to PG, 10–1–[1882], NYPL; HJSr to HJ, 9–21–[1882], H; *JW1* 1:335.

497 Father and daughter: *YE* 84; AHJ to WJ, 12–22–[1882], H; *MAH* 144–45; unpublished missing fragment of HJ to WJ, [12–28–1882?], found by R. A. Sheehan.

497 Last will: AHJ to WJ, 12–22–[1882], 12–11–1882, H; Will and Schedule of Personal Estate, probate records, Suffolk Co., MA, vol. 544, p. 250 (2–26–1883).

498 Unless otherwise noted, the source for HJSr's last weeks consists of AHJ's almost daily letters to WJ, from 11–30–[1882] to 12–25–1882, H.

498 "signally beautiful," "our ordinary unannealed suicides": *NCI* 29:267.

498 Isaac Edwards: HJSr to Anna McBride (James) Edwards, [1879], C. Edwards has been confused with Dr. William Prince, who probably died a natural death.

498 "by the manner": *YE* 88; *JW1* 1:343–44.

499 "It is weary work": *STR* 207.

499 "life is sustained": *MAH* 145.

499 "passed through death": *MAH* 145.

499 "haunted by the terror," "he must eat": *JA* 79, 125.

499 Alice and opium: AHJ to WJ, 12–25–1882, H.

500 "Oh, I have such good boys": *JW1* 341.

500 The daughter: *JA* 149; AHJ to WJ, 12–18–1882, 12–22–[1882], H; *STR* 209; JJGW to HJSr, 9–18–1847, SL.

500 Henry Jr. left England: *ED* 3:57; AHJ to WJ, 12–6–[1882], 12–22–[1882], 12–27–1882, H.

500 Henry's letters: *JR1* 229; *NSB* 62; unpublished fragment of HJ to WJ, [12–28–1882?], Sheehan; *JR2* 3:28, 21; *JR1* 18–20; HJ to HJSr, 1–14–1870, H.

501 HJSr's will: Probate records; *JW1* 1:341; *MAH* 150; WJ to EVW, 12–18–1859, H.

502 WJ's letter: WJ to Sarah Butler Wister, 12–24–[1882], Papers of Owen Wister, MS Div., LC; *JW2* 1:219–20; unpublished fragment of HJ to WJ, [12–28–1882?], Sheehan.

502 "make amends": *JW1* 1:344.

502 William was to be: *NCI* 27:312; Cornel West, *The American Evasion of Philosophy* (Madison: University of Wisconsin Press, 1989), 54–68; *MAI* 383.

503 For some thinkers: WJ to Papini, 7–3–1906, H; WJ, "G. Papini and the Pragmatist Movement in Italy," *Journal of Philosophy* 3:340; A. James Gregor, *Young Mussolini and the Intellectual Origins of Fascism* (Berkeley: University of California Press, 1979), 143; 1926 clipping, "Philosopher from Albany Prompted Mussolini's Climb to Fascist Power," UC; HJSr, *NYTr* 8–26–1856, p. 5. Also see Papini, *Sul Pragmatismo* (*Saggi E Ricerche*) *1903–1911* (Milan, 1913), 81.

504 One of the ways: WJ to Kitty, 12–24–[1884], C; AHJ to Kitty, 10–3–1884, C; *JR2* 3:62, 73.

504 Copies of *The Literary Remains*: *PE* 1:117; *Nation* 40:60–61.

504 The disciples James attracted: Kellogg, *Philosophy of Henry James* (New York: Lovell, 1883); Ontological Society flyer, H; Ilsley to Harold A. Larrabee, 9–11–1928, UC; *New Republic* 56:22; *PE* 1:118; Sechrist to HJIII, 10–27–1929, H.

504 But who can trace: Edward Younger, *John A. Kasson* (Iowa City: State Historical Society of Iowa, 1955), 70, 128, 158; Samuel C. Eby to Austin Warren, 11–8–1929, H; *Encyclopedia of the History of St. Louis* (New York, 1899), 2:1205; *Journal of Speculative Philosophy* 19:53–60.

505 pillow story: Michael James to author, 1–30–1992.

CHARTS OF THE JAMES FAMILY AND THE ROBERTSON-WALSH FAMILY

The following charts show the affiliation and vital facts of some of the people mentioned in this biography. For the James family chart, the principal source is the genealogy brought out by Katharine Hastings in 1924, "William James of Albany, N.Y., and His Descendants." The few corrections and additions that are silently entered here are mandated by various unpublished materials. The sources of the Robertson–Walsh family chart are William Walsh's *A Record and Sketch of Hugh Walsh's Family* (1903), Mr. and Mrs. M. B. Streeter's *The Wyckoff Family in America* (1934), some manuscript genealogies in the Houghton Library, and various probated wills. Neither chart pretends to be exhaustive.

Robert 1765–1823

William d. 1855
John 1793–1866
Robert 1797–1841
Henry 1808–73

Robert b. 1840

William James of
Bailieborough, Ireland
1736–1822
m. Susan McCartney
1746–1824

William of Albany 1771–1832
m. (1)1796 Elizabeth Tillman
1774–97
m. (2) 1798 Mary Ann Connolly
d. 1800
m. (3) 1803 Catharine Barber
1782–1859

John 1785–1813

Charlotte
m. 1832
John Ward Birge

JAMES FAMILY

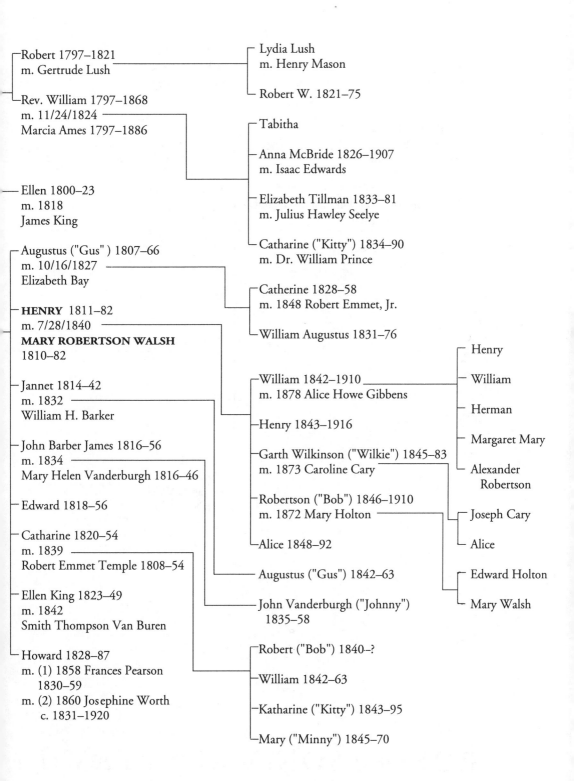

Robert 1797–1821
m. Gertrude Lush

- Lydia Lush
  m. Henry Mason
- Robert W. 1821–75

Rev. William 1797–1868
m. 11/24/1824
Marcia Ames 1797–1886

- Tabitha
- Anna McBride 1826–1907
  m. Isaac Edwards
- Elizabeth Tillman 1833–81
  m. Julius Hawley Seelye
- Catharine ("Kitty") 1834–90
  m. Dr. William Prince

Ellen 1800–23
m. 1818
James King

Augustus ("Gus") 1807–66
m. 10/16/1827
Elizabeth Bay

- Catherine 1828–58
  m. 1848 Robert Emmet, Jr.
- William Augustus 1831–76

HENRY 1811–82
m. 7/28/1840
MARY ROBERTSON WALSH
1810–82

- William 1842–1910
  m. 1878 Alice Howe Gibbens
  - Henry
  - William
  - Herman
  - Margaret Mary
  - Alexander Robertson
- Henry 1843–1916
- Garth Wilkinson ("Wilkie") 1845–83
  m. 1873 Caroline Cary
  - Joseph Cary
  - Alice
- Robertson ("Bob") 1846–1910
  m. 1872 Mary Holton
  - Edward Holton
  - Mary Walsh
- Alice 1848–92

Jannet 1814–42
m. 1832
William H. Barker

John Barber James 1816–56
m. 1834
Mary Helen Vanderburgh 1816–46

- Augustus ("Gus") 1842–63
- John Vanderburgh ("Johnny") 1835–58

Edward 1818–56

Catharine 1820–54
m. 1839
Robert Emmet Temple 1808–54

Ellen King 1823–49
m. 1842
Smith Thompson Van Buren

Howard 1828–87
m. (1) 1858 Frances Pearson
     1830–59
m. (2) 1860 Josephine Worth
     c. 1831–1920

- Robert ("Bob") 1840–?
- William 1842–63
- Katharine ("Kitty") 1843–95
- Mary ("Minny") 1845–70

Hellen d. 1818
m. Dr. John Richardson
Bayard Rodgers
d. 1833

Alexander Robertson
1733–1816 _____
m. Mary Smith

Mary ("great-aunt Wyckoff")
1778–3/3/1855 _____
m. Albert Wyckoff
1771–11/16/1840

William Smith of Dumfries, Scotland
d. New York, 1768

Robert Smith
1779–1866 _____

Elizabeth
1781–12/22/1847
m. James Walsh
c. 1780–1820

ROBERTSON-WALSH FAMILY

Alexander Robertson b. 1807
m. Mary Ridgely Darden d. 1888

Anna S. 1839–94

Katharine O. ("Katy") b. 1841

6 other children

Alexander Robertson
1804–49
m. 4/30/1840
Mary Russell d. 11/16?/1840

Albert ("cousin Albert")
b. 11/?/1840

Helen Rodgers 1807–87
m. Leonard Perkins d. 1869

Henry A. 1815–90

Alexander Robertson

10 children

Alexander Robertson
1809–4/17/1884
m. Emily Brown

William 1842–1910

Henry 1843–1916

MARY ROBERTSON
1810–82
m. **HENRY JAMES**
1811–82

Garth Wilkinson ("Wilkie")
1845–83

Robertson ("Bob") 1846–1910

Catharine ("Aunt Kate") 1812–89

Alice 1848–92

John A. Robertson
1813–4/15/1852

Hugh 1816–59
m. Elizabeth Hall

Hugh McKenzie
2 other children who did not
reach adulthood

James William 1819–72
m. Margaret Ruth Lawrence

4 children in all

Index

∎ ∎ ∎